How "Not" to Travel North Africa, Middle East, Israel & Malta and "Still Enjoy Yourself"

Jack Glass

Published 2010 by arima publishing

www.arimapublishing.com

ISBN 978 1 84549 431 5

© Jack Glass 2010

All rights reserved

This book is copyright. Subject to statutory exception and to provisions of relevant collective licensing agreements, no part of this publication may be reproduced, stored in a retrieval system, or transmitted in any form or by any means, without the prior written permission of the author.

Printed and bound in the United Kingdom

Typeset in Garamond 10.5/12

This book is sold subject to the conditions that it shall not, by way of trade or otherwise, be lent, re-sold, hired out, or otherwise circulated without the publisher's prior consent in any form of binding or cover other than that which it is published and without a similar condition including this condition being imposed on the subsequent purchaser.

Swirl is an imprint of arima publishing.

arima publishing
ASK House, Northgate Avenue
Bury St Edmunds, Suffolk IP32 6BB
t: (+44) 01284 700321

www.arimapublishing.com

A Travelling Man's Thoughts

To each and All my fellow travellers on whatever road you are travelling the Wide, Wide World today and all my family and friends either at home or at work.

My heartfelt Thanks to everyone for keeping in touch with my Greatest Thanks going to Sandralita who reads and types my scribbled handwritten travel notes and her Mum and Dad who received the post as without your help it would have been nearly impossible and Janine the worlds greatest proofreader.

Not forgetting Lonely Planet Guide Books which without them it would be a very difficult hard slog travelling the World.

www.lonelyplanet.com

"A thought about your thoughts"

Don't wait until Manyanna and say "I wish"
Manyanna never comes and "I wish is too late"
So "do it now"

To each and All my fellow Travellers wherever life's road takes you on your World Wide travels today Wishing you All a safe and Happy days travels today, manyanna and always.

al de bes

Jackboy

Map of Morocco

1) MOROCCO with its Elegant Royal Cities of Rabat and Fes then as you walk about the myriad full of life labyrinthine taste and smell Souks of Marrakesh seeing the herbalists, perfumers and all types of craft sellers with sights you will never forget and then make it to the lively never forgotten town of Casablanca all inclosing the full History of Arab North Africa then its sandy Mediterranean Coast cultures driving past the unmissible High snow covered Peaks off the Atlas Mountains high in the sky as you drive through sandy windy deserts it's a pleasure to stop and have a sweet mint tea enjoying watching maybe the snake charmers but everywhere is a pleasure with the always friendly people of Morocco.
2) Capital; Rabat
3) Morocco achieved Independence in 1956
4) Climate; Ave temp Jan-Mar; 20c
5) Language; Arabic, French, Berber, English
6) Currency; Dirham, 1$US = 8 Dirham
7) Visa; Not required, 90 day issued on arrival
8) Return flight £51 + £154 ATM, hotel, food, train to Gatwick
9) Today's ongoing update of day to day accommodation, travel, food, drinks costs = £0

Day 1, Sunday, 27-12-09, Aldershot – Ifield, Crawley; England

Woke up at 0730hrs and up for a piss then naked in my cold kitchen I made a bowl of instant porridge with hot milk and enjoyed my first eats of the day. Turned the radio on and back to bed and being there in the lovely heat I drifted off to sleep again dreaming vivid dreams of my Kelly Rose as we had a great couple of days together over Christmas. She cooked turkey, spuds and veg with me under her strict orders that I was not allowed in her kitchen. Good fun and great cook as we enjoyed our turkey Christmas dinner me doing the washing-up!. Woke up thinking where is she as she had Boxing Day with her Mum and all her family but we had arranged to meet for a few hours today. Finally pressured myself to get up and into the bathroom and had a full dobhi drop, (crap), wiped my ass and a nice wet shave. Got two eggs into a pan ready to boil them then had a lovely hot shower, wow, I was now feeling great!. Turned shower off, cleaned washhand basin and bath, turned my cooker on to heat my boiled eggs and dried off, deodorant on, got dressed and into my kitchen for my delicious three slices of bread, two hard-boiled eggs, mug of Rosy Lee five-star breakie. Feeling good so done a little more of a final pack of my shoulderbag then suddenly remembered I needed to get my deadlock key to Dave Bronlie in Farnborough so checked wallet, cash and car keys in pocket and out into my car. I was panicking a bit as needed to get back before the Churchgoers take up all the car parking spaces along Victoria Road as I was leaving my car parked up in the residents parking area on Victoria Road. Quick no traffic drive to Dave's house in North Camp and Jo his wife answered the door so I gave her the deadlock key plus a new lock, wished her Good Morning and I was away back into my car and back to the Shot. Turned into Victoria Road and seen a space so parked up breathing a sigh of relief as 5 minutes later all the empty spaces were full. Back into my flat and had a text from Kelly and the next minute a knock on the door and in my beauty Queen sweetheart came with big hugs to each other. Great to see and be with her as unluckily her job commitment in Hayling Island prevented her from coming with me but that's life. More eats, more orders, make sure you text, phone, e-mail me and big hugs and kisses and at 1430hrs my beautiful Kelly Rose and I had our last final loving kiss and with tears in my/our eyes she was away her Mum picking her up. It was heartbreaking knowing that I wouldn't be with or see my beauty Queen sweetheart for three months so with moist tears running down my cheeks I was back up the stairs doing a final pack then an e-mail or two and then with a great big in and out breather I went out for a very brisk walk hoping it would calm me down. Walked through the Shot heading towards Tesco's on Queens Road then left and down York Road then left again up Church Lane East which took me out onto Grosvenor Road. Knocked the sex kitten Joan's door but no answer so left a note for the sex kitten and then away along Grosvenor Road calling into Mick's to shake his hand and wish him a great New Year telling him to tell Tony that I had called then that was me back in the Wellington Centre. I had a slow walk about reading today's papers headlines in W H Smith's then just passing time had a browse in the 99p and £1 stores then checking my watch it was 1615hrs so back to my flat I went. Changed all my clothing and had a 4No cheese sandwich din, din with a mug of tea, cleaned teeth, took all the sheets off my bed, dumped them in a pillowcase and nearly there, checked and printed train times from my computer so ready to go, it was 1815hrs. Turned water off at the stop valve and drained the CWSC down, turned the switchboard electric off and with my very bright torch down the stairs I went trolley shoulderbag and all, opened my front door and out, it was 1840hrs, my train was at 1906hrs. Deadlocked my front door and trolley roller shoulderbag with me pulling it I passed my good friend Maurice the barber both saying our smiling Good Lucks to each other and on up across Windsor Way to the train station. Seen the automatic ticket machine so keyed in single to Crawley and it came up £12.20 so put a £20 note in and out came my change and ticket, oh la, la what a great feeling of elation. Into the train station and checking the screen I seen the London Waterloo stopping at Woking and Clapham junction was on time and was stopping at Platform 1. Out to the Platform and five mins later toot, toot in came the four carriage London Waterloo train and stopped, I and a few others got on and no waits we were away. Got a seat, ticket Inspector came along so showed him my ticket and sat back smug and laughing to myself with a big smile on my face I knew I was on my way. We stopped once at Woking then into Clapham Junction which was my stop so off I got and up the stairs not a clue which of the 20 platforms I needed to go too. Kept walking past them as nowhere did a screen show Crawley until at the very last one I seen the screen showing Bognor Regis via Crawley and the platform was 10 deep with people. Down the steps I went and 5 mins later the half full Southern train pulled up and like a football crowd we charged forward and on I got and God be my Saviour I managed to get a seat, Mama Mia, it was 2010hrs. Off we went no room to breathe and first stop was East Croydon where half the train got off and double the amount got on, I didn't care, I still had my seat. Stopped at Purley where lots got off then more got off at Redhill and it was back to normal so we were all able to breathe. Getting near Crawley I telephoned my Hotel and guy said he would come and pick me up, £4 which was good value. Got off at Crawley and over the bridge and down to the waiting room and 5 mins later a car drew up and a guy got out asking me Mr Glass?, I said yes and he put my bag in the boot and in I got and we were away. It was a good run and in we drew to Da Vinci Manor Guest House, Ifield Green, Gatwick Airport, Crawley, RH11 0WU, 01293-511938, davinciguesthouse@googlemail.com. The driver kindly took my bag and in we went to reception where he and a lady showed me a lovely big double bed ensuite room where I put my bag. Out and sat down at reception, paid my £24.20 + £4 +£7 for taxi to Gatwick Airport tomorrow at 0930hrs, wow oh wow everything looking good. Got a receipt and the lady showed me the breakfast room with hot tea/coffee pots saying to help myself so I had a big mug of tea and into my room where I had a packet of chocolate biscuits sitting on my lovely soft bed enjoying my 2140hrs late tea break. Had a read of my Lonely Planet Morocco and that was me, into bed and dreaming of my sexy Kelly Rose I fell asleep, it was 2240hrs.

Date: Sun, 27 Dec 2009
Subject: The start of Jacks 2009/10 travels
Hi All

Just had a walkie around the Shot this afternoon and now ready to make a move by train to a 5 star £24 nicker a night hotel called the Da Vinci Guest House 10mins drive from Gatwick Airport in Ifield village just outside Crawley. My flight is at 1200hrs tomorrow and I could have got a train at 0638hrs to arrive at Gatwick at 1000hrs but not worth taking a chance so will get down near it and at least no upsets if trains are not running or late. Fly into Marrakesh, Morocco, N Africa and land at 1525hrs and will hopefully find my Riad Rahba Hostel with a single ensuite for £10-88 a night for 3 nights then?. More snow and blizzards forecast in Blighty for New Year so just hope my flight details go ok as just need a relaxing sunshine walk and a few night-time antics to keep me in shape and happy.
al de bes
Jack

Day 2, Monday, 28-12-09, Gatwick Airport; England – Marrakesh; Morocco

Woke up once for a piss but had a great night's sleep then woke up for good as the alarm went off at 0710hrs. Stretched my muscular limbs smiling into the dark room and fully refreshed turned the alarm off, threw the covers back and up. Had a piss and a nice wet shave with a soapy face wash, dried off, deodorant on, kit on and that was me. Little final pack of bright red roller shoulderbag and double checked that Passport was in my neckpouch and put it around my neck inside my shirt as the best thing about a neck pouch is you can have a crap or do anything and you don't need to take it off. Out of room and lady was just setting out the breakfast table and invited me to sit down on any chair so I took the top end seat, it was 0820hrs. A full egg, sausage, bacon, beans and tomato English breakfast came and I buttered two slices of bread and got stuck into, yum, yum my lovely breakie, it was delicious. Had three mugs of Rosy Lee in total with another marmalade jam slice of bread and that was me a full and happy breakie man. Back to room and first things first I had a full empty belly dobhi drop, wow, that was a dream come true, wiped my ass, cleaned my teeth and final study of my handsome looks in the mirror, that was me. Little final check of shoulderbag, put lock on it and opening my room door I put it halfway along the hall, guy said you are ready, I smiled saying yeah. He took my bag and I slung my China beachbag over my shoulder and followed him out to his car saying my thanks to reception come breakie lady as we passed her getting a lovely smile in return, it was 0930hrs. Into the front seat of his car/taxi with roller shoulderbag in boot and we were away on the frosty road through Ifield Village then a few major roads following signs for Gatwick Airport then following signs for Gatwick North terminal and passenger drop-off. He stopped, out we both got with him taking my roller shoulderbag from the boot and putting it on the pavement, we shook hands me wishing him all the best and he was away. Pulled handle up and followed signs for departure hall and in I went quickly looking at the departure boards I seen Marrakesh 1200hrs, check-in Zone F. Followed sign for Zone F and came to Royal Morocco Airlines check-in desk with no queue so up to the desk giving the young guy my Passport, he swiped it and said window or aisle seat, I said aisle and put my roller shoulderbag on the escalator beside him, he put sticker on it, gave me my boarding pass and that was me nearly there. Seen departures so over to it, emptied my pockets and putting my China beachbag and everything in a plastic box tray and it and me through x-ray, no hiccups and I was in, what a very smooth start to my day I was thinking. Collected all my stuff, put my neckpouch back on checking it for Passport and happy as a lark over to a cash machine, put my card in and punched in €100, 2 mins later out it came then over to a money changer and had another €120 left over from a previous trip to Malta so gave him €220 in total and after him taking £3 commission I got back 1900-00 Dirham in Moroccan currency. It looked above board so stuck it in my neckpouch and had a walk around the departure area with lots of cafes on its first floor, done my usual 10 minute Internet then having a latte coffee it came over the tannoy all personnel for Flight AT0673 going to Marrakesh please proceed to Gate 102, wow, what a no hassle day.

Finished my lovely sweet coffee thinking Kelly would love this and just followed directions to Gate 102, showed my Passport and Boarding pass, got a stub and that was me, sat down in the lounge thinking this is the life. Only a 10 minute wait and we were invited to start boarding which I did and got my seat 12D an aisle seat. The plane got completely chocka full so booking my £51 return flight last September paid dividends as I know I won't be using the return but for £51 what did I lose. Next we had the usual Captain's flight talk and stewardess checking safety belts and seats upright and at 1200hrs spot on out we taxied to the main runway and hip hip hooray off we went into the clear bright English sky my eyes misting over thinking of my Kelly Rose and brightening up I wished her in my mind to have a wonderful time without me. The plane warmed up then at 1330hrs the dinner refreshment trolley came along and there was no choice, sorry, yes you had, take it or leave it. It was a smallish portion of tasteless meats with cut onions and peas with another portion of brown thick meaty gravy not forgetting the brown bread scone so ate the lot with a can of Coke and a hot tea, very nice. Flapdown back of seat tray cleaned at 1415hrs so had a read of my photocopy Lonely Planet Marrakesh trying to work out where my Riad Rahba Hostel at Rue Rahba Lakdima was, sort of found it on the map so will take a petit taxi from the Airport. Bus looked ok but first-time landing in Morocco someone has got to treat me!, we shall see. Tried to find a mention of my supposedly second move and stop at Ouarzazate on the 31st but it was not even mentioned in my Lonely Planet not forgetting my LP was Africa on a Shoestring. Great views of the Atlantic coastline as we flew along it and also the barren brown Atlas Mountains then up for a piss and back to my seat, lucky I didn't need a crap as no toilet paper in the toilet so I informed the attendant. Sat down in my seat again and the lady in the window seat gave me a customs declaration form to fill in, so getting near. Had an interesting read about Morocco in LP then at 1500hrs as UK time and Morocco time are both the same it came over the tannoy fasten seat belts, seats upright and prepare for landing so today was a fantastic no drama, no rush day, Mama Mia, bless the Lord. Landed spot on 1530hrs and taxied over to arrivals and not long we were getting off and I and everyone went into arrivals. I had already filled my Immigration form in so up to Passport control kiosks, handed mine over, the guy had a two minute look and bang, Moroccan entrance stamp and I was through into the arrivals and lucky again only a five minute wait and my bright red blue ribbon shoulderbag was nearly first out so I grabbed it and trolley handle up I was away outside. Seen lots of Petit brown cabs as they are known and as I approached them 2-3-5 guys came towards me one guy saying I take your bag. I asked how much he said 150 Dirham I said no, 100, he said 140 Dirham, I said no, 120, he agreed and said ok. Shoulderbag in front seat, me in the back, I quickly locked the front door and we were away going into the centre of Marrakesh. He stopped and said this is as far as he can go so I said ok I will walk. He said pointing at guys with deep square wheelbarrow type pulleys, they will take you to your hotel. So out I got, gave him the 120 Dirham and pull handle up I was away into the packed mayhem of the Muslim chanting Mosque Square thinking to myself you're in the shit now as I didn't have a clue where I was. A guy only 20m from where the taxi dropped me off was sitting beside his pulley wheel barrow so I quickly showed him my hotel, he said ok 20 Dirham so with no arguing I said ok, he grabbed my red bag, put it in his barrow and we were away. He took a short cut along an alley way with Hotel Atlas, Hotel Cecil and probably another six hotels in it then came out and into the melee of the full of cooking tent huts and hundreds of fruit stalls with the area fully packed. Down another packed alley we went and there it was, Hotel Riad Rahba, got to the door and he took my bag inside and I gave him 20 Dirham and he was away. The young fellow at reception opened his book and said William, I smiled saying yes, he took me into the lower sitting area and another young fellow gave me a small pot of tea and they said wait here, room nearly ready, so I sat over my sweet tea just relaxed and glad to have made it without any drama. The young guy came over and gave me Room 12 key and pointed up the second landing at an open room door, that's your room. Shoulderbag being carried up two flights of stairs I went into my decent sized single bed ensuite room which smelt a bit as if a sewer was backing up and there was evidence of damp all over the back two walls, not to worry, dumped shoulderbag in the corner and opening my China beachbag I had two Mars bars just happily sitting on my bed, yum yum, really nice. Thinking what do I do, up I got, locked door behind me and I was away downstairs. As I was going out I told the young fellow about the smelly room, he reached under reception and got out a tin of freshener and said use this, I said I will when I come back and I was away going left just following the packed full of hawkers, shops of every kind alley. I turned back after 50 minutes and back into the melee of the square getting busier by the second as hundreds of cooking stalls and fruit stalls were going full blast with thousands of people walking around it and everyone was so friendly. I think I was in the Medina which was a Fort wall enclosed area of Marrakesh. Had a walk here, had a walk there and the next thing I knew it was getting dark so final circle in my walk around the so friendly and so amazing packed area of the square with lots of eating stalls packed full of backpackers I slowly made it back towards my hotel and into a French cafe for another latte, the fourth one I have had tonight. Sat down and feeling peckish I ordered chicken and chips and when it came it was so delicious so just took my time and ate the lot and that was me, paid my bill and out. Eventually found my hotel and in I went saying hello to 3 new guys at reception and only one thought in my head as it was 2220hrs I made it upto my room, stripped off and with no hesitation straight into my soft mattress bed and asleep dreaming sweet dreams of nights to come.

Date: Mon, 28 Dec 2009
Subject: Rm 12. Riad Rahba, Rue Rahba Lakdima, Biyadine, Marrakesh

Hi All

Took train to Crawley early last night and picked up at train station and stayed the night in the Da Vinci Guest House, Ifield, Crawley as did not want any hiccups with train or roads this morning. Great English breakie this morning and taxi to Airport all included in the £35 nicker total hotel bill, v good value, www.davinci-guesthouse-gatwick.co.uk. Good flight, 3hrs then taxi 120 Dirham from Airport and he dropped me off in centre of mayhem Marrakesh with Moslem prayers chanting from de Mosques, I thought I was back in Bazaar, sorry Station Rd in de Shot. Eventually found my £10er a night Hostel as above, not a badish den. Now out in the 1000s of people Djemma El Fna Sq with snake, belly and all sorts of dancing plus 1000s of stalls so gonna have a bite to eat, do you think I will wake up manyanna. Must make the souks an a few carpet shops, what's a carpet as us single Shotty hood do not understand. Must go, belly dancers are calling, staying 3 nights den?

al de bes
Jack

Day 3, Tuesday, 29-12-09, Marrakesh; Morocco

Was woke up at 0330hrs by the 4-5 Muslim chanters from the 4-5 Mosque Minarets surrounding my hostel in the Medina area, cor blimey they made some noise trying to outshout each other on loudspeakers. I tried to go back to sleep after it went deadly silent and I think I did but not a good one, finally up at 0915hrs. Had a quick under arm and face wash using my own soap and towel as nothing in the room then long cargo and Thai sandals on with pocket T-shirt and no plans only a breakie. Out locking my door behind me and down the two flights of stairs to the elegant seating breakfast, dinner eating area. There was quite a crowd all sitting so asked are you all waiting for breakfast, the ones that could understand my English nodded smiling and saying yes. I asked how long does it take and a guy said may be upto 1 hour, I was shocked but sat down on the nice soft seat. About 15 minutes later the breakfast trays with a big round bap, a full teapot full of sweet tea, butter, sweet thick honey, lubbly dubbly and I got stuck in pouring my tea into a small tumbler then buttered the 4 cut slices of the bap then lashing it with the thick honey and first bite it was lovely. I just sat there enjoying my first Marrakesh breakie as young travellers kept coming into the hostel looking for rooms. Finished my lovely breakie and upto my room and had a lovely full empty belly dobhi drop then cleaned ass, cleaned teeth, oh la la and nearly ready to go out but where. Sun cap in Chinabag and out I went, it was 1030hrs and the sun was blazing down so turned left going along the inside of the Medina Fort walls on the fully packed Riad (Road), good fun. My plan was just to walk the Riad and sort of follow the Fort walls on the inside and see its ancient history. Lovely day and it was great sightseeing as I came to a Fort entrance on the walls I could see the ice and snow peaks of the Atlas Mountains, wow oh wow. Walked at least 1 mile then turned right past a school as the previous high wall was down to 3m high then another right and left and I was in a very old part of the Medina going through ancient Fort Arches at every turn I made, really fantastic. It was a fun long walk and had now got back to the pedestrian area of the Medina where the taxi driver had dropped me off so doing well. Walked over and close up around the Koutoubia Mosque then into the quiet and peaceful green neatly planted area of the Koutoubia Gardens, really nice. Went left past a few upmarket Hotels then right and in through another Arch of the Medina Fort walls and slowly got along the fully packed Riad with all its ancient antiques and other shops. Kept going but ole left knee giving me grief then took a right don't know why but it was straight out to the square with all its fruit stalls but no food stalls set up yet, it was 1350hrs. Walked across the empty stalls square and seen half a dozen cafes along its outer edge and picked the Glacier Cafe and sat down as it had a very cheap menu. Picked omelette and chips and a Fanta from it and when it came it was absolutely delicious so I ate every last crumb, really enjoyable. Sat for another 30 minutes enjoying watching the thousands of holiday Europeans enjoying the lovely Morocco sun then paid my 18 Dirham bill and I was away, that was cheap for Morocco!. I still had £80 cash in £20 English pound notes so into a money changer and changed them at 12 Dirham to the pound and I got 985 Dirham, done well so stuck it in my sky and I was away. I had left a pair of cargo trousers at Riad Tailors to have the cargo pockets made bigger so into it and he had done a great job so paid him 100 Dirham, got my cargo trousers and I was away back into my hostel, dumped my cargo trousers and out again. Just a slow walk up around the square as they were just starting to set up their food stalls. Had brought my travel notes out with me and went into a photocopy shop and done two copies of each so if any one set gets lost at least I have a backup. Time even doing nothing marches on and checked my watch again, it was 1640hrs so nearly back at my Riad I went into a Cafe and had sausage and chips with a mint tea, really delicious. I sat outside the cafe in the heat of the day seeing all the hooded even their eyes covered over Muslim women who as they stared at me eating my chips I smiled offering them one but all refused many breaking out in laughter. Finished my second or third big eats of the day, paid my 35 Dirham bill, said my thanks and only a short hectic motorcycles everywhere walk I was back in my hotel and upto my room. Quickly stripped off and had a full empty belly dobhi drop then a lovely shower and ready to fall asleep, I put on my clothes, setting the alarm for 1930hrs and had a little lie on top of my bed siesta, this is the life. Woke up as alarm went off and up, face splash, cleaned teeth and out downstairs in no rush as there was not really anywhere new to go. Turned left outside the Hostel main door and just followed the Souk which at times the tourist crowd nearly blocked it but I thought I had seen most of the Souks but this one was really something with big large antiques and all sorts of shops as I turned every corner but seen one seen them all. It took a while but I eventually found my way back to The Square now fully packed with eating stalls. I didn't want anything to eat and just walking past an excursion sign I enquired of the young lady how much was the trip to Ouarzazate. She said €35 which was return by Minibus and a full sightsee tour of three ancient ruins, very good value I thought even if I went down and stayed there. She said if I came up to her office she will talk me through it so up we went and she introduced herself as Naima and showed me pictures of what was in the day's sightsee so with nothing to lose I paid a 200 Dirham deposit, got a receipt and agreed to meet the driver outside the Malbrouk Hotel at 0700hrs manyanna morning. Shook Naima's hand and I was away thinking that saves me taking a 4-5 hour bus then having to do the tours myself which I like doing but sometimes it makes sense to follow the crowd!. Marrakesh was packed solid so just enjoyed the night-time music vibes following the crowds to the end of the pedestrian area then turned back and into the Luna Cafe to have a nice sausage roll and Rosy Lee sitting enjoying the night time heat and vibrant crowds showing no sign of abating, it was 2200hrs. Stayed for another 20 minutes then up, paid my 15 Dirham and a slow walk back towards my hostel passing an Internet shop so in I went for my usual 15 minutes even booked a room in Agadir for the 31-12-09 for two nights as now thinking of doing a runner and having New Year's night in Agadir, same, same, we shall see. Paid my 5 Dirham Internet and bought some scones for breakie manyanna then into my hostel and upto my room greatly satisfied after a great day. Set alarm for 0600hrs, stripped off and into bed and asleep thinking is their such a thing as a Habit veiled Marrakesh hooker!, we shall see!.

Date: Tue, 29 Dec 2009
Subject: Marrakesh, Morocco

Hi All

Great day thinking I knew where I was and getting lost in the Souks but its amazing how these alleys stretch for miles around the Medina where my £10er a night digs are and the Souks are full of great antiques and 100s of other shops. Had a walk around the Koutoubia very high Mosque who along with 4 others at 0330hrs this morning where seeing who could shout the loudest through their loudspeakers, its garden was a lovely quiet area. Having an early start manyanna as going to Ouarzazate for the day or maybe stay the night, we shall see.
al de bes
Jack

Day 4, Wednesday, 30-12-09, Marrakesh – Ouarzazate; Morocco

Woke up at 0500hrs for a piss then back to bed for approximately a 45 minutes snooze then the Muslim chanters started at 0545hrs but not as loud and not as many as last night so up at 0600hrs as alarm went off. Face splash, long cargo, pocket T-shirt, pullover and Thai sandals on and sat on my bed having my four scones and Fanta brekkie all set out from last night, just the job. Into toilet for a mini dobhi drop, cleaned ass, cleaned teeth and nearly ready to go, it was only 0620hrs. Final check of China beachbag with bottle of Coke, knee bandage in it, camera in pocket and that was me out my door locking it and down the stairs to reception saying see you later and out I went into the dark cold sky not liking walking up the dark, empty, morbid no life square. Made it up to the empty square not a Muslim sinner to be seen and across it to outside the Malbrouk Hotel my pickup point. No one about so went into a just opened cafe and had 2 croissants and a tea, 13 Dirham, enjoyed my early breakie and out to the dark cold Riad again and the young fellow was there, we shook hands. He went across to the Malbrouk Hotel and as a Chinese girl came out he smiled and we all walked up to the end of the pedestrian area where there were 4-5 large Minibuses lined up and five minutes later we all got on one. It started up and we drove along to near my hostel just at the edge of The Square and parked up, it was 0720hrs. Driver got out to have a chat with about six other Minivan drivers parked up. There was now 6-10 fresh orange juice stalls open on the square, the Chinese girl said goodbye and three Spanish girls got on then a Belgian couple and in the driver got and we were away again. The first stop was a petrol station, it was 0745hrs, waste of 45 minutes already I was thinking. The driver came over and done a quick headcount and we were away passing quite a few brightly traditional dressed armed guards along a sort of Fort battlement walled area so it must be some sort of Palace/Government offices, it was 0755hrs. Driving out of Marrakesh was fun as it was a bright red brick render built city, the Red City as legend had it as blood ran deep when it was being built. Not long and we were soon on its grassy tree planted outskirts, no nose to nose traffic spewing petrol fumes into the now daylight but still cold Moroccan air. Stuck behind a large truck but great scenery as the Majestic huge in the blue sky snow capped Atlas mountain range which was on my right as I lay back on my seat and dozed off listening to the Spanish girls yapping and laughing away as the sun was now brightly coming out. We stopped at a little village called Touf built at the highest point of our road as we cut through the Atlas Mountains and it was very cold nearly freezing not what I was expecting. I had a piss, then a Mars bar, 10 Dirham in the cafe then at 0920hrs we were away again along the no safety barrier, bendy cut through Atlas mountain roads and looking down 1000m sheer drop to the valleys below was scary to say the least. Past a signpost, Ouarzazate 123klms, it was 0940hrs so not doing very good as total distance from Marrakesh was 158klms. We were now down in the valley again the road just a nightmare of hairpin bends even down in the bottom of the valley was scary but he was a good driver doing his best. Stopped again at a ladies corporation shop next to and facing the Le Tajune Cafe Road where they made olive oil from nuts. Signpost showed 111klms to Ouarzazate but it's getting warmer, oh la, la. Got friendly with the three Spanish chics who asked me my name and gave me theirs which was Patricia, Julia and Loles, mama mia, this is a traveller's life. Back on our Minibus again and the hairpin bend road was a nightmare as now we were going up towards the snow covered Atlas mountain tops again looking down the sheer drops down the brown dusty mountain sides, one slip and your dead man. Stopped at another cafe called Les Cascades and the wind was freezing but lucky we only had a five-minute photo shoot looking down the mountain valleys, it was 1030hrs. Got near one of the snow-covered peaks then started going downhill again, thank God. Seen a signpost for Ouarzazate, 87klms and Telouet 20klms and now going steeply downhill but could see through the valley in front more heavily covered in snow Atlas mountain peaks, I am shivering now at the mere thought of what's to come!. Passed through Agelmous a mountainside village with all the young kids in thick jacket hoods going to school with their mum in their Muslim fully covered face shawls. Another stop at cafe, restaurant Rafik where I had a Twix and a Mars bar, 10 Dirham roughly each, it was 1115hrs. Signpost Ouarzazate 58 miles and still going downhill but the full of life Spanish chics were great company. Going further downhill and now it looks like the road is levelling out and passing a road sign 51klms with a not heavy but still flowing river on my right every turn we made on our road. It's very amazing to see how these Berber people live as we pass through little square stone hut villages all without any crops or fields or greenery or livestock so they must import all their food. Just now coming into a fertile village with grass and planted fields and livestock, sheep mostly, in small barren fields. On a flat road now and we took a left turn on a very bumpy one lane tarmac road mind you the river was still on our right hand side although the whole area stretching for hundreds of miles as far as I could see was just pure rocky gorge desert until the Atlas mountain peaks with their snow-covered peaks adorned the far distance horizon. It was 1210hrs as we stopped for another photo shoot at an ancient Fort like town called Tamddakhte with its ancient Fort wall old town on top of the hill so off we all got me first and the driver telling us to be back at 1300hrs, it was 1220hrs. Off I went as the girls I think were looking for a toilet and straight through the oldish village and across the first flowing river bridge and Morocco guys on donkeys were offering transport across the second flowing river without a bridge I had no time so quickly walked approximately 150m to where the ancient Village came all the way down from its Fort like top of the small mountain walls and had a photo shoot. Donkey ride upto the Fort closed walled village on top was 100 Dirham so as I didn't need it I did not even attempt a haggle. Real good fun and a pity I did not have the time as if our driver had not stopped so many times getting here I would have had plenty of time to go up the winding ancient paths to the Fort. Not to worry, made it back near our Minibus and had a cheese baguette and a tea at a cafe along with two packets of crisps as a full belly filler. The three Spanish chics came back at 1300hrs then the Belgian couple, Bert and Sophie who were covered in sweat but so elated as had made it right to the top by foot even crossing the knee deep river, they showed us all their great photos from the Fort looking down, wow oh wow, they were a dream. Back in the Minibus and we were away going back the way we came and even having done nothing all day I dozed off waking up to signpost showing Ouarzazate 20klms so slowly but slowly we are nearly there. Reached Ouarzazate at 1340hrs and driving into it through the main highway the street lanterns were a lovely spectacle to reach one's heart before we had even got into the lovely red building town itself. Then the vividly coloured brick pavements were such a work of art and who ever thought of it the striking roundabout features deserves a medal for forward thinking to endear this town before we even get into it. Drove through a very basic town centre and parked up in the Kasbah parking area and out we all got, it was 1400hrs. The driver said we all had to be back at 1530hrs so the Spanish girls went into a nearby restaurant, I went straight over and into the Kasbah paying a 36 Dirham entrance fee and explored all areas we were allowed access too seeing its old timber tree branches as ceiling lintels was really good. Out from there and a walk into the public area of the Kasbah I turned back as it was just full of hoods and numerous hookers but I felt unsafe and shouted hello, hello my friends waving my arms and turned back saying to myself I was so lucky I never strayed down one of the narrow side Souks as I know I wouldn't have come out in one piece. I seen the three Spanish chics as I was leaving and warned them not to go down any alley or souks as full of hoods, they said thank you and went into the Kasbah. I turned left going downhill around the rear of the high Kasbah taking a few photos of this bygone 18th Century City and I had plenty of time so I waved down a Petit taxi and agreed a 50 Dirham fare for a taxi ride around the centre of Ouarzazate, jumped in the front seat and we were away. It was an interesting ride but to me a very drab city centre and he as I asked drove upto and passed the Raf Raf Hostel where I was going to stay but cancelled my request for an £8 ensuite single room. There were lots of fine buildings and hotels in and around the town centre but that's life, same same, next time!. He dropped me off at the Kasbah, I paid him the agreed 50 Dirham and as he tried for more I said my thanks jumped out and away, it was only 1505hrs. Seen the museum/cinema and went in paying my 20 Dirham fee as it's no good saying I wish when I am away as this is where they shot scenes from Lawrence of Arabia, Alexander the great, Abraham, and Gladiator so in I went. Walked through the Roman times Senate area then the Geole (Jail), then the Salle du trone (Throne area), Salle des Prieres (Prayer Ward), Salle de L'Hopital, (Hospital Ward) and finally The Woman of Pharanon room. What a great feeling as I left this area the caretaker smiled at me saying you want to see the films room and I said yes and he took me to a very large room, opened the door and all the old cine cameras and film making sets were still all left as when they finished the last film, what great history. I gave him 10 Dirham and was away making it back to our Minibus just as everyone else came back, it was 1535hrs as we all said are smiling hellos and in we all got and two minutes later we were away going through the city centre and out of Ouarzazate, what a great day. The driver pulled up at an elaborate walled village with Phorth at its huge wooden gates telling us this is where they shot the film The Phorth so we all got out and took our posing photos the Spanish girls wanting me in theirs so being a shy chap I was happy to pose doing my usual thumbs up for their photo. Back in the Minibus again and we were away as it was now a full straight run all the 188klms back to Marrakesh. The girls invited me out tonight for dinner in the Square and sightseeing with them tomorrow so I told them I would see them tonight but tomorrow I am catching a bus to Agadir, same

same we shall see. Going well when one of the girls wanted to be sick so we stopped on the outskirts of Alguim and she had a little spew and stretched her legs then back on board with 134klms to go, still a long way and it was coldish already it was only 1700hrs. I could not believe the drops down the mountainside as looking down you could see 2-3 hairpin bends 100-1000's metres below where we still had to go down, it was unbelievable but our driver was doing well. Kept going then at 1800hrs he pulled into a roadside restaurant with toilet and everyone glad to get off as I was. In I went, had a piss then bought a tea and a packet of chocolate biscuits trying to entice Patricia to have one but no the sexy chic was watching her curvy figure and only having a tea, next minute all in the Minibus again and we were away in the pitch black night, it was 1825hrs. It was a long drive but eventually we made it and the driver pulled in at the end of the pedestrian way where I got off wishing all my Moroccan friends as I called them a sad/happy goodbye and off I got thinking they were following me but no they stayed on telling the driver he is to take them to their hotel so thumbs up I wished them all Goodbye and I was away cutting into and across the square and into my hotel it was 2020hrs. Had a quick wash and shave then plenty of deodorant on and I was out and up past the completely full square and found a restaurant to have and enjoy a chicken sandwich and chips with a tea, really nice. Sat there for a while, paid my 32 Dirham charge and away and into an Internet shop for a 15 minute one e-mail and then out down to the square looking for Patricia and the girls who said they would be out having their din, din. Looked everywhere but no sign of them in their bright orange T-shirts and checking my watch, it was 2245hrs, maybe I had left it too late. It had been a great fun and wonderful day so back to my Hostel room, stripped off and into bed and asleep dreaming Patricia was beside me giving my ole legs a Sponola massage.

Date: Wed, 30 Dec 2009
Subject: Ouarzazate City, Morocco

Hi All
Paid 450 Dirham and jumped a minibus 0730hrs this morning with 3 sponola chicos for a 188klms ride over the Atlas Mountains which where snow capped peaks and it was freezing and one mistake and we where down 1000m along the sometimes no safety barrier mountain road, never been on such a road ever on all my travels. Great history in Ouarzazate as that's where they filmed Lawrence of Arabia and other famous films but its famous old city is still intact with the famous Kasbah still intact but the area around it was real big time dodgy as full of real hoods and full veiled hookers even I felt out of place? Got back 2000hrs and out in full of life and so friendly Marrakesh and its people. Heading for Agadir down the coast manyanna.
al de bes
Jack

Day 5, Thursday, 31-12-09, Marrakesh – Agadir; Morocco

Up at 0700hrs as alarm went off, face splash, long cargo, pocket T-shirt, pullover, socks and Thai sandals on and nearly ready. Had a soft bap roll and two slugs of Coke, cleaned teeth, final pack of shoulderbag, neckpouch on checking Passport in place and out I went locking door behind me and downstairs to reception. No one there so left key on desk telling 3 backpackers waiting for a room if the guy comes back tell him I had left my key, they smiled with the girl saying French, French, me smiling saying no, no Ingleterra, Ingleterra and out the front door I went. Walked up the Souk and Petit taxi driver seen me and came over taking my bag putting it in the back seat with me telling him bus station, him saying yes, in I got and we were away. He drove a long way past the brightly Ceremonial dressed guards at the Royal Palace and I said, shouted at him bus station, bus station and he mumbled something in French and turned around and drove me to a very large kiosk and said ok, out I got and gave him 10 Dirham and I was away into the kiosk. I said to the guy Agadir, he said this is train station, bus station is 50 m up the road all in French so cursing the Moroccan taxi driver out I went in the now raining day and up to the Supratour bus station. The ticket office was not open until 0800hrs so I stood outside its door, it was now 0745hrs. Quite a crowd lined up and it was good fun chatting to other travellers then the doors opened and in I went. Girl said where, I showed her Agadir on my photocopy Lonely Planet, she said today, I said yes. She looked it up on her computer screen and said 95 Dirham so I gave her 100 Dirham and got 5 Dirham change with my ticket and direct bus was at 0900hrs so no planning Jack had not done to bad. Went into the Cafe kiosk and had 2 croissants and a hot tea, 16 Dirham then out to wait beside the Agadir bus talking to a young girl from Malta and a young guy from Chile all travelling which talking to other travellers is always a laugh. I had registered my roller shoulderbag and got my stick on ticket at no cost so as guy opened bus luggage boot I gave him my shoulderbag, he checked the register stick on ticket and put it in the boot. I was elated as I climbed onto the bus, showed my ticket to the driver who signed me off and on I got taking my seat No36 just behind the Maltese girl at No32 so nearly there. Bus quickly filled up then at 0900hrs spot-on we drove out of the bus station and slowly made our way out of Marrakesh and I knew and could feel this was the real true start of my North Africa travels, oh la, la, I was one bigtime happy travelling man. I had some croissants in my China beachbag so took them out and enjoyed my 0915hrs bus breakie just glancing out the window as we passed through little villages with lots of planted green vegetable fields all around them. Very surprised I didn't doze off as just watched the sky turning blue and the hot sun coming out so that was a bonus. It was a very flat farmers fields landscape all each side of the road then we pulled into the complex Kasbah Chichaoua for a toilet, tea, eats stop, it was 1015hrs. Off I got and into one of the cafes and had a pot of tea with a large bap buttered with cheese and an egg omelette, really tasty and filling as I could only manage half of it, stuck the other half in my China beachbag for afters and back on the bus. Took a seat beside Sharon the beauty queen Malta Chico going down to Inezgane to be with her mates for a few days. Next minute at 1045hrs the driver pumped his horn and sort of checked that everyone was on, backed out and we were away, oh la la. It was really beautiful scenery with first of all the Sahara 20m high sand dunes then medium-sized rocky cliffs all each side of the road as me and Sharon had a good chat about our plans for ourselves and the world, great company. Next the cliffs got really high then it all went flat again with farmers green fields and I sort of nodded off. Woke up and the road was now a three lane highway with a new two lane highway being built alongside it and the Atlas mountains were behind us as we drove closer and closer to Agadir and then we went across a series of roundabouts and at the 5th one we turned left and into the way outside town bus station, stopped and we all got off. Sharon asked was this her stop as well, the driver said no, get back on saying Inezgane is the next one so a hug and cheek peck and my lovely Maltese Chico was back on the bus me sad to see her go. I got my roller shoulderbag out of the bus boot and into and out the other side of the bus waiting/ticket/cafe building, to the taxi rank. The drivers wanted 45-50 Dirham so I walked away and just then a German couple said to me are you going into the centre. I said yes showing them my reservation for the La Petite Suede Hotel, Ave Hassam, Agadir and they said let's take a Petit taxi together so I said ok as one drew up, they chatted to the driver as I put my shoulderbag in the boot and got in the front, they in the back and we were away. Got not very far to an Ibis Hotel, 250 Dirham a night and driver stopped. I gave them 20 Dirham for my agreed taxi fee and they started haggling with the driver who after 5 mins turned the engine off as it was getting stupid and nasty. They gave me back my 20 Dirham and agreed some sort of fee with the driver as they only wanted first of all to give him 5-10 Dirham. Out they got doors slamming and driver revved up and we were away to my hotel where I gave him my 20 Dirham, got my shoulderbag from the boot and he was away still in a bad mood cursing the Germans!. Into the hotel I went and showed the guy my booking and paid 300 Dirham for two nights, got my receipt and upto my Room 62 a double bed, shower and washhand basin but no WC, it was outside my room. Not to worry, dumped kit in room, pullover off and checking I had credit card and Agadir photocopy map plus my upto date handwritten story of my travels in an envelope ready to post to Sandralita who types my poor handwriting notes, a pure genius if there was one as I will never know how this lovely girl can read my handwriting. Previous Post Office building was blocked up so asking directions 10 times and getting lost 9 times I had a good sight seeing walk around town eventually finding it and in I went. Guy in front of me in the queue said how are you doing Jack and I was totally flabbergasted as I did not immediately recognise him. He said he used to work with me in Hammersmith and Fulham in the 1990s so as he delivered and put stamps on his letters we shook hands and he was away, what an unreal coincidence. I gave my letter to the lady who weighed it and said 19 Dirham so I gave her the money and she gave me two stamps. First one I licked and stuck on came off immediately so she used a glue stick to half stick it on me saying Oh my God as I pointed out it was not stuck, she saying in her Muslim head piece and laughing, Oh my god, and sticking it correctly this time so first travel writing post on its way. Going back towards the entrance door I said to the lady 'thank you very much', everyone in the queue smiling and as I left, 'bye, bye' the whole Post Office curling up but I was gone. I had a slow walk around town with its hundreds of shops then into the Marche Central Mall just having a lookee at all its many different clothing, antiques, food and incense shops. Out the other end I seen the Le Valle Des Oiseaux (Birds Valley) so in I went and just followed the path seeing the sort of one legged geese then the many different coloured penguins. It was fun as many families were out with their children and the comments about the birds and the amazement on the little kids faces was worth a million dollars. Kept slowly walking and came to the parrots all colours cages then a kangaroo, wallaby enclosed park then a full herd of deer in a large field, wow oh wow, it was all free. Next a herd of llama and finally a field full of the most vividly coloured sort of big turkey birds. It was a just amazing and happy walk and I came out on the sort of edge of the full of restaurants walking area along the seafront, man oh man. The sandy beach was full of sunbeds and I was tempted but will wait until manyanna as straight into a good ole Macdonald's for a beef burger, fries and a Coke, 40 Dirham, lubbly dubbly as I sat outside in the sun. Had enjoyed today's walk so finished my 1630hrs din, din and a slow walk in the lovely sun back towards my hotel passing a beautiful facade Mosque not far from my hotel, Oh God no I was thinking, we shall see. Passing a cash point I drew out 1000 Dirham then in and done some Internet and finally that was me, back to my Hotel and upto my room. Stripped off and had a shave, shower then set the alarm and had a little one hour snooze, woke up, face splash, cleaned teeth, kit on and out, it was 2100hrs, oh la, la, loud music I could hear already from the centre of town. Took the road from my hotel towards the centre of town but loud music and drums was coming from the beach area so I followed the ever increasing crowds going down the beach. Got there and it was one huge heavy mass of all ages, all kinds of dress be it traditional veil or miniskirts, it was a sight to see with all the brick and tented cafes and restaurants along the beach and the promenade blasting out every conceivable type of happy music, some drums only. Still following the crowd it looked like they were going towards the harbour docks lit up area with the mountain slope behind it a mass of lights and a lit up inscription! in French or Moroccan wishing everyone a Happy New Year but that was me. I picked a cheapie restaurant and sat down ordering a coffee and a chocolate scone and just sat back enjoying the happy crowd vibes everyone so full of smiling and laughing life it was a real pleasure to be on Moroccan African soil to celebrate the New Year 2010. Fireworks were starting up as I ordered and paid for a Coke and out I went then in one huge crescendo all the bands and drums and fireworks overhead with the cheery and happy full of life Moroccan people in the full moon I was hugged, I had my hands shook and everyone laughing into the full moon sky with a final boom and bang we all celebrated our 2400hrs New Year, what a grand joyful feeling me a little sad thinking of my happy curvy Kelly Rose. The music never stopping as I was dancing with three Moroccan girls but knees starting to go I gave up after only about 30 minutes, said my smiling thanks and away. Slowly made it back to my hotel the whole area full of blasting out loud music with 1000s of happy people celebrating New Year, what a truly marvellous sight. Upto room, stripped off and into bed I went and asleep a very Happy and fulfilled Moroccan 2010 New Year man, yeah man yeah.

Date: Thu, 31 Dec 2009
Subject: Rm62 La Petite Suede Hotel, Ave Hassan, Agadir, Morocco

Hi All

Jumped a bus, 90 Dirham, 0900hr from Marrakesh and 4hrs later jumped off in Agadir down on the Atlantic Coast facing the Canary Islands and got above 7nicker a night, lovely place so will stay 2 nights? Just had a walk in vibrant town centre and the Birds Valley with all its vivid coloured all types of birds and wild animals. Now treating myself to a MacDonald's, wow, someone has got to treat me? then back to hotel for a shave, shower and out on de town for New Years night, its looking good. Wishing you All wherever you are in the wide, wide world A Very Happy and Great New Year.
al de bes
Jack

Day 6, Friday, 01-01-10, Agadir, Morocco

Great sleep and woke up at 0530hrs and no en-suite wc so had a piss in the wash hand basin, turned the water taps on for a second then back to bed for a nice relaxing snooze the sole of my feet giving me grief as I think going from heeled shoes to flat Thai sandals it has hurt the arch!. Not to worry, up at 0800hrs, long cargo and pocket T-shirt on and out for a lovely dobhi drop, wow oh wow, that's cleaned the system, cleaned my ass and back to room. Had a nice face splash, heeled Thai sandals on and upto the roof cafe area saying Good morning to 2 pairs of travellers and sat down with brilliant views from the external roof seating area. Cafe girl asked me what I wanted in French so I just nodded yes, she smiled coming back 5mins later with a Moroccan pot of tea, six sliced portions of a crusty baguette with one saucer each of jam, butter and a glass of orange, Yum Yum, no Ingleterre breakie today. Buttered and jammed my crusty slices, poured my tea, drank my orange juice and sat back now relaxed and ate my full Moroccan continental breakie, wow, belly full, me happy. Had a read of LP about sightseeing plans for today and the sun was now stifling hot, oh la, la. Back to room, cleaned teeth and first things first I will walk up to the bus station and buy a ticket to Essaouira for tomorrow as well as checking bus times, today looking good, it was 0900hrs. Had my small beach towel with swimming trunks, Mars bar, Kit Kat in China beachbag and out I went into the lovely hot sun. Petit taxi was just dropping someone off so as he said taxi to me I asked him how much to CDM bus station as now it's a must sure thing for me to do as these taxi drivers are Class A con men, he said 30 Dirham, I said no, he said 20 Dirham, I said 20 Dirham, yes, he nodded and in I got and we were away, I was real glad I didn't try to walk it as it was a big-time far. Got there, paid him 20 Dirham, he was away and in I went to the Gare Routiere Voyageurs, Agadir, (CDM) Bus station and downstairs following the sign for Dochitts but first of all went down another floor to the 2 Dirham charge toilets and had a piss. Backup and there was at least 20 bus companies with their offices here and approximately 4-5 I could see went to Essaouira all at different well posted times on notice boards. Supratours had a bus at 0900hrs taking 3hrs so up to their office telling the young fellow single to Essaouira 0900hrs manyanna. He checked and said 65 Dirham so gave him a 100 Dirham note and he gave me my ticket with seat number and change so that was me all signed, sealed and delivered. Stuck ticket in my driving licence wallet and back out onto Ave des Forces Royales Rd thinking will I get a Petit taxi or walk it. Walked it going downhill I now did with a big grin on my face and feeling so elated as now getting a travelling rhythm going. Walked on down Forces Road and at Rue De Mars went into the enormous huge open-air merchandise/food stalls market behind an elaborate Fort wall and had a nosey but no stops lookie and out at the end of the fruit market stalls. Carried on down Forces Road then just took a right past hundreds of Petit cars parked up in a car park then passed Cafe La Fontaine in a lovely full of cafes pedestrian walkway along Boulevard Hassan II, it was 1045hrs so doing well. Next thing I knew where I was as I came to the huge Place De L'Esperance, Hope Square with only 4-5 kids playing football on it, last night it was chock-a-block. Crossed the Road and walked down the side of Birds Alley and came out at Boulevard du 20 Aout and spot-on as that's where I wanted to be as going to do a motor trolley tour around Agadir. Paid my 18 Dirham and guys said it will be another 20-25mins so feeling a bit peckish in I went to the Welcome Café. Sat down facing the lovely blue sky and sea and ordered omelette, chips and a tea and it didn't take long and as soon as it came I sat back enjoying my lovely cooked 1145hrs din, din. Just barely finished it trolley train came along and everyone waiting got on and I took a seat beside two French girls and with a train toot, toot we were away on our sightseeing journey all around Agadir. It was a long sightsee and the full-size of Agadir was unbelievable with its many touristy areas all I would never have seen if I hadn't taken the train tram trolley. Finished our great tour we were now back at our starting/finishing point and shaking hands with the two full of life French girls we all went our own way. I had been keeping a close eye out but had not seen the places I wanted to see close up so as a Petit taxi stopped I showed the driver on my LP photocopied map the Protestant Church, St Anne's Catholic church and the Jewish Synagogue Beth-El. He said yes he knows and fare would be 120 Dirham so I said okay and got in the front seat and we were away. First of all he took me to the Englaise Protestant church with its notice on the wall but it was locked and it was more of a Square dwelling than a traditional church but had seen it. Next we went to and stopped outside the Jewish Synagogue with 24-hour police guard at it but it also was just a small Square dwelling type with nothing to say it was a Synagogue. Then the final stop as I got out this time was St Anne's Catholic Church and it also was a small Square dwelling but it had a front square with lots of notices on it and if one wanted one could make a donation and light a candle to the Lord to help one's life and the poor of the world so I donated 10 Dirham and lit my proddie candle saying a little prayer for the poor of the world. Out I went back into my Petit taxi and we were away passing the big signs "English Pub" with a large sign beside it; "Standup for England", good on ya cobbers I thought thinking I will come here tonight. As we drove back I asked the driver what the large sign on the side of the mountain hill overlooking Agadir said and was that a Fort above it on the brow of the mountain hill. He said the sign says; "Allah is good" and the Fort and building on the top of the mountain hill were the first Kasbah town of Agadir pointing at a signpost 'Agadir Oufella 1st'. So there, really true good history from a taxi driver not many tourists would find out about as we drove on up the mountain him pointing out at each side of the road there was Islamic, Catholic and Protestant Cemeteries some stretching for miles, just amazing. He then drove into a full walled Cemetery telling me this is the English/European cemetery, wow oh wow. We got out but only for a five-mins walk around it as lots of French names but if I had more time I am sure I could have found true blue English, Irish, Scottish, Welsh history as there was a burial book in an alcove, fantastic true history. Into the car and we were away and as he dropped me off I gave him another 20 Dirham, shook his hand and he was away. So time for deserts as I crossed the road and down onto the beach promenade walkway. Went into a toilet, stripped off and put my swimming briefs on then everything and all my clothes in my China beachbag I was straight into and paddling along the lovely coldish sea me thinking at last. Just took my time, it was only 1530hrs and walked/paddled along the beach seawater edge towards the dock area then turned back and paddled all the way back to facing McDonald's then beachbag out of reach of the sea I made it through two heavy breakers and done a 5mins breaststroke then quickly back out as the current was very powerful and no lifeguards anywhere but had done my first sea swim. Grabbed beachbag and only another five mins beach walk and that was me, swimming trunks off, long cargo and pocket T-shirt on and up to Mackie's for a cheeseburger and fries with a coffee, 45 Dirham din din, it was 1640hrs, what a great day. Took my time and walked not far back to my Petite Suede Hotel, got my key and upto my bed made, room cleaned room and had a nice shave and shower, set alarm and plonked myself naked on my lovely soft bed and straight to sleep for a nice one hour siesta, just the job. Up as alarm went off at 1830hrs and one thing I do notice since I put on my heeled Thai sandals is that my left lower leg is now giving me grief so I can't win!. Not to worry I will survive, cleaned teeth then shiver me timbers had a lovely dobhi drop, cleaned ass and out cutting down the lane beside Birds Alley then left and into the English pub which was a lovely pub full of joke murals and lovely soft seats. Had a sprite, 20 Dirham so not cheap but great friendly service and atmosphere. Got a big armchair seat at the pavement and just watched the Agadir world go by for an hour then up, said my thanks and along the road and down to the beach full of life and live music promenade just enjoying my night time stroll. Walked far enough so turned back and had a Coke sitting outside McDonald's listening to the night-time music from all the surrounding restaurants and clubs then that was me, it was 2215hrs. Slow relaxing walk and back into Hotel, got my key and upto room, final pack of nearly everything, stripped off and into bed thinking where are the Moroccan Desert ladies of the night and sleep dreaming sex in a Desert sand dune!.

How "Not" to Travel North Africa, Middle East, Israel & Malta and "Still Enjoy Yourself"

Day 7, Saturday, 02-01-10, Agadir - Essaouira; Morocco

Loud car door shutting and shouting woke me up at 0530hrs then as it went quiet the Moslem chanters from one loudspeaker started then a little doze and up for good at 0650hrs as alarm went off. Had a milky dobhi drop to clear the pipe works, cleaned my ass and back to room, face splash, long cargo, socks and pullover on, neckpouch on checking Passport, final pack of shoulderbag and out upto roof terrace for early breakie I hope as got to be at CTM bus station 0830hrs, we shall see!. No movement from anywhere in Hotel, it was 0735hrs so called it a day and back down to room, cleaned teeth, final check and downstairs I went, said my thanks at reception, handed key over and I was away with the full handle up pulling my Trolley roller red shoulderbag along the nearly no cars streets until a Petit taxi driver seen me and pulled in. I said CTM bus station, how much, he said 20 Dirham so shoulderbag in the boot, me in the front, we were away and it was a long way but as we got there he pulled in, out I got getting my shoulderbag from the boot, gave him his 20 Dirham and he was away. Went into and down to the ground floor and got a sticker for my shoulderbag, guy said 5 Dirham so thinking it was a con I gave it to him anyway and he stuck it on my bag and my ticket. Up I went to the cafe area, no great choices so had 2 croissants and a tea, 16 Dirham and enjoyed my great 0810hrs breakie no Europeans to be seen anywhere. Buses were coming and going from the bus stops so still early I went down to the bus stop, put my shoulderbag beside a seat and had a circle walk around the bus stop area just keeping an eye on my watch. Dead on 0855hrs an empty bus drove in with the sign Agadir-Safi and about 15-18 of us waiting passengers lined up, guy took our luggage and put it in the bus boot and on we got. Only a 2mins wait then with no horn pumping we were away out of Agadir me saying, see you Agadir, I liked you and wow oh wow we took the mountain road directly up along the Kasbah. What a dream route as looking down into the docks and Harbour and looking up not far was the walled Fort of the Kasbah then over the Kasbah mountain hills we went now following the very, very great scenery coastal road. What a lovely dreamy start to my day as we drove along it seeing all the surfers out in the high waves as for miles and miles it was just a 50-100m wide beautiful sandy beaches with sometimes little villages with parking for campervans, that's the way to do it. Seen a signpost for Essaouira 158km, it was 0930hrs and slowly, slowly I dozed off. Woke up to see a line of camels on our left crossing a large area of desert sand dunes, it was 1015hrs as everywhere people were riding horses or donkeys. Next we went up and over a huge mountain with the most fantastic views of real life Morocco as now we were going through inland fertile green valleys and seen a signpost showing 107km. Had to laugh as we passed two herds of goats that were climbing bushy trees up to and along their branches eating the leaves or fruit from them, truly amazing sight. Passed a large inland lake on our right signpost 85km it was 1040hrs so no stops and doing well. Then at 1052hrs at a police roadside checkpoint we were pulled over and the driver had to show his licence and bus mileage was checked with the armed police officers walking through the bus, we were just outside the town of Oued Tamanar. Drove not far to the other side of the town and pulled into the cafe-restaurant Aragana where I had a tea, 8

Dirham and some of my own chocolate cookies having a chat with two Holland ladies called Jessica and Monica just going to Essaouira for a day or two as had been trekking in the mountains for seven days. Their LP book was 10 years old and they asked me for my photocopy to check for accommodation as they did not have any booked and just wanted to check so I lent them my copy as we got back on the bus and away, it was 1120hrs. Only 63km to go as up and over a high covered in cloud and mist Mountain range we went and kept going downhill on the other side me hoping it will start to get warm, it was 1150hrs, so much for 3hrs. Time now 1217hrs and we are back alongside the sea on a coastline road only 8km to go thank God as my ass plus me was getting fed up. Into the centre of Essaouira at 1225hrs seeing the surfers along its full-length beach and can't wait to get off this bus. The bus stopped at the Tour's office and wheelbarrow guy said 20 Dirham to take you to hotel, I said ok, Hotel Samara and put my shoulderbag in his barrow as the two Holland girls were going with another guy who also offered me a hotel but it was outside the Medina walls so we parted saying our Good luck's and Goodbyes. Not a long but not a short walk we finally got to Hotel Samara and I gave him our agreed 20 Dirham, got my shoulderbag and he was away. Into hotel but they had no rooms so out, turned right, tried 2 hotels but they wanted daft prices then into Dar Alouane (House of Colours) Hotel, www.daralouane.com and the lady showed me a single room, not en-suite for 130 Dirham so took it as couldn't be bothered to look anywhere else today. Dumped kit in room and out turning left then right straight up and onto the original Fort battlements full of 17-18th Century cannons, what a truly magnificent sight and had my photo taken a few times as I walked along its full facing the sea thick battlement wall length. Back down and peckish so into a restaurant, sat down and ordered beef burger, chips and a tea which is becoming my favourite meal and sat back watching the never ending touristy world walk by enjoying my lovely cooked lunchtime meal with mint tea. Finished, paid my 35 Dirham meal charge and across the big main Square and into the harbour area with all its small and big timber fishing boats tied up and the fishermen it looks like waiting to go out!. Had a nice relaxing walk around its full-length and had my photo taken outside the restaurant Du Port Chez-Sam, La Taverne, us posers like our thumbs up!. A slow walk taking another path leading me outside the Medina Fort walls and I seen a guy cutting a snake in pieces and feeding it to 5-6 cats, not a pretty sight but that's true life in Morocco. I was now going along the covered in tree debris main beach, must have been a storm recently and seen a Spire Cross thinking it must be a real Church so crossed the road and walked up to and inside it. It was called the Eglise Notre Dame De L' Assumption and had Mass times on a notice board so it was obviously a Catholic church but it was a lovely little Christian Oasis so stood facing the altar and said a little prayer for the poor and homeless of the world wishing the Lord will help them in their every day search for true life. Left taking another direction as I like to explore and got to where the Supratour Bus had dropped me off and went into their office booking a ticket to Safi for the day after manyanna, paid my 65 Dirham, got my ticket and out back through an Arch into the famous Souks again just getting lost but sort of had an idea which way led me back to near my hotel. It was real fun walking the Souks as these narrow then sometimes wide alleys had every conceivable sort of shop under the sun I even found a Square with every stall selling second-hand clothes, good fun. In my walk I was thinking about my non-ensuite room so passing Hotel Tafraout, 7 Rue Marrakesh, 024466276, www.hoteltafraout.com in I went enquiring any rooms with ensuite toilet and shower for tomorrow, the girl said yes, 150 Dirham so thinking that was a good deal I asked for and got a card saying I hope to see you manyanna and out not far to my hotel, it was 1800hrs. I spoke to the manager just explaining I need an ensuite and said I would only be staying tonight, could I have a refund for tomorrow, she said yes asking the girl receptionist to get some change and the girl left the hotel. Next thing the guy who had pointed out the hotel to me came in smelling of drink telling me I should not have booked if I had intended to leave. I told him it was my business what I do and go away or I would give him an Arthur St one which he did shouting abuse from the door. The lady said sorry and gave me 100 Dirham back and I went upto my room then into the shower room and had a wash and shave and ready to go out, it was 2000hrs. Out I went and turned right and followed the Souk along the Fortress high battlement not well lit walls until I came out on the main Square with a few restaurants open but nowhere had any good street lights. Just carried on and along the promenade no light but the beach had well lit areas with sometimes large crowds of young ones milling about enjoying themselves. Went into a well lit up Souk with lots of stall shops still open just more or less having a walk then into an Internet shop for my usual 15min e-mail also checking accommodation for Safi as thinking I will go there manyanna I've seen all I wanted in Essaouira. Printed off 2 maps of Safi, paid my 12 Dirham bill and away now I must admit completely lost. Had a sausage roll and a tea, 25 Dirham sitting in the cafe then out and asked a guy in a shop does he know where Dar Alouane Hotel is showing him my hotel card and he said yes, follow me as he grabbed his bike and we walked along a fairly lit up Souk. Got to a smaller unlit Souk and he said go up there to its end then turn left so off I went into a no shop partially lit up slum alley Souk and hands out of pocket swinging shoulders like an Arthur St hood I walked quickly along the Souk and turned left into a nearly unlit one thinking I am in serious trouble as the corner hoods were getting more and more in groups until turning a corner I seen two café's come Hotels that I knew. Seen my Hotel front door, quickly opened it and in slamming it shut behind me and laughing out loud thinking I was real lucky that time. Up to my single bedroom, stripped off, had a nice slug of orange juice and that was me in bed and asleep dreaming their must be Moroccan sex somewhere.

Date: Sat, 2 Jan 2010
Subject: Dar Alouane Hotel,66 Rue Touahen, Essaouira, Morocco

Hi All

Jumped a bus, 65 Dirham this morning, 0900hrs and 3hrs! later going along the sandy beach coast then up and over the mountains which was great scenery I jumped off at Essaouira and after 3 tries for a cheapie charlie hotel bed I took above (www.daralouane.com), 130 Dirham non en-suite. Essaouira is a lovely beach medieval Fort town with a never ending path of souks, I am still lost. Staying 2 days then will jump a bus upto Safi, dats de plan?
al de bes
Jack

How "Not" to Travel North Africa, Middle East, Israel & Malta and "Still Enjoy Yourself"

Day 8, Sunday, 03-01-10, Essaouira – Safi; Morocco

Had a good sleep even on my concrete pillow not even up once for a piss and woke up for good at 0745hrs as other travellers were talking and going into the toilet. Up, face splash, long cargo, pullover on and out just checking if I had a free breakie or had to pay or find a place, it was 0815hrs. Went down a flight of stairs and the lady owner from last night speaking in French said tea, baguette, jam and butter breakie will be served to me on the roof terrace, so that was good news. Up I went out to the sunlight of one of the highest roof terraces in the area with fantastic views into the town and along the coast, great start to my day. Breakie came and I cut the hot baguette into slices, fully buttered and jammed them, poured my Rosy Lee and that was me, enjoyed my crusty baguette tea breakie for 20mins then took the tray down to the first floor, back upto my room then next door to toilet, washhand basin, had a nice dobhi drop, cleaned my ass, cleaned my teeth and final pack of shoulderbag and out down to reception saying I want to leave my bag here and go for a walk. The girl put it in a lockable room and I was out and away. Turned right this time a different direction from yesterday and last night and I must admit it was a great sightseeing walk and experience. Passing through a shoe Souk I bought a pair of rubber heeled shoes for 20 Dirham, put them on putting my Thai sandals in my China beachbag and the relief I felt as my western feet heels had now real heels to walk on, my both feet felt over the moon and new again, oh la la. Had a coffee, 10 Dirham and who did I bumped into only the two Holland full of life ladies and we had a laughing chat for 10mins. Shaking hands and hugs I was sad to leave them but that's life on the Travellers road then passing near the Supratour bus station I went in and changed my ticket from manyanna to today as had seen all of Essaouira that was there to see and didn't want to waste another full morning manyanna so today's travels all signed sealed and nearly delivered. Slow walk back to hotel, got my roller shoulderbag, said my Goodbyes to the lady and the girl and just strolled all the way back along the harbour walls to the Supratour bus station. Got a 5 Dirham luggage registration sticker, stuck it on shoulderbag and that was me all set to go to Safi, it was 1210hrs, the bus to Safi was at 1230hrs so took a seat in the shaded reception area as the sun was big-time hot. The bus drew in at 1220hrs and quite a crowd got off then about eight of us, me the only Westerner, got on and after driver done a head count we were away. It was a lovely four lane highway then we turned left at signpost 358km to Casablanca, it was 1305hrs. Part of my plan is to see Safi and also to cut my journey time to Casablanca in half. Girl in Supratour office this morning said in answer to my question Supratours have no buses from Safi to Casablanca but other bus companies have so no problem for bus to Casablanca manyanna. Fell asleep and woke up at 1410hrs passing through flat no hills green fields and mint leaf trees everywhere so only 20-30mins to go. Turned left off the main road at a bus station village with a sign stating Safi, 25 km, it was 1415hrs so it's looking good. Just hope I can get cheapie accommodation as Safi is not mentioned in my LP Africa, we shall see. The bus stopped at Supratours office not far from the main bus station and out we all got, no touts or barrow pullers anywhere. I waved at a taxi on the other side of the road and he turned and came over to a stop, I showed him a hand written list of hotels I had and he said Hotel Farah in French and I said ok but how much, he said 10 Dirham so in I got and we where away. It was quite far but very upmarket so I showed him Hotel Majestic, Zenka Binsou, Safi, Tel: 024464011 and he said Medina, I said yes and he drove downhill to it, parked up, got my shoulderbag out from the back seat and I gave him 10 Dirham and he was away. Carried my shoulderbag up one flight of stairs to reception and old guy speaking perfect English said only double rooms left, I said ok, how much, he said 120 Dirham so I said ok giving him my Passport. He done all the paperwork and took me up another flight of stairs saying its an inside quiet room and showed me room 218 with double bed and a washhand basin so I said yes and gave him the 120 Dirham, he gave me key and off he went. First things first, had a piss in the washhand basin with taps running then shoes and socks off putting Thai sandals on as it was big-time hot so had a good slug of orange and out I went, it was 1505hrs. I turned right along the pavements fronting the Medina walls then right again in a main pedestrian only Souk with market stalls all along it. I walked up it seeing a sign on a small narrow Souk stating Cathedral Portuguese so went up it seeing a very old Minaret in an old Mosque then went left into a large timber door in an old stone built very large Spire tower with sign; 10 Dirham entrance fee. Went in as an old guy was giving 2 Westerners a run down in French on who and when it was built and introduced myself as Jack from Belfast and the two Westerners were from the USA driving around Morocco and one could understand French so he acted as interpreter. Where we were standing was built in 1519 by Jewish settlers and it was the Spired part of a larger hall as the Jews welcomed every one and anyone to join them in prayers. In time it became the Portuguese Cathedral and standing in it with its original large brownstone emblems fixed in the ceiling of the Spire was great Medieval history. Finished our lecture and I gave the old guy 10 Dirham, shook hands with my full of life Yankee friends and I was away them asking me was there anything up the Souk, I said yes but it gets narrow and narrower but have a look anyway so away they went. I walked on down towards the industrial harbour with lots of big container ships then a right following the unbelievable Medina Fort walls and moat which was just a work of pure medieval history as it was so big and elaborate and went under a huge Arch but the Medina Fort walls stretched for miles. Next went through a small Arch and along a narrow getting narrower Souk then low and behold I came out not far from Hotel L'Honneur which was only 50m from my hotel and 3-4 others. Needed something to eat so into a pizza cafe and had a tea and a cheese roll which came with chips and salad so enjoyed my late din din, paid my 22 Dirham charge and away. I walked across the road and under the road along the original undercarriage and up to the Chateau De Mer a very old Royal Fort. The guy at the gate said no one is allowed in as it was falling down and dangerous so I said can I just have a look through the gate. He walked with me and opened the gate and we both went into the inner compound and I could feel and sense it was a Royal building as it had great vibes. We walked around it then woosh, a full steam roar of seawater went right up 20-30m from an old Well as everywhere all under the Chateau the sea had eroded and undermined it as he pointed out old sea walls were falling down. I waited and then as the next ocean wave came out the well I got him to take a photo with me posing as usual thumbs up and out we both came and I gave him 10 Dirham and I was away very happy to have made it. Walked up the hill from the Chateau and along the edge of the 100m drop cliff which was real fun as there were large crowds out enjoying the lovely hot sun. Back into town again and it must be a market day as stalls along the pedestrian only Souk were stretching for miles. I turned back then thinking about manyanna I needed to buy a bus ticket to Casablanca so waved a Petit taxi down and agreed a 10 Dirham fare to the Gare Routiere Des Voyageurs bus station, jumped in and we were away, got there, paid him and into the bus station. Started checking all the different company buses to Casablanca then picked Transport Jadar Chekkouri bus Company as they had a bus at 0900hrs and to Casablanca from Safi takes 4hrs so lined up and when I got to the pay point I said 0900hrs to Casablanca, Guy said 80 Dirham, I said its advertised at 50 Dirham so he said ok 50, paid him, got my ticket for tomorrow and that was me a happy and fulfilled man. Back out from the bus station and hailed a taxi and he drove back down to near my hotel as I wanted to draw some money, what a fiasco as not one of the five bank ATM's were paying out any money to anyone not just me. Lucky I had still 400 Dirham on me so it will have to see me through to Casablanca where the ATM will be filled and working I hope. Back to hotel and had a chat with the well spoken English receptionist bloke then up for a wash and shave. Tried for a dobhi drop in the squat toilet but couldn't manage it, then out for a long walk along the brightly lit pedestrian market stalls and turned back as it went on and on for miles and into an Internet cafe. After that I made it down to a cafe near my hotel called the Restaurant de Safi in Rue La Poste and enjoyed a big bowl of soup and chips all for 8 Dirham, Safi is so cheap. I finished my late night 2135hrs din din and into its western toilet for a quick full blast dobhi drop, cleaned ass with my toilet paper and a slow relaxed good vibes walk back to my hotel and upto room. Set alarm for 0645hrs, stripped off and into bed dreaming Casablanca's hookers look out the hunk is coming and asleep thinking I have been a good boy too long.

Email Sent: Sun, 3 Jan 2010
Subject: Hotel Majestic, Safi, Morocco: Tel024464011

Hi All
Jumped a bus 1230hrs today and 2hrs later jumped off in Safi on up the Atlantic coast as heading for Casablanca manyanna on the 0900hrs bus which takes 4hrs from Safi. Booked into the above, 120 Dirham non ensuite just on the edge of the Medina walls Had a great time in Essaouira but seen one Souk seen the lot. Safi is really interesting as into the 1509 century Jewish church for all doms then converted to a Portuguese Cathedral and its spire is still standing. Then into the Chateau De Mer which is falling down as the Atlantic sea gushes up 20m into the sky from its original fresh water wells, good fun. Nice walk along the cliffs top with the great scenery.
al de bes
Jack

Day 9, Monday, 04-01-10, Safi – Casablanca; Morocco

Woke up once for a WHB taps on piss but had a great sleep then finally up at 0650hrs as alarm went off, face splash and going to try for my first squat dobhi drop. Put shorts on, no socks, Thai sandals and pocket T-shirt and out locking door behind me to the one and only squat toilet. Shorts down, knees bent and hand against the back wall and let go with a full dobhi belly blast and didn't hit the squat hole once just splattered the walls and area around it but not to worry, good full empty belly job done. Cleaned my ass and used some paper to clean the walls and floor, filled the bucket from a tap, water cleaned the splatts then bucket flushed the squat and that was me a one empty belly man. Back to room, soaped and cleaned under arm pits, dried off, long cargo, socks and pullover on and out for breakfast but no one about to open the front door so back upto reception and seen a guy sleeping in the room next to it. Rapped the door, he woke up and I smiled making hand movements I go to eat and downstairs we went and he opened the main entrance front door and out I went into the dark street, turned right and into the second cafe full of smokers and ordered a tea and two croissants. Sat down and my order came within 2mins so gave him 10 Dirham and he gave me 2 Dirham change so sat back and enjoyed my lovely 0720hrs Safi breakie. Good fun as watching the smoker seller selling one or two cigarettes to anyone as it reminded me of my Belfast youth days when we used to buy 1 or 2 or feeling rich 5 cigarettes from John Brown's shop in Dover Street, they were de Belfast days. Finished my breakie and out up the now sunny morning and pressed the hotel entrance bell and guy opened the door and up I went to my room, cleaned teeth, final little pack, neckpouch on checking Passport in place and out downstairs giving guy my key. He let me out so went left to the traffic lights and waved a Petit taxi down, told him CTM bus station and we were away and 5mins later he dropped me off at it. Paid him 10 Dirham, grabbed my shoulderbag and into the bus station. I asked guy at Jadar Chekkouri kiosk did I need a luggage ticket, he said no, so sat down watching out for a green and white bus and seen one drive-in so up and walked over. Showed driver my ticket and he put my shoulderbag in the luggage compartment asking for 5 Dirham, I only had 10 so gave it to him and said change, he smiled saying no change so robbed of 50p. Got on bus and eventually found my No10 seat and sat down in it as people getting on were checking and taking their ticket seats, the bus was getting very packed, it was 0850hrs. Driver got on at 0855hrs and at 0900hrs a toot, toot of his horn as we backed out and then away on the road to Casablanca, wow oh wow. Going well as I nodded off then woke up as we stopped in a petrol station cafe car park and driver got out and had a tea!, it was only 0950hrs. Back on again and one by one some people got off and beggars and sellers got on, what an early waste of everyone's time not to mention it was now raining and overcast, 4hrs to Casablanca, I am going to say 5hrs plus. Really glad I took the 0900hr bus as it looks like being a long drive as seen a signpost 201km to Casablanca, its 1010hrs. Green farmers fields each side of our now two lane each way highway with local transport appearing to be donkeys. Just passed a signpost for Casablanca, 50km, its 1155hrs so now doing really well and should make it by 1300hrs unless we have a Naafi break 20mins stop, hope not. It's still slightly raining and overcast and I have no umbrella or rainproof jacket as I thought I would be in a desert country, live and learn. The bus turned off the main highway taking a narrow very busy slow road and stopping to let people off and I seen a signpost Casablanca 12km then 5km then into somewhere near the centre it was 1250hrs. I asked and showed conductor CTM bus station, he said get off at the next stop and take a Petit taxi so off I got at a taxi rank and over to the first taxi and said CTM bus station showing him it on the map, he said ok and we were away. It was quite a long way but we got there and he showed me the meter, 18 Dirham so gave him 20 Dirham and out I got on Boulevard Mohammed V fully chock-a-block with Hotels and all sorts in the centre of Casablanca. Tried one hotel, they said full, then into Hotel Mon Reve, 7 Rue Chaouia, Casablanca, Tel:0522311439 and the guy said double with shower, WC, 150 Dirham so overjoyed at last to have shower, WC and everything in my room I said ok and he gave me room key 18. Up I went 2 flights again and into a very large classy room, dumped shoulderbag and glad to have made it, checked what I was going to carry in my beachbag and out I went, it was 1400hrs. Walked up and in and around the cafe, fruit and all sorts of stalls big central markets then out and along Boulevard Mohammed just in no rush as it was a very busy town centre area then got to Place des Nations Unies having a look at the Clock Tower and Mosque Minaret in the Medina so crossed the road and in for a walkie. It was fun but it was not for a night time walk as full of hoods by the look of it but all very friendly. I poked my head into the great Mosque and away and must have walked out of the Medina as I was now walking alongside a Naval training base and seen an enormous Mosque Minaret in the distance and just kept going and reached it. It was the third biggest religious Monument in the world called The Hassan II Mosque so got up to it and it was certainly worth seeing as it towered over the area all along the beach so poked my head in three times at three different doors and it was a truly magnificent sight. Had a photo shoot outside it but young fellow let on he did not know how to use my camera so no picture with me taken. Feeling very peckish and feet a bit sore so jumped a cab back to hotel and into a cafe having 12 slices of liver, chips and tomatoes and a tea, 31 Dirham, so that was a good finish to my day it was 1800hrs as I got upto my room. Stripped off and changed all my kit, had a nice shave and shower and then out I went and up along Boulevard Mohammed, it was 1925hrs. Strolled along the boulevard in a no rush relaxed walk as Casablanca had great vibes and up to the Place des Nations Unies and done a left away from the Medina thinking later. Found a very good Internet cafe, Cyber club, www.ciga.com at 38 Rue Moultakio Abdelkader, Tel: 022475758 and done my usual 15-20mins then out and across into the well lit area of the Medina as needed a relaxing hooker massage. Didn't get very far as first one half veiled full dress Chico said come in but I smiled and kept going as their was quite a few about. Seen one petite neat figure Chico even in her long cloak dress and looking into each other eyes I knew it was true love to last a Casablanca lifetime. She smiled saying cum so over I went as she slipped her arm around me smiling I was totally now in Casablanca love as we embraced she said short time rubbing her hand everywhere exciting for me. I said yes me darling how much and where we go, she pointed up the hall saying my room and with a sexy imploring look in her love struck eyes she said 200 Dirham and so much in love myself I said ok and with a squeal of sexy delight we both arm in arm and so much in love walked up the timber creaky floor corridor and into a large double bedroom. I quickly got out her money and putting it on a dresser we kissed and exploring each other sexy bodies we where naked deep love kissing and fondling are love struck heat in Casablanca night bodies on her soft bed I was in heaven in Casablanca as we where making wild sexual exotic lust filled Casablanca sweating love the tingling sensual sensations everywhere in my hot body down into my firm rocker thighs I knew we would be together forever in Casablanca as changing positions she was biting my breasts screaming in lust me ripping her back and breasts and as are gasping sensual passions reached a crescendo of Casablanca randy sexual lust love we climaxed together biting each others necks and breasts and screaming in pleasure I was totally lost in the nighttime clouds of Casablanca ecstasy as holding each other tight and panting hard as the sexual spasms tore through each other's hot sexy scented bodies we gradually or I came back to normal lieing in are sweat scented soaked bed I knew I would never leave my true Casablanca lover as we where so much in love. She moved her arm pinching my bum saying "You good man Papa but we go" and opening my eyes she smiled as she give me a quick peck kiss and we both rolled off the bed she grabbing her money as we both got dressed. Happy as a true Casablanca lover she held my arm as we walked to the front door and one final peck kiss and a wave she went back up the corridor so feeling on top of the Casablanca world I made my smiling happy face way out of the Medina across to the Place des Nations Unies and back along the Blvd and breathing like a true happy lover I made it into my Hotel. Upto my room and stripping off I was into my bed and asleep a one happy sexy Casablanca happy man and asleep dreaming Casablanca love in the Medina all night long.

Email Sent: Mon, 4 Jan 2010
Subject: Rm 18, Hotel Mon Reve, 7 Rue Chaouia, Casablanca, Tel: 0522311439

Hi All
Safi was really good with great vibes but up early and had my evil 2 croissants coffee frenchie breakie then caught the 0900hrs, 50 Dirham bus from Safi to Casablanca and arrived Casa 1300hrs and took petit taxi to Blvd Mohammad/Central Market area and got above, a d-ensuite, oh la, la, my own inside loo and hot water for 150 Dirham. Had a walkie into and around the sleazy hooker/druggy Medina peeping into its Mosque then down to the 3rd biggest religious monument in the world the Hassan 2 Mosque, done my peep show and away as they don't like us proddie boys looking in. Its raining here and I though it was a desert country. Will stay Casa manyanna then Rabat?
al de bes
Jack

Day 10, Tuesday, 05-01-10, Casablanca; Morocco

Great sleep only up once for a real WC piss and back to my lovely bed and woke up for good at 0820hrs and up at 0830hrs feeling top of the world. Face splash and all new clean kit on, wrapped and rolled my dirty shirt, long cargo and pullover and put them in a plastic bag hoping to find a laundry cleaning shop. Went downstairs with an envelope for Sandralita, said my Good morning to the receptionist guy saying I will stay one more night, he smiled saying good. I asked him for washing laundry shop, he said turn right above the Post Office so that was a bonus. Got to the Post Office, got my queue ticket 807, seen 806 already at the counter and 2mins later it flashed 807 up on the screen. Up I went giving guy folded envelope with days 5-9 writing in it, he weighed it and said 20 Dirham so I gave him a 100 Dirham note, he gave me change and stuck stamps on it and put it in the behind the counter post box so smiling I said my thanks and out and away. Turned right and right again and seen the laundry shop, went in saying washing, young fellow said yes, laughing and said tomorrow, I said today, he said ok, 1800hrs and unrolled my filthy shirt, long cargo, pullover, underpants and socks writing out a receipt for 45 Dirham and giving me it saying ok, see you 1800hrs and out I went the day looking good. Tried 6-7 cafes and although all open no one was or had started to do any cooking but eventually I found a lovely hot little upstairs cafe, pointing at eggs saying omelette, tea, bread and potato roll and sat down, it was 0930hrs. Lovely one thin egg omelette with bread and potato roll along with a pot of tea came to my table and I was over the moon enjoying my first Casablanca breakie thinking where will I start for my walkie today as I have an overall plan but nothing rigorous. Up, paid my bill smiling and saying my thanks and back along the young no washed kids in second hand clothes sitting smoking at street corners road me thinking this was the lower Shankill Road Brown Square days 40-50 years ago I was having a laugh to myself. Back into the hotel, cleaned teeth and out again making my jolly way along Boulevard Mohammed V to the Place Des Nations 5 Road roundabout and got across it and turned left down Avenue Hassan II Road, wow oh wow I was now a Casablanca expert map reader already. Enjoying my leisurely walk I reached Place Mohammed V with its so beautiful Moroccan French architectural impressive facades all different wonderful shaped building. First one I went into was the Post Office and bought a stamp and posted my late Marrakesh postcard to my sexy curvy Kelly Rose freezing to death in snowbound Ingleterra and wishing her Love and Happiness I kissed it before putting it in the post box. Had a walk past the impressive Hotel de Ville now the Town Hall then the law courts, Palais de Justice but seen a pair of twin Spires on a high building to my right across a park which had a road up to it. Walked towards it and it was such an extraordinary shape but got to its open iron gates and asked security is this the Cathedral du Sacre-Coeur, he nodded yes and I said ok to go in, he nodded yes. In the gate I walked looking and admiring its many 6m high by 350mm wide stained glass colourful windows from the outside and in I went at the entrance Arched door. Shock oh shock as the complete interior had been gutted, not one piece of wood anywhere and the floor was a flat base exposed concrete. Got quickly over the shock and just walked up its centre admiring the many stained glass very colourful windows many with names coloured in them, really nice then back out the front side door and having a look at my photocopied map I made it to Rue de Algiers Road. Got to roundabout and took Bvd Moulay Youssef Road back past the rundown derelict sort of runners stadium with lots of runners doing its circle as I then came back onto Avenue Hassan II at De St Exuperry roundabout with a lovely facade fronted building on its right beside Rue d Agadir Road. It was still early so had plenty of time so going right and right again down the Rue Hadi Amar Riffi Road and low and behold and the Saints above I came to a Brassiere Saint George so stopped and had a St George for England tea and two chocolate rolls tea break. Seeing the clouds building up so paid my 22 Dirham and I was away after an enjoyable St George for England nice 20mins knees up rest. Kept going and the area seemed to get a little downmarket but made it through the slum and den of the long bearded Ayatollahs as they looked at me I wondered what they thought of de Arthur Street shotty den hood!. My plan this time was to make it and see the Royal Palace and as I crossed the Bvd Mohammed Zerktouni main drag I could see large gates in the distance so must be near. Next min as I quickly put on my plastic lightweight poncho with its hood the sky opened up and the rain poured down for 10 full mins but I was nearly watertight and made it through the very upmarket area along a tree planted Road and I was at the main huge big timber Gates of the Walled Fortress of the huge one mile square Royal Palace. The rain stopped, the hot sun came out so stripped off my poncho, rolled it up and stuck it back in my China beachbag. Armed security guard guy came out of the side gate so I wished him Bonne Annee, Happy New Year and he smiled saying Bonjour Monsieur. I pointed at the gate saying, can I go in, he said no, so wishing him well I took another road going back towards my hotel. It didn't take long but next min I was in a built up area passing 10-15 sewing shops then 10-12 luggage shops then passed the Washington Hotel then a large corner sign Champs Elysees above a cafe and got to and past Rue Baghdad and next min I was lost and knew it. Took my time in the sunshine day and walked along until I found a road sign to the main two lane highway of the Bvd Mohammed Zerktouni Road and crossed back to where Rue d'Agadir Road ended and walked back up it to De St Experry roundabout and happy as a lark I knew where I was and slowly sauntered back up Avenue Hassan II towards my Hotel area. I was really elated after a great day so now time for eats and picked a cafe beside my hotel and had quarter chicken, chips, rice, bread and a pot of tea just sitting in the pavement sunshine thinking this is the life. Finished my meal, paid my 28 Dirham charge and back across the road and into my hotel, upto room and bang, a lovely full empty dobhi drop, just the job, cleaned ass and back out upto the laundry, collected my dobhi all neatly cleaned, ironed and folded up, 45 Dirham. Back to Hotel, stripped off and had a lovely shave and hot shower thinking I had not made a bus booking for Rabat manyanna so had a read of LP and it said that the train is quicker and goes directly into the centre of Rabat so will catch a train, wake up and see. Out I went and along Rue Allah ben Abdellah Road this time to Place des Nations Unies and had a stroll up along the Medina wall at Bvd Houphouet Boigny Road as he made Casablanca famous and justly so as it's a full of vibes happy city. Came back and into the full of life market area of the Medina saying to myself I will be a good boy tonoche but the Medina is always so full of life. Made it out onto the packed full of cafes all blaring out music at the Ave des Forces Armees Royales cesspit Road which was packed full of still open stalls but I wanted somewhere to sit down and be safe for a tea or coffee. Got across 2 roads and heard shouting and screams behind me with people running as a car had hit a woman who was now lieing in the middle of the road with a crowd gathering around her all trying to help her. I felt sorry for her but didn't want to get involved so carried on and into a digital photo print shop and got the guy to print eight photos of thumbs up Poser Jack on his Moroccan travels as who knows, camera could get lost, missing or stolen so touch wood, touching my forehead!. It only took 10mins, the guy charged 32 Dirham, paid him and away. Had a walk along the pedestrian only street and finally treated myself to a large milky coffee with a chocolate cake thinking my Kelly Rose would love this. I phoned her getting gasps off where are you and we had a laughing chat and with a few loving phone kiss's my Beauty Queen was gone. Sat for approximately 40mins just watching the Casablanca nightlife happy crowd go walking by and funny enough did not see one Westerner yet the Place des Nations Unies is surrounded by the most upmarket hotel groups in the world. Maybe their clients come to Casablanca to sit in the hotel cafe! or maybe use the many nightclubs all around their area, anyway, it's their money, their life. Not even thinking of Medina Casablanca Morocco love tonight as feet, knees and legs fully gone it was 2240hrs so paid my 18 Dirham bill, said my thanks and a nice slow stroll back along Boulevard Mohammed V Road. Turned left at the closed market and into my hotel saying my Good Nights to the reception guy and gasping and grunting made it up the two flights of bendy stairs and into my room. No packing, no nothing, just stripped off and into my lovely soft bed and asleep dreaming more exotic sexy love in Casablanca.

Email Sent: Tue, 5 Jan 2010
Subject: Casablanca

Hi All
Nice place to visit and some great architecture especially around Place Mohammed V and got lost in some of Casa's dives with de white robed long beard Ayatollah hoods giving me a once over but us Shotty den Arthur St. hoods, who cares who dares. Tried a squat toilet today but missed, swine flue epidemic now sweeping Casa??
Heading for Rabat manyanna by train? when I wake up as no sleep for de sexy boy along Blvd Humphrey Bogart tonite!.
al de bes
Jack

Day 11, Wednesday, 06-01-10, Casablanca - Rabat; Morocco

Seemed to be more car noise than yesterday but checking clock it was 0710hrs so up for a piss and back for a lie in snooze then up for good at 0745hrs. Face splash, long cargo, pocket T-shirt, socks and Thai sandals on and out up to Rue Allah ben Abdellah Street turned right and into the tiny little cafe just passed the Royal Morocco Airlines office and girls and blokes said omelette, bread and tea same as yesterday and I smiled saying yes and upstairs to the tiny cafe area. Not long and my breakie came so I sat back enjoying it all talking to a young Moroccan girl who spoke excellent English. Then paying my 12 Dirham bill we both left I had a walk past my hotel down to Boulevard Hassan Seghir the main road at the huge Sheraton five-star Hotel only 50m from my neat smaller five-star. Had done my legs stretch so back upto hotel room, cleaned teeth, final pack of shoulderbag, neckpouch on checking Passport and out I went thinking reception are going to try a con and charge me again, same same, we shall see. Down the two flights of stairs and no one at reception but the cleaning lady shouted up the stairs and the guy came down saying ok, so smiling I said bye bye and out into the road I went. Flagged down a Petit taxi, shoulderbag on back seat, me in the front telling the driver Casa Port Train Station, he said Casaport and off we drove but not far and stopped outside a small train station, out I got giving him 11 Dirham, he smiled taking his money. I grabbed my shoulderbag from the back seat and handle up I rolled it into the train station and up to a no queue kiosk. Told the guy, Rabat, he said second class, I said yes and he gave me a printed ticket, 2nd, Train 15, Casa-Rabat Ville, 35 Dirham. It looks good as I gave him 100 Dirham note, he gave me change and I was nearly there, it was 0945hrs, next train was 1000hrs. The platform door was locked so we had to wait then as a train drew in with many people getting off coming in another door then the platform guy opened our door and everyone went onto the platform. I seen second-class so into a carriage, got a seat and that was me a one happy Morocco train man and at 1000hrs spot-on we were away. It took a while but we eventually got out of the very big Casablanca container Port all on our left with many big huge container ships anchored up along the shore line. The train got up a very good speed then we had a two minute stop at a station then away again passing through slum area ghettos on each side of the rail lines then finally it was neat flat green fields and forests to admire as we pulled in for our second two mins stop. Ticket collector came along checking and penning a mark on all tickets then a third very fast stop at Rabat Agdal and looking at my LP photo copy I knew Rabat Ville is our next and my final stop. Lots of people stood up as I did and out we went as the train stopped, it was 1100hrs. Just followed the crowd as out we went onto Avenue Mohammed V and orientating myself I turned left heading into the full Rabat town centre then passing Rue Soekarno I knew exactly where I was. Tried one hotel but it was full then into Hotel Berlin, 261 Avenue Mohammed V, Rabat, Tel:0537703435 and the guy showed me a big double ensuite, Western toilet at 200 Dirham so took it as not hunting around looking for a cheaper one for the sake of a fiver. Showed Passport, gave him a 200 Dirham note and he gave me key to Room 28 so took my shoulderbag down to it, dumped it in the room, that was a good quick deal, it was 1145hrs. Put shoes on as will be doing a good walk today by the look of it and out onto Mohammed V Road turning right and into the fully packed stalls and all sorts of the Medina and having a look at my LP photocopy I turned right along a main Souk which was real good fun and now seeing the river and the Medina walls of Sale in the distance. Kept going and came out where the rowing boat plied across the river and looking left seen the Kasbah des Oudaias Medina in the distance and it was a very impressive sight. No hesitation just followed the road upto it with touts trying to get me into the Museum but turned right through the huge blocks Arched overflow in Bab Oudaia gate with more touts but done a few lefts and rights and they got the message and I was left on my own. Had a very interesting walk around its ancient narrow Souks and walls then down a ramshackle path and there it was the full as far as the eye could see the Atlantic Ocean, what a truly memorable sight. Walked down the 1195-1300 Battlements having my usual thumbs up photo shoot and was tempted to go fully down to the sandy beach but had a few plans so turned back. I took a different route back along the empty very narrow blue and white painted walls Souks all very neat and no piled up rubbish anywhere. Came back out the main gates and into the Museum grass tree area but only for a walk around it and out the same Bab and just followed the very full of all sorts stalls along Rue Souika Souk to the great Mosque. Had another look at my Rabat LP map and knew my next stop which would be the Tour Hassan which is Rabat's most famous landmark as I had seen it plainly high in the sky from the Kasbah des Oudaias battlements. Back out onto the main road and took my top shirt off as it was now really hot in the lovely sun and slowly made it upto and in the open air very big Tour Hassan Mosque very impressed with its splendid size. Went over and into the huge Mausoleum of Mohammed V Seeing his Marble Coffin below and was allowed to take photos with all the 6-8 brightly coloured Uniformed guards around the outside and inside of the Mausoleum, very good. Back out really impressed and turned right going along a very upmarket area with lots of Foreign Embassy's legs and feet starting to give me grief but only get one chance so kept going. Came to Place Abraham Lincoln then took a short cut along Avenue Fes passing the Fort Alchary USA Embassy then a right down and I was at another Medina big walls. Crossed the road and down Ave Yacoub al-Mansour and came to the Medina walls of the ancient Roman City of Sala Colonia which inside was the original ruins from Roman times so paid my 10 Dirham fee and in I went. It was well kept and a very remarkable size of a full Roman settlement all dwellings built from stone blocks in the original site. It was obvious there had been many Islamic add-ons but really chuffed to have made it. I had my usual poser photo shoot with a party of girls from Canada doing a two-week charity help in a hospital nursing the poor of Morocco so very proud of the very spirted young Canadian Chico's we had a laugh as we walked back to the really impressive Medina Arched entrance. They got on a bus and we all waved as it pulled away then I cut through the Medina walls and now on my own I very, very slowly made it all the way to the most impressive Archways all over the 2, 4 lane stone Highway. How they built those splendid Towers and Arches so perfect thousands of years ago defies belief. Hardly able to walk I made it past the railway station then along Ave Mohammed V and wow oh wow into my hotel. Took shoes off, put Thai sandals on and oh what a relief and out for a 30 Dirham beef burger, chips and a tea lovely 1710hrs din din and oh did I need it bad and my legs and feet getting better by the minute. Finished my lovely din din and a slow walk back for shave and shower and out again into the always full of life Medina just strolling around its very colourful Souks. Back out the way I came in and upto a middle of Rabat cafe to have a Coke and a 2145hr bedtime tea. Sat for 35mins then legs saying bed, back to hotel, got my key and into room, stripped off and dead as a doornail asleep as head hit de pillow.

Email Sent: Wed, 6 Jan 2010
Subject: Hotel Berlin, Mohammed V, Rabat, Morocco, Tel: 0534648546

Hi All
Jumped a Casablanca train 1000hrs and 3 stops later got to Rabat middle of town train station 1100hrs. Tried one hotel but full then into above and got lovely d-ensuite western toilet, 200 Dirham so took it and out for into the Souks and upto the 1159 AD Medina overlooking the Atlantic Ocean. Then a nice sunny walk to the huge open air Mosque and Mausoleum with the Mohammed V marble coffin still in view then a further walk to the fully open Roman remains in another huge Medina, great day. Will go to Sale manyanna as it's only a rowing boat away across the river.
al de bes
Jack

Day 12, Thursday, 07-01-10, Rabat – Sale; Morocco

Up at 0100hrs my right leg in severe cramp and I was in agony trying to smooth the big bulge muscle cramps away. Needed a dobhi drop as well but sitting down caused more pain but frantically rubbing water on it and also drinking lots of bottled water I managed 2 No dobhi drops, cleaned my ass and cramp was gone, phew, that was a nasty wake up. Back to bed and asleep as if nothing had happened and woke up as people leaving and a high heeled women clip clopping along the marble floors with doors slamming everywhere, turned over a few times enjoying my lovely bed then finally up for good at 0910hrs. Face splash, long sleeve shirt, cargo trousers and shoes on and out across the road to my only L'Alsace cafe and had an omelette with crusty baguette and 2 mint teas, very enjoyable. Had a look at LP Sale where in bygone days it was the base of the Corsairs so will be going there later today. Paid my 24 Dirham bill, back to room, cleaned teeth, had a nice dobhi drop, cleaned ass and sellotaped an envelope for Sandralita with more bad handwritten notes in it then upto reception and paid 200 Dirham for one more day. Out into the overcast Ave Mohammed V and went left upto the Post Office to post my travel notes (days 10-11) to lovely Sandralita the greatest handwriting decipherer in de world. Eventually found where they take the post and sell stamps, Lady said 19 Dirham so paid her, she put the stamps on, ink stamped them and dropped it into a post bin and I was away giving her a postcard with a stamp already on it for my Kelly Rose my curvy Beauty Queen sweetheart and it also went in the bin so today looking good. Had a look at LP and it had the Granda Taxis (shared) rank to Sale up by the Medina wall so walked up and having a chat a guy pointed at one row of Granda Taxis saying Sale Medina. In I got, third one on, two males in the back seat, next min a fattish long robed guy and one large robed woman got in the back so no room to breathe but we were away over the bridge linking Sale and Rabat and he dropped the man and woman off then stopped saying Medina and off I got, paid him the 7 Dirham charge and he was away. In through the main 11th Century gate and turned left just following the ancient Medina walls with its internal timber walkway stand along the battlement as I sometimes took a good look at the arrow/musket holes in them. Got down to near the Atlantic Ocean and these ancient battlement walls were just so amazing to be near and walk alongside them. It started pouring down so poncho on and back in towards the 11-12 century Souks and found the stalls in place and well-kept Merenid Medersa built in 1333 AD, tout said fee for foreigners so paid my 10 Dirham entrance fee and in I went to first of all it's lovely internal hall full of so fine woodwork and stuccos, all so neat it was a joy to see. Upto the first floor on the 500mm wide winding little stairs and along each side of the balcony looking into many little rooms, good fun and history. Had a piss in a Western toilet definitely not five years old never mind 500 but next upto and on the roof with grand views over the rooftops of Sale and that was me, back down and out. Well dressed guy said Mosque pointing at its fantastic built facade which was built 14th Century, do I want to have a look inside so said yes wondering how much he would try and con me. He took me to one large Arched gate which was open telling me there were 18 gates in total and at one time this Mosque was the largest in Morocco.

In we went and it was very big about the size of a football pitch then going out the same gate I gave him 10 Dirham saying my thanks. He said come to my house for tea and look as its 13th Century insides as it had been in his family since then so a bit dubious and concerned would I make it back out alive I said ok. He took me into a dwelling with an open courtyard saying this is Roman architecture as all the rooms with windows are built up from it and said to sit in his open living room as I did. Couple of mins later he bought a kettle and two tumblers and poured two tumblers of tea saying he lived here with one sister and brother. We chatted about Morocco him telling me there are five local accents Berber, Rif, some places Hindu, Portuguese, English, Arabic and French but everyone speaks French and Sale was home and hiding place for the Corsairs, English Christian pirates and all sorts of the Jackals of the nights. On my second cup of tea I said it's been a pleasure to have met you but I will now go as we both stood up I gave him another 10 Dirham coin but he said coins no good could I give him 100 Dirham note. I was half prepared for it and as I got outside his door into the souk I said I have no money on me only coins and gave him another 5 Dirham but he said no good he needs at least a 50 Dirham note so getting the last of my loose 5 cent, 10 cent Dirham change I dropped it in his hand and I was away. Took my time and got into the main Souk of the Medina just browsing the many stalls and shops then out one of the Arched gates and across the railway lines turning right going down towards the river. There was a massive new development being built but going right I found an access through it to where the rowing boats crossed the river and got one with 4 singing, dancing and so happy lively Moroccan girls, one who taught English as a foreign language. We took some photos as it started pouring down again as off we got on the other side I paid my 2 Dirham charge with two 1 Dirham coins getting a 'you cheap foreign git' comment but I was away in the rain and made it into the always full of life Rabat Medina, quite recently built in the 17th century. Walked up the many second-hand shoe stalls and tried on a pair of Adidas air sole trainers and haggled the price from 200 down to 60 Dirham as badly needed a decent lightweight shoe for my poor ole aching feet. Put them on and away finding my way out off the Medina with no problems and into Ave Mohammed V and into my hotel, it was 1600hrs so another good day. Dumped shoes and out across the road to Cafe L'Alsace to have a pizza and a mint tea, just the job, paid my 30 Dirham charge and back to hotel room for a lovely shave and shower, my ole legs and feet thanking me to the high heavens. No rush went out at 1900hrs and into the Medina for a stroll along the lit up main Souks having a regular coffee inside a cafe as it was getting cold but seeing the news of England, cor the snow was feet thick by the look of it. Paid my 10 Dirham coffee charge and back out of the Medina and into Rabat town centre and low and behold found a good ole Macdonald's but not tonight as finished my stroll having a tea in my favourite cafe and that was me back to the hotel and upto room, stripped off and into bed and asleep a one happy feet happy man.

Email Sent: Thu, 7 Jan 2010
Subject: Rabat

Hi All

Had a good day in Sale which in bygone years from the 11th to the 13th Century was the home of the Corsairs, English rogue Christian and all sorts of heathens enjoying themselves, probably a bit like ole Arthur St? The Medina walls recently built in the 14th Century are a fantastic sight along the Atlantic coast path as you can walk along the battlements. Went into the Merenid Medersa a sort of residence built 1333 AD and even was invited into the Grand Mosque which centuries ago was the biggest in Morocco so had a peep saying Allah is Good and away. Got a rowing boat, 2 Dirham across the river back into Rabat Medina and Allah is Good found my way back to Hotel. Heading for Fes manyanna by train.
al de bes
Jack

Day 13, Friday, 08-01-10, Rabat – Fes; Morocco

Woke up by 0700hrs as alarm went off but said to myself its too tight to have breakfast and catch the 0812hrs train to Fes my destination today so turned over in my lovely double bed just relaxed and happy. Seen daylight coming through the window blind so checked my bedside clock and it was only 0750hrs, so up, face splash, long cargo, Thai sandals and long sleeve T-shirt on and out for my Cafe L'Alsace omelette crusty baguette, 2 mint teas breakie which was really lovely except for the crusty baguette, you would think they would start enjoying soft bread, not to worry, paid my 26 Dirham bill and out back upto hotel room. Cleaned teeth and had a lovely dobhi drop, cleaned ass so all set for my 3 1/2 hour train journey. Had a little final pack of shoulderbag, neck pouch on checking Passport and out I went shaking hands with reception guy and handing my room key over down the stairs I went and out. Their was a drizzle of rain from the overcast sky but I went straight up Ave Mohammed V and into Rabat train station checking boards and the next train to Fes was 0917hrs at Platform 2, it was 0900hrs. Showed ticket at gate and down the temporary platform walkway I went as major refurbishment works were going on and onto Platform 2. Stood for about 10mins and then it came over the tannoy in French but it showed 'retard 25mins' on our Fes board so everyone moaning I wheeled my shoulderbag back from the open cold platform and up the moving stairs into the warm of the station and stayed in the heat for 15mins then back down to the platform. Only a 10min wait and the Fes train came in and on I got at second-class. Got a seat in an eight seater cabin as each carriage was divided into eight cabins and my cabin had five people in it including me, all French speakers and one min later we were away through a long tunnel with no lights in the train, good fun. Out we went into the now lovely sunshine daylight going through Rabat me seeing all the places I had walked. Got up a good speed into the grass fields neat forest countryside sometimes through white painted walled towns and villages. Stopped three times at towns for only 2mins each time then I fell asleep listening to the Arabic music from one of the two old fellows radio. Woke up and looking out the window I seen a signpost for Meknes 29km, it was 1130hrs so going well considering I lost 25mins at Rabat. We were now going through sorts of green field hilly valley areas with mountains in the distance with lots of low lieing areas appearing slightly flooded as the rivers were running full blast so maybe it's the rainy season. Mind you it seems to be getting colder as I put on an extra sleeved top or it could be cold air conditioning on the train even on a cold morning day!. Into Meknes main station at 1155hrs for the usual two-min stop, some people got off, some got on and we were away again the skies clouding over in the distant horizon. Went for a piss 1225hrs and low and behold it was a western WC so that's a bonus if you needed a dobhi drop. Mountains in the distance now covered in mist and thick clouds so will maybe have a shorter stay in Fes than I planned, just see the sights and away as don't want rain ruining my silky hair!. Next min the two old guys stood up, one took my shoulderbag from rack putting it on the seat facing me and both said Fes, I looked at my pocket watch and it was only 1300hrs so could not figure it out how we started 25mins late yet arrived 15mins earlier than the 3 1/2 hour journey. Not to worry as the train stopped I seen a big sign Gare de Fes so off I got pulling shoulderbag and we crossed the makeshift walkway across the railway lines as looking down the underpass it was flooded so carried on and out the big huge brilliant entrance Arched facade of Fes station. I stopped and looked at my LP photocopy, mistake number one as 2-3 touts said they'd take me to hotel showing me cards, I said how much, they said 250-300 Dirham so I said thank you very much and I was away with them still trying it on bringing prices down for another 50m then they gave up. Got to Rue Chenguit then a left down Ave de France and I was looking over a very busy main square full of restaurants, a post office and banks all within walking distance of the Medina so looking around I seen a very old but smart facade of Hotel Amor, 31 Rue Arabie Saoudite, Fes, Tel: 35622724. Nothing to lose so upto it and in and asked guy how much for room looking around at all its old but in great shape internal reception and dining room. He said 160 Dirham, so I said Western toilet, he said yes so gave him my Passport, he done his paperwork, I signed it and gave him 160 Dirham. Got key to room 204, Porter took my shoulderbag and up the lift we went into a lovely double ensuite bathroom room, he put my bag in room and away he went. Didn't want to hang about so checked China beachbag had bottle of sprite and 2 Mars bars in it and out I went downstairs, handed key in at reception, got 2 hotel cards and out and away thinking what a great true blue day. Orientated myself and went up the Ave Hassan II then Bvd Moulay Youssef and just completely amazed as I admired the former main entrance to the Medina walled Royal Palace and what size and view it was, it was called The Bab Dekkaken. Carried on and came to one of the fantastic entrances to the Medina and in I went at Bab Sammarine truly magnificent Arched entrance which dated back to the start of Fes-Jdid when work to build the inner area was started in the 13th Century. I was really over the moon to be here and up close to all this 13th Century great architecture and building. In I went to the main Souk walking past ancient buildings and narrow little Souks I think I would have trouble squeezing through but kept on the main drag just admiring all and every building each side. Next got to Rue Fes Jdid Avenue where previously it had Turkish Baths and didn't stop but kept going and reached the next Arched entrance called Bab Chenis. A few touts offered themselves as guides and I am sure it would have been worth it but I like to do my own thing and said no thanks. It was I must admit the most fantastic Medina I had been in as every step was a step back hundreds maybe thousands of years and even on my short walk so far I must have passed 5-6 Mosques. Next reading the walking blue sign I came to Talaha Sghirs, (the little slope), all dwellings around and in it go back to the Merinid Era, 14th Century, truly amazing seeing it up close. Next got to Souk Et Fondouk Chemmaine beside the Qaraouiyine Mosque all built in the 13th century and I peeped my Christian head in to view all its vast open Mosque praying area with lots of worshippers on their knees on mats praying to Allah, so good luck I said and away. This Mosque built 859 AD is the most ancient Mosque in Islam and one of its biggest for hundreds of years. I was still following the main Souk not a clue where I was then came to Place Sieffarine a Square with all the buildings surrounding it being originally the oldest workplace in Fes which was the brassware makers area, great true history. Touts and hustlers were getting worse but I kept going getting offered massage and all sorts but didn't even stop as I could tell they were real hoods then got to Medina Suffarine, 1270 AD but I was not allowed in!. I was getting concerned as I knew I was in the middle of the Fez El - Bali Medina but didn't have a clue how to get out and it was 1645hrs, wouldn't like to be lost in this place when it got dark. Sort of followed the thin Moroccan crowd and with a big sigh of relief I came out on to a main Souk at Bab Bou Jeloud a very main entrance to the Medina built in the 12th century, it was so marvellous and I had my usual thumbs up photo shoot. My poor ole legs nearly gone again I waved down a Petit taxi and jumped in and showed him Fez Ville Nouvelle from my LP map, he put on his meter and we were away. It was quite a long way and as he dropped me off outside my hotel I paid him the 11 Dirham his meter was showing and he was away. Into Hotel and upto room, had a piss and back out and into a little cafe for a hamburger, fritters and a tea, really lovely, so belly full, me happy I paid the 30 Dirham bill and back into my hotel, it was 1835hrs. Got my key and said to the bloke, hot water, he said give it 30mins so upto room just having a read about places to go and then checked for hot water. It was lukewarm but not hot so had a shave and face wash, kit on and downstairs saying to reception guy no hot water, he said yes, it's hot water so thinking that's what they call hot in Morocco I didn't argue and out I went for a good walk, seen a cafe and had a hotdog and tea, it was 2140hrs. Enjoyed my late bedtime tea, paid my 30 Dirham bill and a walk around the empty dark Square thinking there might be a hooker about but no luck tonight so called it a night and back to the hotel. Got my key and up the lift into my room, stripped off and into bed me knowing for some reason this is a hooker area and asleep dreaming Fes jig a jig manyanna noche.

Email Sent: Fri, 8 Jan 2010
Subject: Rm204, Amor Hotel,31 Rue Arabia Saoudite,Fes,Morocco,Tel35622724

Hi All
Had a lie in then up at 0750hrs and out for lovely omelette breakie spoiled by these crusty French baguettes, why can't they get nice soft white bread. Anyway jumped the 0945hrs train from Rabat and arrived Fes 1300hrs and it had a western toilet so that was a bonus. Walked into town and got above d-ensuite, 160 Dirham so done well and out into I must admit the greatest Medina town I have been in so far as every step was just an amazing walk back to the 12-13th Centuries, nothing changed with 350mosques and souks I couldn't even squeeze through and people still live a normal life.
al de bes
Jack

Day 14, Saturday, 09-01-10, Fes; Morocco

I was up a few times for a piss during the night but nice and warm in my five blanket bed I had a good sleep. Woke up for good at 0835hrs then up at 0900hrs no plans, no rush. Face splash then 3 small plasters on my left foot cuts by my shoes and new trainers and also an ankle support bandage with a new support bandage on my right ankle and stood up, hip, hip hooray, all pain gone. Put on 2 tops then long cargo and out downstairs telling guy that I was staying one more day then out for breakie. It was 0930hrs but no cafes doing omelettes open yet so had a 2 croissant, tea, 14 Dirham breakie in Cafe next to hotel. Enjoyed it then back to room for a lovely dobhi drop, cleaned ass, cleaned teeth as they are getting browner every day then a look at LP about my no rush no long walk plan for today. My hotel was at the top end of Fes Ville Nouvelle so decided to walk down into the what looked like busier centre just for a look then the Catholic Church and the Jewish Synagogue and Jewish cemetery which without seeing I think I passed yesterday so that's plan A. Out I went my head as I looked at my LP photocopy of Fes Ville Nouvelle a complete blank, didn't have a clue which direction the train station or the Medina was which I had easily come from and got to yesterday. Walked left but road sign was in Arabic but then seen Gare Fes away in the distance but mind still refusing to orientate my head to which way I should go. Went away from the train station anyway and into a full of life very busy area and looking left I seen Hotel Central down at the roundabout at Ave Mohammed es Slaoui and Bvd Mohammed V so now knew where I was. I turned right up Ave Mohammed es Slaoui and passing three streets on my right I seen 2 prominent Crosses on a building but no names on it but the front gate was open so I went in. A black African lady smiled saying she was going out as I said is this a Church so smiling she knocked a door at the side and a middle aged Moroccan guy came out. I said I am passing and just wondered if this was a Catholic Church, he smiled saying yes and we shook hands him giving me a little run down on the Church as he said back in French times there was 20-25,000 Catholics many French in Fes and its area. Now the only people who come to his Church are black African people who worship, sing and dance on Sundays and it's a pleasure to see and be with them. I said in a lot of Churches in England it's the same and if it wasn't for these people lots of Churches would be closed for good as people don't seem to want to go to Church now . He said he learned his priesthood in Ireland just outside Dublin and invited me as we shook hands to come to the Church for Sunday service tomorrow at 1030hrs. I said I am leaving tomorrow or I would have come then saying my thanks I was away. I knew where I was now so made my way up to Ave De la Liberte and into a cafe for a hamburger, fritters and a tea, 30 Dirham and enjoyed my 1240hrs lunch having another no rush tea. Left there and just followed the same way I had walked yesterday touts asking do I need a guide, I did but said no. Asked discreetly a few times and eventually down a Souk I seen a sign on a big double gate, 'Israelite Cemetery' but it was locked so had a quick thumb's up photo shoot. Discreetly asked again about the Jewish Synagogue and was directed down a very busy Souk then directed into a very narrow little Souk and there it was with a Moroccan guy as doorman. He said 20 Dirham to walk inside so only get one chance so in I went paying him the 20 Dirham saying Shalom, him laughing but his 2No Veiled women friends looked shocked as he said are you Jewish, I said no, Shalom, I am Irish and everyone saying Shalom and laughing he showed me the pulpit which was engraved with a sign: Robby Aben Danan, 1847-1928. It looked as if this was the Rabbi but don't know when the Synagogue was built as the area it was in was and is known as the Jewish quarter but no Jews live here now as far as I could make out. Had a walk around it and it was very well kept and clean with everything in spotless order and well preserved as the sign at the door stated American Express funded the restoration not long ago. Had seen everything and slowly left and we all laughed and wishing each other Shalom out I went into the always lively Souk thinking there must be the most fantastic history buried around this area as even in the Synagogue there was 2 flights of dark stairs going down underground into the basements vaults. Time never stops, it was 1630hrs so slowly made my way past the unbelievable sight of the original Palace gates and slowly back into the Fes Ville Nouvelle area and into a pizza cafe for a full margarita pizza and 2 teas, 32 Dirham and enjoying sitting in the Cafe watching football on telly as that seems to be all that is on. I think it's an African tournament as a team from one country got ambushed and shot as they were travelling to a match on a bus, sad. Back to hotel hoping for hot water and it was not too bad so had a quick shave and shower, kit on and out again as no heat in the rooms, it was 1920hrs. Had a full circle walk around the Ville Nouvelle area and a final tea having a read of LP knowing I will make the move manyanna to a town called Meknes which was the capital of Morocco in the 17th century so should be interesting for a day, we shall see. It was 2205hrs so legs feeling good I called it a night still not seen a hooker, into hotel, upto room, stripped off and into bed and asleep dreaming of my sexy girlfriend Kelly Rose in the freezing English cold and wishing she was with me keeping me warm in my 4 blanket bed.

Email Sent: Sat, 9 Jan 2010
Subject: Islam Fes Churches and Synagogue

Hi All
Had a nice sunny walk in Fes today and first stop at a Catholic Church where Vicar told me only black Africans use it now, approx 400 singing and dancing at Sunday service. I said it's the same in England near enough. Then next stop along a narrow little Souk I went into a well kept by American Express small Jewish Synagogue, 1847 called Aben Danan just outside the Medina where I greeted the Islam caretaker and his veiled sweethearts with Shalom my friends getting shocked looks and asked am I Jewish, I laughing said Shalom, no, I am Irish, everybody laughing. There is a Proddie church but couldn't find it in de Souks. Will head for Meknes manyanna but only for a day?
Shalom, al de bes
Jack

Day 15, Sunday, 10-01-10, Fes – Meknes; Morocco

Woke up 0730hrs lovely and warm and didn't want to move so turned over a few times enjoying my bed but knew I had to get up, it was 0835hrs. Up I got, face splash, soaping armpits then dried off, long cargo, long sleeved T-shirt, ankle support on right ankle, socks and trainers on. Final little pack of shoulderbag and out for breakie. Had a little 5 min swinging my arms walk down to the Cafe beside my hotel for a 2 croissant, 1 tea, 15 Dirham breakie, really nice. Had another little around the Square walk then back upto hotel room and felt it stirring so looking good. Had a big time full empty dobhi drop which cleaned my system for todays travelling fun. Neckpouch on checking Passport, checked wallet and out down the lift, handed my key in shaking hands with the reception guys and out I went into the drizzle rain. Was tempted to get a taxi but kept walking and 15mins later walked into Gare de Fes rail station just hoping to catch the 0950hr train to Meknes, it was 0945hrs so no more walks and straight into the train station. Into ticket office and bought a 20 Dirham single, second-class to Meknes and out into the main hall. Next thing at 0950hrs a train drew into the station and lots of people got up so I followed them over to the platform door showing and asking 2 Moroccan girls was this the train to Meknes, they laughed saying we don't know in English. They got to the ticket inspector who nodded at them so they said yes to me so I followed them down the not flooded underpass and onto the train taking a seat in a six seat cabin with one other beautiful girl in it. We all had a laughing chat as the three girls had studied English at college and they were real fun to be with. A lady and two children took the two other seats in our cabin and at 1000hrs spot on we were away. It was fun to chat and answer all the questions then with a three stop journey along the cow and sheep green fields in we drew to El-Amir Meknes train station and off we all got in the cold drizzling rain, it was only 1030hrs!. Shook hands with my 3 girls as 2 went one way and the big beautiful girl waited for someone to pick her up. I did a right then a left and came to Hotel de Ville but the security guard said it was not a Hotel. The next one I tried was Hotel Nice that they wanted 400 Dirham, I asked the girl any cheapies about, she said go right and take the second street on the left and there is one. This I did and came to Hotel Palace, 11 Rue de Ghana, Meknes, Tel: 0535400468 so straight in and asked for a room for one, guy said 180 Dirham so took it getting room 103. Showed Passport, paid for one night, got key and up only one flight of stairs and into a bit bare but westernised toilet ensuite, two large single beds room and was happy, it was 1130hrs. Dumped kit and out making my way to Avenue Hassan II then along Avenue Moulay-Ismail towards the Medina and not that far as now in the no rain day I could see the Medina walls in the distance on top of a hill with 5-6 prominent Mosque Minarets dotted across the horizon, a really good sight. The Meknes area I was now in was upmarket from what I had been used to but slowly got out of it thinking it will be nice tonight. I got to the bottom of our hill crossing the bridge to start my uphill walk to the Medina walls. The road took a turn to the right then left and then I seen the very prominent Arched fully decorated Bab el Mansour gateway to the old 17th Century City. Very impressed so in I went a few horse and cart touts offering me a ride around. I asked how much, they said 120

Dirham for a full grand tour or 80 Dirham for a petite tour so I said my thanks and kept walking. Came to Moulay Ismail Mausoleum who founded and made Meknes his Capital in the 17th century and it was a so beautiful and great place, it was a joy to see. Don't know which direction I took but walked along a roofed large Souk for quite a while thinking how did they build such enormous and fully stable structures all built in the 14th century. Enjoying my walk I passed and looked into the Royal Golf Course with lovely green grass which looked open to anyone!. Was going to do a full walk of the internal ring road inside the Medina but it started raining so turned back and into the Jar Darnall Museum seeing and admiring all its jewellery, ceramics and a pipe smoking kip which is the Moroccan name for marijuana, all housed in a really up market 19th century original Palace. Still raining so into a Medina cafe and had a tea and 2 short bread cakes, sat for 50mins and the rain did stop. No other plans for today so out the Bab Bernima gate and downhill I went into a few winding Souks but eventually came out just before the main bridge with a Macdonald's across the roundabout, it was 1605hrs. Was tempted but kept going as it was packed and passing lots of traditional cafes all empty so I went into a cafe selling pizza but had a beefburger, fries and a tea, 30 Dirham and sat enjoying my full plate until 1720hrs just watching the Meknes world go by. Up, paid my bill and away back to Hotel and into my room, it was still early so had a read of LP with reference to my plans for tomorrow and decided to have a day out to Volubilis a third Century Roman town and roads. Had a nice shave in the lovely very hot water and turned the actual room heating on and it did work, oh la, la, it was 1910hrs. Out leaving the heating on and had a nice stroll around Meknes with its plenty of decent bars, clubs and cafes including good restaurants and I liked its vibes. Had a tea, 7 Dirham sitting outside a cafe then still plenty of time decided to walk down upto and around the main car road at the Medina and I was away. It also had many packed cafes with all the local clients watching football on TV as I don't think they had TV or running water in their tiny Souk dwellings. Took a right then left up a Souk at a closed Mosque and carried on following the Souk as it got narrower and narrower and more empty and just about to turn back when I heard cars in the distance, turned a corner and out I went to the main road directly facing Musee de Antnes and breathed out a great sigh of relief, it was an experience following those Souks. I turned right at the Bab el Monsour at the big Square then that was me I knew where I was. Happily walked back and had a Moroccan soup with a crusty baguette, 5 Dirham then into my warm room, stripped off and into bed and asleep, another day of adventure over.

Email Sent: Sun, 10 Jan 2010
Subject: Hotel Palace, 11 Rue de Ghana, Meknes, Tel 0535400468

Hi All
Jumped the 0950hrs train from Gare de Fes and arrived Meknes 1030hrs so had a little walk towards the Medina and seen above so got a d-ensuite for 180 Dirham, dumped kit in room. Then out for a good walkie first of all through the Massive Bab el Monsour the very impressive arched gates then around the Souks of Moulay Ismail the first Sultan who made Meknes Morocco's capital city in the 12th Century. Just passed a McDonalds, wonder how many Centuries it goes back?,
Will have a think of plans for manyanna later on, the centuries pass to quickly.
al de bes
jack

Day 16, Monday, 11-01-10, Meknes - Volubile; Morocco

Woke up twice during the night for a piss but back again to the greatest best soft firm mattress I have slept in so far, it was just magic. Finally up at 0830hrs in my warm heated room I washed my armpits with hot water, had a face splash, long cargo, trainers and two long sleeved shirts on but looking out the window it was a bright blue sky, hope it stays that way. Downstairs and out with quite a few cafes open but having a look they didn't appear to cook an omelette so back to the hotel and asked the very helpful guy was there anywhere open that would serve an omelette. He took me outside pointing up just past Hotel Ville and the post office, he said Cafe Dinachk does a good selection so up I went and into its upmarket seating area, sat down and one of four immaculate dressed waiters came over and I said omelette and 1 tea, he nodded and away. About five mins later the omelette came with four crusty sections of baguette so got stuck into my Meknes lovely breakie finishing off the lot with another tea and that was me a full belly happy man mon. Paid my 32 Dirham bill, not bad for the neat immaculate very good service cafe and out over to the post office to post a letter to my sweetheart curvy Kelly, but it was shut today. On down and into my hotel and upto room having a lovely dobhi drop, cleaned ass, cleaned teeth and ready for today's wander to Volubilis, it was 1010hrs. Out I went after asking reception guy where Place de Foire was as that's where I would catch a Grand Taxi which are large taxis that wait until they are full. He said go down our street and taxi rank is facing the police station. Got down to it okay passing touts who said no Grand Taxis to Moulay Idriss a town nearby where the grand taxis delivered to and where I would catch another grand taxi to Volubilis. Tout wanted 200-250 Dirham for trip there and wait 1-2hrs then back but I eventually got away from them and over to a rank of Grand Taxi's. One bloke who seemed to be organising people coming for a taxi said you, pointing at me and pointing at a half full taxi said Volubilis so in I got, one min later five large blokes got in and we were away. I watched as they handed the driver 10 Dirham so I did the same and he stuck it in the dashboard compartment as we easily got out of Meknes and onto a nice country road with cows and sheep and farm fields, sometimes with forests of mint trees alongside it. Finally after a 26km ride me like a sardine in the back seat we reached Moulay Idriss a fairly big 2-3 story high building village and stopped in the main square. We all got out, all the other passengers were locals and disappeared but I was surrounded by touts offering transport and tours for 100 Dirham but I said no. One Grand Taxi driver said 30 Dirham so tried haggling but no other tourists about so I was stuck and finally gave in and said okay giving him the 30 Dirham. Into the back seat and we were away and Volubilis was not that far from Moulay Idriss maybe 4km at the most and as we turned off the main road I could see the huge 200-295 AD Roman remains with large big majestic Arches and big stone Columns about another 1 km away. Wow oh wow, it was a sight to see as it took over a full 2-3 km square low lieing Hill 1 km down the road. We stopped at the car park area and out I got saying good luck and over to the entrance kiosk and had to pay 10 Dirham entrance fee, got my tickets and in I went, it was 1140hrs. Decision, decision, do I start in the middle at the big Roman

Archway or go one side so took the right edge and I was away and slowly got into the great large stone paving De-cumanus Maximus Ceremonial Road built 217AD, what a feeling walking it and looking at its gully's and drainage, marvellous. Many large dwellings had been built all along the road and all had names with a description and the first one which was 1235m sq was the Big Pilasters with its own swimming pool then stopped for a long time admiring the House of Venus so-called because of its exceptional full coloured mosaics, what a lovely sight and all original. Next was the House of Sundial with its thermal baths and latrines which as I took my time could trace where they were in the ruins as every wall had at least a fraction coming out off the ground some only at ground level, others up to 2-3m high. Kept going enjoying the lovely sunrays and was now at the House of Marble Bacchus named after him as a large statue of Bacchus was found on the garden area. I was only stopping at the sign reading dwelling and probably missing lots as the full site stretched for 1-2km in each direction and got to the House of Discipline which had a parade of shops under the houses. It was so amazing the size of the stone blocks and the big huge Pillars as now I was in the Gordon Palace which was a full 4488m sq and was the home of Emperor Gordon in 238-244 AD. I was now completely over the moon just walking and stepping over the little walled Roman ruins. Stopped for a while at The Labours of Hercules House studying and admiring the lovely coloured 12 object mosaics a) The Kidnapping of Ganymedes, b) The 12 Labours of Hercules, c) The Four Seasons, fantastic history. Getting near the huge Centre ruin I came to the House of the Rider then finally for me the Arc of Triumph built by the town of Volubilis to honour Emperor Caracalla and his wife Julia in 217AD for granting the people and the town Roman citizenship and tax exception, what full great history. Kept on walking and up the steps onto a large pillared stage then along to a big well all fully original and in good order. I could have taken a guide but just wanted to walk and enjoy it at my own pace and did have a chat with fellow travellers and a few photo thumbs up Roman Jack pose's. As far as I was concerned my full walkie was now complete so back along the dirt track path I made it back to the entrance a fully chuffed Roman man. The guy wanted or I assumed he wanted 10 Dirham to let me have a piss in the toilets so I said no thanks and walked about 20m and had a piss in the 5000 year old Roman remains as no doubt over the years a few Romans had also done their duty. Out I went into the parking area turning left to go towards main road about 1 km away thinking in the lovely sunshine day I will do a Roman trek and walk back along the main highway road to Moulay Idriss and off I went, it was 1545hrs. Got up to the main road and done a right just strolling along the big Rocky face of the mountain cliff on my left with green fields and small forests sometimes on my right with cows, goats and sheep grazing, me thinking I will be an easy neck cut for any Corsairs on the prowl but enjoying my sunshine walk lorry drivers driving past me smiling and waving, it was fun. It was a good 40mins walk and I came to the turn off for Moulay Idriss where armed police had set up a roadblock so said my Good Afternoons getting a smiling hello and I said, Meknes bus pointing down the Meknes Way Road, they said yes, no problems so I stood in the sun by the bus stop watching the traffic go by. A few fully packed Grand Taxis did pass me then a couple of blokes came down the hill and stood near me and five mins later a Voyager Ismailia single decker bus came along and stopped and we all got on. I got a seat and we were away on our 26km journey to Meknes, paid my 8 Dirham bus fare getting a ticket and not long after 2-3 roadside wave the bus down stops the bus was a chock-a-block sardine can but I had a seat and was happy. Got into the centre of Meknes and I seen a sign for Hotel Malta so jumped off laughing out loud glad to have done it my way, it was 1710hrs. Walked towards my hotel and into the same cafe as yesterday to have a cheeseburger, fritters and a tea, 34 Dirham and belly full I said my thanks and back to hotel. Stripped off, shave and wonderful hot shower, kit on and I was ready for my walkie tonight, it was 1905hrs. A bit sad knowing this is my last night in Meknes I walked up to the area at Place el Hedin and had a laugh seeing the jugglers, musicians and magicians performing, all good fun as it was still warm. Had a tea and two scones in a cafe then slowly but slowly made it back over the River Valley Bridge and up the hill into the feast of restaurants and café's area on the other hill the other side of the river from the Medina and had a bowl of Morocco and Soup with bread and one more nice tea and a scone and that was me, night over. Back into Hotel, upto room, stripped off and into my lovely bed and asleep dreaming more sex in Morocco.

Email Sent: Mon, 11 Jan 2010
Subject: Volubilis 217AD Roman Ruins;

Hi All

Jumped a shared taxi, 10 Dirham and jumped off 25Klms later and got another for 4klms to Volubilise which is a huge Roman remains site approx 2klms sq all built 200-230AD.

www.trekearth.com

It was fantastic seeing the still in place brightly coloured Mosaics in the ground and wall plaques still in position with lots of wall still going up 2-3 meters high then the big Roman Arches and Pillars.

The main Roman ceremonial stone block road is still their and still with all its gullies and drainage built 217AD, the Shots is blocked and not working.

Got a sardine bus back so saved 2 Dirham.

Heading for Rabat manyanna.

al de bes

RomanJack

How "Not" to Travel North Africa, Middle East, Israel & Malta and "Still Enjoy Yourself"

Day 17, Tuesday, 12-01-10, Meknes – Rabat; Morocco

Awake at 0500hrs for a piss and back to bed but turning over a few times then woke up as alarm went off at 0800hrs. Up, face splash, long cargo, two long sleeved T-shirts and trainers on and out downstairs telling guy I was going for breakie. Nice slow walk in the nice fresh blue sky air and into Cafe as yesterday and had the same omelette and a tea. Enjoy my hot crusty baguette breakie, paid my 20 dirham bill and over to Post Marco to post one love letter to my Kelly Rose, my darling curvy sweetheart who I hope is warm in freezing cold England and some travel notes to Sandralita who I also hope is warm and wears her ice skating shoes when she collects her post from Aldershot main post office as posties cannot deliver as it's too cold. Paid for stamps, stuck them on and putting card and letter into post box I was happy now the job is done. Off I went back to Hotel and upto room and bang, a full clearance dobhi drop, cleaned ass, cleaned teeth which are getting browner by the day and little final pack of now getting heavier shoulderbag then out downstairs to reception and handed key over. Said my good luck's and goodbyes and out going left and got lost. Standing at street corner I met a French lady who I spoke to in Volubilis yesterday who was staying in Hotel Touring, she said it was a bit rough with no hot water but at 80 Dirham a night what could she expect. We walked together down to Gare Abigail train station, said our bye byes and in I went. Notice board had Rabat train at 1129hrs, it was only 0950hrs so out and got a Petit cab to Gare de Meknes Train Station, paid him 10 Dirham and into train station, it was 1000hrs. Seen Rabat train 1021hrs so bought a ticket, 60 Dirham and out across the steps underpass and upto platform 2 and looking at the notice board it had depart 1021hrs, retard 50mins. Swearing out loud I was very annoyed but calmed down and sat down on the cold platform chair as what else could I do, just my bad train start to the day but that's life. Train arrived at 1115hrs and on I got taking a seat which there was plenty and we where away and sat back watching the hilly green fields sometimes older villages and towns passing by then at 1320hrs in we drew to Ville Rabat train station. Off I got carrying my roller shoulderbag up and down the temporary steps and out on to Avenue Mohammed V and along its bright stores and shops and into Hotel Berlin, 261 Avenue Mohammed V, Rabat, Tel: 0537703435. The guy smiling shook my hand and I said room, he said okay, 200 Dirham and gave me room key 28 a ground floor room so gave him 200 Dirham and Passport. He filled in his paperwork, gave me my Passport back and off I went down to room, dumped kit and out for a little walkie as Rabat had great walking scenery sights to see but first things first, I needed eats. Went across the road to my only previous visit cafe and two waiters smiling brightly welcomed me back both shaking my hand, one said omelette laughing and I laughing said omelette and sat down to watch the never-ending African Nations cup on telly which I must admit was really good exciting football. Breakfast omelette the second one for today came with fritters and a tea so I happily devoured the whole lot, sat back for 10mins then paid my 24 Dirham bill and out I went. No plans so into the Medina and just went straight through the packed Souk stalls ending up walking sometimes narrow empty Souks which are a robbers dream as no way could you escape as although I knew where I wanted to go, where was I now, lost, I think. Came out at Bab el Alou just facing the cemetery so crossed the road and just happily followed the path leading outside the Kasbah des Oudaias Medina huge Atlantic Ocean walls seeing the surfers in action then up the stone steps into the Kasbah at Almohad des Oudaias having a look over the Atlantic Wall, great sights. No plans so followed the path and out of the Kasbah turning left going downhill along Boulevard Tariq al-Marsa passing the rowing boat Anchorage where I had the last time came back across the Oued Bou Regreg River saying my smiling good lucks to Sale as I stopped. I was looking and seeing how I had walked when I done this the last time and it was an unbelievable trek as it must have been a good 12-15 km. Must slow down I promised myself and crossed the road into the Medina just following the as usual very busy stall Souk and came out at Avenue Mohammed V and that was me, into cafe L'Alsace and treated myself to a hamburger, fritters and a tea, 36 Dirham and sat back having indulged myself in a no rush no walk day, it was 1710hrs. Paid my bill and out upto a digital photo shop and printed all my remaining photos ready to send to Sandralita manyanna as it's my last day in Morocco. Early tomorrow morning I am heading for Algeria, that's the plan. Back over to Hotel and upto room just having a shave and a face wash, tidied up my shoulderbag then out for a walk, it was 1900hrs. No plans so walked up and around the Villa Nouvelle area where my Hotel is then into the well lit still going strong Souk stalls of the Medina and feeling a little bit sad back out and into my only cafe and had another tea watching the telly football. One thing I do notice is the lack of Westerners or maybe it's me but I thought there would be plenty about. Had my usual 20mins Internet then called it a night and back into Hotel and upto room, it was 2205hrs. Stripped off and into bed thinking I am looking forward to hopefully seeing my sexy Casablanca sweetheart manyanna and asleep dreaming Casablanca in de Souk sex.

Email Sent: Tue, 12 Jan 2010
Subject: Rm28 Hotel Berlin, 261 Ave Mohammed V, Rabat, Tel 0537703435

Hi All
Jumped a train 1115hrs and into Rabat Ville at 1320hrs and walked down Ave Mohammed to the above and got same d-ensuite room, 200 Dirham. Staying tonight then heading for Casablanca. Danka Sandralita.
al de bes
Jack

Day 18, Wednesday, 13-01-10, Rabat – Casablanca; Morocco

Great sleep dreaming of my Kelly Rose and her curvy curves then woke up at 0700hrs for a piss then back to bed for a 20min snooze then up for good at 0735hrs. Face splash, long cargo, trainers and two long sleeve shirts on and out for breakie having an omelette and a crusty baguette which is doing my gums and teeth in, how these people eat this crusty monstrosity all their lives is unbelievable. Enjoyed breakie anyway with 2 mint teas then paid my 32 Dirham bill and out drawing 1000 Dirham from a Marco bank ATM and back upto room. Cleaned teeth then felt a great stir and had a full blaster dobhi drop, cleaned ass and final pack of shoulderbag and out handing key in and saying my Good luck and Goodbyes to reception. Slow walk pulling my trolley shoulderbag as don't know how we can do without them trolleys or am I just growing old!. Into Rabat Ville train station and bought a one way, 35 Dirham to Casablanca and down the steps to platform 1, it was 0920hrs, train was due at 0930hrs. Train came in so on I got getting a seat and sitting back a one early on the road happy man just keeping an eye out for Casa Port on my Casablanca train as we passed through green fields with cows, goats and sheep herds on a nice bright sunny day. We stopped approximately 5 times and the guy sitting next to me laughing said next one Casa Port so relieved I said thanks. Drew into Casablanca proper as I couldn't miss it with all the big huge ships anchored off the Casa Port and I and everyone got off and I followed the crowd out of the station, it was 1040hrs. Taxi touts by the dozen touting everyone but I agreed a 10 Dirham over the top charge to drive me to Hotel Mon Reve so shoulderbag in boot and away we went, not far as I could have walked it but wanted to save time. Welcomed by handshakes and big smiles from the reception staff at Hotel Mon Reve, 7 Rue Chaouia, Casablanca, Tel:0522311439 and in I went showed Passport and got room 21, 150 Dirham. Upto room, quick change of kit, rolled up my one week old dirty not changed cargo trousers, shirt and out upto Rue Salah Ben Bouchaib to the laundry shop just past the cafe with photocopy on its front door, in I went and guy smiling said olla and took my kit counting it, gave me receipt saying 1800hrs and out I went for a no plans walk towards the Medina. There were lots of good decent hotels along the way passing the huge old Cinema then got lost and came out on Place Mohammed V. I knew where I was so no rush back and into the Medina at the Arch near Humphrey Bogart. It was fun being in a real Medina and as usual got lost but slowly made it to the Port side of the Youth Hostel. Needed a piss so in asking reception guy could I use their toilets, no problem he said and I had a nice piss and out asking him the price for a non-ensuite, he said 135 Dirham, a rip-off I thought. Out from there having a look across into the harbour at all the big ocean going ships then a slow walk passing a sign above a locked door; Dar Rabbi Hairm Pinto, 1895 so don't know if he was a Jewish Rabbi but kept going until I came out at the big huge Medina Arch at Place Jamaa Souk. Getting an expert at crossing Morocco's roads as now I do as everyone else does just walk across the road ignoring the traffic as they all stop, must admit it's frightening at times. Seen a decent cafe called Romano so sat down outside and had a beef burger sandwich and two teas just watching the Moroccan fun world go by, it was 1605hrs. Time to go so paid my 36 Dirham bill and saying my thanks I was away and last stop into Post Marco and posted my last Moroccan notes to Sandralita, 34 Dirham stamp. Back to Hotel and had a nice shave and shower so feeling like new again went up and collected my dobhi, 62 Dirham and back dumping it in my room. Out again and a nice walk to where the bus station was as may be catching an early bus manyanna to the Airport then a walk past all the upmarket hotels which was good fun and a tout no hassle walk and that was nearly my night over as not even thinking of Medina Chico's tonoche. Back towards my hotel and had a nice hot tea and 2 sweet scones sitting thinking hope I make the Airport on time manyanna, paid my 20 Dirham bill and back into Hotel, it was 2225hrs. Up to room, packed and checked everything then back down telling reception guy to give me an early call at 0500hrs, he said okay. Back upto room, stripped off and into bed dreaming Casablanca sex is not for the fainthearted but wishing for more and asleep a warm and happy Casablanca man.

Email Sent: Wed, 13 Jan 2010
Subject: Casablanca again

Hi All

These French keyboards are a pain, why can't they learn ingliise?? Jumped a train, 35 Dirham and 1hr later got off in Casa, great lively place and booked in the same hotel as last time, Rm 21, 150 Dirham d-ensuite. Just having wander around de Medina. Manyanna at 0800hrs I fly to Algiers in Algeria as no land crossing from Morocco and have booked for 4 nights into Hotel Dar-Tlidjene, 01 Rue de L'Hopital, Ain Taya, 16611, Tel 0021321867600. Any hoods in Algeria want a meet up for a Naafi session let me know
www.hoteldartlidjene.com
al de bes
Jack

Day 19, Thursday, 14-01-10, Casablanca – Khouribga; Morocco

Up at 0430hrs ready for my exciting trip to Algiers, Algeria as it's supposed not to be safe in areas but Algiers was okay I had read. Face splash, cleaned teeth, final little pack of shoulderbag and out locking door behind me and carried shoulderbag down to the bottom of the stairs where the reception guy said taxi, indicating at guy in Hotel Hall, I said yes, and he opened the lobby doors. Taxi driver came in, took my shoulderbag and me saying all the best to reception and out I went seeing taxi driver putting shoulderbag in boot, I got in the front and we were away in the slightly drizzle rain. I got a bit worried as maybe it was a plot to slit my throat and take my money but watching the signposts I seen the sign for Aeroporto so sat back relaxed enjoying the no tooting horn car drive. Had a chat with the driver and checking my e-mail ticket I said Royal Maroc, Terminal 3, he said okay and we drove to outside the Terminal 3 Departure Doors where he stopped, out I got, paid him the 250 Dirham, said my thanks, shook his hand and I was away upto the entrance doors but they were locked, it was 0540hrs. Left shoulderbag by the door and had a circle walk just stretching my legs. At 0600hrs the entrance doors were opened and in I went putting shoulderbag and China beachbag through x-ray and I was in. Royal Maroc check-in desk had opened so joined the small queue and when it came to my turn up I went giving Lady my passport and e-mail ticket. She went on her computer but said your name has not been booked. I don't know why I said it's the 15th isn't it, she said no, it's the 14th so I smiled saying sorry, I have got the wrong date. She said go upto the executive check in empty desk and lady will change your dates so I said my thanks and away but over to the cafe seating area. I couldn't change my tickets as my Passport Visa didn't start until the 15th so I wouldn't be allowed in anyway so what a rollick and how had I managed to drop it as had been keeping my daily dated travel notes and the date on the start of this one was Thursday 15-1-10, my flight date. Not to worry, live and learn as also I did not have a penny of Algerian dinars and not one money changing kiosk in Terminal 3 so will also get some dinars today for manyanna, still can't believe my day and date mix up. Asked security guy can I get a train or bus to Casablanca, he said go to Terminal 1 and catch a train to Gare Voyageurs then catch Petit cab into Casa centre so out I went and a short walk with my shoulderbag on an airport trolley and into Terminal 2 walking through it to Terminal 1 seeing signs for the train. Went down moving escalator and bought a 40 Dirham ticket to Gare Voyageurs at kiosk, it was 0710hrs, train was at 0800hrs. Sat down on some seats and nearly falling asleep as train came in at 0740hrs, passengers got off and us waiting passengers got on and at 0800hrs spot on with a toot of his horn we were away. Train stopped twice then at Casa Voyageurs station lots like me got off. Taxi touts wanted 5 euro then 20 Dirham but I walked over to the main road and waved a Petit taxi down and he said, pointing at it, meter, so in I got with two other guys. He dropped me off at Hotel Mon Reve, my previous hotel and the meter showed eight Dirham so I gave him 10 and into Hotel. Had to wait for a room so left shoulderbag at reception and upto the tea selling kiosks across the road at the market corner and had 2 large egg rolls and 2 teas, 8 Dirham as they are really good value. Back to Hotel and got room 21, same room, dumped kit and out to bank to try for some Algerian dinars. Tried 3 banks but all said no but at the last one guy took me out to the street and pointed up to Air Algeria shop and said try there so in I went and asked the young girl where could I get Algerian dinar. She said nowhere in Casablanca but use credit card when I land at Algiers airport. I being unsure said are you sure they have ATM, she smiled and with her eyes said, yes, are you thick and I said laughing thank you very much and away very relieved as LP says not many ATMs in Algeria. Out I went thinking where to now and a slow walk back to Hotel dumping Passport in shoulderbag and had a look at L P Morocco for a town near Casablanca that I could go to by train for a days outing and picked Settat or Khouribga writing them in my pocket notebook and out again to jump a Petit taxi to Gare Voyageurs train station, 10 Dirham. Got there and into station and looking at departures seen a train for Khouribga departing 1016hrs so running upto kiosk I bought a single, 31 Dirham and running out onto platform 3 I jumped on the train as it pulled out and got a seat, phew, that was neat. Didn't take much notice at first then really started to enjoy going back in time as looking out the train window to very flat sometimes green fields, sometimes ploughed fields all done with blokes with donkeys pulling a wooden plough with very old barren farmhouses, good real history. After two stops and 1hour 30mins later I was back 200years in time as there were no proper roads anywhere and the rail line was a single track but we were still going really fast. Next stop was Sidi Hadjay at 1215hrs then after another fast journey next stop was Mrizig and I was bigtime worried as how was I going to get back as with the heavy rain all the dirt track roads were flooded and impassable that's if I needed to take a bus or car!. Finally everyone standing up we drew into what looked like the very nondescript town of Khouribga and still worried I got off the train and into the not open ticket office, it was 1300hrs. I asked Guy for the next train back to Casablanca, he wrote, 1 train goes at 1530hrs, don't know if it was last one but didn't care as I was catching it and out into Khouribga I walked taking a few market stalls streets then slowly enjoying my new town walk made it all the way into the centre. Kept going and across to the other side of town at Zamkat at Meknes Road beside the Mosque with fresh fish, live turkeys and fresh meat hanging on poles in the indoor market enjoying my walkie keeping an eye on the time. Needed something to eat so into a cafe and had a plate of chips, nice thick sweet scone and a tea and although no Medina, no Port, no nothing to brag about I had seen and had a walk in a New town, so back to the train station, it was 1515hrs. Bought a one-way back to Casablanca, 31 Dirham as train drew in so out onto it and got a seat and at 1530hrs spot on with a toot toot we were away out of Khouribga train station and still enjoying watching the back in time flat landscape as we picked up a good speed. Fell asleep a few times and woke knowing we were near Casablanca, it was 1710hrs. Drew into Gare Voyageurs train station as it was getting dark and off I got, it was 1740hrs. Thought I would walk back so done a right and into a dark slum area but kept going as they can't see me in the dark and out of it thinking I knew my way and turned left and came into the biggest street stall market with lots of Souks filled with stalls that I have ever seen in my life so had a tea and a scone, 9 Dirham. Kept going taking a few lefts at roundabouts but legs starting to go I knew I was lost, so gave in and flagged down a Petit taxi. Told him central market and he took me on a dark sightsee tour of Casablanca but I didn't care. Got there eventually and his meter said 16 Dirham so I gave him a 20 Dirham note and jumped out. Just wanted to go to bed so into a cafe and had a lovely big sausage roll, chips and a tea, really delicious having a laugh with waiter, waitresses and everyone practising their ingleterra I paid my 20 Dirham bill and out, it was 2120hrs. Back to Hotel telling guy to order me a taxi for 0545hrs manyanna and saying my good nights I went upto my room, had a shave, cleaned teeth, final pack of shoulderbag and fell into bed dead to the world and asleep hoping I hear my 0515hrs alarm in the morning.

Email Sent: Thursday, 14 Jan 2010
Subject: Head Gone in Casablanca

Hi All

Up early and got a taxi to Airport and when lady checked my ticket she said your flight is manyanna so there, that's what Casa does to your brain!!. Had a think and jumped a train and now in an end of the railway line town called Khouribga and only train back is at 1530hrs so better not miss it as not many Westerners visit this town by the looks I am getting. Jimmy, Thanks had a look and can't see any problems for Shotty den hoods in Algiers.
al de bes
Jack

Map of Algeria

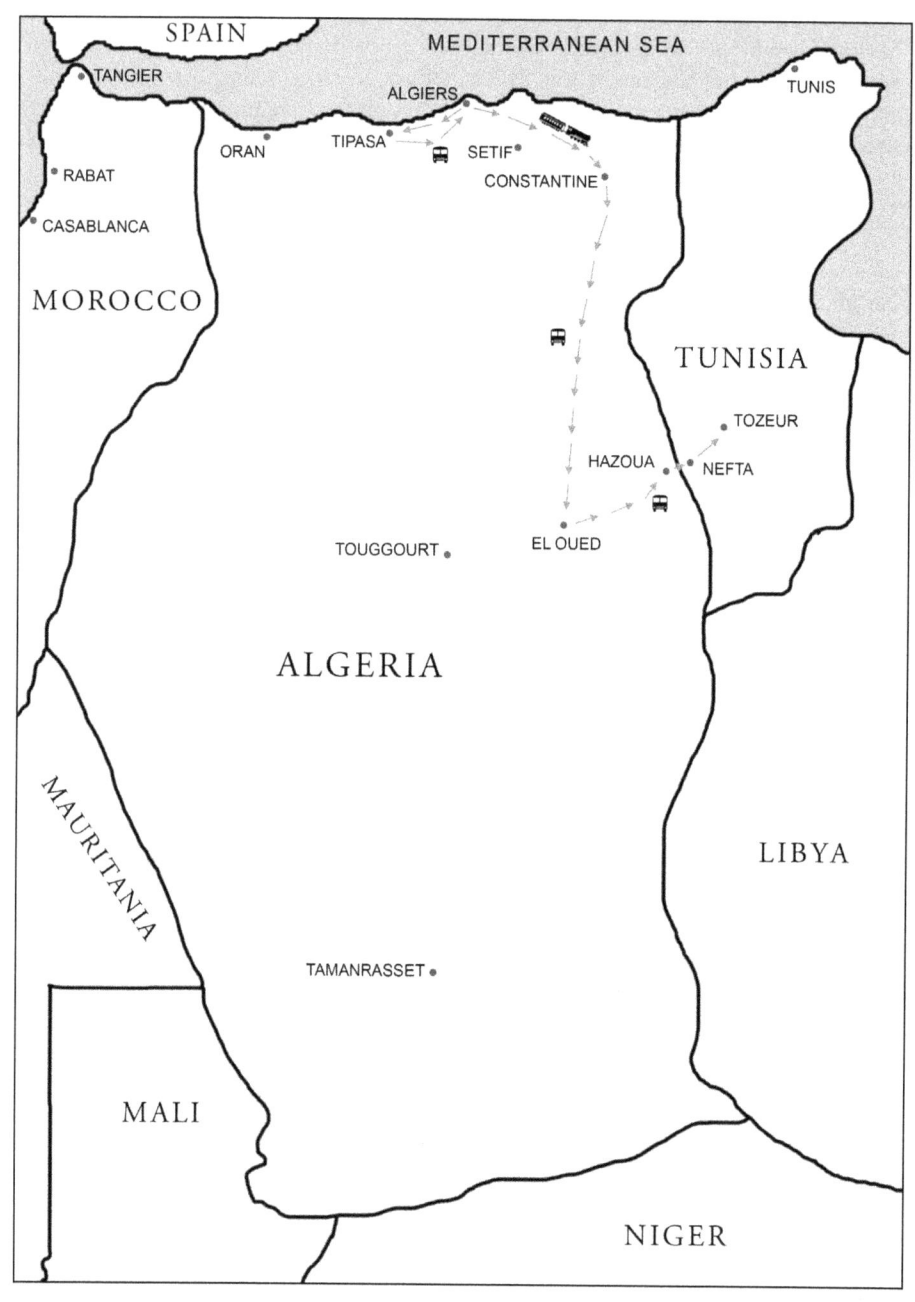

1) ALGERIA is a gem of a so friendly people Country with not many Western travellers on its roads. The real sand and sand dunes of the true Sahara desert area covering 75% of Algeria is a fantastic eye catching sight you will never forget as one drives through its blowing sand clouds listening to the Algerian beloved vocal wailing music. Algiers founded in the 10th Century by the Romans is a step back in time walking its exotic Souks and old city Medina walls but never in your walks anywhere in the world will you meet so honest and a joy to be with the happy Algerian people.
2) Capital; Algiers
3) Algeria achieved Independence in 1962
4) Climate; Ave temp Jan-Mar; 20c
5) Language; Arabic, French, Berber, English
6) Currency; Algeria Dinar, 1$US = 70 Dinar
7) Visa; Required before arrival
8) Return flight £51 + £154 ATM, hotel, food, train to Gatwick
9) Today's ongoing update of day to day accommodation, travel, food, drinks costs = £619

Day 20, Friday, 15-01-10, Casablanca; Morocco – Algiers; Algeria

Woke up once for a piss hearing the drunks shouting outside, it was 0340hrs so back to bed and asleep waking up as alarm went off at 0520hrs. Got up, face splash, underarm wash, dried off and kit all on with Thai sandals. Checked Passport in place, put neckpouch on and out I went down the steep winding stairs giving reception guy 10 Dirham for knocking on my door at 0530hrs and out I went putting shoulderbag in taxi boot, me in the backseat. Wished the driver good morning and we were away in a nice no rain, dark, no cold morning. It was a different driver and we picked up a good speed along the motorway until in we drew to Casablanca Mohammed V Airport and I told him Terminal 3 and he stopped outside it. Paid him the agreed 250 Dirham and he was away and in I went going through Airport security with a bottle of orange and a carton of milky chocolate which in today's world could be any sort of petrol or explosives. Lined up at Royal Maroc Airlines check-in desk and got to the front, girl took my Passport, looked at it and said, window or aisle, so I said aisle. Got boarding pass, flight 560, seat 11c so really chuffed I went over to a cafe and had a lovely tea and 2 croissants enjoying my Frenchy breakie . Next into customs and bang, exit stamp on Passport and in I went through to the departure lounge and had another tea with one more croissant sitting back happy as a happy Algiers lark. Finished my tea seeing our Algerian flight at a separate part of the lounge so went up and sat near it, it was 0805hrs, my flight was 0850hrs. Boarded at 0830hrs and got my seat 11C with plane only a quarter full and walking from the lounge onto the plane I passed a very nice in really good order a 4 propeller Hercules what a surprise they are still going as the last time I was in a Hercules was perhaps 1970 which probably was my last Airborne Parachute jump. Sat back happy in my seat and I could feel tiredness and sleep coming on so had a nice Moroccan snooze then woke up to take off safety demonstration and then we were away, it was 0910hrs. Got up into the sky and after a while it was a most unbelievable sight as we were now flying along the Mediterranean coast with the huge Atlas Rif mountain range with sometimes little white walled villages nestling in the mountains higher slopes all on a lovely clear sunny day, truly fantastic scenery. Had our one croissant, one butter, jam roll plane breakie with a glass of orange and a tea, just the job and settled back sometimes watching the Med Sea coastline below or trying to snooze, good fun. Was given an Algerian Visa customs form to fill in which was all in pure French even I could not understand it so asked a bloke sitting across the aisle from me does he speak English, he said yes and showed me how and what to put on it so another landing in Algeria hiccup out of the way. I had my stamped in my Passport Algeria Visa which most people need to visit Algeria which I had got in London from the Algerian Consulate which was rigmarole in itself taking 2-3 A4 Algeria filled in sheets with proof of Hotel who I had to ask to send me a stamped invitation plus the visit and interview at the Algeria consulate. Entrance date for my 15 day Visa was 15-01-10 but it's now looking good and nearly there, 15 mins to go. Landed and off plane going into Passport control, it was 1150hrs, no one at Passport control and everyone lined up in first of all one queue, then two, then 3-4-5 as queue was now moving fast I reached the Passport kiosk, handed Passport over and two mins later no hassle, bang, Algerian entrance stamp and I was in. Walked through into baggage and seen my bright red shoulderbag with four blue ribbons on its hand straps, grabbed it and out into the main hall getting hassled by money changer and taxi touts but ignored them all and kept going. I looked everywhere in the main hall, even into Arrivals but could not see one MasterCard ATM, all had Visa signs. Went to 2 Airport information enquiry desks asking for MasterCard ATM but both said no, not on Airport, only in the centre of Algiers. Lucky I had a Visa card with me as well but I had not used it on this trip so praying to Allah I put it in and typed out 14,000 Dinar as working it out thats approximately £100, US$200 and out the money came, so lucky there. Tried 2 banks in the airport but they would not change Morocco Dirham so I was so lucky. Asked at Airport information enquiry desk how much is a taxi into Algiers, they said they didn't know. Went out to the sign saying taxi and 3-5-7-9 taxi drivers said where you go, I showed them Hotel Dar Tlidjene and they all let on to not know where it was then one said 1500 Dinars in French, I said no 1000 dinars but they said no. I'd walked away then young English speaking guy said I have one taxi driver to take you for 1000 dinar and I followed him to an old guy and got in the taxi with all the drivers muttering, some shouting and opening the cab doors but I said Good Luck, see you as the ole guy drove off. I gave him the address of the Hotel and watched the road signs and it was not in Algiers as I had thought or website had stated, it was a village suburb way outside Algiers in Ain-Taya. Got to Hotel Dar Tlidjene, 01 Rue de L'Hopital, Ain–Taya, Algiers, Tel: +213 (0) 21867600, www.airtaya.populus.ch / tlidjenegroup@hotmail.com at 1225hrs after quite a long drive and gave the ole fellow 1000 Dinar. At 70 dinar to 1 US dollar he didn't do too bad I thought as he asked for more, I said no money grabbed my shoulderbag and into hotel. Gave girl my booking e-mail, she smiled saying William and took a copy of my Passport and gave me key to Room 7 and up I went. It was a beautiful, very large, very upmarket double ensuite and looking out my window the beach and sea was only 100m away, oh la, la but it was overcast and cloudy. But first things first, I dumped kit in room, changed Thai sandals to trainers and then downstairs for a chat with the lady owner putting 4000 dinars in my driving licence flat wallet. She was so friendly and such a happy person and then I met her husband who was also such a knowledgeable person and gave me very good advice about places of interest I should go. Took his advice about doing a car trip today to the centre of Algiers to see the very distinctive Martyrs Monument which dominates the full skyline above the city and also the Basilique Notre Dame D'Afrique which takes over the lower North End of the sky above the city. He said today's charge for the guide and use of car would be €10 so could not find anywhere as handy or as cheap as that and his English speaking young son would be driver and guide. Out myself with the young 21 year old chap and into a small 4 wheeler and away going first of all along the coast road overlooking the Med all along our Ain Taya village suburb of Algiers. It was a lovely sandy full beach stretching for miles with lots of beach kiosks but weather being overcast and cloudy there was no one only locals walking the actual beach itself. Went out to the outskirts of Ain Taya and down to the beach again at Plage Decca and drove along the beach for 50m or so then back on the main road and into and through the unbelievable close together high rise flats area, all it looked to me built 50-70 years ago. Next it was a joy to see the very old building, many Turkish Palaces designs all along the offside of the Port Road as we passed the Naval Base and along the very nice promenade area, now very upmarket. Good fun seeing the big waves crashing into the huge boulder rocks at the beach front. Young fellow said we will stop and go into the Notre Dame Cathedral as he drove up a very bendy hill and we got to the top and parked in the Cathedral car park and out we both got. First we had a walk along the hill looking across the harbour then into the Basilique Notre Dame D'Afrique Cathedral which was such an amazing and so colourful (Our Lady of Africa) Church full of true history it was such a dream to be here and walking its floors, first foundation stone laid on 14-10-1855. Out from there and I was so elated to have been in it we got back in his car then drove slowly past the full of Turkish Palace ancient buildings with the narrow Souks of the Kasbah nearby then the Grand Post Office a magnificent building and passed a full open garden area in the middle of Algiers, it just defied belief. Passed a very busy street market then all the way up the narrow original road to the full taking over the sky Martyrs Monument and stopped in the car park! with hoods looking after the car and we walked up and around such an imposing and meaningful structure and I had my usual thumbs up photo shoot. Some of the best sights so far in Algiers I walked along the cliff top path looking down, really interesting as the Port and the huge container ships were all over the sea to the horizon. Back into his 4 x 4 he giving the Hoods a cash payment and we were away him telling me their Friday and Saturdays are the weekend when no one works and the roads are empty so that was a bit of a bargain as he said all major roads are chock a block on Sunday the start of the working week. Good day nearly over and not far we went onto the ring road through Algiers and turning off at the signpost to Ain Taya and followed the road to my hotel, said my thanks and said I am going for a walk, it was 1815hrs. He said turn left and it will take me into the centre of Ain Taya so I did and there were loads of shops and cafes just past the two roundabouts and although lots of hoods about everyone was so friendly. Came back passing a full 3m high marble Arabic Inscripted Memorial and about another 200m I came to my hotel and into the restaurant and sat down, young fellow brought me a menu and I had a salad tuna plateful then a bowl of soup filling my belly with the cut crusty baguette pieces, had a cup of tea and that was me. Young fellow then brought me a steak with mashed potato but I said I didn't order and lady said it's the full menu. I said I only pointed at 2 items on the menu so she said ok, I knew I was half wrong as can't understand or speak French, it was now 1950hrs. Went back into Ain Taya large village centre with an old fashioned pedestrian square with still lots of pizza and chicken takeaway shops open then a bit lonely called it a night and a slow walk buying 3 different chocolate bars and back into hotel. Asked lady if I could have a cup of tea, she said Lipton, I said yes and sat downstairs in the dining area enjoying my with chocolate tea break and after a good start to my Algiers day I called it a night at 2225hrs. Said my Goodnights and up to my very warm room, opened a window, stripped off and into bed and asleep dreaming of Algerian friendly passionate love.

Email Sent: Fri, 15 Jan 2010
Subject: Rm7, Dar-Tlidjene Hotel, Rue de l'Hopital, Ain Taya, Algiers, Algeria

Hi All
I booked above in England as needed a hotel for Visa, its very upmarket and half the price again if you book it on their website www.hoteldartlidjene.com Jumped a plane from Casablanca to Algiers this time and haggled the taxi touts at Airport down to 1000 Dinars for taxi to the Ain Taya suburb of Algiers as I thought the hotel was in the centre. Out again with driver, 10 euro for a 2-3hr sightsee of Algiers but out at the Notre Dame D'Afrique beautiful Cathedral and the Martyrs Memorial high on the hill, very striking. At Airport their is not ATM that takes MasterCard, only Visa so was really lucky I had 2 cards with me as nowhere in Morocco changes Dirham into Dinar, Rate is 70Dinar to 1US. Staying 4 days with driver trips to a few places as I could not have done it so cheap and so quick by myself but heading of on my own to Constantine then train across the Tunisia border in 4-5 days time.
al de bes
Jack

Day 21, Saturday, 16-01-10, Algiers – Tipasa; Algeria

Up at 0445hrs for a piss and back to bed but no sleep as large wall clock was ticking loudly and as I heard the Islam loudspeaker chanters in action I knew their first performance was at 0600hrs, the loud ticker showed 0500hrs. Had a think, thinking we probably lose an hour on world time clock from Morocco time but had a sort of snooze anyway. Up at 0830hrs by the loud ticker, shave, underarm and face wash, long cargo and trainers with only pullover on as looking out the window it was a lovely sunny day and then downstairs to the restaurant area. All clocks showed 0900hrs so got speaking to a German guy working in Constantine and he said yes its 0915hrs now as I had my 2 teas, 2 croissants, 2 crusty pieces of baguette and cheese then back upto room for a nice dobhi drop, cleaned ass, cleaned teeth and back down to the restaurant waiting for my driver for today's trip to Tipasa. Not long and young fellow full of life came in smiling and said ok we go and I said you been to disco, he laughed saying no disco in Ain Taya and we got in the 4 x 4 and away. As we drove out of Ain Taya and Algiers we passed through at least 10 Police road checkpoints but traffic was horrendous and chock a block everywhere as we eventually got out of Algiers and into the green fields sometimes tree forest countryside. Got out of the packed traffic and going fast now passing 20-30 squashed together tower blocks, not a pretty sight then out again on the many choked with tower blocks towns each side as we stayed on the motorway following signs for Zeralda. Now seen signs for Tipasa, 49km, which is our destination so approximately 1hrs drive still to go, it was 1105hrs. We were now in full view of the Mediterranean Sea on our right with its rocky sea edge coastline getting nearer to Tipaza or Tipasa and road signs spelt differently on every odd one but the nearer we got it was now spelt Tipasa!. About 11km from Tipasa as just outside Ain Tayourait we turned left going up a very steep bendy mountain road with the most fantastic views from its hillside hairpin bends then inland to Wilaya de Tipasa. Came to and drove into the car park and parked up, it was 1200hrs, had a walk around the magnificent huge 185m circumference 60m dia, 32m high, 4 high door, 2 floors all approx 500 x 300m sq stone block built in a round circle Dome, what a truly fantastic sight but I said to the young fellow, I wonder how many lives were lost building it. We done our walk around it and I said it's a pity we could not get inside. Back in the car and down the great hill going left at the bottom and into Tipasa stopping at a Roman burial place, in we went me paying the 2No 20 dinar entrance fees to Les Necropoles de Tipasa, a burial and incarnation Site and had a walk along the many large slab burial graves. We then walked along the cliff edge path with it looked like Roman dwelling places then that was it after another good sightsee we went back to the car and into the tourist centre of Tipasa and parked up. Checked a few restaurants then had a pizza and drinks sitting outside at Romano restaurant and I thoroughly enjoyed my hot half a pizza and a Fanta. I paid the 200 dinar bill with a 1000 dinar note getting 4 x 200 dinar notes back so now have plenty of change. Left there and into the big full town size of the Roman remains town of Tipasa, entrance fee 25 dinar each which I paid but it was truly very well worth it. We started our walks at the big, half a football pitch size with its 2m thick sliced brick wall, the

L'Amphitheatre and I was in true elated happiness walking across the level lawn inner section thinking of Gladiators with swords killing each other on this actual spot 2000 years ago. Real true history looking around at the seating areas and the Arched entrance to it. Out over the steps from it and around the also thick block brick walls of the Le Nouveau big Temple area but all around it for what looked like miles there were fully intact block ruins of many different sizes. Came to Les Edifices Prive which appeared like a row or rows of Roman Villas and we were still walking on a fraction of the original city. Turning back towards Tipasa touristy centre we had a walk around La Villa des Fresques I think a rich Roman Nobleman's villa. Next we got to Les Thermes we both said it looks like a swimming pool then the Les Petit Thermes de Tipasa which appeared to be private small baths then that was us after a great amazing true Roman history day we walked back and into the car. In our walks we came across many 8-10-12m deep fully constructed round wells now empty but whistling or shouting down them I could hear an echo. The young fellow started up his 4 x 4 and we were away and he was a great young man and a fantastic driver with a great sense of humour, a true credit to his lovely parents. Signpost as we drove out of Tipasa said 67km, it was 1600hrs and I was just hoping no severe traffic jams but with only two little 10min hold ups we drove into central Algiers and parked up near the Kasbah area as I wanted just to orientate myself from where it was from the Bus Station as manyanna I was doing a walking tour of Algiers on my own as although the young lad and his 4 x 4 were priceless for my first 2 days in Algiers I now wanted to be left alone to be happy and get lost. We parked up and walked up to the front of the Ketchaoua Mosque and the young fellow pointed out where the Algiers Bus Station was and I was happy for tomorrow so back in the car and we were away and not long we were in Ain Taya so got him to drop me off in the village centre. Had a look into Hisia Restaurant and young man said, look, and took me into the kitchen showing me 4 big pots of hot food so picked a thick large bean soup, a plate of mashed spuds and sat at a café table enjoying my very filling 1830hrs din din. Finished and very impressed I paid my 150 dinar bill and away and into Hotel and upto room, trousers down and bang, a full happy dobhi drop and that was me, cleaned ass. Had a nice shave then shower and out for a long walk right through and past the pedestrian roundabout and small park area until no more lights and turned back and into a café for a tea and a scone. Fully happy and no plans paid my 30 dinar bill and in the nice warm night made my slow way back to hotel and up into room, stripped off and into bed asleep dreaming Kasbah hookers manyanna.

Email Sent: Sat, 16 Jan 2010
Subject: Roman town of Tipasa

Hi All

Made it 68klms to an ancient Roman town of Tipasa depending on whether you like Z or S. I must admit the Romans where great builders as it had everything from great roads to big amphitheatres, temples, thermal baths, burial grounds and their own private dwellings then the fascinating round tower 60m dia by 32m high. I think Muslim Jack will jump a bus manyanna from Ain Taya and explore Algiers by foot by myself so tell the Kasbah hoods the Arthur st shotty den hood is on his way, anyone about?
al de bes
Jack

Day 22, Sunday, 17-01-10, Ain Taya – Algiers; Algeria

Up 3 times from 0530hrs for runny dobhi drops but enjoyed my I think, vivid nightmares dreams sleep and up for good at 0820hrs. Face splash, long cargo, trainers, pullover on and down to the restaurant breakie room. Had 4 slices of crusty baguette with butter, cheese and jam and 1 croissant with 3 cups of milky coffee and felt really good. Back upto room, cleaned teeth and checking I had map and details of Algiers I dropped key in at reception and out turning left down the main road and only a 100m walk got to the small bus station, it was 0945hrs. Tried in Ingleterra to tell about 6 conductors touting for buses that I wanted to go to Algiers but no one spoke English as I done a circle then the first bus tout said we go to Algiers so on I got paying him 10 Dinar fare, got a seat and we were away out of Ain Taya on the main road. Not far and we stopped, he said, change and pointed at a big bus so out and onto it paying a 15 Dinar fare, got a seat and again we were away. It was a very long journey and I was getting worried as some of the tower block areas we drove through were not a good sight but then seen the sea and Port D'Algier on my right and 20mins later as I seen the Tower Clock Mosque in the far distance as we parked up in Gare Routiere Tafoura, it was 1105hrs. Off I got very pissed off as Hotel was long way from Algiers City Centre but that's life. I walked happily along Bvd Zirout Youcep, turned left and came to Grand Hotel Arago, 06 Rue Haffaf, Nafaa, Tel: 021739493, checked prices and d-ensuite was 1300 Dinar. Out from there then along Rue Bouzrina Ahmet full of market stalls and on down the narrow Rue Freres Elayachi then lost completely I was into and along Rue Hachemi Hamoud and back on the upmarket sea road, phew, I breathed with relief. The sea road was a very picturesque scenery wall as I reached Place des Martyrs a very large Plaza and full of life. Seen the harbour lighthouse in the distance so walked down towards it looking down at all the old harbour and the colourful fishing boats all anchored up but the views of Algiers from the sea angle were just a fantastic sight. Came to a fenced off sign, "Zone Maditarie", "Access Denied" but just glad to have made it this far I turned back enjoying the views and back upto Place des Martyrs and across the packed shawls on the ground market and looking straight at the very imposing very old Ketchaoua Mosque on Rue Hadj Omar the start line for the Casbah. The Mosque was ongoing refurbishment but I still forced myself into it having a look as the front twin Minaret and Arched entrance were so beautifully sculptured it was a joy to be close up. Out from it and up a stepped narrow Souk going uphill no idea where I was going but knew I was going deeper and deeper into the narrow souks of the Casbah as the faces of the young and oldish people were getting more rigid, sterner and eyes more wickedly staring but wished them, "olla my friend" I kept going. Got to the top of Rue Professeur Soudah then along Rue Ben Chereb turning right along Rue Arbadji Abderahane and turned right again thinking time to get out and went down and wow oh wow their they where my lovely darling of the day/night and I knew I was not getting out of here without paying hard dosh but in the mood I felt a stir but this time on the other side. One lovely beautiful figure black haired girl came out from a small Souk standing smiling with her arms out and no room to go past I looked directly into her lovestruck eyes I knew it was

Algerian love to last until the last dawn as she said "You like me" and cuddled up close my heart beating loudly I said yes putting my arms around her. She said you want boom boom rubbing my front rocker as I quickly said yes but where we go and how much. She giving me a tight cuddly saying 40$US and I jumped back a little letting to be surprised she said holding me tight 35$US so caressing her lovely bum I was so much in love I didn't care about the price I said ok getting a happy scream she saying my place taking me up a narrow Souk and in we went under a small Arch door into a neat very small room flat and in true love we kissed caressing each others sexual vibes bodies I got out her money in 25US$ the rest in Dinar putting it on a very small dresser we both stripped of. Oh my god she was so sexy beautiful as we now where in each others arms again French kissing and exploring each others sex aroused bodies I was in heaven in Algiers as we where on the small double bed she was eating me then me on top making pure heavy pounding Algerian style sexual lust passionate love she was biting my neck and wrapping her legs around me as our love sweat drenched each other the bed sheets now sweet scented smelling soaking wet as we changed positions me nearly biting her nipples off as our love vibes reached new heights she was screaming in lust and then with a final fulfilling rush of sexual exotic spasm sex curved naked Algerian love we both climaxed stuck together on are scented sweat wet bed sheets she was ripping my back to pieces in lust I was screaming in passion as the electric tingling sensations all over my body I knew our love would never go away as we slowly but slowly came to a rest I slid off my true love to lie deep up close are heavy contented breathing slowly but slowly coming to a rest I knew I would wake up tomorrow morning in my true loves bed she tickled my bum then my ribs and as she rubbed my face cheeks saying "I like you Papa but we go" and slid of the bed me giving her lovely ass cheek a gentle pat as up we got and got dressed both smiling in contentment and as she took my hand out we went Oh my God into daylight I could hardly believe it. Quickly bending under the small Arch Souk entrance she said go right and I did and with one blowing kiss and a smile to each other she was away. Now it was real fun as I was into a very narrow ancient grubby Souk with small entrances to dwellings you would have to bend to get into at Rue Ayadi Said. Seen this imposing Arch entrance with a security guard and popping my head in he invited me in telling me originally it was the Palace of an Ottoman Turk King 1793, so in I went. He gave me a guided tour telling me and showing me the walls all decorated with Italian, Spanish and Tunisian 500,000 mosaic tiles, really impressive. Next he took me to the Kings shower area all decorated in his sailing boats, descriptions of his 4-5 large sailing boats and the King's own private wide entrance stairs. It was a very imposing Palace with its separate section for servants and guards with big kitchen for cooking all surrounding an inner courtyard topped by a big, huge dome. Had done my full walk so offered him some cash but he said his thanks but no as we shook hands. I asked him directions to the Museum of Popular Arts and Traditions which also was now housed in a previous Turkish Palace, he pointed up the dirty grubby Souk telling me go up, turn right and right again and down some steps and you will see its Archway entrance so I was away back into the Casbah grubby alleys thinking and smiling to myself about my daylight lover thinking will I see her again. Found it more by luck, paid my 20 Dinar entrance fee and in having a walk around its 2 floors very neat mosaic tiled walls seeing the paintings and then out onto its upper balconies with great views over the vivid roof tiles narrow Souks alley dwellings and then out I went saying my thanks. Feeling thirsty and laughing at my earlier daylight sex antics I had a nice hot tea and a scone in Café Dada then kept going on down to the Place des Martyrs, it was 1530hrs. Knew I wanted to go towards the City centre and passed another very old imposing Mosque along Rue Abane Ramdane facing Rue Haman Cherub. Now seen Central Touring Hotel 09, Rue Abane Ramdane, Tel:021736903, 1200 Dinar, single ensuite and also Hotel du Palais with singles for 800 Dinar also on Rue Abane Ramdane with a few other neat hotels nearby all with lots of Police about but it was to me an ok area. Slowly in no rush walked back into the city centre to the Grand Post Office structure which was a very imposing sight and went in for a look at its splendid 8 column high round Dome with its lovely stone carvings all over its walls and Dome ceiling. Out and over to the little going uphill park for a 10min sit down Fanta swig or two on the marble park benches. Feeling peckish so into the Saloon de Pizzeria Fast Food underground café for 2 croissants and a tea, 100 Dinar, just the job, said my thanks and away up the wide marble steps and tarmac path to a large two clenched fists on one side of the 2m sq Stone Memorial, the other side it looked like an engraving of General De Gaulle, don't know as it was old and no names anywhere. There were lovely views from this far up and the huge 12 storey flat building each side as I looked down added a great people feeling to the views. Took my time going down and came to a lovely but elegant hotel called Hotel Djurduro, 6 Rue Lounes Merar, Tel: 021 635455, 1800 Dinar single ensuite, 2200 d-ensuite and was truly sorry I had not made it here for my Algerian trip but the only hotels I could book in England for my Algerian Visa were on the internet and my hotel was the cheapest I could find. It stated it was near Algiers City Centre but it was 27km outside, 2-3hrs by bus and a rip off cost. Seen Hotel Tipasa, 4 Rue Rachid Kessentim, Tel:021 736515 a bit nondescript but decent prices. Kept going on down to the railway station and tried to find times for trains to Constantine on the outside train time board but no luck, didn't try to go in as armed guards everywhere and searches were ongoing. Took my time and over to the bus station where I had been dropped off and seen sign Ain Taya so after a 10min talk in French! I got on the 8 seat only big single decker bus, 70 Dinar fare. Conductor gave me the what used to be the conductors seat as the bus filled up with approximately 40 people on it and we were away. Stopped 6 -7 times going out of Algiers and bus had 60 plus sardine people in it as hitting road bumps I thought the axles or chassis was going to snap, it was 1725hrs. In the dark at 1900hrs we stopped for the 20th time at a small bus station and conductor took me across to a smaller bus and said Ain Taya and on I got, fare 10 Dinar. Got talking to an Algerian fellow who spoke very good English as we travelled on our 1hr journey to Ain Taya and shaking hands off we got. I went into my local restaurant and had thick pea soup and crusty bread and belly full I paid my 160 Dinar bill and back into hotel. Met the owner and paid my 20,000 Dinar 4 night rip off bill then the 50 plus 24 Euro day trip bills and all bills paid I went out for a walk. First stop into an Internet café to do my usual 15-20 mins and laughed out loud as had went into www.shankillmirror.com as wanted to look at its January issue I seen my photo and story of just before Christmas when I was working in Angering, West Sussex I went back to a site I had worked on about 5 years previously where West Sussex County Council who had run out of ideas for street names and I, the Site Agent and Site Manager had to answer one question each picked from a hat. My question was; What is the name of the Football team I support so told them Linfield but before any street names where put up I had left the site and there it was in a full story photo me standing over Linfield Close, great history as I paid my Internet charge and out. Went for a not far nighttime hood walk then called it a night, back to hotel, upto room, stripped off and into bed and asleep a good daylight walking Souk lover Belfast Linfield Algerian man.

Email Sent: Sun, 17 Jan 2010
Subject: Algiers Kasbah and de hoody jack

Hi All

Great day sightseeing in Algiers and made it into 2 No Turkish Palaces up behind the Ketchoua Mosque in the Kasbah. I could tell the Kasbah was a very rough hoody area but they kept their distance from de Shotty Den Arthur St hood but saying that the Algerian people are so friendly and so honest as no tourists yet they have yet to learn the London, Bangkok, Bombay touristy con tricks. Found 4 Hotels I wish I had knew about as directly in middle of Algiers City but that's life. Still enjoying my walkie but heading out the day after manyanna to Constantine by train it looks like, still have to check times etc. Traffic is horrendous on the roads so don't know what time I will make it back to my Ain Taya Hotel on public bus tonight.
al de bes
Jack

How "Not" to Travel North Africa, Middle East, Israel & Malta and "Still Enjoy Yourself"

A little bit of Linfield

Ex Shankill man Jack Glass wanted to share this interesting story with Shankill Mirror readers. About 5 years ago Jack was working in West Sussex about 65 miles from Aldershot on the outskirts of a village called Angmering. As Clerk of Works he was supervising the construction of a large block of semi detached homes. The area was being built up with a massive development of flats, detached and semi detached houses stretching for miles. The County Council had run out of ideas for names for the many roads, closes, drives, parks etc. Jack was nominated to be asked to name a road in the development and was asked a very simple question, 'What is the name of the football team I support?' Coming from Belfast and the Shankill Road the answer was pretty obvious! – Linfield. Jack never heard any more about the development and as he had finished his inspections he left the area.

Towards the end of last year Jack was offered another job on a building site on the outskirts of the same village. Curiosity got the better of him and he went on a search of the original site. Jack takes up the story, 'I eventually found the original site and there it was – Linfield Close, a lovely surprise and I almost had a few tears in my eyes. So there it is a bit of Belfast history in the wilds of West Sussex a road named by me after my favourite football team. So I went and gave it the thumbs up as you can see from the photograph."

Linfield Close named by me

Day 23, Monday, 18-01-10, Ain Taya – La Perloes – Algiers; Algeria

Up at 0800hrs after a very poor restless legs aching sleep, face splash, long cargo trousers on and downstairs for the usual cheese, crusty baguette, coffee breakie, no wonder I'm not sleeping. I said good morning to Toupik the owners' son getting ready to take his Dad to the Airport, finished my 4th cup of coffee and back upto room, cleaned teeth and a sort of dobhi drop, cleaned ass but in no hurry as no firm plans for today. Put bottle of Coke in China beachbag and out turning right and up to the top of the hill enjoying the lovely views over the bay and the clean sandy beaches. Back along the beach road sometimes having to come inland as Villas had taken up the beach but back into centre of Ain Taya on any of its sandy beach come rocky shoreline and had a tea in one of the lots of cafes as it looks a very popular holiday village and area, it was only 1105hrs, where to go now? Back to hotel and talking to reception guy he said jump a bus, 10 Dinar and go to La Perloes a village about 10km along the coast that is a good walking sightsee fishing village and so not even a second thought I said my thanks and walked down to the bus station as had asked reception guy to write it on a sheet of paper for me. Got to bus station area and showed guy La Perloes and he said yes, get on his bus me thinking that was handy. As usual waited until the bus was full and standing room only and we were away. It was a good little run as I paid my 10 Dinar fare and at end of run in a fishing village the conductor gave me a thumbs up, village was named Tamerfoust. Had a walk down to its lovely sandy beach but covered in the most unimaginable debris, it was unbelievable. Had a slow enjoyable walk into the small fishing boat harbour seeing a small Fort in the hills above the village so up through the very old dwellings in the village and into the fence gate to the Fort entrance but guy said I was not allowed in as it had just closed. I said could I just have a look but he said no, come back later so out I went seeing on my left a very old Church with a big concrete cross engraved on its Fort like front structure so walked up to it passing it looked like a sort of Naval Base Accommodation. Guy at gate said ok as I said I look but it was completely derelict the whole inside just a building site mess but in its time it must have had some history but no names or anything. Out saying my thanks and back another way into the village centre and had a tea and 2 scones thinking do I want another night in no nightlife Ain Taya or should I fork out a few bob and get a hotel in the centre of Algiers, see a bit of nightlife and be near the train station for my 0800hrs start tomorrow. Yes, that's good thinking so waiting for a bus I said to myself that's what I will do and knew the hotel I was going to go to. Nine buses stopped at the stop but the 10th one was for Ain Taya so on and got a seat and we were away, fare this time 15 Dinar and got off at Ain Taya bus station. Bought four bananas and an apple and upto room, had my 1450hrs din din and packed my kit then back down chatting to the lovely girl and the owners son Toupik saying I will be leaving shortly, is Maria about, they said she had gone out. Back to room, grabbed shoulderbag and China beachbag then downstairs agreeing a 1000 Dinar fare for Toupik to drive me to Algiers as no chance of even thinking of catching a 2-3hr bus. Shook hands with young, very helpful girl, kit in the 4 x 4 and we were away, me sad and glad at the same time to be leaving Ain Taya but it was too far out from Algiers. The usual Police road checks but no major hold ups and we found Hotel Djurdjura, 6 Rue Louis Meyer, Algiers, Tel: 021635455 easily enough as I directed him from the Grand Post Office, he stopped, I gave him 1000 Dinar, shook hands, I grabbed my shoulderbag and he was away. Into hotel, paid 1800 Dinar, showed Passport, got Rm 12 and up to first floor I went with shoulderbag, dumping it in d-ensuite but toilet was a squat. Back down and asked very helpful staff any western toilets, they said no so dropped key at reception and out across the road to Agha Train Station to buy my ticket to Setif for tomorrow. It took a while but very helpful lady attendant told me in French and then wrote it down I was at the wrong train station, the one I needed was Alger Train Station about 1-2km away nearly facing Place des Martyrs so Plan A to walk out of hotel into train station up de creek. Back to hotel and explained the circumstances, could I have a refund as I wanted to go to a hotel near Alger Train Station, they said if I had booked 2 nights I could have 1 night back but sorry, not refundable. Not to worry I said as I went for a walk in and around the full of life area then into an upstairs café and had 2 cheese burgers and a tea watching part of the first half of Algeria in the Africa Nations Cup, just the job, paid my 220 Dinar bill and back to hotel. Felt a stir, so stripped off completely, bent slightly forward and bang, it hit the back of the shower wall as the shower was directly over the squat toilet so cleaned it as best as I could, cleaned ass and had a shave and shower which cleaned everything!. All clean kit on and out having a walk down to Algiers Train Station checking times then a slow walk around Place des Martyrs with hundreds of young flag waving and cheering people plus cars pumping their horns and flags out their windows as Algiers celebrated getting into the next stage of the Africans Cup. Good fun as I slowly walked back towards my hotel then had another cheese burger and a tea in the same café, it was 2220hrs so another good day/night now over. Went into a Pharmacy and asked do they speak English, young girl came out and I explained I wanted anti bacterial tablets, she said what for and I explained my left testicle was sore, she said has it any lumps, I said yes, she said I needed to go to a hospital but she will give me a drug to stop the infection but it will not cure it. She was very knowledgeable and I paid her the 500 Dinar for 3 packets of Oxafon tablets and out. Back into hotel and agreed an early call with reception staff, upto room, stripped off, set alarm for 0640hrs, took 3 tablets and feeling good I was happy asleep in bed.

Day 24, Tuesday, 19-01-10, Algiers – Constantine; Algeria

Felt a lot better as I woke up at 0440hrs for a piss then back to bed thinking I will go all the way to Constantine today which is a 5hr 30min journey as I was going to do it with a stop after a 3hr journey for the night at Setif but couldn't be bothered to stop now, don't like long runs but its on a train so it will have toilets. Finally up at 0630hrs, tried for a dobhi squat drop, no luck but ball pain now gone so I'm happy. Face splash, Thai sandals, long cargo and pullover on then out downstairs and into little breakfast room for a free pot of milky coffee and one croissant. Quickly back to room, cleaned teeth, zipped up shoulderbag and out down to reception handing key over and saying my thanks and out on to main road and starting to panic a bit I finally flagged down an unoccupied taxi. Got in and he in French said, Airport, I said train pointing up the road and we were away. He went to turn into the docks but I said no, train and finally pointed at Gare Alger Train Station him laughing saying train we drove down the two hills and stopped outside the train station. Paid him a 50 Dinar note but he said one more so gave him a 20 and a 10 Dinar coin, said my thanks, grabbed my shoulderbag and into train station, it was 0710hrs. Found the ticket kiosk with no one queuing and got a ticket to Constantine, 950 Dinar, him pointing go left. Went left and ticket collector at entrance to Platform checked my ticket and pointing at train on I got taking a seat not far from the refreshment, coffee, eating carriage, so that will be handy. Not many people got on and dead on 0735hrs with a double toot toot we were away out of Algiers, me saying good luck Algiers, I liked you. Train was very fast and after the first two stops my carriage was full but I still had my double seat to myself. Went up to the refreshment carriage for a drink and another bloody croissant and enjoyed my strong coffee watching the main road and river mostly on my right as we passed through rocky deep gorges then hill mountain grassy sloped valleys, it was great free sightseeing scenery. It was good fun as well seeing the roads twisting and hairpin bends turning going up the mountains as we went straight through the mountains in long tunnels coming out the other side looking down the untouched small tree valleys as the now glaring sun was half blocked by flimsy clouds. Stopped at a main ongoing full market in the town of Bouira, some got off, some got on, it was 1000hrs. Each time we stopped it was only for a min or two then away again train driver toot tooting as we went through no barrier road crossing and as the mountains were getting bigger and bigger it seemed to be getting colder as we drew into and stopped in the town of Benni Mansour, it was 1040hrs. Next stop was M'Zita, it was 1110hrs so doing well and ass not too sore yet I had another coffee from the cafeteria and he filled up a large glass so it was not the tiny strong one gulp cup end brew. Mountains were now disappearing into the sky but the sun was now nice and strong as we stopped a couple of times then went through a tunnel and it took 6mins to get through even though we were going at a good speed then 15mins later we drew into the very large town of Bord Jbou Arreridj, it was 1150hrs. The ground each side of the railway track was now getting very barren like a desert as ticket inspector came along checking tickets and he looked at mine, stamping it, I was glad as I had been looking at LP map of Algeria and could not see any of these towns on it that we had passed through but my ticket said Constantine so I must be on the right train!. Fell asleep and woke up at 1240hrs as we drew into the train station of the major city town of Setif I believed checking the time as no signs in English, all Arabic, only 1½ to 2hrs to go to Constantine I hope as ass not grieving but still sore. Had a piss in the no seat western grubby toilet and back to seat having another coffee and a packet of creamy biscuits. The landscape was now flat with sometimes rows of trees along the rail lines barren isolated sometimes green with flocks of sheep rocky desert. Another stop at an Arabic name only station, it was 1330hrs but Constantine is the last stop at 1410hrs if I remember right or was it 1510hrs. Will it have signs in English, I hope so but it's a very major City so I can't miss it!. Very surprised but we stopped at a little isolated village called Chelghoum Laid but then another train came along and passed us very slowly. We then went backwards and on to the other line and then forward so its only a single line track, it was 1405hrs when we picked up speed going forward again, rail sign showed 383km to Algiers. Another 2min stop at El Gourzi, a few got off, it was 1430hrs. The ground was now soil with grass growing with also rocky hills but I could see mountains on the distant horizon. I felt we were near as movement started in the carriage many people getting their cases and bags ready and then I seen the station with the end of the train line at the buffer plates and in we drew to signs only in Arabic, Constantine, it was 1510hrs spot on. I let everyone get off and just followed them and outside the station we all went having to hand over my ticket to exit gate ticket inspector. Outside there was a sort of taxi rank with 2-3 Police directing it and all traffic and most people took a taxi as it drew in. I was last with Police using whistles and shouting and pointing at me to a taxi driver who had just dropped someone off but he said no and attempted to drive away and they stood in front of him making him go over to the pavement, everyone was shouting at each other then next thing a Police van drew up and he was forcibly restrained as I was pointed to another taxi, I jumped in and away. I had no map or any details regarding hotels as LP did not publish them in their 2004 Africa on a Shoestring Edition but had a photocopy of a page from the 2000 Edition which gave me areas of hotels and mentioned the Grand Hotel, 2 Rue Ben M'Hidi,, Tel: 031642201, Constantine on the edge of Place de Novembre. I said Grand Hotel, he said ok and I cannot remember the route he took but he dropped me off at Grand Hotel Gusta, I paid him 100 Dinar and he was away. I knew it was way above my budget but went in anyway and it was very old and very posh and tariff was 70$US for a single en-suite, not bad really. I seen a Tourist office just off the reception and went in and asked if there was another Hotel Grand in English, girl said, you speak French, I said no, she as they all do feigned surprise. A guy sitting at the next desk said only English smiling, I said yeah. He said come with me and outside we went and he pointed across the roundabout and said go right and when I get upto the end at the Square go right again so saying my laughing thanks I was away crossing about three roads and up to Place de Novembre. Looking right, yeah man yeah, I seen it and over and up the stairs to the first floor reception. I said room and two reception guys said yes in French, I said shower indicating shower with my hand, they said no and speaking to each other one got a key and took me to Room 2 which was a big double bed with what I thought was a WC and WHB so I said ok. Back to reception and I gave him my Passport and a 1000 Dinar note, he gave 150 Dinar change so I had done well I thought. Got Room 2 key and took shoulderbag down to room and WC pan was only a ladies sit down wash H & C hose tap with a pisshole plug, not a full western WC as I had thought but that's life. I checked corridor outside room and found a communal squat but other than that, it was perfect. Dumped neck pouch and extra wallet in shoulderbag and out giving key into reception and down for a walk about which was really good even without any info or map but the only bad thing was all street and road signs were in Arabic. Found the powerful looking Palais de Justice ok but these buildings especially the ones looking down the Rhumel Gorge battlements were a totally overwhelming sight to see, they were so big and so grand from every angle. I was so enjoying every different visual treat as every hill, every corner had fantastic spectacular views I forgot I was hungry. Tried to print off a map in an internet shop but no luck so back towards my hotel and into a narrow muddy alley and into a little café which I could see sold beef burger and chips. I pointed at chips and one beef burger and an orange drink and 5mins later it was on the table and I enjoyed my 1910hrs late din, din. I paid my 150 Dinar charge and out back upto hotel the reception guys who signed me in had gone and now an old guy said you want room, I said no, my room is Room 2, he said no, show your Passport. I said Passport is in Room 2, so he looked at hotel resident signing in sheets and said what's your occupation?, I said Building Inspector so he gave me Room 2 key and along to room I went laughing to myself. I must admit I don't carry my Passport about but I do carry a photocopy of it and a photocopy of my travel insurance. No shower as room didn't have one, didn't have a shave so just cleaned my teeth and back out handing key in to the same guy, it was 2030hrs. Everywhere had shut and the whole area was deserted but I had a walk about anyway but it was sometimes eerie to be walking the well lit and sometimes dark street not a sinner about, no drunks, no nothing. I made it up along the battlements but didn't go too far then hopefully now well orientated for manyanna I walked back up the slight hill passing two street vendors, one selling single cigarettes, the other hot meatballs and came to my entrance door locked hotel, it was only 2215hrs. Had a look down the street and other hotels had their front entrances shut and locked. I pressed the buzzer and old guy came out onto balcony above the hotel door and waved at me. A couple of mins later he opened the big two timber doors and in I went and waited for him to close and lock the 4 No entrance doors. Back up the stairs and he gave me my key muttering to himself and I smiled saying my Good Nights and back down to room. Changed into shorts and out into squat toilet and had a near miss dobhi drop so cleaned the squat bowl with today's local newspaper, cleaned my ass and back to room, how these old people use these squats I will never know. Nothing to do but not really tired I took two tasty pills pain in my left testicle nearly gone, stripped off and oh God into my concrete mattress bed and dreaming WC's and a soft mattress I fell asleep.

Email Sent: Tue, 19 Jan 2010
Subject: Rm2; Grand Hotel; 2 Rue Larbi Ben, Constantine, Algeria

Hi All

Jumped a train; 950Dinar from Algiers at 0730hrs this morning and got into Constantine 1510hrs. Train had buffet car and sloppy Western WC so had a few snoozes and enjoyed my sightsee. Got taxi to Grand Hotel from train station not a clue as had no map of Constantine and he dropped me off outside Grand Hotel Gitor who wanted 70US so nearly fainting I managed to find out where my Grand Hotel was and they charged me 12US or 850 dinar so guess which one I took? Anyone any info or map of Constantine email it to me as original plan was I was going to have a day in Setif but its only Roman ruins so seen one seen the lot and didn't have time to do updates on Constantine as had and stayed last night in centre of Algiers which was good fun. I thought the hotel I was staying in was near the train station but my good planning I had picked the wrong train station, don't follow my footsteps. Also LP say don't come to Algeria so don't give any info in the LP on a Shoestring. Its a very old place Constantine as I can see on my first walkie but staying manyanna so plenty of time
al de bes
Jack

Day 25, Wednesday, 20-01-10, Constantine; Algeria.

Surprised me but had a good night's sleep waking up at 0530hrs for a piss, then it was hard to get back to sleep as I could now feel the concrete mattress and pillow which caused cramping pains in my legs. Not to worry, turned over and stretched a few times as well as dozing then checked bedside clock and up at 0745hrs. Had a drink of lemonade and two creamy biscuits and felt a stir so had found a small newspaper in the street coming home last night so gently ripped off one page and folding it over I put it in the women's H & C inner thighs washer come pisshole WC pan, sat on it and had a lovely dobhi drop. It felt so wonderful actually sitting on a bowl and relaxed for a change so cleaned my ass using minimal toilet paper putting it on top of the dobhi drop, wrapped the lovely mess up in its one page of newspaper and left it in the bowl. Had an underarm wash, face splash, kit on including trainers and grabbing my wrapped up dobhi drop and out of room across to the communal squat and opening the newspaper I dropped all my early morning stomach residue down the squat hole along with the wet one slice of newspaper and with one full bucket of water my relaxed happy asshole dobhi drop was gone. Back to room, washed hands and out towards reception and had the free 1 croissant, small pot of coffee and milk breakie, just the job, it was 0900hrs, I will now start my Constantine walking tour. Out I went and it was slightly drizzling so light poncho on and away going downhill into the centre of town as I knew it, still had no map. Went left then turning right I was on a lovely designed and beautiful looking arched bridge crossing the De Rhumel Gorge. Looking each side I yelled with joy as looking up the De Rhumel Gorge there they where 3-4 spectacular bridge crossing, one a pedestrian and looking right from it there was the railway station so well orientated now. Went along the side of the Oued Phumel and onto the Mellah Slemane 100m long big 2.5m wide walking suspension bridge and it moved and jolted with us people walking either way on it and great fantastic views down each side of the Gorge. I walked from the railway station side and got to a lift on the other side which was the old town of Constantine. The lift was packed so gasping heavily I walked up the winding timber stairs treads and out into the cobbled streets of Old Constantine with its very old shops and dwellings all along it. Turned right going downhill and enjoyed my walk looking down steep steps to ancient building entrances and alleys all along the edges of the Gorge. Only a 100m walk and I reached another elaborate stone, brick Arched road bridge across the Gorge and just took my time admiring the great getting better every mins views down and along each way of the now 150m drop of the De Rhumel Gorge. Railway station was now to my right so walked down and into it and very helpful staff said there is no train to Touggourt where I hoped to go tomorrow so maybe Plan A up the shoot. Out from the train station turning right then right again and into a corner Travel Agents who as I asked gave me very good advice regarding bus station and times of bus tomorrow to Touggourt, thanked them and away. Going uphill through a dodgy area but everyone was so friendly and the sun was out so poncho off and into Café de Union des Sourds just near the famous 160m long Sidi M'Cid road suspension bridge. Had an egg, beef burger roll with 2 teas enjoying my 1200hrs din din, paid my 150 Dinar and smiling my thanks I was out walking past the huge Hospital and cable car end with the unbelievable views looking down the 175m drop at each side of the bridge directly into the rock precipice slopes of the Rhumel Gorge ravine, what a truly unbelievable sight. Had a photo shoot then up the steep stepped path on the Sidi M'Cid mountain and panting and swearing way above the Sid M'Cid Bridge I turned a corner and their I was at the big stone Arched Monument to the dead built especially for the valiant people of Constantine. On top of the magnificent stone Arch was the statue of the Winged Victory, an Angel with Wings. Up I went and through the big Arch and I was so excited being there looking down past the Kasbah into the roads, streets and alleys of so friendly Constantine it was a joy just as the 1300hrs Muslim chanters echoed up from the Mosque in Constantine way below, what a feeling. Gently walked the little cliff edge path back down to the Sidi M'Cid Bridge and feeling on top of the wide wide world I walked along its 150m length looking and seeing the most fantastic views as I now reached the other side at the Fort like army Kasbah walls at Blvd de la Yugoslavia. Turned around and could not even see the mountain the other side of the gorge as it had suddenly been covered in mist. Had a walk into the Kasbah market stalls everywhere area and asking the question of two young lads, "where is the Palace of Ahmed Bey", one said come this way and only one block I was there, I said my thanks and he was away. The Palace was built by Haji Ahi Ahmed in 1826 as he was the boy ruler. They were putting fencing up around it but in my imploring French Irish lingo I got an ole guy to let me in and gave me a walking tour and it is one of the finest Ottoman build type buildings ever built with every courtyard wall fully tiled in many different French and Tunisian type tiles of all colours and its lovely large inner gardens with orange and olive trees, really peaceful and quiet. Old knees now gone after looking around the five beautiful courtyard upstairs and downstairs with lovely painted walls I said my thanks and went out past the large swimming pool I think!. Another great remarkable Constantine day nearly over, I shook my old friends hand and I was out and away, it was 1715hrs. Back down to my alley café from last night and had same beef burger, chips and an orange 140 Dinar then tried three banks with my MasterCard but no luck as they were all in French or Arabic so might be in trouble. Tried the last one putting my number in and a voice came out saying thank you for banking with us so don't know if I actually transferred money!. Need money urgently so back to hotel and got Algeria's it seems only in use card the Visa out and lucky drew 10,000 Dinar so hopefully that will see me through for the next few days. Tried to look inside the Grande Mosque but not allowed, not to worry, said my thanks and away. Back again to hotel and had a nice shave and standing in the tiled floor I done a hand splashing shower from the WHB and now happy, put kit on and lay on my concrete bed and pillow as nowhere to go anyway. Went out for a good long but very slow walk at 1925hrs having two teas and a scone in two cafes but everywhere was shutting by 1930-2030-2130hrs and town centre and everywhere was dead at 2200hrs. Back to room hoping I will sleep well and hoping for an early rise manyanna to catch a nice early bus to Touggourt thinking I had not seen one traveller for days now. Kit off and into concrete bed and dreaming soft dreams I was asleep in Constantine the land of the Roman Gods.

Email Sent: Wed, 20 Jan 2010
Subject: Constantine bridges and de Rhumel Gorge

Hi All

Had a good history walking today as I was ok once I seen the first bridge I knew where I needed to go and made it across the lovely Mellah Slimane bridge then upto the Monument to the Dead on the top of the mountain then across the Sidi M'Cid Bridge not forgetting a little 2m wide pedestrian bridge. All bridges cross a 150m gorge ravine then past the Military Fort in the Kasbah to the Palace of Ahmed Bey, great day. Manyanna catching a bus and heading out down towards El-Oued the town of a Thousand Domes on the edge of de desert so getting near you Jimmy, bus journey is supposed to be 5hrs, we shall see. Even credit card details are in French so no travellers to work it out for me as have pressed the wrong French button twice now?? Its funny here, I have not seen one other single traveller in Algeria so is it only mad dogs and shotty den men who travel. I think a Bomb killed 4 and injured 50 in Algiers yesterday so keep low and move fast??
al de bes
Jack

Day 26, Thursday, 21-01-10, Constantine – El Oued; Algeria

Great sleep and only woke up as first chanters started early at 0515hrs. Was tempted to go for a full sleep but just turned over a few times dozing then alarm went off at 0545hrs and up I got having a chocolate biscuit and a drink of orange hoping it would do a stir. It did, 2mins later a fully empty dobhi drop in the women's piss toilet bowl with a WHB plug WC with my half slice of newspaper at its bottom, cleaned ass leaving paper on top of the pile. Face splash, cleaned armpits, Thai sandals, long cargo, pullover on and had another chocolate biscuit with a drink of orange so nearly there. Out for breakie dumping dobhi drop down the squat and dicing it with a bucket of water but old guy praying to Allah on his prayer-mat said breakfast starts at 0730hrs. I tried to bribe him with a 50 Dinar coin but no luck so back to room, cleaned teeth, final pack of shoulderbag and shaking hands with the old fellow and his wife I was out into the overcast Constantine streets looking for a taxi. Tried 2 taxis but they did not understand, then got to 5-6 taxi guys and saying St Juins Station Bus Station they finally got the message and in I got and we were away. It was an interesting drive going downhill to the bottom of the gorge looking up the full battlement height of the Constantine precipice gorge then into old streets and finally reached the bus station. Out I got grabbing shoulderbag from the back seat and tried to pay him a 50 Dinar coin but he wanted 100 Dinar so gave it to him. Some bus's parked up in the dark were Universe Space (luxury) and 3-4 guys when I was walking towards the ticket office asked where I wanted to go, I said Touggourt or El-Oued and one guy pointed at his big bus, took my shoulderbag putting it in the hold and on I got, it was 0655hrs. Couple of guys got on with tickets looking for their seat numbers so I got up to get off and guy said no problem I give you ticket so sat back down again, con 2 on its way. Bus was warm and good seats and slowly filling up then only sort of half full at 0730hrs spot on we pulled out of St Juins Bus Station and oh la la I was on de road again. Slowly in the Constantine traffic we trundled out of Constantine passing it looked like a row of Roman Arches, very big and very splendid just as it was getting light. Not long and we were on a good main highway getting up a good speed so seat back I wished Constantine Au revoir. Closed eyes and no thoughts, no dreams, I gently said I will miss you Constantine as we went up and over a small mountain hill heading for a new town. Roads coming into Constantine were now chock a block but we were doing well and I seen a road sign for Biskra so knew we were on the right road. At 0755hrs the conductor came along and I paid him 500 Dinar getting a ticket so sat back in the nice warm Algerian music bus as we passed through green field hilly valleys each side of our road and I was looking forward to our first Naafi break stop. Snoozed off and woke up at 0850hrs with the no public trains railway on my right and large Rocky Mountains in the distance and on my left was sometimes green sparse flat grass areas. We were now going really fast on 2-4 lane highways and I definitely liked the idea of a coffee, croissant stop. No luck for a feed as sometimes now we were in small forest valleys with the mountains getting closer and the only time we slowed down was to trundle through a Police checkpoint at mostly small towns or villages.

Stopped at 0935hrs to let 5 people off at a very large town surrounded by mountains and now all window curtains fully drawn closed on the left as the sun was blinding. Now passing through glorious high rocky barren mountains and it was really fantastic to be near and see them all close up. The single line railway was still on our right with sometimes lots of new work going on but marvellous how they built the original in the first instance. Its now 1030hrs and not even one piss stop, very strange and mountains have come down to sparse barren with shrubs large round hills and I would love to know where we are but all window curtains now closed to keep out the sun and I am sitting on the left which is the wrong side to spot road signs beside the road on our right. Just passed a huge lake on our right and coming into and through a very small village, its 1042hrs. Very slow progress now as new highway being built and all traffic has to use a dirt track beside it but now starving and would sell my life possessions for a croissant and a coffee and although the bus is AC it's still warm and everyone else is nodding off to sleep. Now coming into the large town of Biskra and we did stop but nowhere near any toilets, cafes or shops and 2mins later we were away. I called the conductor and in sign language French and English I tell him I want something to eat and a piss, he said ok 30mins I think as he told me in French we arrive at our destination at 1445hrs, I said my thanks and said I will wait and see. We were now on the edge of the Sahara Desert as it was very plain to see with no mountains at all, just flat shrub, hard sand desert stretching across 100s of miles to the horizons in every direction, what a feeling as I am now in the Sahara with not a cloud in the bright blue sky to be seen. Finally we stopped at a makeshift petrol station and a café along a mile long row of corrugated and concrete roof cafes, restaurants and shops. Off we all got and I followed the crowd of young fellows out through the back of the café to two squat toilets and we each took our turn for a piss. Some of them then kneeled to pray on a prayer mat place beside it. I went into the café but they had no tea so I ordered a coffee and he gave me a thumb thick filled small tumbler but I said no give me a big glass and fill it with water which he did, 2 scone buns, 2 bottles of orange and a packet of creamy biscuits, I went outside to sit in the shade with flies, cats and the dust filled hot air off the desert blowing everywhere, yeah man yeah, Jack of Arabia is home at last. Everyone else had ordered thick, soup, chips and crusty baguettes but still had another 2-3hrs to go so will keep my belly safe until I find a toilet nearby. Still thinking will I stay in Touggourt or get a bus or shared taxi straight to El-Oued but will wait and see. Took my creamy biscuits and orange back onto the bus and listening to the Arabic music I enjoyed the rest of my desert snack until everyone back on board and driver pumped his horn a few times and we were away through this medium sized but many street lights desert oasis and away on our road through the flat hard rock shrub desert sand of the Sahara again. Funny enough the only things blocking the horizons were cable pylons. Came to and stopped at the crossroads in a large town called Poumi with road signpost looking back the other way was saying Biskra 120km, it was 1321hrs, two people got off and we were away again with it getting more and more sandy desert with Nomads camping out in the palm trees. Stopped at a crossroad very large village town at 1400hrs to let two young lads off, one got on all signs in Arabic now so not a clue. Changed a 1000 Dinar note down to 5 x 200 Dinars with the Conductor as only have 3000 Dinars and thinking no banks or

ATMs in the desert might have if I need too try and borrow something from a traveller if I see one as its Friday manyanna, all shops, banks close for the weekend, same same, will wait and see, bad planning by planner Jack. Again it's a truly amazing sight to see the barely started, quarter – half – three quarters nearly finished empty dwelling blocks of flats everywhere be it towns or villages, don't know but its an Algerian icon!. Stopped at Cite El Fir, one got off and two got on and we were away now into the most amazing true sight of the no shrub sand dunes blowing hot dust everywhere along each side of the road, it was 1420hrs so not far or long to go. Drove into Touggourt bus station and as I was going to get off the driver said where I go in French and have a chat with him he told me he goes to El Oued so couldn't believe my luck I stayed on my bus. Only a 5min wait and out we drove through Tourggourt a sort of stone crossroads town and into the pure raw sand dunes blowing sand Sahara Desert again I was so happy so sat back and 2mins later dozed off. Woke up having a good long slug of water and seen water towers and Minarets in the long way horizon distance then into the outskirts of a large town. In we drove along what to me was a beautiful boulevard with covered walkways then came to a huge Monument in the centre of a roundabout and turned left and guy sitting behind me said its El Oued and if your looking for a hotel as he had seen me looking at my photocopy LP there is Hotel Si Moussa pointing left and the bus stopped about 50m from it and most people got off as I did saying my thanks to the driver, it was 1505hrs. Said my thanks to the guy who got off with me as LP didn't have any info or maps in its Algeria section and crossed the road and into the hotel just as another guy with a taxi driver came in. After discussion with the guy's taxi driver, reception guy said to me and the backpacker young guy from Barcelona, Spain, you look, so we went up one flight of stairs and guy showed us a 2 bed double room with a WHB and pointing at the squat toilet down the corridor, 1000 Dinar for room, if you want to share, 500 Dinar each. I said my thanks but don't want to share, Spanish guy said he will go into the centre of town for a look. Back down at reception I said I will take the room, Rm 3, Hotel Si Moussa, Cite Belle Vue, El Oued, Algeria, Tel: 0773788205. Guy said 1000 Dinar so gave it to him as didn't want to waste any more time looking for a cheaper hotel as I knew there would be but for the sake of 5$US my time at this stage was more valuable. He gave me Rm 3 key and up I went, dumped kit in room and out along the main boulevard towards the city centre. El Oued the 'Town of a Thousand Domes' was definitely the most original and most gracious town I have ever been in as I pictured its originality thinking about when it was newish with its wide Squares and One thousand Domes with such original architecture it was a joy to walk around it as I was joyfully doing. Every turn, every angle of every alley, Souk and street there was always more ancient architecture to see and admire all built hundreds of years ago but even the Souks and alleys were wide and full of light. Passed beautiful old Mosques then old schools then into the Kasbah area through its open large wide Arched Gate all built 1425 AD and just had a dander as everywhere was full of space. Came out the same entrance I went in and whatever way I took I came to it must be a War Memorial as it had approximately 1000 names on it with the year they died, the earliest was 1895 and greatest number was in the 1930's but everything in Arabic so could not understand it. On the gable wall behind it was a few very vivid coloured tiled Murals, one had Vive La Gerie. It was now getting dark so checking money I knew I was in very serious trouble as Algeria speaks and uses pure French so my MasterCard Credit Card was no good and my other credit card I did not want to use it without a person who could understand French beside me as all banks all closed now until Monday in three days or Sunday in two days time, I had 2000 Dinar on me. Enjoying my walk but thinking ahead I photocopied a few pages of LP Tunisia and asked guy for any info regarding getting to Tunisia. He said and wrote it in Arabic on a sheet of paper, go to market 2 Liba and there is a shared taxi rank which when taxi is full will go to the Frontier at the Tunisia Border approximately 80km away and taking 1 hour. Shook his hand as I think my best bet is to head into Tunisia with what I have as their banking and ATM system is 100% better than Algeria's I think!. So Plan A now in place for manyanna, didn't want to spend anything so bought 3 bananas, 1 apple, 2 packets of biscuits and a large bottle of cheap coke, total bill 225 Dinar. Walking back I seen a small very clean hotel called Hotel Central, Av Taleb Larbi, El-Oued, Tel: 032248825 with singles for 600 Dinar, double for 800 Dinar, toilet in corridor. Lovely walk and great feeling for El Oued I had my 1 apple, 1 banana, 6 chocolate biscuits and coke din din sitting on my bed wishing I had some money as there were dozens of cheap cafes and restaurants everywhere along all the main four boulevards but that's French for you. Cleaned teeth then putting bedside table on its side I sat on the WHB putting a half sheet of newspaper in the WHB and had a nice relaxing dobhi drop, cleaned ass, putting toilet paper on top, rolled it up and out to the squat dumping it down the hole then a bucket of water following it and that was today's squat problem over and done with. Time was marching on so no shave just went out hoping to bump into the Spanish guy as was going to ask him for 1000 Dinar so had a lovely walk along the full length of the boulevard to the main traffic lights at the crossroad junction passing still open cafes saying I wish to myself but no sign of my Spanish friend so turned back. Enjoyed my still in my Thai sandals walk then into an Internet café for my usual 20mins and that was me, it was 2140hrs. Slow walk back and into hotel, upto room and after a great vibes El Oued sightsee very impressed about the town walk I stripped off and into my one sheet squeaky bed and asleep dreaming I need some money honey dreaming of the £1000s of nicker I had given to de lovely Ladies of the Night Hookers all over the world and not one here to bail me out, that's a travellers life!.

Email Sent: Thur, Jan 21 2010
Subject: Rm3, Hotel Si Moussa, Cite Belle Vue, El Oued, Tel0773788205

Hi All

Plan A working ok as got up and upto Bus Station and got bus, 500Dinar at 0730hrs to El Oued with only 1 piss or eating stop at 1230hrs so would have sold the world for a french croissant and thumb cup coffee.

Got to El Oued at 1505hrs and took hotel, 1000 Dinar with outside room squat toilet, not to worry WHB in room.

El Oued is the most fantastic architechial town I have ever been in for a long time as each Ave or alley is different and so magic and got in and out of the Casbah no problems as us Arthur St Casbah hoods all look alike.

Running out of Dinar, only 2000 left and no banks open as their WE starts on a Fri and probably card not working now but heading for de Tunisian border manyanna by shared taxi as thats the only way you can go so hope their is a few Algeria or Tunisians going AM.

al de bes

Jack

Map of Tunisia

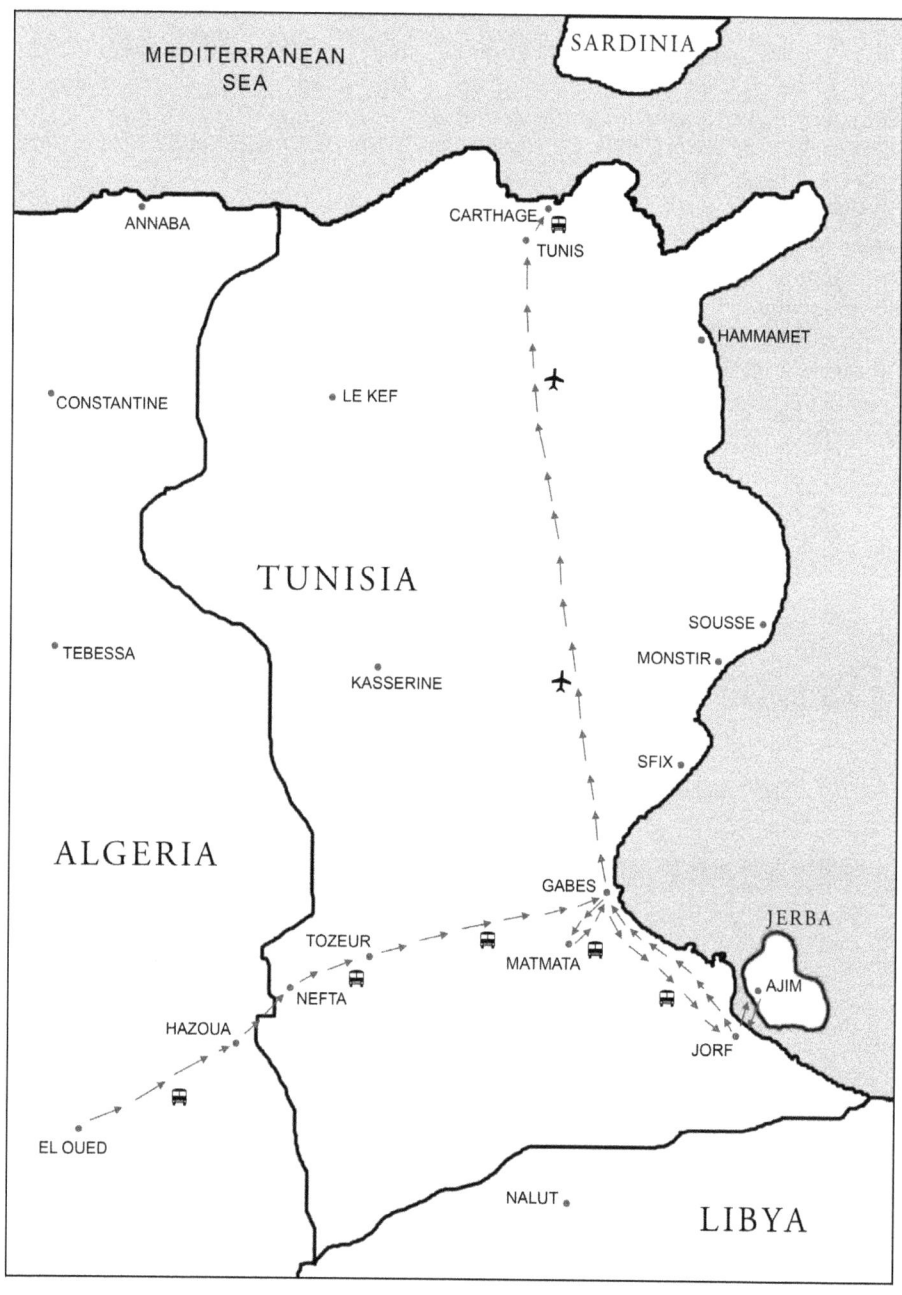

1) TUNISIA with its wonderful mix of Modern and Ancient with its true full of life taste's and smells of the Medina's, Forts and Bazaars new and old culture's has beautiful sun kissed vibrant sandy beaches along the Mediterranean Coast to swim and soak up the sun with Camel Rides into the Sahara desert for the adventurers and everywhere the always friendly people will make your stay a time of happy Memories.
2) Capital; Tunis
3) Tunisia achieved Independence in 1956
4) Climate; Ave temp Jan-Mar;19c
5) Language; French, Arabic, English
6) Currency; Tunisia Dinar, 1$US = 1-5 T Dinar
7) Visa; Not required, 30 day issued on arrival
8) Return flight £51 + £154 ATM, hotel, food, train to Gatwick
9) Today's ongoing update of day to day accommodation, travel, food, drinks costs = £873

Day 27, Friday, 22-01-10, El Oued; Algeria – Tozeur; Tunisia

Was woken up a few times by turning over and the bed creaking loudly and nearly fell out a few times as the single bed had a fall on it to the right. Lots of people leaving from 0600hrs onwards so up for good at 0730hrs. Had my two creamy biscuits breakie and as I felt a stir I lined the washhand basin with a half sheet of Arabic newspaper, got my bedside table, stood on it, sat in the washhand basin and bang, a lovely empty belly dobhi splattering drop, cleaned ass, cleaned the sides of the wash hand basin, face splash and a new reborn man I was ready to go. Kit on with Thai sandals and had my one banana, six creamy biscuits and lemonade breakie and out of room with my rolled up dobhi drop and dropped it down the squat toilet and pouring a full bucket of water on top it was gone, it was only 0800hrs. Had a walk down into the old town centre with the hundreds upon hundreds of bric a brac stalls, old clothes stalls, fresh meat and vegetable stalls with hundreds of people doing their walk around their famous Friday markets. I got lost a few times and was hoping to see the Spanish bloke and borrow or beg some money from him but no luck so back to hotel, it was 1030hrs. Final pack and out with old boy who got me a taxi to the shared taxi parking area, jumped in, and paid him the agreed 50 Dinar and out with two guys saying Tunisia, I said yeah and one put my shoulderbag in the back. Driver said go now showing me 4 x 200 dinar notes, I said no as I only had 1800 Dinar on me. I questioned him about the fare, he said 800 Dinar as one passenger so I knew I was in serious trouble. Had a sad serious think and decided I will have to stay in El Oued today and tomorrow until Sunday as if I pay the 800 Dinar that leaves me with 1000 but I will need taxi fares and accommodation in Tozeur and LP states it has no ATM's so sick as a pig it looks like two days are going to be wasted. Got my bag and a taxi to Hotel Central which I had seen had singles for 400 Dinar and he dropped me off outside it. Went in and all rooms full so out and passing the photocopy shop with the very helpful English speaking Algerian chap I went in and asked him could I leave my shoulderbag in his shop as I wanted to go up to the bank area. He said no problem and off I went still hoping but only found one bank with an ATM and it didn't take either of my credit cards, so very sad. Back down to Benbordi Faycal mobile telephone shop telling him my woes and problems with French. He said he would walk upto the bank with me and check I was doing the ATM correctly so locking his shop up we went trying 2 banks ATM's but neither would accept my cards. Chatting to each other as he had a cousin who married an English girl living in London and his favourite English football team was Portsmouth who had two Algerian players I asked him had he ever visited England. He said no and not for the future as his wife was expecting their first baby and then he offered to help me with a cash loan and got 1800 Dinar out saying; "You are Christian, I am Muslem, we are brothers," "when you get a chance, post it back" and I was so totally amazed and so proud to have met a person who would trust a total stranger and thanked him from the depths of my heart. We exchanged addresses, telephone numbers and outside I went with my shoulderbag still hardly believing people like Benbordi exist in our world today. He then flagged down a taxi, told him where to take me and paid him with his own money and a last shake of his hand I was away to the shared taxi Minibus area where driver dropped me off at the Tunisia parking area, it was 1215hrs. Nice guy in Arab dressed robes said Tunisia and spoke a little English saying and pointing at taxi ready to go. I said ok, Frontier Algeria, he said okay, 150 Dinar so in I got with five other guys with shoulderbag and all sorts in the back and we were away out past the Teapot and Coffee Tumbler Monument getting into the 20-30m round high pure sand of the deepest sand dunes each side of our road I have ever seen and I whispered" I loved you El Oued" as I dozed off. It was a good road journey with sometimes palm tree forest all shrub field desert stretching for hundreds of miles then into the Algerian border control post we drove, it was 1350hrs. Paid my 150 Dinar bill and into Passport control completing the paperwork and handing Passport over with Passport officer filling in my details in Arabic then bang, an exit Algerian stamp, everyone is so friendly. Had to wait for the one and only taxi that was completely falling to bits with some of its doors not even closing, never seen anything like it in my life but then with six persons in it he drove us across the 5km no-man's land between Algeria and Tunisia and I paid him 50 Dinar as we got there and everyone got off, it was 1445hrs. Completed my in English Tunisia Visa form and don't think many English came through this checkpoint as he asked me where UK was so I told him England but had a good laugh as I waited then bang, Tunisia arrival stamp and I was into Tunisia. All the guys that had travelled with me come from Tunisia and so very friendly as we sat about waiting for Louages, (shared Minibus or taxies). I had only Algerian Dinars on me so talking to two very helpful Arab robed guys they called a chap over from a cafe and he and two robed guys went over and I gave him 3200 Algerian Dinar and he gave me 40 Tunisian Dinar back. Then back out my friend and I went to the pickup Louage area on the road surrounded by the never ending waves of desert sand dunes I only then worked it out that I was conned out of 20 Tunisian(T) Dinar I believe, as it was 18 Tunisian Dinar to 1000 Algerian Dinar but didn't care as I now had enough to pay my fare and first night accommodation I hoped. Minibus came and on we got and it took us a good desert journey into a small town and everyone had to get off and I paid 2 Tunisian Dinar and was told Louage Taxi sitting ready to go outside a cafe called " Restaurant de Palmer" it's stated hotel above, could take me but no room for my shoulderbag. Driver wanted to go, I wanted to go, everyone wanted to go so putting my shoulderbag on my knees in the front seat we were away on our signpost 24km sardine desert drive to Tozeur, it was 1545hrs. I dozed off and woke up in the glaring desert sun and we were on the outskirts of Tozeur and in we drove and parked up on its outskirts at the Louages car park and out we all got, I paid, I think 3 T Dinar, very cheap. Got taxi into Tozeur centre ville and he dropped me off as I asked at Hotel Essada just up the street off Ave Habib Bourguiba directly in the centre but guy said compleat, means full. Out from it pulling my trolley shoulderbag through the packed stalls I got to Hotel Khalifa but they were compleat so thinking my luck had run out guy directed me up an alley to Residence Ahlem, Ave Habib Bourguiba, Tozeur 2200, Tunisia, www.residenceahlem.com, Tel: 76463556 a very, very upmarket and clean place. In I went thinking this is going to be a rip-off so asked prices and young girl said 26 T Dinar. I said any cheaper, she said 20 T Dinar and said have a look and took me up to Room 2 a big really fancy d-ensuite with western toilet and shower so saves me doing a dobhi drop in the washhand basin so with no hesitation I said ok as won't get better than this. Back down to reception, filled in the paperwork, paid for one night, got key and upto room dumping shoulderbag in room and out downstairs handing key over and smiling into the sky above I was out for a walk, oh la, la, I had made it. First things first I found a row of banks and ATM's and tried both cards in two different ATM's and drew out 100 T Dinars from each ATM so Jack is an Arab rich boy again. Checked my LP photocopied map of Tozeur and walked down past the very elaborate Hotel de Oasis and into the Archway gate of the Medina old town called Ouled el Hadef which was a totally thrilling experience walking through the nearly deserted tunnel like Arched Souk alleys with every corner a different very old 50mm thick brick face work. I got lost but was enjoying the so clean and so neat little and big buildings sometimes peeping into gaps at big thick timber doors into old court yards all built hundreds of years ago and not a soul about. Just by luck I eventually got out and it was now 1850hrs so time for eats as no wash, shave or shower today. Into a pizza cafe and had a full margarita with two teas, 4 T Dinar and out I seen Hotel Nipper, Bab El Hawa, Tozeur (www.hotelnipper.com) so in and checked prices and single ensuite was only 13 T Dinar but was not even thinking of moving. I must admit Hotel Nipper was in a prime position as all along its road was dozens of cafes and at least 4-5 banks but that's life. Had a walk the other end of town down by the lovely coloured lit up Hotel de Oasis as facing it along Ave Abdulkacem Chebbi there was approximately 30 x 1m sq old photos of Tozeur so just took my time enjoying seeing life as it was in a bygone era. It had already gone dark so done my usual 20min email then into a cafe for a tea and 2 scones, 2 Dinar and slowly but slowly all shops, stalls and everywhere were starting to shut down, not as quick or sudden as El Oued but that's life. Out of cafe, it was 2125hrs and town except for area around Hotel Nipper was now dead so no plans and thinking about my room's big soft bed I made it into my hotel and upto room. No rush had a think and a read of LP about my plans for the day after manyanna, put my rich boy ATM money safe in my neckpouch in my shoulderbag and that was me ready for bed. Stripped off and into bed and enjoying the soft mattress and plenty of leg room I fell asleep dreaming bad dreams of veiled hookers giving me money, honey.

Email Sent: Fri, 22 Jan 2010
Subject: Rm2, Residence Ahlem, Ave Habib Bourguiba, Tozeur, Tunisia, Tel 76463555

Hi All

Jumped a bus 1230hrs after English speaking guy in photocopy shop lent me 1800Dinor as I was telling him I had been to Louage bus station and they wanted 800dinor for shared taxi to Tunisia border and banks ATM would not pay out on my cards so he came with me to banks ATMs to check as all in French and he said your right, no loot for skint jack and offered me the money or else I would have had to stay in El Oued until Sunday when their Mon starts and banks open.

His brother had married an English girl so he said he trusted me so brothers in arms with my Muslim mate I said my thanks and upto the louage minibus shared taxi station, this driver charged 150 Dinar and away to the border. Great fun journey from El Oued to border on our tarmac road through 20-30m high round untouched sand dunes stretching as far as the eye could see with the sun blazing out of the blue sky.

Through border checkpoints and 5 mile no-mans land all on different taxis and finely made Tozeur.

Tried 3 cheapies but no luck as too late in the day so took above www.residenceahlem.com 20 Tunisia Dinar with money I had changed at border then first thing first I tried my 2 cards in ATMs and both worked so now an Arab rich boy again.

Very friendly town and had a great amazing walk around the Medina old town old quarter late PM but a few plans for manyanna then next day head out towards the Tunisia Med coast at my ole El Adem airfield mate Gadaffi's border.

al de bes
Jack

Day 28, Saturday, 23-01-10, Tozeur; Tunisia

Had a most fantastic sleep and remember turning over a few times sighing in great contentment in the soft, big, lovely blanket bed not even up for one piss. Lots of movement outside and at 0800hrs alarm went off so up, face splash, under arm wash. Put long cargo, Thai sandals and pullover on as its cold in the early mornings and at night. Only second different adapter I had used on my travels so far so put it in the plug in the wall and charged up my phone as carrying a four piece travel adapter kit. Out I went downstairs to the breakfast room, guy showed me table so I sat down and 2mins later he brought one big pot of coffee, one of hot milk, plate of crusty baguette pieces, butter, jam and a cake so buttered and jammed six pieces of baguette, poured my coffee and ate the lot enjoying my final delicious piece of cake thinking someday civilisation will come to these foreign countries and they will learn how to cook a sausage, egg, bacon, beans, fried bread and tomatoes English breakfast, long time yet I can imagine. Back upto room as something was stirring and into the western toilet and bang, a full English dobhi drop splatter, so cleaned ass, cleaned toilet bowl, cleaned teeth and ready to go out, where, so had a read of LP and Plan A going into action. Went a short walk only into the old town Ouled el-Hwadef, (Old Quarter) and I do love seeing all this 100s of year old history as I just walked its old mud brick dwelling Souks enjoying the eerie experience of noone about only me then back out and up towards Hotel Nipper and turned left towards the bus station. No rush and seen a digital photo shop so into it looking across the street at the Louage shared taxi station and agreed with the two smiling girls as we looked at smiling thumbs up Algerian Jack's sexy photos which one they will print so that was 2nd part of Plan A in operation as agreed to come back after one hour. Out and looking at my LP photocopy of Tozeur I made my way I hoped towards the Palmeraie as I was sure I could see a palm tree fence fencing off huge palm date trees as a horse and a 4 seater cart stopped in front of me. Horse driver got off and in English said one hour for drive around the Palmeraie, 10 T Dinar so said to myself I might as well treat myself and got on and we were away. We soon got into the dirt track lanes all surrounded by palm date trees and 10-15mins later seen one, seen the lot, I was bored stiff and nearly falling asleep we done the full circumference of this green Oasis in the middle of the desert and off I got giving driver 10 T Dinar and he was away. It was now very warm in the no clouds sun so walked back into the centre of town to the bus station checking bus times for a few places to head for manyanna as heading out first thing in the morning. Next into the two smiling girls at the digital photo shop and they gave me 20 photos so had a look at smiling Jack's happy photos, paid my 6 T Dinar bill and out into cafe for a crusty with meat baguette and tea, 3 T Dinar. This time I was heading for Lake Chort el-Jerid which was on the edge of the Palmeraie and is the largest salt lake in Tunisia. Walking for a good 1km or so I eventually flagged down a taxi showing him it from my LP and he said 20 T Dinar so I said no. Fed up walking through run down villages I flagged another taxi and showing him Lake Chott el Jerid from my photocopy LP he pointed at meter so I jumped in and we were away. We drove all the way into the Palmeraie following the Chak Wak path/road signs and he dropped me off at the Fort Well Cafe in its centre, I paid him the meter 3 T Dinar and he was away as it was obvious he did not understand. I don't know what the cafe and everything inside was about but girl wanted 10 T Dinar entrance fee so said thank you and upto the camel, taxi and horse and cart parking area and a horse and cart driver came over to me as I had a camel photo shoot and asked where I wanted to go. I showed him salt Lake Chort el Jerid and a bonus as he spoke English he said it's 6km away and he will give me a one-hour tour for 20 T Dinar so had a two second think and said ok thinking God help the poor horse and on I got and whip crack we were away following the tarmac road I had been driven in on. Then we went left on a half level dirt tarmac road and again passing through untidy, half derelict villages with all the kids shouting hello, hello. Palm trees disappeared altogether and out we went on to a muddy but firm track with stretching for miles upon miles the firm but muddy ground was just a white salt topped sometimes green shrub growing very flat ground. He kept going directly into it as it looked like shimmering waterway in the distance then stopped about 300m from it. He said, you walk, and I was glad to stretch my legs as I just strolled along the top of all the salt topped ground hoping to get closer to the salt lake Chort el Jerid which my driver had told me was a mirage, it didn't exist. I did get nearer and nearer but it seemed to go further and further away the closer I got to it then gave up before I could either prove it was a lake or just a mirage and came back over my muddy footprints engraved on the salt crusted ground. Driver said smiling, mirage, so I smiling said yes and had my usual photo shoot with the snow like ground behind me. Really glad to have been here to see and walk over the largest salt lake in Tunisia as it was a very extraordinary sight in the desert sands. Back on the cart and we were away driver stopping at a few farm labourers at a green growing area and said to me follow him so off I got. We walked over to the labourers cutting green plants and he said the plants are Spinach so there, said my thanks and back on my Wells Fargo cart feeling sorry for the old horse and whip crack and shout from driver we were away. Told him Hotel Nipper and he said ok and as we passed Hotel de L'Oasis I said ok, said my thanks, gave him 20 T Dinar and he was away. Seen a live market and had a walk in and around the fresh meat dripping blood stalls and the fish with flies and fresh apple/bananas going black stalls and out needing a chesty cough thinking its a bit like my Arthur St den and into a cafe. Had a nice soft omelette, big roll with 2 teas, 4 T Dinar, belly and me happy I had a slow walk back to hotel. Had a read of LP and it looks like Gabes on the Med coast manyanna but we will see. Stripped off, teeth clean, shave and a lovely hot shower. Socks stinking so need to buy some more, so dressed with stinking socks on and out, it was 1850hrs and things starting to close down already. Made my slow way in the dark upto the bus station checking times for a few destinations then back into town centre for a coffee and 2 scones in my favourite eatery just to the right outside my hotel thinking what else I can do as nearly everything closed. Paid my 2 T Dinar bill as getting to know how much T Dinar is worth, back to room having another read of LP then stripped off and into my lovely warm bed thinking Tunisia Chico's where are you.

Email Sent: Sat, 23 Jan 2010
Subject: Tozeur in a day

Hi All

Went for a walk around a great old town Ouled el-Hwadef with no stalls or it looked like anyone living in it but fantastic old brickwork only a walk from my hotel then a horse and 4 seat cart around the Palmeraie, a huge Palm tree area but seen one seen the lot and out. Tried walking to the Lake Chott el-Djerid but give up and got another horse and 4 seat cart to it which is a huge desert salt lake which stretched flat as a pancake right out into the desert for 100s of Klms and no lake as far as I could see but the whole area was pure white salt like snow, good fun.

Heading out for 3hrs on bus manyanna to an underground city built to escape the heat called Matmata just inland from Gabes on de Med coast, that's Plan A.

al de bes
Jack

Day 29, Sunday, 24-01-10, Tozeur – Gabes – Matmata; Tunisia

Great nights sleep with vivid sexual dreams and woke up as it seemed a crowd was talking and laughing as they left, it was 0605hrs. Finally up with no rush at 0730hrs, face splash and 2 chocolate biscuits and with a 2 min stir a full dobhi drop so one hurdle over and done with, cleaned ass, kit on and down for breakie. Had 5 crusty baguette pieces with butter and jam the only way I could eat or enjoy them was to dip them into my coffee cup as I am sure half of France and all these baguette countries do as no one could enjoy eating this crust every day. Had my small piece of cake and that was breakie over and done with. Back upto room and undecided whether to wait for Post Office to open or hit de road, it was 0830hrs so decided to take letter with travel notes out with me and go for a walk. Had a nice little sun shining, but still a bit fresh walk then back to Post Office at 0850hrs, it opened at 0900hrs and I paid for stamps at kiosk giving lady my envelope, said my thanks and back to hotel. Upto room, cleaned teeth, neckpouch on checking Passport in place and shoulderbag zip up I was down to reception handing key over saying my smiling thanks and out up past the stalls all open pulling my shoulderbag and walked upto the bus station. Kiosks I had looked at yesterday with times on them were not open but guy waved me over and I showed him Matmata and Gabe from my photocopy LP, he said no Matmata only Gabe at 1430hrs but pointing down the street he said, catch a shared taxi. Down to shared Louages taxi showing shouting taxi touts Gabe they pointing at a fairly large taxi so over I went driver putting my bag in rear bag section, it was 0920hrs. Slowly but slowly our Louage taxi filled up but driver explained in French to me it was only going to Kebil, I would catch another shared Louage taxi from there, not to worry I said, then Holy Smoke and Allah above, 2 more ladies got on and we were away, 8 in total passengers, it was 1005hrs so bad planning cost me a 2hour wait!. We took the sign posted Gabe/Kebil road with the thick Palmeraie on our right heading out towards a mountain range in the distance then the Palmeraie as we turned right went onto our left hand side with now the flat sparse shrubbery desert stretching for hundreds of miles on our right, all a truly wondrous sight. Got within 5km of a barren huge mountain range and took another right and within 2km we were now in the completely flat brown sand desert, what a dream sightsee as we drove along our tarmac road with a running river directly on the right of it. I could see a shimmering haze in the distance thinking was this Lake Chott el-Djerid and low and behold the road we were on was the Causeway Road across the salt lake with one side shimmering in the Chott el-Djerid lake the other side a 10-20-30km white salt flat desert land, yeah man yeah, I was in a true happy Tunisia heaven. Eventually the flat shimmering in the sunlight lake disappeared altogether leaving only as far as my eyes could see flat sandy desert with sometimes tiny brownish shrubs everywhere as the sun beating down appeared to glisten as you looked at it in the distance, Jack of Arabia is at home at last, it was 1050hrs and most passengers sleeping. We then drove past large palm branch fenced off areas sometimes parallel with our road, other times at right angles so somebody either owns or claims it. Each side of our road was now trees as we passed through a very large town which I can't find on my map, it was 1105hrs as I seen a signpost Tozeur 18km. Out the other side of the town the desert turned to many green isolated shrubs all over it with many Palm tree and Palmeraie villages along our road. Must be going into Kebil as everyone and I paid our 6.5 T Dinar fare and at 1120hrs in we drove to Kebil Louage taxi parking area and we all got off. I didn't follow the other passengers quick enough as they went straight across the 20 parked Louage Road and upto a pay kiosk and came back straight into a Louage taxi and away. A helpful girl from my taxi pointed up at the kiosk so up I went buying a ticket for 6.5 T dinar and showing ticket I got into a Louage taxi waiting for it to get full. It was full at 1135hrs and then we were away, signpost Gabes showing 115km. Kebil looked and appeared a lovely little town as we drove out its large stone Arched gateway into the big mound sparse green shrub desert. Our next stop will be the Berber people Port town of Gabes where I have no maps, info or anything regarding hotels but Plan B is to find a hotel, dump my kit and out to catch a Louage taxi to Matmata as all I want is a few hrs sightsee of this only recently discovered Berber stronghold, all dwellings built underground to escape the heat town. Have a look then back to Gabe's for the night but could be in trouble regarding cheap accommodation in Gabe's, same same we shall see. Signpost 68km to Gabe's and low and behold seen a herd of 8 wild camels trekking and searching for food in the shrub desert along the side of the road. Louage taxi was full so no room to get out my camera for a photo, not to worry, early days yet and looking right at the big tooth shaped mountain on my right thinking people do live on it. Went into and passed through El Hamma, 54km to Gabes to go and listening to the Arabic Tunisia music on our smooth Louage taxi ride I was happy as doing well. Started seeing signposts to Matmata first then Gabe's but life is a journey with different turns as each day and each year goes by so will wait and see. Drove into Gabes and not far arrived at Louage taxi area and out it was 1255hrs. Seen a girl and I took a chance asking her does she know any cheapie hotels in Gabe Centre, she said Hotel Houda writing it on my map of Tunisia page and said pointing across the road, catch taxi. Saying my thanks I crossed the road and into a parked up Petit yellow taxi showing driver Hotel Houda and he said ok and we were away. I asked him is it in Centre Ville, he said no, if I want to go to the centre I will have to catch a Petit taxi and stopped outside Hotel Houda pointing at taxi meter 600 cent so gave him 1 T dinar and he was away. In I went to lovely big Hotel Houda, Ave de la Republique, Gabes, Tunisia, Tel: 75220022 and asked reception guy any rooms, he said in English, yes, 18 T Dinar got a key and said look. He carried my shoulderbag up two flights of stairs and in we went to Room 205, a lovely big double ensuite western toilet. I said ok and he said Passport so gave it to him and he said pay now so I gave him a 20 T Dinar note and he gave me back 2 T Dinar and said collect Passport at reception so I said ok. Dumped whatever I didn't need and down to reception, got Passport and back to room putting it away and that was me downstairs handing key over asking the best way to get to Matmata the famous Berber tribe town after it was filmed in Star Wars and still has its original underground dwellings some now being used as Hotels. He said take a Petit taxi to Matmata Louage taxi area and take one but I will have to wait until it's full so flagged down a yellow Petit taxi, jumped in telling him Matmata Louage taxis and we were away not that far and off I got paying him 600 cents as per his meter. Into a waiting Louage taxi and not long we where full and away and after a good 20km drive we stopped at a crossroad town and out I got paying him 2.5 T Dinar with him pointing across the road at a brown Louage taxi saying Matmata. Went across the road saying Matmata to driver, he said yes, and in I got and 2mins later we were full and away, it was 1355hrs. It was a lovely scenic route going higher and higher up the mountain road in the very warm lovely desert heat seeing the desert barren 20-50m high mound hills then sometimes seeing isolated bunches of palm tree small forest areas. It was fun as I could see little donkey dirt track paths going far up the full mountains. Fare time and did what everyone else did I passed a 1 T Dinar coin upto the driver getting a 100 cent coin back so that was cheap for a 20-25km ride. It was so satisfying seeing the true desert then my first sight of white painted door frame blocks in the centre of a 20m high desert rock mound I knew we must be coming near and in we drew to the lovely village of Matmata with a big white block welcoming sign; Matmata, Genevieve, Welcome, on the side of a hill. Off I got with touts giving me grief saying, guide guide and if they had been a bit civil I would have said yes but they were so annoying I walked away them following me until they got the message and pissed off, it was 1435hrs. Didn't have a clue but asking a couple of Westerners they said go uphill and I did going off the main road seeing dozens of little door entrances tunnelled into the big solid desert mounds and it was fun walking around them on the outside as they were not in use any more by the look of it. Went everywhere I needed to over the desert mounds then seen one of the most famous ones now called Hotel Sidi Driss which was filmed in Star Wars and was so thrilled looking at its entrance. The round door entrance was open and a flight of stone stairs led steeply down so I went down them in the dark and came to its reception but no one about so carried on into the first daylight opening round crater with at least six little entrance doors around it, popped my head into 2 or 3 and they were all bedrooms. Kept going still going down steep steps to the next round entrance crater opening out its top on the ground appox 30m above was the toilet area with approximately 6 western toilets. Laughing to myself I kept going still going downhill in the tunnel joining each round formatted crater and came to the final level which was deep in the ground but light still coming from its opening at the ground level above and that was my film Star Wars walk over and done. Truly chuffed to bits for seeing it all I slowly made my way back upto reception seeing reception guy there and we had a chat. Said my thanks and got him to take some photos of me at the Hotel Sidi Driss entrance, said my thanks and I was away. Luck was on my side as I seen a Musee sign and followed it into another 3-4m bright tunnel to an open to daylight crater and walked around looking into the five bedrooms and cooking areas with beds and all sorts including vividly clothed statues of the Berber men and women from a bygone age, really chuffed I paid my 3 T Dinar entrance fee on leaving. The Tourist Office was closed so just had a walk around the large village but touts at every turn were very annoying. Brilliant day so how do I get back to Gabes and eventually found where Louage taxi had dropped me off and it looked like same taxi was parked up but had only one person on it. Seen the French couple who had directed me earlier and told them about where Hotel Sidi Driss was as they were driving but said afterwards they were going to Jerba so we parted with good lucks. Had a Fanta and a full packet of chocolate biscuits then the driver started up and I waved at him and on I got and we were away only half full, it was 1635hrs. It was a real eye opener driving out of Matmata as I now seen dozens and dozens of small cave like doors all over the mountain mounds so that was a bonus and then down the hairpin bend mountain road we went me thinking that was a real big-time bonus seeing all that today. Signpost said 40km to Gabes then at signpost showing 25km to Gabes we stopped. I paid my 1 T Dinar and changed Louage taxis and we were away again all the way into Gabes and out I got paying driver 1 T Dinar getting 250 cents back, that was a bonus, it was only 1720hrs. No hesitation, flagged a Petit taxi down telling him Gabes Centre Ville and he was away driving into the full of life cafe centre and stopping to let me out, paid him 1 T Dinar, got 200 cents change as all Petit taxis are on meters. Looked about me but didn't have a clue so walked sort of downhill passing Hotel Tacapes, 163 Bis Av Habib Bourguiba, Gabes, 00216 75270701 so went in and double ensuite was only 16 T Dinar. Not far seen Hotel Atlantic, 4 Ave Habib, Bourguiba, Gabes, Tel: 75220034 went in and it had double ensuites for 16 T Dinar so that was a bonus in the centre of town near the beach. Finally got to the old Sailing ship roundabout at Restaurant Casino at the entrance to the Port but straight through the seating area of Restaurant Casino I seen a lovely big two mast old 1800s schooner, what a lovely sight but looking over the near wall was another truly fantastic beautiful sight, yes the Gabes Beach on the Mediterranean Sea. Out of the side back entrance of the restaurant and shouting I got you, I got you out loud I got all the way down to the sea water edge and stuck my big toe in it shouting loudly into the 1800hrs starting to get slightly dark Tunisian sky, yeah man yeah, I was absolutely so thrilled to have made it here. Had a photo shoot and away into Cafe restaurant El Cornish directly beside Restaurant Casino and had 3 scones and a coffee, yeah man yeah, oh I felt so elated. Paid my 1 T Dinar Bill and out but no taxis this time I just walked it the full way back towards my Hotel passing Rue Le General De Gaulle then came to Place 2 Mars then went up Rue de Palestine facing the Post Office and I could feel I was nearly home so into a cafe not far from my hotel and had a big piece of lovely cooked chicken, large portion of chips and a Fanta and I and my belly were happy, paid my 2 T Dinar bill and out and upto hotel just across the road, what a day, it was now 2215hrs. Still a bit early so dumped China beachbag and out for a dander seeing 2 other hotels around the area but one more coffee with a chocolate scone and that was me back to hotel and saying my goodnights to reception I was up to my room. It was only 2255hrs but after a read of LP I stripped off and into my big double bed and asleep dreaming sex on the rocks on a Berber cave bed, that would be a good one!

A real underground Hotel with cave rooms

Real cave rooms

Email Sent: Sunday, 24 Jan 2010
Subject: RM205 Hotel Houda, Ave De La Republique, Gabes, Tunisia. Tel 75274053

Hi All

Jumped a shared taxi from Tozeur and 3hrs with one change arrived in Gabes on the Med coast.

Got hotel as above, 18 T Dinar, dumped kit in room and out to shared Louages taxies and got one to Matmata 40klms away through the desert where the original Berber tribes dwellings are which are dwelling dug and tunnelled into the solid rock desert mounds and go underground so no desert summer heat penetrates.

It was good fun walking around looking at the original 100s of little opening all in the mountain mounds and hills then into a famous one now a hotel called Hotel Sidi Driss and went down its 2 floors looking into its 22 rooms all featured in Star Wars but it was good fun just wandering about in the penetrating desert heat

Jumped another taxi 1 T Dinar AND 24klms later changed taxies and paying another 1 T Dinar was now back in centre of Gabes. Sometimes have French problems with computer, why don't they learn English and use an English keyboard never mind drive on the wrong side of de road.

Knew I was near the sea so walked down to it and shouting yeah man yeah I stuck my big right toe into the Med sea, wow oh wow, what a feeling

I would say I am heading for Jerba down towards the Libya border manyanna but with my strict planning I will wake up and see.

al de bes

Jack

Day 30, Monday, 25-01-10, Gabes – Jerba; Tunisia

Another great sleep in my double blanket bed as it gets cold at night then checking my bedside clock it was 0745hrs so got up still thinking of plans. Underarm and feet wash, shave and face wash in the hot water, kit on including pullover as it was coldish and out downstairs. Asked the two girls if any cafes open for breakie, they pointed down the corridor at their cafe so into it I went and sat down. Only a min or two wait and 6 cut sections of crusty baguette, butter and 1 jam cube with a pot of coffee and a pot of hot milk arrived. Buttering and jamming my baguette slices and plenty of sugar in my milky coffee I sat back enjoying my Frenchie breakie, ugh!. Finished the lot and offered to pay but they said its in hotel room price so up to room, teeth clean and thinking about Gabes I went out for a nice walk into and around the lively town centre then back to hotel, it was 0930hrs. Final pack of shoulderbag and out flagging down a Petit taxi telling him in French, Louages Jerba, he said, Louages Jerba and we were away not far and stopped at a very huge Louage Taxi area. One bloke touting for Jerba, Jerba so I said Jerba, he said yes and put my shoulderbag in the back but there was no one in his taxi so pure luck I seen the bus station nearby. Went up to it thinking I can only try and tried a kiosk asking guy Jerba and asking him the time buses went but he said French, French then young girl came over asking him in French and he told her and she told me 1015hrs in English so looking at clock it was 1010hrs. I said ticket so she said to old guy ticket and price was 5-50 Dinar so gave him the money, got ticket and quickly back 30m to Louage taxi still with no one in it I grabbed my shoulderbag and back showing ticket at turnstile and onto bus which as I sat down started up and we were away, wow, that was a close one, it was 1015hrs. We went right out of Gabes with the sea on our left but didn't realise Gabes town or city was so big as we trundled through its in good order suburbs. Slowly but slowly then getting up a very good speed we got out of Gabes into the Palmeraie planted palm tree areas then sparse brown desert with shrubs and finally out to the hot no clouds blue sky blowing dust from the browny shrub desert so sat back thinking New day, New town and happy on my travels I nodded off. Woke up a few times as we slowed down going through nondescript large villages then shocked woke up for good, it was 1150hrs as we were in a Port called Jorf and my bus was driving down to a ferry and got preference as soon as all the vehicles drove off our bus at front of the queue drove on. I must admit I knew Jerba was an island but thought a causeway drove across it from the mainland, not to worry, great views along the coast as 5mins later after all vehicles where on we were away so I got off the bus for a big stretch and sightsee lookee. Had a read of LP photocopy and the ferry I was on was a 24hr ferry between Jorf and Ajun on the Island of Jerba, its capital is Houmt Souk towards the middle of its North Coast so it looks like I am going there. Jerba is famous for and known as the Land of the Lotus Eaters where the honey drugged fruit as you taste and enjoy gets you addicted to it and you sit back in a stupor and don't want to leave so will have a few good sessions and see how I enjoy it. We drove off the ferry 1215hrs through a nice white building fishing port, it looks good and stopped in the bus station and off we all got, me grabbing my bright red shoulderbag with blue ribbon on its straps. Had been having a look at LP Houmt Souk map and bus station appeared a bit far out from the centre so hailed one of the 30-40 Petit yellow taxi drivers showing him Hotel Arischa directly in the centre of Houmt Souk. He pointed down into centre saying only a 2-5min walk and I was flabbergasted as had never met a truthful honest taxi driver before especially abroad as most taxi drivers would have driven me around for 10mins then drop me off at hotel charging six times the rate. Shoulderbag trolley wheels going full steam I walked down towards the town centre seeing a Hotel and although it seemed a bit outside the centre I decided to take it so in and had a look at price which was 12 T Dinar for one person, all rooms are the same size for 1-2-3 persons. Girl showed me a lovely big double bed room but no WHB as toilets and WHB's were outside so I said, any with toilets in room, she said no, so said my thanks as I now know I need my inside room toilet and out down the stairs and into town centre. Seen Residence Compartments and guy said look, they had WC inside rooms but they were all 4 single bed apartments and price was 40 T Dinar. Said my thanks and away and just on down a Souk in a very lively full of all sorts of shops, stalls and cafes I seen Hotel Des Sables d'Or, Centre Ville, Houmt Souk, Djerba, Tel: 7560423 and it had such a beautiful facade and reception area. Asked guy if any rooms for one person, he said yes and took me up the original old stairs to a round inner courtyard on a first floor balcony and into Room 4. It was so nice with a big double bed, WHB and a shower, he pointed outside and said toilet but me knowing WHB will do for a piss I said ok, back down to reception and paid 14 T Dinar for one night, got my key and took shoulderbag up, dumped it and Passport and other wallet in room. Out straight away and down around the so neat internal areas and handing my key over I was out into the melee of the constant right and left turn Souks trying to orientate myself for first look at the Bavy Gharge Mustapha 13th Century Fort. Two or three turns later I was in Place de Algeria and knew where I was in the vibrant busy Souks and kept happily humming "You take the high road, I'll take the low road and I'll be in Scotland before you" in the now bright hot sunny day as I could see the big stone walled Fort in the distance. Had a sort of walk around it then in the main gate paying a 5 T Dinar entrance fee and up the original big stone steps to the battlement overlooking the sea coast looking left and right. Great sights so just took my time walking all the areas even under the dark stone Archways and one final look at the 2 big 3 mast original schooners anchored up in the yacht fishing port that was my great Fort visit over. Said my smiling thanks and out going left along the seafront of the Fort and along the beach in a no rush walk up to the fishing Port seeing its 50 or so fishing boats and yachts. Time for a coffee so sat down in a cafe and had a scone 1.5 T Dinar so happy enough, where to now. Had another read and look at my fotocopy LP Houmt Souk map and following it I went into a very newish well kept Museum, paid my 5 T Dinar entrance fee and in. Very surprised as nothing much to see as just followed the circuit with no mention of the original Jewish settlement. Out of the newish part and into the old dwelling with its domed ceiling and old inner courtyard with lots of old neat timber ceilings which was the best in the Museum and out I went thinking not much thought went into showing Jerba's past great history in that Museum. Time as usual had marches on, it was 1710hrs so picked a barber from one of the many and had a very neat No1 where he done my hair then my nose, ears and eyebrows so very pleased I paid him 3 T Dinar and out. Belly complaining it wanted something to eat, so into a small cafe for quarter chicken, chips, veg and 3 teas and enjoyed my 1735hrs din din thinking I never asked the price. Finished it and was happy, asked for price and he wrote 7 T Dinar so paid him without arguing as no French so cant argue and out back along the Souks to my hotel and upto room. It had as usual got cold as the sun went down so no shower, just cleaned teeth and out with everywhere closing down and into a digital photo shop getting 19 snaps printed and charge was 6.60 T Dinar, guy said pick them up in one hour so off I went still getting lost and lost and lost again but found an internet shop and did my usual sprightly email letting family know where I am as if the worst happened no good saying I wish. Everywhere except a few restaurants and tea shacks were now closed and the Souks deserted so had a final last tea and a chocolate cake and that was me, collected my photos and a slow walk back to hotel getting two extra blankets from reception and up to room as it did seem colder but coming from inland desert to Mediterranean sea coast it probably was colder anyway. Only 2140hrs so had a read of LP regarding a day out manyanna so had a few plans formatting I felt a stir and over to communal loo and had a nice full bang dobhi drop, cleaned ass and back to room. Stripped off and into my lovely warm bed thinking Tunisia is not a hooker country but surely some must be under the veils and white robes, time will tell and dreaming taking a veil off a naked desert hooker I happily fell asleep.

Email Sent: Mon, 25 Jan 2010
Subject: Rm4, Hotel des Sables D,Or, Centre Villa, Houmt-Souk, Jerba, Tunisia, Tel75650423

HI All
Upto Bus Station to catch the 1015hrs bus which in our drive took us across the sea in a ferry onto the isle of Jerba and another little bus ride to its Capital, Houmt Souk at 1215hrs. After 3rd attempt got above at 14 T Dinar for a WHB and Shower in room but you know what. Fantastic old original hotel so staying for 2 days as Jerba is the Land of the Lotus and even Ulysses men got a taste for it and tried to stay but it tastes like coke????, ha ha. Had a great walk through the Souks then upto the 13th Century Fort then a walk along the beach to the fishing port with old 18th century 3 mast schooners still anchored up then back into town to the musee but all mention of the Jews have been removed as it once in bygone years was a Jewboy town. Will have my Lotus manyanna then head out for a day to an old town for a sightsee, plan A?? Have tried for a Libya visa but it takes 7 days and still does not give me free travel so it looks like I wont see our old mate Gadaffi and our old El Adem Airfield from 1969? again. Egypt is getting closer as it looks like I will fly instead of crossing de desert; any hints anyone let me know.
al de bes
Jack

Day 31, Tuesday, 26-01-10, Jerba; Tunisia

Had a decent sleep but woke up a few times by either cats or penguins screeching outside somewhere then up at 0730hrs ready for my planned day. Face splash, under arm wash, changed all clothing rolling my dirty dobhi linen up, kit on and out downstairs to the always very helpful reception staff. Lady owner/cleaner smiled saying washing rubbing her hands together in a washing motion and me laughing said yes so she put it behind reception. Owner/day reception guy said you stay, I said yes, one more day and paid him 14 T Dinar and said breakfast cafe. He took me outside pointing go left and straight on until you come to main square and Ben Yedder Cafe does good breakfast so saying my thanks I was away. Walked on and on thinking I was lost as it's very easy to do but came out and shouted yeah man yeah as there it was the Ben Yedder nearly fully packed with Tunisian guys already. Went inside and they had big hot rolled up baguettes omelettes so said pointing, one and one indicating with my two hands a large coffee and sat down. It came within 5mins and I sat back happily devouring my nearly first time English breakie, had another coffee and that was me, no rush but paid my 4 T Dinar bill and out turning right and spot on found the Post Office just opened, it was 0910hrs. Took a while but eventually got to the counter and paid for stamps for airmail to UK and posted a few travel notes and some more thumbs up poser Jack's photos to Sylvialita, Sandralita's Mum who saves my life by accepting my travel writing post. Out and a gentle walk back to hotel passing a few lovely named Mosques then a sit down banger dobhi drop in hotel, cleaned ass, cleaned teeth and ready for today's sightseeing antics. Walked upto the bus station feeling a frightful stirring in my belly and knew I needed a watery dobhi drop urgently. Into the usual Bus Station 15mm deep full of piss floor WC and it had a western WC with no toilet seat but trying to keep my socks dry in my Thai sandals I sat on its full of piss rim and had a full empty belly squirt, cleaned ass with my own toilet paper from my Chinabag and out trying to keep my filthy hands from my trouser belt. Found a washhand basin and washed my hands then tightened trouser belt and no piss on my socks I had only another 10min wait then caught the 1015hrs bendy bus, 900 cents to Guellala a pottery making old town 15km away on the other side of the island. Jerba was an island Oasis with lots of trees and it was a neat cheerful 30mins journey to Guellala as we stopped only about 5 times to let people on and off the final stop in the middle of the very colourful Guellala pottery shops area I got off. I went left looking at all the new and sometimes looking into old derelict shops very old artefacts and very old pottery of all shapes and sizes be it small cups to 1m high round storage urns, www.artpoterie.com, good fun and I went into two pottery making shops watching one guy on a wheel making the urn and others painting them all not changed in 500 years, fantastic sights. No hassle as no rush so walked around the fully really colourful village full of the most amazing colourful items of all sorts of pottery then into a cafe near where the bus had dropped me off at 1050hrs, bus back was 1305hrs, it was only 1235hrs so Plan A working well. Had another little walk trying to find the Musee but no luck then back to bus stop and caught the 1315hrs bus paying 1 T Dinar back to Houmt Souk Bus Station. It made me really laugh out loud on the bus as in my Lotus filled brain I had been pointing out to a few girls, a few blokes and the bus conductor, Jerba on my LP photocopy and they with sometimes amazement and others laughing said yes now really laughing to myself I realised why, Jerba is the Island I was on, I had been trying to get back to Houmt Souk the capital of it. No wonder they thought I was a bit crazy so a word of warning, don't take Lotus seed when you want to try and map read. Arrived there at 1345hrs and checking times next bus to Tourist Zone was 1400hrs so just hung about at Bus 11 stop and got on it as it parked up at 1355hrs. The Tourist Zone area I was told by my hotel owner was full of big hotels along the large beach so I just wanted to have a look and sat back as we first drove along Houmt Souk very nice promenade then out and onto a dirt track road as on one side they were constructing a large new road the first hotel we passed which was an amazing size was the Radisson Complex and from there onwards it was just one large hotel complex after another all blocking the sea. We did go through a few villages but no promenade or sea walking footpath as it looked as if we were miles from the sea as we went through two golf courses without any visible sign of a beach or anything but passed a Grand Casino then I seen a large high in the sky Red lighthouse and conductor said tapping me on the shoulder, my stop, so off I got, it was 1430hrs. The stop was directly facing Apartment Hotel Siad so I walked upto the big Red lighthouse then cut across to a road leading down toward camels, horses and neat 4 person horse carriages all for I presume tourists. Kept going in the direction of a fantastic Spinnaker towers Fort wall which looked a very ancient very large dwelling but gave up as shouting "I got you" "I got you" into the sky blue sky I was at the sandy shore sea edge as big breakers were rolling up the sandy beach at a cafe/restaurant called The Chicha Restaurant Pizzeria. Over to empty restaurant and had a coffee and a slice of cake, 2 T Dinar then across the road and across the sandy beach to the sea's edge and although it was still early I knew I was going no further but happy as a lark I started going back upto the main road bus stop at the big Red lighthouse at least 1km from the sea edge!. Got upto the bus stop facing Hotel Siad with sign pointing down the road Plage Sidi Yati and another underneath stating Yati Beach Club but sat down hoping for a bus, it was 1545hrs. Waited 15mins and knew a bus would eventually come along but no patience so walked up the road to two Petit yellow taxis parked outside a hotel and asked how much to Houmt Souk and they said 8 T Dinar so not a bad price for a taxi, I took it, got in and we were away. I said to driver, stop as we passed a 50 year old French lady who asked me in French for directions to her hotel and she was as I could see very tired but she said thanks, no, she was ok and wouldn't get in so off we drove. It's very amazing but there is groups of middle aged French Ladies in 2-4-6 and sometimes 10 or more everywhere all enjoying their holidays, I don't understand it but wishing them well as you only get one chance. Got back into Houmt Souk and I told him Tunis Air Travel Agency and he dropped me off outside it, gave him the 8 T Dinar and he was away. Mind made up so asked lady times of flights to Tunis tomorrow and she told me 0800hrs, 1630hrs or 2030hrs and price was 118 Dinar so giving her my card and copy of Passport I said book the 0800hrs flight. She did, so punched my credit card number into machine, got a receipt and 2mins later a printed out copy of my flight details with her telling me be at Airport desk 1 hour before flight and taxi from

Houmt Souk to Airport takes 15mins so thanking her and all the staff for the excellent service I was out down the road and into Ben Yedder Café. Had 2 small pizzas and 2 large coffees, 6 T Dinar, just the job and well filled I slowly made it back into my hotel collecting my dobhi and upto room, sorry to be leaving but final pack of shoulderbag then stripped off having a lovely hot water shave and shower then kit on and out. Had a good little wander but everywhere nearly shut so into the internet shop behind the Post Office doing my usual 20mins then checked for hotels in Tunis for 15mins then that was me, had one final coffee then back to room, stripped off, set alarm and into bed asleep, no sex, no dreams.

Email Sent: Tue, 26 Jan 2010
Subject: Houmt Souk and area around Jerba

Hi All
Woke up smiling and lazy for a change, I blame it on de Lotus seed?, wat yu tink. Up anyway and jumped a bus to Guellala a very colourful pottery making town to see how they actually make from cups and saucers to large urns so good fun. Jumped another bus to the tourist zone about 12klms from Houmt Souk full of Radisson type hotels all grabbing long stretches of beaches not anything like real Tunisian life but that's life for some. No chance of Libya visa so booked a flight to Tunis for manyanna, 118 Dinar, so will have a few days exploring Tunis and the area around it then fly Egypt Air to I hope to a town just near the Libya border and bus it into Cairo, that's plan A?, anyone about???
al de bes
Jack

Day 32, Wednesday, 27-01-10, Jerba – Tunis; Tunisia

Woke up at 0545hrs as the first chanter started then 3-4 more joined in one very near so turned over a few times joining in letting a few good well loud farts off making sure everyone in the hotel was woken up, then up at 0630hrs. Had a face splash, underarm wash, kit on and out to corridor westerner loo and a lovely full wack farting dobhi drop so job well done, cleaned ass and back to room. Final pack, cleaned teeth, neckpouch on checking Passport and Airline ticket and time and out downstairs handing key over and saying my thanks, handle of trolley shoulderbag up and I was away through the dark but not forbidding Souks and came out at Ben Yedder Café so done a right and across the main road to the taxi rank outside the Post Office. Taxi driver seen me and putting my case in boot I told him, Airport, got in the front and we were away and what a dream 10-15mins drive as me having phobias about getting to Heathrow or Gatwick it was so unbelievable driving a road without traffic. He dropped me off giving me my shoulderbag so paid him 5TDinar and he looked at me sort of implying tip please but saying my thanks I was away into the Airport, it was 0710hrs. There were at least twenty check-in desks which surprised me so went over to a Tunis air ticket office saying Tunis, guy said this is the International Airport, the Internal Airline desks are the other Terminal pointing through the very upmarket well tiled lobby so pulling shoulderbag behind me off I went into the Domestic Terminal looking for any open desks but none. Seen departure board with three Tunis Air Flights, 0900, 1530 and 2030hrs, so it's looking good. Over to a café and had a rip off coffee and tasteless meat Panini, 6 T Dinar, worse than Heathrow but sat back enjoying my sort of breakie awaiting check-in to open. It finally opened so checked in my shoulderbag getting Seat 10F and had a walkie around the Airport waiting to board. We boarded at 0840hrs and I took my Seat 10F and sat back waiting for take off. Tannoy as usual came on and we had the usual seat belt emergency exit and life vest demonstration then at 0910hrs we started up and with a surge of power off we climbed into the blue Tunisian sky me looking down at Jerba Island saying, loved you Jerba, bye bye and got my photocopy LP Tunis out from my cargo pocket to have a read about Tunis and places to stay. To orientate myself I picked Hotel Maison Doree, Rue el Koufa as one side it had Tunis Centre Ville and the other it had the Medina and next thing, I nodded off. I woke up as we were coming into land and landed at 1000hrs. Taxied over to arrivals and everyone got of and I just sauntered into the main hall looking for arrivals luggage, but nothing. I asked at the information desk and they pointed back at where I had walked along the corridor as I got off the plane so I walked back and there was my bag sitting on its own at small luggage moving escalator so grabbed it and out. Followed the signs for taxi being in one instance nearly accosted as bloke tried to make me take his large cab for 10Euro but said piss off and took a yellow Petit cab. Shoulderbag in back seat with me beside it we were away not that far to Hotel Maison Doree and he stopped outside it and said 15 T Dinar, I said where is your meter, he said, no meter, so didn't argue just paid him as I didn't know the price. Into Hotel and well dressed reception of a bygone age showed me tariff which was 44 T Dinar for single person in a d-ensuite so I said my thanks and out as had seen and passed 3-4 hotels so went back for a look. Next one wanted 34 T Dinar then into Hotel Salammbo, 6 Rue de Grece, Tunis, Tel: 21671350732, www.hotelsalammbo.com which inside was so clean and so old but had great vibes. Guy said 28 T Dinar for room with shower and WHB so up I went and had a look and it was perfect, ok no WC but WHB, who cares. Back down, paid for one night, showed Passport and got key to Room 19 and took shoulderbag up, dumped it in room with the 2-3 old colonial type faces of Frenchmen cleaners just completing their cleaning. No rigid plans so thought I would walk the Medina as I knew where it was as had passed it coming in then have a tour of Carthage the original Roman City manyanna, that's Plan A, it was 1100hrs. Handed key in and very friendly reception guy in answer to my question was very helpful regarding where to catch transport tomorrow, so saying my thanks I was out upto Ave Habib Bourguiba town centre road and turning left I seen the big 2 dramatic with Crosses Spired Church across the road so crossed the road at Place de Independence and into as I read its notice; St Vincent de Paul Et St Olivia Cathedrale. It was a very beautiful interior with many high inscribed painted Domes and stained glass windows and it had three old plaques along the left hand wall, the first one was St Victor 189-198AD, second one was St Miltiades 311-317AD and the third was St Gelasius 492-496AD. I didn't fully understand what the numbers thinking is it when they where made Saints but carried on enjoying my walk until I had done and admired all the beautiful interior of the Cathedral, really good. Then standing in the middle aisle I bowed my head looking at the altar saying a little prayer for all the poor and hungry in the world today and may the Lord above be with them all to help them and out I went. Went over to a large statue in the pedestrian walkway of Ibn Khaldun 1332-1406AD, philosopher and historian then turn right just a short walk along Ave de France and through the very big impressive stone Arch gate of L'Victoria and I was in the packed main Souk of the Medina, it was only 1200hrs. I enjoyed my packed Souk walk, getting many "look, just look" from the hundreds of stall guys trying to sell every and anything as it must be a very frustrating job standing there 12hrs a day. I didn't stop once but thought I would go left into the no one about Souks and what a truly marvellous sight and journey it was as these narrow little Souks (alleys) sometimes had 2-3 storey high big stone walls each side and there wasn't one, there were hundreds of little Souks at every turn. I got completely lost but had a wonderful time and came out at nearly the top of the Medina Hill at Rue Said Ben Ziad just beside a very large hospital. Kept going on up the hill to it would appear a really nice Government Buildings many with prominent big round Domes and there was a neat square Tower Clock in the middle of a roundabout, this avenue was called Ave Bab Bnet. Started to go downhill along the very packed with people hill road and passed the large imposing Palais de Justice and then the area got very rundown and I stopped at Place Bab Souka. Feeling very peckish I bought 3 bread rolls and as I ordered them the guy cut the rolls filling them with potato, red sauce and fish so got a bottle of Sprite as well, paid my 4-50 T Dinar, took a seat at the side of the not in use water fountain in the middle of the roundabout and enjoyed my tasty dinner. Belly full, me happy I went straight into a second hand shoes and clothes market just walking through its 50 or so stalls then out the other side completely lost and couldn't believe it but I had done a full circle and was now back at Place Bab Souka again, cor that was magic or maybe my map instincts. Taking another way this time I seen the lovely well kept St Georges Anglican Church and of course went in through the open wide pavement entrance steel gates having a look at the many burial slabs and Memorials, pure old real history. First large Obelisk Memorial was to Officers, NCOs' and men of the 4th Indian Division who lost their lives in the battle for Tunisia 1943 and it was so sad to see so many names who never made it home. Saluted the brave India boys and was completely shocked at a large enclosed grave with headstone; Frank Ritchie, The Grove, Belfast, Ireland, died 14 Nov 1873 aged 23 years so saying all the best you wee Belfast Boy I just walked along the wall reading the many grave plaques upright on it. Some were Italian, some USA, Germany, Swedish and the oldest was 1868-1750, 82 years. One was Samuel Davis Heap, Consulate General born in Carlisle, Pennsylvania USA, 1780, died 1853. All great history as next I came to a plaque; To the Memory of the Officers, Warrant Officers, Non Commissioned Officers and Men of the 1st Batt Irish Guards killed in action at Djebel Bou Aoukaz 27-30 April 1943 so saying out loud into the blue Tunisian sky;" God be with you all my Paddyboy soldier bretheren" I saluted and on to the next one. In Memory of Our Comrades who made the Supreme Sacrifice, 2nd Batt Coldstream Guards, Dec 1942 – May 1943 and there were approximately 120 names below it so saluting them all in the lovely well kept Church I said "God be with you and your families my brave sons" and I was out and away. It took a while but eventually found my way out of the Medina and knew where I was again at the Le Victoria Arch thinking I need to go back in again to the Medina but this time stay left and in I went. Walked a good distance but thought to myself I was lost and luck was on my side as I seen a Police Officer so over to him and asked him the way to the Grande Mosque and he pointed left and its only 50m away. On I trundled and turning a corner there it was with its many, many beautiful round Columns all in full view as they were borrowed! from the ancient Roman City of Carthage on the outskirts of Tunis. Visitors of any religion could go in so I did but only at the entrance marvelling at the perfect round architecture 100s of years old. Smiled my thanks at the bare foot Muslims and away and time was marching on so back out of the most wonderful fantastic Medina and into a pizza shop along Rue De Hollande and enjoyed a full pizza and a coffee, 4 T Dinar. Finished my lovely din din and back to hotel just making it as had a lovely dobhi drop so cleaned ass, cleaned teeth and had a nice rest reading LP Cairo thinking when am I going to go and panicking a little, it was 1720hrs. Had passed a travel agent a few times not far away on Ave Habib Bourguiba so quickly crossed its packed with cars road and into a Travel Agency. Girl looked at me and said you need help, I said yes I want to book a flight to Cairo for Friday so she looked at her computer and said only one flight at 2200hrs, arriving Cairo 0200hrs so thinking its not for me and trying it on I said any flights tomorrow. She looked at her computer again and said yes, the only one is at 1500hrs so without a thought or hesitation I asked how much, she said 342 T Dinar so I said book it as it was a bargain and gave her my credit card. Only 5mins later she got me to sign the stub and gave me my printed out ticket so that's the start of my Egypt trip all set and ready to go. Out from there and into an internet shop and booked a 20$US a night supposedly en-suite room for 5 nights in Cairo and got my printout so that's sealed and delivered.

Met my Korean friends for the third time today who where staying at the same hotel as me and it was a father and daughter on a Middle East and European trip and it was a great pleasure to talk to them and we parted they were going to Rome manyanna, I was going to Cairo. Took my time walking about and Tunis it would appear is full of gay boys but the women are the most attractive Chico's I have seen on my travels as they are so beautiful and in a league of their own. Went into a few noisy bar areas getting a few full eye inviting you want sex looks from no veils short skirt flashing their boobs girls walking about which got a stir on my trouser working parts and now feeling like a rampant dog I knew it was love to last a Tunisia lifetime as one smiling beautiful figure lovely boobs chico stood in front of me saying where you go sexy. I said my heart beating loudly and my trouser parts sticking out I go with you my lovely darling as she curled up into me giving me a tight hug her hands all over me and down my front, oh God, I was so much in love. She pointed at a door beside a full music blasting out bar saying my place and no hesitation with my arm cuddling her we went over and as she pushed the open door fully open in we went along a hall and she unlocked a door and in we went to a large double bedroom me now quickly saying how much as so excited in my true loves arms I had not asked. She said giving me a Tunisia full tongue hands exploring kiss, 80 T Dinar and so truly and so much in love with my sexy lover I didn't care and got out the money in 20 T Dinar notes and leaving it on her dressing table we smiling into each others love struck eyes stripped off naked and fondling and caressing each others sex fuelled bodies we where on her bed making wild sexual grunting gasping sensual Tunisian love, I was in heaven in Tunisia. Changing positions are hands everywhere with her legs around her neck we where like 2 dogs on heat pounding into each others sex crazed bodies and changing positions again her legs rapped around me are true love sexual burning passions rose to new heights and as are sex spasms exploded we climaxed together like two honeymoon lovers she was screaming with passion and biting me everywhere and raking my back and buttocks with her long finger nails I bit her breasts grunting in pure sexual ecstasy are sexual spasm's passions going on and on until slowly but slowly are vibrations sexual spasms subsided down and me breathing heavily and she whimpering in the joys of her climax we came to a rest tightly clasped together on her sweat soaked scented bed I knew I would never leave my Tunis true love ever again she smiled rubbing my face cheek saying 'I like you Papa but we go' and me giving her belly and tits a tickle we both smiling rolled off the bed and got dressed me still in heaven in Tunisia. It was only 2150hrs as we said our Goodbyes with a hug and a cheek peck at her front door and I with a final wave was away along the many Rue loud bar street, Gor was I sweating happy. Finally after a glazed eye round and around the Rue's walk I eventually found my hotel, got my key and upto my room, stripped off again and into bed dreaming of Tunis noisy love all night long and asleep a Tunis true love back and buttocks ripped to pieces happy man.

Email Sent: Wed, 27 Jan 2010
Subject: Rm19, Hotel Salammbo, 6 Rue de Grece, Tunis, Tunisia, Tel71350732. www.hotelsalammbo.com

Hi All

Jumped a plane 0900hrs and landed Tunis 1000hrs and into city centre and got above with WHB and shower, 24 T Dinar, done well I think as it's directly in city centre just out of the Medina. Had a good afternoons walk around the Medina and I will never know how they build it as its pretty special.

Going to Cairo manyanna as plan?? was to go Fri but only flight on Fri was at 2200hrs and arrive Cairo 0200hrs so got a flight, 232 T Dinar manyanna leaving Tunis at 1500hrs so I will visit Carthage in the morning and then upto Airport.

Tunis is really worth a visit as it has great vibes so just going back for shave and shower and who knows tonight???

al de bes

Jack

Map 1 of Egypt

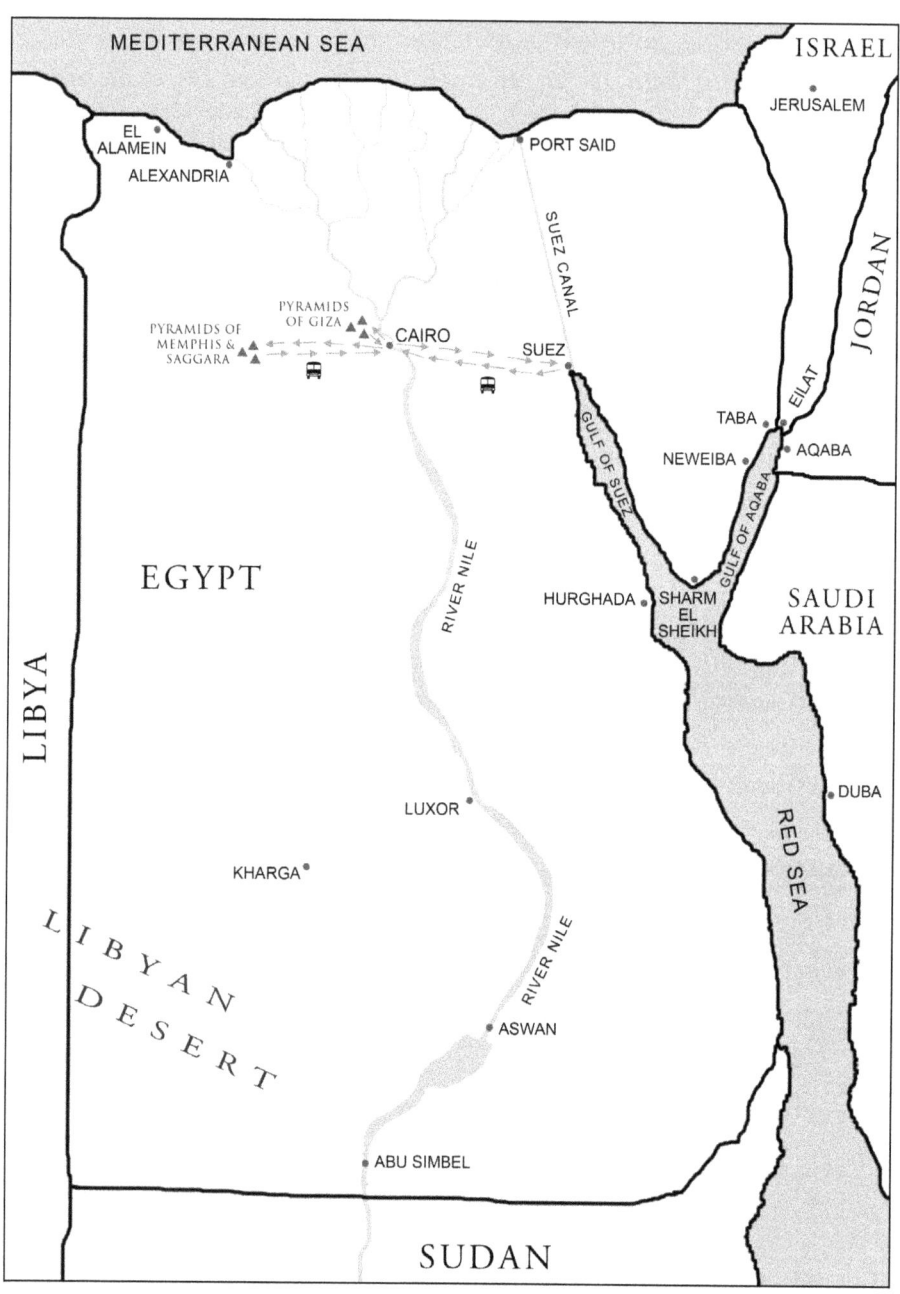

1) EGYPT is the oldest tourist attraction in the world with even the Romans and the Ancient Creeks coming to admire the awe-inspiring wonders of the Pyramids but every turn including the Valley of the Kings with the Tomb of King Tutankhamen Tomb and a sail in a Felecia up the Nile then the exciting hustle and bustle of Cairo before having a relaxing soak in the Red sea is a unique atmospheric sense exploring trip back in time not forgetting a walk along the banks of the famous Suez Canal then a trip to walk and explore the full of history Mediterranean seaport of Alexandria before a climb up Mose's Mt Sinai. Egypt is a never ending trip to enjoy as everywhere you go it's a pleasure to meet the true friendly hospitality of the happy Egyptian people
2) Capital; Cairo
3) Egypt achieved Independence in 1922
4) Climate; Ave temp Jan-Mar;21c
5) Language; Arabic, English
6) Currency; Egyptian Pound, 1$US = 5 E Pounds
7) Visa; Not required, 90 day Visa issued on arrival
8) Return flight £51 + £154 ATM, hotel, food, train to Gatwick
9) Today's ongoing update of day to day accommodation, travel, food, drinks costs = £1167

Day 33, Thursday, 28-01-10, Tunis; Tunisia – Cairo; Egypt

Woke up feeling good and glad I woke up as half of my ass was hanging over the edge of the single bed, it was only 0650hrs so no thought of getting up yet. Lieing in happy contentment thinking the earlier I start the longer I will have exploring the ruins of Carthage the original Roman city so up at 0730hrs. Face splash, underarm wash, kit on and down one flight of stairs to breakfast room for free half baguette, butter and jam and coffee breakie saying good morning to all and everyone. Finished breakie saying good morning to friendly Korean guy then back upto room, cleaned teeth, final pack of everything and out locking room behind me and downstairs handing key into reception telling guy I would be back 1130hrs as checkout was 1200hrs. Downstairs and out upto Habib Bourguiba turned right and a good walk past the big Clock Tower and I was in the TGM train station and showing kiosk ticket guy my large handwritten CARTHAGE HANNIBAL on my photocopy of LP, he said 800 cents so gave him 1 Dinar, got a small blue ticket and out onto the platform. Not long and train drew in with everyone including me got on and we were away, it was 0840hrs. Got a seat ok but my back was facing the front so up and stood by the large glass window door. We stopped quite often but train stations were well illustrated with large station signs so watching them and after approximately 16 stations watching the destination board above the entrance/exit train door I knew where I was. Carthage itself had 6 stations but finally seen Carthage Hannibal, train stopped and off I got. No signpost anywhere and the area was very upmarket with large villas along the road running across the railway lines up the hill one side and down to the sea the other. LP states wander upto the top of Byrsa Hill to enjoy the fine view of the sprawling Carthage so the only hill was on my right so off I went. Got halfway up the tarmac road hill and seen sign for Villa Didon but many large villas along the road then came to sign for Museum so followed it which took me up a large shrub covered hill with the most elaborate imposing huge building I have ever seen so reading LP I was now going up to the 19th Century previous neo-gothic Cathedral where next to it the large open remains of Carthage are in view with also the Museum nearby. Went up the steps and into the Museum on top of the hill paying a 9 T Dinar entrance fee. It was so wonderful just walking around and over huge walls, big 1m diameter round Columns, underground viaducts and vaults with a Basilica Church under the fully marble and big stone sometimes mosaic ground slabs with big fully lifelike statues of clothed men and women all built and constructed in 814 BC, what a truly wonderful sight. I went up one flight of stairs coming to a glass covered tomb with a full skull all bones skeleton, wow oh wow. I walked all around the large open site so happy to have made the City of Carthage as mentioned in the Bible then next stop I went into the Museum. Thought I had seen it all but the Museum was unbelievable with big 10m long by 6m wide mosaics of all types of colourful scenes and so finely made Roman statues 3m high with hundreds of, some very small, some large all types of artefacts, it was a thrilling walk. The only thing that sort of spoiled it a bit was all descriptions of any or everything was in French or Arabic but did get a sort of indication that Dido, a beautiful lady was Queen of Carthage. Had not expected such wonderful sights but had to watch my time, had a chat with a US lady doing her lonesome walk so wished her well and out. Next I went into the big in bygone years Cathedral paying entrance fee of 5 T Dinar but well worth it as its high large Domes and surrounding walls were full of paintings and mosaic colourful life scenes then out from there my great morning nearly over. Walked back down the shrub hill which I didn't have time to explore which has many 814 BC original remains and along the tarmac road back down to the railway station. Crossed the lines and on down the lower road to the Carthage sea edge and quick dip of my big right toe in the sea I was Caesar Jack de Carthage King so laughing with joy I had a slow walk back upto the train station. Paid my 700 cent fare at Kiosk, got a ticket and lucky enough caught the 1055hrs train back into Tunis TGM Station, what a great morning. Posted yesterday's notes back to Sandralita and walked past the big clock and into hotel, it was 1145hrs. Quick final pack, neckpouch on checking Passport, Air ticket and Cairo hotel details which I had booked last night, put other credit card wallet in left leg cargo pocket and out downstairs wishing reception well, handed key over and I was away. Walked down final flight of stairs to entrance door and it was pissing down but doorman went outside and flagged down a taxi for me so dumped shoulderbag in back seat, me in the front and we were away, it was 1210hrs. After a couple of holdups at traffic lights we made the Airport at 1230hrs I seen his meter showing 3.90 Dinar so gave him a 5 Dinar coin, grabbed my shoulderbag and into check-in area of Airport thinking the taxi driver who had driven me from the Airport had well conned me for 10 T Dinar, laugh and learn. Looking at check-in board I seen Cairo, check-in Desk 13 so over and I was second in the queue. A bit wary I don't know why I handed Passport and ticket over, put shoulderbag on moving escalator and 2mins later got my check-in card and Passport back, yeah man yeah, nearly there. Upto Customs giving them Passport and 2 mins later, bang, an exit Tunisia stamp and with a final x-ray I was through having a laugh with a Russian couple as I had a ham roll and a coffee in a café, 7 Dinar. Got my LP photostat copies of Cairo from my China beachbag and sort of had a read for a while in Gate Area 56, it was only 1350hrs. As usual getting fed up then at 1440hrs we were called forward to check-in, got stub and onto the plane taking my seat 10A a left hand window seat. Plane sort of filled up then at 1515hrs out we taxied on to the runway and a lovely final roar we were off into the Tunis now blue sky as I looked down I whispered, loved you Tunis which I did as it was a such a wonderful place. Sat back and 2mins later fell asleep only waking up as the food trolley done its rounds and I and everyone had a rice, meat, chocolate biscuit cake meal, just the job. Flight was 3-4hrs as we land in Cairo at 1900hrs but don't know if we lose or gain an hour on the world clock so had another read of LP. Looking out my left hand window we flew up the Med directly next to Sicily shores as I could see Kelly's Mafioso family waving at me saying we know you Jackboy and wait for you and Kelly Mafioso to visit next year. Had another snooze then checked pocket wrist watch, it was 1715hrs so either 45mins or 1 hour 45mins to go, we shall see. Next thing stewardess handed out Egyptian landing cards and I filled mine in as best I could as some of it was in Arabic. Fasten seatbelts came over the tannoy, it was 1735hrs but looking out my plane window in the darkness I could not see any lights then as I looked again 2mins later we were flying over a coast with a large town or city lights below so it might be

Cairo so its now looking good. We got lower and lower with wheels coming down and it was 1800hrs by my pocket wrist watch so we lose an hour by the World's time clock as its 1900hrs Cairo time as we done a very light landing and taxied over to Arrivals so here we go. Off the plane and bus over to the Arrivals Hall and into Customs I was behind two Swedes and nearly last in our one of 4 queues but watching the priority queue I seen it had gone down to two persons so catching the Police Officer's eye he said ok come over and join which I did and up to Passport kiosk. Bloke took a quick look and said you need Visa so I said where do I get it, he said at Bank Kiosk just back from the queue so a bit annoyed over I went to the Bank Kiosk and said to bloke Visa, he said yes, 15$US. I said do you take Tunisian money, he said no but I noticed an ATM behind the Kiosk. Quickly went over to the ATM and put card in having worked it out at 5-6 Egyptian pounds to 1$US I punched in 1000 Egyptian pounds and within 30 seconds out it came so stuck it in my tee shirt breast pocket and back to Bank Visa Kiosk. Guy said give me a 100 Egypt pound note which I did and he gave me an Egyptian small Visa and 20 Egyptian pounds change, so stuck it in my sky and back over to now nearly no queue Passport kiosks as nearly everyone had gone through. One guy waved me over, took the back tape off the Visa, stuck it on a page of my Passport and bang, entrance stamp Egypt and I was in. Seen my red shoulderbag, grabbed it and out through nothing to declare lane and into main hall. Seen taxi kiosk so went over and asked price for a taxi, one guy said 26$US, I said taxi for one, he said ok, 15$US and they were all so polite and no hassle so I said ok, paid him saying lets go. Guy gave me his card telling me he will do an all day tour for 20-30$US so I said ok maybe tomorrow as that to me was a very cheap price. Out we went to the parking area and a big taxi came in and in I got to the back seat with my bag and we were away guy telling driver New Garden Palace Hotel. It was an ok drive with sometimes 5-10min hold ups at roundabouts but the other side of the road going out of Cairo was solid and not moving for miles not forgetting it's the start of their weekend tomorrow. Driver took me to one westernised backpacker area but my hotel was not there then to another area stopping and asking if anyone knew the New Garden Palace Hotel and I was very annoyed as hotel had not sent a taxi as part of their contract and now Airport taxi driver who said he knew the hotel was now supposedly lost so I got my mobile and phoned the hotel giving my phone to the driver who had a chat in Arabic and gave me my phone back. We then went out passing big 4-5 Star Hotels then down a road with the Nile in full view then into a melee of little streets and with a sigh of relief from me he stopped outside New Garden Palace Hotel, 11 Moderiat Al Tahrir Street, Garden City, Cairo, Egypt, Tel: 0227964020, www.newgardenpalace.com and out we both got. He lifted my shoulderbag from taxi onto the pavement, I gave him a 10 Egyptian pound note and he was away and porter from hotel took my shoulderbag into hotel at reception. I gave guy my booking form asking why did you not pick me up at the airport, he said he sent someone but when I leave a taxi from hotel to the airport will be arranged for me so I said ok not believing a word. He then said I pay for one day in cash so doing his calculation and I checking it it worked out at 17$US as he said 1$US was 5 Egyptian pounds so not arguing I paid him for one day saying I pay for tomorrow as well, he said no, only one day at a time. Got key 65 and porter took my shoulderbag and up the lift we went to Room 65, a huge big, two large single beds room with 2 large chairs, wardrobes, dresser and checking bathroom it even had a real bath plus a WC western toilet so it looks really good. Dumped kit in room putting Passport and surplus money in shoulderbag and out back down to reception, it was 2130hrs. Asked guy were there any internet shops about, he said go left and left again and there is one on the main road so out into the dark but not forbidding neighbourhood and got to a two double lane highway seeing an Internet shop across the road and done my usual 15mins letting everyone know where I was, paid my 3 Egyptian pounds and out for a walk along the very busy main road with buses and cars flying past with not any sort of lights on, crazy world. Had a good walk towards I think the centre of the backpackers area then back buying some chocolate buns and a bottle of lemonade and that was me, made it across a couple of suicide roads no problem and back to hotel. Had a chat with another very helpful reception guy who offered me tours then had a read of my photocopy Cairo asking a few questions and enjoying my buns and lemonade until I looked at the clock, it was 2300hrs. The horn pumping cars slowly died off as Egypt had just beaten Algeria so I said my goodnights and upto room, stripped off and into bed and asleep dreaming an Egyptian belly dancer beauty queen will give me a massage soon to soothe my heavenly muscles.

Email Sent: Thu, 28 Jan 2010
Subject: Rm65, New Garden Palace Hotel, 11 Moderiat Al Tahrir St, Garden City, Cairo, Egypt

Hi All
Had a great Tunisian morning as took a 20min train ride, 700cents from Tunis upto the remains of the famous Bible town of Carthage with all its old Roman statues, artefacts, walls, mosaics with a real Basilica under ground, it was just so interesting and unbelievable true 814 BC history. Even an old skull and skeleton in a tomb but the sometimes 3m high real life statues where so lifelike I could have spent a day just browsing but had to make Airport by 1300hrs but enjoyed my Caesar Jack day by putting my big toe in the Carthage beach sea and away. Now planning on spending 5-8 days in same place, good Lord and the heavens above, what is the Suez canal world coming to. Will start my Cairo sightsee manyanna so any hints let me know.
Flight on time at 1505hrs and landed 1900hrs (lose 1hr on world time clock) then taxi from Hotel was not at Airport so paid 15$US in Egypt Pound which was 70 pound then Airport taxi couldn't find hotel so I phoned it with my mobile and at 2100hrs I finally got to my hotel above with d-ensuite for 17$US is not bad and I am out on de town not a clue where I am near although the Nile is only round the corner. . www.newgardenpalace.com Tel 0227964020
al de bes
Jack

Day 34, Friday, 29-01-10, Cairo - Egyptian Museum & Pyramids; Egypt

Bed was lovely and only woke up once for a piss then back for a snooze then up for good at 0745hrs. Face splash and underarm wash, kit on and upto the 9th floor for a 4 roll, 2 hard boiled eggs, butter, jam and tea breakie, very nice and filling. Back down to room, cleaned teeth and out downstairs handing a pair of long cargo in to be pressed. I knew where I was going so out, turned right and right again onto Oasr al–Ainy Road and happily sauntered along the now shops opening up main drag towards I hoped the Egyptian Museum, we shall see, it was 0915hrs. Walked past lots of armed guards at it looked like a Government building and wow oh wow I was in the Midan Tahrir roundabout area with the Sada Mosque on my left along with lovely all coloured types of buildings with the brutal tower block architecture of the Nile Hilton Hotel catching my eye. Across the roundabout in the distance there was a lovely one storey Domed red building so it looked like the Egyptian Museum, I shall see. Went leftish crossing the busy road and looking left I seen a large two enormous lions each side of a very long bridge and thought it cant be. Had a quick look at my LP photocopy Cairo map and it was, yes, the River Nile and with moist tears in my eyes I walked onto the wide Tahrir Bridge shouting, yeah man yeah and looking down and along at Felucca boats on the Nile River I was so happy and felt on top of the Egypt world. Walked halfway across then back passing well guarded Arab League Building and went left towards the big Domed Red building still feeling over the moon, it was 1000hrs with real bright sunshine and very warm. Crossed a road and onto a side road with sign stating Museum where I had my first walk through x-ray check then upto the bright Red building Museum entrance and x-ray check No2 and seen fee for entrance was 60 Pounds and mind in the Pharaoh sky I said to myself I am not paying 60 nicker to look in a Museum and turning back I remembered I was in Egypt and it was in Egyptian pounds. Laughing out loud sweat oh sweat I got out a 100 Egyptian pound note, handed it in at kiosk, got ticket and change and I was walking along with hundreds of other tourists past all the outside original Egyptian statues and upto and in the main entrance for x-ray check No3 then I was in, thank the Mummies above. I just walked the different big halls each the quarter size of a football pitch full of all kinds of artefacts with each room having its own name like Greco Roman and New Kingdom with everything having a description in Arabic and English. Came to but the place was full of them a lovely statue torso with her head and a crown of Queen Mary Tamum 1279-1213BC. Then the full statue only for her legs of the wife of Waktamum 1327-1323BC, it and everything made to perfection. Now going upstairs I paid 100 Egyptian pounds to go into the Mummies Room and counted 12 Mummies on show and details on a board how they Mummified them so will give a copy to Kelly!! so she can do a good job on me. First one was the Mummified body of King Seguenene, Taa II, 1550-1539BC and his full face, skull could be seen then King Rames II 1279-1213BC and everyone was a King or Prince and it described why they were Mummified as it was part of their folklore that would come back to live another life. Next into the Mummified animals as the Egyptians loved their animals of all species and there were Mummified crocodiles, hippotamus, birds, deer and dogs all thousands of years old. Next into the 50-60 big huge Coffins Room all brightly painted, some square, many life like designs and it was truly magical as they were all removed from excavated tombs. Next into the Archaie Period with all sorts of jars, plates and necklace stones, one exhibit that caught my eye was two different exhibits of marching soldiers, one was 4 rows of Nubian Infantry marching in line, really interesting then original sailing ship models all thousands of years old and just a joy to see. Finally came to the Tutankhamen's original tomb 1336-1327 BC from the Valley of the Kings which was a huge 4m high x 10mlong x 4m wide brightly coloured original tomb and a full description of when and how it was found, I was loving this. Everywhere there were exhibits of big solid gold necklaces and bracelets then my God in the Mummies heaven above I came to the Gold shaped Coffin of Tutankhamen's with all around it gold daggers, amulets and necklaces. It does say wonders for the people who excavated and found all these gold objects as in today's world, would we keep them!. Next big room was the show of after life beds, then a Jewellery Room and going into the next room their was small and large statues of servants at work all 2500BC then an old statue of the Alexandra the Great era I was over the moon, what a truly fantastic unbelievable place. I was tempted to do another walking tour as I only noticed the hall had numbers on them so you could follow a number sequence but was well happy so out I went into the packed seating area hot sunshine of the grassed area garden full of every Nationality in the world. Had a sit down and a slug of orange then Plan A still in operation I walked down towards the River Nile and asking prices for taxi to Old Cairo some wanted 50, some 30 then an old well dressed guy said 25 Egyptian pounds so I said ok and jumped in his car and we were away. He was happy explaining everything and telling me I should do the Pyramids of Giza and Sphinx today as Friday is a Holy no work day and no traffic on the road so asked him how much. He said 60 Egyptian pounds for there and back with him waiting 4hrs so said to myself why not and said ok, it was 1210hrs. Not that far as we went along the Alexandria Desert Road him telling me Giza was a different, better and cleaner area than Cairo as it has no tower blocks. It was a good drive without traffic and turning a corner I was over the Egypt moon as there in the distant desert sand was 3-4 huge way up in the sky Pyramids and again I was over the Pyramids moon as I had finally oh finally made it. In we drove and there in the front was the massive 50m long Sphinx constructed out of one solid stone, driver parked up telling me to wait which I did and came back with another guy who said he will give me a camel ride tour. I said my thanks but no and away I went to the entrance into the Pyramids paying 60 Egyptian pounds, got a ticket and in I went and with no dwelling or any sort of structure in front of me I was looking directly at four of the Pyramids and the Sphinx rising directly out of the blowing sand hot desert in front of me. "I got you" I shouted smiling and laughing to myself as I walked up a desert sand path upto and around the huge 50m long Sphinx which had a sort of animal woman's appeal to its shape. Carried on getting nearer and nearer until I was standing directly close in front of the right hand Pyramid another of my life's ambitions achieved. It was totally amazing seeing the sometimes 1m sq size of the actual stone all neatly in rows and all laid to fall back right up to the Spired Pyramid point, great 1000 year old architecture. Had a walk around the two nearest big 50-75m high Pyramids then into the second one just peeping into its darkish tomb base floor and really chuffed out I went again into the deep blue sunny sky with occasionally gusts of wind blowing the dusty desert sand across the pyramids but overjoyed and happy I made my way over the sand path to the entombed oldest sailing ship in the world. Met a US lady who said don't pay to go in, come up and stand on this rocky mound which I did and I could see the sailing ship through the Museum window, wow, saved 50 Egyptian pounds. Said my thanks and away going into a small Pyramid and down its small 1.5m tunnel to the large stone 200mm thick coffin, no one in it so out and camel and horse drivers giving me grief to buy a ride I made it along the dusty path going past the Sphinx and out the exit gate, it was still early, only 1520hrs me thinking I must come back for a longer sightsee. Seen my driver having a smoke with his taxi friends, he seen me and over we both went to his car, got in and we were away me putting my safety belt on as I now say to myself as I get into these suicide drivers cars its no good saying "I wish" at least it gives me a chance. He wanted to take me to old Cairo but I said no, drop me off at the Nile riverside where you picked me up and he did, gave him 60 Egyptian pounds, he said tip so gave him another 10 Egyptian pounds, said my thanks and out going over to the many river boats all anchored up. Guy said you want River Tour, 30mins or 1 hour, I said 30mins so he pointed at an empty boat but I said no pointing at the nearly packed one next to it, he said 20 so I said ok and got into the very loud Egyptian music with two girls and 1 bloke doing a bum moving dance on it, good fun as we waited for the boat to get really full. Only another 10mins everyone all laughing at the 2 girls still dancing then anchor rope off and we were away out into the middle of the many boat Nile River. Done a good 3-500m sail down the Nile River then across it and back the way we came passing really, really big boats that could never sail as could never get under the low road bridge but all used as restaurants and night clubs. It was fun seeing Cairo from the river looking at all the buildings from the river view point then everyone clapping including me the music stopped, the girls stopped dancing and in we went to anchor up. Got off wishing all my new Egyptian friends good luck and I was away seeing a Church Spire Cross in the distance behind a Muslim Mosque Minaret so tried to follow it from the road but lost it. I knew I was heading in the sort of direction of my hotel and seen a well dressed Victorian Statue in the middle of a roundabout so dicing death I made it across the mad driver road and it was a statue of Simon Bolivar, 1783-1830. I knew he was South American and couldn't figure out what or why his statue was doing here but will do a Google maybe tonight, his statue was in Simon Bolivar Square. Seen the Church again as I went up El Shokh Youssif Street and enjoyed having a walk around its very old stone facade and Police Officer on guard said go in and opened the front gate. Caretaker let me in and everything even the hymn books were in Arabic but it was a very beautiful very old Church as I had a walk around it only seeing in French two names that might be what it was called, one was St Jean, the other was St Marie la Paix but wishing the poor and needy a happy life I was out and away back towards my hotel, it was 1740hrs. Seen a fish shop and had 3 small fish and a packet of hot chips with a large bottle of lemonade, paid my 4 Egyptian pounds and away. Made it back to Hotel, upto room and had my lovely 1800hrs din din eating every last chip and feeling really great so stripped off rolling all my dirty dobhi up and had a lovely shave and shower, just the job. New socks, underpants and shirt on I felt like a new man and at 2050hrs I was out and away up Oasr al–Ainy Road across the bridge to the Midan Tahrir roundabout doing a left along seeing plenty of hotels some good, some rough and enjoyed my walk around the sort of backpackers area. Had a cup of tea and a Mars Bar really enjoying watching the crowded street walk by then knees and head gone I took 30mins to walk slowly back to Hotel and upto room having a Mars Bar and Fanta drink. Glad to be doing it so stripped off and into bed dead as a Pyramid doornail I was asleep no dreams in Cairo.

A Dream come true at the Sphinx and Giza pyramids

Date: Fri, 29 Jan 2010
Subject: Cairo and de Pyramids

Hi All

Had a dander up de street watching the suicide drivers try for 100mph in the streets then made it across a few roads seeing a bridge in the distance and up to it and Allah be praised it crossed the famous River Nile so down the boat steps and stuck my big toe into the Nile shouting I got you and I was so overjoyed. Then not far and into the Egyptian Museum and it was so unbelievable looking at statues and Mummies and Artefacts some 2500BC and Tutankhamen treasures from his Tomb including his gold mask and other gold objects but the Mummies where just amazing. Out from their and took a taxi to the desert Pyramids of Giza and the huge Sphinx and as we turned a corner their they where, I was overwhelmed, parked up, paid him and out into the blowing sand in the heat of the Egypt sun I had a 100m walk and I was up close to and into the 1000 year old Pyramids and had a great walk around the 2 closest ones. Back from their and final 30min boat cruise up and down the Nile and that was a truly great day over. My Hotel is a 10-15min walk from the back packers area but don't think I will be changing as it's a bit classy with hot water, western wc and a great breakie. My plans take me upto manyanna so will have a think tonoche.
al de bes
Jack

Day 35, Saturday, 30-01-10, Cairo - The Citadel/Islamic Cairo/St Sergius Church; Egypt

Up as alarm went off feeling a bit weak and not upto scratch but half hearted face splash, underarm wash and all new kit on, it was 0815hrs. I was going to wear yesterday's smelly kit for my Cairo walkabout but smell even put me off so fresh man on de fume filled Cairo streets today. Up the lift to Floor 9 the breakfast area and buttered 2 rolls, had 2 teas and 2 hardboiled eggs and another roll with jam with one more tea thinking after today where will I got but it looks like Alexandria by train, we shall see. Finished breakie and girl wanted 5 Egyptian pounds for extra tea, I offered 1-2-3-4 pounds but she said no and other tea girl laughing I gave them 5 x 1 pound Egyptian coins saying robbers and laughing myself I was down the lift into room. Had a teeth clean coughing up big black-green mucus from my chest but everything now clear I was ready to go, first stop old town I was thinking. Felt a stir so had a good dobhi drop, cleaned ass and out. Taxi driver sitting outside hotel said where you go pointing at his taxi so instead of my planned walk along the Nile into centre of Cairo I said to myself someone has to treat me and agreed 20 Egyptian pounds fare to Islamic Cairo where the Citadel and 3-4 famous Mosques plus Bazaar and the infamous Northern Cemetery are. In our drive he tried to as they all do talk me into a round the area package with him a guide but I like to do things my own way and said no thanks as we stopped not far from the entrance to the 1176 AD built Salah Al–Dir–Citadel. Paid him his money and in its big huge walled entrance I went paying I think a 60 Egyptian pounds entrance fee and I was in. First stop after following the road up the hill I went into the Ottoman Turkish Mosque of Mohammed Ali with its enormous 90m high in the sky Minarets. The internal area was full of bus tourists but well worth the walk in my socks around its floor looking upto its centre High Dome with below it six other Domes, marvellous designs looking at the Chandelier lights hanging down, great vibes. Then outside I went too look down over the 1m x 500mm thick stone battlements into the old alleys, Souks and crumbling dwellings of the ancient Islam area of Cairo with directly below in the middle of the old town was two close together very old Mosques, one the 1362AD built Madrassa of Sultan Hassan and the other called the Rifar Mosque where interred inside is a previous Shah of Iran. Seen signs for Military Museum and went in through its Corinthian Columns dated 856AD and just took my time strolling past old 19th Century artillery and coastal guns lots made in England and Russia. Came to the big imposing statue of the famous Egyptian General, Abraham Pasha, 1789 - 1848 who led Egypt to its many famous war victories. Passed lots of this Century tanks including 2 Sherman tanks so history wise it's a good walk and next came to rows of head statues including one of King Menes 3000BC, fantastic history, I was so happy. Into the internal Military Museum and it was really good showing colourful old uniforms and paintings and the first cannon ever made!. Passed the Justice Room which was so beautifully decorated it was just a dream to see and walkabout. Next up the big 3m wide marble steps to the first floor and into the Islamic era in Egypt, 641-1517AD Hall with more fantastic history just reading and looking at the vivid paintings especially the painting of the Battle of Alexandria,

1801 when the English - Ottoman troops defeated the French. Enjoyed my Citadel Wall views and thought about walking down to the two Mosques but entrance/exit gate was on the other side so walked back and down the hill and out to the taxi touts wanting to take me on various rides. Agreed a 60 Egyptian pound ride into the Northern Cemetery area then the Mosque of Ibn Tulan and away we went agreeing another price of 100 Egyptian pounds for him to wait then take me to Old Cairo. Got to the 879AD Ibn Tulan Mosque and he said 30mins, I said ok and in I went and it was massive and supposedly is one of the biggest Mosques in the world but had a good walk around it then out and directly right and into the Gayer–Anderson Museum given to the Egyptian Government by a British Army Major, John Gayer-Anderson. Had a very enjoyable back in time history walk seeing old rooms, furniture and artefacts as they were then plus photos of him and his own history, good fun as it went up three storeys as I peeped and walked through old bedrooms, dining rooms and internal courtyards and that was me, out and back to my taxi. Driver said we go to the City of the Dead so didn't argue and we drove into the most run down area I have ever been in with buildings falling apart and every alley, every Souk, walking space with large and small grave stones everywhere as originally built in the 14th Century with lots of Mausoleums some used for indoor singing and club areas the spare spaces around the thousands of graves people built dwellings so now the dead and the living live and sleep side by side. He stopped in the middle of it and said follow me so I did walking up the grave stone alley Souks we sort of done a round in a circle walk which was so funny I laughed out loud a few times as people were cooking beside graves in 2m wide dusty desert Souk alleys but there, real Egyptian life as it is and me still laughing back to our taxi through the dusty graves silent alley Souks we went. Got into the taxi and we were away him saying, Old Cairo and he would drop me off no wait as I can catch a metro so agreed new price of 100 Egyptian pounds and we zoomed across Cairo then came along a road with a 3m high wall with many Arches alongside it but lots had been built up but the ones I could see through had old Mausoleums and big and small Grave stones everywhere. He said Old Cairo Jews Graveyard and stopped at a narrow alley so I got out and paid him the 100 Egyptian pounds asking for 20 back but he laughed and drove off. I was only trying it on but laughing to myself I now tried to find the entrance and after a bit of a walk I seen a sign pointing down which first of all looked like an underground stone subway stating; St Sergius, Baptistery, Jewish Synagogue so went down the steps going left and first stop into St Sergius Church and into the Crypt of the Holy Family under this Church. I as other tourists did I got on my hands and knees looking further down into the lighted crypt below where the Holy Family lived for 3 years 6 months after fleeing Jerusalem from King Herod, what a truly overwhelming experience to be actually standing in the actual Christian Church where Mary and Joseph and baby Jesus had lived. Said a little prayer Thanking the Lord above for letting me do my travels and to look after my Kelly Rose when I am away and help to the poor and homeless the world over and still in a trance I was away through the lovely many coloured paintings Church and out going left just following the quiet lane and into the Church of St George. What a feeling as also in this Church everything was original and so full of true living history. I felt so lucky and so proud to have made it as I rubbed the actual chain as a notice with pictures above it states and show how this actual chain was used to torture St George the Roman and I also in this lovely history Church room lit a candle saying a prayer for good and help for the poor of the entire world and again so happy I left. All writing everywhere to describe everything was in English but all Church notices were in I think Jewish script. Next into an old Church and old Tomb which had Kasrit Elrigian Virgin Mary Church and everywhere was so old but so cared for. Next into Church of St Sergius and Bacchus with many old Saints paintings and one of St Gabriel but everywhere I walked I was so full of true happiness and joy as have never come across history like this ever in my life. Reading the notices it stated a 7 Century Church was found under this Church which itself dated back to the 11th Century and the bones of St Bashnoune were found in 1996. Next church I came to was St Barbara Church which was really old with lots of really vivid old paintings in it. Into I thought was another Church but it was the Ben Ezraa Synagogue and more unbelievable history as at the back of it was where Moses basket with his remains is, what an unbelievable feeling this gave me as even thinking I knew my history I never believed I would ever come or be as close to real history as this and stood thinking God is kind. Out from there still in a daze and still going left I went into a 300 year old Jewish Cemetery and a small Jewish Synagogue and had a small walk around the thousands of Jewish writings Mausoleums and headstones but the earliest gravestone I could see was 1837 and the latest 2005 but I am sure I did hear one guide saying there is still either 400 or 700 Jews still living around the area. Out from there and next into the very huge big Domed Jewish Synagogue, said a prayer for all my family and out. Going left again I came to the Coptic Museum and walking in its gates I walked around the huge big Fortress Towers of The Round Towers of Babylon, 300 AD, my God I said this is never going to end as I walked all around there then into the Coptic Museum for a look. It was very interesting and full of every conceivable sort of artefact from Egyptian Roman, Jewish, Turkish and all the worlds Conquerors who over the Centuries came to Conquer and live in Egypt. Had done the full circle walk just amazed and so thankful the Egyptian Government and people have without a doubt really went out of their way to keep safe all this priceless history and saying my Goodbyes to the two security guards I was out and even thought I knew there was more history places to look at I came back out onto the main road near the Metro Station as it was 1600hrs. Walked over to the Metro showing guy where I wanted to go, paid 3 Egyptian pounds for a oneway ticket and in the turnstile and up and over the bridge where he had directed me him telling me to get off at the 4th stop. Metro arrived within 10mins and on I got to the not packed but standing room only Metro and at the 4th stop me peering out of the window many Egyptian people said get off here and I did as the Egyptian people are so nice and so friendly. Walked up and out of Rabat Metro Station and yeah man yeah seen the Nile Hotel across the roundabout so nearly home. Got across the main suicide highway and just took my time walking back down to my hotel buying a tin of corned beef, 6 soft rolls and a bottle of coke for my dinner. Got into hotel, paid for one more night then upto my room and Thai sandals off I ate my lovely 5 star corned beef dinner, wow I was happy. Belly full, me happy I had a 40min nap siesta then up, face splash, cleaned teeth, a tiny dobhi drop, cleaned ass and out, it was 1845hrs. Into centre of town and had a check for information about getting into Israel and info was that I was ok to get into it from Egypt but if my Passport was stamped I could not travel in Lebanon or Syria. Had a look at a map on the computer and decided to fly to Beirut in Lebanon and bus/train backpack through Lebanon, Syria then Jordan then go into Israel passing through Palestine so that's Plan A. I had my usual walk and 2 coffees in two cafes as it was a really enjoyable and friendly place then a slow walk back along the fume spilling suicide road and back into my hotel. Got my key and up the lift into my room, it was 2240hrs. Stripped off, had a read of LP and into bed dreaming I think I know where the belly dancers are hiding out so hoping I will be belly dancing man manyanna night I was asleep a truly happy Holy man.

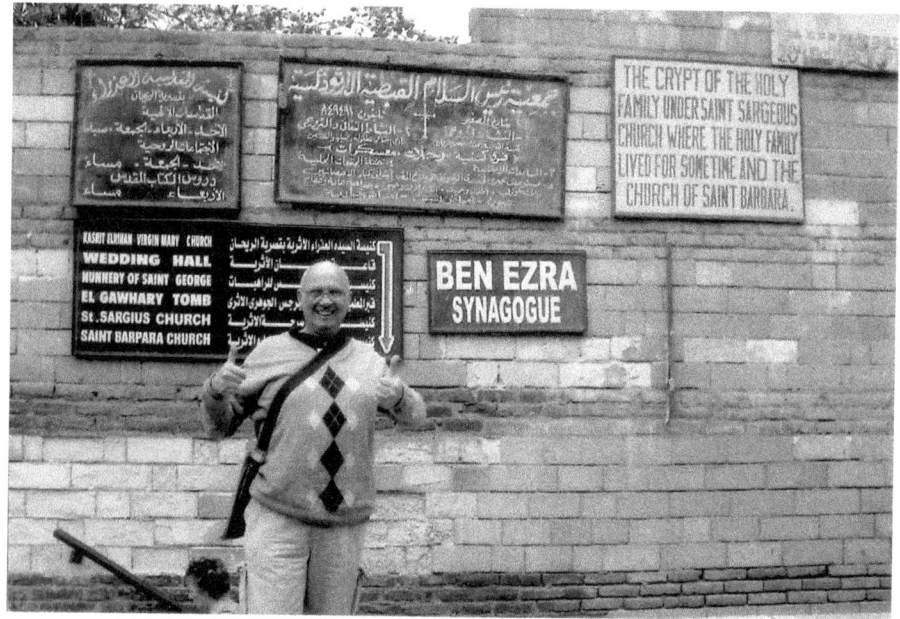

Home of Mary, Joseph and baby Jesus for three years

Date: Sat, 30 Jan 2010
Subject: St Sergius Church in Old Cairo

Hi All
Great history as in the ancient Coptic Christian cobbled alleys of Old Cairo with lots of ancient Churches I went down to the crypt below the Church of St Sergius where Mary and Joseph and baby Jesus spent 3years 6months when King Herod forced them out of Jerusalem, what a wonderful feeling and I said a prayer for all you heathens the world over Wishing You all a Happy Life.
Then a wander around the Islamic Cairo into at least 3 Mosques.
al de bes
Jack

How "Not" to Travel North Africa, Middle East, Israel & Malta and "Still Enjoy Yourself"

Day 36, Sunday, 31-01-10, Cairo - Memphis & Saqqara; Egypt

Up as alarm went off at 0800hrs feeling a bit better, face splash, underarm wash, kit on and down to ground floor, head I think is going so back upto 9th floor breakfast room with the 2 girls serving 2 Chinese guys and one European girl. Got a plate and had my usual 2 hardboiled eggs, 3 rolls, butter and jam and girls made me 2 cups of tea and I sat back eating my best breakie yet on my travels. Had another roll with jam having a laugh with the two girls especially the young 18ish sparkling eyes girl who I think was new and could not speak English, every move I made, every time I spoke my usual daft patter she laughed. Stood up and said I go and as usual the other girl said you pay 5 E Pounds for extra cup of tea so I gave her a 25 cent note saying pointing at the 25, you keep change and tried to get away but they screamed no 25, no 25 me laughing I gave them another 25 cent note and let on to go but they laughing said you no go so gave them one by one counting 5 x 1 E pound notes and after another round of laughing I finally got away. Back down the lift and into room, cleaned teeth and out knowing I was first of all going to the Post Office then Memphis and Sakkara which are former Pharaoh great Cities and Pyramids not the fancy US. Turned left and left again onto Qasr al-Ainy and happily walked on down going South and seen the Post Office on the other side of the suicide highway, waited for a gap then across and in. Guy didn't even weigh my travel notes letter just stuck 4 stamps on it and I paid him 9 E Pounds as he pointed outside saying letterbox and out I went posting my Friday and Saturday's travel notes. Stood at the side of the road and flagged down a taxi showing him Memphis and Saqqara heading on my LP photocopy and saying how much, he said meter so I said ok, got in front seat, safety belt on and we were away. We went out of Cairo beside a lovely tree lined walking footpath along the small River Nile with quite a few neat bridges across it and just followed it until it branched into the full Nile River again, great views. Turned right and over the Nile on an approx 1km long bridge with the most fantastic views of Cairo in every direction from the tall bridge, really good. We were then on a 3 lane highway going really fast passing and looking down on the dust filled sort of Cairo slum Tower blocks no room to hardly breathe between them never mind inside them. Told taxi driver again I only want to go to Memphis and Sakkara as signpost said Giza and he turned off the main highway and we followed a piled up debris each side of a small river from the main river as we then passed through two or three rundown walls falling down village with guys riding donkeys with donkeys and carts everywhere as its Tower block Cairo life one min, real life the next. Reached Memphis a nondescript rundown village but in its heyday 3100BC it was one of the most ancient and greatest cities of Egypt and was a Pharaoh times Capital but only a few remains spread over the desert remain but it is supposed to have a great Museum. Driver parked up and out I got agreeing a 30min – 1hr wait paying 35 E pound to go into the Museum but it was well worth it seeing the 20m long carving of Ramses II and 50-60 large King statues all named with the year of their reign and mostly all 1200-1400BC, the Egyptians definitely liked to sculpture. I went out into the open air Museum having my usual thumbs up photo shoot at the lovely huge sculpture of the Sphinx of Memphis, Dynasty 19, 1200BC. Had done and enjoyed my Memphis walk so out looking for my taxi driver and where was he and the car only having a tea by an Egyptian souvenir shop so didn't even have a chance to say lets go when I was invited into the large shop. I said no thanks and sat down on a seat beside a table having a chat with a French lady who now lived in Egypt owning the shop with her husband an Egyptian!!, it was called Mena Papyrus Factory. Had a tea and enjoyed my chat to everyone then just being polite I went into the factory and was shown how they make the paper which souvenir maps, symbols and all sorts of Egyptian souvenirs are printed on, really good and I bought a 100 E pound paper souvenir. Said my Goodbyes to everyone as taxi driver and French Woman disappeared around the back of the shop no doubt to get his commission then he was back and we were away, everyone including me waving at each other. We followed a road with lots of carpet making schools along it with quite a few big Tour buses parked up in front of them. Only a 2-3km drive we reached Sakkara and I paid 60 E pounds entrance fee to the driver as we parked up in a parking area as he had missed the pay kiosk. He drove back to pay it but I was allowed into the first attempt the Pharaohs made to build a Pyramid and it was a hot sunny desert day as I began my desert sand dunes walk. Just followed one path leading up to the steep Pyramid of Zoser the Pharaohs first attempt at Pyramid building in 2650BC and it still looked good even though it had a few timber scaffold structures where they were doing repairs, me laughing to myself I wondered what sort of scaffold they used in 2650BC. In my walk in different directions I passed 25-30m very deep 6-8m square holes in the ground all surrounded with large 1m x 500mm stone 1m high block walls sort of dwellings and guy said they are Tombs pointing to a 1m sq hole at its side saying that is the way down and I laughed. It was real fun as all I did was trek across the sandy hot desert in any direction I felt like as many tour groups were following a set path and funny enough met a US lady who said she was fed up following the tour guides as all she wanted was just to see what was here not stand like a prune to hear its detailed history and I sympathised with her as we parted. Got to and into the level on the surface Tomb of IDUT, Dyn V, 2362 BC and went in and it was just a miracle of large and small carvings on its 3m high stone walls all different colours, magic, I was really impressed. Out from there telling Tomb tout I have no change and into the Tomb of Unas Ankh, Prince & Son of King Unas, V Dyn, 2400 BC and just took my time looking and admiring the wall carvings, marvellous. Out going right and into the Tomb of Inerft, V Dyn, 2430 BC and really pleased after my walk in the shade of the Tombs I came out into the desert sun and Sun cap on as I needed to shield my silky hair!. Made a good long walk passing lots of ancient stone block cubicles and needed a piss so soaked the ancient sand standing in the shade of one of them thinking they have probably been christened a few times over the years. Came out as a lovely lady was coming over to them and I said they are now gents piss holes but originally they housed little sculptures in the 200mm little enclosures along the walls, she laughed and asked where I came from, I told her good ole Belfast, where do you come from, she said, good ole Texas, US, so I said let me shake your hand as I have always wanted to meet someone from Texas as we had a chat walking back to a parking area, she got in a car and away, I think she was also wanted a Texas piss. Wondering where to go now I could see lots of tourists so followed them into the very elaborate Tomb of Mereruka then the Titi Pyramid Tomb and finally the most fantastic climb down having to bend steeply over frontwards down a little 1.5m high tunnel going steeply downwards and into the beautifully carved and coloured wall carving of The Kagimni Tomb meeting and shaking hands with the lovely Donna from Texas again, small world she said. We had another chat with me telling her how I had mostly come overland from Morocco but Gadaffi wouldn't let me into Libya so laughing we parted again. This Tomb buried deep in the ground was big and the actual Tomb Marble Grave was 3m x 2m long by 300mm thick and the top lid marble had been broken off at the corner so I climbed up to look in but no luck, the Pharaoh had gone. It was good fun making my way slowly up the tunnel until with a great sigh of relief I straightened my back and out into the desert lights, wow oh wow. Had a slow walk back towards the parking area and as I was passing it I went in saying last Tomb but it was well worth it as the carved wall colourful carvings were a joy to see. Back out and now along a desert path and finally made the car park and mistook two blokes for my driver until he shouted and I looked and remembered him, it was 1550hrs. Jumped in his car and we were away and I enjoyed my taxi ride back into the fumes of Cairo again as we agreed a 220 E Pound run to the Suez Canal tomorrow pickup 0800hrs at my hotel and I paid him 200 E Pounds for today, his meter for all of today showed 150 E pounds so I think I had done well, it was 1610hrs. He dropped me off in the centre of Cairo as I wanted to clarify some Passport and Visa requirements with Lebanese Travel Agency I had noticed last night and went in. I asked the English speaking receptionist if I could fly into Lebanon with a one way ticket, she said no I have to have a return which I knew from checking the web so thanked her and into a Travel Shop and the girl done all the homework for flights Cairo – Beirut/ Beirut – Damascus/ Damascus – Amman and Amman – Cairo and totalled it up at 720$US so not in the mood to check for cheapies I said ok and got out my credit card and offered it to her. She phoned up the different flight Airlines that I was flying with but only one took MasterCard so I was a bit annoyed as thought a Travel Agency would take any credit card. The girl told me not one travel agency takes credit cards, they phone up the Airlines and the credit card details are given straight through to the Airlines so said my thanks and out. Went up around the corner to another Travel Agency not far from J Gropi the famous café in Talaat Harb Square. Asked the guy do they take credit cards, he said yes so gave the girl all the details from my earlier travel agency and she put them all into her computer and said 620 $US so I had saved 100$US. Ok, I said giving her my MasterCard and she phoned up the airlines and said sorry they all don't take MasterCard. I said pointing at the bloke he said Sunshine Tours takes credit cards, she said only through the airlines. Stuck and wasting time I was ready to go upto a bank but the banks had closed, she said go to an ATM and draw the money. I said my credit card would not allow that amount but take the Damascus – Amman/ Amman – Cairo of the total and I might be lucky. She did so and said Total is now 415 $US and she would take 1500 E pounds as a deposit and I could pay the rest tomorrow so off I went with the young fellow who took me to the nearest ATM where I keyed in my number and tried for 1500 E pounds but no luck, tried for 1000 E pounds, no luck, tried 4 other ATM's but not one would pay so called it a day and back to Sunshine Tours, 6 Talaat Harb Sq, Tel: (202) 25757060, sunshine@hotmail.com saying to the very helpful girl I will come back tomorrow. She said no problem and told me flights are now confirmed and printed out my flight details on a A4 sheet and gave them to me so I informed her I had booked a trip to the Suez Canal for early tomorrow but would make it to Sunshine Tour Offices tomorrow PM and we both parted shaking hands. Off I went and into the famous J Gropi bakery large café and had 2 large sweet scones and a pot of tea thinking this will skim the bank book but enjoyed my 1815hrs snack until 1845hrs and out, it was half time in the African Football final between Egypt and Uganda and still nil each. I knew I didn't want to go back this late to my hotel as wanted to be around Central Cairo for the final result and in my walk I heard 2-3 loud cheers then an explosive loud cheer so I knew that was an Egyptian goal and checking my pocket watch it was 1940hrs and approximately 5-10min later the Cairo sky erupted with the loudest cheer I have ever heard and that was it, Egypt had won. I was waiting for the fun to start and it didn't take long as hundred upon thousands of mostly young people cheering and carrying flags were making their way into the centre of Cairo and all traffic was being brought to a standstill as they paraded in hundreds on the main central roads of Talaat Square, it was real big time fun but God help anyone trying to get home. I hung about enjoying the singing, dancing and happy vibes then into Hardees for a chicken burger, fries and a Coke, 19 E pounds and sat watching the still thousands of people now blocking every central road in the centre of Cairo with Police hiding away from it all it seemed to me. Out of Hardees with belly full and walked back towards my hotel along the packed full of nose to tail traffic of Oasr al–Ainy Road 4 lane highways road and traffic could barely crawl as the whole of Cairo was it seemed trying to come into the centre to celebrate, it was 2220hrs. Got into hotel, paid for my room and sorry I had come back this early as at 2330hrs the noise from Central Cairo was getting louder and louder with every car in Cairo pumping its horn so no sleep tonight but I will try. Finished my read of LP, tried to phone MasterCard but their office in UK was closed so stripped off and into bed wishing I had some ear plugs and don't know how but sort of fell asleep thinking I was so lucky to be here and see it all for Egypt's big football day.

Date: Sun, 31 Jan 2010
Subject: Memphis & Saqqara; Egypt

Hi All
Had a great day in Memphis and Saqqara in the desert seeing the first attempt when they built the first Pyramid 2400BC. Just me being a Clerk of Works but some of the levels were not to good and pointing was poor so I want it demolished and rebuilt correctly!!!!.
Heading for a look at de Suez Canal manyanna.

al de bes
Jack

Day 37, Monday, 01-02-10, Cairo – Suez; Egypt

Was woken up at 0600hrs as the workers laying a new pavement along each side of the Street outside my Hotel were hammering but fell into a snooze until alarm went off at 0700hrs and up I got feeling good. Underarm wash, face splash and up to breakie room as girl had just opened, said my Good Mornings and had 3 bread rolls, hard boiled egg, butter, jam and 2 cups of tea and enjoyed it all, left her a 5EP tip and back to room. Cleaned teeth and a nice dobhi drop which I was glad to do as will be in a car for a 2-3hrs for two journeys later. Little pack of China beachbag and out downstairs to waiting taxi driver from yesterday, it was 0800hrs. We said our Good Mornings and into taxi, he said Suez, I said yes and we were away. Bit slow getting out of Cairo as we took the tunnel under the Nile at the Azhar Bridge this time and coming out of it I counted 8 Mosque Minarets around the skyline. Passed along a road with hundreds and thousands of Police along it as I think the President of Egypt was about then just about to nod off when I seen a sign, Suez 119km, it was 0830hrs. I nodded off as we got in the hundreds of pylons with attached cables taking up the desert horizon sky then woke up to see signpost, Suez 62km, it was 0915hrs. Each side of our two lanes either way highway was now pure desert sand with sometimes sandy hills and sand dunes but cables still followed our road. Now close to a big huge mountain range on my right with a railway on my left and stopped at a toll gate, signpost Suez 22km, it was 0940hrs. The bleak but startling beautiful mountain range got closer then as we drove into the far outskirts of Suez with sign showing 10km they disappeared as we where now in the hundreds of 6 storey tower blocks Suez suburbs, it was 1000hrs. We drove into the Port area of Suez and parked up at the furthest Public point near the Suez Stadium and out we both got. I had a walk along the sometimes sandy beach waterfront dock area with one side having a few big passenger ships anchored up, the other side was a sort of yacht marina but I passed Moon Beach Resort and all along the promenade area was a rundown touristy stall area. Back again to the taxi and we drove around the complete area with me seeing signs Suez Shipyard then back to the big stone Monument covered in graffiti where driver stopped and I got out. Had a little walk up along the wide sea canal and took a marble seat sit down beside two old Policemen who both spoke excellent English and we had a laughing chat. Said my Goodbyes and back to the Monument having a bottle of lemonade and a packet of chocolate biscuits having a chat with two other Police Officers and they told me the first ship passing through today is at 1400-1500hrs so well snookered as it was only 1210hrs. Had a photo shoot with all the huge tankers anchored off the port and that was me back to taxi and a told him Town of Suez and we were away. Drove through the nothing touristy town of Suez and out onto the main road and we were away. As usual I didn't last long and fell asleep which I like as it halves the journey time. Woke up with signpost 60km to Cairo and it was fabulous looking on my right seeing the different colours of the desert in the far horizon with sometimes black, sometimes gray and right on the horizon sky a white line of desert cliff dunes. Ass is fed up and cant wait to get off and just wondering how much he will try for. I know I agreed a 200EP for both going and return journeys which even to me seems well under par but we shall see, it was 1325hrs. I soon fell asleep again and next thing as I woke up we were in the 10-12 storey inner suburbs of Cairo but as usual traffic was horrendous and we were crawling along. Got further in and I started recognising places and in we came to Talaat Roundabout and I said stop at J Gropi Café which he did and I said wait one moment as I hoped to draw some money from my other credit card. Over to ATM, keyed in my pin asking for 2000EP and sweating like a camel's asshole, click, out it came, wow oh wow, so over and gave him 200EP. He pointed at meter which I knew said 400 but no way had it done 400km. I said you said and we agreed 200 EP for all of today's trip, he said that he said it was 200 there and 200 back so letting on to be annoyed I said ok and gave him another 100 EP then smiling and saying my thanks as he was a good lad, we shook hands and he was back in his taxi and away, con 1 accomplished I said to myself thinking I got off light. I then put my MasterCard in again but no luck so phoned up England saying I am running out of money, why wont your card work and girl was very helpful asking me all the usual security questions and me having to keep asking her to repeat herself in the inner street Cairo noise then she said your card will now work. I said my thanks and over to the same ATM, 1000EP, click, Allah is good as out it came and with a great sigh of relief I stuck all my money and cards in my cargo pockets and up the road to Sunshine Tours shop. The girl from yesterday welcomed me and said is your card now working, I said yes, I have the cash and she done her calculations again with the copy of my planned journey to 2No Middle East Countries and showed me the cost of 2500 EP. I said ok, counted out the money and as she got a guy to check it said smiling sit down and have a coffee while she does the ticket which I did. Two mins later guy brought me a coffee and I sat back greatly relaxed and about 10mins later she stood up smiling saying here is your ticket Mr Glass and showed me a printout of the 2 Airline times and destinations I would be going on then gave me a detailed talk about getting to the Airport 2hrs before each flight and a final shake of her hand and I was away. Yeah mon yeah, I was really chuffed and smiling as I dodged the suicide drivers crossing the road as I got to El Rabat Square. Seen Hardees the restaurant takeaway so in and had a beef burger, fries and a coke, 18 EP and full of laughing joy enjoyed my meal as nothing left for me in Cairo so only tomorrow when I will have to find somewhere to visit. Finished my meal and out along Qasr al-Ainy Road and some sort of demonstration was going on and road was chock a block with poor souls stuck in the no moving traffic. I made it back to hotel after photocopying my travel itinerary and it was only 1720hrs. Had a read of LP then a nice hot water wash and shave and out walking my 10min dander back into town. Tried a few other streets just slowly walking and some of the buildings were such brilliant fantastic architecture it was a joy to see even in the dark. Had a nice scone and a tea in J Gropi great atmosphere old time large café and that was me a one very happy Gippo man. I went back towards the nightclub area with plenty of money in my sky and yeah man yeah I could see there in the dark of the night and said olla to a big smiling girl with Gippo belly dancer ass cheeks as I could feel it in my bones as we caught each others eyes it was true Gippo love to last longer than when the first Pyramid was built. She and me smiling into each others love struck eyes she deliberately blocked my path and smiling with tongue out coming up close saying "you want good time sexyboy" and thinking of Cleopatra naked I felt at home at last in Egypt and said "I go with you babe". She cuddling up and rubbing her hands over my stiff rocker and looking me in the face with her love struck eyes said, "500 E Pounds and holding her close knowing she would be with me until the dawn of the next Pharaoh King I said OK, where we go my Cleopatra Queen. Laughing she pointed up a Souk saying my place and arm in arm off we went the vibes of true Gippo Cleopatra belly dance love vibrating through all of my body as she caressed my lower bits we walked up the Souk and into an open corridor. Up one flight of stairs and she opened her door and in we went to a small flat and into her bedroom me quickly getting out a 2x200 & 1x100 E Pounds notes and putting them on a cabinet we where kissing and groping each others love aroused sexy heavenly bodies. We both quickly stripped off naked and kissing and French kissing we where on her lovely soft big double bed she was eating me like no tomorrow as I fondled her belly dancer curved body then me on top we lustfully pounded into each others sex crazed bodies she was screaming with delight as I was grunting in pure pleasure the scented smell of our love penetrating deep into my lungs she ripped my sore back with her nails as then in one final surge of panting exotic sexual depraved Cairo lust love we climaxed together I screamed in lust biting her neck to pieces as she ripped my buttocks apart holding one in each hand her nails going in deep below my skin we surged and surged into each others uninhibited pure lust bodies I was lost in the spasms of my Cleopatra Queens sex fuelled body as after what seemed a lifetime of love pure sex spasms we slowly but slowly came to a rest tightly embracing each other's true love bodies I just knew we would never be without each other ever again she run her hand up between my thighs and squeezing my footballs I yelled in pain and let on to bite her breasts she smiled saying "You are a sexyman Papa but we go" and giving each other a quick peck we both slid of her sweat soaked nice scent bed and got dressed. She collected her money and holding my hand she led me out down the stairs to the Souk and with a final hug and kiss we waved each other bye bye and I was away up the Souk and out past the lots of beautiful girls of the night and laughing and giggling to myself I walked back along Qasr al-Ainy Road and into my hotel feeling over the Cairo moon. Got my key, upto room and smiling to myself and stripping off I was into bed and asleep dreaming of more sex in the Cleopatra grip as what a wonderful end to my Cairo night.

Day 38, Tuesday, 02-02-10, Cairo – Imbaba – Pyramids; Egypt

One of the best nights sleep so far and didn't even want to get up and had a sleepy think about where to go today but well stuck as seen and done everything in Cairo that tourists do and no way was I doing any more long ass hilly car/taxi journeys. Had big time really enjoyed the Giza Pyramids and Sphinx thinking I didn't do enough the last time so it will be a good half day no rush to go back as they are not far and have a closer no rush walk about so everything planned for today. Up, face splash, underarm wash, kit on and upto Floor 9 breakie room for breakie saying my smiling good morning to the two sexy girls especially the lovely smiling 'eye' one and had 2 teas, 3 rolls, butter, jam and 1 hard boiled egg breakie, really nice having a laugh and trying it on with the dark eyed girl who did not speak English. Finished all and gave her a 25 cent note and run out the door her chasing me saying 10 EP for extra tea and I smiling gave it to her thinking 2$US wont kill me but it keeps these poor people going for a day, I blew her a kiss and back in the lift and upto room. I had time now with no rush so wrote a letter to Benbordi in El Oued in Algeria the most kindly person I have ever met saying my thanks for his great help in lending me the 1800 Algeria Dinars so I could keep moving and put 300 EP and 10 Tunisian Dinar in it, sealed it and just hoping it makes it through the Algerian post. Put my Pyramid photos and some travel notes in another envelope, sealed it and it was ready for posting to Sandralita. Cleaned teeth feeling a stir so had a neat dobhi drop, cleaned ass and nearly ready to go stuck my Middle East LP in my China beachbag as want to photo copy a few pages of Beirut then changed my mind as I can do it tonight and left it on my bed. Out I went and up Qasr al-Ainy Road fully packed with cars and buses and me thinking this Cairo Road access is crazy as you can walk 50-100m and see empty roads! but their was lots of Government Buildings everywhere!!. Got upto the still shouting demonstration people area all surrounded with Police and turned left down passing more very imposing white Government buildings and into the Post Office, gave them my two letters, they weighed the Sandralita one then stuck stamps on the both, total cost 7 EP, approximately 1 $US, defies belief. Outside and posted them in postal box then tried at least 10 taxis to catch a taxi to Burqash Camel Market as changed my mind about going to the Giza Pyramids. All taxis looked at my LP photocopy but said they did not understand then into El Rabat Square and showed it to 6 No Travel Agency Shops but they did not understand then one said the Camel Market is only on Fridays and it is in Imbaba. I said LP states Imbaba is not the camel market no more but no one knew Burqash so gave up and out to the main street, flagged a taxi down telling him Imbaba, jumped in and we were away. Got into the smelly full of debris streets of Imbaba with an on fire refuse dump in a square surrounded by small and large tower blocks and everywhere around the Railway Station there was flocks of sheep and herds of big goats, unbelievable. Guy drove around and then stopped at a line of Minibuses and out I got, paid him our agreed 30 EP and he was away. Tried to talk and show Minibus drivers Burqash but breathing in the lovely smell of the refuse dump fire and blood dripping of the fire ash cow meat carcasses hanging out along the main street I called it a day as going nowhere fast. Stopped a taxi and agreed a 70EP fare to the Giza Pyramids, jumped in and away and my God oh God I was in the front with no safety belt and we were going 500mph swerving in and around traffic like a lunatic racing driver then he nudged me saying Pyramids and oh my Lord there they were in full view from the motorway. Coming off the motorway onto a side road we drove up the hill to the entrance to the Pyramids parking area and two touts jumped in the back of the taxi saying you need a guide, you need horse, you need a camel as you are not allowed in so I said winking at the taxi driver, thank you very much, got out, gave him the 70 EP and walked away upto the pay kiosk entrance. Paid 60 EP for entrance ticket to walk around all the three Pyramids and 35 EP to inside Pyramid 2 and up on the sandy paths as more touts said show ticket, I said piss off and walked on upto the first middle unbelievable size Pyramid as there are lots of tourist Police about but these touts I suppose pay them buckshee so they can con tourists for horse/cart and camel rides. Great feeling as the chanters below in Cairo started their loudspeaker chants and their Allah holy prayers were vibrating all over the Pyramids desert, wow this is real life, it was 1210hrs. I really, really enjoyed being near these unbelievable sized Pyramids plus the whole area was an exploring walking zone of small Pyramids and Tombs and small desert dwellings carved out of stone where the labourers who built the Pyramids used to live. Made the full circle around the biggest Pyramid called the Chephrene and could never imagine how they built it and it was so perfect in its shape. I had bought a 35EP ticket for access into Pyramid No2 called the Cheops Pyramid, these two plus the other one close by were just enormous and I believe connected as Father, Son and Grandson Tombs. Got to and had a walk around the Cheops Pyramid and over I went to a 1.5m high little access door with a security guard me thinking the access would go up but no, it disappeared steeply into the ground. Showed my entrance ticket to the guard who ripped off an end section gave me back my ticket saying no camera so I got out my camera, took the flash card out and gave it to him as don't trust anyone so at least I can buy a new camera and still have my photos. In I went to the dark abyss 1.5m sq walkway if that's what they called it but at least the Egyptians had put a flat timber base with 20mm steel uprights steps every 200mm so bending right over, my back scraping the stone ceiling I stumbled down the lighted chamber swearing, cursing, panting and praying to the good Lord I made it all the 30 metres right down to the bottom passing other access holes each side but grilled off. Got to the bottom walked across a flat 5m square hole and then up the same gradient of another 1.5m" 30m long chamber and really panting I was directly in the middle of the Pyramid looking at the big stone empty coffin of a Pharaoh King. It was a very magic feeling as on my own and not a noise from anywhere so had a piss at the left hand side of the coffin, zip up and away down the way I had come up. I had started going down when 2 girls and 2 blokes started coming up and as we met in the middle I said breathe in and we squeezed by each other all laughing at our daft antics. Got down then up the timber path and out getting my camera back and away walking across the desert sand in the direction of the next Pyramid in which there were supposedly 8 in total the touts had said trying to sell me camel rides but I could only see 4 large ones plus a few smallish ones. Got sort of close to it in the stifling desert heat then turned back and into the Cheops Boat Museum paying a 50EP entrance fee. It was well worth it as although I had seen it from the outside it was well worth seeing it close up. It had the original large boat which carried the coffin up the Nile and was buried usually in a Pyramid at the same time and the 50m long by 6m deep, 3m wide big stone block original area was open to look into and see. The Museum had great photos and descriptions of when it was found in and how it was excavated as the original large timber boat, the oldest in the world was still inside it and was now in full view over three levels of walkways to see and get up close to, fantastic great 5000 year old history as I walked around the three levels just admiring the great strength of this big timber boat. Many Egyptian people as they see me all catch my eye and I always greet them Good morning, Good afternoon Mum/Dad/Grandpa, Babe, Boy and always get a smile in return as everyone in the Boat Museum wanted to talk to me and shake my hand. Another great sightsee over I was out just strolling the desert sand through the labourers dwellings as not one tourist was doing but I found it really exciting seeing and being up close to ancient dwellings carved straight out of the rocky mountain face as I made it downhill to the big walled off Cemetery. Went left being passed by camels and horses then another photo shoot at the Sphinx and after another great fantastic Pyramids day I made it into the old sort of slum village outside the gates. The old village was fun as I just strolled past all its very old souvenir shops then into an old café for a scone and a tea, just the job to quench my thirst. Paid my 6 EP charge and out again into the blinding glare of the hot sun and taxi driver said where you go, I said downtown, he said 50 EP so didn't argue just jumped in and we were away. Good run, no drama and he dropped me off at El Rabat Square so paid him the 50 EP getting buckshee, buckshee, I said I have no other money and closed his door and I was away. Walked slowly back going into areas away from the main road passing the still shouting demonstrators, bought one tin of sardines and one tin of corned beef, 4 bread rolls and a bottle of Coke and into hotel, got my key and upto room, it was 1710hrs. Opened my luxury 5 star meal tins and devoured the lot, wow, I do know how to treat myself. Had a lovely shave and shower, changed all clothing except long cargo and out for my last dander, first of all away from the downtown centre into a very busy local area with lots of cafes and not one sign in English as I love to get off the beaten track. Made my way back into centre of downtown Cairo and really chuffed about today I had 2 teas in J Gropi Cafe sitting enjoying good ole Cairo vibes then that was my night over. Had a short stroll back along the usual fully packed pavements and not much traffic roads and I was in my hotel. Told guy I was leaving tomorrow and don't forget they had promised me a free taxi as they had not sent one upto the Airport for my arrival and he said no problem, ha ha, I laughed, we shall see and upto my room I went. Checked everything, final pack and had a read of Beirut LP and happy enough I stripped off and into my lovely bed and asleep dreaming and hoping Lebanese chicos in Beirut are night lifers to look after my nightly instincts.

Coming out of the Cheops Pyrimid

Email Sent: Tue, 2 Feb 2010
Subject: Imbaba today

Hi All
Last day in Cairo and tried for the Camel Market about 35klms outside it and reached Imbaba ok which was a smelly sewer hole as they even burned food debris in the Sq beside the railway station so chest cleared of any fungi I tried but Minibus drivers didn't understand English so called it a day and back upto the unbelievable Pyramids just walking about any and everywhere, the whole area has wonderful vibes.
Manyanna taking a plane one way to Beirut and make my way back to Egypt via Shalom as if I go into Shalom first the other Middle East countries won't allow me into their countries, crazy but that's life.
al de bes
Jack

Map of Lebanon

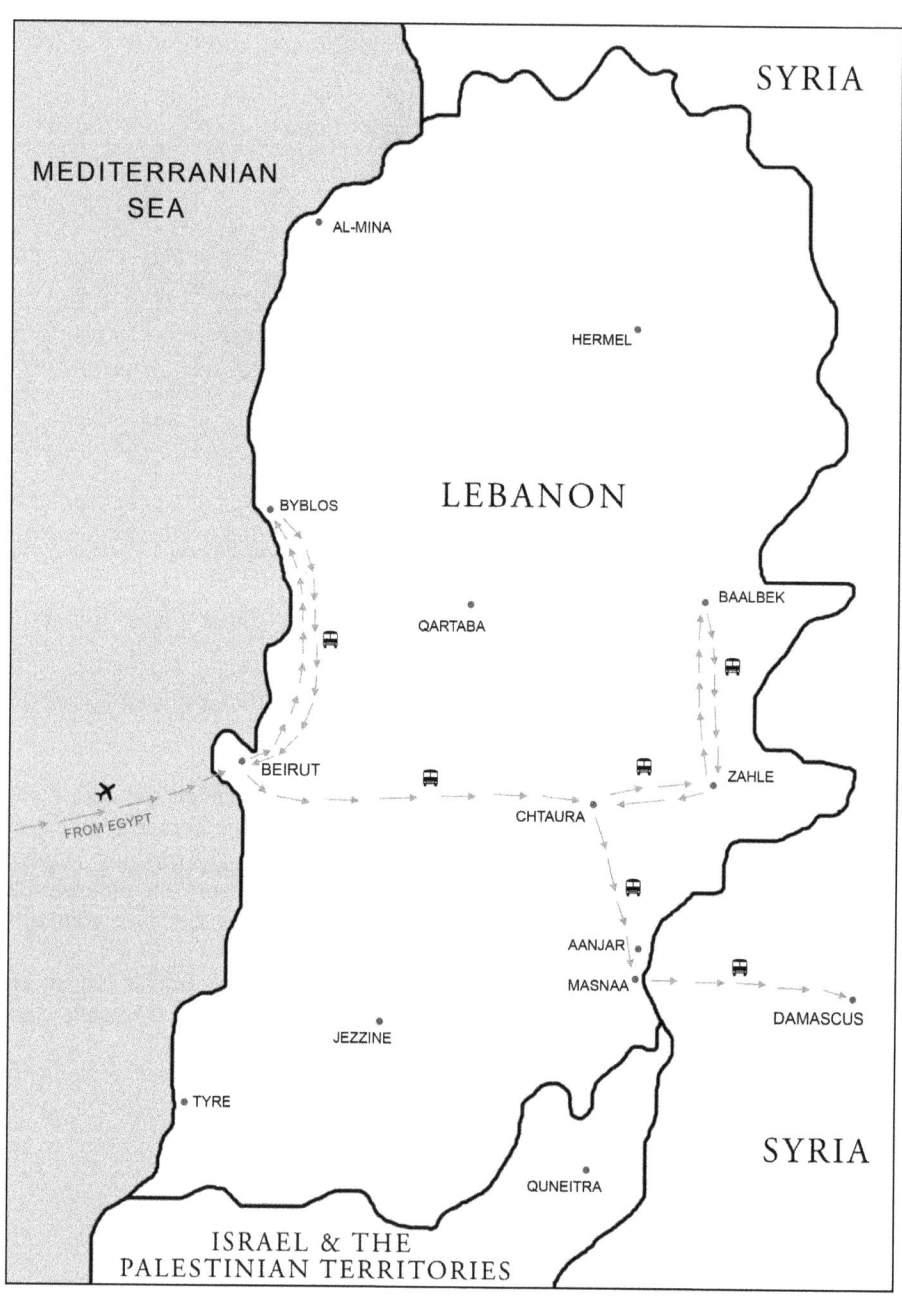

1) LEBANON the "Land of Milk and Honey" goes back 3000BC when it was first settled by the Phoenicians is one of the most fertile and green countries in the Middle East with each part of its countryside having its own local Culture and flavour where you can take fantastic trips by bus to visit very well preserved ancient Roman, Crusader Castles and Ottoman ruins. Beirut its Capital once known as the "Paris of the East" is a vibrant City combining budget lively Hotel market areas with upmarket rich Arab Villas sometimes seeing old shell blitzed Hotels but every turn you will be welcomed by the ever so proud of their country Happy Lebanese people.

2) Capital; Beirut
3) Lebanon achieved Independence in 1943
4) Climate; Ave temp Jan-Mar;19c
5) Language; Arabic, French, English
6) Currency; Lebanese Pound(Lira), 1$US =1500 L Pound
7) Visa; Not required, 30 day issued on arrival
8) Return flight £51 + £154 ATM, hotel, food, train to Gatwick
9) Today's ongoing update of day to day accommodation, travel, food, drinks costs=£1505

Day 39, Wednesday, 03-02-10, Cairo; Egypt – Beirut; Lebanon

Great nights sleep and woke up as the horn pumpers were starting at 0715hrs then had a little well pleased with my plans doze and up at 0735hrs. Alarm off and put it into shoulderbag then face splash and underarm wash, dried off, kit on and final little pack of shoulderbag and out down for breakie. My dark eyed always smiling little beauty queen was not working today so felt sad but enjoyed my 3 rolls, 1 hard boiled egg, butter, jam and 3 tea breakie thinking all plans are working just hope I get into Lebanon ok. I gave the other lovely breakfast lady money for tea and 20EP tip saying for you and Ditty and shaking hands I was away down the lift and into room. Cleaned teeth and a lovely belly stir so had a good milky dobhi drop, cleaned ass and ready to go, it was 0855hrs. Checked Passport, neckpouch on and wallet in left hand cargo pocket and out down the lift, handed key over and shaking hands with everyone I asked for my free taxi to Airport. The bloke at desk said he didn't know anything about it, I said it had been promised the day I arrived and twice yesterday, he just shrugged his shoulders as if he had heard it many times before so I said good con and pulled my trolley shoulderbag down to hotel entrance door thinking its not the money that is the problem, it just a deceiving con. Doorboy flagged down a taxi and in I got, door boy saying to me only pay 60 EP at Airport and we were away, it was 0910hrs. Allah is good as we even drove up Qusr al-Ainy Rd without a traffic jam and were soon going into I think central Cairo passing over a large cantilever bridge with fantastic views of Cairo and I counted at least 6 Christian Churches some with really outstanding architecture then we had 2-3 minor 5min traffic jam holdups but following the Airport sign road we were making good time at a good speed. Seen the Airport and I got a 100EP note ready for him as he dropped me off at T1, out I got with shoulderbag and beachbag, gave him the 100 EP note, got 20 EP note back, he said thanks so smiling I said thanks and into Departures, it was 1010hrs. I checked the Departure Board and seen MEA Middle East Airlines at Gate 4 so found customs, showed Passport and Airline ticket, put shoulderbag and beachbag through x-ray, guy done search of my shoulderbag but when he came to my smelly sock and underpants he closed bag and said ok and I was in. Went upto Gate 4, showed Airline ticket and Passport, put bag on moving escalator and got aisle seat 28, shoulderbag was away and as I was upto Passport control, showed Passport and check-in Airline card, bang, exit Egypt stamp on Passport and I was in, it was 1055hrs, yeah man yeah I am nearly there. Had a walk around the many upper floor cafes and downstairs shops and save my life from Allah above I seen a Thomas Cook Money Changer so over and said you change E. Pounds to US$, he said yes so counted out 1500 EP that I had left over, gave it to him and he gave me back 273$US so happy enough now as reading LP it stated Lebanon money is the Lebanon pound but everywhere takes $US so I was happy as have enough US$ for my first few Beirut days. Time was marching on so upto Gate 3, put China beachbag and me through x-ray, showed Passport and ticket and I was in Gate 3 departure lounge, wow oh wow it's really looking good. Had a seat for only 10mins then bus drew up and out of our now crowded with people Gate 3 lounge and onto the bus and when it was full we drove out to the plane, off the bus, onto the plane and I took seat 28H an aisle seat beside a very friendly Korean guy. He was good fun as we had a chat then safety demonstration film and next thing taxied out to runway and with a muted roar off we sped into the hot Cairo sky. Seeing Cairo from above was certainly a wonderful sight and I whispered "Thank you, I love you Cairo" and sat back enjoying my conversation in English with my Korean friend. We had a nice 2 roll and biscuits, coffee, orange juice snack as I had a look at the TV screen in front of me about information for Beirut and Lebanon then tannoy on we were starting our descent, it was 1235hrs local and Lebanon time. Great to see Beirut and Lebanon as we circled the by the sea Beirut Airfield then in we went for a nice soft landing so New day, New town, New country here I come, it was I think 1250hrs. Off the plane, through Passport control and bang another new stamp, my ole Passport must be pissed off with all the banging it gets. Lost the Korean guy but kept going up to arrivals baggage, seen my bright red shoulderbag with its blue ribbon straps, grabbed it, met the Korean guy and we shook hands as out I went through the 'Nothing to declare' zone and out into the main hall. Seen a tourist office so over collecting a few Lebanon and Beirut leaflets and asked the girl how much for taxi, she said 25$US. I was a bit shocked and said that's expensive is there a bus service, she said where do I go, I said Hamra, she said there is a bus into the Beirut Bus Station but not to Hamra so called it a day and out towards the taxi's. One big fat guy said, taxi, I said yes, he said this way and I said to myself here we go and he took me towards 4-6 taxi drivers who all came towards me. I asked him for price, he said 40$US, I said no good, too expensive and he started shouting in a threatening manner as did some of the taxi drivers so I started shouting back calling him and them a shower of Bastinos and if they want trouble I will give it to them and walked back to the Tourist Office. A Police Officer and manager of the Tourist Office had come out as the shouting was going on and they said we will get you a taxi for 25$US so I followed them past the scumbag now silent taxi drivers and Police Officer said to a taxi driver 25$US to Hamra, he said ok and in I got and we were away. Good 30mins run with taxi driver saying 40$US, I said, no, 25$US and as we got to the Embassy Hotel, Makossi St, Beirut, Lebanon, Tel 01-340814, he dropped me and my shoulderbag off, it was 1350hrs. I gave him 30$US saying 5$US you owe me and as he was going to give it to me I smiled saying ok and into hotel. I gave the girl a copy of my booking through www.booking.com and she said ok, looked it up in her computer and said 100$US for 2 nights, I said yes, ok and she gave me Room 201 saying any problem getting here, I said only the threatening Airport taxi drivers, she shrugged. She showed me where the lift was, so shoulderbag and me in lift, up we went to the 2nd floor and out and into a lovely big 2 bed single ensuite room with a balcony, it was 1405hrs. Dumped kit including Passport in shoulderbag and put LP photocopy of Beirut in left hand cargo pocket and out I went, it was 1415hrs. Walked one block away onto Hamra St and turned right going downhill hoping to see some cheapie hotels but no luck and kept going seeing the breakers from the Mediterranean Sea on the seashore coastline only a few hundred metres away. Got down to General De Gaulle Ave and only a short walk was facing the tall Manava Lighthouse with a little boat harbour one side and a beach club the other but no sandy beach, everywhere was either rocks or man made beach clubs with their own swimming pools as with the size of big waves coming in from the Med Sea no one stood a chance of swimming. Walked left uphill in no rush but a bit sad as no sun and came to the Rawsheh Rock which is where 2 large rocks towering above the sea in a small bay and I am sure on a good day the nutters would be diving or jumping of them. Kept going downhill and save my soul and the heavens above it started raining so quickly on down the hill and into a good ole Burger King Restaurant. It lashed down as I ordered a chicken burger, fries and a coke, 7500 LPs, got my meal and over to the red soft seats by the window and watched the brief heavy deluge of rain then the sun came out as I finished my lovely last chip, one last slug of coke and I was out back down to and along the beach road. I thought I had seen it before making a run to Burger King and yes I was right as down in the round bay below was a beautiful 2-300m long by 50m wide stretch of lovely sand called Ramlet Al Bayda Beach and I bet to myself that there is not much room left on that beach on a sunny day as all and everywhere behind beach road was lots of massive multi storey some very new Tower blocks with lots more being built. Thinking that's enough for the day as my watch was still in Egypt time me thinking it should go forward 1 hour but it was time to go back to hotel. I ran across the General De Gaulle Ave two lane each way highway and just sort of went left to hopefully see somewhere I could recognise but finally gave up facing the very posh I think La Bristol Hotel Restaurant with its top hat, dickey bow tie doormen and asked a barber just across the road and showing him my LP map. He said pointing downhill, go that way and it will take you to Hamra St so off I went walking through a very busy packed with restaurants and shops area and first stop was at Hamra St. I knew my hotel in Makossi Street was the next one down so walked down to it and stood looking each way hoping I might see it and God is kind as there it was approximately 100m on my left the big sign of the Embassy Hotel. It was now very dark so just walked down Makossi St and into hotel, told new bloke receptionist my name, got my Room 201 key and up the two flights of stairs to my room feeling good after not a bad first afternoon day in Beirut, it was 1815hrs. Had a good dobhi drop, cleaned ass, cleaned teeth and no shave, had a read of LP seeing in Centreville of Beirut there is loads of bars and nightclubs as in bygone years before the troubles it was known as the Paris of the East. Time was now 1900hrs so out downstairs, left key at reception and out of hotel and went left at Hamra St hopefully into the good vibes of Beirut Centre, we shall see. Walked a good distance and got to the Bank of Lebanon Road then Mchau St going past an Army camp along Street of the Army and doing a turn I was in a pedestrian only area with dozens of well lit restaurants and cafes all full of young people out enjoying their Beirut night time vibes. Had a coffee in an internet café, 6$US and done my usual 15-20mins internet, 2000LP. I was happy now as I knew where the main Roman ruins and Old Quarter are as I slowly had a dander back towards and into my hotel as two girls with rucksacks came in looking for a room. Reception guy showed them a room but they didn't like it or the price so I followed them out showing them the Mace Hotel around the corner and wishing them good luck as we Travellers have to try and help each other I was back in hotel, got my key and upto room. Stripped off and into bed wishing I should have offered the 2 lovely girls the spare bed in my room and dreaming threesomes all night I was asleep in Beirut a lonely man.

The Thumbs up Poser at Rawsheh Rock, Beirut

Date: Wed, 3 Feb 2010
Subject: Embassy Hotel, Makossi St, Beirut, Lebanon, Tel 01-340814, Rm 201

Hi All
Made Beirut the Paris of the East as its known, 1300hrs and got above, 50$US a night as Beirut is expensive for us cheapie Charlie's.
Had a walkie down the lovely beach area then Rawsheh Rocks then the Lighthouse and suddenly it got dark.
Good nightlife area in centre of town but machine gun soldiers everywhere, don't know how they knew I was coming!!!.
Even passed through a hooker area but as a good Christian Arthur St boy I kept moving!!!!.
Lots to see and visit so will enjoy my next few Beirut days then maybe head towards de Syria border. !!!
al de bes
Jack

Day 40, Thursday, 04-02-10, Beirut; Lebanon

Up at 0800hrs as alarm went off as had enjoyed my nights sleep, face splash, underarm wash, kit on and downstairs asking girl was breakfast included in price. She said no, breakfast is 8$US. I said that's expensive, I will go to an outside café, she said go left then right onto Hamra St and there is plenty of cafes so out I went. I went left on Makossi St then right on (Ru 76), Ru Ibrahim Sevail Abdel-Al St and walking past a little café called Fly Coffee Café I stopped and looked at the menu and prices which were really good. Walked on up to Hamra St but didn't see anything open so back down to Fly Coffee Café and in having a seat. Told and pointed at cheese on Menu with 1 tea and 2 girl customers and girl behind the counter had a discussion about what I meant so all laughing I pointed at a large soft baguette roll and said cheese so everyone laughing, all said ok. 2mins later it came with a large tea and I enjoyed it asking for another and enjoyed it too then breakie finished up I went to the counter and girl said 5000 LP, (1500LP = 1$US) so I had a good filling my belly breakie for 4$US, paid my money and back to hotel and upto room. Cleaned teeth and felt it and had an explosive dobhi drop, cleaned ass and now ready to go so China beachbag over shoulder I was downstairs and had a chat with the very friendly, very helpful girl at reception who told me which way and how to get to Serail in centre so saying my thanks out I went. I had seen a sign Pavilion Hotel when I was out in the morning near the Fly Coffee Café so walked up Rue 76 and across Hamra St and into Pavilion Hotel, Hamra St, Tel: (01) 350160/1/2/3 and asked price of room, guy said 40$US for a single so I said see you tomorrow as that was a decent price with looking at his card it had breakfast for 5$US. Got on to Hamra St and headed into centre ville as I had done last night and past Hamra Star Luxury Apartment Hotel and went in and they said 50$US a room so it looks good. Done a left and sort of got into the Serail area of town and came to the lovely stone block of the St Elias Maronite Church and went in and it was marvellous just to walk its 12-16th Century Church floors and its still in use today as could see the hymn books sitting neatly in the pew seats. A Statue of Jesus was on the right of the pulpit so bowed my head saying a little prayer for the poor and the hungry of the world wishing them happiness and I slowly walked out and not far I came to Eglise St Louis Capucin Church and in also just having a little walk around it admiring the massive stone round Columns and big Dome. Reading an Arabic sign it said St Louis IV, 1214-1270 AD so finished my always fascinating walk and out. Everywhere it seemed there were rifle and machine gun carrying soldiers but they were always very friendly and always said hello. I turned right up the no cars allowed to Park hill road seeing the Ottoman built Gran Serail which was so Majestic on top of the hill looking down over the city, it's the offices of Government now. Kept walking and glancing left, wow oh wow I was looking down on the Roman Baths so just took my time having a gentle no rush walk around the full circumference. It was great workmanship as everything was in closeup full view and I enjoyed being here and so close to real true history. Now into an upmarket area with a Clock Tower and checking my map I was in Nejmeh Sq so had done really well and not having lost too much time. I walked around the old Clock Tower and into the beautiful St

Ellie Cathedral and admired the old paintings, really good then out. Only 5m away to the next door and I was in St George Orthodox Cathedral and what a truly great colourful Cathedral this place was with every wall and all the ceilings full of many descriptive great paintings all painted hundreds of years ago when this Church was built in the time of the Crusades. Went slowly out of the side back door and wow oh wow there was a huge Roman remains site between St George Cathedral and a beautiful Mosque. Kept going saying good luck St George and a slow walk around the Roman remains site seeing 3-4-5 large round stone Columns fully upright and in prime order. I wanted a coffee but every time I came out of one historical Church I would see another Spire Cross in the distance and didn't want to say I wish. Walked up hill past St Vincent de Paul only its walls standing Church saying to myself that's enough no more church's I looked left and what an unbelievable sight as in the distance there was a beautiful Dome 2 Cross Pinnacle Spire Church with many level roofs and Arches it was a joy to see so one more I said and walked uphill towards it. Got to its front entrance door and it was the Cathedral Armeniene Catholque St Gregoure St Elie vivid lovely Church. Went inside it and it was lovely and very clean then out going downhill I seen it also had a Church below ground so went down a few steps into it and was so chuffed as it had big wall paintings of all the original Church's and Monastery's in mountain valleys all over Lebanon and these paintings were just a joy to see as some of these original 12th -14th century Churches were built in so inaccessible areas you would need an organised tour to get anywhere near them but really enjoyed seeing their photographic history, Armenie was mentioned in 80% of the photo pictures. Out from there and going downhill I came to the Martyrs Memorial and stood in silence and sadness in front of it as it was a sad Memorial to ordinary people killed or massacred in the indiscriminate bombing and shooting through the years of Muslim – Christian conflict and thought about the innocent 4000 Protestant people of all ages in N Ireland indiscriminately bombed and murdered by the cowardly Catholic Irish Republican so called army and stood with my head bowed saying a little prayer that God will look after them and their families and I was away. Didn't even walk 25m but seen and went into a Dunkin Donut Café and had a soft meat baguette, large coffee and a chocolate donut, 10,000LP and enjoyed it sitting looking out the rainy street for 30mins until the bright warm sunshine came out again and I was away. Went on downhill to just facing the Port then turned left and had a look peeping inside at the Muslims on their prayer mats praying to Allah in the Mosque Emir Munzir, built 1620 AD saying good luck my brothers. Really enjoying my walk I turned right along General De Gaulle Ave and no rush strolled along The Corniche as it's known to just past the Lighthouse where I had near enough started my round self led tour of Beirut and uphill and spot on I came to Hamra St, turned right and into Fly Coffee Café for another meat baguette and a tea, 4000LP. Enjoyed it and out around the corner and into hotel, got my key and up to room with legs, knees and feet nearly gone I stripped off and into bed, it was 1720hrs. Woke up 1905hrs and decided to get up as had a little plan so nice shave and lovely hot water shower, kit on and checking money out downstairs handing key over and out towards centre ville. Went the same way as last night and came to a dark road rundown area and there they were the Loves of my Life's heart. Walked slowly along a darkish alley all girls smiling at me and looking into the eyes of a deep black haired petite chic I knew it was Beirut true love to last until the end of the next Lebanon Century and chatting in English her cuddling up to me giving me a front section massage she said we go together. I looking into her love struck eyes was so much in love I said yes, how much my beautiful darling, she using her hands said 40$US and I also needed to pay for a hotel room only one block away so my love so strong I agreed cuddling her tight. It was wonderful to be with a true life lover and so much in love and arm in arm we strolled up to a rundown hotel and I paid 10$US for Rm 4 and in we went to a scruffy sheet double bed room kissing and fondling each other it was sheer magic love on a nice hot Lebanon night. I quickly put her 40$US on a table as we quickly stripped off naked kissing and caressing each other as she was so beautiful and as my love vibes heightened we where on the bed making hard pounding sexual intense no bounds Beirut love she was a Lebanon dream of the night as we changed positions 3 times she was screaming in Ecstasy biting my neck squeezed her legs tightly around my back with me in sheer Beirut lust biting her firm lovely breasts and as our sexual exotic spasms passionate pleasures rose to mountain heights we pounded each other into our sweat soaked scented bodies we climaxed together she and me screaming and yelling in pure sexual ecstasy I was lost in the delights of my true Beirut lovers arms until slowly but slowly are vibrating pleasures slowed down then stopped I slid off my true love to lie close up beside her as she held me tight wimpering in naked sexual joy pleasure on our sex scented bed knowing our love would keep us together for ever she giggled then rolled up and on top of me saying, " I like you Papa but we go" and smiling to each other we rolled off our love bed and both laughing we got dressed her putting her money in her bra and out we went to the door of our love alley and with a final cheek peck she saying see you manyanna nocha giving my ass a slap I was away waving my true love goodbye and into the glazed lights of Hamra St. Into a pizza shop I went buying a takeaway pizza and a large tea and legs about to go made it into hotel. Upto room and devoured my 2315hrs feast then body aching all over I was into my lovely soft bed and asleep dreaming true love is "real" true love in the Paris of the East even when the bed sheets are brown and crusty as in my Beauty Queen's arms I was in Heaven in Beirut.

Email Sent: Thu, 4 Feb 2010
Subject: Beirut centre walkie

Hi All

Good sightseeing walk around city centre into about 6 old 12th century Churches all still open for worship, marvellous, then more Roman ruins.

Multi storey buildings going up by the dozen but its amazing still to see huge empty 30 storey buildings still in place with lots of shell holes all over them as its quite a few years since the conflict ended.

Manyanna heading out of town up the coast for a day by public transport about 30klms to Byblos supposed to be the oldest city in the world.

al de bes

Jack

Shelled Hotel

Day 41, Friday, 05-02-10, Beirut – Byblos; Lebanon

Woke up 0430hrs for a quick piss but loving my bed so back in and asleep and no horn pumpers too early as its Friday the day of Prayer and everywhere closed as I keep forgetting their weekend starts today. Up at 0740hrs, underarm wash, face splash, kit on and out downstairs trying it on for a breakie discount but no luck. Dropped key at reception and out upto Fly Coffee Café for 2 cheese soft baguettes and 2 teas, really nice and filling and had a read of LP regarding Byblos first inhabited 7000 years ago and named Byblos by the Greeks in 333BC. Then the Romans took it over in 64BC doing all their usual great building until in 1104AD it was conquered by the Crusaders so great history, plenty to see so that's Plan A today. Tried to find the Pavilion Hotel after leaving the Coffee Café but gave up and back to Embassy Hotel paying for one more rip off 50$US night, upto room, teeth clean and a nice dobhi drop, just the job, cleaned ass and now ready to go. Lights went out and I cheered with a yeah man yeah as I had now experienced a famous Beirut power failure, no problems pulled the curtains and I had real light as the power came back on. Back downstairs and girl gave me detailed instructions of how to travel to Byblos by service taxi and Minibus so thanking her out I went and walked upto Hamra Street and stood by the side of the road and taxi stopped and I said, service, Dawra Bus Terminal thinking what con is now going to be tried. Taxi driver said 10$US so I said no thanks and walked on down Hamra St. In total about 10 taxi drivers stopped and all wanted 10$US until one stopped and said 10,000 LP so I said ok as no good hanging about, jumped in showing him a 20,000LP saying you give me 10,000, he said ok and we were away. It was a very long way across the town past upmarket shopping Malls that were big time rich then we came to Dawra Road roundabout with buses, taxies and Minibuses all parked up around it and out I got giving him the 20,000 Note, he gave me back 2 x 5000LP note's, so I was happy. Didn't get a chance to walk 2m when taxi touts were saying, where you go, I said Byblos and I catch Minibus everyone saying no Minibus or bus now only taxis so laughing I kept on walking and asked a couple of Minibus drivers who pointed at a bus with no number on it so I asked the driver, Byblos, he said yes, so on I got, it was 1000hrs. It didn't fill up quickly and 2-3 young fellows got off and up the road I think catching a shared taxi but at 1020hrs with a toot toot we were away along the well signposted coast main road which was good fun seeing the snow covered mountains high in the sky on my right and sometimes sunshine sandy sunny beaches on my left. I kept my eyes open for signposts for Byblos but nothing then checking my LP map I seen that it had (Jbeil) next to Byblos and next signpost had Jbeil above Tripoli so now happy I was on the right bus I sat back enjoying my people watching as the very friendly Lebanon people are a pleasure to be near and interact with. As people got off I seen they paid the driver with 1 or 2 1000LP notes so got out 2 x 1000Notes ready for sign of Jbeil but never seen it and as bus stopped driver turned around giving me the eye saying Byblos and as I got off I gave him 2 x 100LP notes and got a 500 cent coin back so 41km for 1$US was not bad. I stood at the side of the busy highway and even with my map of Byblos I hadn't a clue but knew it must be towards the sea and was going to walk along the highway when a taxi driver came up a flight of steps and said taxi to Fort, 5000LP which wasn't bad but I said no thanks, I want to walk. He said long way 2-3km as I was walking away a young girl came up the steps. I said Fort, she pointed down the steps and said go under the road, smiling I said my thanks as hadn't even seen the underpass from where I was standing on the main highway road. Down I went and under the underpass going into a very busy centre by the look of it and I could see the top of a Fort Battlements in the distance towards the sea so kept going then seen six Roman stone Columns by a path so only get one chance went back and up to them. It was so beautiful looking at the hills surrounding the town and seen a path going past it looked like old Roman remains then directly into the town centre and its very busy Souks so followed it. No signs pointing anywhere but seen a tourist office so in and asked girl what was the Fort. She said it's the old 12th century Crusader Castle and gave me a detailed tourist map so yeah man yeah I now knew where I was, said my thanks and on through the old cobbled old stone building Souks and finally reached the not signposted or advertised entrance to the Crusaders Castle and wow oh wow the whole ancient 5000 year old Byblos town site. As I went in guy said you have to pay, no problem I said, how much, he said 6000LP so gave it to him, got my ticket and in I went, it was only 1145hrs. Walked up the wide open stone path to the large very imposing wide open big timber gates and was in the 1104BC Crusader Castle and up into the huge central area all built by the Crusaders. I felt so truly overcome and at time's so amazed at this Fortress Castle as the outer walls were 2-3m wide all constructed with stone blocks, truly amazing. Had a gentle walk up and around it looking down sometimes into the Moat from the Ramparts then out and followed the signed path. I walked past and looked down and around the King Well, a very low in the ground spring, went another way and came to an old 218AD Roman Theatre and stood on its stage singing "It's a long way to Tipperary" and everyone near or looking in amazement burst out laughing and I said 1$US for the stage show then away laughing to myself. The tourist leaflet was very good and easy to follow if you wanted but I just went left or right reading the notice board of what the ruins were. I stood and admired the six full 3m height Roman Colonnade, (cols) and followed the path to the Temple of "Lady of Byblos" from 3000BC. Walked around looking down the deep 20m x 5m2 Royal Tombs from the 2nd Millennium all with the original stone coffins and every coffin was open, fantastic just touching it. Now on the Temple of Baalat Gebal, "The Kings Mistress" so even in 3000BC they had bad boys and it must be said, bad girls as well but life is too short, hope they enjoyed it. Still on target I made it on to the original Roman Road and up to the remains of the City Gate, 3rd Millennium BC and I could and felt like I should have come down and stayed the night to give me more time to walk and explore. Next came to the "L" Temple foundation built 2700BC and everywhere there was big large stone artefacts I think stone baths but cant be sure as the whole area was just full of 35 great interesting sites of pure history all described on 1m sq boards on site as well as in the www.destinationlebanon.gov.lb tourist leaflet. Sad but happy I left the site and went left hoping it was and I was spot on as I came to and went into the Church of St John the Baptist, (Eglise St Jean Marc), built by the Crusaders in 1115AD and it was just being decorated for a wedding in it tomorrow as its still in use but enjoyed my walk in and around it. Came out and down around the small dock/boat area seeing the Tower still in place built by the Crusaders to halt any ship intruders then went right and right again going uphill and seen a Bocadillo which is a McDonalds type restaurant. Time for deserts so had a beef burger, fries and a coke, 9000LP, so sat down and enjoyed my lovely meal, just the job. Finished and out and upto and a nice slow walk in and around the plenty to see centre of Modern Byblos then a final walk around the old Souks and that was me, seen a shop selling wristwatches for 8000LP so bought one and it works. Asked and lady directed me towards bus stop for Beirut and up the hill path I went at a road just before the motorway and as a No6 bus came along I waved at him and he stopped. On I got paying the driver 1000LP and getting a ticket stating 500LP but no 500 cent change, not to worry as we stayed on the narrow beach road seeing real Lebanese people passing through small villages and sometimes large beach resorts with one area it looked like the Russians had moved in as everything advertised was for Russians. It now got dark and we were only on the outskirts of Beirut and I was thinking I am in big bad trouble as did not spot or see one place I knew. Didn't realise Beirut was so big but at our last stop I got off in the dark asking driver how to get to Hamra, he pointed at taxis, so off I went thinking here we go. Taxi driver said where you go, I said, Hamra, he said 10,000LP, I said ok thinking that was a quick good deal and into the front seat. It was only a 20min drive and he asked me for my hotel and I told him Embassy Hotel and low and behold 2mins later he dropped me off outside it, I gave him the 10,000Note and he was away, it was 1835hrs. Into hotel and reception guy said you pay for today so I give him a 100$US note and got back 2 x 20$US and 70000LP so I was happy. He said you go Byblos by bus, I said yes, he said you have done well, so there, praise from the experts. Upto room, had a nice shave and face wash and legs overjoyed as not walked that far today. Went out for a dander into two cafes for 2 teas and 2 scones then buying some chocolate biscuits and a bottle of orange I headed back towards hotel. Nearly forgot but stuck my card in an ATM and click, out came 200$US so card working well as Plan A is to head out towards the full of history Bekaa Valley manyanna. Stripped off and into bed and asleep saying sorry I missed you my big girl Beirut chico but you never know, us Roman Jacks might cum again.

Email Sent: Fri, 5 Feb 2010
Subject: Byblos in Lebanon

Hi All

Service taxi from Hamra St, 10,000 LPs to outskirts of Beirut to Minibus terminal and jumped a bus, 1500 LPs 41Klms to Byblos a 7000 year town who Alexander the Great held sway until 332BC then the Romans built their famous baths and roads and theatre all still in place as I was on its stage singing "Its a long way to Tipperary" getting a clapping cheer from many different travellers of today's world.

Its the place where are lettered alphabet was first used.

The Crusaders took it and built a still standing great fortress in 1104AD.

Some of the ruins date back to 2700BC, fantastic live history.

Out from their and into the St John the Baptist Church, 1115AD and still in use today as flowers where being set up for a Wedding.

Came back in de dark not a clue where I was but got a 10,000 LPs taxi from bus drop off point and got to Hotel.

Jumping a bus manyanna to the Bekaa Valley for 2 days sightseeing of Sun City as it has vast huge still in place Roman Ruins, it's near the Syria border so its a journey I have to make anyway as second day heading for Damascus, that's de plan, will wake up and see!!!

www.destinationlebanon.gov.lb

al de bes

Jack

Day 42, Saturday, 06-02-10, Beirut – Baalbek; Lebanon

Horn pumpers awakened me early but just lay in my lovely warm bed not even thinking of moving, had another snooze then checked alarm, it was 0740hrs. Up I got, underarm wash, face splash, kit on and out with my beautiful Kelly Rose's Valentines card and over to the Post Office, it was 0805hrs. Post Office had just opened so gave guy the envelope, he said 2000 LPs so gave it to him, he put stamps on and bang, ink stamped it and my Lebanon Paris of the East sexy curvy Kelly Rose's Valentino's card was away and yeah man yeah I was happy now. Up the street and into Fly Coffee Café having my usual Paris of the East 5 star 2 cheese soft baguette rolls with 2 teas and really enjoyable it was so finished my last gulp and up to counter. Paid girl 6000 LPs, said my usual "Thank you very much" which always gets a huge amazement in the face smiles and back to hotel, got key and into room. Final little pack of everything and felt a nice stir so had a smallish dobhi drop, cleaned ass, cleaned teeth, put neckpouch on checking Passport in place, other wallet in left hand cargo pocket and out with shoulderbag downstairs to reception. Had as usual a great smiling chat with the lovely girl receptionist then shaking hands and her telling me to come back again I was out waving Goodbye and upto Hamra St, it was 0910hrs. Tried 2-3 taxis but they wanted 10$US, tried haggling with this guy in an old rundown taxi and sort of got a price for 6-8-10,0000 LPs, shoulderbag in back, me in front and we were away to the Minibus station at Kala roundabout. Got there and gave him 3$US and 3000 LPs, said my thanks, grabbed my shoulderbag and Minibus driver said Kala, grabbed my shoulderbag, put it in the back of the Minibus and on I got, it was 0930hrs. Three young fellows already on the Minibus asked me where I was from, where I go etc, etc and I told them Zahle, it was 0935hrs. They said they lived in Zahle but worked in the American University in Beirut and were going home but it was snowing in Zahle, I was shocked thinking they were taking the piss as it was nice and sunny now in Beirut. Had a laugh and a chat them telling me of cheapie hotels then at 1000hrs, Minibus full, driver started up and we were away me seeing the snow capped huge mountains on my left as we eventually drove out of Beirut me saying "loved you Beirut" as the people were always so polite and friendly. Settled back enjoying my Tower block flats scenery ride until we eventually got out of Beirut going higher and higher and higher up a twisting hairpin bend road and looking down into Beirut was the most fantastic feeling and scenery it was a fun and a joy to see. We were very high and passed a lovely two Spired with Cross's Church but no snow yet. It was not raining but there was water from it must be the snow running down the roads until we did reach the but not deep snow and carried on our climb upto the top of the main mountain road overlooking Beirut, what a dramatic start to my day, it was 1020hrs as we pulled into a petrol station for a petrol fill. Only 5mins and we were away again higher and higher with deep snow everywhere each side of the road sun shining brightly. I was a bit confused as never realised Middle Eastern Countries got snow but the mountains each side of our road were just all just pure white snow peaks, not to worry sun, sea, sand and snow, what more could I want. Going along the mountain two lane icy road along the mountain top our driver was crazy overtaking on hairpin bends until we came to a near halt as something was wrong as we now crawled 3 cars side by side going up on the one lane taking up more than half off the road leaving just enough space for one car to go past on the other side. Took some photos then guy motioned to me pointing at a sign "Welcome to Bekaa" so hopefully if we can move as we might go down into a valley but is Bekaa a Plateau, we will see eventually as nearly stopped now on the thick ice road. Seen our problem as it was an Army road checkpoint so one by one we went back down to a one line of cars and through the checkpoint, it was 1050hrs. I was really dreading the next part of our journey as looking ahead we had to go down the mountain on a very very steep hill with snow and ice still on the road. Oh my God and Allah above the driver put his foot down driving like a madman overtaking everything and anybody I was shitting myself as this was a mountain steep downhill road with vast drops down into the valleys below, beautiful scenery but one wrong move and dead beautiful scenery. Next thing we drove into the highway town of Chtaura with a McDonalds, KFC and its town centre was a lively full of action area as our Minibus stopped in the Minibus, taxi parking up area, it was 1120hrs. Half the Minibus got off including my laughable Lebanon friends, driver said Zahle to a few girls/blokes standing waiting and as they got on we were away going through many villages and me dreading it in fear the high covered in snow mountain hills seemed to be getting closer and closer. We eventually got to the outskirts of Zahle and drove into the taxi, Minibus parking up area, nothing much here I said to myself so said to driver as everyone got off, Baalbek as that's my final destination anyway so thinking I might as well go the whole hog. Paid driver 5000 LPs as he pointed at a Minibus directly next to ours so me and shoulderbag off and on to it and 2mins later we were away so today's travelling looking good. Mountain snow covered peaks got very close then in we drove to Baalbek with massive high Columns of Roman remains on our left so I said to myself, no drama, just get a hotel and out, it was 1205hrs as we pulled into the Minibus, taxi rank area and off we all got. I gave the driver a 5000 LPs and 2 seconds later he gave me 2 x 1000 LPs back so took my shoulderbag off, looked up and there was Hotel Jupiter, Rue Abdel Halim Hajjar, Tel: 376, 715, 370, 151, Baalbek. Went upto its entrance and guy came out of a small internet shop next to it saying you want room, I said yes and he took me upstairs showing me a big huge 2 double bed room with sofas, chairs and table and said 60$US with heater. I said only 1 person so he took me to a smaller but decent sized ensuite single bed room and said 30$US with heater. I said cheaper trying it on looking at my photocopy LP, he said yes downstairs and showed me a big 2 large beds room with 6-8 more nearby all coming off a central courtyard and said 15$US without heater. I said I need a heater, any cheaper ones upstairs, he said ok the room you just looked in, 20$US with heater so I said ok. Back down gave him my Passport and signed the address form giving him the 20$US and getting key to Room 11, shoulderbag over shoulder and up the stairs and into it. Passport, other wallet in my shoulderbag and taking only beachbag with a bottle of orange and a half packet of biscuits I was downstairs. Guy seen me and I said the Roman Ruins, he said go straight up the road 200m then turn left and you are at the entrance so away I went really chuffed, it was 1315hrs. Walked up into the sort of lively centre of town then done a left down to the armed guard entrance to one of the most famous Roman Ruins still highly viewable in its full height and size dimension. Paid entrance fee, a cheap 6000 LP, got ticket and in just marvelling at the unbelievable size and pure architecture of everything so started my walk at "The Great Temple of Jupiter" which is now and was the biggest temple ever built in the Roman Empire. To actually be in its entrance standing looking with amazement at the 6No 22m high, huge original columns still standing from 60 AD was a wonderful moment in my life. Now looking and walking the great courtyard with real happy vibes as it was enormous measuring approximately 100m sq with hugh underground vaults beneath it but large columns and many gorgeous carving along stone facades were a joy to relax, study and see. I passed many half Domes and many stone blocks just lieing as they were found but all full of original Roman writing, truly amazing. Done my full walk up the steps, down the steps and all nooks and crannies so over to the full height all walls sort of still in place the Medieval Citadel walking its Fortress wall constructed against the Crusaders, what a feeling. Had to go down past the huge in place Columns to a truly glorious site which was "The Temple of Bacchus" and walking around its external high wall constructed 200AD with huge marble Columns all along each wall was fun but truly great fun was going in the entrance seeing the all in place stone carvings along the inner top wall, I just had to nearly stop every 2-3m to enjoy my looks. Next upto the 50No x 10m wide stone steps to view the full lovely site of The Propylaea so really chuffed and not wanting to leave but knew I had to eventually I went into the Museum and just being up close to the original statues and lots of artefacts was a great end to my great day and out I went. It was still early with a nice hot sun beaming down on my skinhead head although the mountains taking up the sky were full of snow. Walked into town doing a left to right slow circle walk and got up to the Halfia Mosque then belly crying in hunger I wanted a proper enclosed café, not an outdoor one, it was 1725hrs. Found the best one which was directly beside my hotel so had a chicken sandwich, one tea and a bowl of soup looking out the windows at the full snow covered mountains thinking I have sort of dropped a rollick as should have came up here for a 3-4hrs sightsee walk then back down the mountain to nice and warm with lots of fast food restaurants Chtaura but that's life. Went back upto my room with my hotel entrance door key, entrance door to first floor steps key and my own room key as hotel was locked up. Had not a clue how to light the fire so now freezing and it was dark I made it out and next door to a digital shop asking the guy does he know where the owner might be, he got on his phone and talking to an old guy who said his son would be over in 5mins. I was now freezing and as the guy who let me the room turned up I said can you light the fire and we went up to my room and he used a lighter to light some sort of liquid gas I think fire and said give it time and it will eventually heat the room and he was away, it was 1830hrs. No chance of a shave or shower tonight I was thinking so out and up around the now dead as a doornail town with only open air cafes with people in overcoats and full hoods sitting in them but had enjoyed my exercise walk looking down at the floodlit lighted ruins, great sight. No one in any other hotels by the sound of it as when passing them blokes came out offering me rooms but said my thanks saying I have one and kept going. Made it back to the café beside my hotel and in feeling the heat and had a cheese sandwich and 3No teas as didn't want to go near my room yet as it was a bit scary, anyone could climb over the wall to gain access and I was the only person there!. Café guy was very friendly telling me it's always cold up in the mountains this time of year. I had to go to bed sometime so checked my 8000 LP new watch and it was 2155hrs so paid my bill and upto room, stripped off in the now warm room and into bed and asleep hoping I will sleep and fire will stay on and not fumigate me to a long time Heaven maybe Hell sleep.

Email Sent: Sat, 6 Feb 2010
Subject: Rm11, Hotel Jupiter, Abdel Halim Hajjar, Baalbek, Lebanon, Tel 376715

Hi All
Jumped taxi, 5000LPs to Minibus area in Kola and straight onto one going to Zahle which 1hr later after going up 1200m hair raising high snow covered mountain road I didn't think we were going to make it. Nothing their so got another to Baalbek town the site of the very famous Roman ruins and 30mins later we arrived in it high up in the snow covered mountains, its freezing.
Done my usual walk around the very imposing ruins as it was well worth it and will make a run for the Syria border manyanna.
al de bes
Jack

Map of Syria

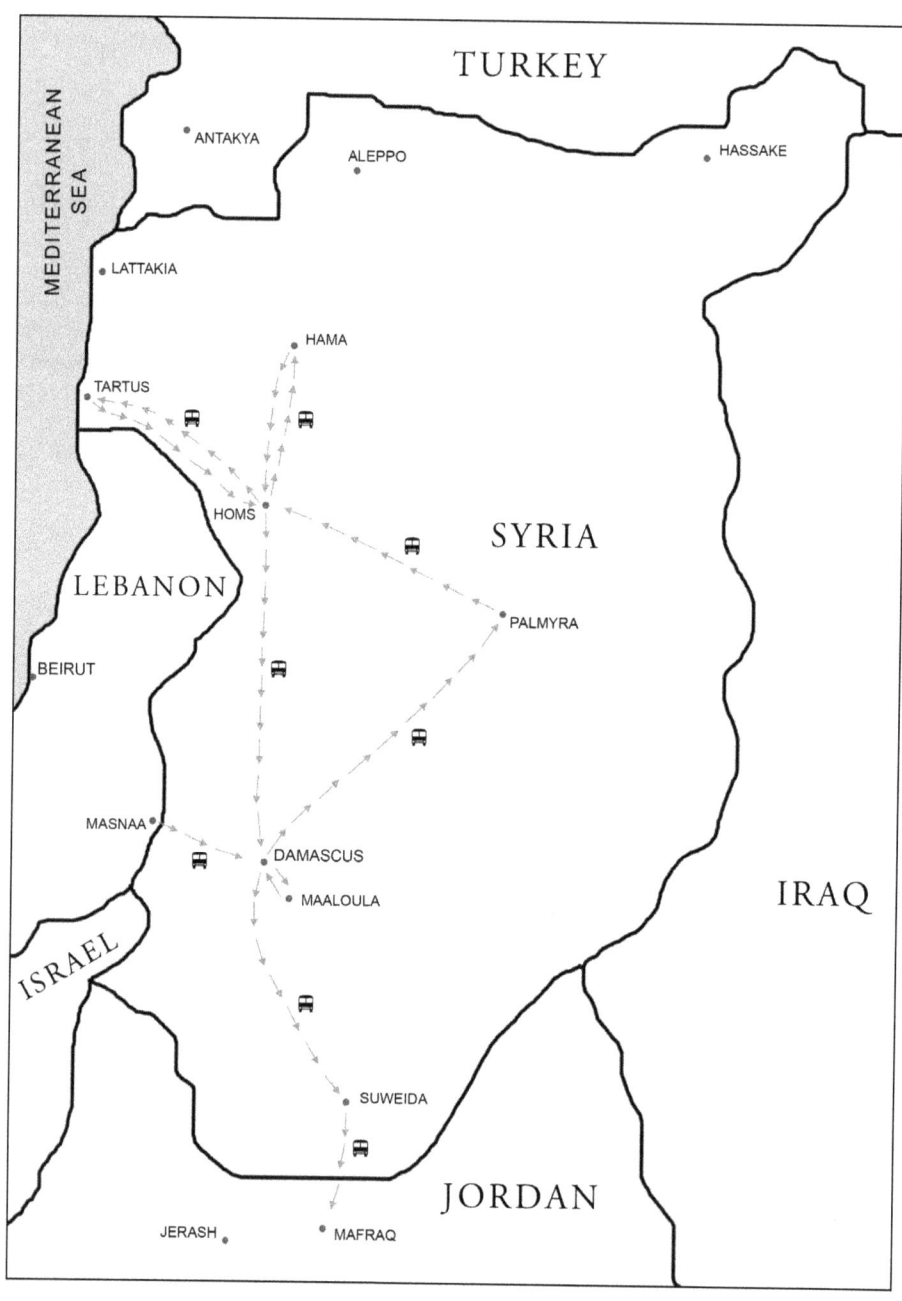

1) SYRIA, once the central part of the caravan and trade route from Asia through Arab people countries to Africa is a country full of so much Ancient History you will need great stamina to go out everyday to view its Holy Bible history, its many Mediaeval Crusader Forts and the great Roman builders world as you walk Damascus the oldest City in the world today to meet and be greeted 'Ahlan wa sahlan', 'You are Welcome' by its so always smiling honest happy people.
2) Capital; Damascus
3) Syria achieved Independence in 1946
4) Climate; Ave temp Jan-Mar;20c
5) Language; Arabic
6) Currency; Syrian Pound, 1$US = 45 S Pounds(Lira)
7) Visa; Not required, 30 day issued on arrival at road border
8) Return flight £51 + £154 ATM, hotel, food, train to Gatwick
9) Today's ongoing update of day to day accommodation, travel, food, drinks costs = £1828

Day 43, Sunday, 07-02-10, Baalbek; Lebanon – Damascus; Syria

Up at 0800hrs and out of my warm five blanket bed, face splash and kit on in the freezing room then out of my room and the sun was warm. Locked my door and opened the stairs door then the main entrance door and into the next door café and had 2 teas and a cheese sandwich which is a flat round bread topped with cheese then heated. Enjoyed my breakie in the nice warm café then paid the 5000LP bill and back upto room and yeah man yeah a lovely jelly baby dobhi drop, cleaned ass, cleaned teeth and little final pack of shoulderbag and I was ready. My biggest worry was I had no hotel booked in Syria as its supposed to be a Customs border requirement that they will ask you for your confirmed hotel booking, we shall see. Left key in door and down and out and across to the Minibuses asking which one for Chtaura and guy pointed so on I got, 4th one on, it was 0900hrs. Small family group got on and only another 10mins wait when a few soldiers got on and we were away me cursing my bad planning as should have stayed in Chtaura, done my day trip to Baalbek and then only a 30min ride to border, live and learn. As we got closer and closer to the bendy mountain road over the snow covered high mountains I said to myself here we go, parachutes on as I could clearly remember our suicide hair raising trip from yesterday. Got to Chtaura which I thought was over the other side of the mountain so we didn't have to cross it so my luck was in today and off I got, it was 0945hrs. Touts surrounded me trying everything to get me into their taxis at 20$US but eventually got a service taxi for 10,000 LPs, it was 1000hrs. Only waited 5mins and we were full and on our way to the Lebanon side of the border going uphill into the snow covered mountains there was 5No in total passengers in our service taxi, 3 in back, 2 in front. Got to the Lebanese border control and I went into the foreigners check line filling in the small pink foreigner's customs card, handed it and my Passport over and 2-3mins later, bang, Lebanon exit stamp then Passport back. Back out with a very helpful Lebanese guy and into back seat waiting service taxi as everyone was waiting for me, 2 Lebanese guys in back seat and 2 Syrian guys in front then we were away on the 3-5km mountain snow no-mans road between the two borders. Got to the Syrian border check point and out I and everyone got, it was 1100hrs. Again I lined up on my own at the Foreigners Passport Control line but guy said you need Visa pointing across behind me at a kiosk so over and Visa was 52$US so panicking a bit I checked my driving licence wallet and I was so lucky, I had a 50$US and a 20$US notes. Guy at kiosk said no change for the 20$US, I said you take Lebanon money, he said no but my taxi driver came in, I gave him 3 LPs and he gave me 2No US dollars back, bought my Syrian Visa and back over to Foreigners Passport Control and two sexy Russian girls were told their 52$US Visa to enter Syria was not valid, they needed a 60$US one so unlucky for them but lucky for me they had to go back over to the Visa kiosk to buy another so quickly handed my Passport with Syrian Visa and Customs Card to Passport guy, he scanned my Passport, quick check of paperwork and bang, Syria enter stamp. Wanting to scream Yeah man Yeah but keeping my emotions in check I said my big time sigh of relief thanks and quickly back out to my taxi waiting in the chock a block queue and in the back seat and we were away me thinking I had got a really good deal as I thought the taxi only took me to the Lebanese Border checkpoint so had done really well one way but had missed out on going to Aanjar. Aanjar was a 660AD Islamic small town only found in 1940 and I was looking forward to spending an hour or two at the most there, it was approximately 5km back from the Lebanese border but in the melee of the hustle and bustle of getting here there and everywhere I had completely forgotten about it, that's life. Had to show stamped Passport at a checkpoint then wow oh wow we were going really fast on our Holy road to Damascus and getting near the outskirts the driver pulled into a big Minibus, taxi and bus parking area and that was his final stop. We all got out me collecting my shoulderbag from the boot of the taxi and I gave the driver 13,000 LPs as didn't need Lebanese money anymore plus he had done me really well. Again taxi touts trying it on and I was tempted to take a bus but got the price down to 200 Syria Lira which 45 Lira to 1$US I thought I had done well as we were well out in the outskirts of Damascus. My destination was Sultan Hotel, Sharia Mousalam al Baroudi, Damascus, Tel: 2225768 so into taxi and away and asked driver to stop at a row of ATM's along a busy street, tried my MasterCard, no luck again, tried my other card and it worked so drew out 5000 Syrian Lira and back in the taxi. He was a decent old guy and dropped me off outside Hotel Cardilie just around the corner from Hotel Sultan, paid him the 200 Lira and he was away. Was tempted to try Hotel Cardilie but said to myself start where you know from LP and around to Hotel Sultan I walked pulling my trolley shoulderbag and in asking for a single room and looking at the prices. Guy speaking good English said 45$US for single and I felt it was a con but price was on the board and after my great day journey getting here I said ok, book me for one room for one night, gave him my Passport and 2200 Lira, got key to room 310 and up the lift I went into a lovely d-ensuite, soap, towels and all the works room. Dumped my shoulderbag in room, took neck pouch off putting it in shoulderbag and that was me ready to start my New Day, New City, New Country exploring, it was 1240hrs. Down to reception and handing key over I said to the three old gentlemen any plans for an afternoon's sightsee, one said yes giving me a map, try the Old City walking route and showing me on the map where to go so that's it, said my thanks and out. It was a fun walk going left past the lovely old Railway Station and on to Sharia Ain Nasr Street with a nearly a straight line to the big Citadel walls and into the full of people and all sorts of shops the covered Souk al Hamidiyya and followed it enjoying the new vibes and new people along it. Came to the Western Gate which is all that is left of the old 3rd Century AD Temple of Jupiter but the full height columns were a lovely history sight and was really glad to see traffic and come out on Sharia Bab Shargi turning right and upto and along Sharia Medhat Pasha Street, (straight street), both streets full of old antique shops and carpet shops, really nice. Going past the Dahdah Palace but it was closed then another right I was now slightly lost in the twisting abrupt turning sometimes very narrow 1000 year old Souks. Took another turn coming out to the Syrian Orthodox St George Shrine, 1836, great history as its still there and very old lady sitting inside it gave me a lovely smile and a vividly coloured old plastic photo of the Virgin Mary so I have her a 25 Lira note which got me an even happier smile. Next into the most beautiful underground St Ananias's (St Hanania Church) Church which was such a lovely gem so said a prayer for all the people hungry and without shelter and left. Made it at last to somewhere on my map which was the Bab Touma Gate, Thomas Gate. Turned back on myself and it was so enjoyable seeing and being in these Souks as I now made it to the Melkito Creek Catholic Cathedral but unlucky as it had just closed, it was 1600hrs. I was now in the Christian Quarter of the Old City with no cars or crowds just gently walking the old Souks, it was just a full joy. Walked past the Convent of St Joseph a very old building and occupied thinking a convent is for women and sometimes checking the street name it was on Al-Abbara. Again knew I had got lost but looking at the street names I knew I was in the Jewish Quarter and these fantastic old buildings built with tree branches as structural cross beams were all still standing but a lot looked empty. I knew I was definitely lost as it got very rundown but came to and marvelled at the huge Umayyad Mosque, 705AD. I was allowed in so paid for ticket then just strolled around it and into the Mausoleum of Saladin, 1193 AD, one of Arabs best loved heroes, what a great fantastic finish to my afternoon and out again coming to the Roman Eastern Temple Gate but still in the Old City and onto Ain Nasr I knew where I was so nearly home, what a great fantastic first day in Damascus, it was 1800hrs. Into a takeaway buying a big egg and chip butty and a can of coke, 75 Lira and back into hotel, got my key and upto my room, half stripped off but enjoyed devouring my 1835hrs late din, din, felt a stir and had a creamy dobhi drop, cleaned ass, cleaned teeth and now ready for tonight. Stripped off and rolling all my dirty clothes up I had a shave and a lovely hot water shower, dried off and full clean kit on I felt like a new Holy man. Down to reception, handed key over and out into the good westernised streets of Damascus and done a full circle night time walk having 2 coffees and 2 scones in 2 cafes, one an internet café doing my usual 20min update. Thinking of my great first day I slowly made it back to my hotel passing many, many hotels some it looked like very cheap but the one I did like was the Karnak Hotel, Alnassr Street, Damascus, Tel: 00963, 11,2216490/ email karnak-hotel@hotmail.com as it was also surrounded by many cafes. Glad my first day went so good so into hotel, got key and upto bed and really chuffed stripped off and phoned my beauty queen Kelly and had a much needed 10min laughing chat until her mobile phone battery went dead and that was me into bed and asleep dreaming that a Syrian Belly Dancer was beside me doing an Arab belly love dance in my arms.

Date: Sun, 7 Feb 2010
Subject: Rm301, Sultan Hotel, Sharia Mousalam al-Baroudi, Damascus, Syria

Hi All

Minibus from Baalbek, 3000LPs at 0900hrs to Chtaura then service taxi, 10,000 LPs from their at 1000hrs right through the 2 borders with stops and min form filling at each side of the 3-5Klms no-mans land border posts.

Got to Leb side and out, filled form in and bang, exit stamp, back onto taxi sharing with 2 Lebs and 2 Syrians and over the snow filled Pass to Syrian checkpost, had to buy a Visa, 52$US and lucky as I had 70$US on me as it does not mention this in LP but he looked at Passport, looked at me probably saying Lebanese hoods, Syrian hoods, Aldershot hoods, same same, bang, enter stamp and I was into Syria.

Back into Taxi and all the way to outskirts of Damascus where that was his final stop as I thought he was only taking me to Leb border.

Got taxi, 200 Syria Lira at 45 Lira to 1$US and into above, 45$US at 1230hrs, what a great approx 150klms action fun drive.

Dumped kit in room and out down into Old Damascus which is 1000S of years old and just a hive of so interesting Souks then into its Christian Quarter seeing old Armenian Churches where guy would not let me use their toilet for a piss unless I paid him so told him to piss off and done my duty around the Souk corner then finally into the Jewish Quarter and everywhere not been touched for Centuries.

Now out on de modern town having a walkie and you never know.

Have a few plans for interesting sights sees over the next few days.

al de bes

Jack

Day 44, Monday, 08-02-10, Damascus – Maaloula; Syria

Up once during the night as blankets had fallen off and I was cold, blankets back on the bed, quick piss and back to sleep until alarm went off at 0800hrs. Didn't want to get up but finally up at 0830hrs, face splash, underarm wash, kit on and out down to Floor 2 breakfast room. I enjoyed my free 1 boiled egg, 2 soft baguette rolls with butter, cheese, jam and a pot of tea having a read of LP. I had given my dirty dobhi to be cleaned to reception last night and they said it will be back at 1500hrs today or else I would have done a runner as on my round trip I have to come back to Damascus anyway, that's life, will have an easy day today. Back to room and a nice dobhi drop, cleaned ass, cleaned teeth and no plans at all I was downstairs and handed key over and walking down the bottom two flights of stairs and out along to the Post Office to post a Valentines postcard to Ms Shannon my beautiful full of life happy niece in Bangor, Northern Ireland. Out of hotel, turned left and left again and into Post Office, bought a 50 Lira stamp, stuck it on and posted it in the postbox and out. Made it along Sharia Mousalam al Buroudi St, turned right and in the gated entrance to the 1554 AD Takiye Mosque just walking around its many Domed exterior with large signs stating The Turkish Government was paying the cost of refurbishment so it was closed. Out the main gate and turned right to the National Museum, paid my entrance fee and in and I could sense it was worth a visit as first I walked around the open garden area full of original old artefacts, statues even an old timber round water wheel. Now inside and it was really worthwhile coming here and I was glad I did as just took my time strolling and enjoying the many, many all sorts of finely carved statues, bracelets and dresses of bygone age. Nearly missed it but down the steps and into the original Hypogeum of Iarhai the Palmyrene which was a dramatic high vault of his tomb, 108 AD. Still amazed, out from it and again nearly missed The Synagogue of Dura-Europos, 300 BC with its original fifty plus all sizes of wall paintings fully describing and showing life as it was 300 BC, I could hardly believe it as I took my time walking around studying and enjoying the paintings. Had enjoyed my museum walk so out and across the walkway bridge across the Barada River and the busy highway road to Beirut St, turned right and just strolled along it into the city centre and had a walk around the Martyrs Memorial grass area large Memorial in the centre of a busy road roundabout. I was now a bit desperate for something to do as it was only 1150hrs and thought about going down the old City again but what's the point. Feeling it a bit peckish I went across the road near my hotel bought a large pizza and back into hotel and into the restaurant soft seating area ordering a pot of tea. Talking to the always very helpful staff about something to do one of the gentlemen said go to Maaloula a very ancient village in the mountains only 1hr away as its got lots of great Christian history so saying my thanks, finished my pizza and out with a written note from him to give to a taxi driver. I had two choices, taxi straight there and drop me off, 600 Lira or take a taxi to Bus/Minibus station 10mins away, wait for a Minibus to fill up then go. Hardly waited 2mins and taxi drew in and I showed him my note, he said Maaloula, I said, yes, how much, he said 800 Lira, I said 600, he said 700 so I said my smiling yes, jumped in and we were away. I enjoyed the great mountain scenery as we got out of

Damascus and was glad I had taken a taxi as it was a long haul 57km and 1600m high and as we got close to Maaloula it was so fantastic seeing the Christian Cross and Holy Mary Statues in and around the now up close stone mountain cliff face with a village half way up it. Up he drove and stopped at the small roundabout in centre of the village and I give him a 1000 Lira note, he said I keep, I said, no 300 Lira and with the usual taxi driver sour face he gave me the full 300 Lira, out I got saying and smiling my thanks he was away. It was fantastic being in this ancient Christian village at the foot of the Qallamoun Mountains so looking around I seen the Convent of St Thekla on the side of the mountain with a small access road leading up to it so that's my first stop as there was at least three other Churches high up the mountain above the many small dwellings. Happy walking up a gravel stone path I took a short cut then was up the stone steps and into the Convent following the signs for the Shrine and in a cave like cavern there was a lovely, beautiful, colourful dark Shrine with an old lady sitting happily in it and three young fellows went in with their shoes off and were given candles which they lit and one by one they knelt at a hole in the linen drapes shielding the coffin tomb and crossing themselves they said a little prayer in Arabic, it was so really wonderful to see. Back down a few steps and into the full of paintings medium sized Church and I just stood there saying a little prayer for all the poor, hungry and homeless in the world today and wish the Lord to help and feed them, then out I went back down. I seen a high mountain stone gorge with a path going along it so just walked up it a little and a girl and a bloke came from nowhere from its twisting path and I said how far does it go. They said approximately 75-100m then it comes out so you can look down on the town below so off I went sometimes passing locals coming down it carrying large bags on a stick over their shoulders. Finally after passing under a bridge and the gorge getting very narrow I reached its end and what lovely views seeing Maaloula from above and the Virgin Mary human height Statue on the mountain looking down into the village, great vibes. I seen a sign Convent of St Sarjioo and made it to the top of a small hill beside the mountains and into the most beautiful Church I have ever seen, said my prayer for the people of the world and left going only 40m to a sign; Temple of the Sun, 175 BC. I followed a new marble path going up to what looked like a new Hotel but seen a stone path and seen a little cavern and in I went and I was just so full of emotion that I had done this, I whispered my Thanks to our Lord above and out. Seen the locals coming from the mountain carrying their belongings or whatever in sacks with a stick over their shoulder all taking the gorge path so I joined them saying Hi all and everyone saying Hi in their own Maaloula language which is one of the most ancient languages in history but great to see and meet them as I galloped my way down the uneven gorge and back up the small hill to below the Convent of St Thekla. I seen another sign St Barbara Church and I was away following little twisting narrow Souks up the mountain village some going underground but I got lost so made it back down into the centre of the village at the tarmac road. Could still see St Barbara's Church but their seemed lots of spired crosses then seen a sign St Lavandius Church and up into the very steep narrow Souks again and actually passed it and it was not until I gave up and turned around I seen it. Back down a Souk and went in its open door to look and stare in amazement at its large Dome and great painting interior, it was a truly great feeling, said my prayer and out taking my time going down looking sometimes into people's dwellings all with steps going down from their entrance doors. Back in the village centre and seen St Georges Church which looked really new so went up and into it and met a priest who as I asked he said the congregation on Sunday's was 600 people. There was a very old Shrine beside the school next to the Church dating back thousands of years so I asked if I could use the toilet and he said no problem and he showed me it and I had a lovely much needed piss. Shook his hand and I was away thinking you need a day here with a good guidebook or a guide as the whole huge gorge was just filled with true history even Jameh Mosque which started its chanting as I looked about for a Minibus. I seen one parked up with no driver but lots of Minibuses where dropping people off at the roundabout so sat near it having a drink of coke and a Twix bar, just the job. Driver came from somewhere getting into the parked up Minibus so over I went, he said Damascus, I said yes and got on. Another 10mins and there were 5 people on it and driver pumped his horn and we were away, it was 1630hrs. I fell asleep and woke up as the guys were passing the fare over to the driver so I said how much and was told 40 Lira, gave him 50 and got 10 Lira coin change. Everyone got off before me as we drove into a Minibus station, out I got saying my thanks and out to the main road flagging down a taxi agreeing 100 Lira to centre of Damascus and after a good 15mins full of traffic run and as he dropped me off at Martyrs Square I paid him the 100 Lira. Slowly walked back towards my hotel buying 3 meat hot rolls and a small pizza and into hotel ordering a large pot of tea and as it came I sat back in the canteen really big time enjoying my 1810hrs din din and brimming with joy after today's great Church sightsee. I paid my tea fee plus my cleaned and pressed dobhi, 375 Lira, which was really cheap and upto room. Dumped everything, had a shave and face wash and out going left through centre of new town to just outside the Old City walls hoping I knew where I was going. Seen them and smiling, whispering yeah man yeah to myself I could see my sweethearts of the night and as I got closer this beautiful figure with scarf around her face Chico said you like Syria and I knew it was love forever in the Holy Damascus sky I said yes smiling and also I love you. She stuck herself into my love struck body and holding me tight rubbing her right hand on my now stiff rocker saying you go with me and totally besotted and so much in love I held her tight saying yes my darling, how much and where we go. She give a lovers yell of joy saying and pointing up the Souk, Love hotel and with a imploring true love look into my eyes she said 40US$. My love so strong I with no hesitation said ok getting a full kiss as we continued into the dark Souk then her caressing my bum she led me into a sort of rundown hotel and I paid 5US$ for a 1hr room we got the key and kissing and cuddling each other in we went to Rm6 a colourful double bed room and quickly getting her 40US$ out I left it on a chair near my side of the bed as we without any foreplay both stripped off and she was so beautiful and lithe as in her arms we where kissing and exploring and fondling each others sex hot bodies then on the bed making instant hot exotic Damascus pounding into each others lust love sex crazed bodies like two heat of the night Syria dogs I never felt so passionate as she was biting my breasts as I bit her prominent hard nipples she screamed with lust raking her long fingernails up and down my back we changed position she going down on me putting her scented legs around my neck I was in love with my tongue then changing positions again her legs behind her head both panting and groaning in passion together I let her legs down as we both continued are heavenly holy sexual thrusting passionate biting each other to holy death lovers Syrian love until as I felt it coming we both climaxed together both screaming in Damascus lust she ripped my tender buttocks to pieces I nearly bit her nipple off as we were drenched in scented hot lovers sweat until with our thrusting vibrating sex bodies going on and on until our sex spasms slowly but slowly died down and I slipped off my true love to lie tightly close up beside her she with her eyes closed was sexually smiling in pure contentment and breathing her lovely breasts up and down I knew our love was so strong we would never ever leave each other as I tickled her belly button she turned over towards me giving me a long lingering Damascus Syrian kiss then sitting up she stroked my face saying "You are one in a million Papa but we go" and slid of the bed as I did and we both smiling at each other we got dressed I made sure she had her loot. Both checked we had everything then out her giving the room key to reception and out we went both holding hands having a smiling laugh together and down towards the end of the Souk and with Bye byes and a quick kiss we parted she going up a narrow Souk just before the road. Sad to leave my Damascus honey I was away galloping across the main road passing one large Dome with about 10-12 smaller Domes all in an ancient wall, don't know what it was but it looked really good with lights lighting up the grass park area surrounding it. Crossed the bridge at Martyrs Square and walked around the big Martyrs Pillar then knees just about to go and eyes hardly able to see I said no more sightsee just make it home and slowly not getting lost I got back to hotel, got my key and into room. Stripped off, heavy hearted and into bed and asleep dreaming true love in Syria with her lithe legs around my neck Damascus girls are not for the fainthearted and asleep a sore Damascus neck happy man.

Date: Mon, 8 Feb 2010
Subject: Maaloula, Syria

Hi All
Had a great half day up in Maaloula at the foot of the Qalamoun Mountains going through little gorges to get upto its old 1000s year old Churches and Shrines and Convent of St Thekla and St Sarkis with St George Church and St Barbara Church all up on the stone side of the mountain and a Cave hole in the stone mountain with an alter in it at a high point is the Temple of the Sun God, 175 BC, great history and a fantastic place.
Jumped a Minibus and now back in Damascus but heading out by bus manyanna to Palmyra for one night then across to the Med coast for one night, that's plan A, will wake up and check it.
al de bes
Jack

Day 45, Tuesday, 09-02-10, Damascus – Palmyra; Syria

Rolled over in my softish/hardish bed and looked at alarm clock it was 0700hrs so gently turned over a few times tempted to go back to sleep but mind made up and neck still sore I got up at 0740hrs. Underarm wash, face splash, kit on and downstairs to breakie room saying Good morning my dears to a party of young girls getting screams of laughter then tucked into my 1 boiled egg, 2 soft baguette large rolls, butter, jam and a pot of tea breakie, really filling as I finished the lot. Back upto room, cleaned teeth, final pack of shoulderbag and out down the lift to 2nd floor reception, handed key over, said my thanks, shook the guy's hand as he wrote bus destination and bus station on a slip of paper and I was away down the lift to ground floor and out. First stop I went to an ATM and being completely stupid punched in 10,000 Lira as I now know if you punch in too much it stops all payments for 24hrs but sweating a bit, click, out came 10,000 Lira and also my credit card, wow oh wow, I was over the Syrian moon. Flagged down a taxi showing him the slip of paper with bus station on it and in I got checking money as we were away and I had only 500 Lira notes so con 1 will soon be on the way. Not that far and got to Harasia Bus Station and out I got giving him a 500 Lira note, he said me keep, I said no, give me change and keep 100. He got out and after trying a few taxi drivers he came back and gave me back 200 Lira, I said pointing at the money he had given me, no, one at a time me pouting in the melee of the taxi packed road I got back 350 Lira, said my thanks and away so robbed again of 50 Lira or maybe 100. Next thing pulling my trolley shoulderbag I was in the 50 or so Agency Bus Station me thinking I thought I was going to Palmyra on a shared service taxi or Minibus!. I asked a few times and was directed to kiosk office of Alrafedain Tours me thinking now I am going to get conned and showing two guys Palmyra from my photocopy LP they said quick, quick, Passport and 200 Lira so quickly gave them both and they grabbed my shoulderbag, gave me a ticket and we went into the bus departure station, he put my bag in bus hold, gave me back my Passport and I was on a big AC soft seat luxury bus, wow, I was really chuffed, it was 0910hrs. Police came on checking tickets and my Passport then we started up and slowly but slowly we finally got out of the Bus Station and were away very quickly out of Damascus passing along big rocky mountain hills on my left with farmers green fields on my right so had been very lucky ref time and transport wise as had not checked one dam thing. Beautiful sunny day as I now pulled down the window shade as my side was the sun side, it was 0935hrs. Now going quite fast on the main highway seeing signposts for Baghdad me laughing to myself thinking should I go that way as it was only 200miles to the border but still laughing said no and settled back watching the girl singing on the Arabic TV. Guy came along giving everyone a glass of water and a chocolate sweet so had my 0945hrs Naafi break happy my detailed planning had worked out good!. I settled back having a read of my photocopy Palmyra and looking out the other side window we were going through a rocky sand mountain desert and pulling the curtain back my side it was a flat desert stretching all the way to the sky blue horizon, wow oh wow, I loved these sights. Next minute I dozed off waking up to Bedouin style tents with camels in the desert dunes and the pure sand desert stretched everywhere but could still see the mountain's on the horizon on my left and now right, it was 1000hrs. Next thing the driver pulled up his front windscreen top curtain cover and what a dramatic exhilarating scene as our road stretches straight for miles as we went through desert mountains each side of the road. Came to and crossed a railway line in a sort of truckers stop village with a couple of restaurants still seeing Baghdad on the road signpost and looking out my right hand window the railway lines carried along parallel with our road I must admit I was sorely tempted!. At 1122hrs we crossed the railway lines again and now they were running parallel on our left as we passed a large industrial probably cement making complex. Happily watching the flat sand desert and mountain in the distance desert landscape I seen a signpost Palmyra 43km. It was 1135hrs so looking good for final stop in approximately 45mins which I know will give me plenty of time to see the 2nd century AD full height ruins of the old town as previous to that it was a travellers Assyrian tent town stopping point for over 1000 years. Road got very bumpy then we passed a very distinct line of shrub trees which was as we got closer was another road connecting from the desert into our straight as a die road. At 1155hrs we came to a roundabout crossroad with Palmyra pointing right, our bus went left to Hom's and I said to myself I have dropped a rollick and got the wrong bus and just about to go upto the conductor when the road started bending to the right and there it was on my right, yes, a full it looked like a city of Roman ruins. The bus stopped on the main highway and lots of Syrians were as baffled as me but everyone including me got off, it was 1210hrs. Not a clue where I was and taxi touts by the dozen I asked where the centre of town is and guy pointed back down the road the bus had come up so trolley shoulderbag handle up I was away leaving the touts for the next bus. Didn't get very far before every taxi was stopping and I asked how much to centre, most said 300 Lira so I kept on walking. I was lost and not a clue as nothing appeared to show that I was getting into the centre of town when a Minibus drew up and a guy said hotel and only have a look. I said town centre, he said, yes, so shoulderbag and me on we were away and into a sort of decent large building each side road and parked up outside a hotel. I said where is centre, he said all around so went inside and he showed me a lovely d-ensuite and said 750 Lira so I said ok as could see the ruins and the Arab Castle all within walking distance. Gave him Passport, paid for one day and up to Room 111, Al Faris Hotel, Castle Road, Palmyra, Syria, Tel: 031-5912514, (www.alfaris-hotel.com). Dumped shoulderbag in room taking neck pouch off and I was ready for today's adventures walk. Met Mohammed the owner downstairs and he said there are four sites you have to see and they are not close together, you will need transport describing them as 1) The Museum, 2) The Valley of the Tombs, 3) The Temple of Bel, 4) The Arab Castle. I looked at LP may and knew if I had a day I could walk it or do it myself but I only had a maximum of 4-5hrs so I asked how much, he said 500 Lira to drive me to each and all the sites, so instant decision I said yes. Ok he said to Minibus driver and in I got and we were away and first stop, The Museum. Into the Museum paying 150 Lira and 75 Lira for look inside the tombs in Museum and in I went. I must admit it was a brilliant fantastic Museum with 75% of descriptions in English of big full life statues and artefacts including colourful mosaics of every description and clothes from the 100-300 BC. The next room I went into was the scary even for me which was the Mummies Room seeing 4No 2000 year old Mummies, two of the Mummies were just bones including the skull and two still had their full white teeth. The other two were still wrapped in their Mummies clothes all from 9-103 BC with only their skulls showing so wished them well and along the corridor thinking not for the faint hearted. Went into an original Tomb with three chambers N, W, E and each had approximately seven 500mm wide large deep neatly cut chambers in the stone wall all with neat 50mm resting edge's for six coffins from top to bottom. Great history as when the coffin was put in the front was sealed with a large marble stone sculpture of the person who died, really interesting 2000 year old history. I done the rest of the very, very interesting museum walk and back out to waiting driver and into Minibus. He said next stop is the Valley of the Tombs and we were away sometimes going along a dusty road and then he stopped and out I got at the Brothers Tomb, 2nd Century AD. First stop I went down approximately 10 steps and into a large Tomb but it was roughly the same as the museum Tomb with many ledges built for the coffins but still very interesting. Back out and into Minibus and away into the desert with now lots of big square stone buildings and he stopped, out I got and everywhere for miles there were these, some small, some large big stone block buildings and into the first one and it was the same as the museum but this one had four floors with many chambers and carved stone coffins. The one I first went into was the touristy one but took my time and went in a 200m circle walk around the desert and into ones lieing sort of derelict and really enjoyed climbing up the 100-300 AD steps looking in the dark recess burial chambers, good fun. Back out to driver and was glad I had taken the Minibus as next stop at 1430hrs I went upto the Temple of Bel, 32AD, paid my entrance fee but just walking out into the so perfect ancient site was a terrific feeling and I just started my journey going right and doing a left hand circle going past 20m marble Roman 1m diameter columns but everything was constructed in a so perfect systematic order and plan, had a few photo shoots meeting Graham from Scotland. I could have stayed and enjoyed another 1-2hrs just walking around but went out and over to the City of a 1000 Columns, 236AD. In through the towering columns every 2-3 metres each side and over and into the bit semi round, with a stone stage Roman Theatre, 100-200 AD, the stage alone was 48m long x 10m wide with 12 semi-circular rows of stone seats and it even had an orchestra area. Just marvelling at every turn I made I then slowly made it back to my pickup point arranged for 1615hrs outside the Temple of Bel and driver was waiting. In I got so happy to have been and seen so interesting true history and we were away up the round hill tarmac road to the Arch Fort a truly high mountain Fort on top of the rocky mountain. Crossed the moat and paid my entrance fee at kiosk then in I went taking my time climbing up and up and up the right angled turn step stair passageway and finally I got right up on to the Fort fantastic view battlements and no rush just walked left in a full circle around the battlements of the Fort seeing the Valley of the Tombs one side then the Temple of Bel and the 1000 columns on another side. Then a view I will always remember was the sunset view looking at the desert hills with the rocky stone mountains behind them on the red sunset sky, truly remarkable and so brilliant a view. Took my time and slowly back down and out into the Minibus and said smiling restaurant and away we went into the lively full of tour bus tourist town centre and he dropped me off outside Pancake Café. Everywhere was full of tour groups eating their 1745hrs din din making sure the driver or guide got commission so I just slowly walked around the town. Back up to Pancake Café and it was now empty so in I went and had a plate of spaghetti bolognaise and two large teas really enjoying my much needed late din din. Just about to leave when I met a young English guy who I had met on the 1000 Column walk area and as we chatted he told me he was a tour guide. I enjoyed my 30-40mins chat and exchanged names, shook hands and I was away as I now know my hotel was way outside the town centre. Walked past the Army barracks with armed guards in jeans and coloured jackets, not army uniforms which seemed very strange to me but finally made it back to my hotel and in I went. Days are sunshine and warm, nights are dark and appear cold so got the young fellow to switch the heating on and I waited for a while for my room to warm up but it didn't get real warm so no shower or shave tonight, it was 2050hrs. Was going to go back into the town centre but said to myself what's the point, nothing their so had a read of LP and an early night for a change. I stripped off at 2200hrs and into bed and hoping my travel plans for tomorrow work out as good as today I drifted off to sleep in my nice warm bed my Damascus sore neck now getting better me dreaming more great sex on de Damascus rocks.

Email Sent: Tue, 9 Feb 2010
Subject: R111, Al Faris Hotel. Castle St, Palmyra, Syria, Tel031-5912514, www.alfares-hotel.com

Hi All

Jumped a Pullman Bus from Damascus, 200Lira at 0910hrs and arrived Palmyra 1210hrs and took a free taxi to above, 750Lira for d-ensuite which now I know is 600m from centre of town.

Had a great day first stop into the Museum saying hi to the 6No 2000year old Mummies and 2 still with his/her full set of teeth and all bones including skulls, great site.

Next stop I was in the Valley of the Tombs where many Large Royal Tombs were built 100-200AC.

Then next the unbelievable Temple of Del as never seen nothing like it in my life as the size of it defied belief.

Then up the main straight street with the amazing Great Colonnade and into The Theatre.

Just finished my day high up on top of a mountain hill in the Arab Fort with spectacular views all around the mountains and down into Palmyra, what a great day.

Jumping a bus manyanna morning to costal town of Tartus!, plan A.

al de bes
Jack

Day 46, Wednesday, 10-02-10, Palmyra – Tartus; Syria

Didn't sleep much after getting woke up by the 0430hrs chanters giving rout from their Minarets for a good 10mins then turning alarm off I got up at 0720hrs, underarm wash, face splash, kit on and took the blanket I had nicked from next room and dumped it back on the bed and back to my room pulling the curtains and what an eye opening view. I could look down and see every tower in the desert sand of the Valley of the Tombs, The Temple of Bel and every high column along the straight road and looking into the bright sun rays the Arab Castle high on the mountain top was a fairytale dream, what a truly remarkable desert morning sight. Out of room and downstairs to ground floor and young fellow had set out my breakfast table so sat down and had my boiled egg, 3 flat portions of bread, with butter, cheese and jam all with a big pot of tea and I must say the ole Syrians make a lovely breakfast and I love their lovely tasting jam as I downed my 4th cup of tea. Back to room, cleaned teeth, nice soft marmalade dobhi drop, cleaned ass, zip up on shoulderbag and I was away downstairs. Young fellow and his dad said Minibus take you to Homs Bus Station for free so got on shaking hands with young fellow and we were away only about 500m to a sort of small bus station and my driver said that one pointing at a small bus so off and gave shoulderbag to driver who put it in the hold. Over to pay kiosk and guy said Passport so got neckpouch out taking Passport from it, gave it to him and he wrote something in Arabic on a small piece of paper giving it to me saying 100 Lira. Gave him the 100 Lira and he said 50 more, I said what, he said ok and I got on the full bus only for two seats saying Good Morning all to all my Syrian bus companions and as usual getting loud bursts of laughter with looks of astonishment, sat down and 2mins later we were away, it was 0830hrs. With truly fantastic last views of the Palmyra Roman Ruins and the Arab Castle we went round the other side of the mountain hill into the desert so sat back looking out the window at the Bedouin tents with camels, goats and sheep all around them and a New day, New town here I come. I enjoyed my sunny sun desert views then dozed off and woke up to lots of green tree, green shrubs and everywhere planted with different types of tree and going into the outskirts of Homs I had a read of LP now thinking of going to Hama, we shall see. In we drove to Homs Bus Station and off I got checking my watch it was only 1020hrs so agreed a 1000 Lira price with a taxi driver to go to Crac Des Chevaliers and come back to the bus station for Hama, he took my shoulderbag, put it in his boot and we were away, it was 1035hrs. There is no bus to Crac des Chevaliers but I could have got bus to Tartus to drop me off at the main highway but this is my lazy day way out of my no walking day. Homs was a transport hub and as we drove through it its only sights were the usual 100s of 4-5-6 storey blocks of flats but it was clean. One thing was very noticeable was the green trees, green fields and no desert anywhere so we must be in a valley plain very fertile area. Seen a sign for Crac des Chevaliers and turning right we drove off the main highway taking the high road to high up in the mountains and followings the road signs going up twisting turning hairpin bends and looking for miles down along the valleys we finally reached the parking area below the most imposing Castle battlement Castle walls I have ever seen in my life, it was enormous. I asked my driver did he want to come with me and smiling he said yes and across the timber plant moat walkway we went into the Castle and I paid 150 Lira entrance fee, driver got in for nothing as I offered to pay but they said no. In we went just following our instincts passing through a huge dark cavern which was the stables then my God and the Heavens above me leading we went up a spiralling round and round steep stair case me hardly able to fit into it and came out breathless way high up in the battlement. Had a great sightsee looking down the bush green valley and over the mountains in the distance then I took my time gently one step at a time down to the bottom. Made it on to the outside moat battlements and met a French couple from yesterday's Temple of Bel walkie and we all greeted each other with smiles and handshakes then along the battlement all built to perfection I was really and truly pleased to be here. Next back into the main castle and this time panting and sweating badly we made it right up the inside tower steps to the top and wow oh wow the views were out of this world. Took a few thumbs uppers then along very dark stone walkways and taking left then right turns enjoying every turn I made I now had seen what I wanted to see of this 12th Century gem and said to my young fellow driver lets hit de road. Down the hundreds of steps twisting and turning until out we went at the main Castle entrance gate, over the moat bridge and into our car, wow oh wow, what a great start to my day, it was 1310hrs. Away we went downhill me tempted to tell him, slow slow but knew I would be wasting my time until finally me real glad we were on the flat road heading towards the highway with driver saying 1000 Lira for taxi to Tartus or do you want dropped off at highway bus stop. I had two choices and don't usually like paying this sort of money for transport but feeling lazy I said ok, drive me into Tartus with driver now smiling happily. It was a good 30km and I was glad I had made my time saving decision looking at LP as I told him Daniel Hotel, Sharia al – Wahada, Tartus, Tel: 312757. We drove into the full of life and great vibes of Tartus and driver stopped asking a few taxi drivers where to go and getting directions he stopped directly outside the hotel so out I got, grabbed my shoulderbag, paid him the 1000 Lira, shook hands and he was away smiling, it was 1340hrs. Into hotel, paid 700 Lira, got Room 10, got key and up to d-ensuite big bedroom, dumped kit in room and downstairs asking directions to The Cathedral of our Lady of Tortosa and the Old City Walls and was given very detailed instructions by the guy at hotel reception and out I went into the lovely hot sunny day. Tartus was full of many small streets all full of shops of every description and I felt so happy here, it felt like I belonged here. Turned another street corner and there it was the full of life 12th Century very large and imposing big block walls of the Cathedral with a sign on its front, "Museum". Over I went to a kiosk seeing price list, foreigners 150 Lira, Syrians free so said to lady in Kiosk, "me Ottoman Syrian", she smiled saying "you Crusader English, 150 Lira please" and both laughing I paid, got my ticket and into the Cathedral which was now a museum but well worth the price and first there was a row of all sizes of stone coffins then a row of body shaped coffins all 100-200 AD, just unbelievable. Walking around it was real fun even though most of the artefacts had no description they were a joy to study and admire. Out from the inside and a walk around the 100+ all different 100-500 AD artefacts all around the Cathedral some like the coins from Alexandra the Great in glass cases, I was in a happy dream. Finished my walk and saying my smiling

Goodbyes to the lady receptionist who said 'be careful Crusader' as I had asked her the way to the old City walls and only a couple of turns down a few packed full of life street I seen the huge stone block walls. Getting closer it was fun as well as residents had burrowed many doors and windows into the walls and were living in many tiny little dwellings all over the walls with twisting stone steps up to their doors, what a sight. No rigid plan just got lost following many little alleys all cut out of the 2-3-4-5m thick walls with people living everywhere in it, I sometimes couldn't stop laughing. Had now seen this colourful living quarter so done a left and yeah man yeah I was now down on the full promenade seafront, what a true lovely sunny day joy. I seen The Cave outdoor café with its indoor section completely in the Fortress wall as it seemed every café, every shop along this section of seafront wall was but happy as a Crusader lark I had a tea and 2 sweet scones enjoying my great day. Up and away after paying 200 Lira and then gently strolled along the rocky seafront promenade with lots of beautiful girls all enjoying the sun sitting on the square timber and marble seats, this is the life. Taking the inner full of life and shops streets I made it back to my Hotel, got key and upto room. Stripped off and had a much needed shave and shower, kit on and sat for 45mins having a read of LP regarding tomorrow and the next few days as will be heading for Jordan soon. It was 1920hrs when I went out but Tartus was a very vibrant place and even got chatted up a few times by 2-3 girls all full of life, what a wonderful world. Had 2 coffees and chocolate cakes in two cafes along the seafront and paying my second bill and away I was waved over by a beautiful big firm curvy chico whose first words in pigeon English was, "I go with you" and as I looked into her love sick eyes I knew our love would survive for many more Syrian Centuries AD and said yes, she said 300 Lira and even as I guessed she was trying it on my love was so rampant I said yes but where, she said cum cum and taking my arm and smiling into each others sex filled lovers eyes she took me up a narrow Souk and quickly knocking a door we where along a hall and into the 2nd room which was a lovely big double bedroom. Quickly getting her 300 Lira out I left it on a small dresser and kissing and fondling each others heavenly bodies we stripped off she was so beautiful and so rampant as onto the firm bed it was like a dream as she was on top we both sometimes foaming at the mouth and groaning in lust filled sexual ecstasy we where or she was pounding me into the firm mattress in exotic Syria passionate true style love I never felt anything like it in my life then she the boss we changed positions me on top and her screaming in sensual Syria love biting my neck and ripping my poor buttocks to pieces I nearly biting her nipple off we both screaming in Damascus full moon high passionate lust filled Syrian love we climaxed together are pounding sexual spasms session going on and on I though I was going to have a heart attack as the tingling love sensation vibrations where like electric shocks all over my body then her falling apart her arms lieing full stretch on her bed we slowly came to a sweat scented rest and I gently slid off tightly beside her knowing in our true love I was here to stay she pulled her arm from under me and raking my breasts said "Yu really good man Papa, I want to see you again" and as I give her ass a lovers gentle slap we both smiling got off the bed and got dressed she picking up her money and arm and arm out to the front door we went. She give me one last hug and as we parted with a smile and a peck kiss said "I see you next day" and waving our Goodbyes I blew a kiss at her and out the Souk and along the main drag I happily went thinking Syria love is a mans dream before he dies. Slowly found my way back into hotel and upto my room I went my heart so Syrian happy, stripped off and into bed and asleep a one happy Tartus Syria Wicked Crusader man.

Email Sent: Wed, 10 Feb 2010
Subject: R10, Daniel Hotel, Sharia al-Wahda, Tartus, Syria, Tel312757

Hi All
Jumped a bus,100Lira from Palmyra 0830hrs and arrived Homs bus station 1030hrs, where I was going had no public transport so got a taxi,1000Lira and away 30klms up the mountains to the Crusaders Castle, Crac Des Chevaliers and I have never seen anything like it in my life, so huge and so perfectly built on top off a mountain, took my time walking around it then back into taxi and down the mountain hill all the way to the main highway where I had 2 options, either take a taxi or get out and flag a bus down so must be getting lazy as paid another 1000Lira and another 30Klms to Tartus.
Tartus has a brilliant 12th Century Our Lady of Tortosa Cathedral with lots of 1-200AD statues and artefacts which I like to browse then had a walk into and around its old thick Fort wall that people now lived in, it was so fun to see the little doors burrowed everywhere into the wall.
Tartus is so friendly and so sunny by the sea as its a dock port and full of life, Hi Sailor.
Great sunny promenade with dozens of so friendly cafes.
Plan A is to head for Hamman manyanna then plan b, we shall see.
Its funny when I take a seat on a bus and even when its full no one wants to sit beside me, I mean I have not showered or changed clothes for a week, eyes are glazed and bloodshot, wonder why!!, no comments please, remember we our British!!!!!!!!!!!!!!!!
al de bes
crusader Jack

Day 47, Thursday 11-02-10, Tartus – Hama; Syria

Woke up 0725hrs happy with thoughts running through my sex happy brain of staying one more night but up, underarm wash, face splash, kit on and downstairs and out towards the waterfront. First café was open so into its neat seating area and had my usual Syrian breakie of one boiled egg, cheese, butter, jam, 4 flat sections of bread and a pot of tea and got stuck in, oh la, la. I do love this Syrian jam and just took my time savouring every last bit and scraping the saucer for a last lick and final drink of my tea I paid my 100 Lira bill and away. One sad last final walk along the promenade area seeing the Island of Award another Crusader stronghold with I could see just below in the motor boat harbour small motor boats going back and forth but not this time and still sometimes sad I made it along the inner streets of my much loved Tartus and into hotel. Told happy smiling guy I was leaving in 15mins so he said taxi to bus station area for Homs, I said, yes, so upto room feeling a stir, quickly sat down on the WC and bang, belly cleared for today's travels, cleaned ass, cleaned teeth, final pack of shoulderbag and out downstairs to reception. Guy said, ok taxi here and shaking his hand out I went dumping shoulderbag on the back seat, me in the front and we were away, me a little sad but thinking New day, New town I was happy again as we got to the bus station. Out I got paying him the 100 Lira rip off price but that's taxi drivers anywhere in the world. Into bus station and save the Gods in the heavens above, I said Hama a couple of times and two guys, one taking my shoulderbag and the other taking me to a kiosk where I paid 100 Lira, got an Arabic scribbled ticket and was put on a medium sized nearly full vividly coloured bus, got a seat and we were away, yeah man yeah, it was 0925hrs. Had a read of my photocopy Hama LP then settled back enjoying my ride and passed the great "Crac Des Chevaliers" Crusader Castle which I could plainly see as we drove along the highway road 10km from it. Got to the sort of outskirts of Homs and into a packed melee of buses and Minibuses Bus Station and we stopped. Driver pointing at me and a Minibus nearby, said Hama, so quickly out saying my thanks and said Hama to Minibus driver, he said Hama, so shoulderbag under seat in the back, me on the Minibus and yo ho ho, bless the Saints looking down, 5mins later we were away, my Belfast luck is running good I said smiling to myself. Paid the driver 40 Lira the usual way of passing the money up to the next seat in front and they pass it on to the driver. I got change back but still can't work out their Syrian coins as no numbers on them as far as I could see or maybe it's in Arabic. Minibus was full but not a sardine can and only approximately a 45min run and we drew into the Minibus station and out I got with taxi touts giving me the usual grief. Took my time reading LP photocopy then said to one guy, taxi to Raid Hotel, how much and the usual palaver of hands up just pay whatever I got in thinking con one coming up. He stopped twice driving around the town asking Police and other taxi drivers where is Raid Hotel me laughing to myself thinking it's a famous backpackers hotel, he is a taxi driver and he is letting on he does not know where it is but eventually we got to it and directly beside it the Cairo Hotel. Out I got giving him 50 Lira, he said more so in no mood to argue I took the 50 Lira note back and gave him a 100 Lira note and saying thanks, slammed the door and away starting my walk up the stairs to reception of Raid Hotel, Sharia al – Quwatli, Hama, Tel: 239512, it was 1050hrs. Couple of guys rushed down, one took my shoulderbag and up two flights of stairs we went to reception, I said, room, smiling guy said, yes, 900Lira, I said I thought you had cheaper rooms, he said yes but all full. I didn't believe him but not going down those stairs again so I said ok and he gave me key to Room 46. Guy carrying my shoulderbag and reception guy with me up we went another two flights of stairs and into a lovely d-ensuite, western WC and it looked good so said ok and gave him my Passport, he said come down later. I quickly put my large wallet with other credit card in shoulderbag along with neck pouch and into toilet and bang, a half treacle dobhi drop so that's one job over and finished as I cleaned my ass. Back down to reception, got my Passport and those stairs were a killer, back upto room putting it back in my neckpouch in my orange beachbag and now I am ready to go out. Slow stepping down the stairs to reception as left knee giving me grief as it definitely does not like these stairs I handed my key into reception and down another two flights of stairs then I was out on Sharia Soukri al-Quwatli St with the prominent Clock Tower crossroads on my right so at least I sort of knew where I was. First thing I wanted to do was post a travel note letter to Sandralita so looking at my LP map I crossed the road at the traffic lights and a gently smiling slow walk upto the Post Office, paid 100 Lira for stamps, stuck them on and put letter in yellow postbox and duty done where do I go now for my todays outing. Seen the lovely Orontes River along the Sharia Jamal Abdel Nassar main road so no plans I smiled to myself crossing the bridge over the Orontes seeing big 10-15-20m diameter wooden Norias water wheels with many square buckets on them as they scooped the water from the Orontes River and as the wheel went its full circle tipped the buckets into the aqua ducts and from there to irrigation channels to continually water all the fields nearby, great sight. Checked my LP map and turned right along the river bank on a paved walkway passing the Sarah Hotel in the remains of the very tidy Old City all with restaurants so one could enjoy nice views having a meal but not for me this time. Went through the stone block Archways on the main road and I was now in "The Citadel" which in many parts was very old, in others quite newish. I got a bit lost but eventually found the very big Orthodox Church, all doors were closed which was a bit strange but went in the main iron gates and followed an alley up the side of the big Church and came to a beautiful small Church called The Church of Theotokos and went in its open door. What a truly lovely place with its big coloured Dome and many large colourful paintings, it was a true joy to see, had a little walk around then really chuffed to have seen it I went left up a very old alley with I could see the old remains of I would suppose the Citadel walls and out. Next I made it into and across the main with water fountain courtyard of a beautiful old Mosque which I think was the Grand Mosque but it had a beautiful mosaic tower and a high towering Minaret and a sign above the Mosque entrance: "Welcome to the Fifth Oldest Mosque in Islam". Wow I said to myself as I quickly opened one of the line of doors and peeped into its fully carpeted large Dome very old but very clean interior and said Good Luck Brothers, closed the door and out another door facing the one I had came in and away really chuffed to have been in there. Was now lost but came to more Norias at least 4-5 I could see some very old and I crossed an old stone bridge across a canal with a sign stating: Al Jaziral Green Island, what a truly extraordinary history sight. Still lost but sort of found my way back to the main drag and up a tarmac road to a park on top of a hill and wow oh wow what great fantastic views from every angle of Hama as I slowly walked around the so peaceful and quiet park which even had a very large kids play area. Came out of the park and down along the old streets passing the small very old Al Noun Mosque, 558-1162 AD I think it said on its entrance wall but it had a great old Sq Tower Minaret. Next I took a road going over another old bridge with 4 Norias which was such a magic sight and was probably the Famous Four Norias of Bechriyyat. I had according to my map and reading about Hama seen and done quite a lot, it was 1220hrs. Tried unsuccessfully to find the Minibus parking area for Minibus to Apamea via Suqeilibiyya as will now head for Apamea about 50km away as Apamea after reading LP is another not to be missed Roman ruins city. Gave up on my map reading so flagged down a taxi and agreed a price of 500 Lira for the 51km to Apamea, jumped in and we were away me thinking that's a cheapie. Good fun with the old driver explaining everything to me in Arabic and me agreeing not having a clue what he was saying then we passed the Citadel of Shierzar on a hill above Shierzar Village and turning right I was flabbergasted at the size of the huge Jabel Mountains on my left, wow oh wow, what a sight. Drove into a small village and up and over a hill with the large village of Qala at al-Mudiq in a Medieval Castle on top of a hill, what fantastic sights at each turning I could see. Next out along our road in an open plain I couldn't miss it as it seemed hundreds of tall marble/stone columns were lined each side going across the plain for it looked like for 2-3miles. Driver pulled into a parking area and out I got giving him a 500 Lira note, he said, more, more and with his finger writing 800 Lira on the car dashboard, I said writing 500 Lira on the car dashboard that's what we agreed, he said ok 700 Lira so it was a good price anyway so I gave it to him saying my thanks. He said one hour, drive back so had a quick think, it was 1325hrs and I was looking forward to taking a 50-100 Lira minibus back to Hama but someone's got to treat me and I said ok 300 Lira as he was snookered if he goes go back without me he has lost a good screw, he said ok, 400 Lira and I laughed shaking his hand saying one hour and I was away towards the most magic beautiful impressive ruins I have ever seen. Over and paid 150 Lira entrance fee and guy giving me the ticket said it's a 2km straight walk on the Roman road pointing down along and between the many 10m high stone/marble columns going east to west each side of the road and I was away on the main street. I had no map of the ruins so first sign I came to was the Church ruins where many big square stone blocks had fallen down then the Asmal Mosque ruins then halfway along this totally amazing main street I came to North Gate. Just taking my time I climbed the big blocks looking at the large Arch all built 2nd Century BC by Seleuars 1, a General of Alexandra the Great until the city was ravished and destroyed by the Persians in 540 AD and again in 612 AD when Syria was overrun by the Muslims Apamea and slowly it became a ghost city and was finally destroyed in an earthquake in 1157 AD. Touts would drive up on motorcycles every 15mins or so and try to sell me Roman coins or small artefacts but I said my thanks and kept going, they might be genuine but I doubt it. It was a very fascinating walk and I finally reached the other end and looking back in the bright sunlight this was without a doubt the most fascinating Roman ruins site I have been to see. Went right on a little path across the plain and then right again having to climb up and over the old Citadel big stone battlement walls which stretched in full circumference for 7km with all the remains of the City in them. Coming back into the main street I came to the Bakehouse Worship Pillar with many inscriptions on it than away across the fields again and up a small hill looking down on the most beautiful scenery lake, which I was lucky to have seen. You without a doubt need a guidebook to follow or trail this enormous site but the 2km long full of columns main street was a joy in itself as I was back on it at the ruins of Zeous Temple. Could have stayed a day but slowly made my way back along the so brilliant and powerful main street and out to the tarmac road where my old Roman Syrian taxi driver was waiting, it was 1550hrs. Greeting each other with ollah's and smiles I got into his taxi and away passing the very imposing Museum in the centre of the small village but it was closed so on we went on our no traffic drive all the way back to Hama and he dropped me off outside my hotel, paid him 400 Lira and he was away so considering everything I think I had done well, it was 1705hrs. Walked back down the street and into Ali Baba small locals only café and had a big rolled in flat bread, a meat, veg, chip sandwich and three lovely teas, wow oh wow, just the job, paid my 130 Lira and away. Seen an empty barbers and in for a neat No1 on my getting bushy silk hair, 100 Lira, not a bad price. Now remembered I was running a bit short of readies so put my card in an Arab Bank ATM, pressed the 5000 Lira fast cash button and sweat starting to browse my forehead out it came, yeah man yeah I shouted, grabbed my cash and card and was one happy no hair man walking the Hama streets. Back into hotel, got my key and upto room. No rush had a nice hot water shave and face wash then out for a walk thinking where will I go manyanna. Hama was a really fun walk with its well lit streets and shops of all sorts open till late and I had 2 lovely coffees in two cafes, one overlooking the Norias Wheels and that was my great history day in Hama nearly over. Slow walk back to hotel, got key and upto room, stripped off and into bed still dreaming where am I going manyanna and fell into a Roman ruins deep Hama sleep.

How "Not" to Travel North Africa, Middle East, Israel & Malta and "Still Enjoy Yourself"

Norias Waterwheel, Hama

Date: Thu, 11 Feb 2010
Subject: Rm46,Riad Hotel, Sharia al-Quwatli,Hama,Tel239512

Hi All
I loved the vibes of Tartus but jumped a Minibus to Hom's, then from Hom's jumped another to Hama, total time approx 1hr40min.
Had a great rest of the morning walking the along the river seeing the Norias rings which are many 10-20-30m dia cartwheels taking water out of the Orontes River then tipping it into irrigation ducts for water for the grassy green fields as now in a very fertile valley.
Then into another Armenian so lovely Church and even into the 5th oldest Mosque in Islam and walking across its hollowed sq and peeping into the Mosque itself saying we our brothers and away and got about 100m when the chanters started, good fun.
Went 50klms to Apamea in the afternoon to the most magnificent full height of col for 2 klms Main St and other Roman ruins all 2nd Century AD, fantastic day.
Now back and had my sandwich roll, don't know what was in it but it tasted ok.
Heading to either Damascus or Amman in Jordon manyanna but Amman seems to far away for one journey and Damascus is only 3hrs away, mind you saying that I keep seeing signposts for Bagdad.
I passed one the other day and Bagdad was only 174Klms away, wat yu tink!!!,keep away or go in and start trouble as yu know what us Aldershot hoods are like!!.
Will wake up in de morning and put plan into action.
al de bes
Jack

Map 1 of Jordan

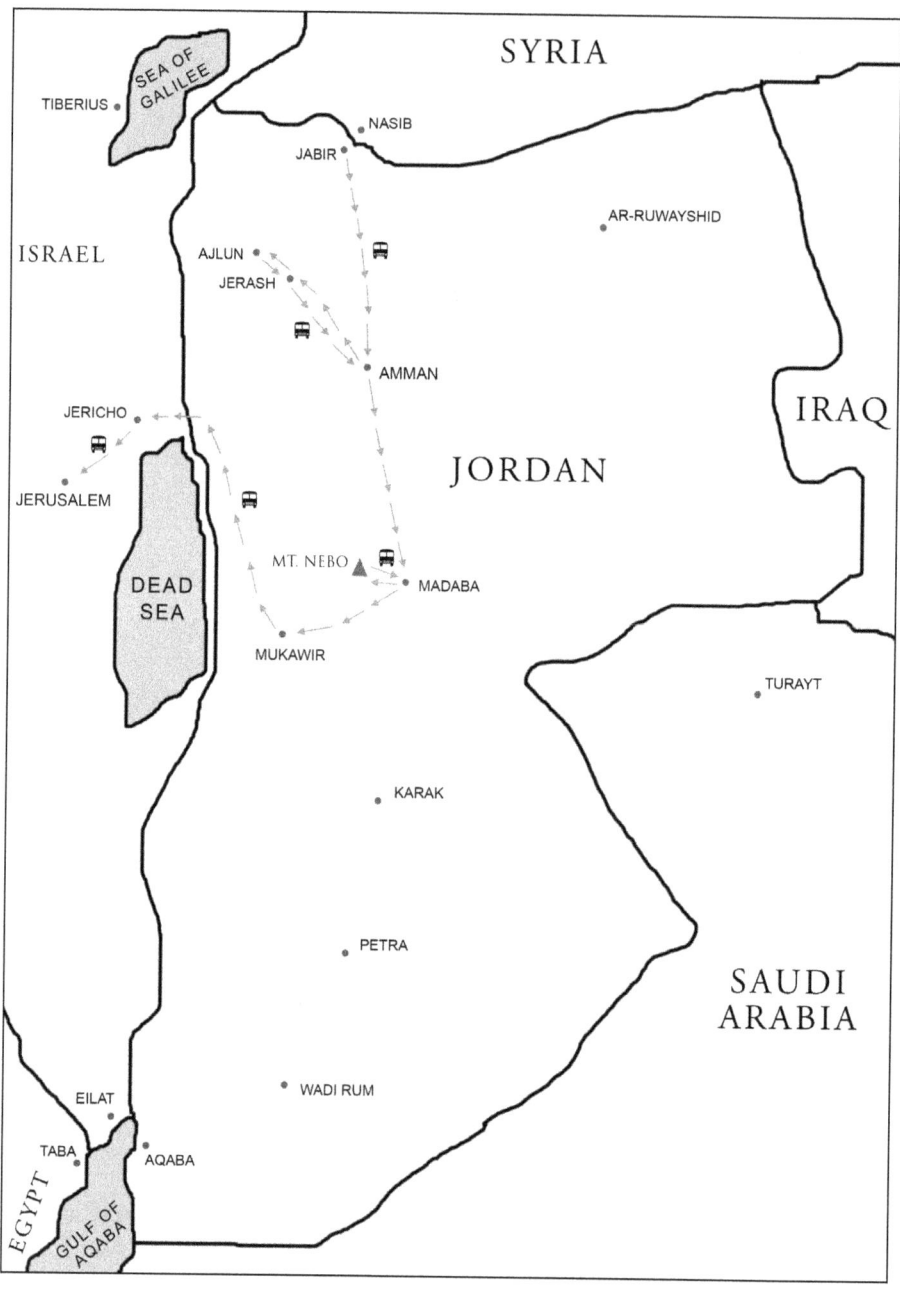

1) **JORDAN** is a modern Country but has great ancient mystical majestic ruins attractions with its main one now 'One of the New Seven Wonders of the World' called Petra a huge stone curved City lost in the mountains for 700 years only finally rediscovered in 1812 is a true walk back in bygone Arab and Bedouins history. Everywhere be it in the deserts or the Biblical folklore towns the Jordanian people are without a doubt a happy people who go out of their way to Welcome and ensure you are Happy.
2) Capital; Amman
3) Jordan achieved Independence in 1946
4) Climate; Ave temp Jan-Mar;21c
5) Language; Arabic, English
6) Currency; Jordanian Dinar, 1$US = 1JD
7) Visa; Not required, 30 day issued on arrival
8) Return flight £51 + £154 ATM, hotel, food, train to Gatwick
9) Today's ongoing update of day to day accommodation, travel, food, drinks costs = £2241

Day 48, Friday, 12-02-10, Hama; Syria – Amman; Jordan

The ole chanters woke me up 0400hrs then drifted back to sleep but not for long as someone was playing loud music from one of the rooms and it was coming up the window well, sometimes I think hotels do this on purpose so you sleep in and don't want to move. Anyway, finally up at 0745hrs, face splash, underarm wash, kit on and down for breakie enjoying my 4 flat slices of bread with a hard boiled egg, butter, cheese and oh la, la, the lovely Syrian jam, life is good. Back upto room, cleaned teeth, final pack of shoulderbag, man oh man the saviour of my life a lovely treacle dobhi drop, cleaned ass, and nearly forgot my dobhi. Went to the balcony drying line, grabbed my long cargo, 2 shirts, underpants and socks and stuck them in my shoulderbag and downstairs to reception giving guy my key. He said you go, I said yes and we shook hands him saying two nights, two breakfasts, dobhi and a tea, 2300 Lira so gave him the money and I was away downstairs and out, it was 0930hrs. Flagged down a taxi on the no cars, no shops open and dead as a doornail street and told him Pullman Bus Station, he said 50 Lira, I said ok, shoulderbag in boot, me in front and we were away. He dropped me off outside at the taxi rank, paid him the 50 Lira, got my shoulderbag from boot and trolley handle up I walked into the nearly deserted very large bus station and seen only one bus company large kiosk with no people in it so over and asked guy for bus to Damascus. He said yes, 1000hrs, fare 140 Lira, so my luck is really good, showed him my Passport, paid him the 140 Lira, got my ticket with seat 36 and only a 5min wait, bus No57 drew into the bus stand, I put shoulderbag in boot, got stub, climbed on the bus and very cheerfully and smiling I took my seat 36 in the www.alahliah-co.com bus. Only another 5min wait as conductor checked tickets and we were away, it was 1000hrs, what a brilliant start to my day. Sat back enjoying driving out of lively Hama then over a long bridge and looking down along a deep valley and we were away going fast on the no traffic road, wow oh wow. Still had not made up my mind whether to stay in Damascus or head straight for the border of Jordan as per my usual planning, but same same, we shall see. Conductor came along giving everyone a plastic cup which he filled with water so had my 1015hrs Naafi break just sitting watching the Syria village world as we drove through along the main highway. Went past a signpost for Homs, 5km, then drew into a large bus and Minibus station and stopped, it was 1030hrs. Half the men got off and I said to myself I better get off then seen them all pulling cigarettes out to have a smoke so sat still. After 20mins, more people loaded baggage in the hold, everyone got back on and we were away. As my usual good trick I fell asleep and woke up as we were travelling fast through the hot sunny bare stone sandy desert and way on my right were huge mountains with snow capped peaks, truly amazing. Passed through Qura and seen sign Damascus 94km, it was 1130hrs. Dozed off again then seen sign Damascus 74km, it was 1200hrs so now definitely thinking of heading straight through to Amman in Jordan. Amman is 3hrs from Damascus so if I can keep my luck rolling and get straight across Damascus to bus station for Amman in Jordan I can check my time from there seeing if its worth it. We finally drew into Damacus bus station and everyone got off, I got my shoulderbag from the bus hold and an old guy said taxi, I said yes, taxi to bus station for Amman, he said 300 Lira, I said that's expensive, he said no, so tried to haggle but no luck so bag in back, me in the front and we were away 25km he said across Damascus to bus station for Amman, Jordan, it was 1240hrs on a bright lovely hot sunshine day. Most we drove was 20km and into a Minibus station he parked up at a barrier with guys all shouting Amman-Lebanon, I said Amman and gave driver his 300 Lira. Guy took my bag into the road Checkpoint building as I had to put my shoulderbag through x-ray, grabbed it and out the door the other side and 2-3 guys said service taxi Amman, I said ok and was pointed to front seat of an upmarket big car with 2 veiled black robed ladies in the back and was offered 1400 Lira, go now, so said ok, lets go mon. Gave driver my Passport and 1400 Lira and he took Passport into an office then out giving me it back so stuck it in my neckpouch and we were away, it was 1310hrs, man oh man, things are looking big time good. It was an AC car and I sat back thinking how much is Visa going to cost at the border and checking my money I had 2000 Lira and a 20$US bill so should have enough, we shall see as with my careful planning I was so well organised. Driver was a looney as we drove out of Damascus on a good 3 lane highway with many signposts for Jordan so sat back enjoying my ride. Had a half packet of biscuits eats with my bottle of Fanta and seen sign; Jordan border 40 km, it was 1400hrs. It was now a grassy lots of good soil flat areas each side of our new two lane highway and I had a look at my photocopy Amman City map and picked Select Hotel for Visa paperwork. Driver said Visa is 500 Syria Lira or 10 JD (Jordan Dollars), he said 1JD is worth 2$US, I can't see that I thought but we shall see. At 5km from border driver had to stop at a checkpoint for a paperwork check, it was 1415hrs then another stop only 100m further on at a big arched Tower when driver got out taking paperwork up to a kiosk, 5mins later back in car and we were away only 50m and into Passport/customs. I filled in the customs form and over to the Diplomats exit and guy filled in his part of the paperwork and bang, diplomat exit Syria stamp on Passport and Consulate Jack was exiting Syria, it was 1430hrs. Back out and into car and it was big time real hot then waiting for driver to come back with about 20 x 200 packets of fags and we all had to get out of the car as he stuffed them under the seats and under the boot and opening one 10x20 packet he give me 3x20 packets saying keep, I said no, you keep as if he was caught he would blame me as us Arthur St hoods know the score so now we are smugglers, it was 1450hrs. Away we went again with one more stop, Passport check and a 100m drive and came to and passed a sign "Welcome to Hashemite Kingdom of Jordan" and upto Jordan Border Passport Control. First I lined up at Visa office then when I got to glass front guy said go to Passport control, I said have you any paperwork he said no, so over to Passport control for foreigners and showed guy Passport, he asked me where I had come from and address in Jordan, I showed him Select Hotel from my photocopy LP, he typed my name into his computer and said ok, go get a Visa so saying out loud to myself they are crazy off I went back around to the Visa office. Lined up behind 3 Turks but it was quite quick and 10mins later he took my Passport, stuck Visa on it and said 10JD, I said you take Syrian Lira, he said no pointing out the door, exchange just next door so swearing out loud calling them plonkers I went up to the currency exchange gaving the guy 2010 Syria Lira and he gave me back 29 Jordan Dinar, (JD). Back to Visa kiosk, gave the guy 10JD, he stuck another stamp on the Visa stamp and said ok, go to Passport Control. Keeping my now livid temper under control I went back to Passport Control and gave him my Passport and one look at Visa, bang, an enter Jordan stamp and he gave me my Passport back so sliding it in my neckpouch I was out looking for my car and found it up the road. Had a piss in the ladies and gents toilet then into car and we were away on the Holy road into Jordan heading for Amman on a hot bright sunny day, it was 1453ohrs. Seen a signpost Amman 86km so at least 1hrs drive to go but sat back relaxing slowly and glad I had done my well planned spur of the moment trip to Jordan so just sat back looking out of the car window at the sometimes green dusty fields each side of our road. Sort of dozed but at 1620hrs we were it must be in the outskirts of Amman with the two veiled women and taxi driver arguing in Arabic then at 1630hrs he pulled into a road full of large taxi cars one side and buses the other and said this is our final stop. Out we all got and I grabbed my shoulderbag from boot, said my Goodbyes to the Jordan ladies and taxi driver then flagged down another yellow taxi, showed him Jebel Amman a sort of backpackers area and we drove there which was ok downtown area but he didn't understand English and we stopped at 2nd circle roundabout. He said have I phone number which I did, he phoned the hotel getting directions then smiled saying in Arabic I now know where to go. We drove quite a way but into a good shopping, cafes and restaurant area and then along Al-Baoniya St until we came to Select Hotel, Al-Baoniya St, Amman, Jordan, Tel4637101. Out I got with shoulderbag, paid him 3JD and he was away, it was 1720hrs, what a marvellous day if you like travelling 300km, crossing 2 borders and into a New town, New currency, thats life, I was so happy. Into hotel and it appeared empty but said to guy at reception, any rooms, he said yes, got 2 keys and up the stairs and showed me Room 24, 2 big d-ensuite rooms with two single beds. I said how much, he said 18JD so trying to work it out but giving up I said what's that in US dollars, he said 22$US so said to myself it will do. Back down to reception, gave him my Passport, filled in the usual paperwork, got my key and upto room with my shoulderbag. Neck pouch and spare wallet into bright orange bag and putting it into shoulderbag I went downstairs too to reception. We had a chat about location, where to go, things to do and he was very helpful and spoke great English so said my thanks and out I went. Just followed his guidance for my first night and turned left at the big Mosque and into the well lit middle street of Jebel Al-Weibdeh and walked its full length sometimes taking rights or lefts seeing plenty of shops, cafes and small sized supermarkets so at least there is some life although it was not in centre of Amman. Into internet café letting everyone know where I was and next stop into a hot food sit down takeaway café and had a big plate of fish and chips, yeah man yeah, I was in the pure heavens above as I did manage to eat every last bit. Drank my last drop of coke, paid my 2-50JD charge and still walking about I now had done the full circle so slowly made my way back towards my hotel. Went into a café for my last tea and two chocolate scones and that was my first Jordan night nearly over, it was 2220hrs. Back to hotel and sat in the lounge with another cup of tea having a read of my photocopy LP about things to do and visit and funny enough I had not done hardly any walking but felt tired so upto room, stripped off and into bed and smiling the hunk is in town yu Jordan chicos and asleep dreaming Jordan desert sexy love.

Email Sent: Fri, 12 Feb 2010
Subject: Rm24, Select Hotel, Al-Baoniya St, Amman, Jordan, Tel :4637102

Hi All
Had my breakie then jumped a bus, 1400Lira, 1000hrs from Hama to Damascus, 1230hrs and put plan B into operation as didn't want to spend half a day in a city I knew so got a taxi across to service taxi station for shared taxi's to Amman and 2 Jordan ladies had just turned up so they took the back seat paying 700Lira and I was in the front paying 1400Lira and we where away. Through Syria border with guards giving a sigh of relief then upto Jordan border all with our taxi driver storing about 20+200 packets of cigs all over the cab but bang, enter Jordan stamp on Passport and back in taxi and all the way along its Holy Rd into Amman to service taxi drop off point and got another Taxi, 3 Jordan Dinar (JD) to above,18 JD for d-ensuite including breakie.
I can't work the JD out it but 70JD = 100$US.
Just out for a walkie but will have a read tonight ref places to visit and take it from their.
Danka Geoff.
al de bes
Jack

Day 49, Saturday, 13-02-10, Amman; Jordan

Definitely heard the chanters but turned over having to be careful I didn't fall out of my 700mm wide bed with its 50mm thick mattress but continued sleeping until checking my bedside clock, it was 0750hrs. Up I got, underarm wash, face splash, kit on including pullover which I don't think I will need and downstairs to breakfast room, guy saying please sit down. I sat down and 2mins later my 3 flat slices of bread, 1 cube of butter, 1 cube of jam, a portion of cheese and a small pot of tea arrived. Got stuck in definitely missing my Syria jam, finished my tea having a look at my LP map for where I am going to go today. Talking to the reception guy he said Rome Amphitheatre and a few other places and he will show me on the big map in reception. I said I just go to room to clean my teeth and I will be back down. Upto room and bang, a lovely full clearance dobhi drop, cleaned ass, cleaned teeth, checked beachbag and had a letter for Sandralita so ready to go I was out locking my door and downstairs to reception, it was 0900hrs. I had a chat with the guy at reception and he showed me on the big map which way to the Roman Theatre and out I went turning right going down the hill I was nearly crying with happiness and was just full of so happy emotion as at 0915hrs in the morning I was sauntering down a hill in Amman, yeah man yeah and smiling broadly at everyone or anything I was so full of joy. Got down to the bottom of the hill and turned right on Al-Malek al-Hussein St and there was yesterday's dropping off point when I came from Damascus and I had shown it to at least 3 taxi drivers and no one knew where it was and I had spent 30-45mins driving around and I could have walked it in 2-5mins. My day ruined I smiled again and was back to my happy normal self and still on al-Hussein Street I drew 100JD at an ATM and passing dozens of hotels, cafes and the place had great vibes. Done a right asking a guy who said next right I went into the Post Office. Took my turn in the stamp queue, got to counter, gave guy my sealed travel notes A5 envelope, he weighed it and said 2JD so gave him a 5JD note saying 2 post card stamps, he said we don't sell them until 1100hrs so looking at him I said ok, he stuck stamp on A5 envelope, gave me my change and envelope and said pointing at post box, post, so I did. Out on street a guy was selling airmail envelopes so put a couple of sheets of LP photocopy in it, put Kelly's address on it, licked a small piece at the bottom and back to post office and queued and up to the desk again and saying stamp for England. He opened a safe with keys and weighing the envelope he gave me a one 850fils, (cent) stamp, I said one stamp for a postcard so he gave me another 850fils stamp, I paid him and was away but a bit annoyed at all this rig moral for a bloody stamp. Anyway in the happy sunny very warm sun I was back to normal and came to the lovely beautiful ruins of The Nymphaeum or Chief Fountain and it was so well built as I had a walk around its round well fountain ruins, great start to my day. Everywhere there were bus tours and it appeared many Germans by the sound of them. Went on down along the full of life streets turning left on Hashemi St and wow oh wow, could see it in the distance, yeah man yeah, the full size curved up the side of a mountain, the Roman Theatre 138 AD with many other ruins near it. Now doing well I made my way upto it marvelling at its size which reading LP it can hold 6000 people. You didn't need to go inside to see it as most of it could be seen from the road but paid my 1 JD entrance fee at the kiosk, got my ticket and in and it was well worth it being on and walking across the high stage all built in the 2nd Century AD in the reign of Antonius Pius who was ruler of the Roman Empire from 138 – 161AD. I went into the beautiful preserved Odeon which was a smaller stage and seating area for musicians. It was just fantastic true history I was seeing and walking on then back liking the huge Columns which once were The Forum the biggest Public Square in Imperial Rome and looking up the rows of curved in a half circle seats going up the face of the mountain hill I said, you only get one chance, and up I went. Got all the way sweating like a donkey's ass to the top then slowly back down having a few thumbs up photo shoots. Back down to the bottom and had a rest seeing a beautiful girl in her tight slacks slowly one step at a time come down the aisle next to my seat and I said, "you're a slow chico", she laughed saying "I don't want to take any chances," I said you are right as we laughed and went out own ways. Out onto the main road and a slow walk around Hashemite Sq and I was tempted to sit down and have a tea but kept going along Ouraysh St then done a right along the packed bazaars with Jordan music blaring out from everywhere. Had a quick peep into the King Hussein Mosque seeing all the Bedouin headdress Arab Jordan bare feet men kneeling on the prayer mats and holy smoke and Allah above, the chanters started from the Minarets loudspeakers above, I looked at my watch, it was 1150hrs. All over town every Minaret was giving it root so I was away looking up the top of the mountain hill I could see prominent old ruins so asking a shop owner how to get to the Citadel, (Castle). He pointed at the steps going up and said 300 steps so off I went, got halfway up still surrounded and overlooked by dwellings then crossed a road and next row of steps the dwellings were left behind until I was sweating and panting really bad my left knee just about staying in place but kept going. Steps disappeared altogether and I followed a small path and turning a corner I was there on top of the mountain hill looking down everywhere at Amman, what a true lovely sight. First stop I made was the Temple of Hercules, 161 AD with its lovely pillars and met Joe a young guy from New York travelling Jordan and we had a photo shoot and who surprised me only the lovely beautiful US chico from the Roman Theatre and as we all shook hands and introduced ourselves, she was Christine also from New York. It was fun as we all chatted then sadly parted as Christine was going down as she had to meet her tour group but it was nice to meet such young travelling people. I was really very impressed with the Citadel as the remains were very imposing as next I strolled over and around the Umayyad Palace, 720 AD which was with its big Dome really very impressive. Out and looking down the Umayyad Cistern then into the Byzantine Basilica a very colour Mosaic from the 6th century but everywhere was a dream on the bright sunny day. Enjoyed my walk and as usual could have stayed all day but had a peep inside the National Archaeological Museum and was tempted but didn't fancy paying 2 JDS entrance fee so kept going on down the hill. Came to a stop and setting on a small wall with people looking at me in amazement I had my tin of corned beef, 2 rolls, a bottle of Coke din din, belly full, me happy on I went down to the bottom of the hill. Orientating myself with the King Hussein Mosque I was away I hoped with my decent map reading in the direction of the Minibus station for Wadi As–Seer and Iraq Al-Amir. I walked quite a long way along the vibrant packed full of shops then past a fresh fruit market and knew I was getting near. Got to a packed full of Minibuses area and seen Muhajireen Police Station so I was spot on. I asked a driver for Minibus to the village of Wadi As-Seer, he pointed across the road and over I went and got on and 5mins later we were full and away. Paid my fare with a 1JD note and got coin change still not a clue what they meant then conductor tapped me on the shoulder as Minibus stopped, pointed at a nearly full Minibus at another roundabout so off I got and onto this one and same, same we were away within 5mins. Paid my fare with coins from change and still had 3 coins left as high up the beautiful valley road we went and it was such great sights looking everywhere down and across the valley. Went downhill then crossing a stone bridge we were going uphill again and stopped at another Minibus station at Wadi As-See and as conductor said finished I got off the Minibus with him pointing up a steep hill saying something in Arabic. Panting like a goat I got 20m up the hill and there was another Minibus station so showing a nearly packed Minibus driver Iraq Al-Amir from my LP photocopy he said ok, pointing get on which I did and 5mins later all seats taken we were away. It was big time great scenery then looking out my right hand window I seen what I hoped I had come here for, yes, a double row of caves high in the mountain cliff. I was tempted to jump off but didn't and 5mins later going downhill we pulled into the village of Iraq Al-Amir and that was our final stop so we all got off. I could see the large ruins not far away which were the Qasr al-Abad (Palace of the Slaves), 2nd Century BC and walked down to it just as a tour bus pulled up and a bus load of Germans by the sound of them got out and we all walked around the perfect old ruins and no wonder as the blocks of stone they were built with were sometimes 3m x 2m x 1.5m and one or two measured 7m x 3m, it was truly amazing and is was built with the largest blocks used in any ancient building anywhere in the Middle East. Done my jumping up and over ancient ruin walls and peeping everywhere as I usually do so had seen it all so back out to tarmac road. Seen two Chico's in a car with their window open and saying lift if you are going back up the hill and they looked at me smiling and saying nothing so I was off going up a very steep tarmac road panting heavily, swearing out loud I managed to reach a stretch of level road and the two chicos in their red car passed me. I shouted, lift lift and smiling and waving at them they drove on without stopping, up yours I shouted into the lovely sunny hot day and kept going. I finally made the road below the caves and seen the red car so up the neat steps to the first row of caves and looking in them there were excavations going on as it looked like their was walls in the ground of the caves, had a piss in one. Seen another row of steps going up to the second row of caves all called Iraq Al-Amir (Caves of the Prince) and up I went stopping at the top final steps seeing and saying my hellos to the two beauty queen driving Chico's and got smiling hellos back. I went into the top left hand cave and it stretched back into the mountain for approximately 30m and the further I walked into the cave the real colder it got so back out and me and the two chicos had a chat asking each other the usual questions and it came about that they were working here in Jordan. Sarah was from Austria and Suzie who looked like a very beautiful Hong Kong girl said she was Jordanian and as we chatted and looked into the final cave going down I was offered a lift back and was put in the front beside Sarah. Me in my usual common sense saying it's a pity the Jordanian's drive on the wrong side of the road both girls laughing saying we all drive on this side of the road, me laughing. They both were good fun and a good laugh and it was Sarah's first time behind the wheel in Jordan but she drove really well and as we got into Amman they dropped me off at the corner beside my hotel, what a lovely good deed. I said my thanks and blowing them a kiss they were away. Into a store just up near the Mosque and bought a tin of sardines and 2 packets of biscuits and back to hotel, it was 1810hrs. Enjoyed my lovely sardine, 2 soft bread rolls, lemonade, din din then stripped off, had a nice dobhi drop, cleaned ass, cleaned teeth and a nice shave and a half warm water shower, just the job. Dried off, new clean kit on and out down to reception having a chat with the very helpful reception guy about a plan for tomorrow and out I went and all the way down Al Hussein St passing the Karnak Hotel in the centre of life area of downtown Amman and went in, guy said yes he had an en-suite room at 10-15-20JD so thinking this would have been a better town centre location, I said my thanks and out. The downtown area streets were really buzzing and full of light and life and I really enjoyed my walk. I had a tea in an upstairs café looking down along the streets then made it back to my hotel via Paris Sq a full of cafés roundabouts then up Al-Karshee St buying some biscuits and into my hotel. Had a tea eating my biscuits then upto room, stripped off and into bed dreaming an Austria & a Jordan chico's were beside me keeping me happy in a threesome love triangle and asleep my vivid dreams trying to keep me awake!.

Roman Theatre, 2nd Century A.D.

Email Sent: Sat, 13 Feb 2010
Subject: Amman and Iraq Al-Amir; Jordan

Hi All

Great hot sunny sightsee day with first the magnificent Nymphaeum fountain ruins then the Roman Theatre, 2nd Century AD with all its seats going up 50 rows cut into the side of a hill and can hold 6000?, fantastic builders and Architects where de ole Romans.

Climbed the 300!! steps that exist and then a small path and into the most magic Citadel which was a dream to walk around on the hill overlooking Amman. Walked around the tall pillars of the Temple of Hercules, 161 AD and around Umayyad Palace then the Umayyad Cistern all 6th Century but every turn was just great pure history.

Down the hill and stopped halfway down for my tin of corned beef and 3 rolls din din, wow it was tasty then a walk and a peep into the King Hussein Mosque, AD 640 and now going for a bus ride. Jumped a Minibus to Iraq Al-Amir and 30mins later after 1-2-3? changes I was walking the Qusr al-Abad(Palace of the Slaves) which was constructed with the biggest stones ever in the history of building with some 3m long 1-5 wide and 2m high, just completely amazing then panting like donkey made it back up the hill to Iraq al-Amir(Caves of the Prince), all caves in 2 rows along a cliff face and they where so cool inside and luck was in as 2 lovely girls one from Austria and one from Jordan who I met in the caves gave me a lift back in their hired car, this is the life.

Just now in the very lively downtown area of Amman so might catch a Valentino looking for love!!!!.

Heading for Jerash manyanna for a wonder about.

Wishing ALL you Lovely Chico's a "Very Happy Valentino's Day and Night" and have a good one.

al de bes

Jack

Day 50, Sunday, 14-02-10, Amman – Jerash; Jordan

Finally up at 0800hrs after a very rough nights sleep as up with diarrhoea 2-3 times then phone ringing at 0600hrs which I answered with guy saying early call 0600hrs, I said no, he said sorry and I went back to bed. Underarm wash, face splash, kit on and downstairs to breakfast room meeting Tai's the very lively beautiful Belgium girl and we had a chat. She was here for two months doing surveys on behalf of Tourism for Jordan to see how it could or might be improved, great chat then she left for work. Finished my 3 flat slices, 1 butter, 1 jam and pot of tea breakie, back to room, teeth clean and out downstairs to start my new day. I flagged down a taxi with bearded round cap old driver and showed him the Bus station for Jerash written in Arabic by reception and he said ok. Got talking or he was talking telling me British TV runs down Muslims and portray them as wanting to kill all Christians but Muslims were not bad people its just British TV. Listening to him and thinking about all my travels through all these Muslim countries he was right and had made a point so as we got to the Bus Station he drove around it then stopped saying and pointing, Jerash Bus. I said how much, he said 1.50JD, I gave him 5JD and said take 2JD as that's what hotel reception said fare will be, he said why, I said "we are brothers" and shook his hand and he gave me 3JD change. Out of taxi and onto bus and it took quite a while to fill but eventually we were away, it was 1000hrs. I checked all my loose coin change and could now see in very small print what they were worth and counted 6 x 5 fil + 4 x 10 fil and 1 x 25 fil coins and gave it to conductor and getting a 10 fil coin back. Bloke next to me gave him a 1JD note and got it looked like 2 x 25 fil coins back so I was well taken to the cleaners for 30 fil, bus robbers never stop. Reached outskirts of Jerash and could see the massive Roman ruins and we went past a huge Arch and up a hill and stopped with a line of columns on my left behind a fence and the biggest and thickest Arch I have seen on my right so off the bus we all got. I knew the pay entrance was back down the hill about ½ km away yet there was another entrance/exit but no pay kiosk facing the Bus station as these Jordanians don't seem to think about making everything central. Must see the huge Arch ruins I said to myself and even looking on the LP map they were not on it so down the old bridge steps I went having a stroll in and around the 2-3 big huge block stone built Arches which was fun then up the steps again and across the road going into the open fence gate of the City of Jerash but guards stopped me saying I must go down the hill to the ticket office entrance so off I went in the lovely hot sun. I passed the huge Hadrian's Arch known also as the Triumphal Arch, AD 129 which was built to honour Emperor Hadrian who was visiting that year, it was something I will always remember as it was so striking. Came to the large original Hippodrome and it had a sign; Gladiators and Chariot Race 1130hrs, it was 1125hrs so upto the pay kiosk, paid 12JD, got my ticket and into the original Roman Hippodrome I went climbing up 60 stone seats stretching for 50m or more until I was on the top one with great views and sat down seeing all the Gladiators and chariots and fully dressed Roman Soldiers across the other side of the large sandy circle of the Hippodrome, wow I said to myself, this will be fun. With a large bugle sound our show started with a 5min talk to all of us approximately 30-40 tourists telling us all that the language used is Roman Latin. Then with every second step a shout, the 6 rows of 4 Roman Soldiers in each row walked grandly across the Hippodrome and Sergeant or Officer giving command then halted in front of us. All carried big spear swords and had armoured helmets with armoured chest vests. We were informed everything we are going to see is how the Roman Army went into and fought its battles. Now in two rows we had the Roman Soldiers doing a spear throw then the many different tactics they used in battle all to confuse and deceive the enemy which was great true history and showed me how intelligent and wise the Roman Generals were. Then in Latin orders the Roman Soldiers marched away to one side of the circle. Next we had 8 Gladiators and were shown the either thumbs up or the thumb to one side as in the next few mins we would be deciding as the Roman crowds did whether the wounded Gladiator lieing on the ground would live or die, the first Gladiator fight started. They were using metal real swords but not obviously trying to kill each other but it was a very fast and brutal fight until with a twist of his leg one of them was on the ground with a sword pointing at his throat and we were signalled from the Roman referee, do we want him to live or die and I put my thumb sideways and the referee done a count and he was allowed to live, he stood up and bowed to us. Next fight was extremely lively until one of them again was on the ground and as before the referee in Latin looking at us said, live or die and again I done my sideways thumb to die as most of our watching crowd did and splurge a red splutter of blood surged out from his throat and he was dead and everybody clapping he after 2mins got up, great fun. Next we had the three different colours, red, green and blue chariot race which was very fast going around the circle of the Hippodrome for 4 laps until red robed guy won. We all clapped as it was so interesting and that was the end as the Roman Soldiers, The Gladiators and the three Chariots lined up in the sand below us and we all clapped everyone smiling and were invited down if anyone wanted a close up photo, marvellous start to my day, it was only 1220hrs. I didn't want a 'Hi sailor' photo with half naked Gladiators or Roman Soldiers so on upto the massive Hadrian's Arch and guy said ticket please, I said I buy one going to get my Mars out and he pointed way back further than the Hippodrome and said ticket office. I said you are a useless bunch of idiots, why don't you have the entrance, the ticket office and the bus station in one compact area and back down buying my 3 JD ticket I was fuming at these stupid Jordanians. Back up and in the South Gate, AD 130 which led me into the very large old 100 AD Roman City. No plans but into and around the South Theatre then the Temple of Zeus, AD162 really enjoying my sunshine walk as next into the beautiful Oval Plaza, what a dream of a building. Next keeping going I was on the lovely Cardo Maximus the Colonnaded Street full of tall graceful Columns. Reached the Fountain lovely round remains called the Nymphaeum, done a left really chuffed and came to the remains of St George and St Theodore Churches. Knew from LP there were two other churches and a Jewish Synagogue remains but a bit lost so I gave up. Got all the way to the North Gate and had my Roman tea break of a packet of cream biscuits and a bottle of lemonade sitting in the shade. Finished my bickies and knew I was looking at the North Theatre and over and in and all around its lovely seating area, 165 AD and every hard stone curved seating area were all in place in rows going up, unbelievable. Just kept moving and next into the gorgeous Temple of Artemis and looking up thanking our one above for letting me do it I slowly made my way back to the North Gate passing many tour groups with their guides but not for me as I would get bored following a given route listening to someone. It was still early, only 1420hrs so quickly asking a taxi driver how much to Ajlun, he said 5JD so thinking that's ok, I jumped in and we were away. In chatting in Arabic and English I asked him how much all the way to Qala'at ar–Rabad the Arch Castle in the hill above the village, he said 6JD total so agreed as really chuffed I had met my first honest taxi driver. It was a long way going along the Jordan St road above the deep valleys and then up and up and up bending hairpin bend roads we went and I could see the Majestic huge Arched Castle built by the Arabs as protection against the Crusaders on its high prominent point above the Jordan valley. The castle also served as one of chain pigeon messenger points that messages could be sent from Cairo to Damascus in one day, marvellous. Taxi driver dropped me off at the car park beside the entrance, paid him getting a plea, one more, so gave him one more as the distance we had travelled it was well worth it. Up the steps towards the Castle entrance and guy said ticket, I said I buy, he said pointing way down the steep road about ½ km away, ticket office down there and I said you Jordanians are shit, crap and useless, stuff your castle as no way was I going to walk down that very very steep road and come back up so I walked the neat path around the castle enjoying the terrific views all over the green valley below. Done my walk and I was away going down the steep road and taxi pulled in saying lift, I said, how much, he said 1 JD so I jumped in giving him 1JD and we were away into the town of Ajlun and he said where you go, I said Amman and he pointed at a Minibus just ready to go and on I got and we were away, I couldn't believe my luck. Paid 85 fils and sat back enjoying the Jordan Valley view then fell asleep a few times before we eventually drove into Amman and he dropped me off at the Minibus/bus/taxi station and out I got. Taxi driver waiting near the bus said, taxi, I said yes, telling him downtown, he said 3JD so jumped in and we were away. As he got into near my hotel I said, stop, paid him the money and out. Into a small café and had 2 large soft turkey baguettes with a coke and really enjoying my 1725hrs din din, paid my 2JD charge and on up the hill and who was coming in only Tais. Greeting each other with smiles she said she had just finished work and was going to have a shower and out with her friends for Valentines night so wishing her all the best I got my key and up to room. Stripped off, nice shave and shower, kit on and out and a nice slow walk down to Paris Sq, a roundabout and on down the steep hill into the vibrant full of life with dozens of cheapie hotels, cafes, clubs, I liked it, drew 200JD at ATM, so rich boy now. Had another chip, sausage roll, coca cola in the quick sandwich café, 2JD then feeling the urge I was on the prowl and knew it and went left towards the Roman Theatre as had my suspicions about a few streets around the area. Turned one corner and a petite curvy figure chico with a twinkle in her eye said I like you and with a twinkle in my winkle I knew in my heart this was true Jordan Amman love to last forever in the Moses sky. I said I like you babe and she cuddling up to me said I go with you and my winkle giving a tinkle and holding my true love tight I said how much babe and where we go. She tickling my tinkle saying 45JD and pointing up an alley Souk said my room so my love now so strong I didn't even try to work it out in $US we where away up the Souk, it was like a Bible dream. Got upto a falling apart door into a rundown corridor and in and she had a key to another door and in we went kissing and holding my true love I managed to get my hand into my pocket to get my wallet out and put the 45JD on a bedside locker hopefully my side of the bed as we stripped off naked kissing and fondling each other's naked bodies her lithe firm body was such a sensual lust filled treat we where on the bed her going down on me then kissing me she was on top her lithe body pushing and pounding mine into the mattress as we made heaving panting gasping sexual groaning uninhibited Jordon exotic love then changing positions I was on top the scented sweat pouring off are love struck bodies I was in Gods heaven in the Jordon clouds as until in one final brutal breast biting nail ripping surge of screaming in sensual passion lust filled Jordanian love we climaxed together like two dogs of the Amman night are sex spasms crescendo reaching new height of full sex rampant Jordan love we both climaxed again and again are bodies glued together both screaming and biting each others necks I was lost in the clouds above the Holy Land until are vibrations slowly but slowly subsided and I slowly came back down to Gods earth and slid of my bible treat beautiful Chico we both lay gasping and breathing heavily tightly beside each other on her soaking with sweat scented bed and knowing I was here in the holy land to stay forever I relaxed in contentment as she rolled up and on top of me feeling my breasts and smiling she said " You are a lovely man Papa" and rubbing my cheek she leaned across the bed grabbing her money saying" we go" and up we both got and having a laugh we both got dressed and hand in hand out we went into the dark night of the Souk. She guided me back to the full lighted area and one last hug we parted smiling with a quick peck and my lovely love was away. Should have got a taxi but so happy I walked all the way back along King Al-Hussein St and nearly home I took a wrong turning and got completely lost in the dark Souk streets. Looking up in the sky I said Allah is good as knew there was a large Minaret Mosque near my hotel and turning a corner there it was its green Minaret glowing in the dark night so Allah was good and I made it back into hotel, got key and upto room. No thoughts just quickly stripped off and into bed dreaming my Jordan true love was holding me close in her arms as we made Amman sensual passionate Jondan love all night in the Bible sky I was fast asleep.

Roman soldiers fighting skills

Gladiator Fight

Roman Chariot Race

Email Sent: Sun, 14 Feb 2010
Subject: Jerash & Ajlun; Jordan

Hi

Jumped a bus to Jerash to see its lovely Roman Hippodrome and just lucky seen their was a Roman soldiers fighting skills show and they where great at it then 2No Gladiators fights and finally a 3 chariot race of 3 Roman chariots, great fun then a stroll around the 2nd Century AD Roman City of Jerash.

In the afternoon jumped a taxi only 30mins away up to the Arab castle of Ajlun on top of a hill and then back to Amman, another great sunny day.

Manyanna pulling out and going to Madaba which is a large town near Bethany, the Dead Sea and Mt Nebo where Mose's is buried, should be a good history day and a crusty one as might have a swim in de Dead Sea, how do you get de salt off!!.

al de bes
Jack

Day 51, Monday, 15-02-10, Amman – Madaba; Jordan

Up at 0720hrs feeling good after a great nights sleep, face splash, underarm wash, kit on and downstairs for breakie sitting at a table with always happy smiling Tais. Enjoyed my breakie having a chat with her and we shook hands touching each other with fists closed as my hand was wet with running butter and wishing each other our happy smiling Goodbyes she went back to her room to clean teeth and then go to work. I finished my breakie and out to reception telling guy I was leaving and he said I pay for 3 teas that I had extra, I said no problem, how much. He said 3JD, I said that's robbery as I can get a meal downtown for the price of one tea, he shrugged so I paid him the robbery price and back to room for my final pack of shoulderbag. Had a nice dobhi drop, cleaned ass, cleaned teeth and me and shoulderbag downstairs ready to go I handed key over, got small section of paper with Bus Station on it in Arabic and out I went seeing 2 Church Steeples down the hill that I hadn't noticed before, flagged down a taxi and agreed 2JD price, jumped in and I was away, it was 0900hrs. Old guy driving said I should go by meter but I said no worry and as we got to the same bus station as yesterday he pointed at meter which said 1.25JD so laughing and shaking his hand I paid him the 2JD. Grabbed shoulderbag and onto the Madaba bus with driver saying put shoulderbag on seat and with only 5 other passengers we were away. I was very surprised as this was the first time I had been on a bus that didn't wait until it was full before leaving, it was 0900hrs. Out we went slowly travelling a few taxi Minibuses stopping points then onto a main highway and boot down we were away getting up a good speed me looking around at Amman saying I will miss you. Having another think I was thinking not really as Jordan if I had known about its semi westernisation would have been my first stop in the Middle East so at least my last stop would have been the Souks and melee of an old real Arab town. Not to worry as I sat back enjoying my sunny day ride the bus driver having a smoke at the wheel, them was the days. Turned right off the highway and a good long run dropping people off then into the outskirts of Madaba, I was looking for the usual Hotel street but didn't see one hotel. Drove into the Bus Station 1020hrs and everyone including me got off and I asked the driver where the hotels are. He pointed and said that way meaning go on from where the Bus Station is so trolley handle up I was away along the many shops melee of the packed bus station area and walked 30m but not one hotel anywhere, very strange. Asked guy and he said go right at the crossroads and all the way up to the top so off I went glancing left and right along streets leading off but nothing. Finally reach the top road and asked again and was directed right where I then seen the Queen Ayola Hotel, King Talaat Street, Madaba, Jordan, Tel: 00962-5-544087 and it was mentioned in LP as a cheapie so upto its front entrance and asked a young fellow at reception how much for a single room, he told me three prices, 15-20-25JD so I said what is the 15JD, has it a toilet inside, he said no, only 20-25JD have toilet inside but have a look. Followed him up the stairs and into Room 6 with a nice big soft mattress d-bed with shower, WC and WHB, he said 20, I said 15, he said no, I said 18, he said yes and back down to reception, paid for one night giving him a 20JD note and as usual no change, showed him Passport then shoulderbag in my hand I was upto room. Dumped shoulderbag in room and taking trainers off I put my Thai sandals on, put neckpouch and other wallet in orange bag, zipped up and out. Reception guy was helpful and we talked through various options and he phoned a taxi and guy came into the big breakfast room reception and offered me a 5hr two Holy sites and the Red Sea with a drive up to the panoramic view looking down into Jericho and Jerusalem in Israel at 35JD. I let on to know what I was talking about and said ok, 30JD, taxi guy said ok so all happy!. Out we went to a nice big white car and I got in the front seat, safety belt on and we were away. The driver was helpful trying to give me a guide as we went up hills and through little villages he then said this village is called Pissalia as we passed a store with sign above it, Baptism Grocery Store. He stopped and dropped me off saying pay 7JD and take the Guided Tour Bus. So out I got, guy saying buy ticket as just ready to go so bought ticket at kiosk and onto the soft seat 3 tonner type bus and we were away. The guide with the bus as we drove along pointed down the valley at Moses Spring as up the hill we drove to Mt Nebo which is near the edge of the East Bank Plateau as he said this is where Moses seen the Promised Land and was later buried here as we drove and stopped at the Moses Memorial Church first built 4th century AD. It was sad but real big time history seeing the Ancient Mosaics describing life in that time as some were on the floor and some on the walls like paintings, very impressive. Back into the bus and the bare stone mountain hills in the heat of the sun was a great sight even passing Bedouin camping areas with large tents and dogs, sheep, goats and camels all running about in and around them, great fun sight then on down we went to the Jordan River passing machine gun checkpoints and stopped at a large car park area and off the bus we all got. We then started a walking tour along a stone pebble path and came to a line of stone marble steps leading down to a small marble square well type structure that is an original part of the 4th Century Church built on the exact spot where Jesus was baptised. I just felt overwhelmed that I had followed and came upon our Lord's life quite a few times now on my travels. We all took photos of each other in our group with Iris from Donegal a full of life lady who it was a great pleasure to meet and be talking to as she told me her husband was working out in the Middle East so she had a chance to see it. Then there was Anton and Enjetice a lively couple on holiday together as Anton was working in Dubai but we all helped each other taking photos as and when required. We walked around to the other side and now we were standing directly on the East bank of the River Jordan, man oh man which was only 10m wide, and my phone rang with a text, 'Welcome to Israel' and I laughed as we could have walked across the river into Israel, no chance as it looked mined and machinegun posts everwhere. Most of us had a photo shoot sticking our feet or big toe in the River Jordan trying to catch the Israel flag across on the other bank in the Israel occupied territory when it was fully out in the wind. I don't know about my 30 JD fare with the taxi but this 7JD tour was unbeatable as I could never in 5 million years found all these spots and walked them so easily and so quickly myself. It was very peculiar as well as at every turn there were New Churches being built everywhere, just amazing as now in our walk I could see the town of Jericho in Israel, what a day. The sun was big time penetrating warm as we strolled back to the big shuttle bus 3 tonner and on we got and away back to the large pick up car park.

Said my Goodbyes to Iris, Anton and Enjetice as we all got into our own taxi transport my driver said we go the Dead Sea and we were away. Quite a long drive but as we went down and down and downhill we turned one corner and there it was stretching as far as my eyes could see, the famous Dead sea and along its each on a main highway road we drove past many hotels plus many more being built and driver pulled into a parking area. He said I can go into a hotel complex and swim in the Dead Sea then use the shower, spa for 15JD or use the one on the left with shower only for 10JD. I said no I only want to paddle along it so he pointed up the road saying walk approximately 100m and there is a rocky path leading down to the sea edge so I was away. Got to a neat rocky slope and walked down it in the company of a Grandma, Grandad, Sons and Wife and ten kids big family as we all made our way to the sea/lake edge. They stripped off, I took off my Thai sandals and socks and stepping on to the 100-200mm thick salt built up all along the sea/lake edge I was one happy man paddling along the Dead Sea with all the grown ups and kids walking and floating in it all around me as large notices stated "Don't taste or swallow the water or swim in it, back float only" and it was real fun seeing the grown ups and kids back floating. I had my usual thumbs up photo and then phoned my Kelly Rose in England and laughing telling her I was in the Dead Sea, she was amazed and giggling as I told her about the salt along the seal/lake edges and we parted still laughing with a kiss. Put my Thai sandals on, no socks now and I was away saying my Goodbyes to the happy family and sweating bad in the powerful sun I made it up to the top of the hill at the road. I had a seat on a stone wall having a good few slugs of lemonade and a nice big chocolate cake roll, just the job as had not eaten all day as too busy enjoying my day. Finished my little Naafi break and back along the road to the driver who said we take the panoramic route so into car and we were away. What a journey as up and up the newish bendy road we went high up in the mountains which were many different colours be it purple, grey, cream, black and green but the as we got higher they stretched for miles upon miles into the horzion. Got as high as the road went and he stopped and out I got but a very dense haze across the Dead Sea stopped my full sight of Jericho and Jerusalem but the views of the mountains each side were terrific. Back in the car and now going for miles downhill and he said he will drop me off at Hotel, I said I want to go to St Georges Mosaic Church. He said my hotel is nearly beside it and we drove to near the Church and stopped, out I got paying him the 30 JD, shaking his hand and he was away, it was 1630hrs, what a great full day. Into the lovely Greek Orthodox St George Church paying a 1JD entrance fee admiring all the lovely wall paintings and most of all the original Mosaic 560 AD floor painting of all the Biblical main sites in the Middle East. When first made in 560 AD the Mosaic jigsaw contained over 2 million pieces but only approximately one third remains but still a truly lovely remarkable ancient site. Time for eats my belly was saying, so out and into a nice empty restaurant and had a beef burger and a tea, 5JD just the job but didn't like the price. Finished my meal and back to hotel and upto room still not got my 2JD change. Had a lovely hot water shave and shower and out, it was 1920hrs. Just took my time having a stroll around the many shops and cafes and restaurants of Madaba which was so full of life then into a café and had a chicken burger, fries and two teas, 3JD and belly really full I called it a night, it was only 2210hrs. Back to hotel with a plan for tomorrow as had enough of rip off Jordan as it's not a true Arab Country for single travellers, more a con but that's life, stop moaning I said to myself laughing. Had a read of LP then stripped off and into bed and asleep dreaming my luck is good, where are you.

Dead Sea

Paddling the Dead Sea

Email Sent: Mon, 15 Feb 2010
Subject: Queen Ayola Hotel, King Talaat St, Madaba, Jordan. Tel 009625544087

Hi All

Jumped a bus from Amman and 1hr later off at Madaba with no map but found above,18JD,d-ensuite,dumped kit in room and got a taxi for 5hrs with agreed price,30JD for 2 Holy Sites and the Dead Sea and we were away.

First stop Mt Nebo on the edge of the east bank at Moses' Memorial Church, 4AD, is were Moses' first seen the promised land and Mt Nebo is where he is buried.

Next in the heat of the desert sun was Bethany and the original site were Jesus was baptised and as I joined a guided tour we walked all the way along the 10m wide Jordan River with Israel flags the other side near the Palestinian border where you could plainly see Jericho, my phone rang to say T Mobile Welcomes me to Israel, ha ha.

Sweating well and with good company of a lady from Donegal we where back to drop off point and I jumped in my taxi to the Dead Sea.

Their was hotels who let you use their seashore for 10-15JD and have a shower but I got taxi driver to drop me off up a deserted area and Thai sandals off I had a walk along the 100-200mm deep thick with hard salt seashore of the warm sea of the Dead Sea, great fun.

Next we went high up the mountain road to the Panorama viewpoint but haze obscured Jerusalem.

Taxi driver dropped me off at 1600hrs and in I went to the Creek Orthodox St Georges Church looking at the Mosaic of all biblical sites in the Middle East constructed 560AD,real great history so my holy day over i walked back to my hotels for a lovely hot water shave and shower, just the job.

Will do one trip manyanna but more of a holy rest day as both knees praying for help!!!
al de bes
Jack

Map 1 of Israel

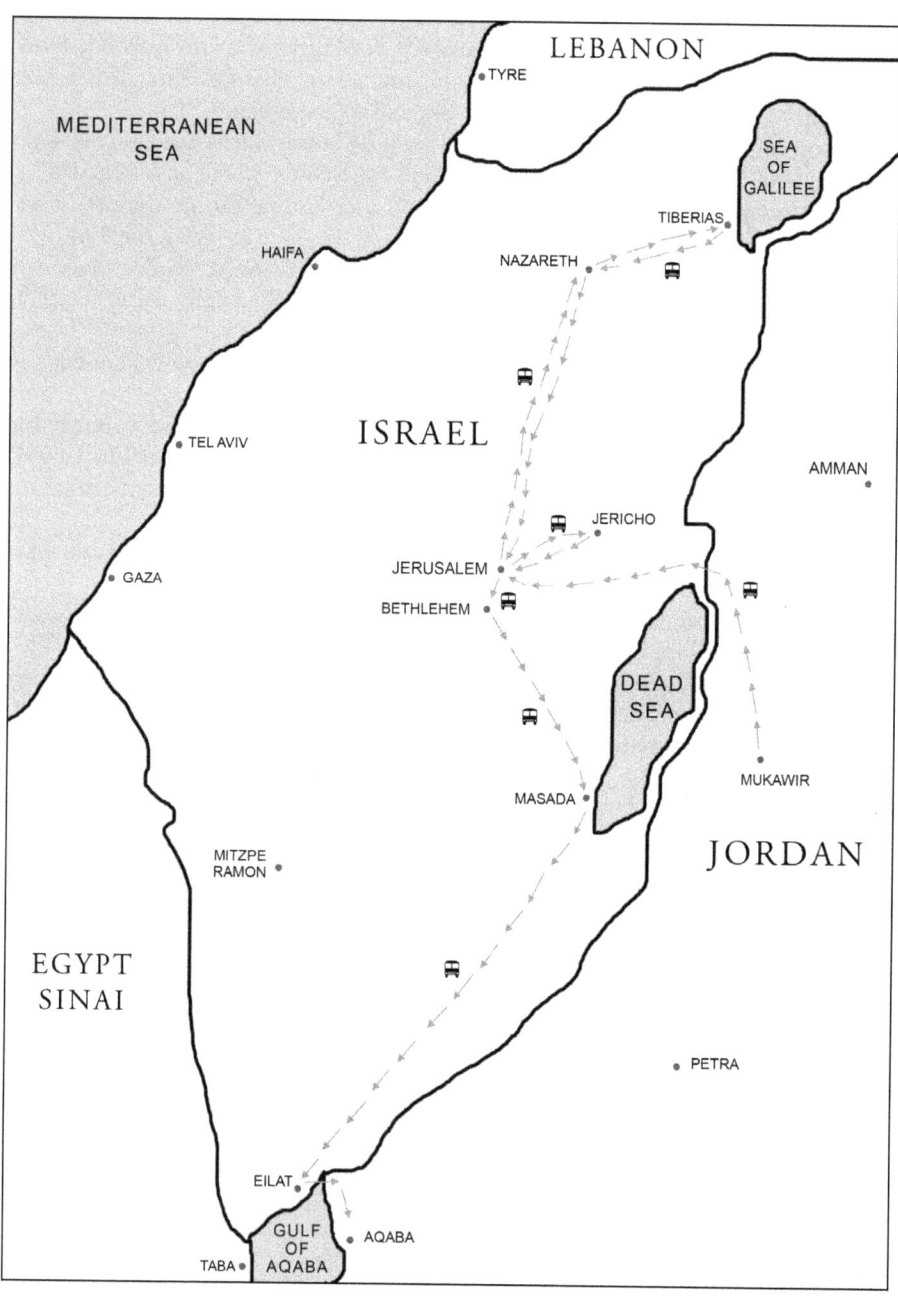

1) ISRAEL the birthplace of Christianity in Jerusalem, Nazareth and Galilee is one step after another going back to Jesus and his disciples life's and is an unbelievable walk back to true life history of the Holy Bible every turn you make not forgetting the Muslims history of Allah and the start of Islam living next door to Christian Arabs all combined and intermingled with seeing the real life as it is today in the old City of Jerusalem as people will go out of their way to help and make your stay a never be forgotten in their happy always willing to help way.
2) Capital; Jerusalem
3) Israel achieved Independence in 1948
4) Climate; Ave temp Jan-Mar; 20c
5) Language; Hebrew, Arabic, English
6) Currency; Shekel, 1$US = 3.5 Shekel
7) Visa; Not required, 30 day issued on arrival
8) Return flight £51 + £154 ATM, hotel, food, train to Gatwick
9) Today's ongoing update of day to day accommodation, travel, food, drinks costs = £2591

Day 52, Tuesday, 16-02-10, Madaba – Mukawir; Jordan – Jerusalem; Israel

Woke up thinking I've had enough of Westernised Jordan and rip off taxi prices and if I wanted to go to Petra I would have to go back to Amman as Petra/Aqaba were down near Taba in Egypt. Lieing their I was thinking if I am travelling Israel I could come out at Eilat which would save me doing the same long journey in two different countries but no firm plans yet. Got up 0730hrs, underarm wash, face splash, kit on and out to noone about breakie room and guy rapping the locked entrance door peeping through the window pointed at a small door and indicated rap it which I did and young bleary eyed fellow came out with key and took a plastic bag full of flat bread off him and then I noticed a row of six plates all with hard boiled eggs, jam, butter sitting on a counter. Went over and touched the tea urn to see if it was hot and it was but young fellow hadn't said one word so poured myself a tea, got 2 flat breads sections with the hard boiled egg plate, sat down and got stuck into my breakie eating the large flat bread sections. A couple came out from the bedroom corridor and sat down we all saying our Good Mornings and introducing ourselves they were from Brazil and were just finishing a two week holiday touring Jordan and their final visit was to the St Georges Church this morning then their flight back to Brazil this afternoon so saying our Goodbyes they went out and away. Talking to young fellow I said I was going to the castle ruins of Mukawir the Castle of Herod the Great first built 100 BC as the caves below it was where Herods brother Herod Antipas beheaded John the Baptist. John the Baptist who was Jewish had criticised him for marrying his brothers wife which is against Jewish Law and Salome, Herods daughter who was a beautiful belly dancer was granted a wish by her mother so she said she wanted John the Baptist's head on a platter, so there, don't trust Chico's!. Agreed a 30JD rip off price for the trip and a quick decision, a drop off at King Hussein Bridge as after the trip I was now going to Israel. Told young fellow to phone up and get my dobhi, wet or dry and I was out upto the Post Office and posted a travel note letter to Sandralita, then back, laundry had come still wet so laid a plastic bag on top of my dry clothes and laid the wet clothes on top. Paid all my bills, shook the new owners hand who had just arrived telling him to put some arrow signs at the bus station then out and with shoulderbag in back seat and me in the front we were away. It was an interesting drive as we went higher and higher up the milky coloured stone mountains which changed to dark brown then black in areas but the views for miles down the valleys and across the mountains was just a pure dream. Eventually I seen the Pillared Column ruins on top of a mountain hill and my driver pulled into a car park on the hill next to it and smiling said, ok see you later, and out I got. I was tempted not to go but as usual said to myself, "you only get one chance" and I was away down the stone steps looking across the hazy mist of the Dead Sea then I came to a decent path going left up the other hill with a small cliff path going right past the row of caves, what do I do. With no hesitation I took the small cliff path but first I went upto and looked inside two caves but no bodies! so back and along the tiny path with one wrong step and it would be a rough rocky tumble down the steep cliff face. Made it to the other side of the hill and up the decent big path to Herod's Castle Column 100BC ruins walking around them with some of the walls 1m wide and looking across the mountains one side and the Dead Sea the other I laughed out loud thinking of Salome saying, "I am keeping my head" and I was away. Went downhill all the way then up the steps to the car park and really sweating bad as the sun was just so unbelievably hot I got to are car. Driver said you like starting up his engine and me taking a full half bottle slug of my lemonade bottle replied great history and we were away just as a tour bus full of Germans arrived. Driver said he'll take the mountain road to King Hussein Bridge, I said yes, but still 30JD and off the main road we went following a smaller tarmac road in a beautiful hairpin bend drive over the mountains, what a journey. At last we came back to the main highway and another good 10km I could see signs for King Hussein Bridge with driver telling me he wait 20mins just to make sure I got through the Jordan Border but I laughed saying don't bother, it was 1125hrs. Drew up at Passport Control, out I got giving him the 30 JD, shook his hand, grabbed my shoulderbag, trolley handle up and I was away being directed by Police into Arrivals. Showed Passport and was told to have a seat in the waiting area for a bus and Passport would be given back on bus so had a seat enjoying a Twix and a Mars Bar with a bottle of lemonade as a happy family of mother, father and 2 sons from Chile sat down, then another two it looked like Jewish guys and we were sitting there for 45mins me getting fed up. Police guy said ok and onto the bus we all got going through a checkpoint and we each got our Passports back with the Jordan exit stamp on it then across the Jordan River we went seeing the barbed wire and look out posts all along the barren brown small mountain hills the Israel side as we drew into Israel Customs and Passport Control. First we had a Passport check then our bags through X-ray and guy made me take off my belt me saying why, don't be stupid you idiot I'm not getting on a plane for goodness sake but finally through and upto Passport Control. Girl took my Passport, looked at it, asked me my name, where was I going to in Israel, why did I want to come and on and on and doing well keeping my temper I answered her daft questions. She then asked me if I wanted my Passport stamped, I said yes and bang, an Israel entrance stamp and I was in, grabbed my red with blue ribbon on the straps shoulderbag and out seeing 2-3 big buses, plus a taxi rank and 1 medium sized bus. I asked the guy at the taxi kiosk where do I catch a bus to Jerusalem, he said pay here, I said bus, he pointed at the small medium bus and said 60 Shekels. I pointed at a sign 13 Shekels, he said that's for Jericho so paid him and on the bus I got. A young girl and a veiled lady got on then 2 young fellows and after waiting for another 30mins I asked when is the bus going. Young fellow said it only goes when full so they had a conversation in Arabic and it was repeated to me in English if we all pay for one seat extra each the bus will go now so I gave the young fellow another 60 Shekels, he took the money over to the kiosk and him and the driver came back and we were away. Only lasted 5-10mins and fell fast asleep only being woken up at a checkpoint by a soldier who wanted to see my Passport, so showed it to him and we were away again. The young girl had an upto date LP Middle East Book and lent it to me as I took some notes of hotels and addresses then she and the lady got off all saying are smiling Goodbyes. Only a few miles and the two young fellows got off then we drove into Jerusalem and along the outside of the old walled city of Jerusalem and stopped along a busy main street and driver said final stop, so off I got thinking this will be fun as not a clue where I was and glad it wasn't dark. Had a look at my LP and asked an old guy sitting outside a shop is there any hotels about, he pointed back up the road and I seen the Golden Walls Hotel. I said cheapie hotels, he said go in Damascus Gate pointing across the road at the Arch opening through the big very imposing walls of Old Jerusalem. Just checking I walked up to the Golden Wall Hotel and asked price of room, girl said 120$US for single so quickly out of there and up the street further along from it into another one and guy said 100$US. I seen there were 4 or 5 hotels all along the street but said to myself I will check the Old City and crossed the road through Damascus Gate Arch and into the melee of every conceivable small shop, restaurant, cafes all it looked like along a tunnel and taking the right hand fork with only a shortish walk I seen a sign Golden Gate Inn, Souk Khan Al – Zeit, Old City, Jerusalem, Tel: 00972-2-6284317. Glad to have made it so up the stone steps then through the café area I was at reception and asked guy any rooms for one. He said yes but it needs cleaning, I said no problem, how much, he said 120 Shekels so working it out at 3.5 Shekels to 1$US it was expensive but reading the girl's upto date version of LP the lowest price in the old City was 24$US for a d-ensuite so said yes I will take it. He said leave kit in room giving me key to Room 111 so down I went and into a 2 single bed bedroom with shower WHB and WC, yeah man yeah. Put neckpouch and spare wallet in orange bag in shoulderbag and I was out with China beachbag and LP. Seen a photocopy place so in and photocopied all of Israel from it, 32 pages in total, paid the robber 32 Shekels and back to hotel dumping my LP in room. I really was feeling big time great vibes for Old City Jerusalem walking through its sometimes narrow tiny Souks and everywhere buzzing with traders and shops it was real life not like westernised rip off Jordan. Walked all the way along Jewish Quarter Road sometimes along old tunnels and came out with great fantastic views looking down a valley seeing a sign, City of David but looking up the valley and reading LP I could see the Tomb of the Virgin Mary all below the huge enormous big Domed Mosque with a Moslem and Jewish Graveyard near to each other. First I went down and along the underground walkway Souk of the Ancient City of David just enhanced with the ancient walls and how did they build such great architecture. Out from there and looking and reading LP the huge Domed Mosque dwarfing the area was the Temple Mount, Mt Moriah where Abraham was instructed by God to sacrifice his son Isaac in a test of faith as part of it is the Wailing Wall. It has two faiths in one Holy site as it is also the Muslims most revered site as it's the site where Mohammed launched himself into heaven to take his seat beside Allah. What unbelievable history so this is No1 for manyanna as looking down then up across the roof tops I could see the Valley of Jesus Baptism and reading LP I could see in the far distance the Mount of Olives, Church of Ascension, Tomb of the Virgin Mary, Russian Orthodox Church of Mary Magdalene to name a few, it was 1730hrs. It was now starting to get slightly dark as the chanters started from the Mosque above so made my way towards the Lions Gate passing many Jewish men in black suits with long beards, black big floppy hats, really good. Into and through Lions Gate passing many young kids with skull caps on my belly now crying out so into a restaurant near my hotel, it was 1755hrs. Felt great so looking at the menu I had a quarter chicken, fries and 2 teas and it was cooked to perfection and tasted gorgeous as I ate every last bit. Finished my 2nd tea, paid my 50 Shekels and away thinking Jerusalem is or appears expensive but only get one chance so will see it all then do a runner. Back to hotel and had a nice holy dobhi drop, cleaned ass, cleaned teeth, face wash, pullover on and out for a walk, it was 1905hrs. Although most shops were starting to close the area along the main Souk still had plenty of life and great vibes as I made my way out Jaffa Gate into a lively café area at Zahal Square and had an outside seat with a coffee enjoying the vibes of the New Town of Jerusalem as its called. Paid 10 Shekels and I was away and a good walk around New Town and eventually found an ATM and head gone drew out 150 Shekels so card in again and drew out another 150 Shekels which in total makes £50, ha ha, laughing to myself I said no more until tomorrow and a nice slow walk back to Damascus Gate and in. Back along the now nearly all closed shops and found an Internet café about 30m past my hotel on the right up a Souk and in and done my usual 20mins, paid my 3 Shekels for the 1hr he charged me and buying a bottle of coke, pint of milk, packet of weetabix and some biscuits as I might try something new for breakie I was back to hostel and into room. Back out again and had 2 free teas from the urn in the lounge area talking to two girls from USA then saying my happy vibes Good Nights I was back to my room, stripped off, finished my tea and into bed really chuffed about my first day in the Holy Land and asleep dreaming Holy Land love!

Temple Moriah, Jerusalem

Email Sent: Tuesday, 16 Feb 2010
Subject: Rm111, Golden Gate Inn, Souk Khan Al-Zeit, Jerusalem Old City.Tel0097226284317

Shalom All

Up and plan A into operation, paid my bill, packed shoulderbag and agreed a taxi price of 30JD for a trip high up the mountain to the village of Mukawir and then to the top of the hill Castle of Herod the Great called Machaerus, locals call it the Gallows Castle. Driver parked up, out I got and it was a high climb as I went past the caves on side of the mountain below the Palace and peeping into them as these caves is where John the Baptist was beheaded by Herod Antipas as that what his daughter Salome de belly dancer wanted so don't trust dolly birds.

Great history their and the Palace above then made it back down to car and away to King Hussein bridge, driver dropped me off and it took me nearly 2hrs to get through the 2 Jordan/Israeli borders and wishing Shalom to all my fellow travellers from Chile we finally got through. Bus from Israel side would not go unless full so we chipped together for the empty 5 seats and we were away and 1hr later after 2 military checkpoints we were in Jerusalem. Got dropped of facing the Damascus Gate at bus stop and tried 2 hotels outside the old city walls but they wanted 100-120$US so into the melee of old city at the Muslim Quarter at Damascus Gate and sweating bad in the heat of the sun I went into above and guy said one room left so took it at 120 Shekels at 3.5shekels to 1$US, dumped kit in room and out. Jerusalem old city is just full of so much history its unbelievable as I walked through the Armenian Quarter no chance of stopping for a piss as Gods knows what they would charge then into the Jewish Quarter and had one as it's free as us Jewboys look after each other. Out the Gate of the Moon Arch and down into the City of David old town then a walk outside the old city wall looking down on the Tomb of the Virgin Mary at the side of the Jewish Cemetery then looking up at the Mount of Olives all with big beards, black suits hard floppy hats or skull caps Jewish blokes all walking about, great vibes.

Coming upto 1730hrs and the chanters just started from the huge Mosque in the old city so made my way back in through the Lions Gate and along a Souk between the Muslim and the Christian Quarter's and into Hostel. Out again and after a good scuff I am out for a dander. Seen a free walking guided tour advertised for manyanna at 1100hrs so will take it but Jerusalem old City is very compact and really amazing so Shalom to you all.

al de bes
Jack

Day 53, Wednesday, 17-02-10, Jerusalem free tour and Mount of Olives; Israel

Great bed and great night's sleep and up at 0730hrs, turned alarm off, underarm wash, face splash, kit on and out to breakfast dining room communal lounge but girl said they don't usually start until 0830hrs or later. She said her and her boyfriend were going out to a Church that only opens a few days a week until 1030am in the morning to have a look and come back for breakfast and they were away. I had a little walk up the large alley Souk with shops of all descriptions beginning to open then back and breakfast was ongoing as you helped yourself. Had 2 boiled eggs, 2 large round pieces of bread, 2 teas and butter on my bread I got tore in and finished the lot just as Marianna a 22year old blond girl from USA who I had met and enjoyed a 5mins chat with last night came from her room with 3 large plastic bags and a laptop in a laptop bag pulling a very large trolley bag behind her. She put the trolleybag in the hotel safe keeping room, said her smiling good morning to me as she had a chat with reception then paid it looked like her final hotel bill. I said are you off, she came over and sat at my table saying yes telling me she had rented an apartment up along Jaffa Road in New Town and was moving out. I said do you need a hand and with relief she said yes, so back to room, cleaned teeth and back to reception. Marianna gave me 2 large heavy plastic bags and her carrying one and her shoulderbag laptop we were away into New Town which was upmarket in areas. Went along a pedestrian only street with lots of cafes and restaurants then cutting across 2-3 traffic lights and down a street between 3-4 5 storey blocks of flats then finally up three flights of outer steel stairs we were at the door of her new accommodation at 800$US a month she had told me as we never stopped talking in our 15-20min interesting journey. Dropped her bags at door, gave each other a hug and I was away thinking she is so brave. Made it back to Old Town only getting lost once in New Town and made my way to Jaffa Gates as that is the start of my free guided tour of Old Town starting at 1100hrs, www.neweuropetours.eu, it was 1045hrs. I seen the Eurotours personnel with their bright red uniform and a large prominent poster on a pole and went over to girl and asked is this the free tour, she said yes and pointing to a seating area smiling said wait there. I joined a happy bunch of all ages travellers most from the USA by the sound of them and waited for our orders in the now bright hot sun. Guy with red jacket emblazoned with www.neweuropetours.eu in an American voice as the US voices were everywhere said ok free tour I am your guide and gave us a rundown on where we going, what we would be seeing and how long it would take and we are ready to go. Approximately 15 of us free tourers followed him across the small Square as he pointed out David Street with the Citadel and Tower of David on our right and telling us Suleyman the Magnificent built them in 1537 AD and the walls were a great fantastic sight in the heat of the sun's rays. Also he told us in bygone history the longest period of Israel rule ever was 586-1200BC now called The Israel Period. As we all got to and looked at the Jaffa Gate he said its name has a reason as it was the approach to the City on the road to and from Jaffa. He said, pointing behind us at the Old City Walls, the spot we were standing on now in 1948 belonged to Jordan and no mans land was along Jaffa Street pointing at the bullet holes everywhere on the old City walls and when I looked closely they were plain to see. Then we were away passing the Mosque of Omar with its old large Minaret and with 2-3 twisting turns in the packed full Souks we turned into the Square of the Crucifixion and resurrection of Jesus. In we went and seen inside the Church of the Holy Sepulchre which is claimed was built over the site of Jesus' Crucifixion so I stood with my head bowed thanking God is good to let me make it here and said a little prayer for the poor and hungry of the world and we were away again, guide telling us we should come back in our own time and see inside the Church. He said the same family had kept the keys to the Church for 800 years but then another family have now had it for 200 years. In his history lesson of the Church he pointed out the White Dome marked the site of the Crucifixion of Jesus and the Green Dome his burial, real fantastic history. Then really getting into it we were away again going into and through the very rough Muslim Quarter and as we walked along its main Souk the chanters started nearly deafening me but more good fun for all, it was 1155hrs. Funny enough at spot on 1200hrs all you could hear was Church bells as we walked along Al Wad Street the Roman road. Got to the Armenian side of the Western Wall going under the 11th Century Arch and had a stop at Temple Mount. Next we were informed about the instructions for the Wailing Wall as we could see many traditional dressed in black suits with big hats and long beards many Jewish men praying with their heads bowed and folded hands against the Wailing Wall and knowing about it and hearing it over the years here I was standing only 50m from it. We were instructed to approach it down the tarmac road and put a skull cap on and if we wanted something from life or wanted to change something in our life to write it on a small sheet of paper and stick it in a niche in the stone built wall as we prayed and do not turn round to come back, walk back 3-4 paces from the wall then turn round. Away I went putting my skull cap on and writing true happiness for ever for my Kelly Rose I put it in a niche in the stone and bowing my skull cap head against my folded arms on the wall I prayed for love and happiness for all of mankind and just about to turn around I remembered and walked back two paces then turned around and passing the skull cap basket I dropped my cap in it and up to our red jacket guide, wow, that was fun. As we all came back our guide said Obama and many Presidents of many Nations had done exactly the same and twice a year all the notes are removed and taken up to near the Israel Cemetery and buried. Everyone happy we were away up the steps of Rabbi Yehudah Halven Ascent Souk and made it to the Quarter Café for a much needed bottle of cold Coke, it was 1250hrs. Next stop was the Spanish Jewish Synagogue in the Jewish Quarter beside the Mosque and he showed us the still in place old flat capped big stones we where walking on used to construct the Roman Road 2000 years ago pointing out the chariot wheel marks, it was just pure amazing. Off again and came to a replica of an original Mosaic map of Jerusalem 1700 years old and we all had a photo shoot. He showed us St Mary Convent, The House of St Mark and The Room of the Last Supper, this was fantastic unbelievable but true history. Giving us a talk he said The Armenian Quarter, 5th Century was where the first people to fully take up Christianity lived. My head burning in the heat of the lovely sunny day that was our Free Walking Tour over as we came walking back to Jaffa Square, it was 1405hrs. Organised paid for tours would go into more details but it was a great introduction to Jerusalem so over to the guide and shaking his hand I gave him a 50 Shekel note and away. I knew I could walk it but time to treat myself and flagged down a taxi telling him Mount of Olives, he said 25 Shekels so not having a clue I said ok, jumped in and we were away first of all going downhill then up a very steep hill and he pointed at the beautiful walled garden of the Mount of Olives and stopped, paid him the money and out. Lots of Tour buses were parked up but went into the sort of Temple of The Mount of Olives paying a 7 Shekels fee and in walking around the colourful Mosaic large panels of every country in the world's language and more of the Lords Prayer, it was beautiful. Out from there and a little walk along the brick wall looking down and through into the Mount of Olives as this is the area where our Lord Jesus took upon himself all the Sins of the World so bowing my head I said Thank You Lord. Went out going up the hill and into the Church of the Ascension which was a large round Domed structure and saying I Thank you my Lord for all my life I was out and going back down the steep road to quickly look from the lookout area point seeing the fantastic brilliant views everywhere all over Jerusalem, it was 1605hrs. Out and slowly clamped my way down the very steep hill and into the Tomb of the Prophets then down the steep path into the Three Coffin Tomb, bowed my head thinking this is so wonderful and saying Thank You Lord in a prayer I was out seeing and passing close to the thousands of Israeli graves on the side of the mountain, some 4000 years old!, wow. Next I was into the Church of the Pater Noster where prayers from the priest were ongoing, really good. Clamped my way on downhill and into the Dominas Flevit seeing a fenced off excavation of four small probably Cremation Coffins in an old stone Grotto then into the people singing small Cross shaped Church, 1st Century. Was doing well so on downhill and into the lovely garden and Church of All Nations with a priest conducting a service in Hebrew or Latin but it was so great a sight to be hearing and seeing it first hand. I was so happy as all behind the Priest were lovely colourful painted Murals on the walls. Out from there and into walking down 45 marble steps into an underground Grotto then bending fully over I was in another little cave seeing in front of me the open stone Coffin with it half filled with a substance it looked like hard clay was the body of the Virgin Mary and closing my moist full of tears eyes and bowing my head I stood there saying 'God, please help the hungry people all the world over and look after my beautiful Kelly Rose'. With the moist tears in my eyes brimming out I was out and up the steps thinking I am such a lucky man to have made it here. Next into The Garden of the Gethsemane Grotto with a beautiful large painting of Jesus on the Cross as this place was so special to Christians the world over as Jesus came here with his disciples on Holy Sunday after the Passover. He was also arrested here and asked for his name, he said Jesus of Nazareth and they fell backwards but he was arrested and led away and this so pure history to me standing here was just totally fantastic. Made it now back up the hill and in through Lions Gate and came to the birthplace of the Virgin Mary, I was totally happy. Happily strolling I came to a sign Prison of Christ Church as this is where in an underground Grotto Jesus was held prisoner for one night, I was totally over the moon thinking about all this history and that was my day nearly over as out I went. Took my time and along the no action main Souk and into the restaurant just up from my hotel having a plate of chips, a meat sandwich and one can of orange, really filling. Paid my 35 shekels, out and into hotel, upto room and one lovely dobhi drop, cleaned ass, cleaned teeth, shave and lovely hot water shower, kit on and I was out again. Went out Jaffa Gate and up Jaffa Street into the centre of New Town with dozens of well lit cafes and onto Ben Yehuda Street and a 1km long pedestrian street full of dancers, buskers and lots of pavement seating well lit cafes even a McDonalds and it was a joy to stroll. I turned right going along King George V Street it also having great vibes with lots of cafes. Great walk then back onto Jaffa Street and had a large coffee and three chocolate cakes I was really chuffed and that was me. Paid my 16 Shekels bill and out and a slow relaxed walk back into the Old City at Jaffa Gate and was unsure in the narrow Souks but still didn't get lost and made my way back to hostel. Got key having a chat with another young US girl then saying my Goodnights, it was 2235hrs. Made into my room, stripped off and into bed, no dreams, just a truly happy Holy Jerusalem Holy man I was asleep.

The Wailing Wall

Birthplace of the Virgin Mary

Email Sent: Wed, 17 Feb, 2010
Subject: Tour of Jerusalem

Shalom All
Great day on my free tour of Jerusalem but a bit sad sometimes when we where in Church's that were Jesus and the 12 Disciples met for the last time and the Church where Jesus was arrested.
Very very sad was walking down the 45 marble stone steps deep into the ground into the Tomb then looking at the open stone coffin of the Virgin Mary.
Got to the Wailing Wall and had to put a skull cap on and write a message and leave it in a niche in the stone high wall with lots of Jews all praying and said a prayer that all yu heathens are granted eternal life and away.
Made it upto and around the Mount of Olives with the Lords Prayer in every langage in the world on Mosaics on a sort of temple looking down at the Mount of Olives.
www.toursinenglish.com www.neweuropetours.eu
Just going into New Town for a walkie
Great history and lots still to see.

al de bes
HolyJack

Day 54, Thursday, 18-02-10, Jerusalem Holy City Tour; Israel

Woke up 0600hrs feeling good and bed was a gem with nice soft mattress and clean heavy sheets, had a piss and back to bed just dozing and planning!. Was tempted to do my own walking tour of the Holy City but lots of areas and Churches mentioned in Eurotours Holy Tour were not even on my LP map so no rush will do the www.neweruropetours.eu so happy now I turned over a few times then got up at 0730hrs. Underarm wash, face splash, kit on with trainers this time as my bare fee Thai sandals march yesterday had given me a few blisters. Out around to breakfast communal sitting room saying Good Morning to Ashley the full of life US beauty Queen journalist getting a full lovely smile and Good Morning back. I asked her when she would know about her Palestine West Bank Visa as she was going in to do a story, she said she will phone up soon and check. Had 4 slices of flat bread, 2 hard boiled eggs, 2 cheese and 4 big spoonfuls of jam and with 4 teas I devoured the lot enjoying my belly start to the day breakie. Ashley was just leaving so saying our Goodbyes she was away trolley bag and all. Back upto room, cleaned teeth and bang, a lovely milky dobhi drop, cleaned ass and final little check of China beachbag with travel notes in it I was out dropping key at reception and made my way through the main Souks to New Gate then into the small Post Office by Jaffa Gate. Weighed 1 letter, got a 4 Shekel stamp and 2 postcards at 2 Shekel stamps each and quizzing the counter girl she said no weight in letter so stuck stamps on, said my thanks, stuck them in Postbox and I was away into the square facing Jaffa Gate. I was early noone about only loads of young soldiers, it was 0930hrs. Had a seat on the steps in the shade of the wall as sun was big time hot and seen Euro Guides coming onto the Square and in the next 10mins approximately 15 travellers turned up. Over I went giving young Euro Guide girl a 100 Shekel note getting a receipt card and my change and was told group will go in approximately 20mins, it was 0945hrs. Next minute a young fellow with red jacket with Eurotours embossed on the back shouted "Holy City Tour" and approximately 8 of us travellers went over to him getting the usual briefing of where we are going, our first stop and his name was Phil. All ready he said and we were away going down the hill on the pavement on the outside of the Old City walls. Didn't walk too far when we stopped between two high Fort walls him explaining one wall was the Old City the other was the Walls of Zion and the tower was King David's Tower and away again passing the Convent Armenian, St Saviour and on we walked past the wide Arch of the Zion Gate with its bullet holes all over the big stone walls. Came to the Church and Abbey of The Dormition King David where Mary, Jesus's mother fell into everlasting sleep, a beautiful old building as we walked around it then into King David's Tomb, 3000 years old and it was marvellous being here in all this history. Up the stone step stairs and I was totally so fulfilled as into the room of The Last Supper, I could hardly believe all these buildings were here and I was walking their holy stone floors the same floors that Jesus and the Disciples had walked, chatted and eaten in. We all bemused had a walk around it and then back down the stone stairs to the massive statue of King David as this area in Medieval times was known as Mount David.

Out we went with the Guide pointing out a large wall way across the valley on a hill telling us that was the original City of David and then we had a nice walk downhill and joined the queue to get into The Temple Mount, it was 1210hrs, the sun was very hot and warm. I left my group and went over to the wall across the road and stood in the shade asking an old guy what time we would get in, he said gate opens at 1230hrs. The queue started moving and soon we were inside after going through x-ray and up some steps looking down at the clapping, cheering and singing Jews with also many praying at the Western Wailing Wall, good fun. Into the Temple Mount we went at the Moroccan Gate all the ladies/girls in our group had to cover their shoulders and knees so some wrapped wide scarves around their waist and in we all went seeing the gleaming Golden Cupola Dome of Haran Ash-Sharif real up close as we were in the compound surrounding it so it was camera shoot everyone posing. This area is the Mt Moriah from the Bible where Abraham was instructed by God to kill his son Isaac in a sacrifice so as to test his faith to God we where looking down from inside the Western Wailing Wall the most revered site in Judaism. Had a walk around the Al-Aqsa the Mihrab a prayer Dome which as they all do indicates the direction of Mecca and dates thousands of years back to the time of Saladin, great Muslim history. We were not allowed into the Al-Aqsa Mosque but had a nice walk around it then in we went to the Dome of the Rock which is on two floors which encloses in it as Christians believe the Rock where Abraham set up and prepared to sacrifice his son and Muslims believe is the Rock where the Prophet Mohammed was accepted into heaven. Its one of Islam's oldest Islamic Monuments built AD588 by Umayyad Caliph Abd al-Malik to keep Muslims from straying into Christianity by going to the older Church of the Holy Sepulchre. It was a joy to walk around its very colourful Mosaics façade and its lovely Arches all built 2000 years ago. Everywhere was so full of stories as we passed the Summer Pulpit, a Domed Arch with chairs all to do with Solomon the Wiseman as we looked towards the Gates of Mercy we looked out through the Gate of the Beautiful at a very lively market along Souk al-Qattanin. Finally we went out a large Arch gate and along a tiny tunnel Souk to another part of the Wailing Wall also with paper messages in the stone niches but no one praying. Only three girls wanted a prayer so all the rest of us went right and came to No: IV Station with the IV Blue sign on the wall which is a marked route of when Jesus carried the cross through Jerusalem and inside Station IV it had a vivid statue of Jesus very weak, nearly on his knees but still carrying the cross. Girls had come back so we went along the street to Station V and Guide said pointing at restaurant, its meal break time but I didn't go in. The Tour Guide was doing his job but he wasn't what I would call a Guide as we would spend 10-15mins at each stop listening to his boring history lesson that went in one ear and out the other as I said to one of the Aussie girls they should have given us a printed sheet of all the history on the route and kept the boring talk to a minimum. Had a seat on top of a drain cover with a bottle of lemonade, a packet of cheese & onion crisps and a chocolate bar, just the job at 1250hrs. A Mexican girl from our team came along to me smiling and asked me had they nearly finished their lunch, I said I will look and looking in the café pointing at my wrist and Guide sitting at table said 10mins so back out telling her 10mins and sat down again well pissed off. Eventually they did come out and we were given the history of Station V as it was one of the places Jesus fell and on the wall was a hand print. Everyone had a photo shoot including me putting their hands over the wall hand then on up the Souk we went. Got to Station VI where Jesus face got torn by a thorn then our final soul Station at Station VII and seen the Judge North Gate, St Alexandra Chapel. I looked on across the Sq and seen the most beautiful Church with Guide saying it's the Church of the Holy Sepulchre which he said pointing at the two Domes one marks the spot where Jesus was Crucified, the other marks the spot where he is buried so this is going to be one or probably the greatest moment of my life. In we went seeing a lovely Alter with a 3 Prophet beautiful painting behind it and all along the wall. Guide said The Hill of Golgara, one side Catholic, one side Orthodox, one side Ethiopian and final side Coptic as all these Churches believe this site marks the spot where Jesus died, was buried and was resurrected. Following the Guide we went down at least two storeys of very old stone steps in an unbelievable very old Church as the lower we got the more stone I could see at the stair edge until we were in a well lit original stone Grotto Vault with many very large and all sizes of paintings along its stone walls. There was a big old stone Tomb with many big candles surrounding it which I and everyone else, 4-5 at a time followed our guide into it and it was the stone Coffin of Our Lord Jesus Christ. I felt shocked, excited, sorry, sad, happy as I touched the stone lid I asked Our Lord for everlasting happiness for my Kelly Rose and the people of all Nations in the world and touching my forehead and the Coffin lid again I was out into the lovely Grotto Vault I was still in a sort of unbelievable shock to be actually here. The Guide took us along and showed us a lovely Mosaic on the wall above a flat stone slab telling us this slab is the original slab where Jesus lay dying and died and I as did most people knelt down in front of it touching my forehead and touching the lid I asked the Lord for true happiness for all the people in the world and I was up and looking around for our team I was in true happy unbelievable shock. We then went up a small winding set of steps to a well lit Alter as I and everyone took our turn kneeling in front of the altar and blessing ourselves with Holy water but no water left when it was my turn but kept my Proddie comments to myself. Out we all went following our guide to St Helena and that was our Holy Tour over so shaking our guide's hand and giving him a 50 shekel note I was away very pissed off about what I though was the general poor standard of the tour, it was 1610hrs and we were supposed to finish at 1500hrs but all the guide wanted to do was rabbit!. Not to worry I had seen a fantastic true lot of Ancient Jew and Jerusalem history today so slowly made my way back to hotel and into room. I had bought a packet of Weetabix, a pint of milk and some sugar so took them into the kitchen area and had my Weetabix din din as the hostel breakfast is not worth missing. Had a great chat with Lisa an US girl who lives in Korea who gave me very good advice about my intended travels most of all I must carry my Passport when I go to Bethlehem manyanna. Really enjoyed our chat then back to room and had a nice shave, shower, cleaned teeth and bang, a dobhi drop, cleaned ass and out. Made it out New Gate and up Jaffa Road into the very vibrant New Town pedestrian area having 2 coffees in the outside seating area and that was me just a slow enjoyable happy stroll back to hotel, it was 2220hrs. Got key and had a chat with Lisa's mate she telling me no buses on Friday night or Saturday so legs, eyes nearly gone I said my Thanks and wishing everyone a Good Night I was upto my room, stripped off and into bed dreaming about one of the most fantastic true History days in all my life I fell into a true Holy asleep.

Email Sent: Thu, 18 Feb 2010
Subject: Jerusalem Holy Tour

Hi All
Great day starting at King David's Tomb then into the Temple Mount and the Dome of the Rock is where Abraham prepared to sacrifice his son Isaac and Prophet Mohammed was accepted into Heaven.
Out from their and into The Church of the Holy Sepulchre and down deep into the grottos of bare stone 2 storeys below it and into the Tomb of our Lord Jesus Christ and touched the stone lid wishing happiness for all the poor and hungry in the world and bending over I was so overwhelmed to be here I was out and back up into the real world.
Along the ancient Roman Rd to the Church and Monastery of the Dormition where Jesus mother Mary fell into everlasting sleep but ever step was so full of history it was unbelievable.
Manyanna taking a bus to Bethlehem for a morning and maybe Jericho PM.
al de bes
Jack

Jesus handprint

Day 55, Friday, 19-02-10, Jerusalem – Bethlehem; Israel.

Great sleep I think but was woken up really early by the Muslim loudspeaker chanter at 0430hrs me thinking this should be made illegal as it never stops and how do people get a decent night's sleep. Up at 0735hrs, underarm wash, face splash and bang an early riser dobhi drop, cleaned ass, kit on and out to very neatly laid out breakfast table, got a plate and had 2 boiled eggs, 4 bread rolls, butter, jam and 4 teas, just the job. Said my Good Mornings to Ashley who sat down, had a tea then straight onto her laptop computer but I was away, back to room, teeth clean, little pack of China beachbag and out going left upto Damascus Gate then turned right going across the road to Suleiman Street Arab Bus Station. Seen Bus 21 nearly full, got on, paid my 6 Shekel fare to the driver, got a back seat and we were away, wow, that was good timing. Enjoying seeing all aspects of Israel/Arab life as we drove out of Jerusalem and only 30-40mins with quite a few dropping off stops and going through the armed Palestine Israel border checkpoint without stopping and next stop on the outskirts of Bethlehem was our final stop and we all got off. Taxi touts everywhere I listened to one old guy giving me a rundown on where, what I should do and then asked him price, he said 200 Shekels so I walked away. He said ok where you want to go, I said Town Centre, he said ok, 20 Shekels so not a clue where I was anyway, I said ok and got in. He said Milk Grotto so I knew it was one of the places I was going to go and see so said nothing as we got to the Milk Grotto Old Chapel, I got out. It was lovely and going down some steps and in a small opening I just wondered around looking at lots of old paintings on the neat walls then down a flight of stone steps to the Grotto itself and Cave as this was the place the Holy Family took shelter when they were on their journey to Egypt. History has it that milk from the Virgin Mary's breast as she was feeding baby Jesus fell on the floor of the cave which turned the cave walls and floor to a white chalk stone. Fabulous history as I bent down touching the marble slab and then just a slow walk back up looking around at all the new area above the Grotto Cave over the last 50-100years then into the small Church bowing my head and saying Thank You Lord. I seen people writing on small sheets of paper and could see lots of small sheets and pens on a semi circle upright bench facing the pulpit and seen people putting their written sheets into an old type letter box and asked an old bearded black robe guy what is it for. He said "it's a Wish to God" so I wrote "Thank you Lord for all your kindness to me and look after my darling Kelly Rose", kissed it and with a truly happy vibrant smile I put it in the Church Wishing Well letterbox and back up to the small bend over entrance and I was back out and upto my taxi driver. Got in saying tour centre, he said yes and we were away. Old guy said Shepherds Field as he drove sort of out of Bethlehem and stopped at a hill looking down all over the area and I got out as he did and he showed me the big huge 10-15n high concrete slab barrier walls saying behind that is Israel, you are now in Palestine giving me a little history rundown and pointing out the Herodion the Volcaio shaped remains of the Palace built by King Herod 24BC and said also there is Solomon's Pools but saying my thanks I said centre and in we both got. Only a short drive he stopped in the village of Beit Jala saying the Shepherds Field and out I got laughing to myself and had a walk around the ruins of the 614 AD Byzantine Monastery and the ruins of a 5th Century Church as I could plainly see the old Mosaic floor and God oh God I found an old well on the hill top and it was full nearly upto the brim with water, I was really, really chuffed. In my walk I passed a long stone seat with lots of small stone seats facing it and on the large stone seat it had inscribed on it; Kitty McGilly, Faith Journey and I loved that name thinking was she an Irish girl and then back upto my driver I was really happy. Into car and he was going on and on about various sites but I said, centre, centre and this time he drove up a very steep winding hill road with the most fantastic Church on it I could see it from my front seat and stopped in Manger Square just facing it. Out I got giving him a 50 Shekel note, he said 100, I said centre, centre and giving him another 20 Shekel note I walked away towards the Church entrance through a 1.4m high hole in the side of it. Lined up taking my turn and doing a good back breaking bend I was in and what a true huge genuine spectacle it was. It was just enormous and all constructed from 325 AD over the Grotto of the Nativity by St Helena, Constantine's the Great mother who as a true Christian came to Bethlehem to investigate the birthplace of Jesus and built it over the Grotto Caves where Jesus was born. I followed a sort of it looked like Russian Tour Group as we went down a small flight of steps and head down I was in the Grotto of the Nativity seeing the Star of David and a sign in Latin; "Here the Virgin Mary Jesus Christ was born" and I was so truly full of such true Happiness to have made it this far as I took my time and bent down on one knee putting my right hand into the Altar and blessing water hole and with a small drop of water I touched my forehead saying into the dark Grotto, "I thank you Lord for all my Life and my Kelly Rose" and crawled back and up and back out into the beautiful Church at the other side of the Church altar. Seen another Church door so went over and it was the Church of St Catherine and a live service was going on with it full of singing people. There was other Grotto caves I went into the first one was The Cave of the Massacre of the Innocents as King Herod in an attempt to kill baby Jesus had all the male infants in the area put to death and another cave is the Cloister of St Jerome which has his Tomb and next to it the cave where he translated the Bible from Hebrew to Latin. Fantastic true history as I walked my way around the beautiful old Church then out the bend over hole entrance door and I was back to real life in Palestine. Seen a Church Cross Spire at the highest point up the hill above the town and made my way up the reasonable sized Souk looking left and right into little tiny Souks some had steps going up, some going down and it was real true Palestine life with lots of Palestine flags flying everywhere. Halfway up the hill I reached St Mary's Syrian Orthodox Church and went in admiring its beautiful on the wall paintings, really superb. Area started getting rougher as I reach the bell ringing Church on the top of the hill it was 1200hrs but not one steel door was open. I had a thought about carrying on over the hill but said no to myself as it looked a bit like Arthur St so back around to the front of the Evangelical Lutheran Christmas Church at Pope Paul VI Street and slowly back down the hill. Halfway down I seen a sign Martyrs Street above Al Fawaghreh Street and turned right and into it and it was big time real old with I could see old stone buildings from hundreds of years ago and peeping into little doors and alleys it was real, real life but quickly back to the main Souk and back down the hill seeing a sign Mary's House, The Bridgettine Sisters. Back up the main Souk and on down to Mangers Square as hundreds of Palestine blokes with mats were on their knees were there and as the chanters started I went into the Bethlehem Peace Centre nice building just to keep out of sight and was warmly welcomed by a lady receptionist who invited me to sit down saying wait 15mins until it is finished so I did. Loud speaker prayers to Allah finished 1240hrs so waited another 10mins for the crown to disperse then had a chat with the very helpful lady at reception who gave me a Bethlehem map telling and showing me the best way to get to Rachel's Tomb the wife of Jacob and mother of Joseph and Benjamin and said don't even think of going over the hill take the long way around it which was the hill I had just come back down from!, what a traveller's tale. Before starting my 2-3km walk I had a rest having a packet of cream biscuits and a bottle of lemonade sitting on a small wall along Manger Street then after my nice din din I was away enjoying my main road with dozens of big tour buses passing many people staring and pointing, look at him, me laughing. Seen an ATM, card in, punched 500 Shekels and with a sign of relief out it came just as a tour bus had stopped and 6-10 people from the Midlands by their accent came up to it saying to me does it work so I showed them my handful of Shekels saying, "God is good to the Belfast boy" and everyone laughing I was away on up the road. Seen a sign King David's Wells but it was pointing up a very huge flight of steps so said no and carried on. Didn't get lost but couldn't see Rachel's Tomb and as the 10th taxi driver tooted me for custom I asked him where it was and he said 10 Shekels so I said yes, jumped in and we went in and around a few tiny not good vibes alley streets all with one side the big 10-15m high full of Graffiti West Wall dividing Israel and Palestine with rough dressed kids all running about. He stopped at a massive big steel gate at the wall and I could see the Dome of the Rachel's Tomb on the other side, out I got and had a walk through a Palestine graveyard this side of the wall from Rachel's Tomb. Their was no doors or access into it so walking along the Palestine side of the wall then out of the graveyard a group of kids were getting violent towards me so quickly jumped in my just stopped taxi and we were away just around the hill and he dropped me off before the border checkpoint. Said my thanks giving him another 10 Shekels and I was away back down to the West Wall on the Palestine side having a photo shoot with a crowd of school kids from Dublin, really good fun, one of the teachers had even worked in the Model School in Belfast so Wishing them All Well I was this time going across and through the West Wall Border. Got upto the border crossing seeing a big crowd of vividly coloured African people just getting onto their tour bus, great sight as the women's dresses where all so brightly coloured. Started off with a CCTV camera walk along an enclosed metal rail walkway then showing my Passport and putting me and my China beachbag through x-ray I was through the Palestine side. Only a short walk meeting Ralph from Belfast travelling Israel for 6 weeks I had to do the same again at the Israel side and I was in. Asked bus driver which bus goes to Jerusalem and he pointed at a nice big clean bus so Ralph and I got on and with only another 4 passengers we were away paying 4 Shekels to the driver. It was a lovely bus and an easy ride and as we both seen Jaffa Gate the bus stopped at Damascus Gate and we both got off, had a photo shoot at the Gate, shook hands and we each went our own way. I walked up Jaffa Road to King George V Street looking for a Bus Tour Company but nothing so back all the way and into Old City and into hostel seeing Ashley still on her laptop and Helen a Japanese girl having a tea reading LP and we all greeted each other with smiles and how was your day and good travellers fun telling each other our today jaunts. Into kitchen and had 8 Weetabix with cold milk and 2 teas and that was my belly full so got key, into room and a lovely hot water shave and shower, I was over the moon. Clean kit on and out thinking about the lively pedestrian area up Jaffa Street and King George V Street so off I went enjoying my walk and laughing out loud it was as dead as a door nail, not one shop or café open as manyanna was Israeli Sabbath Day and everywhere including bus stations closed at 1600hrs today, I couldn't believe it. Walking around I found a McDonalds and it was still open so laughing and shouting out loud "I got you, I got you" I was in and had a beef burger, fries and a coffee, yeah mon yeah. Enjoyed my sort of lonely meal as no one about, paid my bill and away thinking which way. I had already come up Jaffa Street so went left and it did get a little bit seedier as I saw two girls hanging about narrow souks just standing there and knew this could be it. Passed first girl getting an enquiring look but no asking then passing the lovely full figured in tights second girl I got the you want sex on the kosher look and speaking Israel Inglise "you like a good time Papa" I knew in our true Israelite true love we would be together until the last Kosher I said Shalom, yes my beautiful darling as she then cuddled me up close letting her straying hands do the talking as I said, short time, how much she said in her true love voice with her love struck eyes peering into mine, 180 Shekels Papa and as our true intense Israeli love was vibrating between our bodies I said, ok, where we go and she gently pulled me up into the open alley Souk and said up here and my love was so strong I didn't care and followed her into the dark no lights Souk then up a flight of stone steps into a tiny flat and into a small bedroom. Quickly getting a 200 Shekels note out I smiling she rubbing her hands over my aching body I put it on the dresser as we both stripped off naked I was in God's Kosher heaven as she had the figure of the original Queen of the Israeli Jews and onto the bed we went side by side kissing, caressing each other hot naked bodies I was on top French kissing her hot exploring tongue mouth her whimpering in exotic pleasure we where making hot pounding Israeli sex love on her soft bed me groaning in hot sexual lust passion she was now screaming in ecstasy ripping my buttocks to pieces and biting my neck I was savaging her nipples with my teeth we reached new heights of our sadism true Jewish Jerusalem sensual sexual love her legs now twisted tightly around my back we climaxed together her screaming and yelling in pure Shalom love me groaning in sheer Jew passion as our vibrations went on and on my whole body felt like I was being jolted with electric and one more final climax our scented love sweat drenching her bed we slowly but slowly the two of us breathing heavily in pure enjoyment I slid off my together forever for life beautiful Jew girl lover knowing this is where I will stay for the rest of my Jewish life she slapped my bleeding bum and running her hands up my body smiling into my smiling face said "You good Kosherman Papa but we go" and we both slid of the bed standing up I give her lovely ass a gentle slap as she grabbed her money we both got dressed she sticking her money down her right hand sock and out of her room we went. I was still so full of vibes as hand in hand she took me down the stairs to the Souk door and pointing left said Jaffa Gate and I was away blowing a kiss back at my blowing kisses Israelite true love and made it down to and along Jaffa Street to Jaffa Gate then turning left I went down the hill to Damascus Gate and along the Souk and into my hotel. Got my key and upto my room, wow I was thinking, what a session, had a full bottle slug of Fanta, stripped off and cleaning the blood from my ass cheeks I stuck some plasters on the rips and just about to fall asleep I was into my bed and asleep dreaming Kosher Jewish love is only for Jewboys and asleep a one happy Jewboy Kosher man.

Palestine Side of the West Bank Wall.

Machine Guns along the West Bank Wall.

Email Sent: Fri, 19 Feb 2010
Subject: Bethlehem and birthplace of Christ in Palestine Occupied Territories

Hi All

Jumped a public bus, 6 shekel and no check going into Palestine for Glassi the Israeli sitting in the middle seat fitted in with all the rest of the bus's passengers.

Got to Bethlehem and first had a taxi to the Milky Grotto where baby Jesus and the Holy family hid down a cave grotto on their way to Egypt and Mary feeding baby Jesus split some milk and the stone underground grotto turned deep white, still white.

Next stop the Shepherds Field and looking at old ruins and I found a well with water upto its rim, marvellous.

Next into the most fantastic Church I have ever been in called the Nativity Church the oldest Church in the world and down into the cave grotto underneath it to the birthplace of Jesus Christ our Lord in Bethlehem, what a true vibrant feeling and touched the stone and out.

Walked through old town of Bethe upto the top of the hill then turned back as getting a bit like Arthur St but walking through the old town of Bethlehem and looking and peeping into narrow alleys and open doors of the Palestine people with Palestine flags everywhere was a great experience.

Took the long 2-3klms walk all the way from Manger Sq in Bethlehem to the Israel border checkpoint sometimes walking close up along the side of the 10-15m high concrete West Wall which is full of Graffiti but good fun as the Palestine's mostly ignored me.

Made it first to the big steel gate to go in and look in St Rachel's little Domed church which I could see from the Palestine side but big steel gate not open so kept going around the hill and upto the Machine Gun checkpoint and showing Passport both sides I was through and jumped another Public bus, 4shekel straight to the Old City Damascus Gate in Israel, great day.

Manyanna will jump a bus that's if their is any as everywhere in New Town is shut tonight as its Israel Sabbath day manyanna and it started 1600hrs today but their is Arabs who do work.

al de bes
Israeli Jack

Day 56, Saturday, 20-02-10, Jerusalem – Jericho; Israel

Woke up at 0655hrs, quick piss, back to bed for a snooze then up at 0730hrs, bang, a good clearing dobhi drop, cleaned ass, underarm wash, face splash, kit on and out to breakfast communal room saying Good Morning to Ashley on her laptop getting a smiling Good Morning back. Had my usual 2 hard boiled eggs, 4 pieces of half round flat bread, butter, jam and 5 cups of tea and well filled, I was happy. Told Ashley I also was addicted to computers as I always did 15-20mins each day. Me laughing, her smiling her eyes saying Piss off I went back to my room, teeth clean, lemonade, water bottle in China beachbag and out upto reception paying 260 Shekels for Tour Bus day trip to Nazareth and Galilee tomorrow as would not be able to do it on my own as its hundreds of miles away. Checked how many days I had already stayed and paid 300 Shekels for two more so at least my finances are in order, said see you later and I was out and away. Made my way up the Souk to Damascus Gate and took the first street on my right facing it as directed by helpful reception and came to bus station seeing bus No18 and smiling I said to driver, Ramallah, driver said yes so on I got paying him 6 Shekels, got a seat and we were away only half full. He slowly travelled out of Jerusalem picking up lots of passengers and it was now standing room only as we came to the Graffiti West Bank Wall and no stop straight through the checkpoint into Palestine as I think the only checks are when you go back into Israel!. Picked up a good speed and not really far he stopped in the very busy and good vibes centre of Ramallah and off we all got. I said to driver where is shared taxi for Jericho, he pointed down the street towards the Lion Statue crossroads and said turn right so happily smiling off I went. Got to the 6 road Lion crossroads, done a right and 75m on my right there was a fully packed parking area of yellow Minibuses so upto it and asked one driver for Jericho, he pointed up at a yellow Minibus just ready to go and up I went asking Jericho, driver said yes. On I got, so lucky as 5mins later our 7 seater Minibus was full and we were away me paying the 17 Shekels fare. Passed along the heavily armed machine gun Israeli soldiers on guard on the West Bank Wall then we went left away from it but all along on my left I could see the unfinished wall and where it stopped with razor wire barriers going along from it. Slowly we got into the most beautiful high rocky bare mounds of the desert seeing Bedouin tents with camels, goats and donkeys all running about. Great fantastic desert scenery for miles then signpost for Jericho and we went left passing in through a checkpoint and only a short drive the driver stopped at the water fountain roundabout in the centre of Jericho and we all got off, it was 1105hrs already. Taxi touts as usually but knew I needed one because as usual I didn't have a clue and LP book didn't have a map of Jericho which was a bit daft but bluffing my way I haggled a price down from 100 Shekels to 60 Shekels for a drive around a few sites then to drop me off at the Mount and Monastery of Temptation which I believed was high up on the side of a cliff and is where Jesus was tempted by Satan but stayed true to his convictions of Christianity. The driver was polite and said first stop the Jericho Holy Tree and not far we stopped at a fenced off tree, out we both got me looking at a lovely tall, thick, many big branches with plenty of leaves tree as when Jesus was coming into Jericho the Chief Tax Collector for the area called Zacchaeus seen the crowds but being only a small person he could not see Jesus so he went further on up the road and climbed this tree. Jesus seen him and calling out Zacchaeus I stay in your quarter tonight, Zacchaeus welcomed him and the tree was acknowledged then as the Holy Tree and a Mosaic Square was set out describing the meeting and the Holy Tree and its still on view at the side of the tree. Marvellous great old history as I had my usual thumbs up photo shoot turning down requests to buy souvenirs, no chance I said. Back into the car again and we were away out of Jericho passing the ruins of the old City of Jericho which I intended to come back to anyway. It was a wonderful drive as we were now out of Jericho passing through big barren stone hills stretching for miles as this was pure hilly mountain desert area. Wonderful to look at from the car but wouldn't like to be stranded or have to walk it without water as the heat was wonderful but I was drinking plenty of water as I needed it even in the car. Got to the neat large but not huge site of Pillared Columns of The Ruins of Hisham's Palace and driver stopped in the car park and out I got, he said walk it and come back so over to the entrance so paid my 10 Shekels to the very polite girl in the kiosk and in I went to the 8th Century ruins It was an enjoyable walk as looking over the ruins walls all the area of the Palace floor was a colourful Mosaic pattern all so neat it was just so wonderful to see then the Majestic remains of the Monumental Fountain and steps leading down to the bathroom built underground underneath it. In the complex they had built a Mosque which still had its main pillared entrance, great vibes as lots of Niche Reliefs were very plain to see as these old 1000 year old carvings in the stone face were so fine they were just a work of art. Nearly finished my left to right circle walk I bent over and into and stood up in the hole of the Full Imitation Palace and I could see the interior how it originally was, great imaginative thoughts from someone, bent down again and walking bent over I was out, straightened up and smiling I said my thanks to the staff and back into car. Driver said Mount Temptation and we were away him asking me did I want to go up in the Cable car or walk up the full mountain steps path. First question I asked was how much is the cable car, he said 55 Shekels which didn't really put me off but I wanted to do it the real way and said no. I could see the Monastery built directly on the side halfway up the mountain face so saying to myself I will walk up the mountain, this will be fun. He pulled into the parking area at the foot of the mountain cliff face and stopped, I got out, paid him his 60 Shekels, said my thanks and I was away thinking he will wait a long time for a tip from me. First option was to take the steep steps or take the zig zag path so head down I took the steps and out of breath and breathing hard within 2mins I said wrong decision but kept going and sweating heavily in the desert sun I was at my next mountain crossroad decision as I was at the path and steps again so this time I took the path. To be honest it didn't make any difference as both were so steep and kept going thinking will I make it but only a few more heavy gasping breathing steps and wow oh wow God is kind I was at the bottom of the steps upto the Temptation Monastery one way and the café and cable car stop point the other way. No tea, no rest I just done a final gallop and got upto the 2m sq Monastery door with a young African face featured guy sitting to the left of it. I couldn't talk as no breath so heavily breathing for 5mins until my body sort of got back to normal, I said, Monastery. He said, yes, use knocker on the front of the door which I did giving it a 4 knocks, nothing moved behind the door. The young fellow said and using his hand, knock again so I did and again nothing. He then stood up and came over and gave it a good hard knock which got a voice from the side of the mountain and we both leaned over the small parpet wall at the edge of the steps looking up at an old guy with a full beard and skull type hat. He said no and appeared to put his hands together to say he sleep. I said tourist I want to see but he said no and went back off the balcony. I knocked again then 2mins later knocked again, then again then said to myself, no chance, so shook the young fellow's hand him asking for a coin and I searched my trouser pockets but had none so saying no change I was away down the steps. Got to the bottom thinking will I go up to the Café restaurant for a coffee then take the cable car down but said to myself I wont see anything else that I cant see from here and don't want to waste money or time on a coffee so on down the zig zag path I went being careful as it was very steep with loose sand and stone toppings. Got near the bottom and laughing out loud I jumped down the final flight of steps and I was on the tarmac road at the car park meeting two guys and one girl travellers going up. I said its closed but he might let you in so wishing them well off they went up the steep steps me laughing again as I was away on down the steep tarmac road. I looked back a few times and they did make it up to the Monastery door but not sure if they did make it in. Cable cars with plenty of tourists were passing overhead so maybe the old fellow was waiting for a group but now I was down on the main road and I went into the tour bus parking area beside the Old City of Jericho. Seen a lovely fountain called The Elisha Spring Fountain and it had a Mosaic notice at its front; The Old City, The Lowest Place on Earth, 1300 Feet below sea level, 10,000 years old. Wow, what great vibes it gave me reading that. Over to the entrance kiosk, paid my 10 Shekels, got a stub ticket from the three friendly staff and I was in walking along and on top of the old Walls of Jericho, yeah man yeah. Truthfully it was not very big but in the excavation they had found walls and artefacts from 3000 BC. I just followed the signposted path sometimes admiring the 3000 BC still in place walls and got right upto the viewpoint hut and that was me, sat down and had a good big slug of lemonade and ate my pack of creamy chocolate biscuits, what a lovely dinner. Finished my last slug of lemonade, ditched the plastic bottle in the litter bin and down the slope and out saying my Good Lucks to the smiling staff and going left downhill I was away. Said to myself should I get a taxi or walk to the centre of New Jericho so as a good Jewboy without my skullcap I kept walking thinking I was an idiot as sun was big time hot. No stops, no nothing and got back to the centre of the town roundabout small park going to have a seat but asking for Minibus to Jerusalem or Ramallah young guy pointed at 2 yellow Minibuses just across the road one half full so over and guy said Minibus, Jerusalem pointing at the empty one or Minibus Ramallah pointing at the half full one. So I having a laugh said Minibus Ramallah and 4 guys having a smoke ditched their fags and we all climbed into the Minibus along with the driver and we were away as all they were waiting for was one passenger. I paid my 17 Shekels and eating my crisps and bun I fell asleep and was woken up by a couple of guys who pointing at a chock a block Palestine/Israel checkpoint telling me I should to into that one so no worries I said my thanks and off the bus. I crossed the road full of stationery large and small Minibuses with 3 guys telling me to get on their bus as I was not allowed to walk across. Seen other people walking so kept going and followed a girl as we passed the full of Graffiti big 10/15m high West Bank concrete slab Wall then a Machine gun post with 4 heavily armed soldiers and going through two turnstiles I was at x-ray. Put China beachbag through x-ray, me through the upright one and showed girl my Passport, she said ok and I was now going towards the Israel side. Only a short walk and same same at x-ray and showing girl my Passport, she said Visa and showed her two Arabic ones before I eventually found the Israel one at the Allenby Bridge and she nodded and I was in. Lots of buses and asking a guy for bus going to Old City he pointed at one so on I got and 2mins later we were away and only a 10-15min ride we drew into the Bus Station facing Damascus Gate and off everyone got, what a great fulfilling day I smiled to myself, it was 1630hrs. Strolled through the hustle and bustle of Damascus Gate buying two big soft baguette rolls, jar of butter and a pint of long life milk and into hotel, wow oh wow. Dumped shoulderbag in room, got my tin of corned beef that I had bought a few days ago and into the hotel kitchen. Opened the corned beef tin, cut my 2 big baguette rolls filling them with butter and cornbeef, poured myself 4 teas and this is the life sat back eating my 5 star din, din sometimes feeding the meow, meow cat who loved the corned beef. Finished din din and into room having a nice shave and shower, lovely jubbly, new clean kit on and out meeting with Ashley and we went out together but she was going into the restaurant nearby for something to eat which I would have loved to have stayed with her but needed to go into town as wanted to find an ATM to draw some loot. We said our Goodbyes and I was out and checked my watch to see how long it would take me to get to Jaffa Gate as I have to be leaving at 0700hrs tomorrow morning and it took me a 20min walk!. Carried on up Jaffa Road into the many cafes, street musicians and hawkers at pedestrian only Ben Yehuda Street and I loved its lots of shops and cafes fully lighted area thinking how much are hotels around and in it but didn't check as my hostel was near the two bus stations so couldn't get better. Had 2 coffees then called it a night as up really early manyanna and a slow walk back through the full of life new town centre and drew out 400 Shekels at an ATM so cards working well now. Back to Hostel meeting ever so lively and full of life Lisa with Ashley sitting reading and had a good long chat with Lisa who I wont see again as she is leaving manyanna to go back to Korea and start work again so shaking hands I was away. Into room and got the one copy of How Not to Travel South East Asia, Singapore, Brunei, Hong Kong & Australia and "Still Enjoy Yourself by Jack Glass, signed it and back out to Lisa asking her how to spell her name, put it in the book, (www.amazon.com), and gave to a lovely very helpful girl and shaking her hand thanking her for all her great advice I gave her my book. It was fun as she looked at the cover then looked at me saying its your picture but your name is William, I said William on Passport but known as Jack and we laughed. Had another good yarn me telling her don't let her Mum read it and I was finished making my 4 teas so all set, done and dusted I wished my new friend Lisa a happy and safe journey home and I was away back into my room. Had a few scones and drank all my lovely tea, had a little pack of my China beachbag ready for my 0545hrs start tomorrow then stripped off and into bed and thinking what a true wonderful world to always meet some good true honest helpful friends like Lisa and Ashley I was asleep.

Email Sent: Sat, 20 Feb 2010
Subject: Walking the Walls of Jericho

Hi All

Jumped a bus, 6 Shekels to Ramallah then another one,17 Shekels to Jericho and was now on the earths lowest point at 1300feet below sea level and its big time warm, yeah man yeah.

Got a taxi to Hisham's Palace then the Jericho Holy tree where a small guy Tax Collector called Zacchaeus was watching Jesus coming into Jericho give Jesus a bed in his place for the night then Taxi dropped me off at the foot of the Mount Temptation where the Mount and Monastery of Temptation is build all on the vertical side of the mountain and dying of thirst and big time sweating I made it upto the big timber door and the Monks!! wouldn't let me in, this is the spot Jesus was tempted by Satan.

Back down and into the last remains of the oldest city in the world Jericho and walked its walls, they have found remains dating back 3000BC.

Good fun then walked it, 2Klms back to centre of Jericho, jumped Minibus and upto the machine gun checkpoint of the Palestine Israel West Wall and through each side.

Israel is still building the Wall as when in Palestine are road followed it for miles then when it stopped there were fences of barbed razor wire.

First time but have no option as buses don't run to Nazareth from Jerusalem so I am taking a one day tour bus to Nazareth and Galilee manyanna.

al de bes

Jack

Day 57, Sunday, 21-02-10, Jerusalem – Nazareth – Galilee; Israel

Didn't sleep well and the chanters at 0430hrs, the Church bells at 0530hrs didn't help much but up at 0535hrs only one thought in my mind that I need and hope to have a dobhi drop before my 2-3hrs journey at 0700hrs to Nazareth on a Minibus. Had a quick underarm wash, face splash, kit on and out to breakfast room, got my Weetabix and my pint of milk out from my wrapped up black bag on table, put 5 Weetabix in a bowl, poured the milk on it, used my sugar and got stuck into my sort of English breakie enjoying every last bit, cleaned spoon and bowl putting them back on table and overjoyed as felt a stir. Quickly back to room and a small but cleared the system dobhi drop, cleaned ass, cleaned teeth and checking watch still had plenty of time. Had a little pack of beachbag and checking watch again it was 0630hrs so out locking room door and dropping key at reception I was out in the nice fresh air of the main Souk walking upto Damascus Gate seeing the old women and young boys just starting to set up their on the ground stalls!. Turned left out of Damascus Gate and up the hill then left at the top of the hill down to Jaffa Gate and taxi driver smiling said wait there pointing at a row of stone block seats. An old English lady came along and we had a chat her saying she was doing the Masada Tour with the same tour group as me so we waited. Next an Italian guy came along and asked us were we waiting for the Mike Centre Tour, we said yes and the next minute taxi driver standing next to us said there is your driver pointing at a guy walking across the square. I went over saying to him, Mike Centre Tour, he said yes and we all followed him to outside the Tourist Office just inside Jaffa Gate where the Italian guy's girlfriend was waiting and gave him our booking receipts. He told the old English lady sorry but your tour is not until tomorrow then said to another girl, Natasha from Argentina, Stefano from Italy with Cherene his girlfriend from New Zealand and me, ok lets go and we followed him back out to Jaffa Gate to his Minibus and on us four got, he started up and we were away, it was 0715hrs. Didn't take long then we were out along the motorway going through the barren stone hills of the desert stretching for miles with only Bedouin, camel, donkey, goats and tent camps sometimes each side but wonderful views as looking right I could see the Dead Sea glistening in the morning sun. Sometimes we passed through great round sand dunes it was real fun in the cool of the AC minibus as looking out my left hand window I could see a huge barren mountain range, wow, it was some sight as now we were driving straight at it. Went through the mountain valley and looking right I could see double barbed wire razor fence running parallel with our road. Seen a signpost, Tiberias, 54km it was 0840hrs so getting near and had a Passport check at a armed guard checkpoint. We were now on a flat green field green hills valley and in we drew to a tour bus large café and driver said 10mins and we all got out, I only went for a piss the others went into the café, it was 0820hrs. Had a small walk swinging my arms then everyone back, we all got back on the Minibus and away, it was 0905hrs. Passed signpost, Nazareth, 30klm, it was 0920hrs and good fun on the Minibus exchanging traveller's tales with Stefano and Cherene who had been travelling SE Asia before coming to Israel. Now in a big time well organised, well cultivated green valley and lubbly jubbly it's getting warmer. Everyone laughing as we passed a McDonalds Stefano saying it's the place for the last supper as we turned right and I seen a white many buildings town or village on top of a row of hills we were heading for so this looks like Nazareth but no, seen signpost Nazareth, 7km!. Our main road went right across a bridge and through a tunnel and I just spotted a red roof village on top of the hill we were driving to and going left in we drove to the City of Jesus home, the town of Nazareth, it was 0945hrs. Driver parked up and out we all got him pointing up the hill at the huge Domed church The Basilica of the Annunciation which was where the Virgin Mary was informed by Gabriel she would be giving birth to Jesus and we were away myself with sexy Natasha and Stefano with Cherene each twosome going our own pace. We got upto and into the big Church with beautiful Mosaic paintings all around the wall and a huge one behind the altar, really beautiful. Myself and lively full of life Natasha took our time going in a circle around the packed Church as it was Sunday and the morning service with a hymn was just starting then out a side door going down a row of stone steps to below the Church to the original Grotto Cave which was where the Angel Gabriel told the Virgin Mary she would be giving birth to Jesus. It was so moving walking everywhere under and around the Church seeing the Holy Church grottos where the Virgin Mary lived and also the remains off ancient Byzantine and Crusader Churchs all built 4-5 AD. Out from there and into the Church of St Joseph which was also so beautiful inside with many lovely Mosaics all built over the original site of Joseph's carpentry shop in ancient Nazareth, just fantastic history. I really enjoyed walking down and around the Cave Grottos the many remains of large and small buildings with most of the ruins coming up 300-500mm above the ground so every room could be plainly seen. Out from there with so lively and fun to be Natasha and on down Nazareth's main street and into another ongoing hymn singing Church and we turned back us both really over the moon and happy to have seen and walked this unforgettable history. Stefano and Cherene were waiting at the Minibus so on we all got and we were away, it was 1040hrs. Went down a very long steep hill and in we drove to a car park with lots of big tour buses everywhere and parked up and out we all got our driver showing us the way and the first Church was the colourful very old Wedding Church where Jesus performed his first miracle tuning water into wine. Next along the street and into the Greek Catholic Church which in ancient times was a Synagogue where Jesus as a young man prayed and gave lessons in his faith, Natasha and I were so happy visiting these wonderful places. Seen and into another two Churches all full of their congregations happy singing or receiving blessing from the Priest then back to Minibus at the same time as happy Stefano and lively curvy Ms Cherene. Away we went up another large hill and topping the hill was the most fantastic sight of the Sea of Galilee, wow oh wow as looking down on and all around it the bush green valleys was an artists dream. Got into the centre of Taberias then went left driving for miles along the shore edges and came to Tabgha and into The Church of the Multiplication of Loaves and Fishes and all these Churches are just full of Mosaic wall paintings and floors the craftsmanship so fine and skilful it was a full pleasure to be here and see it. This Church and the Rock was where Jesus performed a miracle to feed 5000 followers with 5 loaves and 2 fishes. Next into the Church of the Primacy of St Peter where when Jesus was resurrected he transferred his leadership to St Paul but walking the floor of the Church looking at the vivid stained glass window was a true gem. Back and into the Minibus and we were away not that far to Cafernaum the home of Jesus during his Galilean preaching as all below the Church were the original remains of the house ruins where he lived. It was real good fun walking and chatting and helping each other understand what was in the ruins and why as Natasha was so skilful in her understanding and analysing of the tourist information boards and fun and a laugh to be and walk with. Next a final one on the Banks of the Galilee Sea was The Synagogue, a large fantastic sight and was a so vivid reminder of the great builders of 1-2 BC with all the ruins easily seen coming out of the ground and that was out great day with Jesus and Galilee history nearly over. Into the Minibus and away through majestic bush green valleys until at 1315hrs the driver drove into a restaurant parking area and parked up and out we all got and upstairs to the small restaurant. Natasha and I each had a Fefal Sandwich with a Coke, 30 Shekels and when it arrived I managed to eat all of mine, Natasha could only manage half of hers, great meal, then back in the Minibus and we were away. Drove along the shores of Galilee passing through the very level and full of vibes town of Tiberias and driver said one more stop and in we drove to the Church of Yardenit on the banks of the Jordan River. Had a nice walk up and along the Jordan River banks as this was the place Jesus was baptised and being there I stuck my big toe in the Jordan River having a thumbs up photo shoot. Another great day nearly over we all got back in the Minibus ready for our 3hr journey to Jerusalem and away we went. I and I think everyone else fell asleep and woke up as we had a 10min piss stop which turned out longer as Ms Natasha wanted and had a camel ride around the car park, great fun, everyone curled up laughing. Back in the Minibus again my ass giving me grief then my ears started popping as we drove up the steep hill and into Jerusalem driver parking up facing the Damascus Gate. Out we all got me giving Natasha 25 Shekels for the driver then saying my Goodbyes and Goodluck to Stefano and Cherene we waved each other bye bye and Natasha and I went in the Damascus Gate and along the Souk to my hotel promising to meet again at 1830hrs and I was in my hotel and into my room, it was 1740hrs,. Had a nice shave and face wash then out and 5mins later smiling Natasha came walking down the Souk from her hostel and laughing, chatting and having fun together we walked upto the Ben Yehuda full of life pedestrian café, pub, restaurant area packed with locals and tourists all enjoying their night out. Natasha changed some US dollars into Shekels then looking at her map she said she wanted us to go to the King David Hotel in King David Street as she was a Journalist and that's where when the troubles were on the Journalists would meet up and exchange their stories. Not getting lost but not finding it quickly we did find it and had a lovely coffee sitting in the lounge of the 5 Star Hotel having a great laugh with each other and paying our 36 Shekels bill leaving a 5 Shekels tip out we went after having our second piss in the downstairs toilet. Just before we left we had a walk along a corridor looking at all the Presidents of the Worlds photos who had over the years had stayed in the King David then Natasha laughing and reading them all including Mrs Thatcher we were out. Had a nice fun walk through the upmarket full length Mall all shops still open and finally along the Souk from Jaffa Gate we reached Natasha's Hostel and a nice tight hug, oh she was sexy and a few blow kisses we separated promising to meet up in the morning as we had both planned to leave manyanna. I was a little sad at leaving my full of life beautiful great fun young Natasha but looking forward to seeing her again tomorrow I was into my hotel, got my key and upto room. It was only 2215hrs so had 3 cups of tea with some scones and having a read of my LP I was still planning to go to Eilat manyanna. Little pack of shoulderbag and after a great long full of history happy day I stripped off and into bed dreaming Natasha was on top of me teaching me some sexy journalist tricks I fell into a good happy holy Natasha sleep.

Date: Sun, 21 Feb 2010 16:15:29 +0000
Subject: Nazareth and Sea of Galilee

Hi All
Another great day in Nazareth at the Grotto house of Joseph and Mary below the Christ of St Joseph Church which was such a lovely church seeing where he had his carpentry shop then a walk around the ancient village of Nazareth.
Left their and a drive out to Cana to the Wedding Church where Jesus done his first miracle turning water to wine, I would make my comments but you know what I was going to say !!!!!!!!!!!
Next all the way to the Sea of Galilee to the spot where Jesus was baptised and what a fantastic day just walking along its shores dipping my big toe into the Holy water. Might make a run for Eilat manyanna, don't know, will wake up and see!!.
al de bes
Jack

Day 58, Monday, 22-02-10, Jerusalem – Eilat; Israel.

Up at 0600hrs for a piss then back to bed enjoying my snooze until 0715hrs then up for good, had an underarm wash, face splash and mind made up, will head for Eilat today. Out for breakfast at spot on 0800hrs and good Lord almighty Ashley was not to be seen so said my Good Morning to one traveller and had my usual 4 teas, 2 boiled eggs, 4 slices of flat bread, 2 with lovely jam and 2 bits of cheese and felt full and happy as I finished my last jam bread and slurp of tea. Back to room, teeth clean, final pack of shoulderbag leaving it in my room and down to reception. Told guy I was leaving later and would pay a final bill now, he looked at book and said 450 Shekels for 3 nights, previous 3 nights paid for so gave him the 450 Shekels and out I went turning right at the main Souk and only 50m up to Natasha's Hostel front entrance. Pressed the buzzer and door clicked open so up the stairs hearing my lovely Natasha's voice echoing down from above and got to her at reception with a big smiles and hugs to each other. She said she was staying another day in her hostel but going to Jericho for a day trip today and I really was glad as I wanted her to see the Old City of Jericho. We chatted a bit as she jiggled the keys of her smart small laptop then said 2mins, put laptop in bag and back to her room with the two drinks cartons, tin of sardines and a Mars Bar I had given her. Had a look up at the top roof terrace as Natasha had wanted and this place looked good and was very smart. Back down as my smiling Buenos Aires lovely figure Natasha came out and away we went turning right and upto Damascus Gate and across the road to the second Bus Station on the right and as I said Bus 21 we seen it and she quickly ran over but it was the wrong bus and good ole Jack had also picked the wrong Bus Station. Went back not far to the first Bus Station at HaTevi'im Street and when asked the guy said No18 so Natasha asked the bus driver Ramallah, he said yes and with more smiling tight sexy hugs she was on it and I went back to the Bus Station bus exit and wow oh wow I seen a sign for The Garden Tomb which Protestant Christians believe Jesus was buried and where I was going to anyway. Stood for 5mins then my little sweetie's Natasha's bus came out and waving and blowing kisses at each other she was away and a bit sad I walked up the neat alley and up to the entrance kiosk of The Garden Tomb of Our Lord in Shekham Road and a very kindly lady gave me a leaflet telling me any help or assistance, please ask any member of staff and saying my thanks I was in. No rush as I believed the bus to Eilat ran every hour so had a read of the excellent information leaflet which also informed me the Tomb and the area was maintained by a British Charitable Trust, www.gardentomb.com the Garden Tomb Acc. I followed the signs to Skull Hill seeing a Skull with eyes in the cliff face reading the leaflet it states the Bible says they took Jesus out of the City to the Place of the Skull and there he was crucified. Next stop I was in the Tomb as reading the leaflet the Bible says that Jesus was buried next to his Crucifixion in a Tomb so full of hope I bowing my head and said a little prayer for all the world wishing happiness for all and out I went following the signs. Had a look down the top of Jerusalem's largest rainwater duct reservoir then over too and it was fun looking at an ancient stone wine press. Followed the signs and I was looking and seeing another site of where Our Lord Jesus was Crucified and buried I bowed my head saying "You saved the world" I was out and after another great Jesus history morning I was away back down the small tarmac road to the Bus Station and back in the melee of Jewish Jerusalem life. Was now sad my full of life beautiful Natasha had gone but life must go on. Enjoyed my nice short walk back into Damascus Gate full of fruit sellers area and into hotel. Felt a lovely stir so a good clearance dobhi drop, cleaned ass and final check of everything I was out saying my Goodbyes to staff and always full of life and great smiles beautiful Ms Ashley as we embraced, said our final Goodbyes and I was out and down into the Souk. The Souk was level and had a sort of ramp when it went up the hill to Damascus Gate and out I went and upto the Taxi Rank ready for my New day, New town travel. Taxis wanted 50 Shekels so walking away I flagged one down on the road agreeing a 35 Shekel fee, shoulderbag in boot and we were away to the Central Bus Station. I hadn't realised but it was a long haul but we eventually got there, paid him the money and into the Jewish only, no signs in English Bus Station thinking this is just ignorance and how can anyone understand Hebrew. Finally made it up the two moving escalators to the top floor ticket office and said Eilat showing smiling lady Eilat on my Israel map. She said 73 Shekels so gave her 100, got my ticket and change with lady saying next bus 1400hrs, I was shocked, it was only 1145hrs. Asked her any other buses, she said no so resigned myself to a two hour wasted wait. I asked her what times buses run to Eilat she said 0700, 1000, 1400, and 1700hrs. I was a bit annoyed with both myself and the hostel as I had not checked bus times and hostel knew I was going to Eilat and should have known the bus times or posted them on a notice board but now resigned to a boring bus station wait I went to a café with seats. Left shoulderbag by a table and had a large tea and a big soft cheese hot roll, 16 Shekels, just the job. It was also fun watching the hundreds of 1-2-3-5 and sometimes larger groups of Israeli Soldiers coming and going every destination in the Bus Station some in full civvies but all carrying automatic rifles, not to worry they must be going or coming back from leave, but rifles in public!. Anyway, not my concern as I had one, two, three reads of LP then another tea and some cream biscuits, went for a piss and it was 1325hrs. Looked at my ticket and it said Bus No1 so walked around to Bus Stop 1 but nothing for Eilat then checking the departure gate screen it said Eilat at Gate 4 so checked ticket with a soldier guy and he said yes, ticket ok. Stood nearly in the front of the queue for 15mins then Bus 444 drew in, driver got out and into Bus Main Office, quite a long queue now as the driver came back and opened the bus hold so putting my shoulderbag in the hold I was on the bus showing ticket to the driver. He checked it and I took seat 16 an aisle seat beside a young fellow and 5mins later the bus 90% full we backed out of the Bus Station and were away, it was 1400hrs. I didn't last long and fell asleep, only woke I think because we had stopped at an Army checkpoint but only 50m away was the Dead Sea and the huge mountains of Jordan across the other side all starkly visible in the hot sun's rays, truly marvellous sight, it was 1500hrs. Next moment we were away going up a huge mountain road with tremendous views everywhere into Jordan and as we drove not that far the Dead Sea ended. Only approximately another 10km we turned right away from the signpost saying Border Area and stopped at a bus stop, driver saying over intercom, first stop. Picked up two soldier girls and away back down to our main road and doing a right we were away going full speed again. Everywhere each side of the road was just pure barren desert with the Jordan River on my left as it was the Jordan/Israel Border but looking way ahead it again developed into a huge lake sea. Up the mountain road again then down again to and through an Israeli beach resort with sunbeds at the seashore and every known fast food takeaway along the road set back from the beach. A great scenery run as we were just 5m from the vast sea lake but the great views off the mountains in Jordan were out of this world. Sort of dozed off and fully woke up to the driver on the intercom telling us we would be having our one and only 10-15min piss stop in 5mins and at 1615hrs we drove into a big car park with large fast food takeaway and also a large supermarket so off the bus we all got and first stop for me was a piss stop. Enjoying my nice piss then into the supermarket buying a packet of crisps and a packet of creamy biscuits and outside to the large seating area, got a bottle of lemonade from my China beachbag and sat down eating and savouring my early din din. Finished my crisps, back over to the bus as driver came back and opened the bus door we all got on and I finished my 4 creamy biscuits din din, oh la la, they were tasty. Away we went going through the no habitation no life desert everywhere just sparse sometimes isolated shrubs desert still seeing the great mountains of Jordan high in the sky on my left. Couldn't stay awake, couldn't sleep I was in a sort of daze then seeing sign Taba Border Crossing 95km it was 1705hrs so not doing really good. Looked at time it was 1745hrs and just starting to get dark so put my socks on as it gets slightly cold at night. Got into Central Bus Station at 1810hrs, it was now dark but plenty of lights everywhere and tried to find Bus Station icon on my LP map but no luck so my careful planning well up the shoot. Off bus and around to the hold to collect my shoulderbag and lady with 2-3 other touts was canvassing for hotels and hostels and the nice faced lady wouldn't let me go as I know she was thinking he's an easy touch. Tried to say no without saying no but eventually said ok to and into her car and she drove down through well lit plenty of cafes, restaurants and even an McDonalds area. Next we went right and out of the good part of town and up Argaman Avenue and stopped outside a nice Villa, she took me in and showed me a nice big d-ensuite with kitchen, it was 1835hrs, so said ok. She said you pay now so paid her the 300 Shekels for 2 nights, got key and she was away. Went outside as she left and it had its own deep swimming pool directly outside my room as in all the hurry to show me the room I had seen it but we walked straight past it. Dumped kit in room, neckpouch off and Eilat was big time warm even at night and I was tempted to take my socks off but left them on and out I went locking door behind me and away down the hill turning left at the first roundabout, straight across the second and I was in the Beach Centre of the lively town, really good. Into the big centre Mall and tried 3 ATM's but none paying out on card so rang UK phone number and guy said he/they will activate it again so hurdle one over and done with. Enjoyed my little walk along the still full of life seafront promenade area seeing and hearing the planes takeoff and land all along the Hotels behind the seafront, thats a bit crazy I was thinking to myself. Didn't realise the time, it was 2235hrs already so made my way towards my Villa and into a Pizza Café and had a nice large quarter size pizza with a Nestles tea, 35 Shekels, very enjoyable, paid my charge with a 50 Shekel bill, got my change and away and found my dark Villa, opened door and into my flat noticing one thing that the Eilat Israeli people where very friendly. Only wanted one thing so stripped off and into a lovely soft big double bed and asleep dreaming Natasha was beside me making wild all night Argie love.

Email Sent: Mon, 22 Feb 2010
Subject: Cohava Suites, Haiaziz 2, Eilat, Israel, Tel 0522764412

Hi All
Said and waved my sad goodbyes to lovely Natasha then found my way to the Garden Tomb as gonna catch a bus to Eilat later.
I was now in the Protestant area of Jerusalem where they say Jesus was crucified and buried in the Garden Tomb in Jerusalem, very moving but a little confusing as 2 religions disagree where it all actually happened.
My usual good planning I thought bus's run to Eilat every hour but wrong so only bus left was the 1400hrs so jumped it and into Eilat at 1820hrs, got above 5mins from Centre at 150 shekels a night and it has a big bedroom, bathroom and kitchen, whats a kitchen!!!!!!!!
Staying for a day or two.
al de bes
Jack

Day 59, Tuesday, 23-02-10, Eilat; Israel

Up once nearly frozen to death in my 2 sheets of cover bed, had a piss then duvet on top and back to sleep again. Woke up for good at 0805hrs tempted to lie in as bed was lovely but up, underarm wash, face splash and kettle on as although only 10min walk from Eilat centre there is no cafes around the area so tea bags from packet I had bought last night coming home, swimming trunks on, no sleeve tee shirt and cargo shorts on, I used my sweeteners and made 2 nice big mugs of tea. Took them outside and sat by the lovely swimming pool in the blaring sun heat of Eilat eating my packet of chocolate cookies and drinking my tea I was in pure heaven and couldn't stop laughing at myself!. Back into room as felt a stir, I love that feeling and had a full blast dobhi drop, cleaned my ass then cleaned teeth thinking about Natasha as she was supposed to phone me when she got back safely. I originally had her hotel card but I think I dumped it then looking in my driving licence wallet I found her work card for Buenos Aires but it had no phone number but it had an email address so will try it later. Enjoyed finishing my second mug of tea sitting with my peaked sun cap on as I needed it as nowhere I had been was as hot as Eilat. No plan as just going for a walk up to the Bus Station to check times for buses to Aqaba or Petra both in Jordan as will head that way manyanna. Little pack of China beachbag I was out locking door behind me thinking I will do my walk, have a swim down in the sea then come back 1600hrs for a lazy few hrs at the swimming pool, that's the plan, it was 1000hrs as I left my villa. Met lady from the USA staying in the villa for 2 months and she was fun to chat with and as we parted we introduced ourselves to each other smiling and shaking hands she said, you're a Jacca and I'am a Josleen and we went our own way me laughing as not a clue what she meant. Went downhill seeing the full Majestic high fantastic Jordan mountains fully facing me then went left not right as lady said there is a beautiful beach called Dolphin Beach to the right of the roundabout but its 20 Shekels to go into it and knowing us Jewboys there was no chance of that. Into the shopping Mall and done 15mins internet as found Natasha's business card in my driving licence wallet with her email address on it which she had given to me so emailed her to tell her to get back to me as worried about her not phoning me and hoped she was ok. Had a walk out to the centre's sea front coffee sitting area seeing people on sunbeds and swimming in the sea, lubbly jubbly. Went out and turned right to the next roundabout and up the hill passing many shopping Malls, cafes and all sorts of shops and up the hill to the Bus Station and in. Enquired at the Bus Information Desk about buses to Aqaba, very helpful lady said no buses, I have to take a taxi to the Jordan border then catch a bus to Aqaba so that sounds pretty easy. Next I asked her about buses to the Egyptian Border at Taba and she gave me a printed timetable of bus times starting at 0800hrs and every hour from then up to 2200hrs so all details this time for my trip manyanna!, us planners know how to travel!. Just having a look I think it might have been better just to get a hotel or cheap hotel around the Bus Station as it has lots of good nightlife by the looks of it!. I found Corinne Hostel, d-ensuite with kitchen, Retamin Street, Eilat, Tel: 08-6371472, 150 Shekels for a double bed for me as a single user then only 50m down Retamim

Street I found The Sunset Motel Hostel, d-ensuite 150 Shekels so might have a plan to maybe move manyanna but in saying that my Villa as I know now is central and quiet as anywhere else in Eilat so we will see. Came back passed the Bus Station and into a photo shop printing 47 photos at 1 Shekel per photo and lady said 1 hour come back. I had a nice walk just exploring then into the CoK Café on the Hatmarim Blvd and had a lovely big soft potato and tuna baguette with a large hot tea, really filling and staff were fun to talk and laugh with. Paid my 22 Shekel bill and away smiling and saying my thanks then collected my completed photos, stuck them in my China Beachbag and on down the Hatmarim Bld to the Eilat Museum. Paid my senior 5 Shekel entrance fee telling lady, senior and she smiling said ok and had a walk around its various history of Eilat sections including wars, developments when it was a Port town and all its history from 1000 years BC, good introduction to Eilat. Got to the sunbed area at the beach waterfront I looked again and it appeared a sandy beach but no worries I was just glad to get my kit off and for the first time in 59 days I was in my swimming trunks dipping my feet in the warmish seawater and taking my time over the sometimes gravel stones in the seawater I got upto my thighs, quick knee bend drenching my face and dived into the sea, wow oh wow, I was over the Eilat sea moon. Breast stroked and back floated around for about 20mins then out for a little walk and back along North Beach and plonked myself down on a sunbed one truly happy man, it was 1325hrs. It was so relaxing lieing on the sunbed and the sun was so strong I fell asleep. Woke up and a walk along the beach then in for another dip thinking should I stay a few days here as this is heaven on earth. Had a few good slugs of my Nestle tea enjoying the scenery across the sea of the big huge barren Jordan mountains with the Jordan flag flying at its shoreline as maybe still going there manyanna, we shall see. Got talking to a very friendly young Russian guy and his girlfriend as he told me it was -20 degrees where he just came from in Russia and as he works in the building industry he can only work 7 months of the year. Very lazy now so lay back soaking up the hot sun trying three times to phone my Kelly Rose but no answer. Looking out over the bay and from the Jordan side to our side was lots of small yachts out on the bay with sometimes big containers and small racing boats all so lucky to be enjoying the very hot sun's rays. In for another dip, had another walk, it was 1710hrs so called it a day, cargo shorts and no sleeve tee shirt on and away only 50m to beach town centre. Went into the Pizza cafe from last night and had a pizza and a bottle of Nestle tea, 26 Shekels really enjoying the Margareta cooked pizza, paid my bill and out and upto my Villa and into room, oh la, la, had really enjoyed my swim today. I stripped off and had a nice shave and a lovely shower, just the job, cleaned teeth, checked driving licence wallet and out. Had a slow walk back down the hill passing the Meridian Hotel approximately 75m from my villa and wouldn't like to think what you would get for 150 Shekels, maybe a dog kennel in the cellar if you were lucky. Passing my favourite ATM I drew out another 800 Shekels and kept going passing the big Mall on my right and turned left up Hatmarim Blvd and into the first money changer I seen and there was plenty along this lively full of cafes, restaurants, shopping centres and the Central Bus Station road. I said to guy give me 50$US in US dollars and how much in Israeli Shekels, he said 180 Shekels so gave him 200 and he gave me 2 x 20$US and 1 x 10$US notes and a 20 Shekel note change back.

Stuck it all in my driving licence wallet and I was happy walking up Hatmarim Blvd which had loads of cafes, shops and supermarkets upto the top of the hill and that was me. Crossed the road and slowly window watching, people watching walked back down passing Corinne Hotel and no rush had a nice hot coffee in an open air restaurant. Paid my 15 Shekels bill and away on down the hill and into the big always lively Mall just at the opposite end of the Airport runway as you wont need a taxi if you ever flew from Eilat as the Airport and its runway go right through the centre of town, great idea. Done my usual 20mins internet at the 5 Shekel for 30mins terminals and I had received an email from Natasha telling me she was ok so that was a relief. I had my final walk up and around the 2-3 storeys of shops and food Malls and had one more final coffee enjoying the vibes of people and the hardly dressed beautiful figures of the Israeli girls thinking it would have been a great lively night if Ms Natasha was here. Not to worry I am sure we will meet again, paid my coffee bill and out and a very slow relaxed walk in the warm night back to my Villa and into my room saying hello and having a chat with a Jewish guy from Jerusalem originally from Toronto in Canada. Now retired he now lives in the Villa and that was me, into room, made a cup of tea and had a Mars and a Twix bar and final pack of trolley shoulderbag I was ready for bed. Stripped off and into bed I was thinking of something I had thought about a few sad moments today and that was my ole Da, Stoker George Glass who Died Mon 2-11-09 aged 90 whose birthday it was today. It was sad but it was also wonderful lieing in my bed thinkng and half dreaming of the times he used to take us all down to Greencastle or Whitehouse beaches for a swim or walks up and over Napoleons Nose for a walk. He was a wonderful Dad and great ole Shankill Rd man right till the end and as I sort of fell asleep I remember with Pride the great send-off he had from his Belfast Royal Naval Club and the people of the Shankill on his final walk down the Shankill and my Brother Georges great speech at his wake before my Da finally left us all and was buried and is now in heaven with my Mum Elizabeth Glass and all our great Glass family clan I was asleep.

Email Sent: Tue, 23 Feb 2010
Subject: Sunbed day in Eilat

Hi All

I know you can do it and its in everyone heart but look to the sky and please forgive me as I had a slow relaxing walk around Eilat fully packed with shopping Malls, cafes and restaurants this morning and then paid 20 Shekels and "had a sunbed for the rest of the day going swimming a few times", wow oh wow, I even fell asleep on my sunbed in the lovely 30 degree sun and woke up now a redskin man.
Sometimes I think I am in Russia as I think half of Russia is here or do the Jews look like Russians.
Heading for Aqaba manyanna morning, that's the plan!!!!!!!!!!!!!
al de bes
Jack

Email from my Brother George
Subject; The Funeral of George (Stoker) Glass our Dad.

Hi everyone,
I'd better make it a big inclusive email or my writing hand will be stuffed and I'll forget half of it.
I reckon we gave me Da, Pop, Dad, Granda, Great Granda and Great Great Granda a great send off and I'm very thankful and appreciative of his old shipmates and the Royal Naval Association for the part they played and have passed on our thanks to them and all who attended and those that couldn't make it on the day but were with us in thought.
I caught up with a few of them, Charlie McCullough, Ned McBride and the other "Geordie Glass" at a Royal Irish Rifles Military Band Concert in the Spectrum Centre on the Shankill later in my stay and had a drink and a good old yarn with them in the Orange Hall after the concert.
Your Granda was a bit of a boxing and football hero to them in their younger days and throughout his time in the Navy and all his days on the 'Heel and Ankle" (The Shankill). He was also the oldest surviving member of them all before he died.
We were in very great company at Our Da's funeral with numerous second world war Sailors, Sub-mariners, Royal Marine Commandos, a couple of ex Paratroopers (Jackie & Denver), a former R.U.C Detective Chief Inspector, not to mention the UDA and UVF officers/members present who shall remain nameless.
It was great to see and meet for the first time some of our Glass cousins from Rasharkin, Bertie and Margaret and our old friends Fred and Anneleen Kyle also from Rasharkin and who brought sympathy messages from "the mountain people" as Bobby and Lizzie are fondly known down there and Nessie. Hazel and I went up for a great lunch with Fred and Anneleen later in my stay and caught up with them all, and there's plenty of them still, Bobby Glass, Lizzie, their daughter and granddaughter, Nessie, Lena (both her and Hazel shared plenty of memories of playing together as kids on the farm, where we were banished to for the school holidays every year until Jackie broke a windie then we got sent home pronto)
Caught up with Margaret, Uncle Bobby's daughter and Bertie his son again when we were there. It was a big day.
Lillians' brothers, Tom and Sam and Sams' wife Irene, who lived in Oz many years ago.
Marie and Robert Dennis and son Peter, Lillians cousin and old friends of Pops. Me and Pop always went down to Whiteabbey to see them when I was home and Marie would rustle up the best selection of cakes, biscuits and Irish breads you could get in no time at all too. Marie fondly remembers Big Molly coming into the Co-op in town, where she worked, to sort out the Co quarter and get her 'Divi' in her book.
Davy and Francis, who are coming out to Oz later this year for Johnie's wedding in Narrabri.
My old mates and Pops, John Hamilton and Hughie McCaw and you tried to pay John for the "taxi" out to Roselawn, so funny!!
My very very dear friend and our neighbour forever in Louden Street, Irene Jennings, at 13 we thought we were going to get married. She and her sister

Margaret thought my Dad had Burt Lancaster looks and Irene would visit regularly when he was in Tennent Street home.

Peggy Hanvey and "young" Albert. He used to call Pop "Daddy George" for taking him everywhere as a kid. It was really good to see Peggy again too as she cant get around much these days and she and Gran Weatherall helped us, especially the girls, growing up and later in life. The famous old Penrith Street does it again.

Eleanor (McWilliams) and Alan. David McWilliams, who we hadn't seen in 48 years, and his daughter. Their father Alistair and mother Mary were lifelong friends of Pop and the Glass family and I have very fond memories of going "visiting" to their house at Sydenham on a Sunday afternoon and having "big eats" for tea.

Ray and Edna Johnston, Phil's Dad and Mum and Hazels long time friends.

A person who was at the service on the Shankill spoke to me while we were waiting to get into the into the funeral cars and I said thanks "Trevor" for coming and he said ... "Wouldn't have missed it for Geordie! But I'm Victor", and he was gone! It was in fact Trevor's brother who I haven't seen in 45 years when we went camping together to the Free State (Southern Ireland)

Trevor Robinson and wife Roberta. he wasn't at the Shankill Service but was at Roselawn Crematorium at he and Victor are like twins, but not.

Willie John their father was a great shipmate of your Grandas and neighbours of ours from Greenland Street. Trevor now owns and runs the book binding factory across the street from Grandas flat and owns part of Boundary Street which not too many people from round our way could lay claim to fame to. Anyway, Trevor always tells me about when Willie John died years back Geordie (Granda) wanted to drive up the "Falls Road" to the City Cemetery with the coffin in the hearse still draped in the Union Jack flag. Needless to say he only agreed to it as far as the top of Divis Street but still has a good laugh over me Da's antics. Lovely people.

Johnny Spence, Pops neighbour in Louden Street. He came out in a panic as we were waiting to get into the funeral cars to go up the Shankill as he hadn't realised the time and had to rush to get ready but made it and it was good to see him there. He's a character and knows everything and everyone and said even people in York Street were asking about Geordie after seeing the death notices in the paper. And later he told me there were some "very big high rollers" at the funeral, namely Ned McBride, who was once given a bill for 96,000 pound from the Tax man and promptly signed a cheque for said amount and told them to F'off. Johnny tells it much better than me.

There was one old white haired Lady on her own at the Shankill service who none of us recognised but who I believe spoke to Larissa outside??

Wee Harry Hamilton, another shipmate of Pops, who lived up Tennent Street and called in to see Pop on a regular basis and who was only just out of hospital that week after surgery for bowel cancer, a mighty effort indeed. I met him first when me and Pop were out watching the Shankill District of the 12th parade going down the road and he recalls standing on deck on his first ship in Devonport when he sees this big good looking sailor striding down the dock so cocky and confident and later to find out he was a fellow "Road" man and great ambassador for Naval boxing.

It was quite amazing that day as numerous ones in the parade shouted over to Geordie or others would point and say "hey there's Stoker" to the rest of them as they passed as most would have thought he had already passed away not having seen him around the usual haunts for many years.

I've just remembered about the policeman who, while we were walking behind the hearse, stopped his police car in the middle of the main road, stopping all the traffic in the other direction.... got out....stood to attention.... and saluted Dad till he had passed... such a spontaneous and respectful action hey!

Others, Tony Brown and Annie, Lily Cooke to mention a few just couldn't make it through immobility or the timing being too early but numerous people on the Shankill have expressed their sympathy to me and you all and have very fond memories of Geordie.

And a very special thank you to Rev. Jim Rea, Shankill Methodist Church, for conducting the services and lending me one of his overcoats which fortunately I didn't need on the day.

Hope I haven't forgotten anyone?

Oh! That's right,

Many, many sincere thanks to all of "YOU" for being there.

Jackie, Kate, George, Hazel, Larissa, Michiel, Sian, Wilson, Nico, Xavie, Denver, Chantel, Phil, Shannon, Caitlin, Zoe, Ray, Edna, Kates' friend.

It wasn't possible for all of Pops' other Grandkids and Greatgrandkids, Damien,Fran, Oliver,Thomas, Richard, Julie,Paul,Madisson,Laughlin, Neil,Kylie,Jarrod,Callum,Kaitlin, Sheldon,Paige,Olivia to be there but they were thinking of him and remembering all the fun and laughs they had with him.

Someone will probably tell me what a great time I had at the wake..... No dont!!

But a thank you to Jackie for the Ulster Fry and Denver for the "cupla" pints we had. Great stuff.

It was such a lovely day on the "Sunday after" and very fitting that it was Remembrance Day and what a great turnout of people and the RIR Band at the City Hall.

STOKER GLASS RN would have enjoyed the spectacle.

At The Going Down Of The Sun
And In The Morning
We Will Remember Him

Lest We Forget

Stoker George Glass R.N.

1919 - 2009

Safe Anchorage Old Hand

George and Elizabeth Glass

Ole Stoker's Funeral down the Shankill Rd

Map 2 of Jordan

1) JORDAN is a modern Country but has great ancient mystical majestic ruins attractions with its main one now 'One of the New Seven Wonders of the World' called Petra a huge stone curved City lost in the mountains for 700 years only finally rediscovered in 1812 is a true walk back in bygone Arab and Bedouins history. Everywhere, be it in the deserts or the Biblical folklore towns the Jordanian people are without a doubt a happy people who go out of their way to Welcome and ensure you are Happy.
2) Capital; Amman
3) Jordan achieved Independence in 1956
4) Climate; Ave temp Jan-Mar;21c
5) Language; Arabic, English
6) Currency; Jodanian Dinar, 1$US = 0-70JD
7) Visa; Not required, 30 day issued on arrival
8) Return flight £51 + £154 ATM, hotel, food, train to Gatwick
9) Today's ongoing update of day to day accommodation, travel, food, drinks costs = £3142

Day 60, Wednesday 24-02-10, Eilat; Israel – Aqaba; Jordan.

I woke up 0700hrs after the best night's sleep of my travels as would recommend this Villa for its quietness and lovely big room to anyone. Had a sort of dozy snooze for 30mins then up feeling big time good looking forward to New day, New town and New country. Put kettle on, had an underarm wash, face splash, kit on with no socks and tea bag shared between two large mugs, 6 sweeteners in each I opened my door and sat outside and ate the rest of my chocolate biscuits with my Rosy Lee in the hot sun's rays, man oh man. Finished breakie, cleaned teeth, cleaned mugs, had a little final pack and ready to go I was thinking what will I do with the room door key and out around the villa and seen an Israeli guy that I had met last night staying for a long time in the Villa and said can you take key and give it to Iris, he said yes. He asked do I go to border now, I said yes, he said you want taxi, I said yes, he said do you know the price, I said no laughing as had usual not done my homework. He said I can get you discount and phoned up a taxi firm and 2 mins later said 17 Shekels so cant complain about that and said ok. I asked him about a Canadian lady called Josleen, he said yes she stays here and she is my friend. I said she wanted to go to Aqaba but he said nothing and taxi arrived so saying my thanks and shaking hands I was away putting shoulderbag in boot, me in the front and off we drove. Old taxi driver was good fun talking good English and I felt regrets about leaving the Canadian lady there as I was thinking maybe she was scared of going on her own but that's life and not that far I seen signs for Jordan Border and 5mins later he dropped me off and I paid him the 17 Shekels plus a lot of loose 10 cent coins and he was away. Showed Passport at first Israel checkpoint then upto Exit Charge Desk and had to pay 98 Shekels for exit getting a stamped sheet of paper. Over to very friendly Israel girl Passport Control she saying I wish I could travel all these countries flicking through my Passport and wishing me good travels, bang, Israel exit stamp, got Passport back and I was away about a 100m walk to steel gates of Jordan Entrance for Passport Control. Showed Passport at gate then upto Passport Office handing Passport in and bang, entrance Jordan Passport stamp. Another little 2min walk and final Passport check and I was in Jordan, oh la, la that was really quick. Walked on upto a car park area but only tourist buses and taxi driver said no buses only shared taxis so I said ok, I wait until full, he said no wait, every taxi goes as persons arrives. I asked him the fare, he said 10JD (1$US = 0.70JD) so it wasn't a too bad rip off so I said ok and shoulderbag in boot, me in front with seat belt on, we were away. He asked me hotel name and I told him Jordan Flower Hotel from LP, he said 2-3mins walk from where taxi drop-off. I was going to say drop me off outside hotel but just kept my temper and he dropped me off in centre of Aqaba beside a new Mosque being built facing at least 3 hotels so God help anyone in these hotels in a years time. Had a look at LP and it mentions two of the hotels I was looking at so into Al-Amer Hotel, Raghadan Street, Aqaba, Tel: 2014821 and asked reception guy any single rooms, he said yes, 17 JD, so said ok straight away as not hunting about wasting time looking for anything cheaper. Gave him my Passport, he done his paperwork and guy carrying my shoulderbag up 3 flights of stairs we went into Room 14, guy left shoulderbag on floor, I said my thanks as he left and yeah man yeah I breathed out a big sigh of relief for my very easy start to my day. I had a little think of plans, it was 1035hrs, what a great start to my day I was happy smiling thinking as dumped Passport, neckpouch and extra wallet in shoulderbag. Stripped off all my kit and rolling all my other dirty kit up and putting on all new cleaned kit I was out taking it down to reception saying to guy, you do dobhi. He said no, but two streets away past Ali Babar and walking with me out to Raghadan Street he pointed right saying go down to Ali Babar going left then go right up Bor Said Street and its on the left me thinking theirs no chance of me finding it first time. I said my thanks and away up the street packed with all sorts of shops and after a while I gave up asking an old guy nearly asleep in a chair and he stood up and in perfect English directed me up one more street so off I went and found it no problem this time. Dropped dobhi in at laundry shop at Bor Said Street and guy said it will be ready for 1800hrs tonight so saying my thanks I was away going right down to the right hand side of the public beach, oh la, la, I cant wait for a dip. Had a quick think and it was still early only 1105hrs so stayed on the beach path pavement enjoying all the young ones yelling and shouting as they swam in the sea then got to the Aqaba Museum, paid my 5JD door fee and in seeing old stone and metal artefacts and a very interesting history read of old Aqaba. The old Crusaders had built another Fort so finishing my enjoyable history lesson I was out and into the Aqaba Castle (Mumluk Fort) with its 2m thick outer walls I must say they were greatest builders on earth in those ancient Crusader days as up and down and around the ramparts of this high Fort I walked just marvelling at its so finely built structures. Had a look at my LP Aqaba and out of the Fort and just strolled through the vibrant hustle and bustle of all sorts of shops centre of Aqaba until I was in an upmarket big Hotels area. Youngish girl approached me saying she was from the Philippine's and her friend had the key to her hotel room and she had nowhere to go, could she just walk with me. I said go back to hotel and tell reception you need your room key but she said her friend has it so now what do I do. She said she was hungry and tired could we go back to my hotel room and she will give me her camera and phone as safeguard. I said I am going for a walk around Aqaba thinking is she genuine or is she a con as she was only a thin slim little girl about 5ft high. I was followed my LP map and we came to a fenced off mud brick structure mostly in the ground and reading the notice it was a 300 AD Christian Church probably the oldest church in the world. I took a photo and with my little girl trailing along by my side we got near to the City of Ancient Ayla directly in the middle of all the big upmarket hotels and resorts and after answering her telephone and standing still as I walked across the road I let on not to notice she was not with me and kept going upto the fenced off entrance of the Old City. I had sort of seen her walking away and kept my eyes discreetly on her and she walked on up past the Old City entrance gate and into I think a very upmarket hotel and then she was gone. I tried to work it out and the only conclusion I had was that she was on the game but saying that she wouldn't be carrying a large camera about with her. Did her friend phone her to say she was back, did a client phone her to tell her to go meet in that hotel, don't know and will never know and I must admit I did feel sorry for her and was going to give her 5$US to go and find something to eat!. Went into the fenced off Old City ruins and it was very interesting as I walked the set path reading the diagrams notice board giving a full description of who, why and how it was built, really good fun and then I was back to my starting point and out I went. Turned right and seen a large food Mall called The Gateway with The Rovers Return Pub in it so in I went to the Rovers Return and had a nice plate of chips and a sausage roll with a tea, lubbly jubbly. Enjoyed my Coronation Street din din, paid my 6 Shekels and smiling my Good Byes I was out and only a short walk was back on the beach. Touts were selling glass bottomed boat sails so quick decision I took one at 10 Shekels, got on and out we sailed seeing a large tank on the sea bottom and enjoyed watching all the marine life on the sea base also fantastic sights of the mountains behind Eilat as now looking at it from the other side, Aqaba. Boat driver guy had said he would take me around an old tanker anchored up as not in use no more but didn't but I didn't care as I was now bored. Back to jetty I got off giving him the 10 Shekels he was insisting he wanted buckshee me laughing and away this time along the actual beach. Found a decent enough spot near the high Jordan flag pole, stripped off and in the not cold sea, oh la la as had now swam the Gulf of Aqaba from two different countries. I enjoyed my breaststroke swim and out as now in Muslim Aqaba there were no women swimming never mind in a bathing costume, 90% of women on the beach had big black dresses and veils, crazy man, crazy. Stayed on the no sunbed beach until 1620hrs and that was me, kit on and a slow walk back into the centre and into my hotel. In my walk back I had seen a tailor so into room, emptied my shoulderbag and taking it with me I took it up to the tailor and got him to stitch a stretch of ripped stitching along the seam below one of the shoulderbag handles, 5 Shekels. Back into the room, had a nice shave and face wash and out buying a pizza and a potato pie and back to room eating the lot with a bottle of Nestle tea, yum yum, it was 1840hrs. Cleaned teeth and out and went left and left again and the Aqaba shops were all still fully open as I made it back to the dobhi shop paying 2 Shekels for my cleaned and ironed dobhi, that was cheap. No rush carrying my dobhi I walked back around the city centre then buying some cornflakes and a pint of milk with two spoons and a lunch box I now had my breakfast ready for manyanna as I made it back to my hotel room. Hadn't done that much today but looking forward to tomorrow at Petra I stripped off and into bed asleep a tired but happy no dream Aqaba beach man.

How "Not" to Travel North Africa, Middle East, Israel & Malta and "Still Enjoy Yourself"

Email Sent: Wed, 24 Feb 2010
Subject: Rm14, Al-Amer Hotel, Raghadan St, Aqaba, Jordan, Tel 2014821

Hi All

Jumped a taxi from Villa to border,17 Shekels then paid 98 Shekels at Israel's customs and Passport control, bang, exit stamp Israel.

Walked 75m across to Jordan Passport control and bang, entrance stamp for Jordan and out to shared taxi but no one about so paid 10 Jordan Dinar (JD) and taxi into Aqaba and got above 17JD at 00-70JD to 1$US so not bad I think.

Had as usual a good walk to Aqaba Castle first built by the Crusaders then a loop around the town to Old Aqaba, 650 AD which I enjoyed walking its old walls but lots to see and then into the Rovers Return an English rub a dub for a beef burger and fries with a mug of Rosy Lee, just de job.

Next onto a glass bottom boat seeing an old tank along with marine sea life not forgetting the coca cola tins in the bottom of the sea then time to spoil myself I had a relaxing 2hrs being a swimming beach bum!!!, 2 lazy PMs in 2 days, what is the world coming to.

Just out for a walkie in the full of life seaside resort of Aqaba.

Jumping a bus manyanna morning to Petra and coming back PM.

al de bes

Jack

Day 61, Thursday, 25-02-10, Aqaba - Petra; Jordan.

Worst night's sleep ever as woke up sweating bad on the semi conc mattress and pillow and room was stifling so had a piss and opened the sliding window letting in cold air but also the noise of the main road below, it was 0415hrs. Dozed off a few times cursing myself for not putting the AC on until finally at 0700hrs my alarm went off so up I got straight to wc for a gully empty save my day dobhi drop, cleaned ass then underarm wash, face splash, kit on and ready for breakie. Opened my packet of cornflakes putting the cornflakes in a plastic lunch box, poured the milk, added my tea sweeteners and let it sit for awhile as checked I had my camera, phone, driving licence wallet and then got stuck into my lovely English breakfast really enjoyable sitting on the edge of my conc bed. Washed my plastic lunch box bowl and plastic spoon, cleaned teeth, grabbed China beachbag and out downstairs handing key into reception telling guy I would be back later as going to Petra and outside I went. Went left and left again and straight only approximately 150m into Bus Station and guy standing beside Minibus with Petra – Aqaba on it said, Petra, I said yes seeing 4 people waiting at the stop. How long before full I asked, he said not sure but hopefully not longer than 0815-0830 as it was a big at least 10 seater Minibus. Taxi tout said 30 JD to Petra so asked driver how much on Minibus he said 5JD so instant decision I said ok to taxi tout and we were away over and into his taxi and away, it was 0740hrs as its 1-2hr run and just wanted to get there, see all the sights then coming back wont matter. Not long and we were out of Aqaba on the main Amman Road highway going really well passing through beautiful barren rock mountain ranges which where a joy to see and I very slowly and enjoyably drifted off to sleep. Driver nudged me awake saying Wadi Rum pointing right at a small hill mountain stone village with the vivid rock mountain and sand desert behind it and although we were on the main highway it was a wonderful breathtaking sight even from our road. He gave me a leaflet with 1-2/3-4hr drives and 1-2/3-4 day trips so might take a 1-2hr sunset drive, we shall see. Fun also as we passed through small mudbrick built villages with sometimes herds of goats crossing the highway as we had to slow down and sometimes stop. Then guys on camels, yeah man yeah, I was enjoying my scenery drive as everything 75m back from the road had no water only hilly sometimes rocky outcrops. We then went left off the Kings Highway onto Kings Way signposted Wadi Musa with just pure magic hilly desert landscape for miles down the rocky stone valleys either side, this is the life, it was 0840hrs. Making really good time going a reasonable very fast speed we came over the brow of one high hill and across the full mountain the other side was a mixture of many close together Villas and a small town all high on the side of it and driver said Wadi Musa the town for access to Petra. Wide awake now we drove down a steep hill then up and through Wadi Musa, (Moses Valley) and down a very steep hill it seemed for miles as I then seen lots of big tour buses parked up. My driver stopped near them and said ok, we are here and out we both got, it was 0950hrs. I paid him the 30 JD him telling me he would wait for 4 hrs until 1330hrs and drive me back for the same price, I said no I don't know what time I come back and we shook hands and I was away going to the Petra Centre Entrance pay kiosk.

Looking at prices it said entrance fee, 21JD, horse ride and guide 12JD so I said entrance only, guy gave me two tickets, one for entrance and one for horse ride and guide. I said I don't want a horse ride or guide giving him the ticket back he said its compulsory as per the entrance fee so saying its robbery and fraud, I had to pay 33JD, 12 extra for something I don't want or need. Left the kiosk and went along to the actual entrance gate showing Tourist Police my tickets and showing the horse ride and guide ticket telling them I was forced to buy this but didn't want or need it so its fraud and robbery can he do something about it, he said no, its Government Policy. I said how can it be Government Policy making me buy a ticket I don't want or need, he shrugged his shoulders so I left him, showed my entrance ticket, got a stub back and I was in. Blokes were saying give me your free horse ride ticket and offering me horses to ride but I said no I just want to walk and started my main dirt track walk without a guide down the hill with many caves each side in the stone mountains, wow this is good I was now saying and smiling to myself. I got to Station No1 which was a description of the Nabataean's people who lived here 3rd Century BC and built and carved huge Temples, Tombs, Palaces and places to live out of the base stone mountains and took command of all track caravans passing through from Arabia to Damascus. They were a very clever race starting copper and iron engineering and water irrigation. First stop I stood in the desert heat admiring the Djim block I seen a 2 x 3m sq high big block and caves/tombs above them. Walked on down to the Bab el –Siq the gate to the Siq which led me to the Obelisk Tomb and Bab al Siq Triclinium which was an amazing 4 Obelisks carved high up the side of the mountain with a Tomb cave all surrounded by carved Columns and Arches, what a fantastic sight. Kept going and now in the great vibes Siq the very narrow gorge with viaducts carved into the stone each side of it and as I walked its 2km length I was looking into the niches and as the God Blocks Gorge got wider I was now strolling along on top of a real road made out of semi level big round square and all shapes or flatish boulders laid by the Nabataea's in 3rd Century BC and as I checked levels horses and carts with tourists on board passed me by. There were sometimes many tourists as they were in large groups then maybe in the space of 5mins I would hear or see no one. Looking ahead I could see majestic huge carved Columns in a cliff face but nothing could have prepared me for the full carved face of Columns and a large square opening of the Al-Khazinch (Treasury), it was just a so wonderful unbelievable sight all carved 60 BC and I took 5-10mins walking about it admiring its splendour. On I went and into the Street of Facades with its so much Grand Arch and Column carvings all above and around the many Tombs in the cliffs one side and across the other side the 7000 seat theatre fully carved into the stone and I laughed out loud as how did they do it. Went down steps and into one tomb seeing the stone coffins and the cut out of the stone graves with many perfect square holes in the walls as these places must be an archaeologists dream. Now in the Roman times and on the Colonnaded Street with the ruins of all the shops, restaurants and taverns used by the Romans as their city centre 100 AD, it was fantastic just walking along the Roman Road never mind peeping and stepping into the ruins of these ancient buildings. Had now reached the Great Temple and looking at it from the Roman Road I could only see a flight of stone steps going up approximately 3m high. Up I went and oh my God looking at its area all around it as it was approximately 75m sq with great walls and Arches at its sides and rear. I had to force myself to leave it and keep going on along the Colonnaded Street and through the totally commanding high Arches of the Temeros Gate me trying to figure out where or how or who named these Gates. I was now looking in a huge Square full height building that had withstood many earthquakes and it was the Qasr al-bint a Temple for Worship. Nearly missed it but looking back I could see lots of beautiful so neat carvings in the mountains facing the Great Temple and they were the Temple of the Winged Lambs and a truly unforgettable sight. Now in a village of eating stalls so had a cup of tea, 1 JD, but sat on an ancient stone wall eating my full packet of cream biscuits and enjoying my robbers tea thinking which way will I go, it was 1420hrs and starting to get overcast., I had two choices, one was to go back the way I had come and go up a 1 hour climb of steps to the High Place of Sacrifice or go right and into and up the 1 hour steps climb to the Monastery, what do I do. So mind made up I walked out of the end of the Gorge village of tea huts and into a narrow bushy gorge and just reached the first steps when a few drops of rain started dropping on my silky hair but kept going panting and grunting like a mad dog as the rain got worse. Put on my plastic poncho and looking at the sky I got about half way up and turned around and decision made I was getting out of here and just made the tea huts when the heavens opened up for a fully heavy blast of rain but I was ok, I just hoped the young and old ones high on the mountain tops were also ok. Rain slowly eased so in my bare feet Thai sandals and blue poncho I was slowly treading back the 4km walk to where my taxi had dropped me off and had two stops for Mars Bars and a Fanta drink. Taxi had dropped me off near entrance to Petra Ruins but I knew the Minibus station was in Wadi Musa 2km high above where I was now. Saying no thanks to the many dozen taxi touts I was away going up and up the very steep mountain road panting and grunting passing many hotels and sweating bad I finally reached the small town of Wadi Musa. It had good vibes and plenty of cafes and hotels and taking directions from a veiled lady I could now see the Minibus's parked above the town and desperately waving I ran the last 50m and grunting I got on the bus, driver saying you take bus this time, it was the same bus driver from this morning. I smiled saying yes and plonked myself in a seat and only about 10mins the bus was full and we were away with Peter a young Czechoslovakia bloke on seat 16 next to me. We got talking, it was his first time going to Aqaba, I told and showed him on my LP map where he would get a cheap hotel. He did not have a guide book saying he didn't want one as they were too heavy and asking me what and where he should do and saying he will go with me to Israel border manyanna. He had paid 3JD getting on the bus and as the sort of conductor came around I paid him 5JD, he said 10, I said no, 5 and driver said ok. I said to Peter when we stop in Aqaba I will hopefully show him where the cheapie hotels are and next min I fell asleep, woke up a few times and then finally awake as we came into and stopped at the Aqaba Bus Station. Peter and myself got off me saying Good Luck to the bus driver and I was lucky and found the Jordan Flower Hotel for Peter as manyanna I just wanted to do my own thing not guide someone who didn't event want to buy a guide book so saying my Good Lucks and all the best I shook Peter's hand and I was away. Walking back to hotel I bought a large sausage roll and a meat pie, 1JD and upto my room, ate them both with a bottle of Nestle Tea and belly full, I was happy, it was 1740hrs. Stripped off and had a nice shave and a lovely hot water shower, kit on, cleaned teeth and out for a gentle walk. I did my usual 20min internet then into a café for a 1JD coffee with a scone just watching the Aqaba world go by. I had another walk then it started drizzling rain so bought two cups of tea and back to hotel, paid 30JD for my two nights stay telling very helpful guy I was leaving tomorrow and upto room and thunder and heavy rain started, wow oh wow. Enjoyed my cream biscuits and Mars Bar having a read of LP and just glad to make it I was in my conc bed and asleep dreaming bikini chicks and sunshine in Eilat's beaches manyanna, oh la la, I hope.

Email Sent: Thu, 25 Feb 2010
Subject: The Petra hike

Hi All
Minibus would not move until full so got a taxi, 30JD, 2hrs to Petra and then the famous walk right through the narrow 1-2m wide gorge to the caves and wonderful curving 100 BC all on the stone mountain cliffs walls and also the Roman Colonnade columns along their Roman roads even came to a road laid 100 BC but not by de Romans.
Made it halfway up the mountain steps towards to Monastery but it started raining so called it a day and it lashed down so God help anyone stuck on top of the mountain!!!!!!!!!, hope they made it down.
Jumped a Minibus and back in Aqaba 1700hrs, great day.
Heading back manyanna to the best place yet on my travel which is Eilat and hope the sun shines as want the sunbed for a PM flash of me curves, someone has got to impress de Jew chico's, wat yu tink!!
al de bes
Jack

Map 2 of Israel

1) ISRAEL the birthplace of Christianity in Jerusalem, Nazareth and Galilee is one step after another going back to Jesus and his disciples life's and is an unbelievable walk back to true life history of the Holy Bible every turn you make not forgetting the Muslims history of Allah and the start of Islam living next door to Christian Arabs all combined and intermingled with seeing the real life as it is today in the old City of Jerusalem as people will go out of their way to help and make your stay will never be forgotten in their happy always willing to help way.
2) Capital; Jerusalem
3) Israel achieved Independence in 1948
4) Climate; Ave temp Jan-Mar;20c
5) Language; Hebrew, Arabic, English
6) Currency; Shekel, 1$US = 3.5 Shekel
7) Visa; Not required, 30 day issued on arrival
8) Return flight £51 + £154 ATM, hotel, food, train to Gatwick
9) Today's ongoing update of day to day accommodation, travel, food, drinks costs = £3381

Day 62, Friday, 26-02-10, Aqaba; Jordan – Eilat; Israel

Up 0705hrs feeling really good after a great night sleep sleeping with two pillows which helped my posture as my semi conc bed didn't feel too hard then!. Had an underarm wash, face splash, kit on with neckpouch checking Passport and poured a full load of cornflakes into my lunch box, added sweeteners and milk and let it rest as I done my final shoulderbag pack, things are looking good. Sat down on the edge of my bed and ate my lovely English breakie, cleaned my lunch box and thinking about it I had not even heard the 0500hrs chanters this morning so must have been dead to the world. Thai sandals on and wrote a little letter and with some photos in it, sealed the envelope and out up to the Post Office to post it to my Kelly Rose, oh la, la, sexy chico, I miss my lovely girl. Posted letter and back to hotel and guy came upstairs with me and carried my shoulderbag down to reception, gave him all my loose change and other reception guy phoned up a taxi at an agreed price of 8JD. Only 5mins and taxi arrived so shook everyone's hands, put shoulderbag in taxi boot, me in front and we were away, it was 0830hrs. It was slightly further than I thought but after one Passport/armed police check of bag I was in the Jordan Passport exit and bang, Jordan exit stamp. Trolley handle up and I was away walking the 100m no mans land between the border posts and into a long line at Israel Border Post customs, it was 0920hrs.

Armed guard at Passport line started taking my Passport out of my Passport cover so I took it back of him saying don't damage "my Passport", took it out and give it to him as he didn't even know what he was looking at. Queue took longer as only 1No x-ray kiosk open as they searched an old 70 year old Germans man bag then a Swedish Ladies bag and even searched her handbag annoying everybody as finding nothing. Came to my turn and I was through x-ray guy said we need to open your bag, I said why, what are you looking for as its just gone through x-ray with no problems, he said we are security. I said I know your thick just tell me what you are looking for but he refused. I opened my bag and he searched everywhere in it me saying this is just stupid, you idiot, get me the manager. Another guy with machinegun came over and said we are security, I said tell me what you are looking for as this is a complete waste of everyone's time but he just shrugged his shoulders. Finally I got the go ahead at 1000hrs so all kit back in bag I was out and into Passport line. Only a short wait I gave girl my Passport, she flicked the pages and bang, entry Israel me still fuming but I was in and only a short walk upto the taxi rank. Asked guy how much to Eilat, he said 30 Shekels so bag in boot, me in front and we were away, oh, la, la. Had another Passport check with the same two Israeli scumbags security guards from the border me keeping quiet as all they where trying to do was intimidate me then we where away and I told driver Corrine Hostel, 127 Retamin Street, Eilat, Tel: 6371472. He said good place and 10mins later we were there. Gave him the 30 Shekels and into hostel reception and asked girl for ensuite room, she said 150 Shekels and showed me a detached timber hut with a big double bed, WC, shower so I said really good, paid her 150 Shekels, got key to Hut 10 and took my shoulderbag into hut. Changed into cargo shorts and no sleeve tee shirt, checked my money in driving licence wallet, put neckpouch away in shoulderbag and I was out, it was 1045hrs. Walked down into town going past the entrance to the Airfield and it was cloudy and overcast so really sick about no sunbed today. I turned right going past the big shopping Mall on the Mizrayim Rd then past the roundabout at Argaman Ave where my previous sleeping den was and got to Dekel Beach Resort which looked really good but you had to pay a 20 Shekel entrance fee which was fair enough as it got you a sunbed as well but I kept going. Seen a large Japanese Container Ship and a Cruise liner both docked up in the very small harbour and came to a small ship the size of a tug on top of a hill. I climbed up the steps to SS Dolphin reading the Notice: "May 1967, President Nasser of Egypt announced the closure of the Straits of Tiran to Israel Shipping, 5th June, 1967, Six day war broke out and SS Dolphin broke through the boycott to cross the liberated straits of Tiran to reach the Port of Eilat". I was really pleased to see and be here and look at the sea and the ship with all its vibes history and saying, 'well done you navy boys', thinking of my old Da, Stoker Glass. Back down the steps to ground level and walked a little bit further but still only Port Docks area so called it a day and turned back just enjoying my slow walk sometimes in the penetrating sun's rays, other times in the overcast sky but it was still warm. Made it back to the shopping Mall and took the beach promenade path going passed Rimonim Beach then Leonardo Playa Beach and got to the Royal Promenade now seeing large big elegant 5 star Hotels on my left as I crossed a bridge. It was real fun walking the beach path promenade as the size of these hotels was unbelievable and got to Herod's Cardo. Walked across a little bridge and over to the seas edge as I now was directly facing the big tanker anchored up halfway in the bay between Jordan and Israel standing at the Eilat Ring. Looking and studying the road to my left I could see the 100m no man's land and our Israeli border checkpoint that I had previously come through bringing back the bad memories of the stupid thick customs bloke's deliberately antagonising all Nationalities of the World's tourists searching their bags for no reason only stupidity. Turned back and seeing the 20 storey lovely Herods Hotel great shape from another viewpoint was certainly worth the walk. Walking back it was only then I noticed the many big name, top brand clothes and all different types of upmarket shops, nothing would be buyable for me in this area I thought to myself. Passing a road on my right I seen a high rise Castle but a new one so went down and over to its entrance and it was a Theme Park. I didn't even ask the price but it certainly would be a family thing and seen its name; Kings City. Went another route upto and over the first Arched bridge turning right along the packed full of all descriptions of boats Marina passing Night clubs, cafes and late night restaurants thinking this is Eilat nightlife area so will come over tonight. Took the road past the Eilat Airport entrance and going up the hill I went into my favourite café having a big roll sandwich of potted tuna with a tea, just the job, paid my 28 Shekel charge and away back to hostel, it was only 1610hrs. Had a nice dobhi drop, cleaned ass then had a shave and back out to the kitchen area. Put kettle on and had an instant noodle and 2 rolls with a big mug of tea so belly really full I sat in the communal area having a read of LP and was shocked to death as it seems I was in trouble. LP states if I took the land crossing into Egypt at Taba I needed a Visa before going to the border. My book was 5 years old so checked it with an old guy from hotel and he confirmed LP was true so well up the creek as its Saturday tomorrow and the Middle East weekend is Friday and Saturday. Looking at it another way I will only lose one day's travelling as if it had been Europe I would have lost 2 days as our weekend is Saturday and Sunday. Had a read seeking another route and nearly swearing out loud I seen that I could have got a 1hr ferry from Aqaba at 1200hrs as it runs every day except Saturday so couldn't even do a runner back to Jordan manyanna. I was right sick as could have got a ferry today from Aqaba were I had just come from so there I said to myself you have paid the price for your good planning today. Went out for a walk and my God it started raining so into an Internet shop checking for sights to go and see tomorrow and will go to St Constantine Monastery in the Sinai Desert Peninsula which is where Moses received the 12 Commandments and come back for a beach bum sunbed as checking weather forecast it would be a nice sunny day manyanna. I had a coffee in the very lively night time area at the Leonardo Playa to the Royal Promenade and that was me. Laughing at my mistake I had a slow walk back and into hostel, got my key and into room having a laughing chat as I phoned my Kelly Rose and we had a laughing kissing chat, it was 2150hrs. I stripped off and into a lovely big double bed and dreaming of my curvy Kelly Rose giving those Israelis a Kelly taking too which is not for the faint hearted I was a sleep a happy Eilat Kelly Rose mon.

Date: Fri, 26 Feb 2010
Subject: R10, Corrinne Hostel, Retamin St, Eilat, Israel, Tel6371472

Hi All
Taxi, 8JD from Hotel to Jordan border and bang, exit Jordan stamp.
Walked across no mans land and the hassle getting through customs as they search peoples bags me calling guy an idiot but eventually got through and bang, another Israeli entrance stamp.
Taxi, 30Shekels, and into above, 150Shekels for a d-ensuite hut and hostel is just beside the bus station so handy for manyanna.
Dumped kit in room and its a bit cloudy so a walk upto the model of the SS Dolphin near Dekel beach then another lovely walk along the lovely beach promenade to the Majestic Herods 5 star Hotel enjoying a few coffees along the way as the very hot sun did come out.
Heading for Taba?? the crossing into Egypt manyanna morning but will have a read of LP tonight to see where I fancy ending up, any clues drop me a mail.
al de bes
Jack

Day 63, Saturday, 27-02-10, Eilat beachbum; Israel

Had a good sleep but woke up early about 0600hrs so just turned and dozed until 0730hrs then up, underarm wash, face splash in the cold hut then cargo shorts, no sleeve tee shirt on and out going upto the kitchen with my 1 pint of milk, packet of cornflakes, bottle of jam and 2 soft bread rolls, oh la, la, the 5 star chef is getting ready. Put cornflakes in 2 round bowls with the hostel's sugar then poured my milk on them then left them sitting on a bench table outside the kitchen. Made a large mug of tea using the Hostel's tea bags and sugar, sliced my rolls and out to breakie table. Enjoyed my cornflakes 2 bowl breakie starter then got stuck into my 2 rolls filling each slice with thick jam and sipping my tea I really enjoyed my full belly breakie. Cleaned all bowls, knifes and spoons and sat over my tea having a chat with early morning shift reception guy until the US lady manager arrived at 0910hrs. I explained that I had got my facts about travelling to Egypt mixed up and would stay another day but only had US$ currency on me as I thought I was leaving Israel but would like to pay now as I am going for a walk then the beach. No problem she said and using a calculator she said 40$US so I gave it to her, got my receipt and I was out and away, it was 0940hrs. I knew where I was hoping to find which was the Egyptian Consulate so turned left on Hativat HaNeigev Ave and after 2 more roundabouts got to my other Villa at Argaman Ave and done a right upto the first junction on my right and there it was with the Egyptian flag flying from a flagpole on the roof. Checked my LP and I was spot on and give a smiling wave to a guy on its roof. Walked over to read the notice on the front railing but it just said Consulate closed 1100hrs Thursday. Guy leaned over the roof wall saying can I help you, I said thanks but I will come to see you 0900hrs tomorrow as I need a Visa for Egypt, he said ok and both saying Goodbye I was away back down the hill. I passed the first place I was in and wished I had gone back there although nothing wrong with Corrine Hostel the villa was just more private. I thought about going to Dekel Beach but didn't really know the full price so kept going and got to the shopping centre Mall which was not open. Asked girl setting up coffee tables, she said it opens 1100hrs, it was 1030hrs so I had a coffee sitting looking at 50 -70 small tiny all colour of sails group of yachts close to Israel's shore and the same number with white sails all closer to the Jordan shore, I was just wondering were they both different countries in their own waters, didn't know but it looked like it. The shopping centre opened spot on 1100hrs and I went in, first stop being a dobhi drop, cleaned ass and out around the basement floor looking for a Passport Photo machine or a money changer but no luck and same at ground floor but luck was halfway in at first floor and seen a money changer so over giving girl 78$US and at 3.55 Shekels to 1$US I got back 274 Shekels, said my thanks and away looking at the photo shop but it was closed. Dinner time so bought a packet of potato crisps and out down to the beach and sat down in the sand with my back against a large boulder one of many running along the seashore edge and by God it was hot. Stripped off to swimming briefs and had a walk each way along the now getting packed beach and laughing and nearly crying with joy I watched a crowd of ladies of all ages practicing their dance routines on the sand, great fun. I had to do it sometime so cut my fingernails then my famous butchering course on my toe nails, blood everywhere but walked up and down in the sea along the beach a few times, cleaned all the mess. It was fun watching the bikini chicos all enjoying their swims in the sea then lieing flat out in the shingle sand they were asleep in 2mins. Another must do so in I went to the warmish sea up to my thighs and one splash over my head I was in breast stroking and back floating, oh la, la, I was really happy, came out and had a drying off walk then sat down in the sand with my back against the boulder and 5mins fell fast asleep. Was woken up with a shock deluge of seawater as a big wave from the sea splashed all over me, what a shock awakening, it was 1450hrs. Had a walk then a final face sea splash and that was my lovely day over with me looking out to sea seeing a big with 2 masts timber schooner sailing into Aqaba Bay, what a great sight. Put shorts and no sleeve tee shirt on then brushed the sand off my red bare feet and saying bye bye to the two Caribbean girls reading from bibles I was away. Made it slowly up past the Airfield then up the hill buying 2 bread rolls, 3 shekels and glad to get out of the searing sun heat I made it into the hostel. Dumped Beachbag in room then into kitchen putting the kettle on and when it boiled poured it onto a tea bag mug and a cartoon of noodles, left both simmering for a while as I cut my bread rolls putting the pieces on a large plate then poured the hot veg noodles on the bread and stirring my tea I got stuck into my 1625hrs din din. Really enjoyed it having a 6 pack of chocolate cream biscuits as deserts and belly full, me happy I cleaned the dishes and back to sit down having a chat with some fellow travellers about what money I need for the Visa and crossing the border manyanna. Just going back to my hut I met a young USA guy named Gabriel who was doing the border run manyanna morning as well so shaking hands we said we hope to meet first thing in the morning after breakfast and walk up to the Egyptian Consulate. Into hut and had a shave and lovely hot shower changing kit and done a bit of weight loss of kit in my shoulderbag leaving out my saved my life trainers and one soft jacket as no way will it get cold again where I am heading. Zipped bag up and out I went downhill towards the shopping centre seeing groups and shows at its gable wall with large crowds watching as I did for a while then into the Mall itself doing my usual 20mins internet. Had a full walk and a sit down at the many cheap food stalls area having a scone and a coffee watching the Eilat tourist world go by then paying my bill I was happily but slowly away. Made it halfway up the hill and sat down at an outside seat having a tea and a scone as in no rush, it was 2150hrs. Paid my 5 Shekels bill and and up the hill going into hostel and in I went seeing the 2 blokes still on their laptops which it looks like they stay on 24hrs, don't know but have never seen them out of here. Nobody about to have a chat with so made a mug of tea and a read of LP making my final plans for buses manyanna I had an early one, it was only 2255hrs. Final pack then stripped off and into bed and asleep, no dreams just a stone dead brain.

Date: Sat, 27 Feb 2010
Subject: Still on sunbed in Eilat

Hi All

Good planning and as usual didn't read my LP Middle East until late last night and then double checked it as well and I need a Visa before going to the land border for Egypt at Taba and Egyptian Consulate not open as its their WE so stuck in Eilat until manyanna.

Even reading LP I could have got a ferry from Aqaba to Nuweiba without a Visa as they issue them when you land but that's life, mind you it's only my first hiccup in 63 days.

It's really hot on the sunbed and the bikini set are on de prowl so its good fun.

Just hope no big queue manyanna as wanna hit de road.

Thanks Chantel, really nice of you.

al de bes

Jack

Map 2 of Egypt

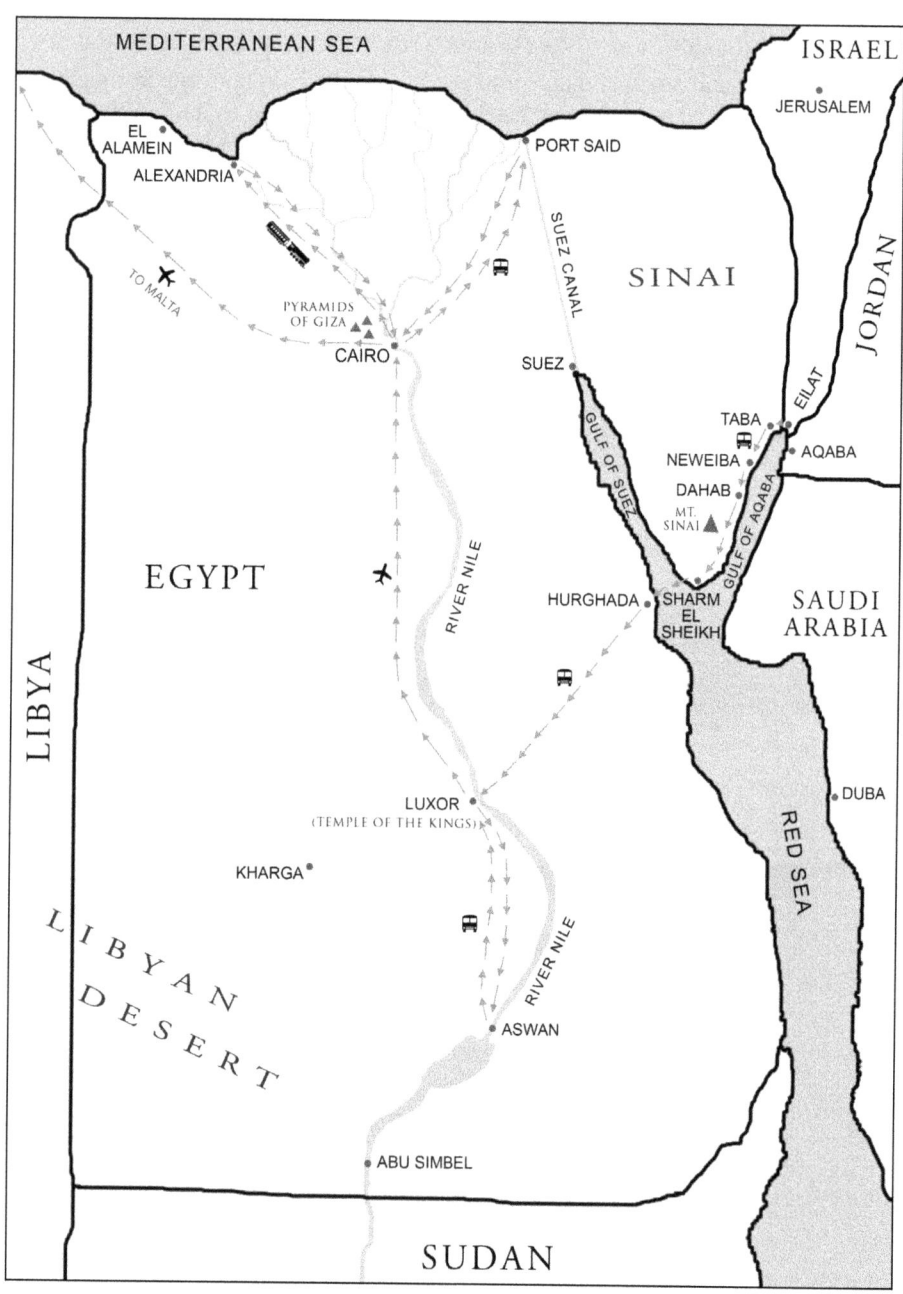

1) EGYPT is the oldest tourist attraction in the world with even the Romans and the Ancient Creeks coming to admire the awe-inspiring wonders of the Pyramids but every turn including the Valley of the Kings with the Tomb of King Tutankhamen Tomb and a sail in a Felecia up the Nile then the exciting hustle and bustle of Cairo before having a relaxing soak in the Red sea is a unique atmospheric sense exploring trip back in time not forgetting a walk along the banks of the famous Suez Canal then a trip to walk and explore the full of history Mediterranean seaport of Alexandra before a climb up Mose's Mt Sinai. Egypt is a never ending trip to enjoy as everywhere you go it's a pleasure to meet the true friendly hospitality of the happy Egyptian people
2) Capital; Cairo
3) Egypt achieved Independence in 1922
4) Climate; Ave temp Jan-Mar;21c
5) Language; Arabic, English
6) Currency; Egyptian Pound, 1$US = 5 E Pounds
7) Visa; Not required, 90 day Visa issued on arrival
8) Return flight £51 + £154 ATM, hotel, food, train to Gatwick
9) Today's ongoing update of day to day accommodation, travel, food, drinks costs = £1167

Day 64, Sunday, 28-02-10, Eilat, Israel – Dahab; Egypt

Great night's sleep and woke up raring to go but it was only 0550hrs so up for a piss then back to bed having a little snooze then finally up for good at 0710hrs. Had my usual underarm wash, face splash then kit on with a little final pack of shoulderbag and out chancing my luck to see if kitchen was open and met Gabriel just coming back from the shop and guy was just opening the kitchen. Into kitchen, got a bowl, filled it with my cornflakes, milk and sugar and told Gabriel to help himself which he did. Enjoyed my cornflakes and a nice big mug of tea with a sliced in half bread roll buttered with thick jam and that was belly full. Quickly back to hut, cleaned teeth and a loud fart dobhi drop, cleaned ass and out putting shoulderbag in reception. I gave Gabriel a shout and 5mins later he was out with his small backpack and out of hostel we went, it was 0820hrs. Having a chat about our travels we made are way downhill along Ha Temarim Blvd to the first roundabout then turned right onto Hativat HaNeiger Ave and going fast having a laughing chat with each other turned right up Argaman Ave and only 100m turned right again and there it was the Egyptian flag above its Consulate, it was 0835hrs. We had a seat on a park bench facing the Consulate me saying get ready to run across the road if we see any other backpackers and only a 10min wait two guys opened the Consulate small entrance gate and over we went. We were greeted with a smiling Good Morning and come in which was a great start to our day not like the surly Israel morbidness. Upstairs we followed the gentlemen and were given a form to fill out which we did and with one Passport size photo and our Passports we handed them over to the very polite old guy. He looked at the Passports and said I being British I have to pay 98 Shekels as a Visa fee and Gabriel who was American only had to pay a 65 Shekel fee. Me as usual being diplomatic said that's blatant discrimination why should the Yanks get it cheaper, old guy laughing shrugged his shoulders saying didn't know and went into his office with our Passports so me and Gabriel sat back in our chairs still chatting about our previous travels. Not a long wait as at 0915hrs the old guy came out and smiling gave us back our Passports just as three USA people came in to ask about extensions, the old guy explaining they have to fill out a form but we were away saying our thanks and took the same road back to our hostel. I got my trolley shoulderbay and saying my thanks to everyone including saying enjoy my cornflakes to two girls who were enjoying them as I had left the still half full packet on the table telling the always happy girl manager to tell any travellers to help themselves. Next thing full of life happy Gabriel a credit to the young travelling world and I were out and into Bus Station checking for bus to Taba for our next journey upto the Israeli Egyptian border, oh la, la. Lined up at ticket office with an Israeli guy rabbiting on at the kiosk and slightly losing my rag as fed up with these bloody Israelies I shouted hurry up there are people trying to catch a bus and after my second rant he quickly gathered his change and away. Got to kiosk and girl said you have to buy your bus ticket on the bus so quickly out at Stop 6 and waited only a few mins and a bus drew up. Driver said to put my shoulderbag on the seat next to me so I did paying my 7.50 Shekel fare as did Gabriel. A few people got on and then we were away, it was 1010hrs as out of the Bus Station we went travelling all around

Eilat then finally along the docks road passing the SS Dolphin ship on its mound hill we were going well only stopping once or twice to pick people up or drop some off and at 1050hrs we had our final stop at the Israel border side. Gabriel and myself got off seeing the three US people who we had seen at the Consulate and Gabriel offered to give a big fat black lady a lift with her two large trolley suitcases but I was away into the Israel Customs Passport border control office putting shoulderbag and beachbag through x-ray I was through without any hiccups and up to the Passport kiosk. Handed Passport and 98 Shekels over and bang, Israeli exit stamp and out into no-mans land I went saying stuff you you miserable thick stupid Israelies and only a 50-75m walk and I was into the Egyptian Customs Border Control Passport Office. Guy gave me a form to complete with the usual name, date of birth, destination, so filled it in, put bag through x-ray and upto Passport kiosk, bang, Egyptian entrance stamp and I was in, hip hip hurray. First tout trying to sell me a taxi to Dahab for 300 Egyptian Pounds (EP) but I said no I will catch a bus, he said next bus is 1500hrs, it was only 1105hrs. I said I will walk and trolley handle up I was out and feeling so happy about the no hassle border crossing I was broad faced joyfully smiling and laughing to myself as I walked along the road. Got to a line of Minibuses and guy said Minibus to Dahab or to Cairo, I said Dahab, he said 100EP, so I said ok, when do we go, he said not long as only 3-5 more passengers required so I sat down on my own really over the moon. A Kiwi couple came along and driver tried to sell them seats for 100EP each but they said no, its to expensive and kept on walking after having a quick chat with me. I said to the driver, what time we go as trying it on I said I cant wait about here all morning and the next minute another guy asked how much do I want to pay for a Minibus to go with only me, I said 100EP, he said 150EP, I said ok and shoulderbag in the back, me in a front seat, we were away, it was 1130hrs. I said there are 2 Kiwi's somewhere and driver drove into Bus Station and pulled up beside them asking them did they want transport at 100EP each, they said no, so I said to them and the driver, do it for 50EP, driver agreed, the two Kiwi's agreed putting their kit in the boot, them on the Minibus and we were away, wow oh wow, that was good. Only another 50m we stopped at Taba Border Control Taxi Kiosk and we all had to pay another 75EP, the 2 Kiwi's argued, me also thinking I had paid it but totally confused now I just paid it as did the Kiwi's and we were away on a good road seeing lovely sandy desolate beaches on my left as we drove along the lovely coastline. Still awake we passed Nuweiba at 1225hrs and next I seen a sign, Dahab, 60km, it was 1230hrs. Going really fast chatting with Jeff and Kirsty my two Kiwi travelling companions with Kirsty offering and giving me a lovely cream biscuit we drove along the Elnaser Rd and into Dahab outskirts at 1315hrs with great views of the sea coastline. I had originally told the driver that I was going to stay at the Auski Camp but listening to Jeff and Kirsty I changed my mind as they recommended The Alaska Camp as they had stayed there before and price for me would be 70EP so told driver and the next minute he stopped directly outside it, it was 1330hrs. We all got off, Jeff paying driver 100EP, driver wanting another 100 but Jeff just walked away. I paid him 150EP telling him he had agreed 100EP with Jeff and I was away into reception of the very upmarket Alaska Camp & Hotel, Dahab, South Sinai, Egypt, www.dahabescafe.com, Tel: +20 (0) 693641004. A very nice English girl behind the desk said, you want single room, I said yes, how much, she said 70EP so gave her the money and Passport which she photocopied, I filled in a form, got my key and that was me into Room 108, yeah man yeah. I was gleefully talking to myself as I changed into no sleeve tee shirt and cargo shorts and with empty China beachbag I was out having a chat with the very helpful Jackie the Essex girl behind reception who now lives in Egypt. I said I compliment you on your hotel, its very upmarket and really lovely rooms as I asked her where I could change Shekels into EP. She told me where a bank was and out I went the other beach entrance and shock oh shock my hotel was directly in the full of life many cafes, restaurants and all sorts of shops in the centre of Dahab, what a joy to see. Slowly just happily browsing along I made it up to the bank but they would not change the Shekels so drew out 1000EP on my credit card sticking 500EP in my waterproof Medical Insurance and Passport photocopy that I always carry and back along the so full of life main beach alley pedestrian street. I walked over the Arched bridge again passing my camp hotel and kept going out of the shops street but still on the beach street I was offered dope and smokes by Bedouins who came out of the narrow Souk alleys but laughing I said too old and kept going all the way to just after Villa Caboodle not that far from the Blue Hole diving area with feet, legs starting to go I turned back. This area was really rough but I was happy so didn't care and feeling peckish I passed my hotel again going over the bridge and into Lavazz Pizza Restaurant and had a Margarita pizza and 2 teas, 45EP, very tasty big pizza but expensive for me. Paid my bill and back to camp hotel seeing and watching the now big waves rolling in and demolishing the front and the seating areas of about 6 beach side restaurants, wow oh wow, something is in the sea!. Into room, cleaned teeth and had a nice little dobhi drop, changed into long cargo and pocket sleeve tee shirt and I was out again, it was 1905hrs. Dahab had really great vibes as I walked a few different paths all full of cafes and shops having 2 coffees sitting watching the world go by then my last final stroll I was back into the open TV lounge of my Alaska Hotel seeing and saying hello to full of life Jeff and Kirsty again, it was 2145hrs as Wales were playing France. Watched it for 5mins then ordered and got a nice tea and saying my Good Nights I was away and into my room, it was 2245hrs as then I suddenly remembered Gabriel and sort of missed his lively conversational company I hoped he was ok as even walking across the border and looking back I hadn't seen him. Stripped off having a read of LP for a plan for tomorrow then into bed and oh my God it was a semi conc mattress but had enjoyed my first day and night in a New town so relaxed and happy I was asleep not even a Belly dancer dream .

Date: Sun, 28 Feb 2010
Subject: R108, Alaska Camp/Hotel Masbat, Dahab, South Sinai, Egypt, www.dahabescafe.com

Hi All

Up to the Egyptian Consulate 0830hrs and they let me in at 0845hrs and 30mins later I had a Visa in Passport for the land crossing at Taba so back to Hostel, said my Goodbyes and jumped a bus upto border, bang, Israeli exit stamp and only a 50m no-mans land walk, bang, Egyptian entrance stamp.

At 1130hrs haggled a Minibus down to 150 Egyptian P(EP)and only me on it we were away picking up a Kiwi couple who paid 100EP between them and at 1330hrs he dropped us off outside above but dozens of Camp/hotels about.

Into above and I paid 70EP for a lovely d-ensuite in above, dropped kit in room and out in the very lively large touristy town with nice beaches and more sunbeds but not this afternoon as heavy seas where ripping all the beach cafes and restaurants fronts and seating areas out, good fun!!!!!!!

Definitely staying a couple of days as going upto Mt Sinai where Moses received the 10 commandments as I do abide by them and have a visit into St Katherine's Monastery at the foot of the Mountain.

Tell Kathleen Mary I was asking and give her ALL MY LOVE.

al de bes

Jack

Day 65, Monday, 01-03-10, Dahab – Mt Sinai; Egypt

Alarm went off at 0700hrs as I woke up so quickly turned it off and up for a small dobhi drop, cleaned ass, underarm wash, face splash, kit on and little pack of China beachbag putting smelly trainers into a plastic bag before putting them in and out over to breakfast floor cushion seats and table area. Guys were still setting out the breakfast buffet table so I had a bowl of cornflakes with milk and sugar then 2 toasts with a large omelette and a final toast with jam eating it with a large mug of tea, wow, belly full, me happy I went back to room. Cleaned teeth and out just as a Bedouin dressed guy came to my room door saying you go Mount Sinai, I said yes, he said smiling its cheap today, only 500$US, I said no, I pay 1000$US for return, he said ok, good price as we got into his Minivan. Me thinking what a relief to get away from the no smile, no joke, thick, sick, stupid Israeli assholes and having another think it was the Israeli border assholes who antagonize tourists as most Israelis are genuine happy people but life is life we only remember the bad things but put it out of my mind as we where away not a far drive to his office. He went in and 5mins later a guy came out giving me a one way ticket for 45EP so I gave him a 50EP note letting him keep 5EP tip for driver. Back in Minivan and we were away him picking up a friend going along the Peace Road out of town, it was 0815hrs. Got outside town on a main highway and stopped at an armed guard checkpoint with a sign stating St Katherine Protectorate. Through the checkpoint and along the valley highway with marvellous views of the big barren stone mountains each side and I still hadn't fallen asleep. Watching the mountains and the road seeing signs at intervals for 55-50-40km to Nuweiba and 90km Taba and it was big time warm even at that time in the morning. Got to checkpoint and junction for St Katherine and we went left, it was 0845hrs. Now passing through large areas of pure desert areas with Bedouin tent camps sometimes each side of the road, good fun and fell asleep. Woke up a few times as driver braked going around hairpin bends and finally woke up at 0930hrs as we pulled into the St Katherine Protectorate Ticket Office and I paid 3$US for a ticket and it was freezing now as we were high up in the mountains. Back into Minivan and upto the drop off point seeing the bleary eyed travellers coming down from their all night sunrise on top of the mountain trip, oh God it was freezing now, wonder what it was like at night, it was 1000hrs as I had a piss and changed Thai sandals to my smelly trainers. Next I walked around to the St Katherine's Monastery entrance and in paying I think a 4EP entrance fee which was well worth it as its 4th Century AD wall paintings and beautiful Altar and all the hanging silver lamps and golden icons were just a true history joy to see. Out from it and touched and pulled at a leaf standing under the Burning Bush which was where God spoke to Moses, I truly felt in Gods hands as I headed out of the Chapel and started my I think already halfway up the 2285m height of Mt Sinai climb up the rocky uneven path, it was 1030hrs. If the wind didn't blow and I was in the sun it was warm but the wind was very cold but now sweating and out of breath and had only made about 3 loops at the bottom of the mountain I knew I was never going to do it on my own as looking down or behind me there were tour groups starting the ascent so I was first one up the mountain this morning. I kept passing camels and

Bedouins sitting in make shift huts offering, tea, coffee, biscuits and camels and I enquired how much. Bedouin guy said 100EP but discount I can have it for 80EP so quick think, I said yes. He saddled up the camel and it got down on its padded knees and on I got and me shouting in fear it stood up back legs first but I hung on and we were away. It was ok but I had no control of the camel as it sometimes went to the edge of the precipice cliff me shouting in fear, stop stop, guy walking behind the camel saying no worry, no worry but no stopping. We passed a tour group of German tourists who I hadn't seen way up the mountain me saying, "you know me", they looking at me in amazement saying no, I said my name is Lawrence. Everyone all silent for a few seconds until a laughing girl said Lawrence of Arabia and the whole group burst out laughing all saying Lawrence of Arabia all taking photos. I was sometimes getting cramp but didn't want to stop as the cliff winding path was still very steep and talking to the Camel guy he told me the Camels name was Oscar, it was aged 13 and that Camels live until they are appox 35years. Finally at the path below the steps he stopped saying we finish me thinking he had said Camel up the steps but I was also glad to get off and I gave him 100EP knowing he wouldn't have any change. He said, no change, I said laughing to myself, ok, on the way down when you see me, call me and give me the 20EP, he said ok, no problem and I still inwardly laughing I was away on up the not steep path and through a little gorge to the bottom of the very steep boulder steps saying to myself this is going to be rough. Kept going thinking no way a Camel could have climbed these steps safely and thinking again the Camel bloke probably said Camel upto the steps. I stopped at least 6-8 times panting and legs and knees sore as the total step very steep climb was approximately 100m but finally and completely out of breath I made it to the little Church on the top of the mountain, wow oh wow, it was 1230hrs. Church was not open which was a shame as it was directly on top of the mountain and their must be some history inside it. I met a Bedouin guy who had a little tea stall but had my coke and creamy biscuits having a chat with him and he confirmed I was the first up today then over to the little wall looking across and down the fantastic mountains and valleys I felt so happy to have made it and stood there shouting into the echoing valley, "Lawrence of Arabia has made it" but looking down it was too steep to see anyone so sat down having another creamy biscuit and coke Naafi break and lo and behold the German group arrived all looking at me and laughing saying its Lawrence. One laughing girl asked me where I was from, I said laughing Belfast and everyone all smiled, it was 1300hrs. Don't know if they were staying for the sunset but it was cold so wishing them all Goodbye I very slowly started making my way down the steep boulder steps all the way down to the bottom of the steps meeting an old English man and lady and wishing them well I was now on the uneven boulder stone winding path. It wound and wound for it seemed miles and I seen another tour group on the extreme face edge of the cliff on a little stone path so that must be the 3000 steps of Repentance which I had not seen but it was a very frightening path so glad I had missed it. Turned one hairpin bend and shouted into the desolate stone mountain valley, I got you, I got you and nearly a third of the way down this was the first time I could see the Monastery, it was 1430hrs. Knees, legs, back and body giving me grief I finally walked past the even path of the now closed Monastery, it was 1515hrs and made my way all the way to the Minibus drop off point. Place was semi deserted only for about six cars and one Minibus and I went to the Minibus driver asking does he go to Dahab, he said go now 200 EP which was probably ok for I think the 100km drive but I said no and had a chat with a few other taxi drivers but they said no, go by Minibus as I could feel the big Minibus Bedouin driver had or was intimidating them. I had a piss hoping for maybe a couple of travellers but no luck and big Minibus driver kept coming over saying, go now. I offered him 100EP but he said no so I sat down in the sun and had some creamy chocolate biscuits and a few slugs of coke. Getting worried as it was now coming up 1630hrs I seen a couple getting into a car and as they passed me I waved them down saying are you going to Dahab, they said yes, I said I will pay you if you give me a lift, they said no, just get in the back and I did and smiling to myself we were away. They were an Italian couple on holiday and staying in Sharm el Sheik. It was a fully beautiful drive through the mountains and the desert valley as I fell asleep and next thing the guy said we turn right at next crossroads to go to Sharm El Sheik so will drop me off and he stopped. Out I got shaking both their hands and they were away. Police Officer at checkpoint said where am I going, I said Dahab, he said do I need transport, I said yes and he flagged down a pickup van and telling the two guys in the front something in Arabic I was invited into the back seat and we were away only about 4-5km into the outskirts of Dahab. They dropped me off in a semi slum area telling me to walk through it and I was a bit apprehensive as although it was still light I didn't like the look of it and flagged down a Minibus and agreed a 10EP run to my hotel. Guy stopped at the rear of my hotel and I only had a 100EP note so tried the three shops for change but no luck then guy said pay me sometime if you see me and he was away. I walked into the centre of town and into a Pizza Café and had my usual Margarita Pizza and two teas, 35EP, really enjoying my 1815hrs late supper. Feeling really tired and legs and back very sore I done my usual 20-30mins internet then had one coffee at the Union Jack flag café beside the Arched bridge and that was my night over, it was 2045hrs. Back to hotel camp having a tea on the cushion area hoping to see Jeff and Kirsty but no luck and at 2135hrs my body dying on my feet I was into room, stripped off, my feet smelling very bad and into bed and asleep not a flicker of a dream.

Email Sent: Mon, 1 Mar 2010
Subject: 2285m Mount Sinai

Hi All

Still cant believe I done it but started it and refused to give in and finally 2hrs later with half the climb on a camel back I made it 2285m upto the little Church on the top praying forgiveness to my feet, knees and legs, back and head.

I was the first one up it at 1230hrs and nearly the first one down but back in Camp at 1800hrs.

Had a walk also around the St Katherine's Monastery with all its ancient paintings and touched the burning bush were Moses' talked to God, great history day.

Not moving manyanna as don't know if I will make it out of my bed.

al de bes

Jack

The Burning Bush

Day 66, Tuesday, 02-03-10, Dahab; Egypt

Was woken up at 0150hrs by I am sure I either heard door rapping or a window being rapped but snoozed off again as probably I was snoring loudly waking some poor soul up. Woke up for good at 0640hrs feeling very relaxed and stretching and turning over a few times I felt in good shape considering yesterday's cruelty to my feet, legs, knees and back so up for good at 0715hrs. Had an underarm wash and face splash putting cargo shorts and no sleeve tee shirt on then out and down to breakie cushion area pouring a tea as they put out the full in honesty 4-5star buffet breakfast. Took my time having a bowl of cornflakes and ordering an omelette then had 4 toasts of bread, butter, cheese, jam and with 2 mugs of tea and as my omelette came I cut it up putting it on my toast and really enjoyed my lubbly jubbly breakie finishing it off with two more jam toast, just the job. Back to room thinking the rapping last night was probably to wake me up to stop me snoring but had a nice full clearance dobhi drop, cleaned ass, cleaned teeth, little check of China beachbag and out, it was 0850hrs. Turned right and over the Arch bridge then right again and upto the main road as directions I had for my first stop was the Bank Misr which was in the Hilton Hotel complex as I just wanted to get rid of my useless Israel Shekels. Pickup Minitruck driver stopped and I said Bank Misr at Hilton Hotel so jumped in and he was away and as we got to the Hilton Resort complex he said no Bank and driving round a roundabout he was driving back into Assalah me shouting, stop stop, him saying he knows Bank and took me to National Bank of Egypt. I said no I want to go to the Hilton Hotel and he was away again and back to and stopped outside the Hilton Complex. I said how much he said 100EP and I was losing my temper I said no, 5EP and tried to open my door but it appeared to be locked. I said open the door my temper boiling over as I told him I will sort him out. He said 50EP, I again said no and he wound the window down and another taxi bloke came over. He was talking to him and me also telling the guy what had happened, the guy said to my taxi driver that he was wrong and then asked me how much I wanted to pay, I said 10EP just to get out and gave him 10EP note and finally got the door open and I was out and away straight across into the guarded entrance of the Hilton Hotel Resort and asked guy directions to the bank. He pointed at door saying go in and its upstairs so up I went but it was closed, it had opening times 0900-1200/1400-1600 and guy came from another room saying it would open at 1100hrs today but can he help me. I counted out 240 Shekels and asked will they change Shekel, he said yes no problem, come back after 1100hrs and downstairs I went and out through the entrance gate thinking what are my plans for today. I had a walk up to El Nasr St thinking how lucky was as I could see the fully sparkling in the bright sun lagoon on my right so yeah man yeah I knew the start of my travels today were going to start and happily sauntered down to its seawater edge. Kit off and put it into China beachbag and China beachbag over shoulder I happily whistled myself across the shallow only up to my knees seawater lagoon swearing out loud a few times as I stood on sharp coral but out onto the crescent narrow stretch of warm sand at the seaside side of the lagoon, this is the life. Walked left then getting near a crowd of Argies I plonked my China beachbag on the shingle sand and paddled only a few steps into the sea and was up to my waist so ducked under the not cold sea and that was me breast stroking and back floating for 10-15mins, it was fun. Out and had a 50m walk each side of my China beachbag then smoothed the sand making a pillow and small towel on it I had another 30mins of the great feeling of doing nothing which felt very strange. The sun was big time hot so up and in for a dip and swim then same same a few times having a few good slugs of my Coca Cola bottle and skin bright red I was up still in my brief swimming pants and away along the 7 Pinnacles Beach and going left at El Gozo Beach it was a dream come true. Went over to the Miracle Lake paddling through its outer edge seeing two girls coming out of it and their skin from waist down were a salty white so I don't know if immersing yourself in a seawater cold lake is good for you or not but my feet and bottom of my legs had now turned slightly salt white. Got onto a very neat wide beach promenade path and happily followed it passing Nubia Village Resort then the Dahab Village "Lagona" both I would say slightly upmarket as now I was into lots of cafes and restaurants each side of the path. Really happy I walked past the Black Prince Pub and Restaurant with sign, free sunbeds and snorkelling in Island Reef but just kept going no pain in legs. Passed the Shots Café thinking I wonder how it got that name then stopped at Hotel Star reading its very good price menu and getting closer to the Arched Bridge I passed the Jasmine Pension and The Christina Beach Hotel both very lively places. Had passed these ancient 100m sq ruins two days ago but read the notice this time; Al Mashraba Hill which was an old lighthouse in an Arabian Port 1BC to 2AD on a spices trading route, I loved that sort of history. Finally made it back and over the Arched Bridge and into my Camp Hotel saying my hellos to Jackie the ever so lovely and helpful English reception lady and asked if I could pay my bill. She checked her books and said two days 70EP per day and 2 breakies at 20EP each, total is 180EP so gave her a 200EP note and got a 20EP note back, it was 1300hrs. Talked with Jackie about my options for this afternoon then saying my thanks I was out and turned right at the main road. Agreed a 60EP 4 x 4 jeep for a ride all the way to the Blue Hole diving reef, jumped in and we were away passing Assalah on its outskirts which was really the area my Camp Hotel was in as it was the original Bedouin camping area and still is but is now a Bedouin enclave of slum housing with goats, dogs and camels all mixing together with the scruffy no shoes little kids running happily about the dusty sand streets, great holiday sights. Tarmac road eventually did stop but driver going quite fast we were up and rolling over large hilly sandy mounds with other 4 x 4 passing us or coming the other way the sun was obliterated by the blowing choky sand and no windows in my 4 x 4 I had to laugh and breathe it in. Went through a very lively ramshackle village with dozens of 4 x 4's parked up and many young westerners dressed in their diving suits carrying their oxygen bottles all going or coming from the Blue Hole sea. Driver stopped and we agreed a 1hr wait and off I went just following the little path seeing lots of divers in their wet suits all going through the safety procedures of testing their kit and stopped at a cliff face reading half a dozen Memorial Plaques to some Westernised young ones who never made it back up, it was very sad. Kept going until I reached the seaside end of the path and had 2 options either climb the smallish hilly cliff on the narrow dirt path or go back so up the dirt track path I went reaching the sort of narrow headland with another option either stop here or keep going along the 2-300mm wide narrow uphill path and looking down the cliffs, one side the sea, the other side the craggy rocky cliff I was away, one slip your dead mon and only a 20m high walk I was at its highest point looking along the coast the other side, yeah man yeah. On the other side along the sort of rocky beach there was a crowd of Westerners all trekking along it on Camels and I laughed out loud into the full heat of the hot sun. Now what do I do as have to go down which was worse than coming up but only taking one wrong path I was happily breathing sighs of relief as made it down to ground level. Walking back I was up close seeing five westerners putting on their face masks and testing them in the seawater then feet first going below the top of the sea until they disappeared completely with one girl without an oxygen bottle only snorkel kit on following them at sea level looking down on them, really good health and safety. Still had 15mins left so had a coffee in the Titanic Café, 8 EP and I must admit really enjoyed it, paid my money and back to driver. He said ok, I said yes and we both got into the 4 x 4 and we were away taking our time slowly passing lots of camels just wandering about on their own as the area had many Bedouin tent camps until we were back on the tarmac highway road and with a good run and only two checkpoints we were back in Assalah and as he stopped at the taxi park, I paid him the 60EP with a 5 EP tip, shook hands and I was away. Went into my Camp Hotel having a piss and a quick chat with Jackie regarding accommodation in Sharm El Sheikh, she tried phoning a few places but no luck so I went out and into an internet shop and booked a 4 Star hotel for 31$US per night including breakfast, www.booking.com wondering what 4 Star means in Egypt!. Tomorrow all signed, sealed and delivered it was 1750hrs so into my favourite café beside the Bamboo Hotel and had a spaghetti bolognaise meal with a tea. It came very quickly and was absolutely delicious as I sat overlooking the pedestrian street watching the travelling world walk by, good fun. Paid my bill saying my thanks and leaving a 3EP tip I was away back to my hotel and into room. Stripped off cargo short and no sleeve tee shirt and had a nice hot water shave and shower then drying off with my tee shirt as had forgotten I had put a pile of dobhi including my towel in the laundry to be cleaned. All new kit on and a nice teeth clean I was out and turned right into the lively town, it was 1905hrs. Went left at the crossroads and all the way along the beach promenade path until I reached the Jasmine Pension and had a coffee in this lively area, great vibes. Paid my bill and a slow walk back seeing the full moonlight shimmering all over the calm sea then done a left through a hotel area into the full light of the of Dahab pedestrian walk area which I really liked. Into an internet café and done my usual 20-30mins emails to everyone and that was me. Back to Camp Hotel and had two teas and even met Jeff and Kirsty again who were just going on their night adventure to climb Mt Sinai so wishing them luck that was my night nearly at an end as nothing for a single man. Into room having a read of LP and back down to reception again to collect my dobhi giving guy 15EP, good value. Back to room, it was only 2220hrs and not tired but stripped off and into bed thinking hookers in Sharm El Sheikh and dreaming there must be I was asleep a one happy Bedouin man.

Email Sent: Tue, 2 Mar 2010
Subject: Lagona and the Blue Hole, Dahab

Hi All

Had a nice lazy day just swimming in the sea in the seaside of the lovely Lagona then a pleasant 2-3 klm walk back into Assalah my part of Dahab which is the Bedouin Camel, goats, donkeys area if you walk to its outskirts.

Then a 4x4 jeep trip about 12klms along the dusty beach road to the Blue Hole which is where all the Divers dive and have fun but saying that their was a few Memorials on a cliff wall to some who never made it up, sad but a fact of life.

Went for another swim then a walk over and along a small cliff tip toeing along the top of its 300mm path, crazy mon crazy but made it back down.

Manyanna jumping a bus to Sharm El-Sheikh de rich Arab boys town, any spare dosh please think of me and don't hesitate to send it.

al de bes

Jack

Day 67, Wednesday, 03-03-10, Dahab – Sharm El Sheikh; Egypt

Woke up and checked clock, it was 0415hrs as I could hear a couple in the room above me talking, walking and moving their luggage about then at 0430hrs the chanters started but I did snooze until 0630hrs. Finally up at 0710hrs, underarm wash, face splash, long cargo, Thai sandals, pocket tee shirt on and ready for breakie. Over to breakie cushion area having my usual bowl of cornflakes, 4 toast omelette, butter, jam and two teas and paying my 20EP breakie charge with 10EP for the 2 teas from last night I said my thanks and back to room, it was 0805hrs. Quick clean of teeth, neckpouch on checking Passport, zipped up my shoulderbag leaving my faithful trainers behind as they had saved my soul a few times I said thanks buddies, I loved you but you now smell bad and I wont be doing anymore marathon walks or climbs, hope someone will treat you nice and I was out of room with trolley handle up. I gave room key to breakfast wallahs and saying and waving Goodbye I went out the big steel iron gate directly at the taxi rank. Guy seen me coming out and said taxi, I said yes for Bus Station to Sharm El Sheikh, he said ok, 30EP, I said no letting on to cross the road he said how much, I said 5EP, he said 10, so I said ok, shoulderbag in back, me in front and we were away not that far but too far to walk where he dropped me off outside the Bus Station, it was 0830hrs. Into Bus Station ticket office and paid 20EP for ticket to Sharm El Sheikh, ticket collector pointing at one of four buses saying my one. The luggage hold was not open yet so had a piss, 2EP charge telling guy robbery and took bag to bus just as driver opened the hold. Put bag in hold getting stub and sticking it and bus ticket in tee shirt breast pocket I was on the bus taking seat No35. Bus got about 25% full then at 0900hrs, toot toot and off we drove out of the Bus Station me giving a little wave saying, bye bye Dahab you were nice to me and settled back to enjoy my 1hr 30min drive to Sharm El Sheikh, what a great start to my day so sat back relaxed and happy. Got well out of Dahab and onto a 4 lane highway going through high mountain barren rock gorges all in the no clouds full heat of the desert sun but nice in our AC bus, what a fascinating sight. Mountains slowly disappeared and we were now going through a flat sandy desert me starting to doze off only when we hit the speed bumps as we stopped at checkpoints, one where we had to show our Passports, it was 1000hrs, only 30mins to go. I could now see the sea as we turned right driving along the coast road and not far drew into a large bus station and stopped. Out I got, grabbed shoulderbag from hold and taxi touts were saying, taxi taxi, I said yes showing them my Hotel reservation for Dive Inn Resort, Ras Um Seid, Sharm El Sheikh, Egypt, Tel: (2069) 3660835 and guy said 50 EP, I said no 20EP, they said no, 40EP, I said ok just wanting to get to the hotel, so shoulderbag in back of pickup van, me in front, we were away. Drove past the St George 3 Corners Hotel then a couple of turns and down El Forousya St and there it was, gave guy 50EP but as usual no change me pointing it out behind his windscreen sunshade and he gave me the 10EP, I said my smiling thanks and away in to reception. I gave guy my reservation, he said I have missed one night as reservation was from 2nd to 4th, I told him it was my mistake but I would be staying another night anyway, he said hotel full. He was not very cooperative as I paid in EP but had to ask for a receipt, had to ask for a hotel card, had to ask for my Passport back as he wanted to photocopy it but eventually got my key to Room 705 and guy pulling my trolley shoulderbag over past the lovely sunbed pool we went and he showed me my 4 star, I must admit, lovely classy, big d-ensuite room. Dumped kit in room, had a piss, changed into cargo shorts and checking China beachbag I was out of room going to go down the beach area as sitting around a pool all day was not for me. Back upto reception, dropped my key in and asked for a map and directions to the beaches but guy said to buy one at the shop next door, had a look but fed up I was away, New day, New town, it was 1110hrs. Turned right on El Forousya Street as could see the sea and kept going downhill and seen bikini clad girls going into a cliff parking area and just followed them past a security guard coming to another desk kiosk where if I wanted to swim I would have to pay a 20EP charge. No options I paid and down the steps to the rocky above sea level sunbed and access into the sea pool and that was me. Took my no sleeve tee shirt and cargo shorts off and taking my time with my ass on the last bit of round smooth boulder I was in the lovely nice sea just breast stroking and back floating but nowhere to stand as it was a very deep cliff edge stone pool. Slowly but slowly I squeezed through the boulders gap and with a final knees up splurge I got my right foot on the seas edge of the boulder pool and grunting out loud I levered myself up onto the stone pad thinking I wouldn't like to be near this area if the sea was rough. Quick decision as the flattish area of the stone cliff was only 10m sq so wanted some breathing space to fart, cough and spit I put cargo shorts and Thai sandals on and I was away back up the steps and through the car park to the road. I didn't have a clue where Sharm El Sheikh was but knew if I got a taxi to the Old Market I would be in the thick of the town centre so didn't need to hail a taxi, they were a never ending horn pumping stopping 'do you want a taxi' maniacs. Finally agreed a 30EP fare to the Old Market and driving there we passed the IL Mercato upmarket area with Starbucks, KFC and McDonalds to name a few and it was only a 50-100m from my hotel on the next street to El Forousya Street so that was a bonus for later on tonight. Went downhill and he stopped at a big Arch with a sign on it, "Old Market". It was a hive and fully packed with loads of people so happily paid him his 30EP and he was away. No rush just strolled everywhere around the hundreds of shops and stalls getting lost a few times which didn't matter then back out under the Arch. Could see a sort of bay so this time brought a map and seen it was Sharm El Maya with Sharm El Sheikh Old City beaches running around it so hoping against hope for a free beach I headed down to it and knew my luck was out. Everywhere along back from the sea edge there were fences with security at entrance and exit points so resigned I asked guy at El Rheima Beach fenced off entrance gate, how much, he said 35EP so sick as a pig paid it, got my entrance stub and I was in. Didn't know if I was allowed or had to pay for sunbeds but stripped off at the left hand fence edge putting cargo shorts in beachbag and I was into the lovely warm sea padding quite a way out before the sea got upto my waist then gently done a head first dive into the sea and that was me for the next 15mins just frolicking about either breast stroking, back floating or doing nothing just watching the bikini chicos doing the same. Eventually came out and over to a soft drink kiosk and bought a bottle of Fanta and a packet of crisps and sitting on its steps edge I enjoyed my 1440hrs din dins. Finished the last of my Fanta and had a stroll around my part of the bay that was not completely fenced off, in for one more dip and that was me as I could see my skin had turned a now brighter red. Had a think so kit on and out and turning right I walked upto and in and around the Tiran slightly upmarket town centre Mall which was fun and it had lovely melody music going then it was time for real eats and I only had one through in my mind which was good ole McDonalds. I hoped I knew where I was going but asked an old traffic policeman and he pointed up the hill so kept walking turning left at the hill top Mosque. Seen IL Mercato Street and turned right going down it passing Banners across the street with www.soho-sharm.com / www.bluelagoonsharm.com and as my eyes misted over I was near a real treat for myself as could see Hardies, KFC, Pizza Hut and good old McDonalds. Yeah man yeah, I was one big happy man and straight into Mackie's ordering a 26EP charge full combo beef burger, fries and a coke and took it outside taking off my no sleeve tee shirt and Thai sandals sitting on a chair I got stuck into my 1705hrs lovely supper, it was gorgeous. Finished it and away only around the corner and into my hotel collecting my key and into my lovely room, stripped off having a nice shave then a quick shower and drying off put on my long cargo and short sleeved pocket tee shirt and out I went, it had just turned 1900hrs. Had a nice walk through the well lit IL Mercato which had great vibes and walked downhill into the Old Market still going full blast. Seen a sign Old Egypt and wow oh wow walked into and along a huge long Bazaar of every sort of conceivable stall doing my full circle probably missing half of it. Seen an Internet shop so in and done my usual 20mins travel story and also booked an en-suite room for two days from tomorrow in a hostel in Na'ama Bay and booked the next three days in a Hurghada Hostel so next five days are taken care of. Kept going around all the fully open and well lit area of the Old Market seeing the Candle Café in the floodlit and waterfall of the cliff face with a Bedouin tent, really amazing scenes and that was me, seen one seen the lot and that was my Old Town little walk over. No chance of me walking up the steep hill so agreed a 20EP price with taxi driver to drive me upto Starbucks my final stop tonight, in I got and off we went and at 2050hrs he stopped outside a motley crew of it looked like travellers sitting around having chats and their Starbucks coffee. I sat down and guy took my order of one coffee and 2mins later he put the large cup on my table so milk and sugar in it, my ole legs were saying thanks for not moving as I had my no rush lovely Starbucks coffee. Final slug, paid my 12EP charge and a 5min walk and I was back in the full of life Dive Inn, got my key and into room, stripped off and back, knees and ankles saying no more you walkie junkie I was into my bed and asleep not even one thought of a dream.

Rich boy

Email Sent: Wed, 3 Mar 2010
Subject: R705, Dive Inn Resort, El Forousya St, Sharm El Sheikh

Hi All
Jumped the 0900hrs bus,10EP, from Dahab and into Sharm El Sheikh at 1030hrs and into above a 4 star upmarket dive for 30$US a night, its just at the rear of the IL Mercato complex with all the many cafes including McDonalds where today I had my first decent meal for over a week!!!!!!!.
Had booked 2 nights www.booking.com but put the 2-3-10 as my first night and they had no other rooms for manyanna so heading for Na'ama Bay manyanna as got a d-ensuite Hostel room for 10$US a night, www.hostelworld.com
Had a great start to my day swimming in Reef Beach then a taxi down to Old Market and into the El Rheima beach, great vibes and sun was hot.
Had a wonder around the Old City, really good.
al de bes
Jack

Day 68, Thursday, 04-03-10, Sharm El Sheikh – Na'ama Bay; Egypt

Checked bedside clock as I woke up sweating a bit as I had turned the AC off going to bed, it was 0620hrs so not a bad one. Turned over and stretched a few times on my creaky lovely soft mattress bed then up for good at 0740hrs. First things first I had a loud farting dobhi drop, cleaned ass then underarm wash, face splash, long cargo, pocket tee shirt on and checking driving licence wallet and bits and pieces I was out upto the large restaurant and my God in the Heavens above this buffet breakfast on order was something I had not seen or ever come across before in all my travels. There must have been 50 different items to choose from be it cereal, bread, cakes, meat, salad, eggs cooked every & anyway so had 4 rolls, 3 teas, small bowl of cornflakes, 1 hard boiled egg and 2 chocolate cakes and happily got stuck in enjoying my 4 star breakie. Finished it all and had another Rosy Lee thinking checkout is 1200hrs but I will make a move about 1000hrs to arrive at Oonas Dive Club, Na'ama Bay, Sonesta Beach, Sharm El Sheikh, South Sinai, Egypt, Tel: +22 224186021 approximately 1030hrs, that's the plan. Back to room having a walk around the Bedouin Tent Café, cleaned teeth and God Help the Saints above, bang, another full dobhi drop me blaming McDonalds. Not to worry, cleaned ass, cleaned teeth, final little pack of shoulderbag, neckpouch on checking Passport and I was out of room going past people on their sunbeds already, they must be crazy as I would get bored stiff in 5mins but everyone to their own and upto reception ready for my next move. Handed key over saying my thanks as it would have been nice to stay for my paid up one missed day and outside to main road flagging down a taxi. Agreed 25EP for ride to Na'ama Bay telling and showing him my Hostel World confirmation sheet, shoulderbag in boot, me in front and we were away in the 1010hrs searing sunshine heat. He drove out of Sharm El Sheikh going up the coast on I think the Peace Rd and we were now in Na'ama Bay going through a many cafes, restaurant area and he stopped at the main front road at the Sonesta Beach Hotel and Casino but I said no showing him Oonas Dive Club Hotel, he asked another taxi driver who gave him directions and we were away. He turned right at the Sofitel Obelisk and we followed the signs for the Fantaja Hotel along a narrow little tarmac road down the walled side of the 5 Star Sinai Grand Casino and stopped directly outside the Oonas Dive Club. Out I got giving him 30EP, he wanted buckshee but I was away into Hotel reception giving guy my email confirmation printed sheet him saying Mr William and asking for Passport which I gave him. I was given Rm35 and with guy carrying my shoulderbag up we went 2 flights of stairs and into room me saying thanks as he left my shoulderbag on the room floor and away. Changed into cargo shorts, no sleeve tee shirt, checked driving licence wallet, put neckpouch in shoulderbag and down to reception, got my Passport back so upto room putting it in neckpouch and back down to reception again. Guy said do I want a beach towel as sunbed, sunshades on the beach were free, I said no not yet as I want to go for a walk in and around central Na'ama town so he said go left onto beach promenade only 10-20m away then go right and follow beach path promenade and it's a 20min walk going past all the big hotels so saying my thanks I was away, it was 1105hrs. Our Hotel sunbed area was in the Sonesta beach sunbed café area which was packed already but turning right I was enjoying my skin getting burnt no rush walk as only had shorts on now, no sleeve tee shirt was in my China beachbag. There was cafes and restaurants along the path and finally made it upto King of Bahrain St which was a very lively full of shops, restaurants and cafes with very expensive prices as no way could I eat at this price, it would probably make me sick but it will be fun to see tonight. I got upto the Peace Rd seeing HSBC, The Hard Rock Café, Fridays and lots of very expensive shops but great vibes. It was Thursday I now know and I wanted to post some travel notes to Sandralita but asking various doormen and finally a policeman I was each time told there is no Post Office in Na'ama Bay the nearest one is in Al Hadoba or El Hadaba depending on your Arabic. I couldn't believe a town this size so upmarket had no Post Office but Policeman told me just hand any post into your hotel reception as that's the norm in Na'ama. I knew the Post Office in Al Hadaba will close PM today until Sunday so instant decision I flagged down a taxi and agreed a 40EP drive back to Sharm El Sheikh to the Al Hadaba Post Office, jumped in and we were away. Got there and finally got it weighed, paid 8EP for stamps, guy stuck them on giving me 2EP change from a 10EP note and I was away back into taxi and got him to drop me off on the Peace Rd facing or in-between the two Hilton Hotel complexes each side of the road, paid him 35EP and he was away. Enjoying the searing sun I kept on the Peace Rd going past the Royal Mall, Playa Mall, Mina Mall, lots of supermarkets and Carrefour Express Store with many casinos each side of the highway road. Came to the Roxy Mall which had a good ole McDonalds on its front then past Sonesta Beach Hotel and knew where I was as I turned right at the Sofitel Obelisk and wandering past many security road blocks I was glad to get into my hotel reception not taking that road again I was thinking. This time got a sunbed beach towel and down to the 4-5 Hotel complex approximately 3-400 sunbeds sunshade Sonesta private beach care area with snorkelling and flippers for hire and plonked myself down on a one of a row of empty sunbeds saying no more moves today you sick walkie junkie. Had a packet of creamy chocolate biscuits with a bottle of Fanta then treat time again I was down to the beach and into the not cold seawater and splash I was breast stroking and back floating, man oh man, this is a great life. Had my usual 15-20mins enjoyable frolic then back to my sunbed lieing flat out and the only thing that stopped me going to sleep was the flies me thinking I have been showering regularly lately, why me. In for another Red Sea frolic and that was the rest of my afternoon chores! as when the flies got to much too handle in for a dip I went. It was 1610hrs, time to call it a day so leaving all my now packed with Russian friends sunbeds as they do like to enjoy life with their skimpy bikini girlfriends drinking Vodka on the quiet I was away and into the Oonas Dive Club reasonably priced restaurant having a cheese burger and fries with 2 glasses of tea, 45EP not bad for Na'ama. Paid my bill, got my room key from reception guy and upto room and had a nice shave and shower, no flies tonight and thinking over my plans for the next few days I put on my long cargo, pocket tee shirt, checked driving licence wallet and down to reception for some advice regarding my plans but the older guy was not back from doing a pickup at the Airport so will check later. Out I went along the beach path and the wind was cold so back to hotel, upto room and put my pullover on and back out. Great walk along the beach path seeing all the hundreds of people eating and enjoying their 1920hrs 5 Star suppers and passing a money changer in I went hoping against hope and asked the guy does he change Israeli shekels, he said how much have I got, I said 320 giving it to him, he said after doing a check on his calculator, 395EP and counting it out, gave it to me. I said I thought it was worth 440EP, he said not today's price but me laughing to myself I said my thanks and away one more chore over and done. Each step I took the area was getting more and more lit up with more shops then done a right up Hussein Salem St and came to one of the most amazing sights I have seen in a long time. It was as I was standing staring up the fully colourful lit up King of Bahrain St a truly great vibes and marvellous spectacle as it was one jam packed pedestrian walkway with along each side there were many large cafes all with their Shisha pipe smokers supposedly being put on another planet by puffing and inhaling the smoke from the pipe. Gently smiling I walked its full length passing fully lit up and packed with people big Malls and Bazaars with long alleys until I came to another semi pedestrian walkway and turned right thinking I had seen and walked the King Of Bahrain St earlier today but nothing could have prepared me for tonight. Had to have a look and went into the vibrant 3 storeys full of life Na'ama Centre Mall just amazed at every turn I made. I seen a toilet so over to it and door attendant guy said 5EP so said robber and back the way I came and out only another 50m and into McDonalds and had my first free piss for a long time, long live Mackies I smiled to myself. Enjoying my walk I passed the Hard Rock Café then turned back and had a coffee sitting on one of its cushion seats in the roadside outdoor area, oh la, la. Time never stops so paid my 15EP charge and gently strolled back all the way along King of Bahrain St having a final tea, 10EP in a cushioned outdoor seating area and that was me for the night it was 2220hrs. Everywhere still buzzing with live stage shows at different 4-5 Star Hotels outdoor areas but feeling the great vibes of the Na'ama night I bought 2 packets of creamy chocolate biscuits and a final slow walk I was back in my hotel, got my key and upto room. Put kettle on, stripped off and had a mug of tea with a full pack of bickies and that was me, light off and into bed and dreaming of more Gippo sex I fell asleep.

Email Sent: Thu, 4 Mar 2010
Subject: R12, Oonas Dive Club Hotel, Na'ama Bay, Sharm El Sheikh, Egypt

Hi All
Sorry to leave my 30$US stay in my 4star Hotel but no beds for next day so decided to go to Naama Bay just over the hill and sleep their anyway and got above for 50$US, B&B as this Naama Bay is big time rich. Good fun as my hotel is on the beach with sunbeds and fantastic rooms with a good cheap dinner menu as laughing to myself walking past the all the big 5 Star hotels into centre of town I seen meals advertised for 200/300 EP as I would choke to death eating at that money.
Staying for 2 days then heading for Hurghada as booked 3 nights in a place their for 18$US a night as us rich boys like to throw a bender now and again, wat yu tink.
Now red as a beetroot.
al de bes
Jack

Day 69, Friday, 05-03-10, Naama Bay – Nabq, Egypt

Awakened early at 0430hrs as could hear the drum disco music from somewhere and it went on until 0530hrs I think but snoozed and turned over a few times then still tired I forced myself up, it was 0735hrs. Underarm wash, face splash and yeah man yeah, an explosive dobhi drop, cleaned ass, cargo shorts, no sleeve tee shirt on and down to next door restaurant for buffet breakfast and checking times I had seen that I had booked the wrong dates for my Hurghada hostel. I had booked for arrival Sunday 7th March but will arrive late Saturday night 6th March as boat does not go today, Friday 5th only goes Saturday at 1800hrs that's if I am lucky taking 1hr 30mins so will have to either log in to www.hostelworld.com or phone up, I shall see. Had a bowl of cornflakes with a fried omelette, 3 teas and 5 slices of white bread with butter and jam and sat back in contentment trying not to listen to or watch the BBC News on the large telly as no news is good news. Must admit sitting in the restaurant bar area my room was the complete opposite end from it as it had music and ongoing noise to very late last night with the revellers and people passing it going back to their hotels so I was lucky where my room is as I had a decent nights sleep. God help the poor souls living above it as they have to put up with loud speaker melody music on now and its only 0830hrs. Finished breakie and back upto room, cleaned teeth, little pack of China beachbag and downstairs to reception with security guy telling me reception guy does not start until 0930hrs, it was 0915hrs so had a seat indoors away from the already searing hot sun, its unbelievable how hot it is. I was trying to get the reception guy to book me a ticket on the Sharm El Sheikh Express Boat for tomorrow night but I am getting the impression he is trying to avoid booking it so I will have to stay 2 extra nights as no boat on Sunday night. Waited until 1000hrs and he had come quickly in once but disappeared so called it a day and out hopefully to find the boats office up by the Hard Rock Café, same same, we shall see. Quick walk and guy in Hard Rock Café said Travel Agent who does boat tickets is facing the Marriot Hotel on Peace Rd so thinking what a bunch of assholes as it makes me think they are intentionally doing this to stop people leaving I was out onto Peace Rd and jumped in a service Minibus taxi getting a back seat and paying my 3EP fare by passing it up over the shoulder to the guy in the front and that was my fare paid as we drove all along the Peace Rd I looked right seeing Tiran Island in the Red Sea. The Minibus stopped and as some got on, some got off and paid either 1-2 or 3EP depending on how far they were going to travel and I maybe paid over the top but didn't ask for a refund as we drove into Nabq Oasis my 12km away destination for today. Said ok and driver stopped and out I got at a line of all sorts of shops on the left hand side of the road and the never ending big and small beach resorts on my right. Good fun walking through not what you would call an Oasis today and came to the Public Horizon Sharm Beach at the roundabout but looking down the access to the beach tarmac road it was a long way so kept going thinking once I see Nabq I can come back. It looked like I was now in the centre of Nabq as came to the elaborate Grand Mall Nabq with near beside it the big huge Jasmine Centre. Looking across the road I could see the huge St Georges Bar on the beachside of the road with a big notice above its front entrance, The Shining Knight of Sharm and unbelievable but it had a large crowd already drinking most looked English so good luck to St George I said laughing out into the Egyptian hot sky, those were the Maltese days. I was tempted to have a Naafi break tea break but no stopping as only another 50m I was walking past a good ole McDonalds, KFC, Starbucks, Fridays and a Hard Rock Café with a sign stating Opening Soon and looking across the road I was laughing like a mad dog as there was a line of tent like tiny bamboo separate shops with one having Primark above its entrance, good fun. Got to the Al Kan Shopping Promenade big sign and turned left up the coloured painted pedestrian road thinking I shall come back here tonight as it has a bit of life different from Na'ama. Had a dander up and around the coloured road shops most closed as the chanters were giving it root and as it was prayer time for my Moslem friends. Back out to and crossed the Peace Rd and took a tarmac road between the Oriental Resort and Laguna Vista all the 100m walk down to the sunbed sunshade beach of Nabq Bay, yeah man yeah, time for a dip. Stripped off on the flat seashore rock beside the empty lifeguard lookout tower and paddled out into the clearest sea I have ever seen with all sorts of smallish fish some stopping to look at my feet as I laughed at them it was so funny. Sea only got up to below my waist even as I walked out nearly 100m so done a few bend over and bending my knees underwater splashes and that was me back to the beach in the lovely searing burn you dead sun. Made it back to the Tower, grabbed China beachbag with my cargo shorts, no sleeve tee shirt in it and of I went in my brief swimming trunks and Thai sandals along the sunbed, sunshade beach as they never stop, it must go on for hundreds of miles as nowhere in the world have I seen tourism like this. Finally all my body areas now bright red I walked back up the tarmac road and back onto Peace Rd, flagged down a service Minibus and taking my seat I paid my 3EP the usual way by passing it to the guy in front. Travelling fast we passed the Airfield and wow oh wow I seen the SS Thistlegorm lieing on its side shipwreck in the Red Sea not far from the Island of Tiran which is a very popular diving area. Not far now and I said ok to driver and he pulled in directly facing an Obelisk and saying my thanks out I got, crossed the suicide road running quickly and along a minor road along the walls of the Grand Casino Sinai I made it into my hotel reception lounge. Asked guy again any luck with phone number for ferry, he said no as I now believe it's a con to make people stay longer. Got a beach towel and only 20m I was in the lovely Yankee ballad records on the loudspeaker at the Sonesta Beach area. Got a sunbed, spread my towel on it, stripped off and I was down into the lovely sea happily frolicking about breast stroking and back floating for 20mins, what a great life. Out upto sunbed and had 30mins on my back then 30mins on my front and could see I was slowly turning into a brown man and had a little doze for 10mins. Had one more dip and a lazy sunbed lie, checked time, it was 1725hrs belly telling me it was time for eats. Put cargo shorts on and slinging towel over shoulder I went back into reception giving him the towel then out into the outside seating area and ordered a spaghetti bolognaise and one tea and when it came on a big plate it looked and tasted gorgeous as I took my first dollup, lubbly dubbly so took my time really enjoying my 1745hrs lovely meal. Finished my tea, paid my 44EP bill leaving a 1EP tip and away back upto room having a shave and a lovely shower, wow I felt like a new man. Long cargo, pocket tee shirt on and I was out upto Peace Rd and found the Travel Agents called Menia-Tours, www.menia-tours.net beside and facing the Marriot Hotel and guy gave me a card saying phone him tomorrow at 1200hrs and he will check for a seat on the Hurghada Ferry. I said can you not do it now, he said no, I said my thanks and left thinking I will try again in centre of town to find the shipping office and maybe go down to the Port area as no one wants to book me a seat on this bloody ferry. Going back to the dark two lane each way Peace Rd highway I heard a long screech of brakes and seen a young girl getting hit on her ass by a car which knocked her sprawling full length onto the other lane so quickly ran over helping her up onto the pavement and with her friend with her a crowd gathered around all offering to help. She could move and had no broken bones or serious injuries as she was so very lucky as these Egyptian drivers I don't know why drive without lights. She was able to walk and her and her friend said they were going back to their hotel and arms around each other they went back into the Novotel only 50m away. I was wanting to go to Nabq so tried flagging down the going passed very fast service Minivan's but none would stop so eventually got a taxi down to 30EP, jumped in and we were away not fun as this is a crazy driving experience. Drove into the bright lights of the first of the three areas of shopping Malls and said ok to driver and got out giving him the 30EP and he was away. Had a little walkie then down to the middle village you would nearly call it having a lookie and a dander around my final stop at Starbucks, KFC, Fridays and the coloured pedestrian street. It was a nice place if you were with company but didn't want to stop so back to the main Peace Rd and same taxi who had bought me here drew up me thinking he was following what he though was an easy screw. Jumped in agreeing a 40EP fare this time and another dark suicide run he dropped me off at a well lit up and colourful street near King Bahrain St, paid him his fee and he was away. Enjoyed my walk along this half pedestrian only walking area then into my favourite King Bahrain St enjoying my walk past all the Shisha and cushion cafes and had a well earned tea in one at the end just crowd watching for 40mins. Paid my 10EP charge and away along the beach Promenade Lane even seeing a 15min free Bedouin belly dancer show her giving her ass, tits and firmish belly a good jingle which was really good. Nearly home so bought a packet of creamy biscuits and into hotel. Got my room key and upto room, it was 2235hrs so put the kettle on making 2 mugs of tea and stripping off I sat on the side of my bed enjoying my bedtime tea when pop my left knee jumped out, oh God, it was agony. Tried to move but found it very hard, tried rubbing it but no luck and tried bending and in agony I could but it would still not go back in. I didn't want to phone reception or ask for help but might need to do so put my underpants on, took 3 painkillers and limped into the shower, spraying it with warm hot water and which definitely eased the pain and tried bending it back in but no luck. Dried off and back into room and sat on the edge of my bed by the phone and said one more time and bent it and forced it to bend really tight and pop, it jumped back in, oh my God I was saying as I quickly got an elastic knee bandage from my China beachbag and slipped it up over my knee. Had a little walk and it was ok but time for bed so only pocket tee shirt and underpants on I took them off and into my lovely bed stretching my lovely sore ole knees saying to myself you are the culprit you walkie junkie manaic. Why don't you just get a sunbed like everyone else and be bored stiff doing nothing all day, so promise promise and with one last stretch I was asleep dreaming sunbed Jack, New day, New life.

Email Sent: Fri, 5 Mar 2010
Subject: Nabq, Egypt

Hi All

Jumped a service Minibus(shared) and only 12klms I was enjoying the shallow beach of Nabq for an hour or so even seen a shop the size of a dog kennel with Primark above its door!!!!!!!!, couldn't stop laughing.

Came back to Nabq tonight as it has the usual Starbucks, McDonalds, Fridays, KFC and all the rest but Na'ama takes some beating as will head back later for my final rosy lee.

Heading for Hurghada manyanna on the 1800hrs boat but they try every trick to keep you in Na'ama telling me no boats, boat full etc as I think its done on purpose, not to worry, same, same.

Its bigtime warm here, hows blighty.

al de bes

Jack

Day 70, Saturday, 06-03-10, Na'ama Bay – Hurghada; Egypt

Great sleep, never heard a dicky bird and up at 0730hrs having an underarm wash, face splash and dobhi drop, yeah man yeah, cleaned ass, cargo shorts and no sleeve tee shirt on and down for buffet breakie. Had my usual bowl of cornflakes then an omelette with 4 slices of white bread with butter and jam along with 3 teas and belly full, me happy I was back upto room, cleaned teeth, little pack of China beachbag and downstairs to reception. Told guy I wanted to stay another half day only and was not checking out at 1200hrs, he said ok saying the price is 10Euros and will I pay my full bill at same time, I said ok and he put my credit card into machine, I punched in my code and 2mins later got a receipt for 619EP, (77Euros) so all and everything paid. I asked again and showed him on his computer how to do a Google for Hurghada Ferries and he got it up, we got the telephone number me also telling him Mena-Tours, www.mena-tours.net with their office facing the Marriot Hotel does booking, he said ok. He phoned Red Sea Jet Ferries office number 0102335209 but no answer, it was only 0850hrs, I said lets give then until 0900-0930hrs then I want to go out and enjoy myself not hang about like an idiot trying to make a single booking. He nodded smiling and I left to go back upto my room as forgot my LP as want to photocopy a few pages and map of Hurghada. Grabbed LP Middle East book and back down and thinking I can only try went left then right up the street beside Sonesta Hotel, running across Peace Rd thinking about the teenage girl last night and hoping she is ok. Seen Thomas Cook and went in just trying and asked for Ferry ticket to Hurghada, guy said only one who does it is Mena-Tours pointing, go right up the road or I can have a flight tomorrow at 1100hrs for 400EP. I said my thanks for the more information in 1min than I had received from anyone else over the last 3 days. I asked him if there are any internet cafes about, he pointed left saying go into the Roza Mall beside McDonalds so really chuffed I was out and into the cafes and shops of the not big Roza Mall but internet 12 seat shop was not opening until 1200hrs. Done my photocopying at the Kodak Express Office in the Roza Mall and its looking good so out and only a short walk I was in Mena-Tours. Guy from yesterday said you go Hurghada today, I said yes, he phoned up and said to me single, one way, I said yes, he put his phone down and writing out my ticket he asked for my Passport, I said only photocopy, he said no problem and got me to write my name and Nationality and said 250EP. I gave it to him and he showed me my ticket for the Red Sea Jet Ferry at 1700hrs, put it in a see through plastic envelope and as we shook hands he gave it to me, it was 1020hrs and time to breathe out a sign of relief, what a malarkey for a simple one-way ticket. Really smiling now I left Mena-Tours and seen an ATM so drew out 1000EP and stuck it in my sky so at least I will have money when I arrive at Hurghada. Back across to hotel putting ticket and LP book and spare dosh on top of cabinet and thinking where shall I go today for a few hours. Down to reception telling reception guy how well I did to get ticket and where I got the ticket from. He said I told you but just smiling at him I was away along the beach promenade path in a no rush stroll going all the way to the turn off for King Bahrain St. Turned back just again amazed at the prices of meals starting at 300EP but mind you all along this promenade was every 5 Star hotel in the history of hotels. Back to Sonesta Resort Beach and a quick 10m walk into my hotel reception, got a large beach towel and back and onto the hundreds of sunbed, sunshade nice music café and restaurant of Sonesta Beach Resort dropping my China beachbag on an empty sunbed. Stripped off to swimming briefs and out to the nice not cold not warm sea and took my time over the coral rocks and splash I was having a breastie and backie enjoying my hot sun frolic for the next 15mins then out back to sunbed, no walks today I was thinking, is this true. Bought a bottle of Fanta and drinking it lieing on my sunbed it was a nice and very pleasant experience seeing and watching half of Russia especially the mini bikini chicos either flat out asleep on their sunbeds or having a laugh together in groups. Had another few swims and another few walks in between my hot searing sunshine sunbed and checking watch it was time to go, it was 1400hrs. Up I got saying bye bye beachie and taking beach towel with me I dumped it in the hotel reception as I got my key and upto room. First things first I done a final pack of shoulderbag not that it needed much packing then stripped off completely and had a shave and a lovely shower no grief at all from my left knee. Dried off then long cargo, pocket tee shirt on and put neckpouch checking Passport around my neck and opened my door and trolley handle up I was out locking door behind me. Guy cleaning rooms took my shoulderbag down the 2 flights of steps so I gave him some loose 10cent coins and trolley handle up I was round to reception and gave guy my key, said my thanks shaking his hand and I was away going left then right and up the street the side of Sonesta Beach Hotel. Got to Peace Rd, taxi stopped and I showed him my Hurghada ticket saying ferry. He said 150$US I said no thinking here we go and next he said English pounds I said no waiting for his next one, he said ok, 150EP and I laughed and went across the main Peace Rd him saying how much but got across the other side and taxi stopped. Driver asked where you go, I said Hurghada Ferry, he said how much, I said 20EP, he said 40EP, I said ok and shoulderbag in back seat, me in front with safety belt on we were away, it was 1530hrs. My ticket said boat time 1700hrs but checking internet last night it said all Sharm El Sheikh ferries go at 1800hrs but better to be safe than sorry. It was a good drive passing through Na'ama Bay me waving saying bye bye Na'ama we were over the bare desert hill and through Sharm El Sheikh me seeing all the areas and roads, streets I had walked including the Old Market and along past the Beach Resort area my eyes misting over a bit we were up a hill and there was the Gated large sea Port to our front. Driver stopped at gate me seeing about six Egyptian blokes with shoulderbags standing at the side of the gate. I gave driver a 50EP note saying my thanks and as I walked towards the gate the guards said wait here until 1600hrs as that is boarding time and 2 guys at a desk waved me over saying ticket. I showed them my ticket and Passport me asking could I have bought a ticket here, they said yes, how much I asked, they said same price you paid 250EP, so that was at least a safeguard. Had a good 15min wait then pistol armed guards arrived saying boarding everyone and everyone showing Passports and tickets we went through the big steel gates then into a departure hall everyone putting their bags through x-ray and that was me in. Had a little bit of a walk then up the gangplank and putting my shoulderbag in the luggage racks I went into the AC lounge and had a seat, it was 1635hrs. Not long at 1650hrs engine revved up then spot on 1700hrs we backed out and going forward we were away out of the Port passing big Cruise liners one called the Costa Europe then a big Catamaran yacht marina and slowly chugged our way out into the Red sea at the Gulf of Aqaba, what a wonderful feeling. Giving a quick wave to Sinai and this side of Egypt we were now out in the full ocean sea, yeah man yeah, it was 1705hrs so sat back as now a sailor on de high seas. Had a little walkie and there was approximately 350 seats on the first deck and approximately only 40 passengers, 2 Male, Female toilets and a coffee, tea food kiosk as 2No films were showing. There didn't appear access on to the main deck and I didn't care as I had a lovely soft seat with plenty of leg room and a table in front of me for my first Rosy Lee at 1735hrs looking out the large window to the flat sea horizon. Enjoyed my 4EP tea with 4 cream bickies as it slowly got dark and at 1810hrs you could just about distinguish the horizon line between the dark sea and the slightly lighter sky and 10mins later nothing only pure black darkness, man oh man, but not long to go and I fell asleep. Woke up and it was 1920hrs and no sign of docking so I was thinking I had caught the wrong boat but remembered the 2-3 ticket and Passport and baggage checks then the final ticket check as I boarded so checked LP again and it did say 1hr 30mins. Had another 4EP tea with a packet of crisps and a Mars Bar and asked a guy sitting near me how long does the boat take, he said 3hrs so there, glad we did start at 1700hrs as it will be 2000hrs docking time, not bad I suppose. Treated myself to another tea and had 6 creamy biscuits so belly not needing any meals tonight when we reach dry land. Bit of movement on board with guys putting jackets on and then engine slowed down a little and wow oh wow I could see lights on my right out the right hand windows so must be getting near, it was 1940hrs. Yeah man yeah looking out my left hand window there were lights all along the coast and in we sailed to the Port of Hurghada and docked up. A quite orderly queue as everyone collected their mostly shoulderbag luggage and off the boat going across a flat large concrete might be a parking area but nothing anywhere in the dark night and out the dock gates I walked. Old fellow came towards me saying taxi, I said how much, he said where to, I said Sea View Hotel, Hurghada as I knew the Port we were in was 5-10km from Hurghada itself, he said 40EP so no haggling I said yes and as we got to his taxi, shoulderbag in boot, me in the front and we were away. He told me its only 35 years since hotels started to be built in Hurghada as when he grew up there was nothing here only little villages as we drove past massive hotels and Resorts still being built around the existing ones everywhere I looked. Passing a large Mosque he said was only 30 years old then pointing out the main roads to Old Town and New Town he stopped outside the very imposing and neat Sea View Hotel, El Cornish, Hurghada. Out we both got him putting my shoulderbag on pavement as I gave him a 50EP note saying ok, shook his hand and back into his taxi he was away. Into hotel giving reception guy my printed out www.hostelworld.com booking email, at 18$US a night for a single use, d-ensuite room. Guy done his calculations on his calculator and I had to pay 270EP so gave him 300 and got a 20EP note back him promising the other 10EP manyanna, me laughing, same same we shall see. Filled in and signed the usual form and got key to Room 218 and guy took my shoulderbag up only one flight of stairs, wow, what is life coming too but I was so happy to have made it. Guy unlocked my door and into a lovely big AC double bed, TV, fridge, ensuite large bathroom room he turned the lights on and saying ok he was away. Very pleased I took neckpouch off putting it into my shoulderbag, had a piss and out locking door behind me and down to reception. Asked where Old Town was, guy pointed left, go upto the T junction and go left so I was away, it was 2035hrs. Passing the Cinderella Hotel also on El Cornish or El Kornish I seen an internet shop and straight in doing my 20min update of affairs. Out from it and left along the bright lights and all the shops I think of Karim Sayed St which I happily walked passing the 4 Seasons Hotel with a very lovely café next to it but kept going into the centre of town by the look of it. Reached a very busy area everywhere all shops, cafes and restaurants still open all still touting for trade as I was now on the getting very busy Abdel Aziz Mustafa St with every conceivable shop you could think of. Passed two roundabouts, one with a large police presence then I was in a pedestrian only street market all with their carpet on the ground stalls I could hardly move there was such a big crowd. Followed it on Ali El Garem St for quite a distance hoping to see a lighted road going left but no luck but it had been a wonderful exploring start to my dark night arrival so turned back and made it all the way back stopping in a shop just before my hotel and bought a large bottle of Fanta, 4 packets of biscuits, 1 Mars Bar, 1 Twix, 20EP, so it's a real cheapie place Hurghada. Into hotel and upto room and half stripping off I had a packet of chocolate soft buns and a few slugs of Fanta to wash them down, I was full and happy. Stripped right off and looking forward to manyanna I was into my lovely big soft mattress double bed and dreaming of a belly dancer massage I fell into a relaxing and happy New town, New night sleep.

Email Sent: Sat, 6 Mar 2010
Subject: Rm218, Sea View Hotel, El Cornish, Hurghada, Egypt

Hi All
I was a no walk sunbed beachbum until 1400hrs today today, no walking, this is a crazy world.
Jumped the Red Sea Jet Ferry, 250EP at 1700hrs from Sharm El Sheikh and crossed the Red Sea and at 2000hrs arrived Hurghada and got a taxi and into above at 18$US a night for a single use d-en-suite, really classy.
Just having a dander in de old town.
Will stay 3 nights?? but same same, we will see.
al de bes
brownskinJack

Day 71, Sunday, 07-03-10, Hurghada; Egypt

Very noisy room as it over looked the sometimes busy back road with the car, lorry, bus traffic horns pumping never seemed to stop and doors slamming from any rooms in the hotel vibrated into my room but lovely soft mattress double bed so couldn't complain paying 18$US. Up at 0800hrs, had a piss, underarm wash, face splash and change of kit rolling all my dirty dobhi up and downstairs handing in at reception, guy said ready manyanna. Into breakfast buffet room and no cornflakes or cereals only fruit and green veg and egg omelette so got 2 soft rolls, 2 teas and 4 omelette slices and sat down to enjoy my first Hurghada breakie. Had another 2 rolls with jam and one more tea and that was me, where do I start today?. All information on boards was either in Russian or Polish as far as I could see so asked reception guy any information in English, he sort of grunted and didn't answer. Had a read of LP then back to room as felt a stir and bang, a great empty belly dobhi drop, cleaned ass and I was ready to go out, oh la, la, New day, New town, here comes the Belfast lover. Went downstairs saying to the very abrupt old Egyptian reception guy, do you keep key or will I, he said leave it here so I gave it to him. I then asked him has hotel got a beach or a beach card and he gave me one with Geisum Beach & Sea View Hotel name's on it saying its approximately 100m to the left and costs 10EP or telling me further on was another beach saying 30EP and out I went going right, trust me!. It was a resort only street of El Kornish many only half built and left like an eyesore which they were but passed the nice Hilton Resort on the beach side and got to the single Minaret Mosque at El Estad Street. Didn't have a clue but it was still early so kept going past the two upright Dolphins playing with balls Stature at a nice children's playground then the blue front façade face of the King Tut Resort just past a line of 1930's style blocks of flats. Didn't want to stop but where was I going and came to and walked past the Jardin Café looking out over the flat blue, no waves Red Sea. Taxi drivers pumping their horns as they passed so flagged down the next one and agreed a 10EP run to the Sharm El Sheikh boat departure point at the old port in Sigala so jumped in and we were away not really that far and he dropped me off pointing at the Red Sea Jet Express Boat Office, so paid him and he was away. Just had a look but big dockyard gate closed so kept going and turned right at the nice small yacht monument in the roundabout and into the melee of the rundown area of Sigala seeing a huge one big Dome with approximately 10 smaller Domes Mosque just being built as my final stop after my junky walkie around Sigala will be the huge Hurghada Marina directly beside the Mosque. I was doing well passing many grubby cafes and the service Minibus pick up/drop off point but I didn't know if Sigala had a neat new Resort waterfront as all I passed was oldish areas. Looking in the distance I seen through a dusty side street the opposite end of the Hurghada Marina and a slow walk my legs saying enough is enough you junkie walker I was up at the security entrance gate and in. The Marina dock was full of big Catamarans some the size of small destroyers and all back from the dock was lots of upmarket very clean cafes and restaurants and lots of shops which I suspect the whole great vibes area is the place to be at night so might give it a go tonight. Back out and going past the little yacht roundabout I flagged down a taxi and agreed a 20EP fee to drive me back to Sea View Hotel as its now beach bum sunbed time, jumped in and we were away. He stopped just past my hotel and I paid him saying my thanks seeing a very neat very large sunshade café beach area with no name at the entrance next to the El Sawaky Camp Café but directly facing El Jazeera Café. Off I went towards it and down the steps onto the beach and guy waved me over, I said how much to stay on sunbed on beach showing him my Sea View Hotel, Geisum Beach plastic card, he said no charge but we need your card so I gave it to him, he said hotel will give it back to me tomorrow morning. So no drama he give me a large beach towel and I walked across and took a sunbed under Shade No53, yeah man yeah my ole knees were saying with joy. I stripped off dumping kit on sunbed and a slow walk out into the not cold sea splashing myself I avoided the rocks amongst the sand as I paddled further and further out to sea. I got out approximately 75m but the seawater was only up to my waist so one final splash and in I went happily breast stroking and back floating in pure bliss in the hot sunshine of de Arab day. Had a piss destroying more marine coral life an Archaeologist would say and slowly came back out having a 100m sandy beach walk each way along the beach drying off my sunshine figure. Sat on my sunbed and had 6 creamy biscuits with 3 chocolate rolls with a bottle of Fanta and enjoyed my tasty thirst quenching din din, oh la la, it was 1340hrs. In for a breaststroke swim again and a walk each way on the 75m long private beach then lay fully stretched on my sunbed and woke up, it was 1520hrs. No intention of moving now so in for another few dips and beach walks in between lieing on my sunbed and as the sun was coming down closer to the roof tops of the hotel resorts across the road so checking time it was 1655hrs. I called it a hot red skin day putting on my cargo shorts and no sleeve tee shirt and I was away thinking and hoping my hotel had a restaurant. Walking back up the road I checked the menu at the Valentino Hotel Restaurant which had a pizza and beer for 25EP so I ordered a pizza and a tea and when it came it was very tasty and even got talking to an English bloke just passing which was very strange as not many tourists want to talk to anyone me thinking maybe it's the day to day hassle from the touts that puts them off. Enjoying my pizza and second tea I watched the five fishermen walking into the sea setting their round in a circle nets up, leaving it for 2mins then splashing and thumping the water walking towards its opening and then rolling the net up with their today, tonight's din din! catch. Nearly finished my lovely din din seeing and wondering why the Egyptians don't walk on the pavement as the men, women and children with not a care in the world walk on the suicide roads, madness mon. Paid my 30EP and saying my thanks I was away only a short walk and into my no restaurant hotel. Got my key from the never stop giving orders owner and had a chat with him telling me he has had enough and would like to sell. I said I have seen you working it looks likes 24hrs a day, take a holiday and start enjoying yourself. He told me he cant trust anyone as the workforce as soon as he trains them they leave and go to a bigger hotel chain. Wishing him well I was upto my room, stripped off and had a nice shave and shower and all clean kit on I was in a great clean mood as guy rapped door saying laundry. I opened the door and he gave me my nice clean and pressed laundry back saying 27EP so gave him a 20 and a 10EP note and as usual, no change. He had another look after I said change and found 2 one pound coins so I took it laughing saying ok and closed my door. Dumped laundry and downstairs handing key into reception and out going to Sigala trying to flag down a service Minibus but guy from hotel said walk approximately 100m up to the Mosque and that's the Minibus station so I did and got the last seat in a Minibus just leaving. I could hardly believe the great sight of the Hotel Beirut and Happy Days Hotel complex with dozens of shops along the side of the road me thinking I must have fell asleep coming this way this morning as don't remember them. I was thinking Sigala would be a dive but no it was a lively full of life town centre with plenty of fully lit up shops so today's reflection of Sigala does not rhyme with tonight's good vibes. Stopped a few times on the coast road to Sigala dropping people off then stopped at the Minibus station in centre of Sigala at the El Jaker Café at the Star Fish roundabout and off I got knowing where I was giving the driver a one pound coin as my fare. I went left and only 100m I was at the main security guard gate to the Hurghada Marina Complex and in I went. It was very quiet with all the well lit up big yachts and Catamarans along the harbour path one side and lots of shops, cafes and restaurants along the pedestrian walkway as I hands in pockets just walked its 150m length. Had a tea, 8EP in the Papas HRG pub/café enjoying my quiet walk but had seen Jam/Reggae advertised for tomorrow night in one of the cafes so no peace for anyone when that starts. Paid my bill and a no rush walk and same same, caught a service Minibus just ready to go. Stayed on it all the way into the centre of Hurghada in the Ad-Dahar area and as the Minibus stopped to let some people on I got off giving the driver 5P note and got 3EP in coins back, so had done well for both journeys. Had a walkie but couldn't see the packed full lit market area I had walked last night so maybe its only a Saturday thing, not to worry done a good full circle walk then back passing the Seven Seasons Hotel and on down to El Kornish Street and done a right coming back towards my hotel, it was 2225hrs. I was thinking of stopping for a coffee or tea at a café or restaurant along El Kornish St but said no and made it back into hotel, got my key and upto room having a Mars Bar and a Twix with a bottle of Fanta so thinking what a great day and night I stripped off and into bed and asleep dreaming hot sunshine sunbed, same same manyanna.

Email Sent: Sun, 7 Mar 2010
Subject: Hurghada on de Red Sea, Egypt

Hi All
Nice walkabout this morning then onto Public? sunbed/sunshade, 10EP Beach and enjoyed the rest of my sunstroke day going in for a dip a few times in the crystal clear sea.
Just left the www.hurghadamarinaredsea.com with all the million $ yachts docked up and paid 8 gippo pounds for a rosy lee, mama mia.
Not doing anything manyanna so head must be gone, wat yu tink!!!.
al de bes
Jack

Day 72, Monday, 08-03-10, Hurghada beach bum; Egypt

Woke up early I was thinking and checked bedside clock, it was 0535hrs so just snoozed and turned over a million times then fed up got up at 0800hrs spot on. Nice dobhi drop, cleaned ass then an underarm wash and a face splash, cargo shorts and no sleeve tee shirt on and down for breakie. Got 2 teas and 4 soft rolls, no omelette left so had 2 slices of luncheon meat with 2 rolls and filled the other 2 rolls with jam and got stuck in to my gippo breakie. Finished it quite quickly then had another tea taking it with me out to the fresh air reception area and the owner had just arrived telling me the Egyptian economy was down and he and everyone had to pay higher taxes to keep the Egyptian Government afloat so me just nodding I finished my tea and saying see you later I was back upto my room. Cleaned teeth and little pack of China beachbag and I was out down to reception giving key to guy and out as I wanted to find the Red Jet Express Bus Service to Luxor as reading LP they only allow 4 foreigners per bus and then only 3-4 buses per day as I want to go manyanna. Out I went turning right and right again at the Mosque and asking directions I was pointed further on up the road so kept walking but finally gave in and flagged down a taxi telling him Red Jet Bus to Luxor, he said 10EP so jumped in and we were away and it was further than I thought but two about turns which their road system call a roundabout he drew into Red Jet Bus Company. I and him got out and in Gippo and English it was agreed no bus today, only bus will be here 0700hrs manyanna and bus goes at 0800hrs taking 3½ hrs, price 45EP so agreed with guy I would be coming manyanna I got back into my taxi and he drove back up near the main roundabout to near beside the Zam Zam Hotel and my driver got out telling me to stay in cab. He came back within 5mins telling me bus pointing at it goes at 1100hrs today, charge is 25EP so saying my thanks for his efforts I said I go 0800hrs manyanna so into his driver seat and we were away back to my hotel both agreeing that he will pick me up at 0700hrs tomorrow as I gave him 30EP, he said his thanks and was away so first one of today's chores over, it was only 0935hrs. Emptied shoulderbag slinging it over my shoulder and downstairs dropping key in at reception again then out going left along El Kornish St into Ad-Dahar the centre of town and found a peddle sewing machine guy. Showed him 2 runs of snapped threads along the joints of my shoulderbag all my own fault as trying to force the zip closed I had snapped a row of threads along 2 joints. He said 20EP so couldn't haggle or could but although I know their must be other ones I said ok as he was putting new soles on an old guys shoes he said 30mins. I said no problem leaving bag in his shop and along the main Vibrant Rd thinking this is the place to stay and found a photocopy shop and photocopied some sheets of my travel notes paying 4EP. Back to sewing shop and he was just starting my shoulderbag pedalling the large needle up and down from the pedal beneath the sewing machine and 2mins later gave me my bag back another good job done. Shoulderbag over shoulder and I was away going left past the Seven Seasons Hotel to the Post Office just facing the Hospital but my luck had changed for some reason and it was shut as I wanted to weigh it and buy some stamps to post my travel notes to Sandralita. An old guy seen me looking in the window and told me the Post guy has gone out collecting and will be back in 30mins so saying my thanks I wondered what to do. Seen a postbox across the road at the roundabout facing the Brown Dutch Café so had a dander down to the next roundabout at the 2 Minaret Mosque going past a café called The Seedy Monsour Café having a laugh at an Egyptian Road Sign I took a photo and warning myself no mad dog walking today I went back and into the empty Dutch Brown pub/café/restaurant. Had a 6EP tea enjoying the not much activity anywhere including the traffic and checking my watch the 30mins was up so bought 6No 1.5EP stamps at a supermarket. Stuck them on and upto the Post Office but still not open so with no hesitation this time I crossed the road and put the A5 envelope in the post box, job done I was away thinking will it make it past the collection guy, we will see, it was 1115hrs. Next job I was into an Internet café just behind the Cinderella Hotel just down from my hotel and checked for flights to Malta from Port Said but no luck then checked Alexandria and Cairo and the only place with a direct flight to Malta was Cairo. Alexandria had flights via either Cyprus or Cairo, the same with Port Said so chose Cairo and tried booking a one way for 1100hrs, 14-03-10 but the hassle with the booking as the website wanted over the top Credit cards checks and confirmation of this and that with other Passwords and in the end a simple 10min job taking 25mins it refused to take my card. Back to hotel dumping shoulderbag in room putting neckpouch with Passport in it on then down and asked reception guy where is Egypt Air Office, he said it's the other side of Hurghada and it will take me either two service minibuses or take a taxi, I said taxi as it was 1210hrs. He said I will tell taxi driver and the price is 20EP one way so he flagged down a cab telling driver in Egyptian language where to go, in I got and we were away. We went all the way into the centre of Hurghada and then out the other side going past many half finished upmarket blocks of flats and then drove into a shopping area me thinking all this way for 20EP and stopped directly in front of Egypt Air Office saying I wait. I said I could be 10-15mins how much for the trip here, wait and back, he said 50EP, I said ok, grabbed my China beachbag and into Egypt Air Office getting a number 124 queue ticket. Only one other person at the 4 kiosk front desk and I was called forward near enough straight away telling lady to check for flights to Malta from the 14-03-10 just hoping for 16th. She went on her computer and said one flight 1100hrs, 14-03-10 then next flight is 18-03-10 so I said book me the 18-03-10 flight as I have tried but will have Paddy's day in Egypt rather than Malta as that's life for the travelling Shankill Paddy boy. She said ok, how you pay, cash or credit card, I said credit card giving her mine so she put it on her pay point, tapped in a few numbers and next thing gave me a stub to sign giving me the other half of the stub and 1min later gave me a printed out Egyptian Air Flight ticket. Wow, that was good I said and thanking her I was out and over to taxi, got in and we were away. He told me there was a travel agency near the Mosque that would have done my booking which was half the distance we had travelled as we were now passing the El Jaker Café then the Mosque me thinking he is going to hit me for 20EP first one way then 50EP on top plus a waiting charge as we drew up outside my hotel. I opened door getting my driving licence wallet out of my cargo pocket and give him a 50EP plus a 5EP tip and saying my thanks I got out. He said his goodwill thanks and was away me thinking that was the cheapest taxi for the longest taxi journey I have ever had in all my travels. Relieved about the no hassle I got my room key from reception guy saying ok and upto room putting ticket inside neck pouch and putting neck pouch in my orange cloth small bag in shoulderbag. Zipped up my shoulderbag and back out of room down to reception and with a large smiling sigh of relief I handed key in and said now for the beach asking him for beachcard which he gave me saying 10EP so I give him a 10EP note and out I went, oh my God it was 1240hrs but glad everything was all over and sorted. Little stroll along El Kornish and down the steps giving guy my card getting a large beach towel and seeing my sunbed from yesterday over I went to it. Quickly stripped off to swimming briefs, wow oh wow, what a marvellous life and with no hiccups or drama I was straight down and a body splash with my hands I paddled out avoiding the stone coral rocks then sea at waist level I done a dive and was back in heaven in the clear heavenly Hurghada Red Sea. Done my usual 15-20mins frolics then out at the right hand of the beach down from my sunbed and slowly walked the sandy beach along the seas edge getting a smiling hello from a young veiled Egyptian girl, very strange. I smiled my hellos back to her and her older friend and one bloke all on three sunbeds close together and kept going to the other end of the 100m longish beach. Had a walk up to near the El Geisum Cafe then back along the sea edge with my veiled headdress friend blowing me a kiss saying how are you, me happy to meet for the first time an outgoing Gippo girl, I said fine, life is good smiling as I passed her and going up to my sunbed. Had a 30min lie on it having a good slug of my large Fanta with 8 creamy biscuits, just the job. The sun was searing hot so in for another dip and out passing my now no veil but sunglasses Chico who put her arms out saying and inviting me to come over beside her saying lets have a photo shoot. I did go over me saying to myself this is so very strange and as she put herself in my arms her veiled girlfriend with her took a poser Jack photo and all laughing I left with a stir in my briefs I was getting more blowing smiling kisses as never had I come across anything like this in England, never mind Egypt. Came back along the beach going to my sunbed her this time with her veil and sunglasses off saying we meet tonight and she was a beautiful lovely girl as she asked what age am I. Drawing it with my forefinger in the sand I said 63, she drew 19 in the sand saying me but me looking at her I was thinking she had the confident eyes of a street girl on de prowl. She said can we meet tonight so really in the mood I said ok thinking this is handy and said 9 o'clock at entrance to the left of the El Sawaky Camp facing the Al Geisum Cafe so squeezing up to me giving me a hug and a lovely smile she said ok. I could feel a strong twinkle in my winkle as I walked across to my sunbed then next thing she came over to me in only her minitop and her jeans we wrote each others names and telephone numbers on a sheet of paper me now bigtime feeling the urge said lets meet at 1900hrs. She said ok as her friend and her friend's boyfriend were calling her as their 1700hrs lunch had arrived from the café. I was invited over but saying my thanks putting my cargo shorts and no sleeve tee shirt on I and she waving kisses at each other I was away giving Abo one of the guys from the camp overseeing the beach my beach towel. He said with his dead serious face she is a bad girl, I laughed saying thanks Abo but we are made for each other as I am a bad boy, he looked at me in amazement as I went away up the steps and not far along El Kornish St I was into the Valentinos Hotel Restaurant. I ordered pasta and a tea and not long it came so mixed the meat and large pasta up adding a dollop of salt I thoroughly enjoyed my supper sitting looking over the Red Sea. I had another tea and that was me, paid my 40EP bill, querying the extra 5EP and a slow walk back into my hotel, got my key and upto room. I stripped off having a shave and a lovely shower my skin now a deep brown, unbelievable. I left credit card and any extra cash out from my driving licence wallet as I know what women are like when they see a wallet. Neatly dressed and expecting the best I made it down to the El Geisum Café and sat outside having a tea and seen my sprightly lovely figure beach chico come laughing down from an alley off El Kornish St and we met with a nice embrace. Had a chat in pigeon English and Egyptian and agreed to walk into the centre of Ad-Aadar for coffee or tea having a laugh together we made it past the Seven Seasons Hotel and all the way down and along Abd El Aziz Mostafa St to the Simple Pub just before the entrance to the thriving pedestrian only Market St and into the Simple Pub we went. I had a tea, she had an orange juice still having a laugh together then I paid the bill and we were away. She said, holding my arm, can she come back with me to my hotel, I said sorry but no way could I take a chance asking that bloody owner to let her come into my room as I must admit I didn't know the Egyptian Hotel Rules. We snuggled up close in a few dark alleys me having a big time rocker on knowing I was going to do anything for tonight's pleasure. She said, holding me and pointing lets go up here and it was an alley with two derelict buildings each side with access into them for anyone and we went into the left hand one and up the stairs kissing like two hot night Arab gippo dogs as she was and I was fondling and groping each other everywhere she had my belt and zip undone with her blouse off and only her panties half on I quickly stripped of my long cargo the Egyptian music blasting out from a pub nearby. Quickly nearly ripping my underpants off she was down on me with me pulling her bra up and fondling her lovely big knob breasts I was pounding my lust filled rocker stiffly down her throat she ripping my sore ass cheeks apart she stood up as we where full of sex love kissing again then turning around she stuck her lovely ass cheeks out and in I lunged to her hot scented heaven in a slum cherry lips she screamed with lust shouting more more as now in my true lover grip of her Gippo cherry I was as she was grunting sometimes screaming in pure Gippo hot pure sexual spasms ecstasy I gripped her hot sweet scented thighs pulling her into me and now the both of lost in our Hurghada sheer passionate exotic pounding rampant sexual sex me now slapping her buttocks our sexual pounding sweats rose to a full heat filled sadism screaming crescendo until with one last grunting ripping into her scream of sexuel delight we both sexually climaxed together our screams off passion drowning the Gippo Pub music we kept on and on until heavily breathing and gasping out loud I pulled out from my true and only lover in the Gippo earth I slid down the dark wall as we sat our naked buttocks on the flithy dirt rock floor I knew we would be forever together in the dark hole of the Gippo slum dwelling she smiled giving me a slap on my naked thigh saying "your a bastino Papa Jack" and stood up pulling her other leg into her panties so I stood up getting fully dressed again me now laughing out loud at our mad sex night. Holding her tight and both of us laughing I got out my little digital light and checking everywhere around where we were I held her hand as we walked down the stone steps and out into the semi lit road. Holding her tight and arm and arm we slowly walked having a laugh and chat back towards our

Hotels and I got out my driving licence wallet saying you need any money. She said with a mischievous smile, yes please so give her 200EP getting a half imploring look so give her another 100EP getting a big smiling hug and kiss then as we reached her hotel with alley's and Souks near and around it we promised to telephone each other manyanna and another lovely hug and kiss I was away looking back once but she was gone. Made it back into hotel and eyes glazed like a Gippo camel I got my key from reception and up into room. Still laughing and so happy I stripped off and into bed happy as a gippo dog and dreaming gippo doggie style love is the only way in the heat of the Arab Red Sea dark gippo night I was asleep a truly happy doggie style Arab Gippo man.

Email Sent: Mon, 8 Mar 2010
Subject: Hurghada beach bum

HI All
Cor, getting used to this 6hr sunbed beach bum mentality as done it nearly all day plus swimming as well in the crystal clear with coral Red Sea, good fun.
Now out in centre of Ad-Aadar with its lots of cafes, restaurants and bars.
Jumping a 45EP, 0800hrs bus and heading on the 4hr journey to Luxor manyanna to see the Valley of the Kings, if I had waited until 1100hrs bus would have cost 25EP but big spenders, who cares.
al de bes
Jack

Just say a hedgehog family crossed

Day 73, Tuesday 09-03-10, Hurghada – Luxor, Egypt

Wakened 0450hrs as it was humid and warm and up for a piss, tried to go back to sleep but noise from generator going off and on so enjoyed turning over and doing stretching exercises on my aching muscles in my nice soft bed for the next hour or so then up for good at 0615hrs. Ate 2 chocolate buns with a few slugs of orange and out to the loo, bang, a full explosive dobhi drop, cleaned ass, washed my armpits, cleaned teeth and long cargo, pocket tee shirt on then neckpouch on checking Passport and wow oh wow, I was ready to go. Final little pack of shoulderbag then zips up I was downstairs leaving shoulderbag and China beachbag at seating area in front of reception. Into breakfast room having 2 soft rolls with butter and jam and 2 teas looking out the sunny day window seeing the building workers going full blast at the site across the road, it was 0650hrs thinking early start, early finish for them as it probably gets too hot PM. Finished my breakie feeling a stir and up to the communal loo at the end of the corridor then back to my China beachbag grabbing a section of toilet roll and quickly back to communal WC and splatter, bang, another full belly clearance dobhi drop so well set up for my 4hr bus journey today, I was happy. Cleaned ass then back to dining room to finish my tea and saying my Good Lucks and Good Byes to staff and the owner who had just come in and was giving all the staff their orders again, he never stops, I went outside and stood at the side of the road on the pavement, it was 0705hrs. Taxi with old Arab full robed driver stopped so told him Luxor Bus Station, he said 20EP so no haggle said yes, got in and we were away. He took me to the Bus Station facing the Zam Zam Hotel so just checking I went upto the kiosk and asked what time is the bus for Luxor, guy said 1030hrs here. Back to taxi pointing down the road saying Bus Station lets go, jumped in and we were away. Reached Red Jet Express Bus Station and driver stopped, I gave him a 20EP note, grabbed shoulderbag and over to kiosk taking my turn behind 4 Farang girls who got tickets. It was now my turn and guy said rota full no seats so shouting at him saying I came yesterday and you promised me a seat you gippo's are scum as I knew the regulations supposedly only allow 4-6 foreigners per bus so had missed out their. Over to the main highway and flagged down a taxi agreeing a 16EP fare up to the other Zam Zam Hotel Bus Station and giving driver 20EP I was out over to bus kiosk. I said Luxor, guy said 1030hrs and pay driver, it was only 0735hrs. Had a quick think and nothing to lose so flagged down another taxi and back to Red Sea Express Bus Area and upto kiosk. I said sorry for earlier but you promised me a seat as I spoke to you last night about booking a seat and he said ok, 45EP and gave me a ticket so smoothy boy Jack had got a seat. Spoke to the 4 girls from the USA one of whom was born in High Wycombe and they were good company for 15mins we all exchanging travellers tales then guy said if you want to sit in the café you have to buy a drink, a coke or something and checking my watch it was 0810hrs. I said no thanks as bus is supposed to go at 0800hrs and walked upto a sweet shop kiosk and sat on a large upside down plastic bucket. I got bored as it was now 0830hrs and no sign of any movement and talking to a lively young taxi driver he told me bus never goes until 0900hrs nowdays. I said 0800-0900hrs, same same, we shall see and both laughing he said looking around this bus is exceeding the foreigners rota as usually not more than 4 foreigners allowed on, I said I am not sure how strict the bus companies are. Next min 3 young European backpackers went up to the ticket kiosk but were refused tickets and were standing there looking a bit lost so I went over and explained where the other bus station was and bus goes at 1030hrs so happily smiling we shook hands and they were away up the main highway road. Not a long wait a large bus drew into our parking lot and we were all called forward and putting my shoulderbag in the hold I paid the driver 1EP him putting a stub on my bag and the other half of the stub on my ticket and getting a stub from my Bus Ticket I was on the cold AC bus taking seat 36 and with only 24 people on our 50 seater bus we were away, it was 0900hrs. Didn't take long as we were now out of Hurghada with bleak desert sand dunes on my right and the sea coast still on my left, great views. The conductor came along and I was offered a drink so I had a tea and he gave me a tray with 2 cheese rolls and a large tea on it so enjoyed my 0920hrs second breakie as we travelled along the road then turned right with now the full desert desolate landscape each side me thinking if we keep going at this speed its going to take a day to reach Luxor, hope not. Bus did hot up a little but had a pair of socks and a pullover in my China beachbag just in case the AC turned the bus into a fridge as does happen. Stopped at a checkpoint then we were now going through a rocky pointed mountain valley with sometimes Bedouin tents in the sandy enclaves. Got out of the small mountain range and into now high sand dunes with a single railway line sometimes either side of our road as our only companion and looking out our bus window I could sometimes see for miles across the creamy milk coloured dust blowing desert. Dozed off and next think woke up as we had stopped for a smoke break, it was 1215hrs and the only ones who got off were 5 white women, 3 Egyptian men and me a non smoker as we where in the searing very hot heat of a town or City square. I had a brisk swinging of the arms walk around the bus then back on to its cool interior and 2mins later we were away going into a teaming full of life Town/City centre following a large river on our right with a stop to let 2 blokes off all road signs in Arabic now so not a clue where we where. Mind you the desert had disappeared as out of the town/city we were driving through miles of flat fields growing some sort of bright green vegetable with lots of Palm and other sorts of trees everywhere and still next to the full water river. Conductor guy came along and wrote 18EP for me to pay, I said what for, he said tea and rolls so another con as he did not indicate payment when giving it to me or anyone else and 18EP was more than double the price in a café, but that's life, I will never learn. The greenness and fertility of this valley where a fantastic sight as I have never seen anything growing with such vibrancy anywhere in the world as now we were also driving through brick built slum areas as it is so unbelievable how these people live but also sobering to see real life as it is for the Egyptian poor. Passed over wide Canals full to the brim with swirling water then seen a sign 'Welcome to Luxor', it was 1320hrs so not far to go, oh la, la, my ass giving me grief. A USA girl in the seat in front of me with unlit cigarette in her mouth or behind her ear kept turning around to the Egyptian guy across from me asking how far to go and he kept saying, only 10mins and after each 10mins was up she would ask him again and the 4th time she asked him, I said only 10mins and she said that's the 4th time you/he has said it and everyone laughing we drove onto and along Nile St. Passed along The Avenue of Sphinxes which were rows of human faced stone lions intermingled with beautiful Architecture tall Marble Columns and wonderful old stone walls. Really interesting as wow oh wow we passed the Majestic entrance of the Luxor Temple from my side of the window and I was that interested I never even seen the Nile. We drove through the not excessive traffic and parked near the Railway Station and everyone sighing got off with the young Yankee girls puffing like mad on their cigarettes everyone grabbed their cases from the hold as I did then sort of orientated myself I walked back towards the town centre. Two hotel touts giving me grief but still worth listening to I followed one into a drab Hotel going up 4 flights of stairs to see a room with no bathroom but for 30EP what would anyone expect. Followed the next tout still going in the direction I wanted but hotel could only give me the room for one night so no commission today lads and on I went on my own. I did get lost two times but eventually found the Nefertiti Hotel, El-Sahaby St, Luxor, Egypt, www.nefertitihotel.com, Tel: 002/096-2372886. Asked girl at reception any single rooms she said no, only a 2 bed d-ensuite for 100EP and its only available for tonight, no rooms tomorrow so now snookered I give up saying ok and got key for room 209 and up we both went two flights of stairs and in to it. I said ok and back down showing Passport, filling in the usual address, Passport number etc, paid my 100EP and carrying shoulderbag up the stairs I went to my room, it was 1420hrs. I quickly changed into cargo shorts with no sleeve tee shirt I was out and only across the road I paid 50EP and into the Luxor Temple complex which was a true pleasure to walk everywhere reading its history but being so close to these huge Columns and all the Stone Carvings was just a true delight. Enjoyed my history walk and it was sweltering in the burning sun's rays I said to myself I have always wanted to sail a felucca sailing boat on the Nile so why not now and could hardly get near the Nile as touts of every description were giving me grief, it was disgusting. Eventually along the Nile huge river promenade I got one guy down to 50EP for 1hr sail up and back down the Nile and tip toeing across the little scaffold plank access gang plate I was on a Felucca sailing boat on the Nile, yeah man yeah, I had done it. First of all he got the Felucca out past all the docked up ones then as a motor boat pulling 4 Feluccas up the Nile River passed he threw a rope to the last Felucca and we were away in our 1 tugboat, 5 Felucca towed convoy up the mighty River Nile until are Captain in our Felucca called Lady Jane took the tow rope away. Next thing him and his mate put the massive big sails in place and we were doing a very slow sail as not much wind. It was good fun seeing and being one of the lots of Feluccas sailing around the wide Nile in a circle me now on the rudder having a laugh then we all sort of headed down river for a sail until with the massive oars out, sails rolled up and with the two crews rowing, me on the rudder again we docked up at the side of the Nile, yeah mon yeah, I had done it. Paid my 50EP plus a 10EP tip and narrow scaffold gangplank down I was off the Felucca and happy as a Hi Sailor I had a gentle walk back towards my hostel/hotel, it was 1810hrs and just getting dark. I knew the cafes along the Souk done meals but was totally surprised as all along the middle of the Souk they had put table and chairs for meals so sat down, got the menu and ordered a margarita pizza and a tea. Pizza came and it was delicious so enjoyed my late pizza and two gippo teas supper, paid my 30EP bill, said my thanks, no tip and back upto room happy about my first

Luxor day. Stripped off but only had an underarm wash and a shave then long cargo, pocket tee shirt on and I was out and going left I followed El Souk St right upto near its end but the area got really murky so turned back and had a lovely Souk walk until I got to Nile St saying to myself these Souk touts are a severe pain. Seen Venus Hotel so booked and paid a deposit for manyanna so at least I have now got a bed. Gently and nicely I strolled a less hassle walk along Nile St to the Train Station and had a coke in the Salt & Bread Café at El Mahate Sq at the Railway Station and time never stops, it was 2015hrs. Paid my rip off 7EP for the coke and back up to the Souk and into it again getting the uncalled for grief from all sorts of sellers touts and could hardly believe my eyes and was in shock for an instant as met Jeff and Kirsty the two Kiwis again and we greeted each other with handshakes and smiles, what a true coincidence as who would have believed it. We had a laughing full off life chat about our travels they telling me they were heading for Cairo manyanna and what a small world it is we again shook hands and wishing each other 'safe travels and might see you in Cairo' we went are own way, it was 2050hrs. I did some internet then bought a packet of cream cheddar biscuits but for some reason I was feeling tired so back to Hotel and upto my room, turned AC on and really did need it. Stripped off and having a read of LP ate half my creamy delights, it was only 2235hrs but bed here I come and into bed no dreams just asleep a dead Luxor Hi Sailor River Nile man.

Email Sent: Tue, 9 Mar 2010
Subject: Nefertiti Hotel, El-Sahaby St, Luxor, Egypt

Hi All
Up early and got breakie then around to Bus Station and 4 USA girls plus a few others had already got their tickets for the 0800hrs bus and rules supposedly are that no more than 4 Farangs are allowed on bus's to Luxor so he refused me so called him a few names and taxi to next bus station but next bus was at 1030-1100hrs.
Back to Red Jet Express trying it on saying sorry I am on my own and one more will not make any difference and he let my on, 45EP, what a relief.
Start time was supposed to be 0800hrs but we left at 0900hrs and 4hrs30mins later with WC on bus we arrived in Luxor with only one 5min stop for de smokers, 4yankee girls.
Had a walk about seeing the Nile River and looking at a few hotels and tried 2 others but finally took above at 100EP rip off.
Had a nice walk through the Luxor Temple which a couple of 1000 years old is really something then got my own yacht, 50EP called a Felucca!! and sails up had a trip up and down de Nile for an hour.
Few plans for Manyanna as will stay 3 days but its big time warm here!!! and I must admit I do miss de beach sunbed!!!!!!!!!!!!!!!!!
al de bes
Jack

Day 74, Wednesday, 10-03-10, Luxor & Temple of the Kings; Egypt

Felt good after a great night's AC sleep, it was still early, only 0610hrs so relaxed enjoying the warmth of my sheets instead of the sweat then up for good at 0715hrs. Underarm wash, face splash, long cargo, pocket tee shirt on and down and outside to the middle of the alley dining tables. Sat down and guy brought me a bowl of popcorns in hot milk so added sugar and munched my way through half a bowl before an omelette with sliced tomatoes, cheesy butter, jam and 2 rolls with a gippo tea arrived so finished my munchies first. Got stuck into and finished one of the finest breakies in my travels having another tea to start my day. Back upto room, cleaned teeth, nice dobhi drop, final pack of shoulderbag and down the stairs and handing my key into reception saying my thanks I was out going right with trolley handle up then turned left and only a 75m walk I was in Venus Hotel, Youssef Hassan St, Luxor, Egypt, Tel: 002/0952372625. Showed guy behind counter the hotel card with the booking and 50EP deposit paid, he said ok, Room 204 giving me key and asking for my Passport which I gave him and up two flights of stairs I went into an AC, double bed, ensuite decent room. Changed into cargo shorts, no sleeve tee shirt and went down to get my Passport then back upto room putting it in my neckpouch in shoulderbag then little check of China beachbag I was out for good and downstairs to reception handing key to reception guy. He said, you pay the balance of the room so I gave him a 200EP note saying take for 2 days but as usual he had no change and asked me where I was going. I said the Valley of the Kings and a few other places asking him for any ideas. He said he could do a package of 4-6 sites including the Valley of the Kings and Valley of the Queen's for 150EP so I said ok and he called upstairs to girl and telling her he was going he left the hotel with me first stop an ATM where I drew out 1000EP. Next it was agreed I would give him another 200EP note and he would pay for all the entrance fees to the different sights, seemed strange but maybe he can get them cheaper. I said ok giving him another 200EP note which now he had 400EP from me in total. A good quick walk and he said large passenger boat has just left the East Bank jetty to go across to the West Bank do I want to wait or catch a little fast passenger boat so no good hanging about I said small boat and we walked down the path and onto one that had just docked and on we both got me not wanting him with me but he had organised the 150EP van to pick me/us up at the West Bank Jetty. He paid the fares and 3-5mins later we both jumped off on the West Bank Jetty and up the steps to the parking area where his mate was waiting and they agreed the first stop and we were away. The Minibus was AC and by God did you need it as the searing heat was it seemed actually burning my bare arms as we drove along a road with first of all the mountain with its dozens of tomb caves and many old ruins along it so whatever it had been in is previous life it must have been a very important City or place to live. Got onto and along a slip road in we went to a very busy parking area with lots of big Tour buses and dozens of Minibuses and parked directly to the left of the entrance pay kiosk for the Temple of Hatshepsut and parked up. Me and the reception guy both got out him saying see you here in 1 hrs time and in we went to the pay kiosk paying him the 30EP entrance fee and in. Wow oh wow, what a truly wonderful sight as Hatshepsut Temple was so huge with its very high intact 1m thick wall fully engraved with the famous hank face men, lovely figure ladies plus all sorts of animals, I was truly enjoying my early morning 1495-1475 BC Temple walk. Made it up to the second level with all its colourful painted carved into the stone wall around its Shrine then down to the first level again which was similar but no access to below the ground, lower level. Walking back was a joyful fun walk passing lots of smaller Tombs and one large one all with their colourful carvings and lots with huge, big stone statues of women with thin face beards!. Jumped the little trolley train and off at the exit sign and out having a look for my driver. There were 20+ Minibuses parked up plus 15+ big tourist buses but no sign of my Minibus and the heat in the car park would scorch you. Taxi driver who seen me walk past him a dozen times as I treble checked the Minibuses said he will phone my hotel if I want so I gave him the number and he phoned and hotel promised Minibus would be on its way and 10mins later the driver drove into the car park and giving the taxi driver a 10EP note I was away. Our next stop was the Habu Temple, driver paying my 30EP admission, it was 1110hrs and hot sun would kill you but I must admit it was the biggest and most fantastic sight Temple I have ever seen or been into in my life. I walked through it to the 3rd section passing big huge 1-2m diameter thick stone Columns, how did they do it. Everywhere had the unbelievable true 2000 year old craftsmen famous Egyptian carvings, truly marvellous. Really enjoyed my wonderful walk then back out to the van and away. We stopped but only for 5mins at one of the world's most famous photo shoot at the Colossi of Memnon which where 2 approximately 20m high statues of Memnon who was killed in the Trojan War by Achilles, fantastic true history. Had my usual thumbs up photo shoot then back into the AC Minibus and away and got off at our next stop with all its great true history, The Valley of the Kings. Driver paid my 80EP entrance fee and in with no cameras allowed and the ticket only allowed me to visit 3 tombs of the more than 60 but the most famous one I wanted to go into The Tomb of Tutankhamen was closed, not to worry. Walking up the stone valley floor was like being roasted alive and in I went to Sety II Tomb, Dynasty 19 getting my ticket clipped. I had to walk steeply downhill on a timber ribbed gangplank and then was in the entrance it looked like a 50m 3m sq tunnel corridor with sometimes little rooms off them, maybe burial sites but every wall was full of colourful murals all painted on the carvings out of stone, truly marvellous. As I reached the end with the large open stone coffin I as usual looked inside it but no one about then really great vibes I made it up the timber gangplank saying breath-in to a couple coming down and laughing we squeezed past each other and not far I was out. Walking uphill I picked for my next underground funeral parlour sightsee the Ramese II Tomb, Dynasty 20 and a truly remarkable history look walking its full colourful 50m deep underground length. Only one more so picked the Sons of Rameses II, Dynasty 19 and down into the tunnel I walked and along into some of the biggest Tombs in the Valley of the Kings and enjoyed the coolness of the Tomb me thinking in 2-4000BC how long did it take a workforce to cut and carve these square tunnels and all these marvellous carvings as this must have been undertaken when a King was alive!. Had seen my three Royal Tombs and would have liked to have seen more but only three allowed so out and along the scorching valley stone floor and into as I got into our Minibus we were away me drinking from my 2litre water bottle like no manyanna. Not far and we drove and parked up in the Valley of the Queens, driver parked up and out I got. Driver paid my 35EP entrance fee and in again walking the stone scorched valley with only 4 Tombs out of the 62 tombs open but certainly worth the effort of a visit. Went into Tomb of Titi enjoying my tunnel corridor carvings on the walls walk then out and up the hill to the Tomb of Prince Kha-En-Wast which undoubtedly was the most brilliant and elaborate painted stone wall carving I have ever seen, it was so lifelike and so real. Kept on moving and drinking from my 2litre water bottle and the last one for me was the Tomb of Prince Seth seeing again all the finely curved wall curving of lovely men, lady figures which do tell a story if you had the time to study and can understand it then out I went I was really chuffed. It was something I will never forget and I was so enjoyably happy to have been, seen and walked the Valleys of the Kings and Queens I was one King happy man as I reached my driver and the Minibus, got in and we were away. He took me to an Alabaster shop but I was not interested in seeing how they made the small statues or even thinking of buying anything so back into the Minibus and along to the Ferry. Shaking hands and saying my thanks I left my driver and down the gangplank onto the fast passenger small water boat paying the 10EP fee and only 4 passengers we zoomed across the Nile to the West Bank and off upto and passed the Luxor Temple I walked, it was 1720hrs. Made my way into El Souk then the alley at my previous hotel and had a seat ordering spaghetti bolognaise and a tea. It came within 15mins as I had a great fun chat with a Uruguay guy and his US girlfriend. I enjoyed my lovely din din supper in the Aladdin Café outdoor seating area, paid my 35EP and a slow no rush walk I was back into Venus Hotel, got my key and into room swiftly turning the AC on. Stripped off and had a shave and lovely shower, dried off putting long cargo, pocket tee shirt on and out dropping key in at reception. Had a walk down to and into the train station, lady giving me the sleeper time of 1930-0530hrs or 2230-0830hrs for train times to Cairo as I was thinking of taking a bed in a 2 bed sleeper. Said my thanks and away flagging down a pony & cart and went on a horse & cart sightsee through Luxor seeing 3 Christian Churches even passing a loud trombone beating full of Happy smiling people in the street Wedding, great fun. No plans so had 2 coffees and sweating well I made it back into and upto my hotel room, it was 2240hrs. Turned AC on, lubbly dubbly, stripped off and I was into bed and asleep like a King in a cool Tomb dreaming where is Queen Kelly.

Email Sent: Wed, 10 Mar 2010
Subject: Valley of the Kings, Luxor

Hi All

Great history day visiting the Valley of the Kings 2-3000 BC with its many long tunnels painted wall curving on the stone walls of the big underground tunnels before reaching the Tomb itself.

Each Tomb had its on entrance and all along the valley mountains there was dozens but with ticket you could only visit 3, same with the Valley of the Queens.

Into a few Hugh Temples and called it a day at 1600hrs in the scorching heat of the valleys.

Will do the Temples of Karnak manyanna.

Moved Hotels this morning as all rooms booked up and now in Venus Hotel, Youssef Hassan St, Luxor, Tel002/0952372625, 80 EP d-ensuite, AC.

al de bes

Jack

Day 75, Thursday, 11-03-10, Luxor & The Temple of Karnak; Egypt

Only woke up once to pull the blanket over my sheet as it was now a bit cold but I loved that feeling of snuggling into a blanket, reminds me of England. Woke up for good seeing the daylight glimmering through my curtained window with the horn pumpers starting to give it rout already, it was 0710hrs. Snoozed until 0800hrs then up turning alarm off, had a piss, underarm wash, face splash and cargo shorts with no sleeve tee shirt on having a very serious think about my travel plans as if I have to waste a day travelling to Cairo, do I take the sleeper night rain, do I take a bus, do I fly, do I go to Aswan, decision, decision so out of room down for breakie. The breakfast area was like a restaurant and guy said, breakfast, tea or coffee as I walked into it, I said tea and sat down looking down over the lovely green grass and many little trees of the garden facing the Chez Omar Restaurant, really nice. Breakfast came on a plate with 4 soft rolls, an omelette, butter, jam, yoghurt and my tea, really good and I got stuck into it at the start of my 0815hrs day. Finished it all giving young guy a tip of 5EP, back upto room, dobhi drop stirring and had a nice one, cleaned ass, cleaned teeth, little check of China beachbag and locking room door behind me I went downstairs and handing key over I was out turning left then right at Sharia al–Karnak as heading towards my first stop today, The Temple of Karnak. Didn't really mean to walk it but it was only 2km and passing a bank put card in and drew out 1000EP. Stuck it in my sky and the heat was unbelievable as I bought a 2 litre bottle of water thinking to die of thirst must be a vile tortured death as sometimes I ran out of water and only have to wait 10-15mins to the next café or somewhere but that 10-15mins of thirst was a nightmare in the Luxor valley desert 40° desert paths, but its all part of the fun. Passed the Rezeiky Camp Hostel knowing I was near and turned another corner and could see a massive height stone wall ruins so headed for the modern security guard and ticket office gate for the Temple of Karnak. Bought my ticket, 65EP and another short walk through another security checkpoint where guy took my ticket and gave me a stub back then I was in. Seen the very tall walls and giant Obelisks and rows of large stone Sphinx Lions, yeah, man yeah I was thinking this looks and feels really special. First stop I was at the Temple of Ramses, 1198-1167 BC and entered it at the big 4m high Statues and oh my God I thought I had seen everything but these great big Columns were 20m high x 2m dia, what an unbelievable sight and all 2-4000 BC. Next I went into the Great Hypostyle Hall and it just got more and more amazing with its in total 134 huge thick Columns 1313-1292 BC, how or who designed it never mind how did they build it as everything was pure stone with 1000's of painted engravings from floor up the walls and columns to the ceiling, fantastic. Next I was in the Cachette Courtyard admiring the beautiful more goats beard woman face statues!, truly remarkable. Kept going slightly right but towards the extreme walled enclosure edge of the Temples. Got to the Sacred Lake which appeared shallow as I walked around its 200m x 117m wide banks I would have loved to have had a swim. Everywhere was teaming with tourists mostly big AC bus Tours as carpark was full of them and every turn there were guides explaining, what, where and how to the bored stiff by the look of the tour tourists of every Nationality in the world. I could have spent hours admiring all the statues, carvings and all different types of building but kept going and now I was in The Barque Sanctuary, 1500 BC with its unmissible 30m high and another broken one half its size, the two red granite pointed Pillars full from head to toe of Egyptian carvings and writing. Kept slugging water down my neck as I went into the Akl-Menara Temple, a beautiful many round and square pillor Column hall with vivid coloured Columns and all the curving along its stone ceiling, truly amazing. Still going forward I went right upto the steel rear entrance guarded locked gate where excavations were still ongoing and turned back still going to the right in my sort of circle walk. Reached the Wadjid at the 28m high Obelisks then my next sweating like a pig stop was in the Courtyard of The Third Pylon and by gum I was sweating bad, it was 1235hrs and the numerous Minaret chanters were giving it root again. Crossed The Great Forecourt, 1333-1306 BC and last and final stop I was into and having a look at The Sacred Bank Shrines of Seti II, 1205 BC and thanking our Lord above for letting me see and walk these fantastic Temples area I was out walking across the square to the exit and out. I knew the Nile was on my right so crossed El Karnak Temple St and what a terrific view of the Nile I was looking at with the bright vivid Valley of the Kings mountain range behind it, truly marvellous as I gently walked the footpath at the riverside. I passed big dinner cruise the Nile boats and could feel my swimming trunks starting to rub into my inner thighs so have maybe dropped a rollick putting them on and walking like the walkie junkie I am. I knew where I wanted to go and after a good 2-3km walk I reached the Mummified Museum but luck was out as reading the notice board it closed from 1400-1600hrs, it was 1410hrs so what will I do. I spotted an internet café and into it doing a Google then as it came up with good priced cheap flights Aswan – Cairo on e-dreams I decided to book a 125$US flight and did so using my credit card. The response was sickening and a con as it said I have to confirm with a bank transfer of my money to the Deutsche Bank, UK what a complete fraud con as no mention of this was given when I was making my booking so replied telling them they were frauds and to refund me my full money without any fees, we shall see. Needed to do or go somewhere for the rest of the afternoon so reading my photocopy LP it said the Tombs of the Nobles was a coloured and great vivid must see carving so down the steps at the big river crossing boat paying a 1EP fee but fee was only 50 Pils but didn't argue and on I got taking a seat on the top deck and 10mins later we were away. Great views each way up and down the great wide Nile River and 5mins later we docked on the West Bank and I just followed everyone as we got off. I had a chat with a taxi tout and got price to the Tomb of the Nobles, waiting time 40mins and back to boat for 40EP so not too bad, in the front seat and we were away. The lad spoke excellent English and after quite a long drive he dropped me off at the ticket office saying buy ticket so up I went and said Tomb of the Nobles, guy said 3 Tombs only so I picked Ramose, Userhet and Khaemhet, gave him 35EP, got my ticket, back in the taxi and another good little drive and he dropped me off at a mountain hill full of Tomb caves saying 40mins and he was away. I walked across the desert sand to a dusty path with 3-4 guide touts telling me I was lost and they would guide me and the truth was I was lost but said no and kept walking. My luck was in as the 3 Tombs I had picked were at the bottom of the mountain and well signposted and down the steps I went showing my ticket and into the first one which was the Tomb of Ramose which was a very huge 32 Column underground corridor with 8 Columns around the shrine. All along the walls and ceiling were nice coloured carvings which you can read if you did an Egyptian reading course then out and around a little rocky hill and I was going down steps again into the Tomb of Userhet along a long darkish underground hall with niches where the many coffins had been with Statues of him and his wife and family, very sad but great history. I left there and the only reason I found my next Tomb was because I followed the echoing sound of people talking from its underground tunnel and again down the steps and I was in the Tomb of Kha Em Het. It had three underground fantastic halls and the last one had great history Statues of him and his wife which was all so just amazing and that was my 3 Tombs walk over. Out back into the searing lovely sun and my bathing trunks were causing a severe rubber rash in my inner thighs maybe because of sweating and being tight but needed to get them off urgently and quickly behind a stone entrance to a Tomb, dropped my cargo shorts smiling thinking the Gippos have seen it all before, took them off putting my cargo shorts back on but its my own fault as rash is here to stay as every step was a painful inner thigh pain. Sat down where the taxi had dropped me off, two taxi touts saying my taxi will never come and 5mins later he arrived and on I got slugging the last of my 2 litres of water, I was parched. He was nearly at the ferry and I quickly told him to stop and as he did I paid him and he was away as I shouted Hi High Wycombe to my four smoking Yankee girl mates from the bus journey and we all laughed and shook hands all my pain forgotten just being in their lively happy company for 5mins as we had a chat. They were leaving manyanna to go home so a final handshake I wished them a safe journey back home and a bit sad but happy to meet my fellow travellers again I was on down and paying my 1EP charge, didn't ask for change, I was on the big boat, got a seat and 5mins later we were away. Again only 5mins later we docked on the East Bank and everyone got off and our docking point was only a short distance from my hotel. I bought some rash moisturising cream on my way back to hotel, got my room key and upto room, dropped cargo shorts and rubbed the moisturising cream into my inner thigh and my God did it hurt but cargo shorts up I was out and over to the Omar Jezy Café sitting by the green Oasis Garden I had a pizza and 2 teas for my 1720hrs yum yummy din din. Enjoyed it, paid my 40EP bill and back into hotel and upto room, stripped off, had a nice shave and a lovely shower, dried off and rubbing the moisturising cream into my thighs I cut two snips in each leg of my underpants so no rubbing and long cargo and pocket tee shirt on out I went. Had a slow walk through El Souk and met the guy from the Post Office outside the Post Office as I had been in it this morning buying some stamps him telling me he did not understand written English and had agreed to read a letter sent to him by someone. I had told him in the Post Office when he was doing my Sandralita's stamps I was not going back to his house and as we shook hands he pointed at a motorbike saying lets go and you can meet my wife and family. I said no, he said do you not trust me, I said I have not got the time and walked away making my way down to the Train Station. Took my turn in the queue and bought a first class ticket to Aswan, 41EP for 0730hrs for manyanna morning so big time chuffed to get that over with I was back up Nile St and passing a barber's I went in and got price of 35EP for a No1. Young fellow was good and done my silky hair then got a roll of thread and wrapping one end of it around his left hand forefinger with the other in his right hand he tweaked it very quickly up and down the front of my cheeks and my ears and the thread did catch loose hairs but the sharp pain as it pulled hairs from my ears was sore. He stopped then the older guy who I thought was only going to give me a head rub put cream on my face and leaving it on then gave my head a full massage so thinking con 1 on its way. I then had to sit over hot steam as he rubbed the cream from my face then cleaned everywhere with cool water and one more final splash he then was dried off. I was trying it on as knew their was a con going on so gave him 40EP saying keep the 5EP, he said face clean, head massage, 150EP, I said I never asked you for anything why should I pay, got out a 20EP note, gave it to him saying no more and I was out and away to have a coffee in the Centre Café, it was 2145hrs. Finished my enjoyable coffee paying my 8EP bill and back to hotel. Guy at reception said he would give me an AC car and driver for transport to Aswan tomorrow taking me to any must see sights on the way for 450EP, I said I am on my own, if I had been with 3 friends it would have been ok and saying my thanks I was upto room, AC on and stripped off. Put some more moisturising cream on my inner thighs thinking I need Cleopatra or one of her mates for this sort of massage then nearly falling asleep I set my alarm for 0620hrs and as I lay back on my conc pillow I was asleep dead as a doornail in conc.

Email Sent: Thu, 11 Mar 2010
Subject: Temple of Karnak, Luxor

Hi All
Great sleep in my AC room, you need it out this end of Gypoo.
Went for a half a day walk around the huge town of Temples and they where something special some of the cols 28m high and 2m dia and all built 2-4000 years ago.
Tried to get in to see the Mummies but the museum was locked so had a walkie around the Tombs of the Nobles and that was me, ferry, 1EP back to East Bank.
Plan for manyanna is to make it to Aswan, we shall wake up and see!!!!!!!!!!!!!.
al de bes
Jack

Day 76, Friday, 12-03-10, Luxor – Aswan; Egypt

Woke up cold in only my bed sheet for cover and quickly pulled the blanket over me snuggling into it, lubbly dubbly. Had another good sleep and came awake feeling relaxed and warm so checked alarm and it was 0605hrs so turned alarm off lieing there in quiet contentment knowing I will have to get up sometime so the sooner the better, bed sheet and blanket to one side and up. Had a piss then an underarm wash, face splash, long cargo, pocket tee shirt on and downstairs to breakfast room, young reception fellows had just got up. Sat down and 5 mins later 4 bread rolls, cheese, jam, tea and a small omelette arrived and giving the young man a 5EP note as I enjoyed my happy belly breakie. Back to room and only a tiny dobhi drop so cleaned ass, cleaned teeth, final pack of China beachbag and shoulderbag putting neckpouch on checking Passport in place I was out downstairs to reception, it was spot on 0705hrs. Young fellow said you want a taxi, I said yes as we both went outside him calling taxi to a guy standing beside a taxi, I put bag in boot, me in front and we were away to the Train Station. Got to the Train Station roundabout and he stopped so me out, grabbed my shoulderbag and gave him 15EP, he wanted another 5 but I said I don't have any and away. Into Train Station and young fellow said Aswan, I said yes so let him take my shoulderbag down the underground walkway and up the steps to Platform 2 and up to where Car No3 would stop as although ticket was in Arabic I had got the Tourist Information Office last night to write it down in English. I gave the young fellow a 5EP note and he was away, it was 0720hrs. I had travelled India and thought I had seen long trains but the sleeper train that pulled into our platform at 0730hrs was 120-150m long discharging loads of Farangs probably coming from Cairo. Next train was my train and as it arrived at 0750hrs I found Car 3 and showing a couple of guys my ticket they pointed to Seat 28, a 6 seater compartment so me and shoulderbag into it, I sat down, wow that was easy I said to myself at 0800hrs. At 0810hrs, toot toot we were away into the brilliant stone desert scenery with spectacular sights then green sugar plantations with us going through old ancient stone dwelling villages that have never changed in the past 100-200 years giving me a great feel of real Egypt. I took a pair of socks and my pullover from my shoulderbag quickly putting them on as it was freezing in the AC 6 seat cabin with only me in it. Had a walkie each way along the long 6 cabin carriage and only 2-3 persons in each cabin and one western wc so went in for a piss seeing it was full of dobhi crap with no bins and dirty toilet paper littering the floor and laughing to myself I was glad I didn't have to sit down on that one. Me, the only Farang in our large carriage my carriage window really black with dust so had my usual walks every 15mins looking out of the corridor windows at the always changing real Egypt landscape and villages then we had a stop, our second one I think at a town called Edfu. Only a short 3-5min stop then we were away and I could have stretched out in the 3 large seats my side of the cabin but put shoulderbag under my knees and feet and didn't wake up until we drew into Aswan, it was 1100hrs. Checked my brainbox was still in place and off the train taking socks and pullover off in the searing hot desert sun then 2-3-4 touts were selling hotels so followed one who was offering rooms for 40EP in Horus Hotel, 89 Cornish Eh-Nil

St, Aswan, Tel: 097-2313313, www.arh-zooz@yahoo.com which I had seen in my photocopy LP and it offered a free lift to it. He said you can walk it but why walk with your bag when you can get a lift so into the taxi and along the Nile River Road and stopped outside the Horus Hotel. Out and up the lift to the 4th floor and guy showed me a neat 2 large single beds big ensuite room so I said ok. He said sit down for 1min and he gave me an outline of trips he could do, first one from 1230hrs today taking in The Temple of Philae, The Aswan's and the High Dam at Lake Nasser plus the unfinished obelisk, 70EP, so said ok to that one which would have taken me a day by myself to find these places. In our talk we discussed how long I was going to stay and if I was only staying one night I might want to take a lift in an AC car going to Luxor tomorrow but visiting the Great Temple of Simbel in Abu Simbel and The Temple of Horus in Edfu on the way back for 100EP so as no way I could match these prices and see all those sights myself I said ok and paid him the full amount. He said driver for today will be waiting here in reception for you at 1230hrs and he left, it was 1150hrs. I also went out for a walk just trying to get orientated then back, collected Passport and into room taking glasses off, stripping off my long cargo and pocket tee shirt and putting on cargo shorts and no sleeve tee shirt and sat down and screamed with fear as quickly stood up and picked up my flattened glasses. Tried to straighten them but broke one of the lenses and sick as a pig I searched my shoulderbag until I found my old spare pair, that was unlucky. Short pack of China beachbag with plenty of water and Coca Cola and out to reception and driver was there, he said lets go and down the lift we went and out into his lovely AC taxi, I was happy again. Pain from my rash was gradually going away so that was good and it was a long ride but eventually we got to The Unfinished Obelisk and as we stopped in the car park the driver said 20mins and out I got and over to the ticket office paying 30EP for ticket. Went up the sort of cliff walk just following the path route and looking everywhere I couldn't see a thing only noticing the ground I was walking over was pure stone. Eventually got up to the highest point and there directly in the stone was a full length pointed obelisk approximately 40m long by 1m thick but the final cut to cut it from the stone had never happened me thinking these Gippos probably done it on purpose anyway saying to themselves the thick tourists will visit anything and back down the stone hill path I went and back into the lovely AC car. Driver started up and we were away with driver telling me we will drive across the Aswan Dam Road built by the British in 1902 but over the years it couldn't hold the high water table so President Nasser built the High Dam and the lake it now holds is called Lake Nasser. Enjoying the AC we came up a hill and you couldn't miss it the huge Aswan Dam Walls then crossed the dam on the road and quite a good drive we drove on the road above the biggest Dam and Artificial Lake in the world called the High Dam and pulled in and stopped beside the ticket office. Driver got out and I gave him a 20EP note which he paid, got ticket and only a short drive he parked beside 6-7 big tourist buses me thinking Egypt must live and rely on tourists as there is millions here. Out I got driver saying 30mins so had a walk each side seeing Lake Nasser in all its miles of splendour with it looked like many small islands then over to the other side seeing a small river which is still called The Nile but not the 100m wide Nile that I know, this was only a trickle but thinking about it that's what the dam is all about!. Back into my AC car driver telling me he would now go to the boat for me to visit The Temple of Philae and we were away. I was enjoying my chauffeur driving day, no map reading, no getting lost, no sweating like a pig walking up hills, this is the life as he stopped at the security office for the Temple and guy took his number plate and gave him a copy which he gave to me telling me when I land back on the jetty give this slip to the Police and they will phone him and he will arrive back and pick me up as no parking is the rule at the jetty. On we drove to the ticket office and I paid 50EP for my ticket and was away walking downhill to the many motor boats, some large and some small. Guy said only one, I said yes, he said 40EP so I showed him my ticket, he said you still have to pay for a boat so thinking this was a con I went back to the ticket office and they said yes, I have to pay for boat so back down and climbed over 3 boats to get onto mine and we were away. In chatting he said how long will I be, I said 1hr, he said ok he will wait so as we docked up off I got. Panting a little I went up the hill and into the very big huge Temple of Philae which enclosed in its vast circular walls is the Temple of Nectanelo, the Temple of Isisusred, the Gateway of Hadrian, the Temple of Imhotey and a few more all started in 4th Century BC. It was a truly marvellous structure with the huge 1m thick mushroom head Columns all full of engravings I was completely enthralled happily walking left to right in a circle. I got talking to a security guard and he showed me the steps going down through a locked steel gate where he said when the water rises this is like a well as you can walk down the steps to the water level for any water refill supplies. Went left following him as he pointed up at a British War Memorial neatly engraved on the stone wall of the Temple saying graffiti. I didn't think he meant it as graffiti as he didn't probably know what graffiti meant, probably a superior Officer said it as he was really intent on showing it to me and it was a sad remembrance of a bygone age as how did these men come all the way from England and did the ones that lived ever make it home. It read; Lord Kitchener, Heavy Camel Regt, 1884-5, D & D, Royal Dragoons, Scots Greys, 5 & 16 Lancers with the rank and name of the Officers with only the total number of soldiers killed and someone had neatly inscribed a French name under it saying he served with and died for the British Empire and saluting those great bygone day Soldiers of the Queen and the Great British Empire I said God be with you and all your families and I was away. Gave the guard a 5EP note, shook his hand and he was away so just kept going left to right happily enjoying the great architecture and thinking who drew the plans, overseen it, who managed it as its 2-4000 years old and still a great sightsee. Done my rounds and it was a very huge vast island walk then back to the jetty with 3 young Egyptian girls wanting me to pose with them so thumbs up I gave them my best as my boat drew in at the sea edge jetty. I stepped onto the bow holding tight to the sail mast and boat started rolling over as if it was going to capsize and I screamed with shock shouting My God and boat guy quickly pulled me over the other side of the mast and as I sat down the boat came back on an even keel, cor, I was shocked for a min or two. Away we went back across the no wave sea and as we docked I jumped off and up the hill giving my ticket to Police who phoned the car park and 5mins later my driver arrived, in I got and we were away. Driving back I seen a sign Commonwealth War Graves and asked him to turn around and go back which he did and parked in its car park. Out I got but it was closed and as I looked through the gate it would have been a walk back 1-200 years to read the true life of the Great British soldiers who died for the Great British Empire. Back to car and we were away and he dropped me off near my hotel, out I got giving him a 20EP note and he was away. It was still early so went up and had a walk along the famous Aswan Souk and enjoyed my hardly any tout hassle only shouts and laughs from the Nubian's saying 'Hey Rambo, we like you Rambo' one even standing in front of me smiling and laughing saying 'You want trouble Rambo' but me thinking I hardly look like a Rambo but enjoying the banter I got to the other extreme edge of the Souk and went left. Made it all the way right along it to the Railway Station which was good fun then went left passed all the cafes with lots of hotels about me thinking this would have been an ideal place to stay. Enjoying my nice no sweat walk I made it on down to the small sailing ship road roundabout facing the Alexandra the Great sailing ship on the Nile which was a big Nile Restaurant Cruiser and turned left passing a lovely quiet large very neat park. I crossed the road to the Nile side admiring the fully green little island called Kitchener Island as he had it fully planted with all species of bush and trees, very nice. I didn't want to annoy my rash so took the offer of a horse and buggy ride along the Nile back to facing my hotel. Gave him a 20EP note and he quickly showed me 50 note handing it back, me saying to myself no way did I give him a 50EP note but took it, stuck it in my wallet and gave him another 20EP note and him trying to show me another note off I got and he was away. I watched him go thinking something strange happened then and checked the note he had given me and it was a 50 Pils (i.e. 50 cents) note so well conned of 5$US and had a laugh thinking it was the first one this trip but a good lesson learned. Into the Egyptian Café next to hotel and had curry chicken, potato crisps, bread and a soup with a can of coke, oh la, la, starting to eat now. Paid my rip off 35EP bill and back upto room for a nice shave and shower and out for a walk the same as this afternoon and done the full Souk walk enjoying the friendly Nubian Egyptian music as it had a great rhythm. Had an Egyptian tea in a café down by the Railway Station then into an internet café thinking I will book a room in Cairo for manyanna night as will be arriving late by train so logged into www.hotelworld and booked a 22$US room for 4 nights as even if my plans do make me miss a night, what have I lost. It was real fun walking the Nile pavement path seeing the mountain and the hill all lit up on the other side then another good day over I was into my hotel and upto my room. Little pack of everything then stripped off and into bed asleep dreaming Cairo hookers, the Gippo hunk is cuming home.

Email Sent: Fri, 12 Mar 2010
Subject: Rm122, Horus Hotel, 89 Cornish El-Nil St, Aswan, Tel 097-2303323

Hi All

Jumped the 0730hrs train at 0800hrs, 41 EP for 1st Class and had a not cleanish cabin to myself, toilet was a cesspit but that's life on a 3hr journey as these trains are 100-150metres long.

Got off the train and tout sold me above a de-ensuite for 40EP, took it, dumped kit and out, first stop the 1902 Aswan Dam built by de Brits then Lake Nasser and the High Dam, 3600m long and 111m deep, great show.

Next jumped a boat and out the Lake and onto the Temple of Philae which was in really excellent condition and found a British War Memorial inscription on a block of stone reading; Lord Kitchener; Heavy Camel Regt; 1884-5, D & D, Royal Dragoons, Scots Greys, 5&16 Lancers with the names of the Officers and men who never made it home and on the way back seen a Commonwealth War Graves but it was closed as looking over the walls there must be unbelievable brit toms history on those Gravestones.

Just walked the Souks and never bought anything and came along the Nile passing Kitchener's Island.

Plan is manyanna to be part of a group to go to 2-3 must see sites and then back to Luxor where I am going to jump a 8hr train to Cairo, dats de plan, same,same, we shall see.

Its thirsty work in de searing desert heat here.

al de bes

Jack

Day 77, Saturday 13-03-10, Aswan – Luxor – Cairo; Egypt

Loud noise from AC woke me up a few times in the night but enjoyed my soft mattress no top sheet bed until snoozing and turning over I got up at 0700hrs. Underarm wash, face splash, long cargo, pocket tee shirt on and upstairs to restaurant area and the fresh breeze and the views over the Nile from the open windows were just a superb start to my travelling day. I could hardly walk away from the window seeing the great Oasis of the Kitchener Island and the rocky head of Elephantine Island with it looked like an old Fort on the small mountain peak even an old Mosque but everything was just a magical scenery dream. Guy brought me my boiled egg, cheese, 4 slices of bread and a tea breakie and enjoyed it still having to force myself to stop looking out and over the River Nile starting to come alive with only a few empty motor cruisers plying the river. Finished breakie saying bye bye Nile and back to room, cleaned teeth, had a small blaster loud farting dobhi drop, cleaned ass and final pack of shoulderbag and China beachbag I locked my door behind me and out sitting under the fan at reception and got talking to a German guy also going to Luxor. We were told transport not until 0800hrs him saying typical Egyptian 0730hrs means 0800hrs and both laughing we sat back having a chat about our next few days travels. Next min phone rang and reception guy said transport waiting, it was spot on 0800hrs so down the lift we both went with guy waiting for us at ground floor. We followed him out to the Minibus and luggage was put on the roof rack and in we got taking the long back seat with a Hong Kong couple already in a middle seat. Drove 50m and picked up 2 Japanese guys then another 30m and picked up a single Hong Kong girl and it was all agreed with the driver our drop off points in Luxor and Minibus with plenty of room for a change we were away out along the donkey, goat, hens and chicken road out of Aswan with the never ending River Nile directly on our left. The further away from Aswan we drove the more beautiful it got with only palm trees and desolate rocky hills along its far bank. Stopped at a tree lined river bank and driver got out shouting and crossed the road walking down through the trees towards the Nile and 5mins later came back along with 2 Japanese young guys, 1 Hong Kong bloke, a white girl and guy so either it's a river crossing or probally a camp site. They all got in with driver tieing their luggage on the roof rack and with 12 in our now nearly full Minibus, we were away again, it was 0840hrs. Next we were driving through a built up town and I seen a sign Kom Ombo Temple 2km and 5mins later we turned left along a side road and parked up in a car park with an old ruined mudbrick built village on a hill overlooking it and I knew we would not be going to the famous Temple of Abu Simbel a place I was dreaming and wanting to visit which I thought the guy who sold me the trip had said as it was the completely the other direction out of Aswan towards Sudan, that life, no chance of going back now . Out we all got, driver saying I thought ½ hour and I was away through security and down steps to ticket offices buying my 30EP entrance ticket, it was 0905hrs. Back up the steps to the Kom Ombo fantastic huge stone 2m dia Columns full of carvings opening Arch, wow, this looked good. Looked left and there were 3-4 large river Cruisers docked up so many times I got a free lecture on the meaning of the carvings as I walked past the tour groups. The carvings were really good on lots of big walls as I sometimes took my time to study them then making my way to the exit I had a fantastic view of the River Nile as it went left and disappeared into the hot desert haze, wow, this country never stops. A slow walk back to the Minibus with a 10min wait before all our gang made it back then all on board we were away me having a good slug of one of my water bottles, it was 0945hrs. The road now was very busy but driver doing his best to get us all to Allah above was overtaking and tail gating every chance he could. Stopped again and picked up 2 Canadians, it was 1000hrs and Minibus now full, 15 of us in a no AC hot sardine can, this is the travelling life as I fell asleep. Woke up seeing most of the Minibus rocking asleep then we went left over the Nile and into a town called Edfu, it was now 1055hrs so no chance of reaching Luxor by 1200hrs as we still had one more Temple stop. Seen another sign for Edfu then we went left over the Nile on a bridge and through the town of Edfu and stopped in the carpark of the Edfu Temple, it was 1100hrs. Driver said 1hr and we all got off making our way to the ticket office where I paid 50EP entrance fee getting a ticket. I went in the outside entrance of the Temple seeing the huge 2 Square front walls then next in through the many Column entrance all surrounded by a big thick mud brick wall 2m thick. Got upto the 30m high 5m thick stone block Arched entrance and I was now in the cool shade of the 75m square courtyard with many large 10m Columns along each side, very very impressive as it all takes some believing. I had a little walk about then made it into the dark of the Inner Temple itself and upto the Arched canoe boat Altar wishing Good Luck to all my fellow travellers. Next I had a walk along and around the many rooms from the main Temple all full of beautiful 10m high carvings on them and seen a slightly dark tunnel and went into it just following it and came out near the first entrance and that was my 45mins enjoyable walkie over. Found a shady spot and ate 6 cream biscuits with my bottle of lemonade so belly happy, me happy, it was time to board our Minibus as we all did and away we went, it was 1205hrs. Went back the same way we came crossing the very long Nile Bridge and back to the highway road to Luxor everywhere all along each side was green fields thick with every conceivable growth a farmer would dream off. Had a piss stop me haggling price of coca cola from 10 down to 5EP for Hong Kong girl telling her she now owes me 2EP, please pay now, she laughing saying, no no. Ass getting sore we reached Ista, it was 1310hrs and talking to the German guy he said train from Luxor to Cairo takes 14hrs as he has taken it 3 times before but tourist office and guy at railway station said it takes 8hrs but mind now made up, stuff the train, I am going to catch a plane so will ask driver to drop me off at airport. Reached Luxor 1345hrs the first drop off was the German guy me saying my thanks and also telling driver to take me to Airport which he agreed for 40EP so said ok. Hong Kong guy was next then the Hong Kong beauty queen her shaking my hand and blowing me a kiss as our bus was away, I was in love again!. Next the 4 Japanese guys and the Canadians and only me left we were away to the Airport 8km away. Got to Domestic Departures and in I went but not one Airline selling tickets kiosk. I asked security and was told if I want a ticket I have to go to Egypt Air Office in Luxor so Plan A to hopefully catch a last minute flight up the shoot. Jumped a taxi, 40EP and agreed he wait and off we went back into Luxor to Egypt Air Luxor Office and in I went. Guy said Passport so gave it to him and said Cairo, he looked it up on his screen saying 1 seat on the 1940hrs flight at 650EP or 200EP for a seat on the 2300hrs flight. I said book me on the 1940hrs flight saying do you take credit card, he said no, so I said I will go to the bank just up the road and off I went drawing out 1000EP. Back to the office and he told me pay at kiosk and over I went giving guy 700EP, got my ticket and change back, cor, was I happy. Back out and into taxi and I said I want to check the opening times for the Mummification Museum and he stopped facing it and we both could see the 35° sunshine humid heat glistening from the Nile behind as this is what the Egyptians call winter. Had a look and Museum opening times were 10-2 / 4-9, it was 1620hrs so we agreed he would wait for me for 40mins. In I went paying a 50EP entrance charge and followed the line with vivid wall descriptions of how it started and what they did as first they scrap a Mummies brain and then I seen a real live Mummie close up of a 21st Dynasty High Priest whose face and feet were plain to be seen, really remarkable. Then next a line of 1000 year old Mummies very colourful coffins so there I now know a few Mummie skills and back out to my driver and we were away, it was 1710hrs. Got to Airport, paid him a 100EP note, he was happy and away so in I went, put shoulderbag and me through x-ray then into and sat down in the Airport café facing Egypt Air check-in waiting for my flight to come up on the screen. Had a real big English cup of tea, not a whiskey glass cup with a big ham roll and really enjoyed my 1745hrs din din having a Mars Bar as dessert, wow, I am back in the Shot, total 50EP. Seen my flight MS436 come up on the Departure board and quickly over putting my shoulderbag on the moving escalator. Gave girl my flight paperwork with Passport and 2mins later got my Airline check-in stub, shoulderbag was away and over I went to final x-ray showing check-in ticket and I was in departures, wow, that was big time easy. Sat down facing the departure board screen hoping I didn't fall asleep just keeping an eye on it as the whole departure area was full of white Farang tourists. Getting a bit worried I then seen my flight come up on the screen, joined the queue and 5mins later we were called forward, had our boarding cards checked getting a stub back. Boarded a bus and when it was full out we went to the plane me first off taking my seat 26A a window seat so belt on having a look at the stewardess giving the safety instructions there was not one seat left, every seat was taken up by white Farang tourists so Egypt Air must be making a bomb. Only a few mins with engine roaring we were high in the sky above Luxor me looking out my window saying I liked you Luxor. Sat back in contentment as the drinks trolley came along me thinking this was a good move as the train and boredom would have killed me never mind arriving after midnight so just a little bit sorry I couldn't have booked an earlier flight I had a Coca Cola drink. Had a read of the in-flight magazine and it mentioned Cyprus where I had hoped to make and see Joe Devlin but have now run out of time, that's life. Finished the mag, put it back and woke up to the tannoy going on about seat belts and 10mins later after a great Aerial picture of colourful Cairo at night in we went for a nice soft landing, it was 2100hrs. Off the plane and not too long grabbed my bright red shoulderbag and out with taxi touts all over me and agreed an 80EP fee for taxi to Sara Inn, 21 Yousef El Guindi St from Hoda Sharaway St, Cairo, Egypt, www.sarainnhotel.com Tel: 202-23922940. Jumped in the taxi with shoulderbag on back seat and the traffic was horrendous but guy was a good driver and stopped to phone the hotel up, had a chat then away again all the way to the Egyptian Museum and finally at 2200hrs he parked up beside the Sara Inn. Gave him a 100EP note saying my thanks and I was in the lift and upto the 6th floor at reception. Guy as I showed him my www.hostelworld.com print out confirmation said Welcome Mr William and took me and my shoulderbag to room 716 a big huge d-ensuite with sofas and armchairs saying this one is yours for tonight but we shall move you to a slightly smaller one tomorrow. No problem I said and how much, he checked my outstanding balance and said 442EP so I gave him 440EP with his words pay the 2EP when you have change me laughing and saying to myself that makes a change. Done a 20min internet message letting people know where I am then out to a food kiosk just around the corner and bought 1 Fanta, 1 Coke, 1 large water and a packet of chocolate biscuits, 10EP which was so honest and so cheap compared with some of the prices I have had to pay. Back to room, had a full Fanta, most of the chocie bickies and that was me, stripped of, turned AC on and into bed and I don't know why but completely drained I was asleep not even a feather of a dream.

Email Sent: Sat, 13 Mar 2010
Subject: Rm716, Sara Inn, Cairo, Egypt

Hi All

Jumped Minibus 0800hrs and visited 2 sites on our sardine oven run from Aswan to Luxor, got to Luxor 1430hrs so no chance of a train as German guy on bus said he had took it 3 times and journey time was 14hrs.

Went to Airport and got the only seat left on the 1930hrs Egypt Air, 650EP, could have taken the 2300hrs flight for 200EP but just wanted to get here and got the above Hostel with a nice d-ensuite room with breakie for 20$US at 2230hrs tonight.

No plans manyanna!!!!!!
al de bes
Jack

Day 78, Sunday, 14-03-10, Cairo, Egypt

Sweating like a nightclub Sheila I woke up at 0520hrs, turned AC on and woke up cool again at 0745hrs. Up for a piss, underarm wash, face splash, long cargo on and down to breakfast room come restaurant and sat down. 5mins later a mug of tea, 2 long soft baguette rolls, 1 banana, 1 orange, portion of cheese, jam and an omelette arrived so got stuck in really enjoying it and ate the lot with another 3EP tea asking about a trip I seen they do to Alexandria. They didn't have any information on the trip saying guy would come at 1200hrs, I said I won't be here as going out sightseeing. Back to room, teeth clean, nice spluttering dobhi drop, cleaned ass and where do I go as seen everything the last time so had a read of LP. I had my plans for manyanna and next day in sort of place so out handing key into reception and leaving shoulderbag in lobby as they were moving me to a slightly smaller room at supposedly 1100hrs but I said I'm not hanging about and I was away down the lift and outside, did get lost 1-2 times as its postie time for my travel notes to Sandralita as they close Friday and Saturday as that's their weekend. Finally found the Ramses St Post Office, guy weighed the letter and said 8EP, paid him, he stuck the stamps on and said post box outside so out I went and another one gone thinking about poor Sandralita having to read my scribbled handwriting must be torture, not to worry it keeps her off de booze!. Good fun walking back along Ramse's St as each side of the large pavement for 200m they had a flat mat pavement sale of everything and anything but enjoyed my looking only as I knew I wouldn't be buying anything. Walked my way along Ramse's St and seen a lovely big Church in El Kholek Sarwat St called the Eglise Catholique Cordi Jesu Catholic Church and admired it from the outside as the front gates were locked. Young police security guard said it opens 1300hrs and 1700hrs me thinking that's strange as its Sunday today but maybe the Christians in Egypt abide by the Friday and Saturday weekend, don't know, said my thanks and away. I got to Merit Pasha St staying on my side of the suicide road turning right down El Tahair St passing the American University in Cairo which was really huge. I did think of crossing the Qasr Al Nil Bridge with its most impressive big Lion Statues each side but it was so hot so only strayed about 20m along it and enjoyed looking each way as each side of it up and down the Nile were great views. Back and turned right making my way down to the Nile riverbank path and followed it passing the huge Semiramis Intercontinental Massive Hotel. Followed the path until Resort Hotel took over the riverbank right of way then came back having a seat on a tea urn plastic seat at a Nile makeshift Café and had a tea, 3EP. Enjoyed my 3EP tea looking down the bank at the hundreds of plastic bottles debris floating at the edge of the riverbank and ate about 6No creamy chocolate bickies to help my body get enough weight to keep going!!. Finished my tea and away passing the 50 or more small motor passenger tourist boats all blaring out Egyptian music and declined a few offers for a boat ride. Flagged down a taxi and agreed price of 20EP to go to Abdin Palace Museum, jumped in and we were away and as we got near it the Abdeen Palace itself was a huge Massive Modern white block with armed guard soldiers some Ceremonial dressed all at and along its 100m front white wall with gates and access doors and driver stopped one block away from it and pointing at the left edge said go left and Museum is around the back. Out I got giving him the 20EP him saying buckshee me saying sorry and I was away. Walked a long way but no sign of any entrance and came to a small door I asked a soldier where is the Museum, he shrugged his shoulders calling out to someone and a guy came out saying this is the soldiers barracks entrance, we don't know where the Museum is. I said my thanks and back the way I came thinking this must be the Prime Minister or President Palace residence and got back around to the front asking the soldiers where is the Museum, they said its closed today and pointing I would have had to walk a long way around the side road to reach it so saying my thanks I had a slow walk going back towards my hotel. Had a tea in an open air café as it was only 1535hrs then back into my hotel and upto the restaurant breakie room and ordered a pizza and 2 teas. Fell asleep in the humid heat and 40mins later my din din supper arrived. Paid the 40EP charge and sat back enjoying my cooked in the hotel oven pizza and finishing my last gulp of tea my belly was happy and back to my room I went stripping of all my dirty and smelly clothes, had a new razor shave and hot shower giving my silky hair a shampoo and feeling on top of de world, I dried off. Put on all new sparkling clean kit, checked driving licence wallet and out handing key in at reception and outside my first stop was an ATM drawing out 1000EP. Got sort of lost in the dark night but reached the J.Gropie Café roundabout and knew where I was again. Flagged down at least 10 taxis telling them Train and Railway Station but not one understood then his bonnet held up with a plastic bottle, no windows falling completely apart taxi stopped, big guy nodded saying station so no handle on the door, he opened it and in I got. He took me to the Bus Station but I said no, train station, he stopped saying ask a young guy and me telling young guy Train Station, him telling driver and we were away again and after quite a long drive we got there and I gave him 20EP saying wait 10mins giving him another 5EP. Out I got and into the Ramse's Train Station and over to the ticket office, bought a 2nd class ticket to Alexandra as no 1st class available, paid my 27EP and back out to driver. He let me in the car and we were away again and I got him to drop me off near the Egyptian Museum, gave him another 20EP and he was away. Had a good walk around the women's clothes shops and the men's clothes shops areas both separate then into KFC and had a lovely cold Pepsi, 6EP sitting near the street window watching the never ending night life and the occasional backpackers with massive rucksacks go plodding by and that was my night over. Slow walk back to hotel and upto reception and breakie room area having a mug of tea and a chat with the 3 young lads on duty and as no trains to Port Said I agreed a 420EP all day car trip there and back for the day after tomorrow plus a taxi 20EP at 0715hrs for tomorrow morning. Paid him the full 440EP saying to myself I have done my best and into room, stripped off and taking blanket off bed in I got then remembered my Kelly Rose my darling Beauty Queen sweetheart and phoned her sitting on the edge of my bed. What a joy to hear her lovely voice as we chatted and laughed together for 10mins then kissing over the phone I sadly wished her bye bye and phone was off. Into bed feeling really happy and dreaming vivid dreams of curvy Kelly doing a Gippo belly dance I was asleep in my Kelly Rose's loving arms.

Date: Sun, 14 Mar
Subject: Cairo and a walk along the Nile

Hi All
Had a lazy day today just a walk along the Nile.
Booked my ticket 27EP for a 2nd class seat on a train to Alexandra for manyanna, 1st class was sold out so this should be fun!!!!, coming back later PM I hope!!!.
Wish me well.
al de bes
Jack

River Nile

Day 79, Monday 15-03-10, Cairo – Alexandria, Egypt

One minute hot, next minute cold, blanket on, blanket off, I couldn't figure it out but tried to sometimes sleep as I don't think the room had proper AC, more a cold fan and snoozing away the alarm went off and up I quickly got, it was 0610hrs. Underarm wash, face splash, long cargo, pocket tee shirt on and out into breakie room. The old owner was already in there having a smoke telling the young fellows how to do their job and as I sat down he left the room. Breakfast was 2 large soft rolls, jam, cheese, banana and 2 mugs of tea and an orange, really nice as I ate the lot. Finished breakie giving breakie guy a 5EP tip for my extra 3EP tea then back to room as I felt the restless stir and had a nice full empty dobhi drop, cleaned ass thinking that was a good one. Little pack of China beachbag, cleaned teeth and I was ready to go, it was 0705hrs. Out to reception room giving guy my Arabic ticket and he wrote in English on the back Train 905, Car 9, Seat 28, I said my thanks as he said driver is here and the driver and I were away into and down the lift and outside into his rundown car. He was a young fellow named Akhmed and away we went him horn pumping and overtaking in the inside and outside lanes that's if he found a space but with safety belt on I at least stood a chance. Got to the station and out I got giving him a 5EP tip and he was very surprised saying is that for him, I said yes, we shook hands and I walked into the station. Found line 4 and showing guy my ticket he took me to Car No 1 and pointing at the other end of the train said Car No 9 so off I walked at least 100m and into Car No 9. The seat numbers on the train were lucky enough in English so found seat 28 and sat down and not long a guy sat beside me and in the next 20mins the carriage got nearly 100% full so me thinking I could be in trouble getting a seat to come back. Toot toot and at 0800hrs we were away the conductor came along checking tickets putting a scribble on mine and as no more dramas I sat back in my lovely seat and fell fast asleep as we chugged out of Cairo Ramses Station, it was 0805hrs. Woke up 0905hrs seeing most of the carriage sleeping as we passed through many villages and some large towns but everywhere was green crop fields with the main highway road running parallel with out train line. It was fun also as the Egyptians love it seems to shout as they argue without threat of violence as even on the train different 2-3 blokes were arguing expressing themselves and pointing very loudly until it ended happily. Tea and sandwich trolley came along, it was 1010hrs but I didn't want anything. Next time I checked my watch it was 1020hrs so we must be getting near as total time was supposedly 2hrs 30mins, same same, we shall see. First stop 1025hrs and 50% of the passengers got off and I asked guy showing him my LP Alexandria, he said stop No2 but we were as far as I could make out in the outskirts of Alexandria so near the Mediterranean Coast Sea again, yeah man yeah. Got to the next and final stop and off I and everyone got, not a clue where we were as train station was not on LP map. Went outside the train station and taxi guy said to me do I want a taxi tour, I said yes, how much, he said 150EP for 5 stops and naming some that I recognised so said ok and followed him to his taxi and in we both got and away him telling me the price was now 200EP, couldn't be bothered to argue over 50EP but knew there would be at least another further con. We just followed the tram lines on the road passing Pompey's Pillar then through a maze of side streets to stop outside the Catacombs of Kom ash-Shaqqafa which in ancient times held over 300 bodies. Out I got him saying 30mins, paid 35EP entrance fee getting a ticket, showed ticket at entrance kiosk getting a stub back and just followed the many tourists lining up to go into The Caralla Hale a Circular stone ground level hut with a very deep 20m well inside with steps all the way around it in a circle to below it. Took my time and glad I had the patience as got to the first level with as I walked around its many tunnels there was hundreds of grave coffin niches cut out in the underground tunnel stone walls then down to the next and same same then came to a big glass container which had hundreds of bones and skulls to be seen, ugh, glad I had an early breakie. Enjoyed my really interesting walk and up the steps and out I went and down the steps into the Gram Tomb which was 3 separate Tombs with neat coloured wall carvings, really good. Back upto and out at the area full of large stone Coffins happy to have been down and seen the Catacombs. Back and into car and we were away stopping beside the Pompey Pillar, out I got and in I went paying a 20EP entrance fee but it was a truly fantastic sight with the 30m high Column inside the mudbrick remains of the old Ancient City of Alexandria walls so just took my time walking around it coming out of it at the mudbrick 2m thick foundations of the Ptolemail Temple of Serapiu, 3rd BC just marvelling at all this fantastic history in front of my eyes. Driver waved at me so crossed the road and into the front seat putting my safety belt on as you don't need too but you only get one chance!. Off we went his horn never stopped pumping which is I suppose a stress release as this type of driving requires great skills and out I got and in paying my 20EP entrance charge at the Roman Theatre. What a truly glorious sight as it had the real 4th Century AD Roman Amphitheatre,(Kom al-Dikka), which was great to walk and admire then a slow walk into the old dwellings quarters of Alexandria, 3rd Century BC. Next into the Villa of the Bird, AD117, which was the marvellous remains of a Wealthy Villa, great to see and walk around. Sun beaming down I was back and into my happy drivers car and away we went passing the full height still in use great façade of the Alexandria Opera House but the Salek Salsal Street it was in was just full of 6-7-8-9 storey, some fully Colonnaded Victorian type Architecture buildings. Passed a man begging on the pavement with no face, another with no legs and I wished I could have given them something as it was so sad to see but I had no small change. Next passed the horse riding statue of Mohammed Ali as we then went downhill passing alongside the big touristy Cruise Liners docked up in the Port of Alexandria, truly great sights as with the size of them they must accommodate 1-2-3000 people. Wondered where we were going next as we drove along a pot hole full of debris road with its still in use tram lines then through a cesspit slum area full of 5-6-7 storey some mudbrick tower blocks and stopped outside the Anfoundy Tombs. In I went paying a 20EP charge and down the steps to have a look at the 5No underground Tombs, nothing fantastic just old history but worth a look and back to car, it was 1325hrs. A sort of long drive following the half circle of the Alexandria Bay and he parked near the Qaitbey Citadel, 882AD. Out I got taking my China beachbag with me telling him I was going to have my cream chocolate biscuits and Fanta din din at the promenade seating area in the bay and he could join me if he wanted. He said no, smiling and off I went finding a marble seat, sat down in the nice sunny day and thinking I wasn't hungry I ate the full packet of big creamy chocolate biscuits finishing them off with my last gulp from my bottle of Fanta, great stuff. Over to what I thought was the entrance to the Citadel and paid a 5EP entrance charge and had a walk around the living and dead fish Aquarium then out and into the entrance to the beautiful white Qaitbey Citadel built on top of what was one of the original Seven Wonders of the World, the site of the Old Pharos Alexandria Lighthouse. It was a great walk first of all on ground level going into the Mosque of Citadel the oldest Mosque in ancient Alexandria with its 4 Sects of Islam then down lots of steps to the underground Reservoir which stank of piss, don't blame me I said out loud in the dark and back up the steps. Out from there and all the way down and along the Coastal Passage which was along the front of the Citadel at sea level but this great Castle was such a joy to see and walk. Next I walked the ramparts seeing the yachts and boats docked, anchored up one side and the rocky promenade the other, more great sights on a lovely sunny day. Back to my still awake driver and price had now gone upto 300EP me saying you agreed 150EP at the start him saying time and further sites have now increased it, me saying to myself he's done it before but its just part of Egypt's way as no way was he going to do all this for 150EP so I said ok. We were away passing Mapasha Faruck Residence in front of a big Mosque then the continuous slow marching 2 soldiers in front of the half circle Arched Monument to the unknown soldier. Now back on the fume filled 20km of the inner road of Alexandria Bay passing the huge library which I said no when driver asked me did I want to look inside. After a long drive we drove into me paying a 6EP charge the carpark of the Residence of King Faruk a truly marvellous Architectural building to admire but no one was allowed in at the Armed Guards main gate. It had a very beautiful park with lots of walking paths even along the coast but thinking I had done enough I just had a short stroll and a thumbs up poser shoot in front of the Faruk Palace and back to driver telling him Train Station, it was 1650hrs. Away we went and taking a different way through the throbbing vibrant centre of Alexandria we got to the Train Station and I gave him 300EP as in one way he had done well and the other if I had picked my 5 & 7 sights and had been able to tell him I could have maybe kept the price down but that's life. After taking the 300EP he said 25EP for parking so couldn't disagree with that and his final say 25EP for buckshee, I said no showing him my empty driving licence wallet telling him I haven't even enough to buy a train ticket, got out of the car and saying my thanks I was away. I knew there was an ATM in the Train Station so in, seen it, put card in, 1min later I had 1000EP so over to ticket kiosk and bought a one way to Cairo, 19EP. Guy said go quick and I hadn't even a clue what Platform so into the tourist office and guy looking at ticket said Platform 4 and run quickly as train is leaving now. Ran over to Platform 4 and guy standing at the rear carriage door seen me and took my ticket and into Carriage 8 we went, he said sit at seat 34 and gave me back my ticket as looking at it again I could now see all these details plainly written in English under the Arabic. Sat back sighing with relief and 2mins later we were away, it was 1730hrs. Didn't last long and fell asleep wakening up a few times as we stopped but like everyone else on the very comfortable reclining seats I dozed back off again until 1940hrs when this time I was fully awake. Next stop lots got off then in we went and stopped in Cairo Ramse's Train Station our final stop and I and everyone got off. Young fellow said taxi as I walked out of the station, I said yes how much, he said where to, I said downtown, he said 35EP, I said 30, he said ok and along the car park we went and into his car. I showed him my Sara Inn card with the address on it and he said ok but don't forget 5EP parking in Train Station, I just laughed to myself as it never stops and sat back enjoying my ride back to the hotel. He stopped near the hotel and I gave him 2 x 20EP, he said as usual no change so I laughed saying ok, give me 20EP back and he found 2 x 5EP notes so I took one saying my thanks and into lift and out at reception with guys saying, Welcome home, everyone smiling. Glad to be back I said menu and smiling ordered 2 sausage rolls with 2 teas and while they were being got ready I done my usual 15-20min internet in the Internet 3 computer screen room and that was me, no chance of any movement tonight. Ate my din din supper enjoying every last bit and slurp of tea, paid my 30EP bill and saying Goodnight see you all in the morning I checked with guy to make sure my epic Port Said trip was on and got yes, no problem. Back to room, stripped off, cleaned teeth and into bed a bit sore but Happy man and asleep no dreams, just a Jack of Alexandria Great man.

Date: Mon, 15 Mar 2010
Subject: Alexandria, Egypt

Hi All
Yeah, 2nd class was great with reclining soft seats and a lot warmer than 1st class.
Took 2hr 30mins to get their,27EP and 3hrs to get back,19EP but like everyone on the train I had a nice snooze, so a round trip of app 600klms for 9$US was not bad.
Alexandria was really good with some fascinating history sites and on the North side of the bay beautiful sandy beaches. I would have loved to stay a few days but got some plans.
Heading for Port Said manyanna just for the day as will try and find El Gameel Airfield where 3 Para parachuted into in 1956, I don't think its their now but only get one chance, any clues let me know.
Nite nite, legs, neck, back, head gone!!!!!!!!!!
al de bes
Jack

Day 80, Tuesday, 16-03-10, Cairo – Port Said & Al Gamell Airfield; Egypt

The night was a bit cooler so had a lovely blanket sleep only up once in the night for a piss then up for good at 0640hrs. Had my usual underarm wash, face splash, long cargo and pocket tee shirt with neckpouch on as heading for Port Said later and their might be a few Army security road checkpoints. Out for breakie having 2 small bananas, 2 mugs of tea, 2 soft bread rolls and a portion of jam, belly well filled I was happy and back to room. Teeth clean and a full clearance dobhi drop, just the job for my 3hr 450EP car ride as no trains to Port Said so I was told or read but didn't check at the train station so now paying the price!. Young man driver was waiting as I left my key at reception, he introduced himself as Akhmed and down the lift and into the sort of decent car we both got and away him telling me my journey time is 3hrs each way and first stop he will fill up with petrol, me keeping quiet. Stopped at the petrol station, filled up I hope and away down along the 2 lane highway tunnel then up and over the Orouba Bridge traffic choca block everywhere me thinking we will be lucky doing it in 3hrs. Long queues then now out of Cairo I seen a sign, Port Said, 174km, it was 0915hrs. The first paypoint checkpoint was at 0955hrs, Port Said 112km where driver paid 5EP and we where away on the open desert road again. Each side of our road now had many trees of all sizes and types then we passed the huge Mubarak Peace Bridge with now loads of Thai Tuk-tuks plying the road, it was 1040hrs, 50km to go, 3hr-4hrs, same same in Egyptian time. The Mubarak Peace Bridge crossed the Suez Canal but have not seen the canal or any ships yet although the canal on our right is parallel to our road. Seen a small boat and could now identify the canal only 200m away over a small manmade earth ridge hump. Signpost 15km to Port Said, it was 1100hrs and now very cloudy. Went past sign "Welcome to Port Said Industrial Zone", 5km to Port Said with many factories so doing ok and next thing we were over a bridge and into Port Said itself. A straight road and went past the famous Green Domes of the Suez Canal House built in 1869 for the opening Ceremony of the Canal. At last I could see the Canal as we passed huge waterside cranes then a Public ferry across the Canal port and driver asking directions we parked up facing the Travel Agency Canal Tours and we both got out, it was 1120hrs so not too bad. I said to give me 10mins and went along to the Port Said Tourist Office where guy gave me a great map of Port Said which had on it The Military Museum so saying my thanks out I went. Had a walk along the high path at the edge of the Suez Canal, yeah man yeah I have done it seeing great sights of large ships anchored up waiting to go. Back to driver telling him I would be 2hrs-3hrs maximum doing my walk and I would see him back where he is now, he agreed and I was away enjoying the vibes of the full of life but no hassle Port Said. Good walk then went left up 23rd July St and a happy exciting long walk I reached the Military Museum and in paying a 5EP entrance fee. It was small but I looked first of all at the history of the Canal which mostly was dug by hand with 20,000 Egyptians a month working in shifts in total 720,000 over a year, thousands died until the Canal finally opened in Nov 17th 1869 for the first ship. I found one room full of interesting paintings regarding the Nov 5th 1956 invasion of Al Gameel Airfield,

Port Said by British and French Paratroopers all documented from the Egyptian point of view, it even had a live video showing British tanks and the dead lieing in the streets, very sad. I had seen everything in the small Museum so asked 3 young lads at the reception desk were Al Gameel Airfield was or had it been built over. They didn't know or maybe let on not to know and one went away saying wait and came back with the Director of the Museum and an Army Officer. I explained I was interested in the history of Al Gameel Airfield regarding the 1956 English Army Paratroopers who parachuted on to it and the Directory gave me the full history. He outlined on my map where the original Al Gameel Airfield was and mostly still is but is now called Airport Al Gameel. He highlighted Saad Zaghoul St, Al Manak St, Demashque St and Al NAsar St all just passed the Al Shodadat Cemetary as the now built upon area of the previously old Al Gameel Airfield adjoining he said the new Al Gameel Club at the Mediterranean Sea. Drawing the old Al Gameel airfield on my map across all the roads above he stated this is where 3 Para parachuted into but which is now a many block of flats build up area and if I wished to go and see it, he would organise a taxi for me. I said yes shaking his and the Army Major's hand and we walked out to the main road where he flagged down a taxi telling the driver where to go and fee would be 10EP, in I got saying my true thanks again as that was very helpful and we were away. Got to the Airport Al Gameel Army Security gate and checkpoint for the Airport Al Gameel entrance but didn't stop and turned left driving into a rundown 60's lots of tower block blocks of flats and driver stopped just before another security point and out I got him saying this is the area where the old Al Gameel Airfield used to be. I had a 10min walkabout seeing Airport Al Gameel over the brow of a hill just outside the perimeter of our tower blocks. I was so happy and so proud to make it so stood stiffly to attention and saluted saying "You were the greatest 3 Para and you fill me with pride" and as moist tears came to my eyes I brought my hand down and a slow full of pride walk back to the taxi a proud ex 1966-72 Para myself, five of those years with 3 Para. Into the taxi and coming back we passed the huge Shodadat Cemetery and I told my driver to stop and over I went to where a gate was open. Lady said the Italian Cemetery is next gate and the English Cemetery is the last gate so saying my thanks I went down to the English gate and in and was completely shocked as it was a War Cemetery with 100's maybe a 1000 war graves. I had a walk looking at the names and the old famous Regiments as most died in either the 1st or 2nd World Wars. It was sad reading the headstones, R Hopkin, London Irish Rifles, 15 Dec 1943, Aged 26. Came to a girls grave and I had never seen a girl's name on a war grave before, it read; Pamella Iaa Prichard, Woman's RN Services, 12 July, 1942, Aged 22, I was so sad. Many headstones were to sailors from HMS Stag so it must have been sunk. Just walking the graves it made me feel so proud of the Great British Army as the names of the Regiments were now from a bygone age like: Royal Dublin Fusiliers, Black Watch, Highland Light Infantry, Loyal North Lancers Regt, South & East Lancers Regt, Hampshire Regt, Yorkshire Regt, Somerset Light Infantry, E Kent Regt., Cheshire Regt., Royal Welsh Regt, British West India Regt, Australia Light Horse and it never stopped so standing to attention in the middle I saluted saying "we will never forget and you will always be part and in our hearts" and a slow walk I was out and back into my taxi and we were away. He drove only a short way and I asked him to stop again and out I got and down to the big breakers empty beach making my way to the sea edge and stuck my bare right toe into it saying out loud I have made the Med again and then back to the taxi, jumped in and we were away. Just before Shairo Palestino at the edge of the rundown tower blocks I asked him to stop again as I was so lucky I spotted a Mosaic tiled large Mural of it appeared to be 3 Para jumping in on Al Gameel Airfield on the gable end of maybe the run down Port Said National Museum. Got out taking a few photos and tried to gain access but it had closed up locked doors and windows so saluted the Mural saying Good Luck 3 Para and Gibby our Colour Sargent in C Coy who was the only hero I remember who actually jumped into El Gameel. Back to the taxi, paid him 30EP for his help and he was away. Slowly walked back along past the very cheap shops and cafes enjoying Port Said's happy vibes wishing I could have stayed here. Seen my taxi driver from Cairo and smiled to him saying everything ok, he said yes, do you want to go back to Cairo now. I didn't really want to but I would have to go sometime as it would have been great to stay a day or two so said yes, got in our car and we where away, it was 1515hrs. Stopped at a duty free zone police checkpoint where driver had to open his boot, nothing in it, we were away again. Doing well and being stupid like all young ones he was trying to intimidate, tailgate and go past every other car on the road so I told him to remember he has a paid passenger. Fell asleep and woke up in the outskirts of Cairo and with my good day nearly over and sun nearly set we made it through the unbelievable Cairo traffic back to my hotel me eating half of my chocolate biscuits and never once was I asked for my Passport, it was 1850hrs. Out I got giving him a 50EP note tip, shook his hand saying my thanks I was into the hotel and upto my room. Dumped China beachbag and no wash, shave or anything tonight I handed my key in and out, found a neat café and had a burger and fries with 2 teas, just the job, paid my 11EP bill and out going for a stroll around what I call the centre not crossing the main suicide road and into KFC. Had a large coffee in my favourite J Groppi Cafe at the Midan Talaat Harb roundabout not even thinking of any plans for tomorrow and sat watching the moonlight world go by, it was 2140hrs. Paid my 6EP bill and out and looking forward to a lie in I was up the lift, got my key and into room. Cleaned teeth and a nice spuddy dobhi drop, cleaned ass and had a little read of LP seeing if there is anything I might want to look at manyanna then stripped off and into my lovely soft double bed and curled up happy as a lark and asleep happy in my Port Said dreams.

3 Para in Al Gameel

3 Para the Greatest

Date: Tue, 16 Mar 2010
Subject: Al Gameel Airfield, Port Said, Egypt

Hi All

No trains worth taking so had to fork out 470EP for a private taxi all day and away we went 200Klms to Port Said and getting out of Cairo was a nightmare, never seen traffic like it in my life.

Got to Port Said and got a map at the tourist office and first stop the Military Museum one room showing the 3 Para jump from the Egyptian point of view but asked the question to the Director of the Museum where is Al Gameel and he showed me on my map telling me where 3Para jumped in part of it has now been built over with Tower Blocks and the rest of the Airfield is now known as Airport Al Gameel, their is no Monument of any sort.

It was quite a distance on the Western side of Port Said taking in Saad Zaghoul St, Al Nassr St and Al Manakh St so took a taxi and made it to the Airport Ent at Saad Zaghoul St then into and had a walk around the tower block rough area up the side of it and stood proudly to attention saying 'You where and are the Greatest 3 Para and fill me with Pride' and thinking back to 1956 I was away with moist tears in my proud eyes.

Coming back approx 3 klms from the jump area just by luck I seen a old mosaic tiled large 4 by 2 metre picture of the 3 Para jump on a gable wall and took a few photo's. The date 1907 on the photo is Egyptian Machriki Numeral for 1956 which I knew as on my travels I came across the confusing type of numeral a confusing few times.

Port Said I now know was worth a nights stay as good vibes and plenty to see although the big waves coming in the Med beach where to heavy for a dip.

Lie in and do nothing manyanna. Have a Great Paddys day and drink de Night Away.

al de bes
Jack

Day 81, Wednesday 17-03-10, Cairo, Egypt

Nice sleep only up once for a piss then opened my sliding window to let in lovely fresh cool air, back to bed and just enjoyed the sensation of not having to get up as not going anywhere today, that's the plan. It was sometimes hard but I forced myself to enjoy turning over and stretching my legs and body in my lovely bed then up for good, my God it was 0900hrs, what a truly wonderful experience. Had an underarm wash, face splash and changed my dirty clothes putting on clean long cargo and pocket tee shirt and rolling all the smelly stuff up out I went to reception guy who counted 4 large & 3 small items and said price for cleaning and ironing, 18EP, so paid him. Paid for 1 more night, 110EP and also for taxi to Airport in the morning guy telling me due to traffic jams I have to leave hotel at 0730hrs to ensure I check-in at 0900hrs as my flight is 1100hrs, price for taxi is 60EP. I queried the 60EP but was told if I want to check prices with taxi drivers outside the lowest I will get is 50EP but then I will have the hassle of getting a taxi outside. This taxi was the taxi from the hotel and will be waiting to take me to my terminal which is T3 for Egypt Air for flight to Malta so listening to him I paid the 60EP and that's tonight and tomorrow all signed, sealed and delivered. Into breakie restaurant and had omelette, 3 soft bread rolls, cheese and jam portions, banana and an orange with 2 teas and ordering 2 extra rolls I paid guy 4EP for them and my extra tea and sat back really enjoying a lovely breakie sometimes having a chat with a Japanese girl speaking Yankee Inglaise. Finished my breakie and last gulp of tea and wishing the Japanese couple good luck I was back to my room, cleaned teeth then a fantastic dobhi drop, cleaned ass and nowhere to go I will go for a walk back to my first hotel in Cairo to say hello to my first Cairo friends. China beachbag with a bottle of Fanta, a bottle of water, orange, peaked sunshade hat and out I went handing key into reception, down the lift and out into the melee of car horn pumping and fumes of good ole Cairo. Made my slow way down Mahmoud Bassiouni St getting across the suicide driver main road then went behind the Egyptian Museum and on to the Nile River footpath at the 6th October Bridge and turned left enjoying the cool sunshine breeze. Kept slowly going, then past the 5 Star Four Seasons Hotel at the Tahrir Bridge thinking I will stay on the Nile River path and go left when I hope I see something I know. Enjoyed my late morning walk and as a tributary of the Nile came in from the left I went left passing the Grand Hyatt Cairo Hotel in all its splendour. Wandered past the Italian Embassy and came out on Kasr El Airy St just right of Kasr El Airy Post Office and I liked this friendly vibes area with its lots of cafes and restaurants. Was getting near then done a left and another left and there it was, The New Garden Palace Hotel my first stop all those weeks ago in Cairo. Went into reception and was warmly greeted by the reception guy him smiling saying you come back, I said no as I have a hotel in centre and we shook hands him asking how much but I said I just come to say hello as I am flying out tomorrow and shaking hands again I was away, it was 1230hrs already but where do I go now. Walked towards Tahrir Sq seeing the protesters still all along the pavement many sleeping and had forgot what it was all about but kept going seeing a sign Abdeen Palace Museum just past the lovely façade of the American University in Cairo. Quickly flagged down a taxi and he pointed at his meter in answer to my question how much so in I got and we were away. He went a different direction than what I thought was the way and I pointed go left, he said he will when he gets back on the correct road, me laughing to myself saying it never stops. Good drive around half of Cairo he was telling me Abdeen Palace itself was the residence of President Mubarak the President of Egypt. Drove past the lovely white frontage of the Palace first built by King Farouk then around to the rear at Gamae Abdin St and he stopped at the entry sign, out I got seeing his meter showing 16EP, gave him 20EP and I was away towards the entrance. Guy said ticket, I said where and he pointed across the street at a car park so over I went and bought my entry ticket, 15EP for the Abdin Palace Museum. Back over, showed my ticket and had to hand my camera and cellphone over to security getting a metal numbered stub then through x-ray with China beachbag being searched and at last I was in making sure I had my camera memory card in my breast pocket. Started at the Arms Museum then the Court of Historical Guns and I don't think there is a collection of old guns that could match this Museum anywhere in the world, it was just unbelievable the hundreds of different type revolvers, rifles and machine guns on show. Next onto the Swords and Daggers Museum and it was the same with ancient swords and daggers from every Nation of the world. Enjoyed it and then into the ancient Medals Museum again seeing medals and ribbons from Countries all over the world then a pottery museum and that was me, very impressed, out I walked into the bright sunshine. Had a lovely walk around the massive lawned beautiful garden with plenty of seats and upto an elaborate stone Arch seating area thinking just a pity they didn't have a café as it would have been nice to have a seat and relax, it was 1550hrs. Made my way out and handing my metal numbered stub over I got my camera and phone back then out onto the main El Tahreir St road and a slow walk back towards my hotel. Bought 3 tuna and 3 beef rolls, 6EP and into lobby, up the lift and into reception, got my key asking for 2 mugs of tea and 5mins later it was brought to my room, gave guy 6EP and totally relaxed enjoyed my 1645hrs supper eating 6 more chocolate biscuits as desserts, yeah man yeah, belly full, I was happy. Had a little siesta for 40mins for a change then shave and nice shower, long cargo and pocket tee shirt on I was out handing key in and down the lift, it was 1825hrs. Just had a dander about and around Tahrir Sq feeling slightly peckish I went into a lovely little café called the Mago Takeaway which had a downstairs and upstairs seating area in Mahmoud Basuonee St beside the Religious Francane Primary & Secondary School for girls. It had a great selection of foods so had a beef burger, fries and a tea enjoying my late night meal and that was me, paid my 12EP charge saying my thanks and I was away. Enjoyed my lazy day but have to make a move manyanna so up the lift, got my key telling guy give me a call 0630hrs and into room. Final pack of shoulderbag, checked neckpouch hanging it on the inside door handle and everything in order and really big time sad about leaving Egypt I was into bed and asleep dreaming them was the Maltese nights.

Email Sent: Wed, 17 March 2010
Subject: Cairo and nowhere to go!

Hi All

Forced myself to have a lie in and got up at 0900hrs, that was good.

Had a walk along the Nile to my first Cairo Hotel having a quick chat with the staff then PM went to the Abdeen Palace where President Mubarak stays and he didn't even invite me in for a drop of de black stuff for Paddy's Day, what is de world coming to.

Went into its great Arms Museum having a slow enjoyable walk then out walking back to my Hotel.

Heading for Malta manyanna as them was the Maltese nights in 1969-70 not a care in de world drunk as skunks down de Gut.

al de bes

Jack

Map of Malta

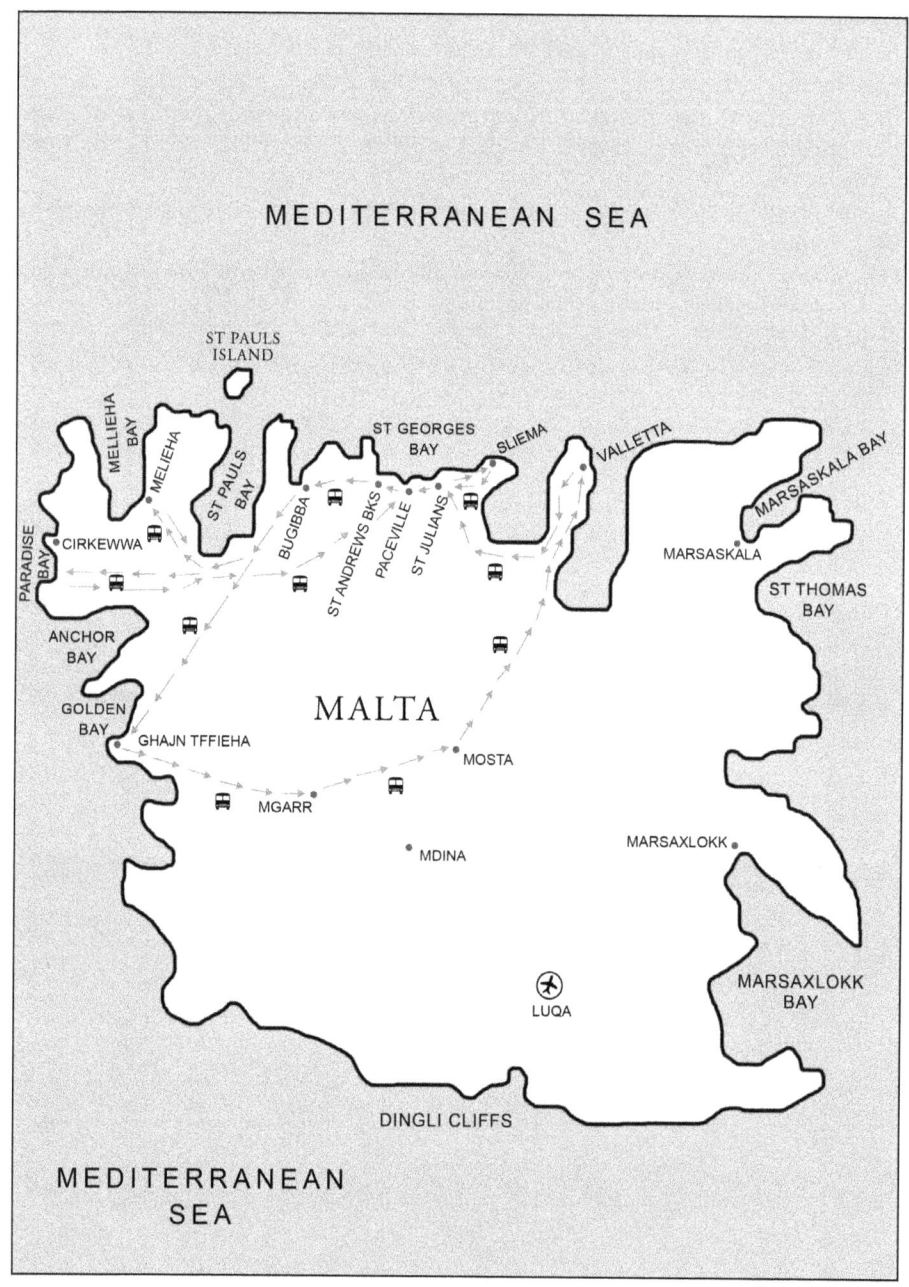

1) MALTA is a small Island but with its full of great impressive stone Fortifications and Building History everywhere all around the Island especially in Valetta its a never ending walk. It's a walkers paradise with hilly walks along the beautiful cliffs and down onto its sometimes sandy beach bays for a swim. If you like friendly nightlife you will never sleep on a weekend as some of the popular coast towns vibrate with late nightlife until the early hours where as you meet the ever so friendly Maltese people your stay on their Island will be an everlasting Memory to never forget.
2) Capital; Valetta
3) Malta achieved Independence in 1964
4) Climate; Ave temp Jan-Mar; 21c
5) Language; Maltese, English
6) Currency; Euro, 1$US = 0-60Euro
7) Visa; Not required, 30 day Visa issued on arrival
8) Return flight £51 + £154 ATM, hotel, food, train to Gatwick
9) Today's ongoing update of day to day accommodation, travel, food, drinks costs = £4462

Day 82, Thursday, 18-03-10, Cairo; Egypt – Paceville; Malta.

Woke up and checked alarm clock, it was 0550hrs, tried to doze or sleep but I was very sweating warm so opened the window letting in nice fresh cool air and dozed off wakening up again as alarm went off at 0630hrs. Finally dragged myself out of bed at 0645hrs, underarm wash, face splash, socks, long cargo, pocket tee shirt, pullover and Thai sandals on I was out upto breakfast restaurant room going out on the balcony breathing in big gulps of fresh air. Young fellow said breakfast with 2 teas, I said yes and sat down, seen the comment book and over to it writing Great place, helpful staff and central for everything, thanks, signing it Mr William. Breakfast arrived, 1 omelette, 3 bread rolls, portion of cheese and jam, 1 banana and 1 orange with 2 teas, wow it was great. Finished the lot giving young fellow 5EP for my extra 3EP tea and saying my thanks I went quickly back to my room as felt a stir and bang, a full discharge dobhi drop, cleaned ass, cleaned teeth and a final pack of shoulderbag I put neckpouch on checking Passport and Airline e-ticket and out to reception. Handed key over saying my thanks and shaking reception guy's hand who said driver for Airport is here and driver taking my shoulderbag into lift, I said and waved my final bye bye and as lift door closed we went down to the ground floor, it was 0730hrs. Into the ramshackle taxi driver's car with him saying Egypt Air, Terminal 3, I said yes as we drove into the not too much traffic of Cairo just following the motorway signs for Cairo Airport. Never stopped for any traffic jams and in we drove to T3 car drop off point and stopped, he and I got out, he put my shoulderbag on the pavement as I gave him a 5EP note, we shook hands and he was away, it was 0800hrs, things are looking good. Into Airport and International Departures putting my shoulderbag and China beachbag with 5 packets of 200 Marlborough in them at 100EP per packet of 200 through x-ray, me through x-ray and I was in. Looked at departure board seeing Malta Gate H02, check-in gate 345 so over to it, put shoulderbag on the moving escalator, give girl my Passport and boarding pass which I had just printed from the self check-in machine. She checked details smiling and saying I don't need a Visa, me saying no and gave me back my Passport and boarding pass and a Passport departure card and I was away saying my thanks. Briefly lined up at Passport Control and bang, Egypt exit stamp, got my Passport and boarding pass back and I was in Departures, it was only 0820hrs. My flight was not until 1100hrs so very impressed with my no hassle Airport departure I had a walk around the massive food Mall thinking and wishing every Airport in the world could copy the Egyptians. Finally sat down in a lounge having a drink of orange and 6 chocolate biscuits I had brought in with me just watching the departure board and listening to the tannoy seeing every Nationality in the world going home from having a holiday in Egypt walk by. Called to Departure Gate G2 and going through another x-ray they took my Fanta and water bottle. Took another seat but only for 15mins when we were called forward and showing boarding pass and getting a stub back out I went and onto a bus which when it got full out we drove out to our Egypt Air, flight 0443 plane. Off the bus and up the steps I took my seat 31A and are 2 seats in a row each side of the plane about 80% full we had our safety demonstration. Spot on 1100hrs with a roar of our jets off we went into the Cairo Egypt sky me really very sad and looking out my window down into Cairo I whispered "loved you Cairo, good luck" and sat back thinking New day, New Town, New country today. Fell asleep straight away and woke up as the food, drinks trolley was doing its round and had a lovely sliced chicken, salad, Coca Cola, tea, 1145hrs meal so sat back feeling top of the world as I finished the lot. Had a read of the Egyptian Air magazine, had a piss and a walk up and down the plane. Sitting back down again it came over the tannoy, fasten seatbelts, seats upright, prepare for landing, it was 1345hrs and at 1400hrs Egyptian time, bump, in we landed at Luqa International Airport, Malta, yeah, man yeah, I loved this Maltese Island. Quickly put my watch back 1hr to 1300hrs as we gain 1hr and off the plane and into arrivals we all went. Not long and my bright red shoulderbag with blue tape on its straps came out severely ripped at the previously repaired handle section, not to worry, grabbed it and out the nothing to declare Arched door. Made my way to my previously booked Airport transfer 14 Euro return which is good as checking the taxi fares they wanted 21 Euro for a single journey but it was only 1330hrs, the next transfer was 1400hrs so you do pay a price one way or the other. Large Minibus didn't turn up until 1410hrs and I was nearly going to take a taxi as fed up waiting but put shoulderbag in hold and we were away. He drove into Paceville but didn't know where the Tropicana Hotel was so I showed him as that was my drop off point, got out, got my shoulderbag and into the Hotel large internet café as I needed to print out my Burlington Apartments, Dragonara Rd, Paceville, St Julian's, Malta, Tel: 3562 3799175 booking form from www.booking.com as had forgot. Seen an ATM and drew out 100Euro then into the internet café paying 5Euro for 180mins, logged on, printed out my booking and next step I had to go to the St Georges Park Resort up on the right past the Black Bull Pub. Away I went a quick walk and into its reception, showed girl my booking and she gave me an envelope with Key to room 903, said my thanks and down to Burlington Apartments directly facing La Vallette Resort. Into lift and up to 6th floor and my room was directly facing the lift door so out, opened my door and in putting my key attachment into the electricity point and click, lights were on as all curtains were pulled, it was 1515hrs. Nice big sitting room, kitchen with full cutlery, Microwave, cups, saucers and plates with large ensuite bathroom and a big bedroom with 2 large single beds as the price 36Euros for 3 nights was for 2 people, not bad, 12 Euros a night for 2. Took neckpouch off putting it in my orange bag in my shoulderbag and where do I start. I knew the area really well as had been stationed here in 1969-70 with 3 Para in St Andrews Barracks and a few of the Paceville Pubs and St Georges Bay were some of our favourite haunts. Out and a slow happy relaxing walk around Paceville full of cafes, pubs, clubs area as this was the Maltese nightlife area. Next I passed the Highlanders Pub, then Dicks Pub and down Spinola Hill into St Julians at Spinola Bay seeing another favourite pub called Tonys Bar as usual packed full all the guys sitting outside. Feeling right peckish I seen a good ole McDonalds so in and had a fish burger, fries and a coke, 5Euros, couldn't have been better and filled me well. It was a lovely sunny day so followed a path around Spinola Bay then along the rocks behind the wall of the Portomoso Marina and into the big huge harbour of Portomoso Marina seeing all the huge Catamarans docked up in it. It was fun looking at them and I just admired the thought of sailing the world, that would be real fun. Made it completely around only on the rocks to the right of the Marina and I was back on a tarmac road. Sun still shining so went right and up and over a small hill along Triq Dragunara and down to St Georges Bay seeing all the young Chico's flashing their curves on its sandy beach and checked the time, it was 1800hrs. It would be dark in Egypt now but I have gained an hour so a final look at the Chico's starting to get dressed I made it back to my apartment and had a nice shave and face wash, that will do me today and out. Went down the hill again and had a tea in McDonalds facing Spinola Bay seeing all the young ones heading up to Paceville then a slow enjoyable walk back to Paceville and into Bay Street's throbbing full of shops and cafes all still open shopping Mall just having a slow walkabout. It was fun as the whole of Paceville was now one big throbbing music dance hall area and it was only 2155hrs. Enjoyed my hill step walk passing all the packed Pub and Nightclubs deafening ear busting sounds upto the head of the steps having one more tea in Burger King at the top of Triq Wilga thinking this will do me. Let the young ones enjoy their night out I said to myself as I made it back to my apartment, gently stripped off and into bed dreaming Malta in them bygone great days was not for the faint hearted and I was asleep in my Holy Euro Island.

Email Sent: Thu, 18 March 2010
Subject: R906, Burlington Apartments, Dragonara Rd, Paceville, St Julians, Malta, Tel35623799175

Hi All
60EP Taxi to Cairo Airport at 0730hrs, Flight 1100hrs and as we were coming into land in Malta the girl flight Egypt Air attendant said its only 18degrees which got smiles and laughs from us Farangs, landed 1300hrs, (gained 1hr) in when God made earth he made a little piece of heaven for people to go to and enjoy themselves and he called it Malta.
Got pre booked Airport bus to Paceville, (return) 14Euro.
Booked above at www booking.com at 12Euro a night, Kitchen, bedroom, sitting rm & ensuite bathroom, don't know what a kitchen is but can use all de rest.
Got key, dumped kit in room and out.
Had a dander past Dicks Bar then Tonys Bar then a good long sunshine walk around the Portomoso then down to St Georges bay having a couple of coffees to relax.
Danka Sandralita, its looking good.
al de bes
Jack

Day 83, Friday, 19-03-10, Paceville – Golden Bay; Malta

Up once for a runny dobhi drop, cleaned ass and back to bed taking one blanket off as it was warm and sort of snoozed or slept then said to myself don't hang about and up I got, it was 0745hrs. Had underarm wash, face splash and another milky dobhi drop me thinking the plane meal, then McDonalds, might have something to do with it, cleaned ass, no sleeve tee shirt and cargo shorts on and out of room. Down the lift and out going left then left again down to Answers a Bulgarian Café on the corner down Triq Ball. Sat in the bright glaring sunshine heat and ordered the 4-95Euro English breakie. It came with a pot of tea, 2 full slices of toasted bread, 2 butter, 2 jam cubes, 2 sausage, 2 eggs, bacon and beans, my oh my, what a lovely start to my day as I enjoyed and ate the lot drinking the last drop of milk out of the milk jug, nothing wasted. Paid my bill with a 5Euro note saying keep the change and away having a think about today's beach plans. Back to room, cleaned teeth, little pack of China beachbag and I was out going upto the bus stop on the main road going past the Drayton Pub and the Highlanders Bar. Lucky I had time as quickly read the bus number and seen my number for Golden Bay was 652 and only another 2mins wait and it arrived me waving it to stop. On I got, the only passenger and paid 1Euro 16cents, got my ticket and really pleased took the back sunlight seat. It was a long way but great interesting scenery with a ticket inspector checking tickets. Got to Golden Bay passing a cycle racing bike race going the opposite way and a crowd of heavy leather big motor cyclists as today was a Maltese National Holiday all shops everywhere closed. Off the bus and it was nice and warm and down the hill I went seeing the lovely sand of Golden Bay below me than took a line of downward steps and I was back again in heaven in Malta. The sand was warm as I stripped off to my swimming briefs so had a full length beach paddle in the cold sea then back to beachbag. I knew I wouldn't last long but had a lie on my small towel in the hot sun for maybe 5mins then up, cargo shorts and Thai sandals on and I was away along the bottom of the cliff which went around to Ghajn Tuffieha Bay and gasping like a sick lover I climbed the rockface cliff and loving the great vibes of Malta I was now on top of the cliff. There were many tourists of all Nationalities walking or sitting admiring the views as I walked the cliff edge to the Sq Lighthouse overlooking Ghajn Tuffieha Bay another beautiful sandy beach and took my time going down the conc steps onto its beach. Tried again to sit still and only be a beachbum but it was way to early for me so cargo shorts and Thai sandals on again I was up the steep hill looking down at the separate nudist beach but only one Ho Chi Mini banana on show, no Singapore slitters or Brazil pumpkins to admire. What will I do now as I looked far across the sea by and down the steep mountain side between me and Gnejna Bay. I should be locked up but slowly bit by bit I took my time one step at a time and went down the very very steep dirt/crusty mud of the side of the mountain which got me to within 3m of the beach but there was a 1m drop between the edge of the dirt soil steep cliff and the rocky beach. What do I do trying to keep upright and to stop slipping on the near horizontal cliff as all I wanted to do was protect my 2 long gone shoulders so gently sat down throwing my China beachbag onto the beach and slid feet first into the air and landed very neatly on my

2 feet, wow I had done well. Followed the rocky beach towards the sandy Gnejna Bay Beach sometime along 100mm steps on the steep big rocky area having to jump down and across a 1m gap so no chance of getting back. It was difficult but something I liked then came to another tiny downhill path which ended at another gap and slowly made my way along the dusty path and looking across I couldn't take a chance as I was on my own so back up the dusty path which was easy going uphill and climbed the full grass bushes mountain pulling the grass for support and across just below it and all the way down again and back onto the path. Had a good few slugs of water and an elderly English couple asked me was it ok to go the way they had seen me as they also didn't want to cross the 1m dusty path gap. I said only if you climb up and over the mountain face rim, don't try and follow the sea path along to Ghajn Tuffieha Bay as there is 2-3 serious gaps and other dangerous climbs which the way you want to go are uphill so they said their thanks and said we will look at getting upto the mountain rim and we parted wishing each other all the best. Finally oh finally legs aching I reached the rough sands of Gnejna Bay, Thai sandals off and a lovely paddle walk along it both ways then up to the toilet and had a piss. Would have paid big money for a taxi as no buses go to Gnejna Bay so what do I do now as my next stop was Mgarr a town inland from Gnejna Bay. Had a think about my choices, do I sit by the road and try to hitch or walk and try to hitch so off I went and when hearing a car I would stop and give a hitch sign but panting and sweating like a pig I walked the full uphill 3-5 km into and past the built by money of selling eggs the big Domed Egg Church the Church of the Assumption in the centre of Mgarr. I am thinking I am crazy mon crazy so sweating like a Gut girl on a Sat night I bought 2 tuna rolls and enjoyed my 1320hrs Naffi break sitting by the roadside at a bus stop waiting for the bus the lady in shop told me that only goes to Valetta. I was going to go to Valetta manyanna for a half day but will do it today so that's sorted. Just finished my 2nd roll and bus arrived, paying the 47Cent fare, got my ticket and sat down thinking about the times in 1969-70 we used to stagger shouting and singing from St Andrews Barracks all the way to Valetta and think nothing of it. Reached Valetta Bus Station at the magnificent Arched Gate entrance at Valetta City Walls, off I got and straight down Republic St seeing The Central Bank of Malta way up on my right which used to be the Forces Vernon Club and kept going passing The Church of St Francis of Assisi built 1598 then the Treasury of The Order of St John, 1744 and a quick look in the Palace but it was half closed. Seen an old history tablet on its inner Arched gate wall; Prince Albert, 2nd Son of Queen Victoria visited Malta as Midshipman on board HMS Euryalus. Turned back and now quite sad but very excited I went right then right again and I was in Strait St, The Gut the day/night residence of the Darling massage Angels of Malta, what happy nights, what happy days 40 years ago as we were the final British Forces Unit to be stationed in Malta as Malta went Fully Independent. Old 60 year old Chico came out giving my ass a squeeze saying you always come back. I laughed saying only to see you and she pouted saying old days are gone and laughing said but you can have one if you like and left me going into her pad. She made my day me laughing out loud then I was sad and happy at the same time seeing the faded falling to bits some of the very old the ones that are left Pub signs over the blocked up old Pub doors starting with the Retainer Bar, then Larry's Bar, then the Smiling Prince

Bar, then Carmen's Bar and finally The Piccadilly Bar me thinking another few years at the most and nothing will be left. Took a few photos and kept going on down Strait St until I reached the bottom and went quickly over to the road walls along the sea harbour as this area was rough. Walked all the way around going past the main harbour then turned right up past 'The Pub' the final drink pub of Oliver Reed still fully open but closed today. Made it all the way down to the Sliema / Valetta Ferry dock and boat had just docked so joined the queue, paid my 93 cents, took a seat and across seeing the beautiful sights of Malta from the sea and in we docked facing Tony's Bar in Sliema another one of our drink stops in those Maltese nights/days. Didn't stop as I knew I would be back tonight and jumped a bus, 47 cents and back to Paceville another wonderful knee breaking day nearly over. Into Paceville Burger King having a fish roll, fries and a tea, 4 Euro 20 cents, and enjoyed my 1745hrs din din supper. Nearly asleep I went back to my studio flat, stripped off and had a shave and a lovely shower. Long cargo, pocket tee shirt, socks and pullover on as its cold at night and out upto the bus stop for Sliema. Good bus service as didn't wait long, paid my 47cents fare and took a seat. Pressed bell for the Manoel Island stop and off I got having a piss in the gent's toilet facing the Brown Jug Bar another old favourite 1969/70 drinking den. Turned right going up Triq L-Imsida St I knew what I was looking for and going past the petrol station I seen 2 lovely Chico's of the night at a street corner but smiling and in the mood I passed them keeping on the other side of the street. Turned left at the next corner then left again and there they were sitting along outside the big rundown block, yes, the happiest and most beautiful girls in Malta as one petite short skirt beauty queen smiled at me looking me in the eye and with her love glazed eyes I knew in my heart our Maltese love would last until the final last Maltese night she stood up blocking my path and as she put her arms around me caressing my aching limbs we both smiling into our both lovesick lovers eyes she whispered " short time Papa" and me holding her close in the vibes of our true Maltese love I said yes, how much My sexy Darling. She said 35 Euro fondling my rocker parts and my love so strong I said yes, where we go and with a squeal of joy she said my place taking my hand as we went into the dark morbid block entrance and laughing together up two flights of stairs and into a nice big Studio type double bedroom. Quickly I got out her 35 Euro putting it on a table we both stripping off naked kissing, caressing and fondling our fully in love firm bodies I was in the heavens above as her lithe curvy body was such a lust filled sensual treat we were on the bed making groaning, gasping uninhabited lustful sex spasms Maltese love she was biting my neck to pieces ripping my scarred back and buttocks skin to pieces and screaming in passion as I also was biting and chewing her firm breast nipples we changed positions she now on top as we pounded each other into are sex scented smelling mattress we changed positions again me on top her beautiful strong legs wrapped around my back we both now screaming in pure Maltese lust our bodies reached a crescendo of breast biting exotic Maltese sexual lust we climaxed together the sexual vibrations like electrical shocks vibrating through my body we where biting and screaming in pure depraved Maltese lust as we kept pounding into each others love stuck bodies I was in the clouds above Malta until it seemed like hours are sexual spasms went on and on until slowly but slowly we came to a sweated sweet scent drenched stop and I slipped of my beautiful lover to lie curled up tight beside my Maltese Star all my body pain now gone just happy Vibes as I knew in my lovers heart we would never move or leave each other she turned over and smiling give my ass a slap and tickling my ribs saying, "You are a star Papa but we go" and me poking and stroking her lovely ass we both got up and dressed she laughing stuck her loot down her bra. Out of room and down the grimy block stairs we went laughing together then one final peck and a smiling wave at the street entrance she turned back and out I went a one happy no pain man I walked down to the bus stop. Jumped a bus, 47 cents and full of life I got off in Paceville and along into my studio, stripped off and the happiest smiling man in Malta I was into my lovely bed and dreaming Maltese sex 24hrs every day is good for the joints and asleep the happiest Maltese man in all of Malta.

Vernon Club now the Bank of Malta

Oliver Reed's last one

Email Sent: Fri, 19 Mar 2010
Subject: Golden Bay, Ghajn Tuffieha Bay, Gnejna Bay, a Maltese dream.

Hi All
What a great crazy day as jumped a bus to Golden Bay, 1Euro 16cents and down on its lovely beach, got fed up after 10mins and up the cliff and down to Tuffieha Bay, both really good.
Bored stiff so down the cliff then along the rocky seashore with no return as jumping across 1m gorges and came to one I couldn't cross so had to climb the cliff and go across it to Gnejna Bay, had a rest then walked it to Mgarr to catch a bus to Valetta.
Tears in my eyes I made it down Strait St,(The Gut) with my 60years old charmers saying you always come back to see us still trying to give me a massage!!!.
Only the faded crumbling remains of some of our night time bars that are still their like Retainers Bar, Larry's Bar, Smiling Prince Bar, Carmen's Bar and the Piccadilly Bar so tears in my eyes I wished Strait St goodbye and came back by ferry into Sliema docking facing Tonys Bar, them was de Maltese nights.
Just out on the town in Sliema going to have a lookee past the Brown Jug Bar and up Triq L-Imsida St as you never know who you find, that's my feeble excuse!!!!
Will head for Paradise Bay manyanna, that's if my knees are still working!!.
al de bes
Jack

Day 84, Saturday, 20-03-10, Paceville – Paradise Bay; Malta

Fantastic sleep only up once for a piss and had to force myself out of the lovely soft mattress and sheets, it was 0800hrs. Underarm wash, face splash and around to Answers Café ordering my 4-95Euro English breakie which was a pure delight when it came with a pot of tea, pot of mil, 2 sausages, bacon, 2 eggs, beans, 2 full slices of toasted bread, 2 portions of butter and jam and in the bright sunny Maltese lovely hot morning I ate every bit of my lovely breakie, magic. Paid my bill and upto Edrichton Holiday Office to pay my 3 nights 36Euro bill and had a laugh with the two girls one who knew me from before saying you not staying long this time. I said no, I made a mistake by not booking longer but that's life, I'll be back end of May. My bill had already been paid from my credit card so got a slip, down the lift and out. Only a short walk and in the lift and upto and into my room having a quick dobhi drop, cleaned ass, cleaned teeth, little pack of beachbag and I was out going up to the bus stop for Paradise Bay, oh la la. Seen a money changer office so asked guy would or does he change Egyptian Pounds, he said yes so gave him 1020EP and got back 130Euro so yeah man yeah, stuck it in my sky and upto catch Bus No 645 to Paradise Bay. Waited a good 10mins this time then seen Bus 645, waved him down and on giving him a 2Euro coin, fare was 1-16Euro so got my ticket, change and sat down. Ticket inspector boarded so showed him my ticket as every bus I have been on there is always a ticket inspector who gets on, must be the drivers trying to swindle. On a notice looking at the partition wall at drivers seat I could have bought a one day ticket for 3-50Euro, a three day ticket for 7-00Euro and a seven day ticket for 10 or 12 Euro which was really good so will remember for my next Maltese trip. Great views over the sea and inwards over Malta as we crested a high hill and down into St Pauls Bay named after Saint Paul who was shipwrecked here in 60 AD on his way to Rome. The lovely huge San Pawl Milqi Church 2klms south of Bugibba on a hill above Murarrad before it was built is believed to be the site where he stayed and converted the Islands helpful and kind people who looked after him to Christianity. We passed lots of shops, cafes and restaurants and it looked a lively fun place. Next we where on the coast road again going past the Red Tower a square type Fort Tower on a hill as we past a road sign pointing left to Paradise Bay me looking for a bus stop but didn't see one as we carried on stopped to park in the Gozo Channel Ferry carpark and everyone including me got off. Gozo was a beautiful sight only 100-200m away across the sea and looked really good but beachbag over shoulder I walked back approximately 100m to the Paradise Bay sign passing a bus stop then turned right up the slight hill and going down the many steep steps I was on the best and most cleanest beautiful sandy beach in Malta. Taking my no sleeve tee shirt and cargo shorts off I enjoyed an each way paddle walk along the sea edge then only me on the beach I smoothed the sand into a sand pillow, laid my towel and with my knees and legs giving a sigh of relief I lay down in the lovely hot sun. Got up after 10mins having a paddle only no swim then only cargo shorts on I was up the hilly steps onto the top of the cliff and had a walk along it with all its spectacular views over Gozo and the sea, really good. Had a rock seat having 6 chocolate biscuits with a few slugs of Fanta and thinking about St Pauls Bay I thought I might as well have a look so a good long sunshine dander along the tarmac road to the blue bus stop and having a good few slugs of water I was there waiting for a bus, it was 1110hrs. I was really sick about leaving Malta and finally made my mind up I will check for a cheap flight maybe for next Wednesday, 24-03-10 when I see an internet café. Bus came and on I got telling him St Pauls, got my 0.55cents ticket me thinking I am crazy not buying a Bus pass but trying to work it out I would have saved nothing. Seen a lovely sandy bay half of it covered in seaweed and our bus going up a very steep hill I pressed the stop buzzer, bus stopped and I got off only to find I was in Mellieha. I had a walk through its happy vibes town area anyway then sat down at another bus stop. Bus No 656 came along and on I got paying 1-16Euro for ticket to St Julian's and got off just past the sign for Pembroke. Thrilled to bits I was in heaven again walking up Normandy Road and came to what used to be our 3 Para Tower Block Guardroom Jail House. Nothing on the outside had changed as all the old road names at the 5 crossroad roundabout were all still the same, Normandy Rd, Anzio Rd, Cassino Rd, Triq Alamein and Trobruk Rd all taking me back 40 years ago. St Andrews full size Barracks accommodation was still in its full glory but now a live in Teaching English as a Foreign Language School. Walked on up past the barracks and looking left there it was a soldiers dream the greatest place I had ever been in my life, the Naafi, a big huge stone built block taking up the full skyline and onto I walked I think a football pitch in our day and stood facing our famous 3 Para drinking heaven. It was in a very poor state of repair with no windows and debris everywhere so I could have climbed in some of the front missing window spaces but went around the back and in through a full of debris door and with moist tears in my eyes I slowly wandered everywhere in and around the internal ruins of what was once a thriving full of life meeting place for all of us 20-30 year old gang of soldiers, our gang nickname from the rest of the Battalion was 'The Click'. In and around the full of debre floor I walked seeing my name "Jack Glass, 3 Para, Forever in our Hearts" painted on a stone block wall I think from me many years ago when I had first come back so standing to attention I saluted saying "You, the Naafi was are CO and best friend for 2 years" and out the back door I went a one happy Naafi man. Went left along Triq Arnhem and crossing the road I went into Jessie's Bar beside the Ploughman's Pub and Jessie's Bar in its hey day was a very famous Royal Marine drinking hole and still every year they come back for Remembrance Sunday. I had a cup of tea speaking to Jessie's daughter and she knew me from old saying you're a Para from Aldershot and saying those were the days. She said you Paras all drank in the Golden Star Pub which is now a Chinese Takeaway called the Pavilion Palace. I said that's correct as it was The Click's gang first stop drinking Den after the Naffi with Tony and Lena the owners having to put up with us shouting, swearing and drinking until we collapsed on the floor most nights. Finished my tea, shook hands and I was away taking a few photos from the outside and went past Triq Dun Gazepp Fariqi St directly facing the Pavilion Palace which was our staggering walk route from the Naafi, what great Memories of those nights and days we had with not a care in the world. Made it across the road and down past the Guardroom thinking I slept there a few times. Took the Anzio Rd down towards St George's Bay as we used to walk a rocky gorge taking us out directly facing the bay but the gorge was now full of bushes and trees so stayed on the tarmac road seeing all the in our time Officers Villas on my left then done a right again and I was in front of St George Bay sandy beach packed with all Nationalities of the world all being taught English in Malta's many English teaching schools. I do notice that in my time 40 years ago English was widely spoken by the Maltese, now you hardly hear it as although they all speak English they talk between themselves in Maltese.. I found a vacant spot of sand but no sunbed, stripped off, had a few slugs of my Fanta eating a few more chocolate biscuits and just lay dozing in my sand pillow sunbed for a good 30mins then up, cargo shorts on and away. Made it near my apartment and had a nice Nugget chicken and chips meal, 3-50Euro and that was my day over, back to apartment, shave and shower and had a nice 45min siesta on my bed. Cleaned teeth, long cargo, pocket tee shirt on and I was out not going anywhere tonight. Made it down into St Julian's having a tea and a chocolate muffin in McDonalds facing Tony's Bar for an hour watching the no clothes Maltese Chico's heading up the hill to Paceville. Paid my 3-60Euro bill and followed the crowd back into Paceville having one more sleepy tea in Answers Café. Remembered I wanted to check my emails so across the street and into the large internet café. First of all I changed my flight, 20Euro, to Wed, 24-3-10 then booked 3 extra nights in Burlington Apartments, 36Euro and now looking forward to really relaxing I was out for another tea in Answers Cafe The noise from the bars and clubs was deafening for me but fun for the 100s-1000s of the so full of life young ones lots prancing about the streets all enjoying their Malta nightlife. Time marched on, it was 2250hrs so bed calling I made it back to my quiet apartment, stripped off and into bed and dreaming true love near the Brown Jug in Malta I fell into a lovely deep Maltese sleep.

The old football pitch & guardroom *Naafi*

Wall inside the Naafi: Forever in My Heart *Golden Star*

Email Sent: Sat, 20 Mar 2010
Subject: Paradise in Paradise Bay, Malta

Hi All
Made Paradise Bay a lovely clean sandy beach with no stones and cheap sunbeds so had a nearly 15mins doing nothing then along the top of the cliffs with great views over Gozo.
Made it back and into St Andrews Barracks now a English teaching college but all the old blocks still their as well as the Guardroom at the 5 Road crossroads at Normandy Rd, Anzio Rd, Casino Rd, Triq Alamein and Tobruk Rd then seen Gods gift to the soldiers of the British Army, the Naafi building.
Had a walk inside its ruins shell and what great memories of Vodka straight from the bottle nights it brought back then out the back and along Triq Arnhem and across the road to what now is a Chinese Restaurant but the ole Golden Star Pub was the final seat for many of the Click gang Para soldiers of the Queen of England.
Its Sat night and the dance halls, pubs, clubs of Paceville make it the loudest place on earth with the 1000s of no clothes Maltese chicos out all night enjoying their life so no sleep tonoche.
al de bes
Jack

St Andrews Barracks

Guardroom

St Andrews Barracks

Jack in 3 Para

Day 85, Sunday 21-03-10, Paceville – Valletta, Malta

I loved my bed and again didn't want to get up but finally fully awake I was up, underarm wash, face splash, cargo shorts, no sleeve tee shirt on, checked driving licence wallet in cargo pocket, copy of Passport and Insurance in back pocket and out around to Answers in Tri Ball St for my usual English breakie, what a lovely meal sitting outside in the sunshine heat. I finished my last gulp of tea, paid my bill and back to room just as the 2 English girls in charge knocked on my door. Caroline told me no problem, I can stay in this room for the next 3 days so all smiling and having a laugh I said my thanks and they were away. Had a nice explosive dobhi drop to clear the system, cleaned ass, cleaned my now brown teeth and little pack of China beachbag out I went to my start of a new day. Walked up to the bus stop for Valetta and only a 2min wait on I got paying the 47cent fare got my ticket and happily sat down. It was good to see the Church going Maltese people all very neatly dressed going to their Churches. Bus was the best way to travel Malta as now ours fully packed we drove into Valetta Bus Station and off we all got. I turned right as I got off the bus and straight into the throbbing packed full of people Sunday stall market selling everything and anything and just took my time walking the full length on the left then back up on the right hand side and nearly bought a brand new trolleybag for 15Euro but had started stitching my ripped seam trolley shoulderbag with unbreakable thread this morning and slowly getting their so I said no. I came out of the market on the pavement by the Valetta Wall and in through the main gate Arch feeling sad and happy as I always do thinking of all the great times and my Click mates 40 years ago. First stop as usual I walked upto the Bank Centrali Ta Malta as previous to it being a Bank HQ it was the Malta Forces Vernon Club and our first stop. Back down and along Republic St turning left at the first street before the Palace and came to the greatest nights of my 22 year old life, Strait St or The Gut as it was known throughout the British Army, Navy and Airforce. Just slowly walked down it passing the Public Toilets now being refurbished as in our day they where our pisshole as the Bars didn't have any toilets. Crossed a small street and seeing the very old faded bar names, all the doors blocked up I was now at the Smiling Prince Bar, then the Piccadilly Bar and crossed another small street looking up I was at the Blue Peter Bar then the Silver Horse, Alex McKay Bar and could hardly read it but reached the Royal Bar and now at the end I crossed St Dominic St at the Golden Eagle Bar and moist tears flowing I went down the final row of steps at Jews Sally Port going across the main road at Marsamxett Harbour. Lovely sunny day and promising myself no more marathons I went right past Fort St Elmo onto Triq Il-Mediterranean and came to where they show the 45min film Malta Experience and it had just turned 1055hrs, next film was 1100hrs so down the steps and oh my God through an underground tunnel to reception. Guy said ticket, I said yes, how much, he said 9-50Euro so gave him a 10Euro note, got my change and ticket and a few steps later I was in the cinema. Put on my over the head ear speakers turning the knob to No2 for English and 2mins later the full screen Malta History show started. It was very graphic starting 4000 years ago and showing the different warlike Nations who over the Centuries held Malta and finished with the

British Rule then Malta's Independence. It was a fantastic film then I was out as the lights came on really chuffed to have seen the great history of Malta and its people. Came out onto Triq Il-Mediterranean and seen across the road The Knights Hospitaller so had a look at what it was and it was a self follow the arrows walk of their history and the underground Hospital. Paid my 2-80Euro OAPs entrance fee and went quite a way down underground reading the walled notes of how and why it was built and the types of medicines used but seeing and being in a 540 bed underground medieval hospital was great real history as I walked the arrow path seeing wards, operating theatres and reading the history notes I finally made it back up little winding stairs and out, what a fascinating experience. Walked on up Triq Il-Mediterranean coming to the Siege Memorial big Bell Square Pillar Arches to Commemorate the award of the George Cross to the People and Island of Malta on the 15th April 2002 on its 60th Anniversary to the 7000 servicemen and civilians who lost their lives 1940-43 and read their Epitaph on a dead mans Tomb. It read; "At the going down of the sun and in the morning we shall Remember them" so saluting the brave people of Malta I said, "God be with you and your families and we will never forget" I was away. Crossed the road and up San Paul St then right on Archbishop St and crossing Merchant St I seen a pub called "The Pub" which was the last drinking hole of Oliver Reed who dropped dead 2nd May, 1999 sitting at the counter but unlucky as it was closed on Sundays, might come back but thinking about it, that's the way to go!. Carried on down Archbishop St passing the Greek Catholic Church Our Lady of Damascus and turned back and went right walking up the peaceful Merchant St and out the main Valetta Arched gateway to the bus station. Had a slow walk down the road into Floriana then seen Bus No68 and I was beside a bus stop so waved him down and on paying my 0-47Euro and sat down pleased with my great morning. Stayed on the whole Hog getting off at the top of the hill leading down into St George's Bay and had a nice slow walk downhill onto St Georges sandy beach full of brief bikini Chico's, oh la la. Found a sunny stretch of vacant sand, stripped of to swimming briefs, laid my Mini towel with China beachbag as my pillow I was a very happy contented man lieing there with my eyes closed enjoying the hot sun on my bare skin, it was 1450hrs. Had my half packet of chocolate biscuits with a bottle of Fanta, had 2-3 paddles along the seafront, lay on my back and as it got hot, my front, sometimes dozing off and checking watch, it was 1700hrs, what a great day. Kit on and upto Burger King having a fish roll, fries and a tea, 5-70Euro and really enjoyed it. Said my thanks and a slow walk back and upto my apartment studio, stripped off, had a shave and lovely hot water shower, long cargo, pocket tee shirt on and out, it was 1920hrs. No plans just had a walk past the Drayton & Highlander Pubs then down past Dicks Bar and the Scotsman Pub all the way down to Tony's bar everywhere quite full and all enjoying their addictive alcoholic drugs. Into McDonalds and sitting near the entrance door looking out I had a tea and a chocolate muffin and wishing my Kelly Rose was here I paid my 2-20Euro and out going up Spinola Hill. Enjoyed my very slow walk all the way into the Baystreet lively area and had a seat with another tea and a chocolate donut, 2-70Euros. My night nearly over, it was 2235hrs I gently made it past the loud throbbing many bars and clubs in Paceville and up the lift and into my apartment, stripped off, into bed and asleep, no dreams.

Smiling Prince Bar   *Splendid bar*

Larry bar   *The Gut*

Piccadilly Bar Carmen bar

Silver Horse, Alex McKay The Blue Peter Bar

Home in Strait Street

Retainer Bar

Piss holes in the wall

Email Sent: Sun, 21 Mar 2010
Subject: Valetta, St Georges Bay, Malta

Hi All

Body slowly getting back to normal as went down to the big Sunday Valetta market then a dander along Strait St again!!, it has so wonderful Memories I feel so much at home in it.

Went into the Malta Experience film show which showed me 4000 years of Malta history which was really good then down underground into the Knights Hospitaller Hospital just wondering the wards and everything built 100s of years ago.

That was my morning over as no 10-15klms hikes and next stop was the bikini chico's sandy beach of St Georges Bay for a beach towel lie down.

When we where here 40years ago it was a rocky inlet sewer outlet and the Maltese's could not believe we swam in it, mind you, full of Vodka who cares who dares and that was my sunshine day finished at 1700hrs.

Head for Bugibba manyanna for a lookee.
al de bes
Jack

Day 86, Monday, 22-03-10, Paceville – Bugibba; Malta

Woke up a couple of times and had a piss but bed was so nice I slept until 0820hrs, seen my bedside clock and quickly up, underarm wash, face splash, cargo shorts and no sleeve tee shirt on. Checking driving licence wallet then out and down the lift and around to my favourite Answers Café for its lovely 4-95Euro no chips English breakie. Ate every last crumb not an egg stain left on the plate and happy as a pig in shit I paid my bill and back to apartment. Cleaned teeth feeling a stir and had a few bananas dobhi drop, just the job, cleaned ass, final little pack of China beachbag and out up to bus stop and caught the No70 to Bugibba. Paid my 1-18 Euro fare and we were away as I sat back enjoying the Malta bright blue sea and sky coastline horizon. We first took the road to the other side of Bugibba and as we turned back onto the coast road to come back to the bus station I pressed the stop buzzer and off I got and my God the sun was hot nearly burning my bare arms. Enjoyed my walk along the busy shops on the coast road then into and a walkie around the many shops, bars and restaurants in the town centre with also lots of Hotels. The only thing missing was a Public Beach which was a shame as all it would take was a bulldozer to flatten the rocks along the sea line, put in some sand and how's your father, a nice sandy beach for the future and saying that they could do it in many desolate bays all around the island. Enjoyed my walkie and into a Western Union office and sent a Happy Birthday message with some loot to my curvy sexy Kelly Rose whose Birthday it is tomorrow and phoned her to tell her I love her and make sure she goes out for a blinder tonight or tomorrow night and kissing and a final love you, I smiling with happiness turned my phone off, it was 1250hrs. Made it back to the bus station having a tea with a ham and cheese sandwich in a café, paid my bill and caught the No652 bus, 1-16Euro back to Paceville. Seen the Military Cemetery so pressed the stop buzzer and off I got and walked left down Triq Sir Adrian Dingle St as wanted to salute and say Goodbye to a young click friend of mine in 3 Para who died in Malta in 1969 and was buried with full Military Honours in this Commonwealth Graveyard. Went in the large gate in the centre of the neat block walls and took my time sadly reading true history from 1900 onwards of the brave Maltese, British and Canadians who gave their life's in honour of peace. I got to Wally's gravestone; Private A J Walton, 3rd Parachute Regt, 22nd Jan, 1969, age 20, In Loving Memory of a Dear Son and Grandson, Rest in Peace. I stood there in sad grief thinking why, then stood proudly to attention I saluted saying, "you were one of the best Wally and we will never forget" and arm down I was sadly away just taking my time sadly looking at the history of the British Empire in a bygone world on the gravestones. Passed many Royal Artillery, Welsh Regt, Devonshire Regt, Dorsetshire Regt, Manchester Regt, Hampshire Regt, Scottish Rifle, Gordon Highlanders, Royal Enniskilling Fusiliers, South Wales Borders, Royal Irish Fusiliers, Green Howards, Royal Malta Artillery, The Buffs, Ontario Regt, Royal Canadian Artillery which were just a few of the many Great British Empire Regiments. A lot of headstones were from the years 1941-42 with the years 1908-18 also having quite a few then seeing an unknown soldier grave:- A soldier of the 1939-45 War, known onto God, 21st Sept 1943, I proudly stood there saying out loud "We are proud of you all and will never forget" and with a stiff arm salute I turned and slowly walked out. I walked back up Triq Adrian Dingle St going past Falaise Rd directly facing the big ruins of The Australian Branch of the British Red Cross erected for the "Benefit of The Soldiers of the Empire" and on down through our old still looking good St Andrew Barracks making my way down past Andrews Bar to St Georges Bay sandy beach. It was Monday so beach was reasonably empty with plenty of room so got a 3Euro sunbed laughing as someone has got to start treating me. Stripped off to swimming briefs and plonked my ass on my small towel and stretched out in Maltese contentment, this is a great life, it was 1420hrs. Had my usual walkie and paddle up and down the lovely sunny day sandy sea edge 3-4 times then sitting or lieing flat out on the sunny sandy beach sunbed enjoying a few sips of my Fanta I checked my watch, it was 1650hrs so called it a day. Cargo shorts, no sleeve tee shirt on and I was away going up the steps into the centre of Paceville. Everywhere inside the cafes and restaurants was empty and darkish and as I attempted to go into Burger King it was closed guy telling me there was a power failure so into a supermarket with its own generator and bought a packet of crisps and a tin of corn beef, 1-60Euro and back to the no lights entrance lobby of my apartment block. Lifts were not working so took my time in the semi dark and climbed upto my 5th floor room and in. Had a small pocket torch so found it while I could still see in the semi daylight then had quick shave and face wash and getting dressed ready to go out it was now pitch black in my room. My plan was to go into Bugibba but as nowhere open and no lights anywhere in Paceville it would probably be the same in Bugibba so just had a night time walk. All or most of the big 4-5Star hotels had lights then I came to the Baystreet Shopping Complex with everywhere lit up so in and had a no rush coffee in one of its many cafes. Paid my 1-60Euro bill and out, it was now 2005hrs and still no lights but walked down Spinola Hill to facing Tony's Bar and into the bright lights of good ole McDonalds and had a tea and a muffin, 2-10Euro enjoying watching the dark Spinola crowds going darkly by. It was now 2140hrs so out and back up the hill into the now lit up Paceville and had enjoyed my dark moonlight night so back up the stairs not needing my torch on and into room. No plans so stripped off and into bed and asleep dreaming my curvy Kelly Rose was in my arms giving me her 27 sexy birthday kisses.

Andrew Bar

St Georges Bay

This is the life on St Georges Bay beach

Email Sent: Mon, 22 Mar 2010
Subject: Bugibba, Malta

Hi All

Bugibba was a great place with plenty of shops, cafes and restaurants so if you want rid of de Miss's for a day or night or two give her a few bob and drop her off in centre of Bugibba and yu can head down the Gut!!.

Was going to go back tonight but we have had a power failure for the past 2-3 hrs so nothing open in Paceville so it probably is the same in Bugibba so didn't bother.

Week End over so Paceville is a bit quieter and theirs plenty of room on St Georges Bay Beach but I do miss the bikini Maltese chico's.

Don't know where I will be manyanna, will wake up and see.

al de bes

Jack

Day 87, Tuesday, 23-03-10, Paceville – Sliema; Malta

Fantastic sleep as no loud 0100-0500hrs early morning shouting screaming revellers as the weekend is over and up at 0800hrs as alarm went off. Pulled bedroom curtains and shock oh shock the sky was overcast and cloudy, no sun anywhere and I looked around my room double checking I was not at home in England. No, I was in Malta so no more 3 day extensions, its now time to face my Kelly Rose music and go home!. Cargo shorts, no sleeve tee shirt on and out down the lift my right tooth now painful and out into the street and by god it was cold so around to Answers my only breakie café and had my 4-95Euro large, no chips breakie sitting inside as it seemed freezing outside. I finished the lot, paid my bill and posted some travel notes to Sylvialita, Sandralita's Mum who kindly receives my travel notes mail, good girl. Back to room, cleaned teeth and had a nice dobhi drop, cleaned ass and changed into long cargo, pocket tee shirt, socks and that was me, where do I go. Had a look at map and finally decided to just walk the route we used to walk from St Andrews Barracks to Sliema as no flashing me timber on the beaches today in this weather. Didn't need my China beachbag so down the lift and out making my way past Dicks Bar then the Scotsmans Bar and going down Spinola Hill I seen a barber next to Tony's Bar so over I went. No queues, no one only the barber there so in I went asking how much for a No1, he said 7Euros so thinking that was expensive I said ok and sat down in the seat as could remember coming here for a haircut in 1969. Guy in chatting to me said his dad had owned and barbered here for 50years as I was telling him he barbered me and maybe a few others back in the good ole 1969-70 Maltese days. He done a good job, paid him the 7Euro and reading a large newspaper cutting on the wall it described his dad being a barber and cutting the Army Boys from St Andrews way back in a bygone time, so there, shook his hand and out. Went right then turned right up the no pavement hill at Triq Il-Kbria then crossed the road onto the narrow little pavement as this was the shortcut way to Sliema we used to walk sometimes pissed as Newts on our midweek Wed sports day or weekend booze day and nights as due to the afternoon heat we only worked 0630hrs to 1200hrs. The street took me out at St Julian's Bay near the Belgravia Auction Gallery where I had two choices either take the Triq Manwel Dimech St which we near enough always did or take the steep hill with steps up it at the side of the Cathedral called Triq Sicilian which we sometimes shouting and laughing we would gallop up. I took Triq Manwel Dimech going under the Arched Bridge across the road which led me onto Triq IL-Prince of Wales 6th June, 1862. Only a few mins walk and I was at the road fork with Sliema Police Station in its centre and could maybe have taken either one but took and went downhill on Triq Manwel Dimech the right hand fork and again only a few mins walk I came out in Sliema waterfront facing the Sliema 1939-45 War Memorial and the docking point for the Sliema, Valletta ferry. Went left only 50m and came to the first Tony's Bar and only 10m separating it and the other Tony's Bar as in our bygone 1969/70 days one of these bars was named the Snake Pit Bar but couldn't remember which one we used as my memory in those pissed as newts days/nights never worked. Had a nice refreshing Rosy Lee in the not many people in the first Tony Bar enjoying the vibes of good ole Sliema watching the tourist world walk by. It was getting warmer but still no sun or sunshine. Crossed the road and just a very slow happy dander I made it along the Sliema harbour waterfront pavement passing the bridge to Manoel Island and had a piss in the Public Toilets facing The Brown Jug Bar thinking it wasn't empty or quiet when the Naafi Click boys were about. Had a quick think of my petite lithe Chico from the other night but said no to myself laughing then a fleeting thought of walking it to Valletta which we used to do but knees saying piss off you walkie junkie I turned back happily walking back into the centre of Sliema. Had another fleeting thought of walking up and around the Point but said no and went left up the hill at St Anne's Sq which is the long haul back, it was 1215hrs. Enjoying every step with plenty of tourists about I made it to Peppi's Cafeteria and took an outside seat overlooking the coast having 2 sausage rolls and the biggest pot of tea of my travels and sat there for 45mins eating my 1300hrs, 3-50Euro din din in quiet happy contentment as no rush to go anywhere today. Took my last gulp of tea, paid my bill and went down the very narrow very winding metal staircase and had a piss in the basement toilet. Back up the winding staircase and away thinking I should retire here and another good walk I was now back in St Julian's Bay passing the Belgravia Auction Gallery again. Changed my reserve fund of 70$US at a money exchange kiosk getting 50Eueo back, stuck it in my sky thinking wont need to draw any more Euros now and kept going on the coast main road. Had to laugh as passed a Unisex hairstylist called Croppers then back into and up the hill at Spinola Bay I was nearly home. Went into the cheapest supermarket in Malta directly under the Portomoso Tower called Arkadia Food Store buying biscuits, tin of corn beef, packet of rolls and a carton of noodles for my night time last feast tonight all items at half or a fraction of the price I would pay in the shops and that was me. Made it back into my Burlington Apartments saying my hellos to the 2 English ladies and one English gentleman who supervise and clean the rooms then up the lift and into my room. It was still warm so had a little naked siesta for 40mins then up making my scoff using plates, knives and forks provided and thoroughly enjoyed my made by the master chef himself 1705hrs supper. Got clean kit out from shoulderbag and sort of done a final pack of it then had my last shave and shower, long cargo, clean pocket tee shirt, underpants and pullover on and checking everything ready for manyanna I was out down the lift. Up to the bus stop and caught a bus to Bugibba getting off at the bus station and enjoyed my good 2hrs walk and 3 teas in 3 cafes as it was a very lively area to be in, pity about it not having a beach. Really enjoyed my last night in lovely Malta and caught a bus, 1-16Euro back to Paceville still thinking about my nightime chico and into the noise of the nightclub and girly bar areas with its many www.darlingsclub.com gentleman's clubs and happy and sad at the same time as this was the final end of my travels. Back into room, got neckpouch out checking Passport and hung it on the inside of my door handle. Done my sad final and last pack of my shoulderbag and stripped off setting alarm and into my last travelling bed I was so sad but thinking and dreaming of my beautiful Kelly Rose I fell into a happy restful rocker sleep.

Email Sent: Tue, 23 Mar 2010
Subject: Paceville and the Clicks route to Sliema
Hi All

Great day as no sunshine but walked the Naafi clicks route from St Andrews Barracks to Sliema, was going to continue to Valetta but knees said enough is enough yu walkie junkie.

Malta is so good as the motorist drive on the correct side of the road, I just wish the rest of the world would follow!!.

One thing that disturbs me is in Paceville at the weekends the young 18 to 25 year old girls run the streets shouting and raving in Maltese lingo, its only me but I think they are complaining about they have no money to buy clothes as they are all half naked, wat yu tink!!!!!!!!!!!!!!

Sorry night tonight as its my last night as head back to Blighty manyanna, 88 days-nights on the loose comes to an end so last email, hip hip hooray I can hear you cheering.

al de bes
Jack

Email Sent: Tue, 23 Mar 2010
Subject: Love Malta and had been back quite a few times and having a read of some of my previous emails from bygone years I had to laugh so have put them together so I can share my laught you. Look at the date of the first one.

Jack Glass Ex 3 Para in Spinola and the Gut; Malta
30/09/05

Chao Boys
Today I am just having a wander back in time 1968-70 and trying to retrace the"Clicks" steps from the Naafi in St Andrews Barracks to the Gut in Valletta. Half pissed we would leave the Naafi and walk past the Guardroom clock tower at the crossroads of Casino, Tobruk, Anzio and Alamein Roads (never knew there was a guardroom there!!!!!!) to make our way to Spinola. First stops included Highlanders Bar and Scotsman's Bar which I had one in each today, next stop was Dicks Bar for one, everybody mouthing off, nobody listening. Next stop was Tonys Bar directly in Spinola which was a great favourite and by then many good click drinkers didn't know they were in it or left it!!! I think sometimes we used to haggle the price for a taxi OR sometimes we would stagger to Sliema but weekends especially we would reach the GUT in Valletta and we always had our favourite corner bar to meet up again. The Gut was a long stepped alley full of hooker bars and fully pissed we were easy meat, there are only two bars left now but all the old bar names are still there, real history. On the way home 2400-0100 fully gone we would sometimes make it to Andrews Bar in St Georges Bay which now is a beautiful sandy beach with high rise hotels, then it was a rocky sewer outlet and the only things that went swimming were rats and 3 Para, the Maltese said the rats where the cleanest between the two!!! Our DZ most days/nights after the Naafi was a bar across the public road from the Naafi called the Golden Star and the Devil if he ever came to earth for company used to use it with us, no other animal in the world would join us (its not there now), up from it was Jessie's Bar which was a Royal Marine place. I finished my walkie today at the Forces graveyard and gave a final salute to a young 3 Para Naafi click Walla, Wally Walton, died aged 20, 1969, a great friend and comrade who went early to the big DZ in the sky, "only the good die young", so wont see you for a while Wally. Some memories today so back to Paceville for din dins ready for tonight!!!
Al de bes
shanko jack

Chao Boys

Thanks to Jimmy Morham reminding me about the Snake Pit Bar in Sliema, I think I found it but all the bars along Sliema waterfront are cafes/come restaurants and different names now, no off their pissed pea/brain?? shouting Paras ranting/raving along the roads, those were the days. Don't forget from 68-70 in Malta we only worked!! 0700-1200 as us poor boys the CO said should not be out in the midday sun so no matter how hard I tried I never made the first one in the Naafi to start our day with a double vodka and coke (no measure, straight from the litre bottle), then we started buying our own black market litre bottles so by the time we left the Naafi 1600-1800 us Click boys had downed a full bottle and were speaking a language very few understood; CRAP, I think its called. I have a cup of rosy lea in Tonys Bar (Spinola) every day to start my wonderings and Tonys Bar always has a few Maltese's sitting, drinking and talking and each time I go in NOBODY MOVES, how times have changed, when the Maltese sitting in Tonys Bar used to see the Click coming down Spinola Hill they USED TO RUN and leave the bar empty, wonder why!
al de bes
shanko jack

Chao Boys

Anyway on my first day I went swimming in Paradise Bay and a kip on the beach for a few hours then St Pauls Bay for a swim, all in one day, something I didn't do in two years the last time!! Today I went to Golden Bay for a swim then up over the cliffs to Ghajn Tuffieha Bay and then along another little bay with approximately 10 nudists but undeterred (ready for anything), swimming trunks off and done a dance, SORRY, prance, SORRY, quick walk "of the flamers and away"!! Mind you, 4-5 blokes did give me the EYE, must have been Ex 3 Para, but too late, away, virgin ass and all!! Back up the cliffs and jumped a bus with my 5ML (7 quid) 5 day bus pass, jump on anytime and back to good old Spinola. Just heading down Tonys Bar, Spinola for a rosy lee and then my last one of the night!!!!!, down the Gut.
al de bes
shanko jack

Chao Boys

Met Geordie Ward in the shot and had a yarn about Malta, mind you I couldn't get a word in edgeways but anyways he told me our best drinking hole was the famous bar across the road from the Naafi called the "Golden Star" and what fond happy memories he brought back when he said that name. i.e. 10-12-20 pissed, shouting (2-3 sleeping) animals with no brains, just double vodka until the early hours, great days and he said there was another bar just down the road from it that was used by the MT?!!!! He also told me we used to get a horse and Maltese carriage from Spinola to Sliema and our first stop in Valetta was in the Vernon Club which was just inside the main arch gates on the left but by that time I told him I didn't even know we were in Malta !!!

al de bes

shanko Jack

Chao Boys

The Italian, who went to Malta, read with Italian accent.

One day ima gonna Malta to bigga hotel. Ina morning I go down to eat breakfast. I tella waitress I wanna two pissia toast. She brings me only one piss. I tella her I want two piss. She say go to the toilet, I say you no understand, I wanna to piss onna my plate. She say you better no piss onna plate, you sonna ma bitch. I don't even know the lady and she call me sonna ma bitch. Late I go to eat at the bigga restaurant. The waitress brings me a spoon and knife but no fock, I tella her I wanna fock. She tells me everyone wanna fock. I tella her you no understand, I wanna fock on the table. She say you better not fock on the table, you sonna ma bitch. So I go back to my room inna hotel and there is no shits onna my bed. I call the manager and tella him I wanna shits. He tella me go to toilet. I say you no understand, I wanna shits on my bed. He say you better not shits onna your bed you sonna bitch. I go to checkout and the man at the desk say "peace on you", I say piss on you too you sonna bitch, I go back to Italy . AND ANOTHER DAY DAWNS!!!!!!!!!!!!!!!!!!!!!!!!!

al de bes

Shanko jack

Chao Boys

Its great here in Fred Zamitt country and he sends his regards, he said we should have got a campaign medal for what we went through in Malteaser land. I said never mind a campaign medal what about catching "NAAFI Syndrome", should I sue the MOD as due to many unexplained cocktails in the NAAFI and other places sometimes my brain!!!!! wouldn't work and my legs didn't seem to be attached to my body, have I a good case, he said depends what's in the case, open a bottle and we will talk it through!!!!!! Enjoyed today's lovely sunshine on my wavy hair?, (Waved goodbye) at 0900 lieing on the beach at St Georges Bay, what's it like in blighty !!! ha, ha. Found a Brown Jug Bar in Sliema just past the bridge to Maneol Island and facing a petrol station and it fits in with one of our stops in 69-70 after leaving the Naafi or the Golden Star head gone and singing. Just around the corner from it past Trig San Gorge is a few big apartments, Sliema hookers, they were rough!!!!, I will check out tonight if they still are and let you know manyanna.

al de bes

shanko Jack

Chao Boys

The good gungee Maltese girls have not changed nor their clothes and still not washed BUT lovely smell and "great, oh la, la" and that's in Sliema. They are like "sisters in arms" to gungee 3 even when she got on top and another sneaked in to rob my trousers but not this time as shanko is an old campaigner and screamed loudly and slid out, she run, kit on, forgot my underpants (gungee 3, underpants!!!!!!, times have changed) and out on to the street full of hookers with my t shirt in my hand and down to the Brown Jug Bar. Another great night and no manyanna!!!!

Al de bes

Shanko Jack

Chao Boys
Two Italians go to Malta and catch a Maltese bus. (Read with Italian Accent)
A bus stops, and 2 Italian men get on. They sit down and start talking. The lady sitting next to them ignores them at first but her attention is galvanised when she hears one of them say to the other; "Emma come first, den I come, den two asses come together, I come once a more, two asses they come together again, I come again and pee twice, then I come one lasta time"!!!!!!!!!!!!!!
The lady stood up, "you foul mouthed sex obsessed swine", retorted the lady indignantly, "In this Catholic country Malta ……….we don't speak aloud in public places about our sex lives." "Hey, coola downa plesea lady," said the man, "whosa talking abouta sex??? I telling my frienda how to spell " Mississippi " And another day dawns!!!
al de bes
shanko Jack

Chao Boys
7 things a "Gut girl" Never said to a Para;
1. Ah……that's cute, 2. WOW and your feet are so big. 3. Are you cold or something. 4. This explains your car! 5. At least this won't take long. 6. But it still works, yeah?!! 7. I guess this makes me an early bird!!!! Manyanna never comes, only gungee 3 with Gut girls.
al de bes
Shanko Jack

Chao Boys

Strait St (The Gut) Valetta;

Met Dom Mintoff, he sends his love and said 3 Para in Malta were a credit to the British Nation in 68-70 but PLEASE, PLEASE, PLEASE NEVER COME BACK!! Found the Vernon Club, turn right under the arches and its now the HQ Central Bank of Malta !!!, still smell the piss!! Carried on down and turned left and into Strait St, a narrow alleyway with steps going downhill, the "Gut" as we knew it, and came to the piss holes in the wall just across from where the bars started, the bars didn't have any toilets!, and the piss holes, no toilet paper, Gungee 3 !, "did it matter! No bars now, most blocked up and grimy area, just the old flaking painted names, first bar I knew but no name then Retainer Bar, then Larry Bar, then Malata Bar then Splendid Bar, then an intersection alley then my heart stood still as I looked up and I was at the Smiling Prince Bar, across the alley was the Carmen Bar and then the Piccadilly Bar, these bars and one that had no name were our heaven on earth piss holes and I just stood there for a while thinking how did we survive making it down here never mind making it home, God was kind or else he didn't want us in that state!!! Carried on over another alley intersection to Blue Peter Bar then Silver Horse Bar (Alex McKay) and now nearly down at the bottom of the Gut, great memories, them was the nights!!!!!!!!!

al de bes

shanko Jack

Chao Boys
Promotion in the Para's.
Life in the Para's is like a tree full of Monkeys, all on different limbs, all at different levels.
Some are climbing up, some are climbing down.
The Para's on top "from their eyes" look down and see a tree full of smiling faces.
The Para's on the bottom look up
And see nothing but ASSHOLES!!
al de bes
shanko Jack

Chao Boys
Manyanna is like a pint in the NAAFI, It arrives, it's gone and will never come back!!
al de bes
shanko Jack

Chao lads
Another one over and 60 next year, who would have thought Shanko would see 60 in the horizon!!!!, Why worry.
There are only two things to worry about; Either you are well or you are sick.
If you are well, then there is nothing to worry about,
But if you are sick, there are two things to worry about;
Either you get well or you die.
If you get well there is nothing to worry about
If you die, there are two things to worry about; Either you go to Heaven or Hell.
If you go to Heaven, there is nothing to worry about'
But if you go to Hell, you'll be so dam busy shaking hands with ex-Paras,
You won't have time to worry.
al de Bes
shanko Jack

1) **ENGLAND** the Land of Hope and Glory, St George for England and God Save the Queen.
2) Capital; London
3) Independent since time began
4) Climate; Ave temp Jan-Mar; 10c
5) Language; English
6) Currency; English Pound, 1$US = 0-60pence
7) Visa; Back home, don't need
8) Return flight £51 + £154 ATM, hotel, food, train to Gatwick = £206
9) Today's ongoing update of day to day accommodation, travel, food, drinks costs = £5172 + £206 = "£5378 total".

Day 88, Wednesday, 24-03-10, Paceville; Malta – Aldershot; England

Very poor nights sleep getting up 2-3times for a piss and finally up at 0700hrs. Pulled the curtain and it was a lovely sunny day, just my luck. The building workers had already started as there is massive excavations and high rise buildings going up everywhere. Going along the coast on my days out there is new high rocky mountain hills inland where once it was flat rocky desolate fields as I suppose the excavations have to go somewhere but its nice to see the lower part of the new hills are now green with bushes. Into bathroom and had an underarm wash, face splash, some deodorant on and got dressed with long cargo, pocket tee shirt and pullover on and I was nearly ready but very sad then thinking of my Kelly Rose I was happy. Out down the lift and around to Answers my breakie stop and had my usual 2 full slices of toasted bread, 2 butter, 2 jam cubes, 2 eggs, 2 bacon, 2 sausage and beans with a pot of tea and enjoyed my last Maltese English breakie, really nice. Paid my 4-95Euro charge with all my loose Euro coins as UK is not in the Euro, said my thanks saying I will see you next time and back upto room, it was only 0815hrs. Cleaned teeth then using toothpick same as last night forced the eats debris from under my sore tooth and same as last night the pain went away. Cleaned teeth and had a nice farting dobhi drop which cleaned the system for today's travels, cleaned ass, and nearly there. Final little pack of shoulderbag then wheeled it out to the inside of the entrance door, turned all lights off and final check of neckpouch checking Passport and as per room instructions left my roomkey on the sitting room table. Also as a laugh I left a "All work and No Play make a Housewife in Burlington" poster on it writing bye bye chicos, see you next time and I was out of my room closing and locking the door behind me. Down the lift and back around to facing Tropicana Hotel where my www.maltatransfer.com pick up was arranged for 0925hrs, it was 0915hrs. Stood there looking everywhere up and down the road but at 0940hrs I went into the Tropicana Hotel reception asking guy did he have Malta Transfer's phone number as I only had an email confirmation. He said no so out again standing waiting and getting worried, it was now 0945hrs. Into the Tropicana Hotel desk again and guy said you want taxi to Airport, 18Euro so thinking that was a good price and didn't want to take any chances I said yes and he phoned up Wembley Taxi's whose office I knew was on Spinola Hill. Only a 2-5min wait, taxi arrived and in I got putting shoulderbag on the back seat, me in the front with safety belt on and we were away. Good no hassle run without the usual Maltese 100mph taxi drama and into the front of Airport departures and he dropped me off, got my bag, paid him a 20Euro note, said my thanks and in I went. Seen the screen, Easyjet, EZY8824 Malta –London Gatwick, check-in at Gate 21-22 so upto gate, put bag on moving escalator, gave girl my Passport and 2mins later my bag was away and I was given my Passport and boarding card, oh la, la, that was easy I thought. Into departures showing my Passport and boarding pass then into Gate 11 showing my Passport and boarding pass again and that was me. Bought a bottle of Fanta at rip off 2-60Euro and sat down eating a few chocolate cakes that I had smuggled in, it was now 1045hrs. At 1140hrs it came over the tannoy all passengers for Easyjet

EZY 8824, 1210hrs please proceed through security and onto Airport bus which I did. Bus got full and out to the plane we drove and off I got going up the gangplank steps onto the plane and took my seat 7D, an aisle seat. Plane fully packed not a spare seat we had the usual safety demonstration, lifebelts, emergency landing etc and at 1230hrs out we taxied and with a giant roar we were away off into the clean sunny Maltese sky me looking out both windows each side of the plane saying "I loved you Malta" and sat back thinking of my sexy Kelly Rose, oh la, la, more treats to come. Had a read of the inflight Easyjet Magazine, had 2 walks, dozed off for 30mins and it came over the tannoy, fasten seatbelts etc, prepare for landing and in we flew to drab cloudy Gatwick Airport and bump I was now back on good ole English soil, it was 1425hrs English time as we gain 1hr. Off the plane, waited not long, grabbed my sewed together red shoulderbag with its blue ribbon straps and looking confident I went through the green, Nothing to Declare walkway and with a sigh of relief I was through with my smuggled 3 packets of 200 cigarettes tobacco haul, Mama Mia. Had a piss then drawing £100 at an ATM I followed the sign for the train station buying a single £8-50 to Aldershot via Guildford, next train, 1603hrs and made it down the escalator to Platform 3, it was 1535hrs. Severe delays on all London trains but mine was the Reading via Guildford so at 1555hrs as it drew into the station lots got off going on their holidays and quite a crowd got on as I did, got a seat and sat back big time breathing a sigh of relief as not long before I am home. Off we went at 1603hrs me for a change admiring the green lovely fields of England's Hampshire countryside. Stopped a few times and at 1641hrs off I got at Guildford, nearly home. Checked departure board and caught the Ascot 1700hrs train and at 1715hrs me smiling and happy I got off in my home town of Aldershot. Down through the underground walkway my faithful red trolley shoulderbag on its last legs and out of the train station admiring the sight of my local Funky End Pub in Bazaar, sorry Station Road. Took first right before the Funky End Pub and down Hood St now known as Arthur St and happy as a hood lark I seen my flat and with big smiles and great vibes I walked down to my front door and unlocking the Dead & Yale locks I was home, it was 1720hrs. Climbed my stairs turning electric on at the meter and water on at the stopvalve and smiling to the world I felt so happy and good. Phoned up my Kelly Rose and laughing, kissing over the phone we arranged to meet for a lovers embrace later. Had a look out my windows, nothing had changed and after my North Africa, Middle East, Israel and Malta 9 Countries, 88 days great exploring expedition fully over and now back to realty it was now time for a real Rosy Lee and I put my kettle on. Made a lovely big mug of sweet tea and wishing all my fellow travellers wherever they are in Today's Wide World Good Lucks and Safe Journeys I sat down on my sofa a very happy and contented man waiting for the Love of my life, my sexy curvy full of life Kelly Rose, oh la la, Happiness never stops.

Email Sent: Wed, 24 Mar 2010
Subject: Aldershot, England

Hi All

Made it up to Luqa Airport with plenty of time and took off 1220hrs landing in London Gatwick 1320hrs English time as we gain an hour.

I think we landed in the N Terminal as took me an hour to get to the Gatwick train station and next train was 1603hrs so paid my £8-50 fare and arrived in the good ole sunshine Shotty Den at 1720hrs.

3hr flight from Malta, 5hr wait and train journey from Gatwick but now home and had a lovely Rosy Lee and the Shot looks like nothing much has changed.

Final and last email so Good Luck to You all and enjoy all your travels.

al de bes

Jack

www.ingramcontent.com/pod-product-compliance
Lightning Source LLC
Chambersburg PA
CBHW051033160426
43193CB00010B/931